CramSession
Approved Study Material

The CramSession Seal of Approval is given to study materials that meet with the requirements of CramSession's review process. The seal is our way of letting you know that the study material you are purchasing will help you pass the exam and provide you with high quality, relevant, and technically accurate information. Our reviewers include CramSession staff and the much larger CramSession community who are knowledgeable authors and technical editors in their own right. We receive early copies of the study material as it is being produced and review the study material before it reaches stores. When we review study materials we make sure the content is relevant to the exam vendor's published exam outline, that it provides technically accurate information, and that it is written with the appropriate audience in mind—you, the certification exam candidate. While we can't guarantee you will pass the exam, we can assure you that the study material you are purchasing meets with our own high standards and expectations.

About CramSession.com

CramSession.com is the #1 destination on the Internet for online certification study guides and related material. With over more than 250 online CramSession study guides, we offer the most comprehensive selection of study material available online. Additionally, our technical articles, newsletters, practice questions, discussion boards, and large IT user community help to ensure that you have the support to study effectively for your exam and gain the knowledge and experience you need to succeed in IT.

MCSE

Windows® XP Professional

Exam 70-270

Gord Barker
Robert L. Bogue

Training Guide

MCSE Training Guide (70-270): Windows® XP Professional

International Standard Book Number: 0-7897-2773-0

Library of Congress Catalog Card Number: 2002104067

Printed in the United States of America

First Printing: July 2002
Second Printing with corrections: November 2002

05   04   03   5   4   3

Trademarks

Warning and Disclaimer

PUBLISHER
Paul Boger

EXECUTIVE EDITOR
Jeff Riley

DEVELOPMENT EDITOR
Susan Zahn

MANAGING EDITOR
Tom Hayes

PROJECT EDITORS
Tonya Simpson
Christina Smith

PRODUCTION EDITOR
Maribeth Echard

INDEXER
Mandie Frank

PROOFREADER
Plan-It Publishing

TECHNICAL EDITORS
Marc Savage
Ed Tetz

TEAM COORDINATOR
Rosemary Lewis

MEDIA DEVELOPER
Michael Hunter

INTERIOR DESIGNER
Louisa Klucznik

COVER DESIGNER
Charis Ann Santillie

Contents at a Glance

Table of Contents

4 Monitoring and Optimizing System Performance and Reliability

7 Implementing, Monitoring, and Troubleshooting Security   485

PART II: Final Review

PART III: Appendixes

About the Authors

Robert L. Bogue, MCSE, CNA, A+, Network+, I-Net+, Server+, e-Biz+, IT Project+, and CDIA+, has contributed to more than 100 book projects as well as numerous magazine articles and reviews. His broad experience includes networking and integration topics as well as software development. He is currently a strategic IT consultant. He's a frequent contributor to CertCities.com. When not killing trees or getting certified, he enjoys flying planes and working toward higher ratings on his pilot's license. Robert can be reached at Rob.Bogue@ThorProjects.com.

Gord Barker, MCSE, currently works as a Senior Consultant for Microsoft Canada Co. in Edmonton, Alberta, Canada. He worked with Telus to complete the largest single rollout of Windows 2000 to occur prior to the product launch. He currently works with large customers to deploy Microsoft technology, including SQL Server, Active Directory domains with Windows 2000 and Windows XP desktops, Content Manager, BizTalk, and Exchange. Gord lives in Edmonton, Alberta with his wife Christina.

About the Technical Reviewers

Edward Tetz graduated in 1990 from Saint Lawrence College in Cornwall, Ontario, with a diploma in Business Administration. He spent a short time in computer sales, which turned into a computer support position. He has spent most of his time since then performing system and LAN support for small and large organizations. In 1994, he added training to his repertoire. He currently holds the following certifications: MCT, MCSE, MCDBA, CTT+, A+, CIW MA, and CIW CI. He has experience with Apple Macintosh, IBM OS/2, Linux, and all Microsoft operating systems. Over the years, he has delivered training on many Microsoft products. He is currently an independent consultant.

Marc Savage, MCSE, MCT, A+, Net+, is a Training Manager and the National Microsoft Advisor for Polar Bear Corporate Solutions—Canada's largest corporate education provider. Marc is a Senior Technical Trainer and consultant with many years of experience in system/network administration. Marc has been working on network designs, server implementations, network management, and designing custom course delivery for many medium to large clients.

Dedication

The best measure of a man is in the quality of his friends.—January 22, 2002

To my friends: Brian and Cindy Proffitt, Lynette and Joe Quinn, Brian and Janie Latka, Betty and Matt Wise, and Julie and Dave Lahr for their love and support during the first few weeks after the birth of my son, Alexander Nathaniel.

—Rob Bogue

This book is dedicated to my wife Christina for her unwavering support during this project.

—Gord Barker

Acknowledgments

No book projects can be done in a vacuum. In fact, the publisher's editorial staff rarely gets enough credit for the work they do to make a book such as the one you see here. The best acknowledgment that I can give to them is that this book—or any other book—would not be the same without their talent. —Rob Bogue

I would like to thank the people most directly involved in this project: Susan Zahn and Jeff Riley, for their assistance, along with Ed Tetz and Marc Savage, who had great suggestions and edits. —Gord Barker

Tell Us What You Think!

As the reader of this book, you are our most important critic and commentator. We value your opinion and want to know what we're doing right, what we could do better, what areas you'd like to see us publish in, and any other words of wisdom you're willing to pass our way.

As an executive editor for Que Certification, I welcome your comments. You can email or write me directly to let me know what you did or didn't like about this book—as well as what we can do to make our books stronger.

Please note that I cannot help you with technical problems related to the topic of this book. We do have a User Services group, however, where I will forward specific technical questions related to the book.

When you write, please be sure to include this book's title and authors' names as well as your name, phone number, and email address. I will carefully review your comments and share them with the authors and editors who worked on the book.

Email: certification@quepublishing.com

Mail: Jeff Riley
          Executive Editor
          Que Publishing
          201 West 103rd Street
          Indianapolis, IN 46290 USA

How to Use This Book

Que Certification has made an effort in its Training Guide series to make the information as accessible as possible for the purposes of learning the certification material. Here, you have an opportunity to view the many instructional features that have been incorporated into the books to achieve that goal.

CHAPTER OPENER

Each chapter begins with a set of features designed to allow you to maximize study time for that material.

List of Objectives: Each chapter begins with a list of the objectives as stated by Microsoft.

Objective Explanations: Immediately following each objective is an explanation of it, providing context that defines it more meaningfully in relation to the exam. Because Microsoft can sometimes be vague in its objectives list, the objective explanations are designed to clarify any vagueness by relying on the authors' test-taking experience.

OBJECTIVES

This chapter looks at the DNS server that comes with Windows 2000 as it relates to the Active Directory. Although it concentrates on how to integrate with Active Directory, the chapter starts with a brief discussion of the basics of DNS. After that, a discussion of the installation is presented along with a look at the roles of a DNS server. After these basics are covered, the chapter turns to how it works with Active Directory.

The following objectives from the exam are covered in this chapter:

Install, configure, and troubleshoot DNS for Active Directory.

- **Integrate Active Directory DNS zones with non-Active Directory DNS zones.**
- **Configure zones for dynamic updates.**

▶ This objective is included to make sure you are able to work with DNS both for Active Directory and for other types of computers on your network. Also, one of the important changes in DNS for Windows 2000 is the capability to deal with dynamic updates. This is important for Active Directory so it can register various services with the DNS server to allow clients to find LDAP servers and domain controllers.

Manage, monitor, and troubleshoot DNS.

- **Manage replication of DNS data.**

▶ In managing replication of DNS, you need to understand the difference between zone transfers for standard zones and Active Directory replication that handles replication of Active Directory–integrated zones.

CHAPTER 2

Configuring DNS for Active Directory

Chapter Outline: Learning always gets a boost when you can see both the forest and the trees. To give you a visual image of how the topics in a chapter fit together, you will find a chapter outline at the beginning of each chapter. You will also be able to use this for easy reference when looking for a particular topic.

STUDY STRATEGIES

▶ Windows XP Professional supports more types of devices than any previous version of the operating system. In addition to the range of devices supported, configuration is made automatic because of Plug and Play. You can expect several questions related to installing and supporting newer hardware devices on your Windows XP Professional computer. Many of these questions will be presented as scenarios in which the capabilities of these devices are used to solve problems.

▶ You also should expect to see questions dealing with new disk capabilities to provide fault tolerance as well as more options in configuring disk storage.

▶ Greater disk storage capacity creates a need for offline storage capabilities. Expect to see questions on Removable Storage Management (RSM) and the configuration of robotic libraries and media pools.

▶ Some new devices that you can expect to see questions on are support for infrared (IrDA) and wireless support, plus support for Universal Serial Bus (USB) devices.

▶ Finally, Windows XP Professional can support an additional processor. You can expect to see some questions that focus on the impact of improving the CPU power of your Windows XP Professional computer and its impact on other resources available within your system.

▶ In short, by focusing on the previously mentioned major areas, you will be well prepared for this portion of the exam.

Study Strategies: Each topic presents its own learning challenge. To support you through this, Que Certification has included strategies for how to best approach studying in order to retain the material in the chapter, particularly as it is addressed on the exam.

INSTRUCTIONAL FEATURES WITHIN THE CHAPTER

These books include a large amount and different kinds of information. The many different elements are designed to help you identify information by its purpose and importance to the exam and also to provide you with varied ways to learn the material. You will be able to determine how much attention to devote to certain elements, depending on what your goals are. By becoming familiar with the different presentations of information, you will know what information will be important to you as a test-taker and which information will be important to you as a practitioner.

Objective Coverage Text: In the text before an exam objective is specifically addressed, you will notice the objective is listed to help call your attention to that particular material.

Warning: In using sophisticated information technology, there is always potential for mistakes or even catastrophes that can occur through improper application of the technology. Warnings appear in the margins to alert you to such potential problems.

EXAM TIP

Extending Volumes Expect questions on the exam about extending existing volumes that are not NTFS volumes. Existing spanned volumes formatted with NTFS can be extended by adding free space. Disk Management formats the new area without affecting the existing files on the original volume or the spanned volume. Spanned volumes formatted with FAT cannot be extended.

Exam Tip: Exam Tips appear in the margins to provide specific exam-related advice. Such tips may address what material is covered (or not covered) on the exam, how it is covered, mnemonic devices, or particular quirks of that exam.

Note: Notes appear in the margins and contain various kinds of useful information, such as tips on the technology or administrative practices, historical background on terms and technologies, or side commentary on industry issues.

NOTE

Write It Down It's always a good idea to document the current and working configuration parameters before you make any modifications. Changing a resource configuration can leave a device in a nonfunctioning state.

MEDIA DEVICES

Implement, manage, and troubleshoot disk devices.

The following sections address configuring and maintaining CD and DVD devices, fixed disks, volumes, and other media devices.

CD-ROM and DVD Devices

Current CD-ROM and DVD devices support Plug and Play and therefore should be automatically configured when you install the devices.

Support for the CD-ROM File System (CDFS) is maintained in Windows XP Professional for support of legacy applications and is used by RSM in storing CD-ROMs in removable storage libraries. CD-ROM devices support 650MB of storage per platter, and although this was once considered immense, it pales against the DVD standard, which currently can hold more than 26 times as much data (up to 17GB of information).

Windows XP Professional provides support for creating CD-R and CD-RW disks (providing your computer has a CD device that can create as well as read disks).

A CD-R or CD-RW disk can be created as a single session or a multisession disk. A session is defined as a lead-in, program data, and lead-out. The purpose of a multisession disk is to allow additional information to be added to a disk after the initial recording. The entire CD-R also has a lead-in and lead-out section that contains the table of contents and addresses for the various sessions recorded on the disk.

In addition, a disk can be written "Disk at Once," in which case the entire disk is written continuously without interruptions, or "Track at Once," in which case a session is made up of discrete tracks written to the disk; and, then, the disk is "finalized" and the session is closed off (by writing the lead-out).

Most pressed CD-ROMs are single-session, disk-at-a-time recordings. Most audio playback units can therefore play only the first session of a multisession CD-R.

WARNING

Manually Adjusting Resources The usual reason for adjusting device configuration is to support a legacy device (not Plug and Play) that requires either jumpers or a config utility to configure the device. These configuration parameters must then be configured in Windows XP Professional.

If you must manually configure a non–Plug and Play device, the resources assigned become fixed. This reduces the flexibility that Windows XP Professional has for allocating resources to other devices. If too many resources are manually configured, Windows XP Professional might not be able to install new Plug and Play devices.

Resource settings should be changed only if you are certain that the new settings do not conflict with any other hardware, or if the hardware manufacturer has supplied a specific set of resource settings with the device.

Step by Step: Step by Steps are hands-on tutorial instructions that walk you through a particular task or function relevant to the exam objectives.

Figure: To improve readability, the figures have been placed in the margins wherever possible so they do not interrupt the main flow of text.

In the Field Sidebar: These more extensive discussions cover material that perhaps is not as directly relevant to the exam, but which is useful as reference material or in everyday practice. In the Field may also provide useful background or contextual information necessary for understanding the larger topic under consideration.

Review Break: Crucial information is summarized at various points in the book in lists or tables. At the end of a particularly long section, you might come across a Review Break that is there just to wrap up one long objective and reinforce the key points before you shift your focus to the next section.

CASE STUDIES

Case Studies are presented throughout the book to provide you with another, more conceptual opportunity to apply the knowledge you are developing. They also reflect the "real-world" experiences of the authors in ways that prepare you not only for the exam but for actual network administration as well. In each Case Study, you will find similar elements: a description of a Scenario, the Essence of the Case, and an extended Analysis section.

CASE STUDY: THE AMARANTH ENGINEERING COMPANY

ESSENCE OF THE CASE

The following points summarize the essence of the case study:

- The back-end database has all the important files on one disk.
- The disk failed with no recent backup.
- Recovery to the previous night required the next day's data to be reentered.

SCENARIO

Although you work at an engineering company, your responsibility is to oversee the computer systems that support the company's works. In this case, you are analyzing the recent events of the company's accounting system. The company uses a commercial accounting system that uses a single server for a back-end database. This was installed more than a year ago and has been working well. However, the database was installed with all the default settings and a single large database file holding indexes, and data was created. The transaction log files are also held on this main disk and full backups are done each night. The incident you are reviewing involves a disk failure on the database disk late one afternoon last week. The disk was replaced but the database needed to be recovered from the previous backup. No transaction logs are available to apply and the entire day's work needs to be reentered. Your task is to prevent this from happening again.

Essence of the Case: A bulleted list of the key problems or issues that need to be addressed in the Scenario.

Scenario: A few paragraphs describing a situation that professional practitioners in the field might face. A Scenario will deal with an issue relating to the objectives covered in the chapter, and it includes the kinds of details that make a difference.

Analysis: This is a lengthy description of the best way to handle the problems listed in the Essence of the Case. In this section, you might find a table summarizing the solutions, a worded example, or both.

ANALYSIS

This situation is quite common. An application system (in this case, an accounting application) uses a back-end database to store data and produce invoices and reports. After all this is set up, there is a tendency to not revisit the initial configuration again until there is a problem.

Having the database tables and indexes on one disk is generally considered a potential disk performance bottleneck; however, the real problem comes when the previous night's backup is restored to disk. There are no transaction logs left to apply to the database in order to bring it

EXTENSIVE REVIEW AND SELF-TEST OPTIONS

At the end of each chapter, along with some summary elements, you will find a section called "Apply Your Knowledge" that gives you several different methods with which to test your understanding of the material and review what you have learned.

CHAPTER SUMMARY

KEY TERMS
- Plug and Play
- Dynamic disks
- Simple volumes
- Spanned
- Striped
- RAID-5
- Mirrored
- Media pools

This chapter focused on devices and drivers that you can add to your computer to customize it for your needs.

First, the Windows XP Professional implementation of Plug and Play was discussed along with resources available in Windows XP Professional and ways of assigning them to devices. The new dynamic disk structures available were discussed along with CD-ROM technology and removable storage.

Second, the new Windows XP Professional feature allowing multiple video displays was discussed, along with the procedures for configuring your virtual desktop.

Third, to support mobile computing and APM/ACPI features of

Key Terms: A list of key terms appears at the end of each chapter. These are terms that you should be sure you know and are comfortable defining and understanding when you go in to take the exam.

Chapter Summary: Before the Apply Your Knowledge section, you will find a chapter summary that wraps up the chapter and reviews what you should have learned.

Chapter 3   IMPLEMENTING...HARDWARE DEVICES AND DRIVERS   251

APPLY YOUR KNOWLEDGE

3.5 Installing a USB Device and Measuring Power Used

This exercise will go through the steps to install a bus-powered USB device and then cover how to measure the power consumed. This lab uses a Microsoft IntelliMouse Optical but any USB device that is recognized by Windows XP Professional will work.

Estimated Time: 10 minutes

1. Unplug any existing mouse currently connected to your Windows XP Professional computer.
2. Plug the Microsoft IntelliMouse Optical mouse into a USB port on your computer.
3. Wait until the Found New Hardware window closes (it should find a Microsoft IntelliMouse Optical and a USB Human Interface Device). The new optical mouse should now function.
4. Click Start, Control Panel and Performance and Maintenance.
5. Click Administrative Tools and double-click Computer Management, and then click Device Manager.
6. In the right window, expand the Universal Serial Bus Controllers item.
7. Right-click USB Root Hub and select Properties.
8. Select the Power tab and you should see a device on the hub identified as an HID-compliant mouse using a total of 100mA. This will vary depending on the type of USB device you have installed for this lab.

3.6 Transferring Files Using Wireless Connection

This exercise will walk through the steps necessary to set up a connection and transfer files between computers using a wireless (IrDA) connection. This lab will require you to have two devices (computers or a computer and a handheld device) with IrDA capabilities.

Estimated Time: 10 minutes

1. Click Start, Control panel, Printers and Other Hardware, and double-click Wireless Link.
2. Select the File Transfer tab and check the Display an Icon on the Taskbar Indicating Infrared Activity check box.
3. Click OK to close the Wireless Link window.
4. Reposition the two infrared transceiver windows until the Infrared icon appears on the taskbar.
5. Click the Infrared icon on the taskbar.
6. In the Wireless Link dialog box, select the files you want to send and click Send.
7. You can also send files using the IRFTP program started from Start/Run or any command prompt.

Review Questions

1. You change the resources your non-Plug and Play video adapter uses in Device Manager, but now the system will not boot correctly. What is wrong?

Exercises: These activities provide an opportunity for you to master specific hands-on tasks. Our goal is to increase your proficiency with the product or technology. You must be able to conduct these tasks in order to pass the exam.

Review Questions: These open-ended, short-answer questions allow you to quickly assess your comprehension of what you just read in the chapter. Instead of asking you to choose from a list of options, these questions require you to state the correct answers in your own words. Although you will not experience these kinds of questions on the exam, these questions will indeed test your level of comprehension of key concepts.

APPLY YOUR KNOWLEDGE

2. Your application currently uses logical drives on which to store some of its data. The application needs to reference these logical devices using drive letters. You have converted your system to use dynamic disks and would like to organize these files into subdirectories rather than on separate devices. Will your application be able to read its data? Why or why not?

3. What devices does RSM manage on a typical desktop computer?

4. You have a laptop that you have configured with multiple display adapters while it is in its docking bay. When you boot your laptop, the multiple displays do not work correctly. What is the reason?

5. You have a device that is not working perfectly. You install an updated driver from the manufacturer's site and find that the device doesn't work at all now. What do you do?

6. You install a new high-speed modem that the salesman said would run at 56Kb. When you dial up to your Internet service provider (ISP), you find you can't get as much speed as you expected. What is the reason?

7. You have just purchased a new desktop computer that has Windows XP Professional already installed on it. You want to ensure that the latest device drivers available are installed and the drivers are all signed. What is your most efficient course of action?

8. You are using Performance Monitoring to display how busy your computer is. You note that the

Exam Questions

1. You have a home computer that originally had Windows NT 4.0 installed. You configured the two disks you had installed on the system as a stripe set. Later, you upgraded your machine to Windows 2000 Professional. Now you want to upgrade the machine to Windows XP Professional. What do you have to do first?

   A. Upgrade the computer to Windows XP Professional and run Diskpart to convert the stripe to a striped volume.

   B. Upgrade the computer to Windows XP Professional and run FTOnline to mount the stripe set and copy the data to a backup device.

   C. Back up the information from the stripe set, delete the stripe sets, and re-create the disk as dynamic with a simple volume, and reload the data.

   D. Convert the disk to dynamic and continue with the upgrade.

2. You own a laptop that you use when you are on the road visiting customers. You would like to be able to put your machine into hibernation while your plane takes off and lands. You look at the power options but do not see a hibernation tab. You determine that your laptop is not ACPI compliant. You visit the manufacturer's Web site and download the latest BIOS which is ACPI compliant. After installing it, Windows XP Professional will not start. What do you do?

Exam Questions: These questions reflect the kinds of multiple-choice questions that appear on the Microsoft exams. Use them to become familiar with the exam question formats and to help you determine what you know and what you need to review or study more.

Answers and Explanations: For each of the Review and Exam questions, you will find thorough explanations located at the end of the section.

Suggested Readings and Resources: The very last element in every chapter is a list of additional resources you can use if you want to go above and beyond certification-level material or if you need to spend more time on a particular subject that you are having trouble understanding.

Suggested Readings and Resources

1. *Microsoft Windows XP Inside Out* (Microsoft Press)

2. *Microsoft Windows 2000 Performance Tuning Technical Reference* (Microsoft Press)

3. *Microsoft SQL Server 2000 Performance Tuning Technical Reference* (Microsoft Press)

Introduction

MCSE Training Guide (70-270): Windows XP Professional is designed for technicians, system administrators, or other information technology professionals with the goal of obtaining certification as a Microsoft Certified Professional (MCP), Microsoft Certified System Administrator (MCSA), or Microsoft Certified Systems Engineer (MCSE). It covers the Installing, Configuring, and Administering Microsoft Windows XP Professional Exam (70-270). According to Microsoft, this exam measures your ability to implement, administer, and troubleshoot Windows XP Professional as a desktop operating system in a network environment.

This book is your one-stop shop. Everything you need to know to pass the exam is in here. You do not have to take a class in addition to buying this book to pass the exam. However, depending on your personal study habits or learning style, you might benefit from buying this book *and* taking a class.

Que Publishing training guides are meticulously crafted to give you the best possible learning experience for the particular characteristics of the technology covered in the actual certification exam. The instructional design that is implemented in the training guides reflects the task- and experience-based nature of Microsoft certification exams. The training guides provide you with the factual knowledge base you need for the exams, but then take it to the next level with case studies, step by steps, exercises, and exam questions that require you to engage in the analytical thinking needed to successfully answer the scenario-based questions found in the Microsoft exams.

Microsoft assumes that the typical candidate for this exam will have a minimum of one year's experience implementing and administering any desktop operating system in a network environment.

HOW THIS BOOK HELPS YOU

This book takes you on a self-guided tour of all the areas covered by the Installing, Configuring, and Administering Microsoft Windows XP Professional Exam and teaches you the specific skills you'll need to achieve your MCP, MCSA, or MCSE certification. You'll also find helpful hints, tips, real-world examples, and exercises, as well as references to additional study materials. Specifically, this book is set up to help you in the following ways:

◆ **Organization**—The book is organized by individual exam objectives. Every objective you need to know for the Installing, Configuring, and Administering Microsoft Windows XP Professional Exam is covered in this book. We have attempted to present the objectives in as close an order as possible to that listed by Microsoft. However, we have not hesitated to reorganize the objectives where needed to make the material as easy as possible for you to learn. We have also attempted to make the information accessible in the following ways:

  - The full list of exam units and objectives is included in this introduction.

  - Each chapter begins with a list of the objectives to be covered.

  - Each chapter also begins with an outline that provides an overview of the material and the page numbers where particular topics can be found.

  - The objectives are repeated where the material most directly relevant to it is covered (unless the whole chapter addresses a single objective).

◆ **Instructional features**—This book has been designed to provide you with multiple ways to learn and reinforce the exam material. Following are some of the helpful methods:

- *Objective Explanations.* As mentioned previously, each chapter begins with a list of the objectives covered in the chapter. In addition, immediately following each objective is an explanation in a context that defines it more meaningfully.

- *Study Strategies.* The beginning of the chapter also includes strategies for approaching the studying and retaining of the material in the chapter, not only particularly as it is addressed on the exam but also in ways that will benefit you on the job.

- *Exam Tips.* Exam tips appear in the margin to provide specific exam-related advice. Such tips may address what material is covered (or not covered) on the exam, how it is covered, mnemonic devices, or particular quirks of that exam.

- *Review Breaks and Summaries.* Crucial information is summarized at various points in the book in lists or tables. Each chapter also ends with a summary.

- *Key Terms.* A list of key terms appears at the end of each chapter.

- *Notes.* These appear in the margin and contain various kinds of useful or practical information, such as tips on technology or administrative practices, historical background on terms and technologies, or side commentary on industry issues.

- *Warnings.* When using sophisticated information technology, there is always the potential for mistakes or even catastrophes to occur because of improper application of the technology. Warnings appear in the margin to alert you to such potential problems.

- *In the Field.* These more extensive discussions cover material that might not be directly relevant to the exam but that is useful as reference material or in everyday practice. *In the Field* sidebars also can provide useful background or contextual information necessary for understanding the larger topic under consideration.

- *Case Studies.* Each chapter concludes with a case study. The cases are meant to help you understand the practical applications of the information covered in the chapter. They also help prepare you for the task-based analysis that is required when answering the Microsoft exam questions.

- *Step by Steps.* These are hands-on, tutorial instructions that walk you through a particular task or function relevant to the exam objectives.

- *Exercises.* Found at the end of the chapters in the "Apply Your Knowledge" section, exercises are performance-based opportunities for you to learn and assess your knowledge.

◆ **Extensive practice test options**—The book provides numerous opportunities for you to assess your knowledge and practice for the exam. The practice options include the following:

- *Review Questions.* These open-ended questions appear in the "Apply Your Knowledge" section at the end of each chapter. They allow you to quickly assess your comprehension of what you just read in the chapter. Answers to the questions are provided later in a separate section titled "Answers to Review Questions."

- *Exam Questions.* These questions also appear in the "Apply Your Knowledge" section. Use them to help you determine what you know and what you need to review or study further. Answers and explanations for them are provided in a separate section titled "Answers to Exam Questions."

- *Practice Exam.* A practice exam is included in the "Final Review" section. The "Final Review" section and the "Practice Exam" are discussed as follows:

◆ *PrepLogic.* The special Training Guide version of the *PrepLogic* software included on the CD-ROM provides further practice questions.

> **NOTE** For a description of the Que *PrepLogic, Preview Edition* software, please see Appendix D, "Using the *PrepLogic, Preview Edition* Software."

◆ **Final Review**—This part of the book provides you with three valuable tools for preparing for the exam.

- *Fast Facts.* This condensed version of the information contained in the book will prove extremely useful for last-minute review.

- *Study and Exam Tips.* Read this section early on to help you develop study strategies. It also provides you with valuable exam-day tips and information on exam/question formats such as adaptive tests and case study–based questions.

- *Practice Exam.* A practice test is included. Questions are written in styles similar to those used on the actual exam. Use it to assess your readiness for the real thing. Use the extensive answer explanations to improve your retention and understanding of the material.

The book includes several other features, such as a section titled "Suggested Reading and Resources" at the end of each chapter that directs you toward further information that could aid you in your exam preparation or your actual work. There are valuable appendixes as well, including a glossary (Appendix A), an overview of the Microsoft certification program (Appendix B), and a description of what is on the CD-ROM (Appendix C).

For more information about the exam or the certification process, in North America contact Microsoft at

Microsoft Education: 800-636-7544

`http://www.microsoft.com/traincert/`

`MCPHelp@microsoft.com`

WHAT THE INSTALLING, CONFIGURING, AND ADMINISTERING MICROSOFT WINDOWS XP PROFESSIONAL EXAM (70-270) COVERS

The Installing, Configuring, and Administering Microsoft Windows XP Professional Exam (70-270) covers the Windows XP Professional topics represented by the conceptual groupings or units of the test objectives. The objectives reflect job skills in the following areas:

◆ Installing Windows XP Professional

◆ Implementing and Conducting Administration of Resources

◆ Implementing, Managing, Monitoring, and Troubleshooting Hardware Devices and Drivers

◆ Monitoring and Optimizing System Performance and Reliability

◆ Configuring and Troubleshooting the Desktop Environment

◆ Implementing, Managing, and Troubleshooting Network Protocols and Services

◆ Configuring, Managing, and Troubleshooting Security

Before taking the exam, you should be proficient in the job skills represented by the following units, objectives, and subobjectives.

Installing Windows XP Professional

Perform an attended installation of Windows XP Professional.

Perform an unattended installation of Windows XP Professional.

◆ Install Windows XP Professional by using Windows XP Server Remote Installation Services (RIS).

◆ Install Windows XP Professional by using the System Preparation Tool.

◆ Create unattended answer files by using Setup Manager to automate the installation of Windows XP Professional.

Upgrade from a previous version of Windows to Windows XP Professional.

◆ Prepare a computer to meet upgrade requirements.

◆ Migrate existing user environments to a new installation.

Perform post-installation updates and product activation.

Troubleshoot failed installations.

Implementing and Conducting Administration of Resources

Monitor, manage, and troubleshoot access to files and folders.

◆ Configure, manage, and troubleshoot file compression.

◆ Control access to files and folders by using permissions.

◆ Optimize access to files and folders.

Manage and troubleshoot access to shared folders.

◆ Create and remove shared folders.

◆ Control access to shared folders by using permissions.

◆ Manage and troubleshoot Web server resources.

Connect to local and network print devices.

- ◆ Manage printers and print jobs.
- ◆ Control access to printers by using permissions.
- ◆ Connect to an Internet printer.
- ◆ Connect to a local print device.

Configure and manage file systems.

- ◆ Convert from one file system to another file system.
- ◆ Configure NTFS, FAT32, or FAT file systems.

Manage and troubleshoot access to and synchronization of offline files.

Implementing, Managing, Monitoring, and Troubleshooting Hardware Devices and Drivers

Implement, manage, and troubleshoot disk devices.

- ◆ Install, configure, and manage DVD and CD-ROM devices.
- ◆ Monitor and configure disks.
- ◆ Monitor, configure, and troubleshoot volumes.
- ◆ Monitor and configure removable media, such as tape devices.

Implement, manage, and troubleshoot display devices.

- ◆ Configure multiple-display support.
- ◆ Install, configure, and troubleshoot a video adapter.

Configure Advanced Configuration Power Interface (ACPI).

Implement, manage, and troubleshoot input/output (I/O) devices.

- ◆ Monitor, configure, and troubleshoot I/O devices, such as printers, scanners, multimedia devices, mouse, keyboard, and smart card readers.
- ◆ Monitor, configure, and troubleshoot multimedia hardware, such as cameras.
- ◆ Install, configure, and manage modems.
- ◆ Install, configure, and manage Infrared Data Association (IrDA) devices.
- ◆ Install, configure, and manage wireless devices.
- ◆ Install, configure, and manage USB devices.
- ◆ Install, configure, and manage handheld devices.
- ◆ Install, configure, and manage network adapters.

Manage and troubleshoot drivers and driver signing.

Monitor and configure multiprocessor units.

Monitoring and Optimizing System Performance and Reliability

Monitor, optimize, and troubleshoot performance of the Windows XP Professional desktop.

- ◆ Optimize and troubleshoot memory performance.
- ◆ Optimize and troubleshoot processor utilization.
- ◆ Optimize and troubleshoot disk performance.
- ◆ Optimize and troubleshoot application performance.
- ◆ Configure, manage, and troubleshoot Scheduled Tasks.

Manage, monitor, and optimize system performance for mobile users.

Restore and back up the operating system, system state data, and user data.

◆ Recover system state and user data by using Windows Backup.

◆ Troubleshoot system restoration by starting in safe mode.

◆ Recover system state and user data by using the Recovery Console.

Configuring and Troubleshooting the Desktop Environment

Configure and manage user profiles and desktop settings.

Configure support for multiple languages or multiple locations.

◆ Enable multiple-language support.

◆ Configure multiple-language support for users.

◆ Configure local settings.

◆ Configure Windows XP Professional for multiple locations.

Manage applications by using Windows Installer packages.

Configure and troubleshoot desktop settings.

Configure and troubleshoot accessibility services.

Implementing, Managing, and Troubleshooting Network Protocols and Services

Configure and troubleshoot the TCP/IP protocol.

Connect to computers by using dial-up networking.

◆ Connect to computers by using a virtual private network (VPN) connection.

◆ Create a dial-up connection to connect to a remote access server.

◆ Connect to the Internet by using dial-up networking.

◆ Configure and troubleshoot Internet Connection Sharing.

Connect to resources using Internet Explorer.

Configure, manage, and implement Internet Information Services (IIS).

Configure, manage, and troubleshoot remote desktop and remote assistance.

Configure, manage, and troubleshoot an Internet connection firewall.

Configuring, Managing, and Troubleshooting Security

Configure, manage, and troubleshoot Encrypting File System (EFS).

Configure, manage, and troubleshoot a security configuration and local security policy.

Configure, manage, and troubleshoot local user and group accounts.

♦ Configure, manage, and troubleshoot auditing.

♦ Configure, manage, and troubleshoot account settings.

♦ Configure, manage, and troubleshoot account policy.

♦ Configure and troubleshoot local users and groups.

♦ Configure, manage, and troubleshoot user and group rights.

♦ Troubleshoot cache credentials.

Configure, manage, and troubleshoot Internet Explorer security settings.

HARDWARE AND SOFTWARE YOU'LL NEED

As a self-paced study guide, *MCSE Training Guide (70-270): Windows XP Professional* is meant to help you understand concepts that must be refined through hands-on experience. To make the most of your studying, you need to have as much background on and experience with Windows XP Professional as possible. The best way to do this is to combine studying with work on Windows XP Professional. This section gives you a description of the minimum computer requirements you need to enjoy a solid practice environment.

You will find that many of the concepts presented in this book explore the use of Windows XP Professional within a Microsoft networked environment. To fully practice some of the exam objectives, you will need access to two (or more) computers networked together. You also will find that access to the Windows server products is beneficial. The following presents a detailed list of hardware and software requirements:

♦ Windows XP Professional (and optionally Windows 2000 Server or .NET Server)

♦ Windows 95/98 and/or Windows NT 4.0 Workstation (this software is required to test upgrade paths to Windows XP Professional)

♦ A server and a workstation computer on the Microsoft Hardware Compatibility List

♦ Pentium 233MHz (or better) (Pentium 300 recommended)

♦ A minimum 1.5GB of free disk space

♦ SuperVGA (800×600) or higher-resolution video adapter and monitor

♦ Mouse or equivalent pointing device

♦ CD-ROM or DVD drive

♦ Network Interface Card (NIC) or modem connection to the Internet

♦ Presence of an existing network, or use of a two-port (or more) miniport hub to create a test network

♦ 128MB of RAM or higher (64MB minimum)

It is easier to obtain access to the necessary computer hardware and software in a corporate business environment. It can be difficult, however, to allocate enough time within the busy workday to complete a self-study program. Most of your study time will occur after normal working hours, away from the everyday interruptions and pressures of your regular job.

ADVICE ON TAKING THE EXAM

More extensive tips are found in the Final Review section titled "Study and Exam Prep Tips," but keep this advice in mind as you study:

◆ **Read all the material**—Microsoft has been known to include material not expressly specified in the objectives. This book has included additional information not reflected in the objectives in an effort to give you the best possible preparation for the examination—and for the real-world experiences to come.

◆ **Do the Step by Steps and complete the exercises in each chapter**—They will help you gain experience using the specified methodology or approach. As noted previously, all Microsoft exams are task- and experienced-based and require you to have experience actually performing the tasks upon which you will be tested.

◆ **Use the questions to assess your knowledge**—Don't just read the chapter content; use the questions to find out what you know and what you don't. If you are struggling at all, study some more, review, and then assess your knowledge again.

◆ **Review the exam objectives**—Develop your own questions and examples for each topic listed. If you can develop and answer several questions for each topic, you should not find it difficult to pass the exam.

NOTE
Exam-Taking Advice Although this book is designed to prepare you to take and pass the Installing, Configuring, and Administering Microsoft Windows XP Professional certification exam, there are no guarantees. Read this book, work through the questions and exercises, and when you feel confident, take the Practice Exam and additional exams using the *PrepLogic, Preview Edition* test software. This should tell you whether you are ready for the real thing.

When taking the actual certification exam, be sure you answer all the questions before your time limit expires. Do not spend too much time on any one question. If you are unsure, answer it as best as you can; then mark it for review when you have finished the rest of the questions. However, this advice will not apply if you are taking an adaptive exam. In that case, take your time on each question. There is no opportunity to go back to a question.

Remember, the primary object is not to pass the exam—it is to understand the material. After you understand the material, passing the exam should be simple. Knowledge is a pyramid; to build upward, you need a solid foundation. This book and the Microsoft Certified Professional programs are designed to ensure that you have that solid foundation.

Good luck!

QUE CERTIFICATION PUBLISHING

The staff of Que Certification Publishing is committed to bringing you the very best in computer reference material. Each Que Certification book is the result of months of work by authors and staff who research and refine the information contained within its covers.

As part of this commitment to you, Que Certification invites your input. Please let us know whether you enjoy this book, whether you have trouble with the information or examples presented, or whether you have a suggestion for the next edition.

Please note, however, that Que Certification staff cannot serve as a technical resource during your preparation for the Microsoft certification exams or for questions about software- or hardware-related problems. Please refer instead to the documentation that accompanies the Microsoft products or to the applications' Help systems.

If you have a question or comment about any Que Certification book, there are several ways to contact Que Certification Publishing. We will respond to as many readers as we can. Your name, address, or phone number will never become part of a mailing list or be used for any purpose other than to help us continue to bring you the best books possible. You can write to us at the following address:

Que Certification Publishing
Attn: Executive Editor
201 W. 103rd Street
Indianapolis, IN 46290

If you prefer, you can fax Que Certification Publishing at 317-581-4663.

You also can send e-mail to Que Certification at the following Internet address:

certification@quepublishing.com

Thank you for selecting *MCSE Training Guide (70-270): Windows XP Professional.*

Exam Preparation

This chapter covers topics associated with installing Windows XP Professional. It helps you prepare for the exam by addressing the following exam objectives:

Perform an attended installation of Windows XP Professional.

▶ As a system support professional working with Windows XP, you will need to know how to install Windows XP. No matter how you install Windows XP, you will find that knowledge of the manual installation process will help you fully understand the installation process and how to troubleshoot a failed installation.

Perform an unattended installation of Windows XP Professional.

- **Install Windows XP Professional by using Remote Installation Services (RIS).**

- **Install Windows XP Professional by using the System Preparation Tool.**

- **Create unattended answer files by using Setup Manager to automate the installation of Windows XP Professional.**

▶ In most large environments, you will want to use automated tools to assist in the deployment of Windows XP. Microsoft has introduced a number of tools to speed up the deployment of Windows XP. These objectives ensure that support professionals understand all the options available for the deployment of Windows XP.

CHAPTER 1

Installing Windows XP Professional

OBJECTIVES

Upgrade from a previous version of Windows to Windows XP Professional.

- **Prepare a computer to meet upgrade requirements.**

- **Migrate existing user environments to a new installation.**

▶ It is very rare that you will be installing Windows XP in brand-new environments. In most situations, you will be installing Windows XP into existing environments and will be required to upgrade existing systems. This objective ensures you understand the issues associated with upgrading existing Windows 9x and Windows NT environments and user profiles to Windows XP.

Perform post-installation updates and product activation.

▶ One of the new requirements for Windows XP is activation, which binds the product key to the hardware. Understanding the activation process is key to understanding how to deploy Windows XP. Once installed, maintaining the installation requires that the appropriate software updates be applied in the form of service packs and hot fixes. Mastering this objective ensures that you can do more than just install the product—it also addresses your ability to maintain that installation.

Troubleshoot failed installations.

▶ Anyone installing a product should be able to troubleshoot problems when they pop up. This objective covers a number of common installation problems that you might encounter with Windows XP.

OUTLINE

STUDY STRATEGIES

▶ When studying the material for this unit, sit down and install Windows XP no fewer than five times. Although the installation process is not the most exciting process in the world, it is very structured. The more times you see it, the easier it will be to recognize the major phases of the installation process. No matter what type of installation you are performing (with the exception of disk imaging), you will always see the four phases of the installation process.

▶ After fully exploring manual (attended) installations of the Windows XP product, you should focus on automating the installation process. Do not try to get too fancy—simply use the Setup Manager to create an unattended text file and uniqueness database file and use Sysprep to prepare a system for cloning.

▶ Read about the RIS and Riprep processes but don't get caught up in the details. To fully understand these services, you need a solid background in Active Directory. This technology is covered in great detail on other exams. For the purposes of this exam, you need to understand only the technology required to support the RIS process—not details about how to implement all the options in every environment.

INTRODUCTION

This chapter covers the installation of Windows XP. The chapter starts with an overview of the Windows XP product line. During the discussion of the installation, a number of questions are presented so that you will be fully prepared to complete the installation of Windows XP. Topics include system requirements, disk configurations, file systems, licensing, and workgroup versus domain model. The installation process is also covered in detail so you will be able to identify the steps involved in installing Windows XP.

Automated installations of Windows XP are also covered in this chapter. We explore the use of unattended text files, Remote Installation Services, and the process of imaging a hard drive. At the end of the chapter, you will be able to identify the Windows XP technologies that assist in the automated installation of Windows XP.

The chapter ends with a discussion of the upgrade process for legacy Windows 9x, Windows NT, and Windows 2000 operating systems.

WINDOWS XP PRODUCT FAMILY

Windows XP represents the latest version of Microsoft's Windows NT technology. Before looking at the products that make up the Windows XP product family, it's important to understand a few of the key features that Windows XP inherits from its Windows NT roots. They are

◆ **Active Directory (AD) support**—With the release of Windows 2000, Microsoft released its new management framework for large networks. This framework, Active Directory, unified all the users and resources on an enterprise network into one hierarchy.

◆ **Symmetric Multi-Processing (SMP)**—SMP allows computers to be built with more than one processor that cooperatively shares processing responsibility. Each processor in an SMP system can run independently of the other, performing operating system or application tasks.

◆ **Kernel and Program Protection**—The architecture of Windows XP, like Windows NT and Windows 2000 before it, protects the operating system kernel from rogue programs. It also protects programs themselves from other rogue programs running on the same machine. This means that one poorly written application cannot, in most cases, cause a Windows XP machine to fail.

The Windows XP product line includes three versions of the product. This section briefly summarizes each of these products and the major differences among them.

◆ Windows XP Home Edition is Microsoft's attempt to move the home operating system market into alignment with the corporate operating system market. XP Home Edition is a replacement for Windows Millennium Edition.

◆ Windows XP Professional is the workstation operating system of choice in a corporate environment. Windows 9x and Windows NT 4.0 workstations must be replaced if companies are to fully utilize the features of a Windows 2000 Server-based network (software deployment, Group Policies, and Active Directory, to name a few).

◆ Windows XP 64-bit is a version of Windows XP Professional specifically designed and compiled for 64-bit processors. The features don't differ from Windows XP Professional. The key difference is a different set of optimizations designed to further improve performance on 64-bit processors.

Table 1.1 should help clarify the differences between Windows XP Home and Windows XP Professional.

What Product Is Right for Your Environment?   Expect questions on the exam that require you to identify the right product for a specific environment. To answer these questions, you must understand the environment that Microsoft intended for its use.

TABLE 1.1

WINDOWS XP PRODUCT DIFFERENCES

Feature	Windows XP Home	Windows XP Professional
Automated System Recovery	✓	✓
Domain Membership		✓
Encrypting File System		✓
Remote Desktop		✓
Remote Assistance	✓	✓
Symmetric Multi-Processing (SMP)	✓	✓

Unlike Windows 2000, Windows XP does not include the server line of products. Despite the fact that Windows XP and Microsoft's new .NET Servers run the same kernel, they are branded differently. In addition to being branded differently, the .NET Servers also have additional features and services not available in Windows XP Home Edition or Windows XP Professional.

BEFORE YOU BEGIN INSTALLATION

After you have determined the version of Windows XP you need to install, you must consider several options regarding its installation. Ensure that you have answers to the following questions before you begin your installation:

◆ Does your system meet the minimum hardware requirements?

◆ Have you determined the optimal disk partition configuration for your system?

◆ Which file system is appropriate for your environment?

◆ Which licensing mode should be used (for server installations)?

◆ Will you be installing your system into a workgroup or a domain?

The following sections provide an overview of these configuration options.

Hardware Requirements

Table 1.2 lists the minimum hardware requirements to install and operate Windows XP Professional.

TABLE 1.2

WINDOWS XP HOME EDITION OR PROFESSIONAL MINIMUM HARDWARE REQUIREMENTS

Component	Windows XP Requirements
Processor	233MHz or higher (300MHz recommended)
Memory	64MB (128MB recommended)
CD-ROM	CD-ROM or DVD drive
Free disk	1.5GB space
Display	SuperVGA (800×600)
Other	Keyboard and mouse

Before installing any of the Windows XP products, you should ensure that your hardware meets the preceding minimum standards.

Disk and Partition Options

Windows XP supports two types of disk storage, both of which use the same hard disks. The first, called *basic storage*, is one you will most likely be familiar with. The second was new to Windows 2000 and is called *dynamic storage*.

Basic storage is similar to disk partitioning found in the Windows 95/98 and Windows NT 4.0 environments. Basic storage consists of disks that contain primary partitions and extended partitions with logical drives. You can have up to four primary partitions, or up to three primary partitions and one extended partition per physical hard disk. You may not have more than one extended partition per physical hard disk.

NOTE

You Must Plan for Realistic System Requirements! You should note that these are simply the recommended minimum system requirements. You will find that significantly higher system requirements typically are required in a production environment. It is recommended that you fully evaluate the applications your system will be running to determine an accurate picture of their hardware requirements. After you have chosen an appropriate hardware platform, you will need to closely monitor it to ensure that you are getting the desired performance.

N O T E **Extending System and Boot Partitions**   Although all volumes can be extended, system and boot partitions are special to Windows XP, and you will not be allowed to extend them in the same way you would extend another disk. You can, however, use third-party tools to resize the partition.

N O T E **Dynamic Disks and the Installation Process**   You do not need to be an expert on Windows dynamic disks to understand the Windows XP installation process. It is discussed in this chapter only, so you don't limit your options when you install Windows XP.

If you partition your hard disks so that 1MB of unallocated space is not available on the end of your drive, you must repartition your hard disk to create the space. In short, if you ever think you might want to convert your disks to dynamic, be sure you leave the unpartitioned space at the end of your hard drive before you install Windows XP.

N O T E **Dynamic Disk and Windows 9x/Windows NT**   Dynamic disks are supported only on Windows 2000 and Windows XP. They are not supported on Windows 9x, Windows NT, or other operating systems. If you are dual-booting your system and you convert your disk from basic to dynamic, you will no longer be able to access the partitions (called *volumes* if converted to a dynamic disk) from operating systems other than Windows 2000 and Windows XP.

Dynamic storage consists of a disk that contains volumes rather than partitions. Although the distinctions between volumes and partitions might seem trivial, the exam is quite likely to ask you to identify whether a volume is associated with a dynamic disk or a basic disk. To create a dynamic disk, you must convert a basic disk into a dynamic disk. Dynamic storage offers the following advantages over basic storage:

- Volumes can be extended to include noncontiguous space on the available disks.

- There is no limit on the number of volumes you can create on a single disk.

- Disk configuration information is stored on the disk instead of in the Windows Registry. Configuration information is also replicated to all other dynamic disks so that one disk failure will not cause all dynamic storage to become unavailable.

Once converted to dynamic, a disk cannot be converted back to basic without removing all existing volumes from your disk. If you want to convert a basic disk into a dynamic disk, you must ensure that a minimum of 1MB of free (unallocated) space is available on your basic disks. This area is needed to track dynamic disk configuration information. Without it, the conversion process cannot proceed.

The advantages of dynamic disks are seen primarily in a server environment where fault-tolerant disk arrangements such as mirroring and RAID 5 are used. Although you're expected to know the difference for the exam, in practice you'll find little need to convert basic disks to dynamic disks on Windows XP Professional.

Managing Partitions on Basic Disks

Basic disks allow for a number of different partition configurations. A *partition* is an area of a physical hard disk that functions as though it were a separate unit. There is a limit of four partitions per physical disk.

A *primary partition* is a partition that can contain the files necessary to boot a particular operating system. A primary partition cannot be further subpartitioned. There can be up to four primary partitions per physical disk.

A primary partition is needed for a Windows XP system partition. The system partition is needed to load Windows XP (it contains NTLDR and NEDETECT.COM). Only a primary partition can be used for the system partition.

Windows XP also uses a boot partition. The boot partition contains the actual Windows XP operating system files. The system partition can be on the same partition but does not have to be.

You are limited to four partitions per physical disk. In some situations, however, you may require more partitions. To assist in breaking the four-partition limit, you have the capability to create an *extended partition.* Extended partitions are similar to primary partitions in that they define areas of space on a physical hard drive.

The main differences between primary partitions and extended partitions are as follows:

◆ There can be only one extended partition per physical hard disk.

◆ Extended partitions must be divided into logical drives.

◆ Logical drives cannot be configured as active (they cannot become a Windows XP system partition).

During installation, the Windows XP Setup program examines the hard disk to determine its existing configuration. The Setup program will allow you to create new partitions. Microsoft suggests that you create only one partition on which to install Windows XP. After Windows XP is installed and operational, you can use the Disk Management utility to manage disk configurations.

Microsoft recommends that you install Windows XP on a partition with a minimum of 2GB. As previously mentioned, Windows XP requires only 1.5GB of free disk space. As a practical matter, Windows NT didn't support boot partitions of more than 2GB. However, Windows 2000 and Windows XP allow you to create a boot partition that is as large as the hard disk—as long as the disk driver supports drives that large.

NOTE **Basic Disks Versus Dynamic Disks** A hard disk must be either basic or dynamic. You cannot combine the storage types on one disk.

NOTE **Reverting from Dynamic to Basic Disks** To change a dynamic disk back into a basic disk, you must delete all volumes from the dynamic disk. After you have done this then, through Disk Management, right-click the dynamic disk that you want to change back to a basic disk, and then click Convert to Basic Disk.

NOTE **System/Boot Partition Nomenclature** Windows NT/2000/XP's naming for the system and boot partition is opposite of what you might expect. The boot files are on the system partition and the system files (that is, \%SystemRoot%\SYSTEM32) are located on the boot partition. Confused yet? Just remember that the names for this are counterintuitive.

IN THE FIELD

BOOT PARTITION SIZE

In practice, it's best to create as large a boot partition as you can. This will allow for the inevitable growth of the Windows root directory that invariably happens as applications are installed.

Remember to leave 1MB of unpartitioned space at the end of the drive if you intend to convert the disk to a dynamic disk.

Windows XP File Systems

Before you decide which file system to use, you should understand the benefits and limitations of each file system. Changing a volume's existing file system can be time consuming, so choose the file system that best suits your long-term needs. If you decide to use a different file system, you must back up your data and then reformat the volume using the new file system, although you can convert a FAT or FAT32 volume to an NTFS volume without formatting the volume (like most disk operations, however, it is recommended that you back up your data before the conversion).

The following sections provide an overview of the differences between the FAT, FAT32, and NTFS file systems.

FAT

File Allocation Table (FAT) is a file system that has been around for a very long time and is currently supported by most operating systems on the market, at the expense of being limited to partition sizes no larger than 2GB.

The primary benefit of using FAT is that it is supported by Windows NT 3.5x/4.0, Windows 95/98/Me, Windows 3.x, and DOS. For this reason, FAT is a good "least common denominator," allowing you to make files available between Windows XP and older operating systems. The version of FAT supported by Windows XP has several additional features that are not supported by systems running DOS. When used under Windows XP, the FAT file system supports the following additional features:

◆ Long filenames up to 255 characters.

◆ Multiple spaces.

◆ Multiple periods.

◆ Filenames are not case sensitive but do preserve case.

For all the benefits of FAT, several of its major limitations should make you stop and think before it becomes the file system of choice on your Windows XP system.

The primary limitations of FAT are as follows:

◆ FAT is inefficient for larger partitions. FAT uses inefficient cluster sizes. A cluster is the smallest unit of storage on a partition. The larger the cluster size, the more wasted storage space there is in the FAT partition.

◆ FAT provides no security. The FAT file system does not support security, so there is no way to prevent a user from accessing a file if the user can log in to the computer.

◆ FAT does not support compression, encryption, remote storage, mount points, or disk quotas under Windows XP.

FAT32

The FAT32 file system is similar to FAT. FAT32 was introduced in the Microsoft product line with Windows 95 OSR 2. The primary difference between FAT and FAT32 is that FAT32 supports a smaller cluster size. Thus, it does not waste as much space with larger partitions. Like FAT, FAT32 supports long filenames, multiple spaces, multiple periods, and preserves case while not being case sensitive. It also has the same limitations in terms of not having a security mechanism and not being able to support compression, encryption, remote storage, mount points, or disk quotas.

Additionally, FAT32 is not supported on operating systems prior to Windows 95 OSR2. As a result, Windows NT, DOS, and some non-Windows operating systems will have trouble reading FAT32 partitions. If you're attempting to dual-boot with a very old operating system, you might not be able to use FAT32.

NTFS

NTFS is the file system of choice on most systems running Windows XP. In addition to the features supported by FAT and FAT32 running under Windows XP, it has the following benefits:

◆ **Recoverability**—NTFS is a recoverable file system. It uses transaction logging to automatically log all files and directory updates so that in the case of a system failure, the operating system can redo failed operations.

◆ **Security**—NTFS provides folder- and file-level security for protecting files.

◆ **Compression**—NTFS supports compression of files and folders to help save disk space.

◆ **Encryption**—NTFS supports file-level encryption. This enables a user to encrypt sensitive files so that no one else can read the files.

◆ **Disk quotas**—NTFS partitions support user-level disk quotas. This gives an administrator the ability to set an upper limit on the amount of space that a user can use on a partition. After the user reaches the limit, he or she is not allowed to store more information on the partition.

◆ **Sparse files**—These are very large files created by applications in such a way that only limited disk space is needed. NTFS allocates disk space only to the portions of a file that are written to.

◆ **Size**—NTFS partitions can support much larger partition sizes than FAT or FAT32. NFTS can support partitions up to 16 *exabytes* in size (this is equal to 16 billion gigabytes) .

Using NTFS gives you enhanced functionality and scalability when compared to either FAT or FAT32.

The main limitation of NTFS is that other operating systems do not support it, and it has high system overhead. If you need to dual-boot your system or have partitions less than 400MB in size, it is recommended you format the partition with FAT or FAT32.

> **NOTE**
>
> **NTFS Versions**   Windows 2000 and Windows XP use a more recent version of NTFS than the version that shipped with Windows NT 4. If you want to dual-boot between Windows 2000 or Windows XP and Windows NT, you must apply the latest service pack to Windows NT 4 before you install Windows 2000 or Windows XP.

Workgroup Versus Domain Models

During the installation of Windows XP, you must choose the type of network security group to which you want to belong. Your choices are between a domain model and a workgroup model. The following list quickly describes each model and the information required to join the security group:

File Systems and the Exam For the exam, you should look for reasons why you have to pick an operating system. If you need file-level security or encryption, you must use NTFS. If you need compatibility with other operating systems, you must choose FAT or FAT32 (depending upon the operating system).

◆ **Workgroup Model**—A workgroup is a logical grouping of computers created to assist in the organization of equipment. Under the workgroup model, each computer that is part of a workgroup maintains its own security database. Because security data is managed at each machine separately, the workgroup model is limited to small groupings of machines. To join a workgroup during the installation process, you need to know only the name of the workgroup.

◆ **Domain Model**—The domain model is similar to the workgroup model in that it creates logical groupings of computer equipment. The primary difference between the workgroup and domain models is that the domain model supports a centralized database of security information.

Joining a domain requires that the following be present:

• The Domain Name Service (DNS) name of the domain (for example, `Microsoft.com`).

• A computer account must exist for the computer you are installing. Before a computer can join a domain, a computer account must exist in the domain. Your network administrator, prior to the installation process, can create the computer account. You also can create the computer account during the installation process if you have authority to add domain computer accounts (see Chapter 7, "Implementing, Monitoring, and Troubleshooting Security," the sections titled "User Rights" and "Built-In Groups," for details on the rights required to create computer accounts).

• A domain controller and DNS server must be available on the network.

INSTALLING WINDOWS XP PROFESSIONAL—AN OVERVIEW

After you have planned your Windows XP installation, you can start the installation process. This section provides an overview of the installation process and emphasizes the configuration information required during each phase of the installation.

The Windows XP installation process is broken into the following phases:

1. Running the setup program

2. Completing the Setup Wizard

3. Installing network components

4. Completing the installation

Phase 1—Running the Setup Program

To begin the Windows XP installation, you will need to start your computer and access the Windows XP installation files. Three ways to start the installation process are as follows:

◆ Boot the system, load the appropriate drivers to access the CD-ROM, and load the setup program from the command prompt by executing the WINNT32.EXE command.

◆ If your computer supports booting from the CD-ROM, you can boot the system from the CD-ROM with the Windows XP CD in the drive. This will cause the setup program to run automatically.

◆ You also can create a network client and attach to the installation files over the network.

The first phase of the installation process is often referred to as the "text-mode" portion of the installation. During this portion of the install, you are asked for the basic installation information. This information is required to prepare the installation partition and copy required installation files to the hard disk.

The text-mode setup process for a new system completes the following steps:

1. Setup loads a minimal version of Windows XP into memory.

2. The text-mode portion of setup starts.

3. You will be prompted to load third-party RAID/SCSI drivers. To load drivers, press F6.

4. You are asked to agree to the licensing agreement. To agree, press F8.

5. The setup program prompts you to select a boot partition for this installation of Windows XP (the boot partition is where Windows XP is run from).

6. The setup program prompts you for the file system you would like for the partition. Whether you select an existing partition or a new partition, you're asked how you want to format the partition. You're offered both quick and "thorough" formatting options for both FAT and NTFS. The thorough option tests every sector on the hard disk. If you selected an existing partition, you're given the option of leaving the file system alone (intact). If the existing partition you selected is FAT, you're given the option to upgrade it to NTFS.

7. Setup copies files to the hard disk and saves configuration information.

8. Setup restarts the computer and then starts the Graphical User Interface (GUI) portion of the installation.

> **N O T E**   **Deleting Existing Partitions**   If you booted from the CD, you'll be able to delete all partitions and start from scratch. If you booted by running WINNT on the local system, you will not be allowed to delete the system partition. If you need to delete the existing partitions, you should boot from the CD.

Phase 2—Completing the Setup Wizard

After the text-mode installation has restarted your computer, the GUI-mode installation begins. This is where a large number of configuration options are specified.

After the setup program has installed Windows XP security features and detects hardware devices, the Setup Wizard prompts you for the following information:

◆ Regional settings

◆ Name and organization

◆ Product key

◆ Computer name and password for the local Administrator account

◆ Time, date, and time zone

Phase 3—Installing Networking Components

This phase of the install process guides you through the configuration of the Windows XP networking components. During this portion of the installation, the following occurs:

1. Setup detects your network adapter. If setup cannot detect your adapter, you must provide the appropriate drivers on disk. After configuring your network adapter, Windows XP will attempt to locate a DHCP server on the network.

2. Setup then prompts you to choose to install networking components with typical or custom settings. The typical installation includes the following options:

    • Client for Microsoft Networks

    • File and Print Sharing for Microsoft Networks

    • TCP/IP

    • QoS Packet Scheduler

3. Setup prompts you to join a workgroup or a domain.

4. Setup installs and configures the Windows XP components that you specified.

After installing the networking components, the setup program moves to the final phase of installation.

Phase 4—Completing the Installation

The final phase of installation completes the following:

- ◆ Copies remaining files to your system

- ◆ Applies the configuration you selected

- ◆ Saves your configuration to the local hard disk

- ◆ Removes temporary files

- ◆ Restarts the computer

If you elected to join a domain, as soon as the system restarts, the Network Identification Wizard runs. This wizard asks whether you are the only user who will be accessing this system or can other users access it as well. You should avoid selecting that you are the only user, unless you want to enable automatic logon. If you indicate that you are the only user, you are assigned administrative privileges on the local machine.

INSTALLING WINDOWS XP PROFESSIONAL MANUALLY

Perform an attended installation of Windows XP Professional.

The next two sections focus on how a technician would install Windows XP Professional at the computer rather than remotely or through an automated process. Two methods are available: installation from a CD or from a network.

Installing from a Local CD

Installing from a local CD-ROM is one of the easiest ways to install Windows XP. This option makes sense, however, only if you are installing a small number of computers or doing a nonstandard configuration, because it is time consuming. You can install Windows XP Professional by booting from the CD-ROM or by inserting the CD-ROM into a system that is already running a previous version of Windows.

NOTE

Deleting the Boot Partition   You cannot delete the boot partition when running WINNT or WINNT32. If you want to do a new installation and want to repartition the hard drive during the process, you must boot from the CD.

EXAM TIP

Command Switches and the Exam
You will need to remember the command switches associated with both the WINNT and WINNT32 setup programs.

If you booted from a Windows XP installation CD, the setup program will automatically run. Alternatively, you will have to run the setup program manually. Depending on the operating system you use to boot the computer, you will run either WINNT.EXE or WINNT32.EXE.

If you are using DOS to access your CD-ROM, you will run WINNT.EXE to start the setup process. If you are installing Windows XP over Windows 95/98/Me, Windows NT, or Windows 2000 (either performing an upgrade or new installation), you will run WINNT32.EXE to start the setup process.

Both WINNT and WINNT32 support a number of command switches that allow for customization of the installation process. Table 1.3 presents the command switches associated with WINNT. Table 1.4 presents the command switches associated with WINNT32. To use a switch, type the command followed by a space followed by the switch.

TABLE 1.3

WINNT.EXE COMMAND SWITCHES

Switch	Description
/a	Enables accessibility options.
/e:command	Executes a command before the final phase of setup. The command is run without a profile loaded, so only applications that update the all users profile and not the local user profile will install correctly.
/i:inf_file	Specifies the filename of the setup information file. The default is Dosnet.inf. A setup information file is used to automate the installation.
/r:folder	Specifies an optional folder to be installed. The folder will be installed under %systemroot%.
/rx:folder	Specifies an optional folder to be copied. The files are deleted after installation.
/s:source_path	Specifies the location of the Windows XP installation files.
/t:temp_drive	Specifies the location where temporary files should be copied during installation.
/u:script_file	Specifies an unattended text file (this will be discussed in greater detail in upcoming sections).
/udf:id, [file]	Used in conjunction with an unattended text file (to be discussed in greater detail in upcoming sections).

TABLE 1.4

WINNT32.EXE COMMAND SWITCHES

Switch	Description
/copydir:*folder*	This option creates an additional folder with the systemroot. For example, if the source folder contains a folder called `Private_drivers` that has modifications just for your site, you can type **/copydir:Private_drivers** to have setup copy that folder to your installed Windows XP folder. The new folder location would be `%SystemRoot%\Private_drivers`. You can use `/copydir` to create as many additional folders as you want.
/copysource: *folder name*	Creates an additional folder within the systemroot (just like the copydir option). `setup` deletes the files after the installation is complete.
/cmd:*command*	Executes a command before the final stage of setup.
/cmdcons	Copies additional files to the hard disk that are necessary to load a command-line interface for repair and recovery.
/debug *level:file*	Creates a debug log at a specified level.
/s:*source_path*	Specifies the location of the Windows XP installation files. You can specify multiple paths to speed up the installation process.
/syspart:*drive*	Copies setup startup files to a hard disk and marks the drive as active. This allows you to move the hard disk to another computer to complete the installation. You must use the `/tempdrive` option with this switch.
/tempdrive:*drive*	Specifies the location where temporary files should be placed.
/checkupgradeonly	Checks your computer for upgrade compatibility with Windows XP. For Windows 95 or Windows 98 upgrades, setup creates a report named `Upgrade.txt` in the Windows installation folder. For Windows NT 3.51, Windows NT 4.0, or Windows 2000 upgrades, it saves the report to the `Winnt32.log` in the installation folder.

continues

TABLE 1.4	*continued*

WINNT32.EXE COMMAND SWITCHES

Switch	*Description*
/makelocalsource	Instructs setup to copy all installation source files to your local hard disk. Use /makelocalsource when installing from a CD to provide installation files when the CD is not available later in the installation.
/unattend[num]:*file*	Specifies an unattended text file (to be discussed in greater detail in upcoming sections). num represents the number of seconds to wait before reboot after the file copy.
/Udf:*id, [udf_file]*	Used in conjunction with an unattended text file (to be discussed in greater detail in upcoming sections) .
/dudisable	Prevents Dynamic Update from running. Dynamic Update automatically tries to update the setup software before running the setup. This will prevent setup from attempting to contact Dynamic Update and get updated setup files.
/duprepare:pathname	Causes setup to download the dynamic updates to setup into the directory specified by pathname. This is useful when you are about to do a large number of setups and want to pre-download the updated setup files.
/dushare:pathname	Identifies the location where you have previously downloaded Dynamic Update files. When run on a client, specifies that the client installation will use the updated files on the share specified in pathname.
/m:folder_name	Indicates the location of replacement installation files. Setup will look first to this folder and then to the source folder.
/makelocalsource	Copies all files to the boot disk so that setup can continue to run if the CD is not available after rebooting.
/noreboot	Setup won't reboot after copying files so that you can run additional commands.
/unattend	Upgrades a previous version of Windows and accepts all existing settings without prompting.

NOTE

Boot Disks   Windows NT users will notice that the /b option is no longer supported by WINNT or WINNT32. Boot disks are no longer supported. You cannot make boot disks for Windows XP.

Installing over a Network

In environments where you are installing a large number of systems, you will find that installing over the network is preferred to local CD-based installations. Generally, installing over the network is easier to manage and is much faster than CDs.

To install Windows XP over a network, run the setup program from a shared network folder. The setup program copies the required file to the local system, and then starts the installation process. This process is similar to the CD-based installation but has the following additional requirements:

◆ A distribution server with a copy of Windows XP installation files must be available.

◆ You must have network client software so that client computers can attach to the distribution server.

◆ Client computers must have an existing 1.5GB partition (at least 2GB is highly recommended). This partition is required so the installation files can be copied from the distribution server to the client before installation starts.

After you meet these requirements, you will be able to start a networked installation of Windows XP. Step by Step 1.1 shows you how to do just that.

STEP BY STEP

1.1 Networked Installation of Windows XP

1. Start the local computer and initialize the client network software.

2. Connect to the distribution server.

3. Run `WINNT.EXE` or `WINNT32.EXE` (and any command switches you require) to start the setup program. A temporary folder called `$Win_nt$.~ls` will be created. This folder contains the temporary installation files required to install Windows XP.

4. Setup will restart the computer. Upon reboot, Phase 1 of the installation will begin.

AUTOMATING THE INSTALLATION PROCESS

Perform an unattended installation of Windows XP Professional.

In addition to manual installation, Windows XP offers you three automated or unattended methods: scripting, Remote Installation Services (RIS), and imaging (often called *cloning*).

In most large deployments of Windows XP, it would be impractical to install each workstation using the traditional CD-based installation. Instead, Microsoft has tools that leverage the fact that most systems can be installed using standardized configurations. Using Windows XP deployment tools such as RIS, deployments will be automated so that the only user intervention the installations will require is to turn the computer on. Some computers might require a key press to boot from the network, although some will not.

Because of the power that these new deployment tools offer and the importance of this technology to companies planning large installations of Windows XP Professional, it is essential that you are able to analyze deployment scenarios to determine the most effective tool to get the job done.

Creating Unattended Installation Files

Although the computers on most networks are not identical, they usually have several similarities. It is possible to create a script file that will automate the installation process so that little or no user intervention is required during the installation process.

Using setup scripts offers a number of benefits for most deployments. The following list includes some of these benefits:

- ◆ Little or no user intervention is required, so the chance of human error is reduced.

- ◆ You can be assured that all machines installed have consistent and correct configurations.

- ◆ Staff with little or no knowledge of Windows XP can complete installations.

Files Used for Unattended Installation

Two different files are used during an unattended installation. The first file is called an *unattended text file* (also referred to as an *answer file*). This file contains all the information necessary to install Windows XP. The second file is called a *uniqueness definition file (UDF)*. Most large-scale deployments have a standard configuration that will be applied to each system. There will always be, however, a number of settings that must be unique to each machine (the computer name, for example). The unattended text file is used to configure all the standard options for each machine (one file for each type of hardware platform in your environment); the UDF file is used to configure the unique aspects of each individual computer.

The UDF file is optional. You can create a unique unattended text file for each computer in your environment. In most situations, however, this solution is impractical because the management of the unattended text files becomes difficult. Most organizations will assess the operational requirements of each computer being installed and categorize them into major groupings. An unattended text file would then be created for each category of system. A UDF file would also be needed so that the unique configuration options for each individual computer, within each category, could be included in the installation process.

Both the answer and UDF files can be created using the Windows XP Setup Manager or using a simple text editor. The Setup Manager is available in the \Support\tools folder on the Windows XP distribution CDs. Open the DEPLOY.CAB file and copy the files to a directory. The Setup Manager program is SETUPMGR.EXE.

The Setup Manager allows you to do the following:

◆ Create answer and UDF files using an easy-to-use graphical interface.

◆ Specify computer-specific or user-specific information.

◆ Include application setup scripts in the answer files.

◆ Create answer files (winnt.sif) that can be used if booting from the installation CD.

◆ Automatically create a networked distribution folder for the installation files.

> **NOTE**
>
> **Manual Version Setup Manager Scripts**   Although it is possible to create scripts from scratch using a text editor, it is recommended that the Setup Manager be used. The Setup Manager is less prone to errors and can be used to create unattended text files that can be used with the remote installation server.

In the next two sections, we will explore the contents of an unattended text file and a UDF file, and the Setup Manager.

Creating an Unattended Text File

Using an unattended text file allows the administrator to start the installation of Windows XP and walk away. The installation process reads the unattended text file and uses the information contained within it to configure the system.

To install Windows XP using an unattended text file, use the /u switch after the WINNT, or WINNT32 command. The syntax of this command is as follows:

```
WINNT /u:answer file /s:source path where the
   Windows XP installation files can be found
```

or

```
WINNT32 /unattend:answer file /s:source path where the Win-
dows
   XP installation files can be found
```

where

◆ /u or /unattend is the switch specifying that this is an unattended installation.

◆ *answer file* is the name of the answer file that you have created (the default name is Unattend.txt).

◆ /s is the switch to point to the location of the Windows XP installation files.

◆ *source path* is the location of the Windows XP installation files (the I386 directory for an Intel installation).

The main purpose of the unattended text file is to answer all the prompts that the person performing the installation would manually enter during the installation. You can use the same unattended text file across several computers. If you use the same unattended text file in this way, however, you will need to revisit each computer after the installation is complete to configure unique aspects of each computer (unless a Uniqueness Database File [UDF] is used—more on this later).

EXAM TIP

Command Syntax Matters You are sure to get a question regarding the parameters to use with WINNT or WINNT32 to run an unattended text file. If you can memorize the syntax, these are easy marks.

Following is a sample unattended text file (you can find a copy of this file on the Windows XP CD in the I386 directory). This file can be opened using any text editor. The information found in `Unattended.txt` is categorized into section headings, parameters, and values associated with those parameters. The sample file contains a fraction of the total number of section headings and parameters supported during unattended installations. At the time of this writing, Microsoft had not yet made available a document that details the unattended options for Windows XP; however, it can be assumed that the options will be virtually identical to those for Windows 2000. You can find more about the Windows 2000 options by searching TechNet for "Microsoft Windows 2000 Guide to Unattended Setup" (`http://www.microsoft.com/TechNet/win2000/win2ksrv/technote/unattend.asp).Microsoft`).

As you review this file, note that information is organized in the following format:

```
[Section Heading]
; Comments
; Comments
Parameter = value
```

The file contents are listed here:

```
; Microsoft Windows Codename Whistler Personal, Profes-
sional,
; Server, Advanced Server and Datacenter
; (c) 1994—2000 Microsoft Corporation. All rights
reserved.
;
; Sample Unattended Setup Answer File
;
; This file contains information about how to automate the
installation
; or upgrade of Windows Codename Whistler so the
; Setup program runs without requiring user input.
;

[Unattended]
Unattendmode = FullUnattended
OemPreinstall = NO
TargetPath = *
Filesystem = LeaveAlone
```

```
[UserData]
FullName = "Your User Name"
OrgName = "Your Organization Name"
ComputerName = *
ProductKey= "JJWKH-7M9R8-26VM4-FX8CC-GDPD8"


[GuiUnattended]
; Sets the Timezone to the Pacific Northwest
; Sets the Admin Password to NULL
; Turn AutoLogon ON and login once
TimeZone = "004"
AdminPassword = *
AutoLogon = Yes
AutoLogonCount = 1


[LicenseFilePrintData]
; For Server installs
AutoMode = "PerServer"
AutoUsers = "5"


[GuiRunOnce]
; List the programs that you want to launch when the
; machine is logged into for the first time


[Display]
BitsPerPel = 8
XResolution = 800
YResolution = 600
VRefresh = 70


[Networking]


[Identification]
JoinWorkgroup = Workgroup
```

Information in the `Unattended.txt` file is divided into main sections. Table 1.5 provides explanations of the section headings and parameters found in a typical `Unattended.txt` file.

TABLE 1.5

SECTION HEADINGS AND PARAMETERS IN A TYPICAL UNATTENDED TEXT FILE

Section Heading	Option (Values)	Description
Unattended This section header is used to identify whether an unattended installation is being performed. This section is required in an Unattend.txt file; otherwise, the answer file will be ignored.	UnattendMode (Values: GuiAttended / ProvideDefault / DefaultHide / Readonly / FullUnattended)	This parameter defines the unattended mode to be used during GUI-mode setup. The default value is DefaultHide when the key is not specified. When this key is specified, text-mode setup is fully automated with or without the necessary answers. GuiAttended specifies that the GUI-mode section of setup is attended. When specified, the end user will be required to answer all questions in the GUI-mode portion of setup before setup completes. This mode is useful in preinstallation scenarios in which the OEM or administrator wants to automate only text-mode setup. ProvideDefault specifies that answers in the answer file are defaults. In this case, setup will display these default answers to the user, who may change them if desired. This is useful in preinstallation scenarios where the OEM or administrator wants to give persons setting up the machine the option to change the predefined default answers (especially network options).

continues

TABLE 1.5   *continued*

**SECTION HEADINGS AND PARAMETERS IN A TYPICAL
UNATTENDED TEXT FILE**

Section Heading	Option (Values)	Description
		`DefaultHide` specifies that answers in the answer file are defaults. Unlike the `ProvideDefault` value, setup will not display the user interface to end users if all the answers relating to a particular wizard page are specified in the answer file. If only subsets of the answers on a page are specified, the page will be displayed with the provided answers. The user will be able to modify any of the answers on the displayed page. This is useful in deployment scenarios where an administrator may only want end users to provide the administrator password on the computer. This is the default behavior if unattended mode is not specified.
		`ReadOnly` specifies that answers in the answer file are read-only if the wizard pages containing these answers are displayed to the end user. Just like the `DefaultHide` parameter, no user interface is displayed to the user if all answers on a page are

Section Heading	*Option (Values)*	*Description*
		supplied in the answer file. Unlike the `DefaultHide` parameter, however, the user can only specify new answers on a displayed page. This is useful in scenarios where an administrator wants to force specific answers on a page. `FullUnattended` specifies that GUI mode is fully unattended. If a required setup answer is not specified in the answer file, an error will be generated. This is useful in deployment scenarios where a complete hands-off installation is required and an unspecified answer is an error in the answer file.
	Repartition (Value: Yes/No)	Specifies whether all partitions on the first drive on the client computer should be deleted and the drive reformatted with the NTFS file system.
	FileSystem (Value: ConvertNTFS/ LeaveAlone)	This key specifies whether the primary partition should be converted to NTFS or left alone.
	NtUpgrade	This key determines whether a previous

continues

TABLE 1.5	*continued*

SECTION HEADINGS AND PARAMETERS IN A TYPICAL UNATTENDED TEXT FILE

Section Heading	*Option (Values)*	*Description*
	(Value: Yes/No)	version of Windows 2000 Professional or Server, Windows 2000 Advanced Server, or Windows 2000 Datacenter Server should be upgraded.
	Win9xUpgrade (Values: Yes/No)	The Win9xUpgrade key determines whether previous installations of Windows 95 or Windows 98 should be upgraded to Windows XP. Yes indicates that the Windows installation should be upgraded, and No means do not upgrade the installation if found. The default is No. This parameter is necessary only when using an answer file to upgrade an existing Windows 9x computer to Windows XP. It is valid only if used in conjunction with the Winnt32.exe.
	TargetPath (Values: * or *<path name>*)	This key determines the installation folder in which Windows XP should be installed. * indicates that setup should generate a unique folder name for the installation. This is usually WINDOWS, unless that folder already exists. In that case, setup will install into WINDOWS.*x* (where X is between 0 to 999) if that folder does not already exist.

Section Heading	*Option (Values)*	*Description*
		`<path name>` is the user-defined install folder and should not include the drive letter. To specify the target drive, the `/tempdrive` command-line option to `Winnt32.exe` or `/t` option to Winnt.exe must be specified.
UserData This section is used to specify user-specific data into the installation process—specifically the user's name, organization, computer name, and product ID.	`FullName` (Value: `<string>`)	The `FullName` key is used to specify the user's full name. If the key is empty or missing, the user is prompted to enter a name.
	`OrgName` (Value: `<string>`)	This key is used to specify an organization's name. If the `OrgName` key is empty or missing, the user is prompted to enter an organization name.
	`ComputerName` (Value: `<string>`)	This key is used to specify the computer name. If the `ComputerName` key is empty or missing, the user is prompted to enter a computer name. If the value is `*`, setup generates a random computer name based on the organization name specified.

continues

TABLE 1.5	*continued*

SECTION HEADINGS AND PARAMETERS IN A TYPICAL UNATTENDED TEXT FILE

Section Heading	*Option (Values)*	*Description*
		The computer name specified should contain no more than 64 characters. If more than 64 characters are used for the `ComputerName` parameter, the computer name will be truncated to 64 characters. You will want to use names of 15 characters or less if you have Windows 95/98/Me or Windows NT systems in your environment.
	ProductID (Value: `<string>`)	The `ProductID` key specifies the Microsoft product identification (Product ID) number. This parameter sets the Product ID for all computers installed using this unattended text file to the same value. This could cause issues when calling Microsoft product support.
GuiUnattended This section is used to specify the settings for the GUI portion of the installation. It can be used to indicate the time zone and to hide the administrator password page.	AdminPassword (Value: `<password>`/`*`)	This key sets up the administrator account password. If the value is *, setup will set the Administrator password to NULL.

Section Heading	Option (Values)	Description
	AutoLogon (Value: Yes/No)	This key, if set to Yes, sets up the computer to auto-logon once with the Administrator account. The default behavior is No. The key is not valid on upgrades. If you specify an AdminPassword, that password will be used to perform the auto-logon process. The password will be deleted from the copy of the answer file left on the computer after the installation is complete.
	AutoLogonCount (Value: <integer>)	This key lists the number of times that the computer should automatically log on using the administrator account and password specified. The value is decremented after each logon and the feature is disabled after the specified number of logon attempts is complete. It is useful only when Autologon = Yes. A reboot is required to decrement the counter.
	TimeZone (Value: <index>)	The TimeZone key determines the time zone of the computer. If the key is empty, the user is prompted to select a time zone.

continues

TABLE 1.5	*continued*

SECTION HEADINGS AND PARAMETERS IN A TYPICAL UNATTENDED TEXT FILE

Section Heading	Option (Values)	Description
	`ProfilesDir` (Value: `<path to profile directory>` Default: `%systemdrive%\ Documents and Settings`)	The `ProfilesDir` key is used to specify the location of Windows XP profiles. This parameter is valid only on clean installs of Windows XP, and it is ignored on upgrades. The `ProfilesDir` parameter is useful in scenarios that require new installations to use the same profile directory as Windows NT 4.0. For example, `ProfilesDir = %systemroot%\Profiles`. The directory specified must contain an environment variable such as `%systemdrive%` or `%systemroot%`.
	`DetachedProgram` (Value: `<detached program string>`)	The `DetachedProgram` key is used to indicate the path of the custom program that should run concurrently with the setup program. If the program requires any arguments, the `Arguments` key must be specified.
	`Arguments` (Value: `<arguments string>`)	The `Arguments` key indicates that arguments or parameters accompany the custom program that should run concurrently with the setup program.

Section Heading	*Option (Values)*	*Description*
		If `AutoMode` is empty or missing, the user will be prompted to select the license mode.
	AutoUsers (Value: *integer*)	This key is valid only if `AutoMode` = `PerServer`. The integer value indicates the number of client licenses purchased for the server being installed. The minimum value allowed is 5 (less than 5 will cause the install to fail).
GuiRunOnce This section specifies a command you want run when the installation completes for the first time and the computer is rebooted. This is useful if you want to install additional software on the computer after the operating system is installed.		
Display This section allows you to specify the display settings you want applied.	BitsPerPixel (Value: <valid bits per pixel>)	This key specifies the `<valid bits per pixel>` for the graphics device being installed. For example, a value of 8 (2^8) infers 256 colors; 16 infers 65,536 to the system. colors.

continues

TABLE 1.5   *continued*

SECTION HEADINGS AND PARAMETERS IN A TYPICAL UNATTENDED TEXT FILE

Section Heading	Option (Values)	Description
	Xresolution (Value: <valid x resolution>)	This key specifies a <valid x resolution> for the graphics device being installed.
	Yresolution (Value: <valid y resolution>)	This key specifies a <valid y resolution> for the graphics device being installed.
	Vrefresh (Value: <valid refresh rate>)	This key specifies a <valid refresh rate> for the graphics device being installed. Be very careful with these settings. An improperly configured refresh rate can damage your monitor.
Networking This section is used to specify network settings such as network adapters, services, and protocols. If this section is not provided, networking will not be installed.	InstallDefault Components (Value: Yes | No Default: No)	When set to Yes, setup will install default networking components. The default networking configuration automatically installs the following: TCP/IP on all network adapters, File and Printer Sharing for Microsoft Networks, and Client for Microsoft Networks.

Creating Uniqueness Database Files

UDF files allow you to specify the unique settings associated with each computer in your environment. As shown in the previous section, UDF files can be created using the Setup Manager. You may, however, want to modify your UDF file to include additional configuration settings (above and beyond unique computer names).

UDF files contain two sections. One section of the file, indicated by the [UniqueIds] header, contains a listing of all unique IDs referenced in the file and the sections associated with them. The second part of the file contains the actual sections that are to be used by each computer when it is installed.

When a UDF file is used in conjunction with an answer file, any configuration setting associated with a unique ID is merged with the contents of the answer file.

The following is a listing of a standard UDF file:

```
;SetupMgrTag
[UniqueIds]
   Workstation1=UserData, Network
   Workstation2=UserData
   Workstation3=UserData
   Workstation4=UserData

[Workstation1:UserData]
   ComputerName=Workstation1

[Workstation2:UserData]
   ComputerName=Workstation2

[Workstation3:UserData]
   ComputerName=Workstation3

[Workstation4:UserData]
   ComputerName=Workstation4

[Workstation1:Network]
   JoinDomain="DomainName"
```

Note the top header of this file. This UDF file is set up to configure four computers (Workstation1; Workstation2; Workstation3; and Workstation4). We see this from the [UniqueIds] section of the file. We also can see that Workstation1 will have a UserData and Network configuration stored in this file. Workstation2 through Workstation4 have UserData configurations stored. In this example, Workstation1 has a custom network configuration. Workstation2 through Workstation4 would receive the network configuration specified in the unattended answer file.

Using the Setup Manager

The Setup Manager is a powerful tool that assists in the creation of unattended answer and UDF files. The utility can be installed by extracting the files from the DEPLOY.CAB file in the \Support\Tools directory on the Windows XP installation CDs.

Once installed, performing the steps in Step by Step 1.2 will run the Setup Manager.

FIGURE 1.1
Windows XP Setup Manager Wizard welcome screen.

FIGURE 1.2
Setup Manager—New or Existing Answer File Options.

STEP BY STEP

1.2 Running the Setup Manager

1. Run Setupmgr.exe from the folder you extracted the Setup Manager in.

2. In the Welcome to the Windows XP Setup Manager Wizard window, click Next (as shown in Figure 1.1).

3. The New or Existing Answer File window will then be presented (see Figure 1.2). Your options are as follows:

    -   **Create a New Answer File**—This option will allow you to create a new answer file based on the information you supply. Use this option when you want to create a new answer file.

    -   **Modify an Existing Answer File**—This option allows you to select an existing answer file so it can be edited. Use this option if you want to edit an existing configuration file.

Depending on the option you select, the Setup Wizard will walk you through the process of creating or editing an unattended text file.

Table 1.6 presents the major categories of information requested by the Setup Manager during the creation of a new answer file.

TABLE 1.6		
WINDOWS XP SETUP WIZARD CONFIGURATION OPTIONS		
Information Category	*Options*	*Description*
Product to Install (see Figure 1.3)	Windows Unattended Installation	Allows for the creation of an answer file for the installation of Windows XP (Home or Professional).
	Sysprep Install	Allows for the creation of an answer file that can be used by the Sysprep mini installer program (see the section "The System Preparation (Sysprep) Tool" for details).
	RIS	Allows for the creation of an answer file for use with a Remote Installation Server.
Platform (see Figure 1.4)	Windows XP Home Edition	Allows for the creation of an answer file for the installation of Windows XP Home Edition.
	Windows XP Professional	Allows for the creation of an answer file for the installation of Windows XP Professional.
	Windows 2002 Server, Advanced Server, or Data Center	Allows for the creation of an answer file for the installation of .NET Servers.
User Interaction Level (see Figure 1.5)	Provide Defaults	Display all setup pages to the user for review. Setup uses the values contained in the answer file as defaults but will allow the user to change to values.
	Fully Automated	Prevents all user intervention. You will create an answer file with all configuration options configured—the user is not allowed to modify these settings.
	Hide Pages	Displays configuration pages that are missing values. The user can change any value presented but only pages with missing configuration values are presented.

continues

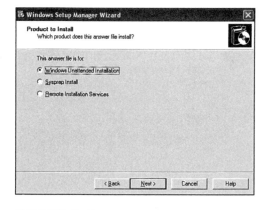

FIGURE 1.3
Setup Manager—Product to Install.

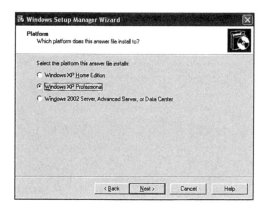

FIGURE 1.4
Setup Manager—Platform Installation Options.

FIGURE 1.5
Setup Manager—User Interaction Level.

FIGURE 1.6
Setup Manager—Distribution Folder.

FIGURE 1.7
Setup Manager—Customize the Software
Options.

| TABLE 1.6 | *continued* |

WINDOWS XP SETUP WIZARD CONFIGURATION OPTIONS

Information Category	*Options*	*Description*
	Read Only	Displays all setup pages that contain missing values but users can provide only missing values.
	GUI Attended	Automates the text-mode portion of setup. When the GUI-mode portion of setup begins, users must provide all configuration values.
Distribution Folder (see Figure 1.6)	Yes, Create or Modify a Distribution Folder	Allows you to create or modify a folder that will contain the files necessary to install Windows XP Professional (or the operating system you selected).
	No, This Answer File Will Be Used to Install from a CD	Doesn't require that you create an installation folder for your unattended installation folder.
Customize the Software (see Figure 1.7)	Name	Allows you to associate a name with this computer (usually a department name).
	Organization	Allows you to associate an organization with the computer (usually the company name).

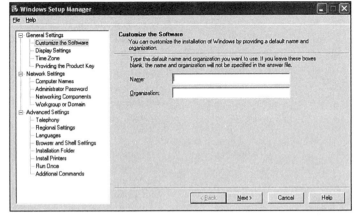

Information Category	*Options*	*Description*
Display Settings (see Figure 1.8)	Colors	Allows you to set the color depth of your adapter.
	Screen Area	Allows you to set the horizontal and vertical screen area.
	Refresh Frequency	Allows you to set the video refresh rate.
	Custom Video Settings	This button will open a dialog box asking for the Color (in bits/pixel), Screen Area on the X (Horizontal) axis, Screen Area on the Y (Vertical) axis, and refresh frequency in Hertz.
Time Zone (see Figure 1.9)	Time Zone	Allows you to set up your time zone and daylight savings configuration.

continues

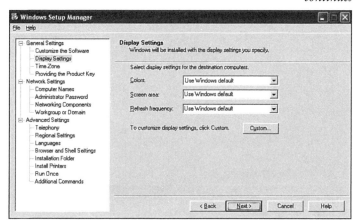

FIGURE 1.8
Setup Manager—Display Settings.

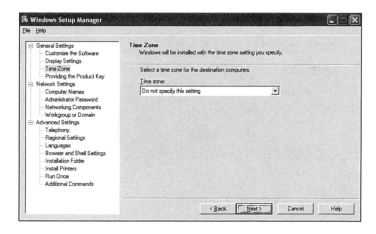

FIGURE 1.9
Setup Manager—Time Zone Configuration Options.

TABLE 1.6	*continued*

WINDOWS XP SETUP WIZARD CONFIGURATION OPTIONS

Information Category	*Options*	*Description*
Product Key (see Figure 1.10)	Product Key	Allows you to enter the product key for the setup. Even though you can use the same product key for multiple installations, you must have licenses for each individual computer. Additionally, because of the activation mechanism that Microsoft is using with Windows XP you must use a product key associated with volume licensing.
Computer Names (see Figure 1.11)	Computer Name/ Computers to Be Installed	Allows you to specify the name or names of the computers you want to install. If you specify multiple computer names, the Setup Wizard will automatically create a UDB file with the appropriate section headings to uniquely name each computer.

You also have the option to have the Setup program automatically generate computer names (it uses part of the organization name and a random number to create unique computer names). |

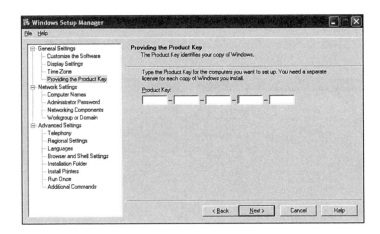

FIGURE 1.10
Setup Manager—Product Key.

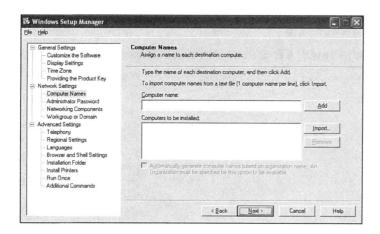

FIGURE 1.11
Setup Manager—Computer Names.

Information Category	Options	Description
Administrator Password (see Figure 1.12)	Prompt the User for an Administrator Password	During the GUI portion of the installation, the user is prompted for an Administrator password. This allows for some degree of security (because the Administrator's password is not written to the answer file), but the installation will not be fully automated as the user must provide the password during install.
	Use the Following Administrator Password	This allows you to specify the Administrator's password. This might be considered a security risk. The password is written to the answer file (it is deleted after the installation is complete, however, so a copy is not left on the new computer), and all computers that use the answer file will have the same Administrator's password. Even with the Encryption option available for XP setups, the option should be carefully considered. This option does, however, allow for a completely unattended installation.

continues

TABLE 1.6	*continued*

WINDOWS XP SETUP WIZARD CONFIGURATION OPTIONS

Information Category	*Options*	*Description*
	Encrypt Administrator Password in Answer File	Encrypts the administrator password in the answer file so it is not available as clear text. Because this is two-way encryption (by requirement), it is possible for someone to reverse engineer the password. However, this will keep most people from being able to determine the administrator password.
	When the Computer Starts, Automatically Log On As Administrator	This option will automatically log into the computer as Administrator after setup is complete.
Configure Network Settings (see Figure 1.13)	Typical Settings	The typical setting installs TCP/IP, enables the Dynamic Host Configuration Protocol (DHCP) client, and installs the Client for Microsoft Networks.
	Customize Settings	The custom setting allows you to select the number of network adapter cards and the network components you would like to install (such as TCP/IP or Client for Novell Networks).

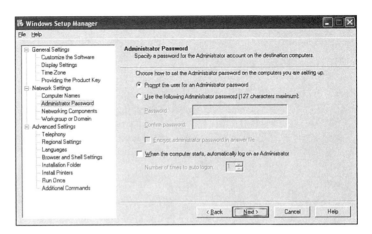

FIGURE 1.12
Setup Manager—Administrator Password options.

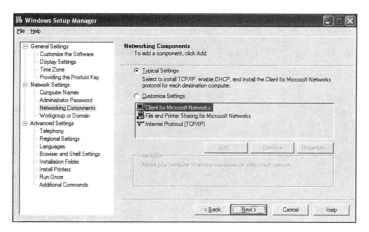

FIGURE 1.13
Setup Manager—Networking Components.

Information Category	Options	Description
Join a Domain (see Figure 1.14)	Workgroup	Allows you to join a workgroup.
	Windows Server Domain	Allows you to join a Windows Server Domain. You are also able to provide the credentials required to create a computer account in the domain. These credentials cannot be encrypted (like the Administrator account password was previously).

continues

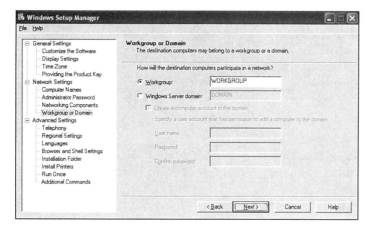

FIGURE 1.14
Setup Manager—Workgroup or Domain.

TABLE 1.6	*continued*

WINDOWS XP SETUP WIZARD CONFIGURATION OPTIONS

Information Category	*Options*	*Description*
Telephony (see Figure 1.15)	What Country/Region Are You In?	Allows you to control the country telephony property. In most cases, this value can and should be set.
	What Area (or City) Code Are You In?	Allows you to set the area code for computers created with this unattended file. Useful if all the computers using the unattended file will be in the same area code.
	If You Dial a Number to Access an Outside Line, What Is It?	Allows you to set a dialing prefix, such as 9, to get out of a PBX.
	The Phone System At This Location Uses	Allows you to control whether the modem will attempt to use tone or pulse dialing. In most cases, this can be set to tone dialing.

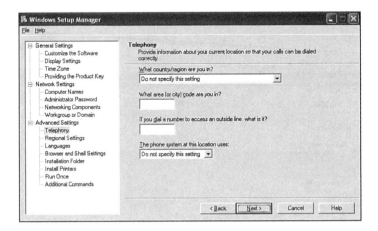

FIGURE 1.15
Setup Manager—Telephony settings.

Information Category	*Options*	*Description*
Regional Settings (see Figure 1.16)	Use the Default Regional Settings for the Windows Version You Are Installing	Allow you to let Windows default to a region based on the type of media being installed from.
	User Can Select Regional Settings During Setup	Allows the user to specify what regional settings they want to use for their computer.
	Specify Regional Settings in the Answer File	Allows you to force a regional setting on all computers that are installed from the unattended file.
Languages (see Figure 1.17)	Language Groups	Allows you to specify additional language character sets.

continues

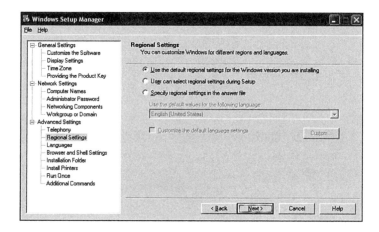

FIGURE 1.16
Setup Manager—Regional Settings.

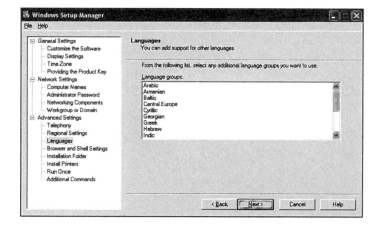

FIGURE 1.17
Setup Manager—Languages.

TABLE 1.6	*continued*

WINDOWS XP SETUP WIZARD CONFIGURATION OPTIONS

Information Category	*Options*	*Description*
Browser and Shell Settings (see Figure 1.18)	Use Default Internet Explorer Settings	Allows the default configuration options associated with Internet Explorer to be used.
	Use an Auto-configuration Script Created by the Internet Explorer Administration Kit to Configure Your Browser	Allows a PAC (Proxy Auto Configuration) file to be specified for the browser. PAC files are script files that tell the browser to work with proxy servers in your environment.
	Individually Specify Proxy and Default Home Page Settings	Allows individual configuration settings to be provided for the browser.
Installation Folder (see Figure 1.19)	Installation Folder	Allows you to specify the directory name of the where Windows XP will be installed. (%WINDIR%)

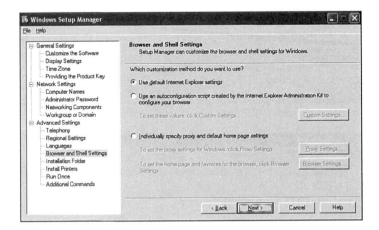

FIGURE 1.18
Setup Manager—Browser and Shell Settings.

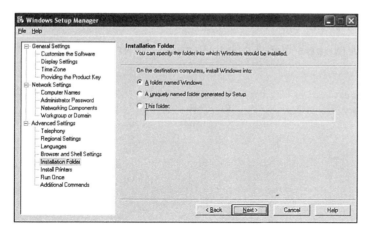

FIGURE 1.19
Setup Manager—Installation Folder.

Information Category	Options	Description
Install Printers (see Figure 1.20)	Network Printer Name/Install These Printers	Allows you to specify one or more printers to install as part of the automated installation. This allows you to have printers enabled as soon as the computer is installed.
		The first printer in the list of installed printers will be set as the Default printer.

continues

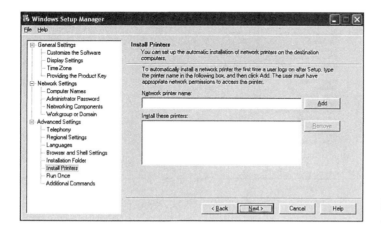

FIGURE 1.20
Setup Manager—Install Printers options.

TABLE 1.6	*continued*	

WINDOWS XP SETUP WIZARD CONFIGURATION OPTIONS

Information Category	*Options*	*Description*
Run Once (see Figure 1.21)	Command to Run/ Run These Commands	The Run Once page allows you to specify commands that should be run upon first logon. The commands will be run in the user's security context, so you must ensure that the first user to log on has appropriate privileges to run the command.

Any printers that you specified in the Printer Configuration page will be listed as part of the Run These Commands page. |
| Additional Commands (see Figure 1.22) | Command to Run/ Command List | These options allow you to list a number of commands you want executed at the end of your unattended setup. These commands are run without a current user profile, which can cause some problems or some application setup programs. |

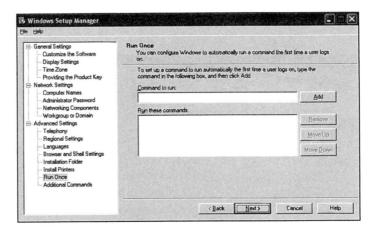

FIGURE 1.21
Setup Manager—Run Once options.

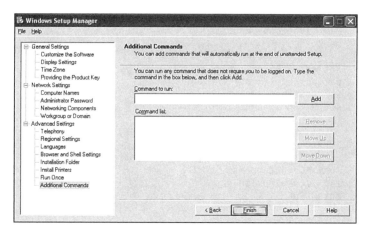

FIGURE 1.22
Setup Manager—Additional Commands options.

Information Category	Options	Description
Answer File Name (see Figure 1.23)	Description String	Provides the text that describes the answer file. It is displayed to users when they run an install using the Client Installation Wizard.

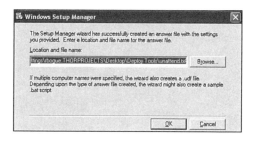

FIGURE 1.23
Setup Manager—Answer filename.

When the Setup Wizard has finished, you will find it has created three files. The files are named as follows:

◆ Answer File Name.txt

◆ Answer File Name.udb

◆ Answer File Name.bat

The first file is the unattended answer file. The second file is the UDF file (if multiple computer names were specified during creation of the files). The third file is a batch file that will allow you to start your unattended installs from the command prompt without having to type the full syntax of the WINNT or WINNT32 commands.

The following is an example of this batch file:

```
@rem SetupMgrTag
@echo off

rem
rem This is a SAMPLE batch script generated by the Setup
Manager Wizard.
rem If this script is moved from the location where it was
```

Remember the Syntax of the Files
The syntax of the unattended.txt and UDF files is complex. Create a sample using the Setup Manager and review them before the exam. The code generated by the unattended.bat file is especially useful if you want to see the correct syntax associated with using the unattended text and UDF file together.

```
generated, it may
rem have to be modified.
rem

set AnswerFile=.\unattend.txt
set UdfFile=.\unattend.udb
set ComputerName=%1
set SetupFiles=E:\i386

if "%ComputerName%" == "" goto USAGE

E:\i386\winnt32 /s:%SetupFiles% /unattend:%AnswerFile%
/udf:%ComputerName%,%UdfF
ile% /makelocalsource
goto DONE

:USAGE
echo.
echo Usage: unattend ^<computername^>
echo.
```

To use this file, you will need to modify the set statements to point to your installation, unattend, and udf files. The syntax used to run the batch and install computer1 (for example) would be as follows:

```
unattend.bat computer1
```

RIS Images   Although referred to simply as images, most RIS images are actual copies of the Windows XP installation files. When a client is installed using RIS, it actually runs the native Windows XP install process. For this reason, the RIS process does not suffer from the difficulties that disk imaging can run into (such as hardware incompatibilities from computer to computer). RIS also supports images created with Riprep, which are like Sysprep-prepared images for disk cloning. When using this kind of an image, the hardware is more important.

Remote Installation Services (RIS)

Windows XP Remote Installation Services (RIS) allows client computers to be installed throughout an enterprise from a central location. This service greatly reduces the effort required to manage the images that are being used throughout your environment as they are stored in and managed from a central location.

RIS provides the following benefits:

◆ Enables remote installation of Windows XP Professional

◆ Simplifies server image management

◆ Supports recovery of the operating system and computer if a system failure occurs during installation

RIS requires an Active Directory infrastructure and has specific server and workstation requirements. The following sections discuss these requirements.

The RIS Process

Remote installation is the process of an RIS client connecting to a server running the Remote Installation Service (RIS), and then starting an automated installation of Windows XP Professional on a local computer.

RIS Server Requirements

The RIS runs on a Windows 2000 server. RIS must be installed on the computer by running the Setup Wizard from the Add and Remove Programs icon of Control Panel. When installed, the Windows 2000 Remote Installation Services Setup Wizard can be used to configure the RIS service.

The RIS server can be either a domain controller or a member server. The following network services do not have to be installed on the RIS server but must be available on the network:

◆ **DHCP Server**—RIS clients must obtain their network configurations from a DHCP server during the initial stages of the RIS installation procedure.

◆ **Active Directory**—RIS relies on the Microsoft Active Directory service in Windows XP for locating existing client computers and RIS servers.

◆ **DNS Server**—RIS uses DNS to resolve the IP addresses of directory servers and client computers on the network.

Remote installation also requires that RIS be installed on a partition that is formatted as NTFS and shared over the network. This partition must not be the boot partition for Windows XP (the drive where Windows 2000 Server is installed), but must be large enough to store the RIS images.

After RIS is installed, it is ready to receive its first image. RIS can be configured to store multiple images on its local hard drive. Although referred to as images (which sometimes infers a single file that represents the contents of a hard drive), the files copied to the RIS server are actual copies of all the source files required to install Windows XP Professional.

NOTE

The DNS Requirement   Saying that a DNS server is required is technically redundant because Active Directory requires DNS—however, Microsoft lists DNS as an explicit requirement.

EXAM TIP

Know the RIS Requirements Know this list for this exam and many of the other Microsoft exams. Microsoft has a disproportionate number of questions on the exam asking about problems with RIS. Invariably, one of the previous is missing. Most frequently, its DHCP is missing.

NOTE

Links Rather Than Files   One of the features of RIS is that it will use links, which can be created only on an NTFS partition, to minimize the amount of space that is used when you have multiple images on the same server. A link is a small pointer to the actual file and consumes significantly less space than another copy of the file.

After the first image is installed, the service can be authorized to respond to client requests. When authorized, clients can download their operating system installation files from the RIS server.

RIS Client Requirements

Client computers that support remote installation must have one of the following configurations:

◆ A network adapter card configured to use the Pre-Boot Execution Environment (PXE) boot ROM

◆ A supported network adapter card and a remote installation boot disk

Computers that support either of the previous configurations can simply be plugged into the network and switched on. When they initialize, they will boot from the network and receive information regarding the location of the RIS server (most machines require the user to press F12 to indicate a network boot). The user then is prompted to log on. After the user has logged on, a listing of the RIS installation images stored on the RIS server is displayed.

RIS servers can also be configured so that they respond only to computers that they are explicitly configured to service. This is called *prestaging* a client. During this process, a unique identifier for each workstation, the Media Access Control (MAC) address of the network adapter, is used to create a computer object in Active Directory. The computer is assigned an RIS server and installation image. Under this configuration, when the client requests a configuration from the RIS server, the client is not presented a list of available installation images. The client is automatically given its preconfigured image.

Using the Remote Image Preparation (Riprep) Tool

Remote Installation Preparation (Riprep) is a utility that enables you to prepare a workstation image that can be loaded on the RIS server. The nice thing about Riprep images is that they can include Windows XP Professional and any applications you want included in your download image.

> **NOTE**
>
> **Booting from a Network Adapter Card** You will need to configure your system to boot from the network adapter card. On most systems, this is done through the system BIOS—refer to your system documentation for details.

> **NOTE**
>
> **Creating Computer Accounts Without Assigning an Image** You also can create computer accounts in the Active Directory for RIS clients without assigning an image. This enables you to control the computer name without requiring a particular RIS image, and allows RIS to respond to all potential clients.

Two systems are required to create a Riprep image. The first system is the source computer (the computer that contains the base operating system and applications); the second is the RIS server.

The steps in setting up the Riprep source computer are as follows:

1. Install Windows XP Professional.

2. Configure Windows XP components and settings to ensure that all settings are correct for your environment.

3. Install and configure all applications you want included in your image. You should verify all configuration settings for each application you install. During most of the configuration of the computer, you will most likely be logged in as Administrator. When all configurations are complete, you should copy the Administrator profile over the Default User profile to ensure that the default user profile is updated to include all settings.

4. Test the source computer to ensure that it is configured properly. After you create the image, it cannot be changed.

After the source computer is ready, you can run the Remote Installation Preparation Wizard. Type `\\RIS_SERVER_NAME\reminst\admin\i386\Riprep.exe` to run this wizard.

The wizard removes all unique information, such as security identifier (SID) information, computer name, and Registry settings, from the computer. A Riprep image is then transferred to an RIS server and an answer file is associated with the newly created image. At this point, the image is available for RIS clients.

Using Sysprep to Image Windows XP Professional Installs

Another popular option for installing Windows XP is to use third-party imaging tools to create installation images. This differs from an RIS image in that the Windows XP setup program is not being used to install Windows XP on the system. Instead, a duplicate copy

Sysprep Versus Riprep   Riprep, which
was discussed in the previous section,
is similar to the concept of imaging
the hard drive for copying. The primary
difference between Sysprep and
Riprep is that Riprep prepares an
image for RIS delivery.

of one computer's hard drive is transferred to other machines. This
type of installation is very fast because the setup program does not
need to be executed on the target system.

Some issues are associated with this type of installation, however.
Because the hard disk is being duplicated, each system that is created
using the image is an exact duplicate. For this reason, issues arise
because computer names and security identifiers are duplicated
across the network.

Sysprep is a utility that gives users the capability to prepare a computer so it can be imaged. Sysprep removes all user- and machine-
specific information from the computer so that the next time it is
booted, it will generate or ask for the missing information. Disk
duplication software then can be used to take a snapshot of the computer's hard drive so it can be transferred to another machine. Step
by Step 1.3 illustrates the use of the Sysprep tool.

You also can use Sysprep as part of an audit process to verify the
functionality of a computer before it is delivered. During the
process, you can, for example, check that the operating system loads
and applications launch properly. This allows you to examine each
computer that has Windows XP preinstalled. You can examine the
computer as it will exist at the user site, and then use the Sysprep
tool to return the computer to an end-user ready state. Then, when
the user receives the computer and turns it on for the first time, the
computer runs Mini-Setup.

STEP BY STEP

1.3 The Sysprep Process

1. Install Windows XP Professional.

2. Configure Windows XP components and settings to
   ensure that all settings are correct for your environment.

3. Install and configure all applications you want included in
   your image. You should verify all configuration settings for
   each application you install.

4. Test the source computer to ensure that it is configured
   properly. After you create the image, it cannot be changed.

5. Extract the contents of the DEPLOY.CAB file located on the Windows XP Professional CD into a temporary directory.

6. Run Sysprep.exe on the computer from the temporary directory. Sysprep will remove all unique configuration settings from the computer. It should not be run on a computer that you are not preparing for duplication because of unpredictable results that may occur, particularly with regard to behavior in a domain.

7. Shut down the computer and run a third-party disk image-copying tool to create a master image of the disk.

8. Save the new disk on a shared folder of a CD.

9. Copy the image to multiple destination computers.

10. When the new machines are started, you will be prompted for computer-specific variables, such as computer name and administrator password. If a Sysprep.inf file is provided, a mini-setup program will manage the install and no user intervention is required.

To assist in the disk duplication process, the Sysprep utility supports a number of command options, as shown in Table 1.7.

TABLE 1.7

SYSPREP COMMAND OPTIONS

Option	Description
Sysprep.inf	A file created with Setup Manager to customize the Mini-Setup routine that will run the first time the target user reboots the computer.
-pnp	The Mini-Setup wizard that detects new or different Plug-and-Play devices on the destination computer and disables those that were used on the master computer but not found on the destination computer.
	You might want to use the -pnp switch to enable legacy device detection or to reenumerate the devices on the destination computer. Using this switch adds a few extra minutes to the end user's experience in order to do a complete hardware redetection.

continues

EXAM TIP

Riprep Versus Sysprep   Know the difference between Riprep and Sysprep. These programs often appear in the same answers list. Knowing the difference between the two utilities is essential. Remember that Riprep is used when you want to deploy images via RIS. Sysprep is used when you want to use disk cloning to deploy images.

TABLE 1.7   *continued*

SYSPREP COMMAND OPTIONS

Option	*Description*
-quiet	Suppresses confirmation dialog boxes displayed to the user.
-nosidgen	Informs the setup program not to generate new SIDs on the reboot.
-reboot	Forces the computer to reboot rather than shut down.
-factory	Allows the creation of an intermediary image on which applications can be installed later. This will not force the next boot to go through the welcome or mini-setup processes.
-reseal	Allows you to finalize preparations for the computer after -factory has been used.
-activated	Causes Sysprep to not reset the activation information because the activation has been performed by the factory for the user.

USING A DUAL-BOOT SYSTEM

Dual-booting is a term used to describe a computer that has more than one operating system installed on it. When the computer starts, a boot manager provides a list of the installed operating systems so the user can choose the OS to be booted.

Users might want to configure their computers to dual-boot if you are in the process of transitioning your users to Windows XP. Dual-booting your systems enables you to retain your original configuration (including software configurations) and still access the new operating system. In some environments, this is useful because it allows you to test new configurations and retain your original configuration.

When dual-booting a system, you must be aware of incompatibilities that can arise between the different OSes you are installing. For example, if you were to dual-boot Windows 98 with Windows XP Professional, partitions formatted as NTFS under Windows XP Professional would not be accessible from Windows 98.

To create a dual-boot system, install Windows XP Professional on the same computer as another, existing operating system but in a different directory. When the system reboots, the Windows boot manager will present you with a list of available operating systems.

> **WARNING**
>
> **Dual-Booting Is Not Recommended**
> Although it is possible to set up a dual-boot system with Windows 95/98, Windows NT, Windows 2000, and Windows XP, it is not recommended. Remember that you will need to install all applications multiple times (once for each OS supported), and no application/system settings are migrated or shared between the OSs.

UPGRADING TO WINDOWS XP PROFESSIONAL

Upgrade from a previous version of Windows to Windows XP Professional.

Windows XP offers several new technologies that help simplify network management. To take advantage of these features, network clients need to be upgraded to run Windows XP Professional. Upgrading clients also allows them to retain their software configurations and user preferences.

The following represents the basic upgrade process:

1. Verify the upgrade path.

2. Ensure hardware requirements are met.

3. Test compatibility with the Windows XP Compatibility Tool.

The following sections explore this process.

Verifying Upgrade Paths

You can upgrade earlier versions of Windows to Windows XP. Table 1.8 presents the upgrade path for older Windows operating systems.

EXAM TIP

Upgrade Paths You should make a point to remember the upgrade paths that are available to you.

TABLE 1.8

WINDOWS XP PROFESSIONAL UPGRADE PATHS

Upgrade From:	*Upgrade To:*
Windows 3.x	Windows 98 or Me and then upgrade to Windows XP Professional
Windows 95	Upgrade to Windows 98 or Me, and then upgrade to Windows XP Professional
	Windows 98 and Windows Me Windows XP Professional (or Windows XP Home)
Windows NT Workstation	Windows XP Professional 3.51 or 4.0
Windows NT Workstation	Windows NT Workstation 3.51 or 4.0 and 3.1 or 3.5, and then upgrade to Windows XP Professional

Client Hardware Requirements

Before you attempt to upgrade your system, you should ensure that it meets the minimum hardware requirements. Table 1.9 presents the minimum hardware requirements for Windows XP Professional.

TABLE 1.9

WINDOWS XP PROFESSIONAL HARDWARE REQUIREMENTS

Type of Hardware	*Requirement*
Processor	233MHz (300MHz or higher recommended)
Memory	64MB (128MB recommended)
Hard Disk Free Space	1.5GB of free space on the boot partition
Video	SVGA (800×600) or higher video card and monitor
CD/DVD	CD-ROM or DVD ROM
Accessories	Keyboard and pointing device

Hardware Compatibility

During an upgrade, a hardware compatibility report is generated. This report shows you the hardware components that are not compatible with Windows XP.

Microsoft recommends that you run the compatibility tools before you start your system upgrades. Knowing the incompatibilities before you start your upgrades enables you to research whether new drivers or fixes have been created for your specific incompatibility.

You can generate a compatibility report using the Windows XP Compatibility tools (also called *Readiness analyzer*) in two ways. This first involves running the WINNT32 setup program with the /checkupgradeonly command switch. This command switch starts the first part of the Windows XP installation program but checks only the hardware.

The second option is to run the Chkupgrd.exe utility. This utility can be downloaded from Microsoft (www.microsoft.com/downloads).

Both the WINNT32 /checkupgradeonly and the Chkupgrd.exe compatibility tools report the same information. The report is a simple text document that can be saved for future reference.

The report documents system hardware and software that is incompatible with Windows XP Professional. It also will identify whether you need to obtain upgrades for software that is installed on your system.

Upgrading Compatible Windows 98/Me Clients

For Windows 98/Me clients that do not present any compatibility issues, you can run the Windows XP Professional setup program (WINNT32.EXE) to upgrade them to Windows XP.

N O T E

Free Virus Scanning   Trend Micro
makes its HouseCall Web-based virus-
scanning tool available free. For more
information, go to http://
housecall.antivirus.com.

Before you begin the upgrade process, you should ensure everything
is in order and that you have a recovery path if the upgrade fails.
The following is a list of suggested activities before attempting an
upgrade:

◆ Uncompress all compressed drives.

◆ Scan for viruses.

◆ Do a complete backup of the system.

◆ Remove (or at least disable) any incompatible software.

Step by Step 1.4 illustrates the upgrade process.

STEP BY STEP

1.4 Upgrading Compatible Windows 98/ME Clients to Windows XP Professional

1. Be sure you have a current backup of your system before
you begin this process. Run WINNT32.EXE.

2. Accept the license agreement.

3. If the computer you are upgrading is part of a domain,
create a computer for the system in the domain (Windows
98/Me systems do not require computer accounts).

4. When prompted, load any upgrade packs required to
bring your software up to be Windows XP compatible.
You should be prepared for this based on the compatibility report generated prior to trying the upgrade.

5. When prompted, upgrade FAT and FAT32 partitions to
NTFS.

6. The Windows XP Compatibility Tool runs and reports
any compatibility issues that might exist. If the system is
compatible, Windows XP will continue to upgrade the
system. If an incompatibility exists, Windows XP Setup
will terminate and the upgrade will stop.

Upgrading Compatible Windows NT Clients

For Windows NT clients that do not present any compatibility issues, you can run the Windows XP Professional setup program (WINNT32.EXE) to upgrade them to Windows XP. Before you begin the upgrade process, you should ensure that you have a recovery path if the upgrade fails (again, back up your computer, run a virus check, and so on). Step by Step 1.5 leads you through the upgrade process.

STEP BY STEP

1.5 Upgrading Compatible Windows NT Clients to Windows XP

1. Be sure you have a current backup of your system before you begin this process. Run WINNT32.EXE.

2. When prompted by the Windows XP Setup Wizard, specify whether this is a new install or an upgrade. Select Upgrade and click Next.

3. Accept the license agreement.

4. Follow the prompts and provide the information Windows XP Professional asks for, such as the product key, and so on.

5. When prompted, upgrade FAT and FAT32 partitions to NTFS. You also must upgrade existing NTFS (4.0) partitions to the Windows XP version of NTFS (5.0).

   Your system will now restart and setup will continue without user intervention.

NOTE **An Upgrade Is Different from a New Installation** If you select a new install, you will need to reinstall all your applications.

NOTE **Compatibility Reports** During the upgrade, the Setup Wizard will generate a compatibility report. The report is saved as %systemroot%\winnt32.log. If the upgrade fails, this is an excellent place to start your troubleshooting.

Incompatible Systems

Computers that do not meet the compatibility requirements of Windows XP can still participate, to a limited degree, in a Windows XP network.

Windows NT 3.51 or 4.0 clients that do not meet the hardware compatibility requirements can still log on to a Windows 2000 network. They cannot, however, use many of the advanced desktop management tools available in Windows 2000.

Windows 95/98 clients need a Windows 2000 Directory Service client installed on them to access Windows 2000 fault-tolerant distributed file systems, search the Active Directory, and change passwords on any domain controller in the domain. To install the service, follow Step by Step 1.6.

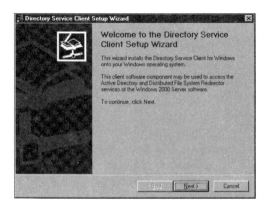

FIGURE 1.24
Direct Service Client Setup Wizard.

STEP BY STEP

1.6 Installing the Windows 9x Directory Services Client

1. Run `Dsclient.exe` from the Clients\Win9x directory of the Windows 2000 Server CD. You will see the Welcome to the Directory Service Client Setup Wizard (see Figure 1.24).

2. Click Next in the Directory Services Client Setup Wizard.

3. Accept the license agreement.

4. Click Finish to complete the installation (see Figure 1.25). After the installation is complete, you will need to restart your computer.

5. Click OK to restart your computer.

FIGURE 1.25
Direct Service Client Setup Wizard—Installation Completed.

Migrating User Environments

Historically, Microsoft has written exams that are much more focused on the corporation or enterprise and much less focused on the small office. However, inclusion of the material on migrating existing user environments to the new installation demonstrates a desire to address the needs of both corporate and small office environments.

Migrating users from other machines and previous versions of Windows can be accomplished via

◆ File and Settings Transfer (FAST) Wizard

◆ User State Migration Tool (USMT)

The FAST wizard is designed to be used in smaller environments where only a few machines must have user settings migrated. The USMT is designed to help corporations that are migrating large numbers of users.

File and Settings Transfer (FAST) Wizard

The FAST wizard is designed for those environments that need to allow a user to copy their personalized settings from one machine to another. This facilitates the deployment of new machines by reducing the amount of disruptive time that is spent reconfiguring desktop settings and locating files.

The following is a list of configuration options that are migrated with the FAST tool:

◆ Internet Explorer Settings

◆ Internet Explorer Favorites

◆ Cookies Folder

◆ Outlook Express Settings and Store

◆ Outlook Settings and Personal Storage Files

◆ Dial-Up Connections

◆ Telephony Settings

◆ Regional Options

◆ Accessibility Options

◆ Wallpaper and Screen Saver

◆ Fonts

NOTE

Migration and Roaming Profiles
FAST and USMT are not as important in the corporate environment where roaming profiles are used as they are in a smaller environment or environments where roaming profiles are not used. Roaming profiles allow the server to keep a copy of the user's "profile" information and provide that information to any workstation into which the user logs.

◆ Folder Options (Default)

◆ Taskbar Settings

◆ Mouse and Keyboard Settings

◆ Sounds Settings

◆ Network Drive and Printer Mappings

◆ Desktop Folder

◆ My Documents Folder

◆ Microsoft Office Settings

◆ Microsoft Office Templates

◆ Microsoft Office Documents

Conspicuously absent from the preceding list are applications and non-Microsoft Office files. This means that you'll have to reinstall applications on Windows XP Professional manually. The FAST tool will not move files that are not in the My Documents folder and do not match the extension of a Microsoft Office file.

The end result of this is that the FAST Wizard will move a great deal of the files and settings on the user workstations, but it probably will not migrate all the information that you need to migrate.

The FAST Wizard is run in two parts. One part runs on the destination (new) workstation and the other part runs on the source (old) workstation. If you need to perform the migration via floppy disks and the old machine does not have a CD-ROM, you run the FAST wizard first on the destination (new) workstation to create a Wizard disk that you can use in the source machine. Otherwise, you'll run the FAST Wizard on the source machine first. Step by Step 1.7 shows you how to run the FAST Wizard on the source machine to capture the settings.

STEP BY STEP

1.7 Using the FAST Wizard to Capture Settings

1. Run the FAST Wizard from the Windows XP Professional CD. The filename is FASTWIZ.EXE and is located in the \SUPPORT\TOOLS directory.

2. Click Next to move beyond the introduction screen and wait until the FAST Wizard progresses to the Select a Transfer Method step, as shown in Figure 1.26.

3. Select the method to use for the transfer. The Direct Cable option enables you to use a special cable to connect the two computers. This cable will transfer all the information. The Home or Small Office Network option enables you to transfer information across a traditional network. This option will be dimmed if your computer is a member of a domain. The Floppy Drive or Other Removable Media option enables you to transfer the information using floppy disks. Use this option as a last resort. The final option enables you to save the results to a directory. This will allow you to move the files across the network, burn a CD, or in other ways move the files. Click Next to continue to the next step, which will display a dialog box similar to Figure 1.27.

4. Select whether to copy files and settings, files only, or settings only. In most cases, you'll want to migrate files and settings. Click the Next button to proceed to the Select Custom Files and Settings step, as shown in Figure 1.28.

5. Add additional settings, folders, files, or file types by clicking the appropriate button. You'll want to do this for other types of files that the user needs moved. For example, if the user uses AutoCAD, they'll need to move all .DWG files. Similarly, if the user stores their work in C:\WORK, this directory will need to be added to the list. Click the Next button to display the Install Programs on Your New Computer step, as shown in Figure 1.29.

continues

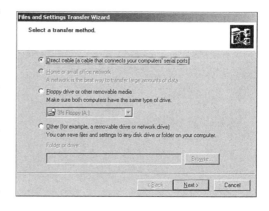

FIGURE 1.26
FAST—Pick a transfer mechanism.

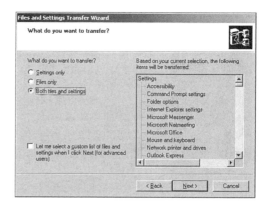

FIGURE 1.27
FAST—Select files and settings.

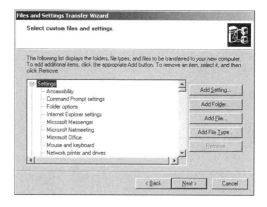

FIGURE 1.28
FAST—Select Custom Files and Settings.

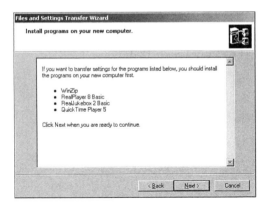

FIGURE 1.29
FAST—Install Programs on Your New Computer.

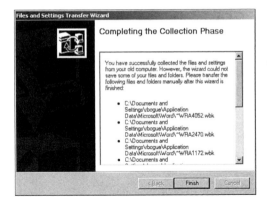

FIGURE 1.30
FAST—Completing the Collection Phase.

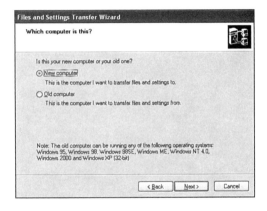

FIGURE 1.31
FAST—Which Computer Is This?

continued

6. Review the list of applications and ensure that they are installed on the new machine *before* running the FAST Wizard to import the settings. Click the Next button to show the Completing the Collection Phase step, as shown in Figure 1.30.

7. Review the errors and messages generated by the collection process. If critical files were not included in the collection, make copies of them and be prepared to manually install them on the new machine. Click the Finish button.

After you've captured all the files and settings, you need to apply those settings to the new computer. This can be done by following the steps in Step by Step 1.8.

STEP BY STEP

1.8 Using the FAST Wizard to Install Captured Settings

1. Run the File and Settings Transfer Wizard from the Start, All Programs, Accessories, System Tools menu.

2. On the welcome screen, click the Next button to reveal the Which Computer Is This? step, as shown in Figure 1.31.

3. Keep the New Computer setting and click the Next button to move to the Do You Have a Windows XP CD? step, as shown in Figure 1.32.

4. Select I Don't Need the Wizard Disk. I Have Already Collected My Files and Settings from My Old Computer. Click the Next button to display the Where Are the Files and Settings? step, as shown in Figure 1.33.

5. Select the Other option and enter (or browse) for the location where you stored the files and settings from the old computer. Click the Next button to start the transfer. When completed, the Completing the Files and Settings Transfer Wizard step, as shown in Figure 1.34, will be displayed.

6. Read the errors and warning to be sure you can manually address the failures. Click Finish when you are done.

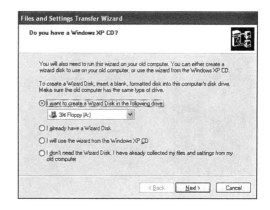

FIGURE 1.32
FAST—Do You Have a Windows XP CD?

That is all there is to the File and Settings Transfer Wizard.

User State Migration Tool

The User State Migration Tool (USMT) does the same things that the FAST Wizard will. However, because it is a command-line utility, it can be automated in logon scripts or Group Policy objects, or pushed through SMS. The USMT is really two command-line utilities:

◆ `ScanState.EXE`—The utility that captures the files and settings.

◆ `LoadState.EXE`—The utility that copies files and settings to the new machine from the information captured by `ScanState.EXE`.

USMT is substantially more flexible than the FAST Wizard because the captured files and settings are controlled via INF files. The provided INF files have the same functionality as the options in the FAST wizard, allowing for most common settings and files to be migrated.

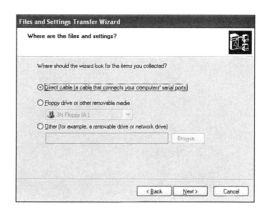

FIGURE 1.33
FAST—Where Are the Files and Settings?

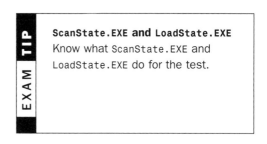

EXAM TIP

ScanState.EXE and LoadState.EXE Know what `ScanState.EXE` and `LoadState.EXE` do for the test.

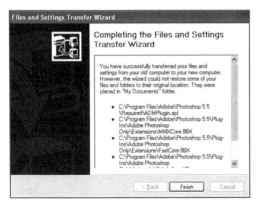

FIGURE 1.34
FAST—Completing the Files and Settings Transfer Wizard.

The USMT tool is found in the \VALUEADD\MSFT\USMT folder on the Windows XP CD-ROM.

POST-INSTALLATION TASKS

Perform post-installation updates and product activation.

After you have Windows XP installed and operational on your network, you will need to maintain it. For the individual user, the primary mechanism for distributing updates to the operating system is the Windows Update feature. This feature allows users to connect to a Microsoft Web site and receive updates to their operating system.

Upgrades come in three basic categories:

◆ **Program Updates**—Some of the programs that are installed with the operating system, such as Internet Explorer, are updated from time to time, and those updates can be downloaded.

◆ **Hot Fixes**—Hot fixes are important, often security-related, updates that fix something in the operating system. Although Microsoft tests hot fixes before making them available, they are not given the same scrutiny that service packs are given.

◆ **Service Packs**—Service packs combine hot fixes into a neat package that has been further tested, and generally should be installed into every workstation in the network.

Windows Update calls hot fixes *critical updates*. In a corporate environment, it's necessary to maintain a large number of computers. Each individual hot fix can be downloaded to be applied to all machines. However, these updates must be manually downloaded. The Windows Update feature will update only the computer from which it is being run.

In addition to the need to keep the operating system updated with service packs, hot fixes, and program updates, retail versions of Windows XP must be activated within the first 30 days of use. This associates the product key that was entered in the setup program to the particular hardware on which the operating system is installed. If you must reinstall Windows XP Professional after you've made hardware changes, particularly network card changes, you might receive a message that the version of Windows XP Professional you have has already been activated on another computer. In that case, you must call Microsoft to have them reset the database so that the operating system can be activated again.

Behind the scenes, Microsoft is creating a pseudounique code based on the installed devices on your computer. In particular, the devices that are assumed to be fixed are things such as the boot drive, the motherboard BIOS, the processor type, and so on. This code is used in conjunction with your product key. If this code differs too much from the code with which you activated, the computer will fail to reactivate and you must call Microsoft.

Corporate users with volume licensing are not required to individually activate each copy of Windows XP Professional.

EXAM TIP

Time Limit on Activation Know that if you fail to activate Windows XP Professional, the computer will stop working 30 days after it's installed.

EXAM TIP

SMS 1.0–Based Questions The location of the SMS.INI file was the root of the C:\ drive in SMS version 1.0, which has been changed in version 1.2.

TROUBLESHOOTING THE INSTALLATION PROCESS

Troubleshoot failed installations.

The Windows XP installation process is relatively simple. There are, however, a number of common problems that you might experience. Table 1.9 presents a listing of common setup problems.

TABLE 1.9

COMMON SETUP PROBLEMS

Problem	Solution
Media errors	If your installation CD has been damaged, you will receive media errors. The only solution to this problem is to obtain a new copy of the installation CD.
Nonsupported CD-ROM drive	If the Windows XP setup program reports that it cannot find or access the CD-ROM, you might need to replace the CD-ROM unit.

continues

TABLE 1.9	*continued*

COMMON SETUP PROBLEMS

Problem	*Solution*
Nonsupported mass storage device	You might experience the situation where the Windows XP setup program cannot access your hard disks. This is usually a problem with the drivers being used to access your hard drives. Remember that if you are running specialized RAID or SCSI controllers, you must specify (and provide) the appropriate drivers during installation.
Inability to connect to the domain controller	You should verify that the domain name is correct and that the domain controller is running. You should also verify that DNS is configured properly and is running.
Failure of Windows XP to install or start	Verify the Windows XP Compatibility report.

CASE STUDY: ABC COMPANY

ESSENCE OF THE CASE

Here are the essential elements in this case:

▶ Upgrading Windows 98/Me/NT 4.0 to Windows XP

▶ Upgrading Windows NT 3.5 to Windows XP

▶ Automating the installation of new computers

ABC Company is in the process of installing Windows XP Professional on all desktop computers in their organization. Details of their environment are as follows:

- Existing equipment
- 200 Windows 98 workstations
- 200 Windows Me workstations
- 150 Windows NT 4.0 (SP5) workstations
- 50 Windows NT 3.5 workstations
- New equipment
- 100 500MHz Pentium III computers (new purchases) with 64MB of RAM and 6GB hard drives

CASE STUDY: ABC COMPANY

Existing workstations need to be upgraded to support Windows XP. New equipment must be installed to support Windows XP. ABC Company uses a number of in-house applications and the standard Microsoft Office products.

Before a budget approval can proceed on this project, a detailed rollout plan is required for the board of directors. The budget is tight for this project and it must be completed with as little use of staff time as possible.

ANALYSIS

The information presented must be broken down into its individual components to fully analyze this scenario.

One of the first challenges for the installation team will be to fully inventory the existing equipment to determine whether it meets the minimum hardware requirements for Windows XP. Any equipment that does not meet the minimum requirements must be upgraded or replaced. From a budget perspective, it is critical that all upgrade/replacement costs are included in the implementation plan.

A standardized method of upgrading each machine should then be developed. Because each machine is currently in production use, you must include procedures to back up all data on the local machines before the upgrade occurs (to limit the possibility of data loss). Windows 98/Me machines can be upgraded directly to Windows XP. You will, however, need to plan for the creation of computer accounts for computers being upgraded from Windows 95/98. Windows NT 3.5 machines must be upgraded to Windows NT 4.0 (SP5) and then upgraded to Windows XP Professional.

New systems must have Windows XP Professional installed on them. You will need to test the fastest method of Installing Windows XP Professional (and required applications) on these machines. You should compare the following installation technologies outlined in Table 1.10.

TABLE 1.10

INSTALLATION TECHNOLOGIES

Technology	Additional Considerations
RIS	Are Active Directory, DNS, DHCP, and a domain controller available?
Answer files	How many different common configurations are required?
Images	How well does a software image work on the new machines?

CHAPTER SUMMARY

KEY TERMS

- Boot partition
- Dual-boot
- System partition
- Primary partition
- Extended partition
- Logical drive
- Basic disks
- Dynamic disks
- NTFS
- FAT
- FAT32
- Bootable disk
- Remote Installation Services (RIS)
- Unattended text file
- Answer file
- Uniqueness definition file (UDF)
- File and Settings Transfer Wizard (FAST)
- User State Migration Tool (USMT)
- Activation

In this chapter, we focused on the installation issues for Windows XP Professional, including the hardware requirements for Windows XP, the requirements to upgrade a machine from a previous version of Windows, the phases of the installation process, file system selection, and the options for installing Windows XP on a large number of systems.

Microsoft has provided a number of excellent tools to aid in the installation of Windows XP: unattended installation, Disk Duplication (Sysprep), and Remote Installation Service (RIS). The unattended installation file can be created by the Setup Manager. The other installation options require more setup and preparation.

We discussed post-installation activities: downloading updates and product activation. The chapter ended with a troubleshooting section to help resolve problems with failed installations.

APPLY YOUR KNOWLEDGE

Exercises

1.1   Installing Windows XP Professional from a Local CD

This exercise demonstrates how to install Windows XP Professional from the local CD-ROM of your computer. It is assumed that your system meets the minimum system requirements discussed earlier in this chapter and that your hard disk is not currently partitioned.

Estimated Time: 50 minutes

We will start this exercise by booting from a Windows XP Professional CD.

1. Boot the system from the Windows XP Professional CD-ROM.

2. Press Enter at the Setup Notification screen.

3. Press Enter at the Welcome to Setup screen.

4. The Windows XP Professional setup program reports whether your computer hard disk is new or has been erased. You are asked whether you want to continue your installation. Press C to indicate that you want to continue.

5. Press F8 to accept the Windows XP Professional license agreement.

6. You are shown a list of existing partitions on your computer (it will be blank). Press C to create a new partition on disk 0.

7. You are prompted to enter the size of the new partition you want to create. Enter **2048** to create a 2GB partition.

8. Once again, you are presented with a list of existing partitions. Press Enter to select the C: New (Unformatted) 2048MB partition.

NOTE **Partition Size**   You might want to create the partition as large as Windows XP Professional will allow you to make it.

9. Setup displays a list of file systems that can be used to format the new partition. For this installation, select FAT. During an installation in a production environment, you would select the file system most appropriate for your environment.

   Setup now examines your hard disk and copies several files to the Windows XP installation folder.

10. Setup now reboots your computer. You should ensure that the Windows XP installation CD is still in the CD ROM drive.

    PHASE II (GUI Mode) of the installation now begins. Complete steps 11–16 to complete this phase of installation.

11. Click Next at the Windows XP Professional Setup Wizard window.

    An Installing Devices page appears. This window tells you that setup is detecting and installing devices.

12. The Regional Settings page then appears. You are prompted to customize your Regional Settings (time/date, currency, and so on) and Language. Click Next.

13. You are then prompted to personalize your software. Enter your name and organization in the prompt boxes.

APPLY YOUR KNOWLEDGE

14. At the next prompt, enter the product license key for your copy of Windows XP Professional.

15. You are then asked to provide a computer name and password for the local administrator account. Enter **TESTMACHINE** for your computer name and **password** for the administrator password. Click Next.

16. The Date/Time settings are now required. Adjust the date and time to your local time and click Next.

    PHASE III (Network Installation) of the installation now begins. Complete steps 17–18 to complete this phase of installation.

17. The Network Settings page appears. Select Typical Settings and click Next.

18. You are now asked to join a workgroup or domain. Keep the default settings and join a workgroup named workgroup. Click Next.

    In step 19, PHASE IV (Final Installation) of the installation, you finish the installation.

19. Reboot the system. After the system has restarted, log on to the system as Administrator with a password of password. This completes this exercise.

1.2   Verifying Windows NT 4.0 Compatibility with Windows XP

In this exercise, you will verify the compatibility of an existing Windows NT 4.0 Workstation with Windows XP.

Estimated Time: 10 minutes

Note: Completing the first part of this lab requires an existing computer running Windows NT 4.0 Workstation.

1. Insert the Windows XP Professional installation CD in the computer's CD-ROM.

2. From START/RUN/OPEN, execute d:\i386\winnt32 /checkupgradeonly (where d: is your CD ROM device).

3. From the Windows XP Professional Setup System Compatibility Check window, note whether any errors have been recorded.

4. Click the Save As button to save the report. Save the text file to your desktop.

5. Click Next. The Windows XP Professional Setup program should close.

6. Use Notepad to review the text file you generated in step 4. This ends this exercise.

Review Questions

1. What are the primary differences between Windows XP Home Edition and Windows XP Professional?

2. What are the minimum system requirements for Windows XP Professional?

3. What are the advantages and disadvantages of FAT/FAT32 versus NTFS?

4. What utility is used to generate unattended text files and how is it installed?

5. What are the four phases of the Windows XP installation process?

6. What is the difference between a local CD-based installation of Windows XP and a networked installation of Windows XP?

7. What is the primary difference between a Sysprep and Riprep installation?

Exam Questions

1. As the network administrator for a large accounting firm, you are developing a Windows XP Professional deployment plan. During the planning process, you learn about dynamic disks and are not sure about the advantages of using them within your organization. In your plan, you document that you will revisit the issue of dynamic disks after the initial Windows XP Professional rollout is complete.

   To ensure the greatest amount of flexibility in the future, what should you include in the Windows XP installation specifications for your environment?

   A. All partitions are formatted with NTFS.

   B. All partitions are formatted with FAT.

   C. All partitions are formatted with FAT32.

   D. 1MB of unpartitioned disk space must be left at the end of each physical drive.

   E. Planning for dynamic disks is not important; you can mix dynamic and basic partitions on each physical hard disk.

2. You are the manager of the software-testing lab at your office. You are testing Windows 98/Me, Windows NT 4.0, and Windows XP. While testing several computers running Windows XP Professional and Windows 98, you convert the system partition to NTFS. Your Windows 98 installation will no longer boot.

   What should you do to fix this situation?

   A. Use the `convert` command to convert the partition from NTFS to FAT.

   B. Use a DOS boot disk to boot the computer and reinstall Windows 95.

   C. Back up any data from the partition, reformat the partition, and reinstall both Windows 95 and Windows XP.

   D. Look for a cause other than NTFS. Windows 95 supports NTFS, so the problem is not related to the partition.

3. You are a support technician for your company. You have been asked to set up a computer to dual-boot Windows NT 4.0 and Windows XP Professional. You have also been asked to install a new hard drive with a large 3GB partition formatted as FAT. You created the 3GB partition on the new drive during the installation of Windows XP. You created the partition using the Windows XP Professional setup program. The user for whom you set up the computer is complaining that she cannot access the new 3GB partition from Windows NT 4.0.

APPLY YOUR KNOWLEDGE

What is the most likely cause of the problem?

A. Windows NT 4.0 is not able to read the file contained on a Windows XP–formatted partition.

B. Windows XP automatically formats FAT partitions greater than 3GB as FAT32. Windows NT 4.0 does not support FAT32.

C. Windows XP and Windows NT 4.0 cannot be dual-booted.

D. You cannot create a 3GB FAT partition on any Windows-based system.

4. As the network administrator for your company, you are planning the rollout of Windows XP Professional for 2,300 users at your company. You are evaluating the various options for deploying these computers. Which option is likely to be best for your deployment?

A. Install Windows XP Professional on each machine using a CD.

B. Create an unattended installation file and uniqueness database. Use this in conjunction with CDs to install the machines.

C. Install one workstation including all the applications. Then, create a SYSPrep image and use a third-party disk duplication program to copy the hard disk. Install the hard disks in the computers.

D. Install one workstation, including all the applications. Then, create an RIS image using Riprep. Use RIS to install the image.

5. As the network administrator for your company, you are planning the rollout of Windows XP Professional for 15 users at your company. You are evaluating the various options for deploying these computers. Which option is likely to be best for your deployment?

A. Install Windows XP Professional on each machine using a CD.

B. Create an unattended installation file and uniqueness database. Use this in conjunction with CDs to install the machines.

C. Install one workstation, including all the applications. Then, create a Sysprep image and use a third-party disk duplication program to copy the hard disk. Install the hard disks in the computers.

D. Install one workstation, including all the applications. Then, create an RIS image using Riprep. Use RIS to install the image.

6. As the network administrator for your company, you are planning the rollout of Windows XP Professional for 200 users at your company. Many of these computers will be dialing into the corporate network via a VPN server. You are evaluating the various options for deploying these computers. Which option is likely to be best for your deployment?

A. Install Windows XP Professional on each machine using a CD.

B. Create an unattended installation file and uniqueness database. Use this in conjunction with CDs to install the machines.

C. Install one workstation, including all the applications. Then, create a Sysprep image and use a third-party disk duplication program to copy the hard disk. Install the hard disks in the computers.

D. Install one workstation, including all the applications. Then, create an RIS image using Riprep. Use RIS to install the image.

7. You are working the late shift at your company's help desk. A frustrated user contacts you and explains that he is trying to install four new workstations in his department; each of the new workstation needs to be configured identically to his personal workstation (the workstation arrived configured with a default installation of Windows 95). Upon detailed questioning, the user explains that he ran Sysprep on his personal workstation to create an installation image. He is now very upset because setup runs whenever he reboots his computer. What should you tell the user? Select three.

A. Sysprep should be run only on a fresh installation of Windows so that a clean version of the operating system can be imaged.

B. Sysprep should be run only on an expendable (nonproduction) machine, because its security identifiers will be changed upon reboot (unless the -nosidgen option is used with Sysprep).

C. The user should have just installed the new workstation manually because the number of machines is very small.

D. The user should have considered using the Setup Manager to create an unattended text file based on the configuration of his computer.

E. The user should have installed Remote Installation Services and created an RIS image of the workstation to be installed.

F. The user should have upgraded the existing Windows 95 computers to Windows XP Professional.

8. You are installing a Windows XP Professional system over the network. The machine you are installing has the following specifications: Pentium 450MHz CPU, 128MB RAM, 16MB SVGA video card, and a 14GB hard drive (currently unpartitioned). You boot from a disk that has the Microsoft network client on it attached to the distribution server.

When you run WINNT, the install cannot complete. What is the most likely cause of the problem?

A. The system does not meet the minimum system requirements.

B. You cannot use WINNT to perform a networked installation of Windows XP Professional.

C. You must have a partition on the machine before you can perform a networked installation.

D. You do not have administrative privileges on the network.

9. As network administrator at your company, you are required to install many Windows XP Professional workstations. Using the Setup Manager, you create an unattended text file that represents a standard configuration file called setup.txt for your environment. You also have shared a copy of the Windows XP source files on a server named dis_server in a share named I386.

APPLY YOUR KNOWLEDGE

What command will use your script file to install Windows XP Professional?

A. `Sysprep—Sysprep.inf`

B. `WINNT32 /u:setup.txt /s:\\dis_server\ i386 /b`

C. `WINNT32 /u:setup.txt /s:\\dis_server\i386 /b /udf:comp1,udf_file1.txt`

D. `WINNT /u:setup.txt /s:\\dis_server\i386`

10. You are responsible for rolling out 600 computers with Windows XP Professional. Approximately 200 of the computers are brand-new and will ship directly from the manufacturer. The remaining 400 are existing computers currently in use across your enterprise. Approximately half of these computers are running Windows NT Workstation 4.0, with the remaining running Windows 98. Many of the existing machines have software and data stored on them that will have to be preserved.

    Your manager suggests that all workstations be installed using a Sysprep image. As the person responsible for this rollout, what is your opinion of your manager's solution?

    A. You agree with your manager and support the suggested approach to the problem.

    B. You are concerned that data might be lost on the existing computers.

    C. You support the proposed solution for the new computers only.

    D. You support the proposed solution for the existing computers only.

    E. You do not agree with your manager and feel the plan should be redeveloped.

11. You are responsible for rolling out 600 computers with Windows XP Professional. Approximately 200 of the computers are brand-new and will ship directly from the manufacturer. The remaining 400 are existing computers currently in use across your enterprise. Approximately half of these computers are running Windows NT 4.0 Workstation, with the remaining running Windows 98. Many of the existing computers have software and data stored on them that will have to be preserved.

    Your manager suggests that all new workstation be installed using a Sysprep image and that existing workstations be upgraded to Windows XP Professional using the setup program and unattended text file. As the person responsible for this rollout, what is your opinion of your manager's solution?

    A. You agree with your manager and support the suggested approach to the problem.

    B. You are concerned that data might be lost on the existing computers.

    C. You support the proposed solution for the new computers only.

    D. You support the proposed solution for the existing computers only.

    E. You do not agree with your manager and feel the plan should be redeveloped.

12. You are in the process of setting up Remote Installation Services (RIS). Which of the following are required to support this service? Select three.

    A. Active Directory

    B. Sysprep

APPLY YOUR KNOWLEDGE

C. DNS

D. DHCP

E. Riprep

13. You are installing new hardware for two users. They have not done as directed and have stored their documents in the local My Documents directory. You need to move their files over to their new Windows XP Professional system. How should you do this?

    A. Run the File and Settings Transfer Wizard.

    B. Run the User State Migration tool.

    C. Run Sysprep.

    D. Run Riprep.

14. You are installing new hardware for 50 users. They have not done as directed and have stored their documents in their local My Documents directory. You need to move their files over to their new Windows XP Professional system. How should you do this?

    A. Run the File and Settings Transfer Wizard.

    B. Run the User State Migration tool.

    C. Run Sysprep.

    D. Run Riprep.

15. What conditions would cause you to use USMT rather than FAST? (Choose all that apply.)

    A. You want to migrate Internet Explorer Settings.

    B. You want to move custom application configurations.

    C. You want to move documents that are not in the My Documents folder.

    D. You want to move the user's mouse preferences.

Answers to Review Questions

1. Home edition supports a subset of the features supported by the Professional Edition. Professional edition can join a domain and supports remote desktop and encrypting file systems. See the section titled "Windows XP Product Family" for details.

2. A 233MHz processor (300MHz or higher recommended), 64MB of RAM (128MB or higher recommended), an 800×600 SVGA video card, and an appropriate keyboard and mouse. See the section titled "Hardware Requirements" for details.

3. One of the primary advantages of FAT is that it is supported by almost every operating system on the market. On the downside, however, it lacks local security and is inefficient on large partitions.

   Windows 95 (OSR2), Windows 98, and Windows XP are the only operating systems that support FAT32. Like FAT, FAT32 lacks local security. FAT32 is, however, more efficient than FAT for larger partitions.

   Windows XP, Windows 2000, and Windows NT (with SP3+) are the only operating systems that support the version of NTFS (5.0) that ships with Windows XP. NTFS offers several advantages, such as local security, encryption, and compression. See the section titled "Windows XP File Systems" for details.

APPLY YOUR KNOWLEDGE

4. Setup Manager is used to generate unattended text files. The Setup Manager utility ships with the Windows XP Resource Kit. See the section titled "Automating the Installation Process" for details.

5. Phase I is the Text Mode of the installation. During this phase, you will provide information regarding the installation partition, file format, and installation directory. Phase II, or GUI-mode setup, is when you configure the following: regional settings, name and organization, licensing mode (server only), computer name, and optional components to install. Phase III of the installation involves setting up the network components on your system (network adapter cards and so on). The last phase of the installation copies remaining files to your computer, applies configuration settings, removes temporary files, and restarts the computer. See the section titled "Installing Windows XP—An Overview" for details.

6. To complete a networked-based installation, you must have the installation files copied to a distribution server, client software so you can attach to the distribution server, and a minimum of 685MB of free drive space on the local machine you want to install. See the section titled "Installing over a Network" for details.

7. Riprep is used to create images (a copy of setup files and corresponding script files) that work in conjunction with the RIS server. Both Riprep and Sysprep remove unique information from a computer so it can be "imaged." Sysprep is for use with third-party disk-imaging utilities. The key here is that Riprep works with RIS, and Sysprep works with third-party disk-imaging

utilities. See the sections titled "Using the Remote Image Preparation (Riprep) Tool" and "Imaging Windows XP Professional Installs" for details.

Answers to Exam Questions

1. **D.** Dynamic disks are created by converting a basic disk to dynamic. The conversion process requires that a 1MB block of free space be available at the end of the hard drive. For this reason, D is the most appropriate answer. Because you are looking into the future, you must ensure that each hard drive has the capability to be converted if the need arises. Answers A and B are incorrect because the file format does not affect drive types. Answer E is also incorrect because dynamic disks and basic partitions (volumes) cannot coexist with each other at the drive level. See the section titled "Disk and Partition Options" for details.

2. **C.** Windows 95 supports only FAT (and FAT32 if OSR2), Windows 98 supports FAT and FAT32, and Windows NT 4.0 supports FAT and NTFS. Windows XP supports FAT, FAT32, and NTFS. Because the Windows 95 operating system cannot support NTFS, you will need to reformat the drive and reinstall Windows 95 (and any other OS on the system). Answer A is incorrect because you cannot convert NTFS to FAT. Answer B is incorrect because DOS does not know how to access an NTFS-formatted drive, so you would not be able to read the drive from DOS. Answer D is also incorrect because Windows 95 does not support NTFS. See the section titled "Windows XP File Systems" for details.

3. **B.** Windows XP will, by default, format large FAT partitions with FAT32. FAT32 is not supported by Windows NT 4.0 and therefore cannot be run. Answer A is incorrect because Windows NT 4.0 and Windows XP are able to read information from the drive as long as the file system is supported. Answer C is incorrect because Windows XP and NT support dual-booting. Answer D is incorrect because Windows NT has the capability to create 4GB FAT partitions. See the section titled "Windows XP File Systems" for details.

4. **D.** In an environment that has 2,300 machines, the additional time and effort to both build an image and set up the Remote Installation Service (RIS) will be returned several times over. Although option C (using Sysprep) is an option, it requires that you physically touch each machine to install the hard drive. This is not necessary with RIS. Option B is a good option for a dozen or so systems when you want to increase productivity but don't have time to create an image. However, this process doesn't save as much time as having images. Option A is the slowest way to install multiple systems.

See the section titled "Automating the Installation Process" for details.

5. **B.** The overhead of creating an image is probably not warranted in such a small network, but creating an unattended setup file will greatly reduce the amount of work it takes to install these systems. Multiple copies of the installation CD and unattended files will make this process even quicker.

See the section titled "Automating the Installation Process" for details.

6. **C.** Because of the large number of computers, creating an image will be optimal for deployment; however, RIS cannot be used because not all the systems will be installed on the corporate network. As a result, the best option is to use Sysprep and a third-party disk-duplication utility.

See the section titled "Automating the Installation Process" for details.

7. **A, B, D.** This user assumed that he could simply copy his existing configuration to the rest of the computers. Remember that Sysprep utility removes the security identifier (SID) from the machine on which it is being run so the hard disk can be imaged using a third-party utility.

Answer A is correct because any misconfigurations or errors on the workstation will be transferred to the new workstations. Answer B is correct because the Sysprep removes SID data from the local machine so it can be imaged to other computers.

Answers C and D are both correct but you must choose (you have been asked to select only three answers)—this is a classic Microsoft question. Technically, answer C is correct because the user could have installed all the machines manually. Technically, answer D is also correct because Setup Manager can be used to create unattended text files based on the existing configuration of a computer. Some might argue that application configuration would not transfer over using the Setup Manager method (which is true) and therefore answer C is the most appropriate. In most cases, however, Microsoft wants you to be able to demonstrate that you know how all of their utilities work. For this reason, I would lean toward answer D because it emphasizes the fact you understand the capabilities of Setup Manager.

Answer E is incorrect because the user most likely does not have rights to install RIS (remember that RIS requires Active Directory, DNS, and DHCP). This would also be a lot of work for such a small number of computers. Answer F is incorrect because the Windows 95 installation that shipped on the computers would not include all the applications required. See the section titled "Automating the Installation Process" for details.

8. **C.** To complete a network-based installation of Windows XP, you must have a formatted partition with approximately 700MB of free space. This partition is required to hold the temporary installation files that are pulled across the network before the installation starts. Answer A is incorrect because the system outlined does meet the minimum system requirements of Windows XP. Answer B is incorrect because both WINNT and WINNT32 support network-based installations. Answer D is incorrect because you do not need administrative privileges to install a system. See the section titled "Installing over a Network" for details.

9. **D.** Answer D is the correct syntax for installing Windows XP with an unattended text file. Answer A is incorrect as Sysprep is not a valid command for installing Windows XP. Answers B and C are incorrect because the /b switch is no longer supported under Windows XP. See the section titled "Automating the Installation Process" for details.

10. **B, C.** Using a Sysprep image to install the computer requires that data on existing hard drives be lost. If you used your manager's solution, you would need to back up the data from each workstation before you installed the image. For this reason, the Sysprep installation is not the best method of installation for the existing workstation. Sysprep images are a very effective method of installing new workstations. See the section titled "Imaging Windows XP Professional Installs" for details.

11. **A.** Your manager's plan is a sound one. Using a Sysprep image for the new machines will allow for a consistent and fast installation. Completing a scripted upgrade on the remaining machines should not affect existing data or applications. See the section titled "Imaging Windows XP Professional Installs" for details.

12. **A, C, D.** Remote installation services require that Active Directory be present on the network. You must install the RIS server on a member server (or domain controller). DHCP and DNS are also required to support the RIS server. DHCP assigns IP Address configurations to RIS clients and DNS allows RIS Clients to find the Active Directory and RIS servers. See the section titled "Remote Installation Services (RIS)" for details.

13. **A.** Although the User State Migration Tool (USMT) will allow you to have more flexibility with the state migration process, it's not necessary for this situation, and the number of computers is low enough that scripting the migration process as is required with USMT is probably not warranted. The File and Settings Transfer Wizard is the easiest way to move most settings and all files contained in the My Documents folder. Sysprep and Riprep are for preparing images of systems for duplication and neither is appropriate here. See the section titled "Migrating User Environments" for more information.

APPLY YOUR KNOWLEDGE

14. **B.** Because there are a number of users that are receiving hardware, it's probably appropriate to script the process of gathering settings and applying them to the new system. This will save some effort over running the File and Settings Transfer Wizard on each system. See the section titled "Migrating User Environments" for more information.

15. **B, C.** FAST and USMT both move Internet Explorer and mouse preferences to the new system, meaning neither A nor D is an appropriate reason to select USMT over FAST. However, USMT will move other configuration information, including alternative file types, and will allow you to move other directories in addition to My Documents. See the section titled "Migrating User Environments" for more information.

Suggested Readings and Resources

Web resources

- Deploying Windows XP, available at
  `http://www.microsoft.com/windowsxp/pro/techinfo/deployment/default.asp`

- User State Migration in Windows XP, available at
  `http://www.microsoft.com/windowsxp/pro/techinfo/deployment/userstate/default.asp`

- Deploying Windows XP Using Windows Product Activation, available at
  `http://www.microsoft.com/windowsxp/pro/techinfo/deployment/activation/default.asp`

- Managing Windows XP in a Windows 2000 Server Environment, available at
  `http://www.microsoft.com/WindowsXP/pro/techinfo/administration/policy/default.asp`

This chapter covers the following Microsoft-specified objectives for the Implementing and Conducting Administration of Resources section of the exam:

Monitor, manage, and troubleshoot access to files and folders.

- **Configure, manage, and troubleshoot file compression.**

- **Control access to files and folders by using permissions.**

- **Optimize access to files and folders.**

▶ File system resources still represent one of the most important services used on networks today. As a network administrator, you must learn to balance the ease of networked access against security considerations. This objective also introduces the importance of designing an efficient directory structure so that access to folders and files is optimized for your environment.

Manage and troubleshoot access to shared folders.

- **Create and remove shared folders.**

- **Control access to shared folders by using permissions.**

- **Manage and troubleshoot Web server resources.**

▶ Shared folders allow users to gain access to folders and files remotely. As a network administrator, you must gain a full appreciation of shared folders and shared folder security.

Connect to local and network print devices.

- **Manage printers and print jobs.**

- **Control access to printers by using permissions.**

CHAPTER 2

Implementing and Conducting Administration of Resources

- **Connect to an Internet printer.**

- **Connect to a local print device.**

▶ The print environment is another heavily used network service. This objective ensures that, as a network administrator, you understand how to configure and manage the Windows 2000 printer environment. This objective includes print security, printer management, and print job management.

Configure and manage file systems.

- **Convert from one file system to another file system.**

- **Configure NTFS, FAT32, or FAT file systems.**

▶ The Windows 2000 file system offers network administrators a large number of configuration options. This objective ensures that you understand the implications of using one file system over another and that you have the skills required to manage the file system you use in your environment.

Manage and troubleshoot access to and synchronization of offline files.

▶ Windows 2000 Professional was the first Windows operating system to support the automatic synchronization of files through the offline files feature. Windows XP Professional offers this feature, which allows traveling users to have access to copies of network files automatically.

STUDY STRATEGIES

▶ The key to understanding most of the objectives for this chapter is your understanding of permissions. Permissions give users abilities to perform specific actions on resources on the network. If you understand how Microsoft applies permissions to the file system (the most complex of the permissions), you will find permissions, when applied to other services, very easy to understand. In short, focus your efforts on NTFS- and share-level permissions. Understanding these permissions makes working with printer permissions easy.

▶ You will need to understand the limitations of FAT and FAT32 with regard to security in the Windows XP environment. You also need to thoroughly understand how to manage these file systems (for example, what file system can be converted to one another versus a required reformat of the hard drive).

▶ Offline files represent a huge step forward in the capability to help laptop users keep the information that they need with them. The leap forward is from the Briefcase feature that was introduced in Windows 95. Offline files can synchronize important files in a nearly transparent fashion.

▶ Printing is a relatively easy section. I suggest you configure a few local printers and play for a couple of hours. I also suggest you focus on the Web-based printer management utilities.

▶ Microsoft's fax service is implemented as a virtual printer and a MMC snap-in that allows you to control defaults and receipt options. The fax service is not complicated; however, it is important that you know how to set up Windows XP to receive faxes.

INTRODUCTION

The primary focus of this chapter is the efficient management of network resources. Specifically, it takes a detailed look at the management of the network file and print environments.

The chapter starts with an overview of the challenges that face network administrators when it comes to the management of network resources. The issues associated with the management of a network file system are then covered. Specifically, shared folders are discussed to ensure that you have a thorough understanding of how shares and share security work. We then look at NTFS security and how it can be used, in conjunction with share-level security, to secure a network file system. The second major service, printing, is then covered. These sections detail how to configure, secure, and then manage a print environment.

MANAGING NETWORK RESOURCES

Networks allow users to share resources. One of the primary goals of the network administrator is to control access to resources and ensure that a resource is accessible to authorized users and secured from unauthorized users. In the world of networks, there are a number of different types of networked resources. Some of the most common networked resources include file systems, printers, and databases. Regardless of the service you are dealing with, network administrators typically use access rights (referred to as *permissions* in the world of Windows XP) to control access to resources. Permissions define the level of access a user has to resources. Depending on the type of resources you are managing, different sets of permissions will be available to control different levels of access.

FILE RESOURCES

Monitor, manage, and troubleshoot access to files and folders.

Manage and troubleshoot access to shared folders.

One of the most heavily used network services found in most environments is file sharing. Microsoft Windows XP allows network administrators to "share" file system resources so that multiple users are accessing a file system remotely over the network. Windows XP also offers a very secure file system (NTFS) that gives an administrator the capability to secure a file system by giving a user permission to use the resource.

The following sections provide details on managing file system resources. Specifically, the skills required to manage and troubleshoot shared folders and NTFS permissions are presented.

Shared Folders

To allow remote access to resources, you must make them available over the network. After resources are available on the network, users—with the appropriate permissions—can access resources from computers found on the network. One of the challenges facing the network administrator is how to provide access to resources and still have a secure environment. Windows XP enables you to control the resources you want to make available over the network.

Sharing a folder in Windows XP means you are making a folder within a file system available to users on the network. After you decide which file system resources you want to make available over the network, you will need to share them out and set user permissions. Shared folders are created at the folder (or directory) level for FAT, FAT32, and NTFS file systems. After a folder is shared, users with permissions to the share have access to all the files and subfolders beneath it provided that they have access to the files themselves if the volume is formatted with NTFS.

Share Permissions

When sharing a folder, you must determine the level of access you are going to assign to different users. Remember that managing access to a file system is a delicate balance of allowing access to appropriate resources for the appropriate users and protecting resources from unauthorized access. To assist in securing shared resources, Windows XP supports several share-level permissions. These permissions define the level of access users will have when they access the file system resources over the network through the shared directory.

Table 2.1 presents a list of share permissions and the level of access associated with each.

TABLE 2.1

WINDOWS XP SHARE-LEVEL PERMISSIONS

Share Permission	Definition
Read	The Read permission allows the user to display files and subfolders within the shared folder. The user is also allowed to execute programs that are contained in the directories.
Change	The Change permission gives the user all the permissions associated with the Read permission and also allows him to add files or subfolders to the shared folder. The user is also allowed to append or delete the information from existing files and folders.
Full Control	The Full Control permission gives the user all the permissions associated with the Change permission and also allows him to change the file permissions or file system resources. The user is also allowed to take ownership of file resources (if he has the appropriate NTFS permissions).

Multiple Share Permissions

Share-level permissions can be assigned to users and groups. Because of this, you might find that some users have multiple permissions assigned to them. For example, a user account named DougH is given the Read share permission to a shared folder. The user DougH is a member of the group called IT_Staff. The group IT_Staff is given Change permissions to the same shared folder. Because the user DougH is a member of the IT_Staff group, the effective permissions on the share are Read (received from assignment to the user account) and Change (received from assignment to the group). This means that the user has both Read and Change access to the share. When multiple permissions are assigned, the least restrictive will be the final effective permission.

The only exception to the preceding rule is if the Deny permission is applied to a user or group of which the user is a member. If you are

WARNING

Assign Only the Required Permissions to Users You must be very careful when assigning share-level permissions. Do not give permissions to users who do not require them. After you have access to a share, the permissions cannot be blocked unless you use NTFS file system permissions.

denied permission to a share, this permission will override all other permissions you receive and you will not be given access to the resource. Specific permissions can be denied. If a user is denied Full Control, the user will have no access to the share. If the user is denied Change permission, she is not able to have Full Control permissions but can still have Read permissions.

Creating Shared Folders

Shared folders can be created in two different ways. This section provides detailed step-by-step instructions regarding the setup of shared folders.

Step by Step 2.1 shows how to share folders from your local hard drive. This means you have access to the local system. In this Step by Step, we will share a folder called DATA from the local C partition of your system to a local group called Accounts. The Accounts group needs Change permissions to this resource. The local Administrators group needs Full Control permissions to the share so the resource can be managed. This Step by Step assumes you have a directory called DATA on your local drive and a group called Accounts created on your local system.

STEP BY STEP

2.1 Sharing Folders on Local Drives

1. Select Start, My Computer.

2. From the My Computer window, double-click the C drive to open the C drive window.

3. From the C drive window, create a DATA directory.

4. Right-click the directory. From the context menu, select Properties.

5. From the Properties dialog box, click the Sharing tab (alternatively, you could have selected the Sharing and Security option from the context menu in step 4).

6. The Sharing Properties tab is presented in Figure 2.1.

continues

FIGURE 2.1

Windows XP Sharing properties tab.

continued

7. Select the Share This Folder option. After this option has been selected, you will be able to provide a share name and description and configure the share. The share name represents the name used when accessing the resource over the network. The Comment field is used to describe the resources being shared (some user views show you the share description when accessing the share). For the share name, enter `ACCTDATA`.

8. Enter `Test of Accounting Data Share` for the Comment.

9. Leave the User Limit setting to Maximum Allowed. This setting allows you to limit the total number of users allowed to access this shared folder at any one time. For Windows XP Pro, you'll be limited to 10 simultaneous connections.

10. To set the share permissions, click the Permissions button. Figure 2.2 shows the share permissions assigned to the share.

11. Note the default permissions assigned to all new shares created in your environment. You should remove the default permissions of Everyone with Full Control permission by clicking the Remove button.

12. Click the Add button to display the Select Users or Groups dialog box.

13. Enter `Accounting` in the Enter the Object Names to Select text box.

14. Click the Check Names button to have Windows XP verify the group name you entered. The display will change to reflect the computer name and group name, as shown in Figure 2.3.

15. Click the OK button to return to the permissions dialog box.

16. Select the Accounting group in the Group or User Names list and check the Allow box next to the Read permission (if it is not already selected).

17. Repeat steps 12–16 to set up the Administrators group.

FIGURE 2.2
Windows XP Share Permissions property page.

FIGURE 2.3
Select Users or Groups.

18. Click the OK button to return to the DATA properties dialog box.

19. Click the OK button to close the properties dialog box.

The second method of creating shares can be performed on both local and remote computers. Step by Step 2.2 demonstrates how to create a share using the Computer Management Microsoft Management Snap-In.

STEP BY STEP

2.2 Creating Shares Using the Computer Management Snap-In

1. Select Start, Control Panel.

2. Double-click Administrative Tools.

3. Double-click Computer Management.

4. Open the Shared Folders node of the Computer Management Snap-In. Click the Shares folder. From this location, you can create and manage shares on your system. Figure 2.4 shows the appropriate MMC screen.

> **NOTE**
>
> **Managing Shares on a Remote Computer**   If you want to manage shares on a remote computer, right-click the computer management node in the tree and select Connect to Another Computer. From the Select Computer dialog box, enter the name of the computer to connect to.

continues

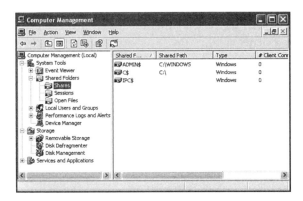

FIGURE 2.4
Computer Management Snap-In with Shares node.

continued

5. To create a new share, right-click the Shares folder in the Shared Folders node. From the context menu, select New File Share. This action will launch the Create Share Folder Wizard.

6. The wizard will walk you through the process of creating the new share. At the first screen, you will need to indicate the physical path to the folder you want to share (a browse is provided so you can find the folder you want). For this example, enter `C:\DATA`. You also will need to provide a share name and description. Click Next to continue.

7. You will now need to set the share permissions associated with the share. The wizard provides three common configurations and a custom option. In most cases, you will need to enter a custom configuration. Entering permissions is identical to the process documented in Step by Step 2.2. Click the Finish button to create your share.

8. Click the No button when prompted if you want to create new shared folders.

Connecting to Shared Folders

After shares have been created, users will need to connect to them. Table 2.2 presents the four common methods that can be used to connect to a share.

TABLE 2.2

COMMON METHODS USED TO CONNECT TO FOLDER SHARES

Method	*Description*
Net Use Command	You can use the Net Use command to connect a share. At a command prompt type the following: **NET USE X: \\COMPUTERNAME\SHARE**

Method	*Description*
	In this command, *COMPUTERNAME* represents the name of the computer where the share physically resides; *SHARE* represents the name assigned to the share; and *X:* represents the local drive letter you can map to the shared location.
Map a network drive from the Tools menu in Windows Explorer	From the Tools menu of any Windows Explorer window, you can map network drives. This tool allows you to select a local drive letter and assign it to a network share location (either by typing the UNC path to the share or by browsing the network to find the path).
My Network Places	By opening the computer icons found in My Network Places, you are able to see the shares that you have recently accessed on other computers.
UNC Path	From the Run option on the Start menu, you can type the UNC path to a share (such as **COMPUTERNAME****SHARE**). This will cause a new window to be opened on your desktop, displaying the contents of the share.

Administrative Shared Folders

Depending on the configuration of your computer, some or all of the following special shared folders are automatically created by Windows XP for administrative and system use. Previously, Figure 2.4 showed the default administrative shares found on a Windows XP Professional computer. In most cases, special shared folders should not be deleted or modified.

Table 2.3 provides a definition for each of the administrative shares found.

TABLE 2.3	
TYPES OF ADMINISTRATIVE SHARES	
Share Type	*Description*
DRIVELETTER$	A shared folder that allows administrative personnel to connect to the root directory of a drive (shown as A$, B$, C$, D$, and so on). For example, D$ is a shared folder name by which drive D: might be accessed by an administrator over the network.
	For a Windows XP Professional computer, only members of the Administrators or Backup Operators group can connect to these shared folders. For a Windows XP Server computer, members of the Server Operators group can also connect to these shared folders.
ADMIN$	A resource used by the system during remote administration of a computer. The path of this resource is always the path to the Windows XP system root. This is the directory in which Windows XP is installed and which locally is available as `%WINDIR%`. For example, `C:\Windows` is a typical `ADMIN$` directory.
IPC$	A resource sharing the resources essential for communication between programs. It is used during remote administration of a computer and when viewing a computer's shared resources.
PRINT$	The Print$ share will be found on any system that has a shared printer installed on it. This share is used for the remote installation of printer drivers.

NOTE

Be Sure You Have IIS Installed
You must install Microsoft Internet Information Services (IIS) for the activities in this section to function. Without IIS installed, the menu options are not available.

FIGURE 2.5
The Web Sharing tab.

Web Server Resources

Another method of sharing information with users is through the Windows XP Internet Information Services (IIS) and the Internet Explorer (IE). You can make file resources available to users through their browsers through the click of a mouse button.

To share a file system resource through IIS, you will need to access the Web Sharing tab of the property page for the folder (as shown in Figure 2.5). You can access this page by right-clicking the folder you want to share, selecting Properties from the context menu, and then clicking the Web Sharing tab.

By selecting the Share This Folder option, you can enter the alias name you want to use to represent this folder on your Web site. For example, if you were to alias a folder as DATA it would be accessible through your browser at the following URL: `HTTP://computer_name/DATA`. This enables you to access the information from the Web folder.

NTFS Permissions

Monitor, manage, and troubleshoot access to files and folders.

An optimal configuration for most Windows XP systems will include partitions formatted with NTFS. NTFS offers a number of advantages over FAT and FAT32—the most significant being folder and file security.

To secure folders and files on an NTFS partition, you assign NTFS permissions for each user or group that requires it. If a user does not have any permission assigned to his user account, or does not belong to a group with permissions assigned, the user will not be able to access the resource.

NTFS permissions can be assigned at both the file and folder level. You use NTFS folder permissions to control access to a folder. You use NTFS file permissions to control access to specific files. Due to the nature of files and folders, the permissions assigned to files are different from the permissions assigned to folders. Folders are used to organize file resources and act as a container where files can be stored. Because folders contain file permissions at the folder level, they give users the ability to create new files or list the files a folder contains. File permissions generally deal with the users' ability to manage the file itself (for example, to read or modify the file).

NTFS permissions can be assigned to both users and groups. Members of the Administrators group can assign NTFS permissions to files and folders on a system if they have full control, or by taking ownership of a file. The owner of a file or folder and users with Full Control permission can also assign permissions to a file or folder.

Folder Permissions

You assign folder permissions to control the access that users have to folders and the files contained within those folders. Table 2.4 lists the standard NTFS permissions that can be assigned to a folder and the level of access each provides.

TABLE 2.4

NTFS FOLDER PERMISSIONS

Permission	*Description*
Read	Allows a user to see the files and subfolders in a folder and view folder attributes, ownership, and permissions.
Write	Allows a user to create new file and subfolders with the folder, change folder attributes, and view folder ownership and permissions.
List Folder Contents	Allows a user to see the names of files and subfolders in the folder.
Read and Execute	Gives a user the rights assigned through the Read permission and the List Folder Contents permission. It also gives the user the ability to traverse folders. Traverse folders rights allow a user to reach files and folders located in subdirectories even if the user does not have permission to access portions of the directory path.
Modify	Gives a user the ability to delete the folder and perform the actions permitted by the write and read/execute permissions.
Full Control	Allows a user to change permissions, take ownership, delete subfolders and files, and perform the actions granted by all other permissions.

File Permissions

You assign file permissions to control the access that users have to files. Table 2.5 lists the standard NTFS permissions that can be assigned to a file and the level of access it provides.

TABLE 2.5

NTFS FILE PERMISSIONS

Permission	Description
Read	Allows a user to read a file and view file attributes, ownership, and permissions.
Write	Allows a user to overwrite a file, change file attributes, and view file ownership and permissions.
Read and Execute	Gives a user the rights required to run applications and perform the actions permitted by the read permission.
Modify	Gives a user the ability to modify and delete a file and perform the actions permitted by the write and read/execute permissions.
Full Control	Allows a user to change permissions, take ownership, delete subfolders and files, and perform the actions granted by all other permissions.

Multiple NTFS Permissions

Permissions can be assigned to users and to groups. Because of this, it is possible for a user to be assigned permissions through multiple sources (for example, you have membership in multiple groups each with permissions assigned). A user's effective permissions for a resource are the combination of the NTFS permissions that you assign to the individual user account and to all the groups to which the user belongs.

Permissions can be denied. By denying permission to a folder or file, you are denying a specific level of access, regardless of the other permissions assigned to a user or group. Even if a user has access permissions to the file or folder as a member of a group, denying permission to the user blocks any other permissions the user has.

When determining a user's effective permissions, you must examine the permissions assigned at the specific resource. Remember that every file and folder on an NTFS partition has a list of permissions assigned to it. For this reason, permissions assigned at the file level will override permissions assigned at the folder level.

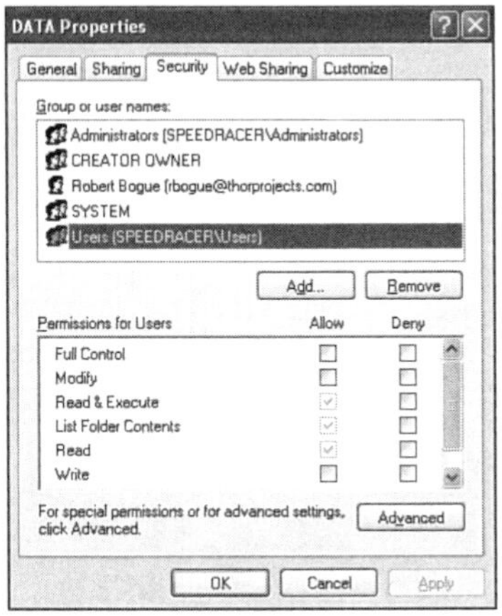

FIGURE 2.6
Folder permissions and inheritance.

> ᴎᴏᴛᴇ **Testing Permissions**   One of the
> notable additions to Windows XP is
> the capability to test the effective per-
> missions of a user or group on the
> object to which you're assigning secu-
> rity. This will help to ensure that you
> are assigning permissions as you
> intend to. To access this new feature,
> click the Advanced button on the
> Security tab and select the Effective
> Permissions tab. This will allow you to
> test the effective permissions of a
> user or group.

Permission Inheritance

By default, permissions assigned to a parent folder are inherited by
and propagated to the subfolders and files that are contained in the
parent folder. This default action, however, can be modified to meet
the needs of specific environments. Figure 2.6 shows the folder permissions of a folder. Note the grayed-out permissions; this indicates
that these permissions are being inherited from the parent.

You can prevent subfolders and files from inheriting permissions that
are assigned to parent folders. By doing so, permission changes made
to parent folders will not affect child folders and files.

When you prevent permission inheritance, you must choose one of
the following options:

◆ Copy inherited permission from the parent folder.

◆ Remove the inherited permissions and retain only the permissions that were explicitly assigned.

Default NTFS Permissions

When you format an NTFS partition, Windows XP will assign a set
of default permissions to the partition. You must understand the
default assignments if you are to secure your environment. Table 2.6
lists the default NTFS permissions.

TABLE 2.6

DEFAULT NTFS PERMISSION ASSIGNMENTS

Default Assignment	*Description*
For new NTFS partitions	When you format a partition with NTFS, Windows will automatically assign permissions to the System and Administrators for Full Control and a series of permissions that allow users to see and execute from the root directory as well as create folders in the root directory.
For new folders or files	When you create a new folder or file on an NTFS partition, the folder or file inherits the permissions of its parent folder.

Default Assignment	*Description*
When a user or group is given access to a file or folder	When a user or group is given access to a folder, the default permissions assigned are Read & Execute, List Folder Contents, and Read.
	When a user or group is given access to a file, the default permissions assigned are Read & Execute and Read.

Assigning Permissions

Users with Full Control access and the owner of a resource can grant permissions to a folder or file. The Security property page can be accessed by completing the following steps:

1. Right-click the file or folder you want to manage.

2. Select Properties from the drop-down menu.

3. Click the Security tab.

Table 2.7 presents the configuration options for NTFS security.

TABLE 2.7

NTFS SECURITY SETTINGS

Option	*Description*
Group or User Names	Lists the users and groups (also referred to as *security principals*) that have NTFS permissions assigned for this resource.
Permissions for	Lists the NTFS permissions assigned or denied for the security principal selected in the Name box.
Add	Opens the Select User, Groups, or Computers dialog box. This allows you to add new security principals to the Name box.
Remove	Removes the select security principal from the name box. By removing a security principal from the list, its associated permissions are also removed.
Advanced	Opens an advanced dialog box that enables you to specify specific permissions, set auditing, and take ownership. Additionally, you can review the effective permissions of any user or group.

NOTE

Domains and the Security Tab
If you are studying with a Windows XP Professional machine that is not joined to a domain, you might not see the Security tab by default. To see the Security tab, you must start the control panel (Start, Control Panel), double-click folder options, select the View tab, scroll down to the bottom of the advanced settings, and uncheck the Use Simple File Sharing (Recommended) option. This will allow your XP Professional machine to behave in a manner similar to how it will behave in a domain.

NOTE

Owners of a Resource Can Manage Its Permissions Remember that if you own a resource, you can manage its permissions. This is a very important concept because administrators always have the ability to take ownership of resources. After you own the resource, you can then manage the permissions on the resource.

You can view the ownership information associated with a resource by right-clicking the file or folder and selecting Properties from the context menu. From the Security tab, you can click the Advanced button to view the advanced security properties of the resource. To view the ownership information, click the Ownership tab.

Special Permissions for Files and Folders

Standard permissions consist of a logical group of special permissions. Table 2.8 presents a listing of the special permissions supported on Windows XP NTFS partitions.

TABLE 2.8

SPECIAL PERMISSIONS

Special Permission	*Description*
Traverse Folder/Execute File	Traverse Folder allows or denies moving through folders to reach other files or folders, even if the user has no permissions to the folders being traversed (the permission applies only to folders).
	Traverse Folder takes effect when a group or user is not granted the Bypass Traverse Checking user right in the Group Policy snap-in. (By default, the Everyone group is given the Bypass Traverse Checking user right.)
	The Execute File permission allows or denies running program files (the permission applies only to files).
	Setting the Traverse Folder permission on a folder does not automatically set the Execute File permission on all files within that folder.
List Folder/Read Data	The List Folder permission allows or denies viewing filenames and subfolder names within the folder (the permission applies only to folders).
	The Read Data permission allows or denies viewing data in files (the permission applies only to files).
Read Attributes	The Read Attributes permission allows or denies viewing the attributes of a file or folder (for example, the read-only and hidden attributes). Attributes are defined by NTFS.
Read Extended Attributes	The Read Extended Attributes permission allows or denies viewing the extended attributes of a file or folder. Extended attributes are defined by programs and can vary by program.

Special Permission	*Description*
Create Files/Write Data	The Create Files permission allows or denies creating files within the folder (the permission applies only to folders).
	The Write Data permission allows or denies making changes to the file and overwriting existing content (the permission applies only to files).
Create Folders/Append Data	The Create Folders permission allows or denies creating folders within the folder (the permission applies only to folders).
	The Append Data permission allows or denies making changes to the end of the file but not changing, deleting, or overwriting existing data (the permission applies only to files).
Write Attributes	The Write Attributes permission allows or denies changing the attributes of a file or folder.
Write Extended Attributes	The Write Extended Attributes permission allows or denies changing the extended attributes of a file or folder. Extended attributes are defined by programs and can vary by program.
Delete Subfolders and Files	The Delete Subfolders and Files permission allows or denies deleting subfolders and files, even if the Delete permission has not been granted on the subfolder or file.
Delete	The Delete permission allows or denies deleting the file or folder. If you don't have Delete permission on a file or folder, you can still delete it if you have been granted Delete Subfolders and Files permission on the parent folder.
Read Permissions	The Read Permissions permission allows or denies reading permissions of the file or folder, such as Full Control, Read, and Write.
Change Permissions	The Change Permissions permission allows or denies changing permissions of the file or folder, such as Full Control, Read, and Write.

continues

| TABLE 2.8 | *continued* |

SPECIAL PERMISSIONS

Special Permission	*Description*
Take Ownership	The Take Ownership permission allows or denies taking ownership of the file or folder. The owner of a file or folder can always change permissions on it, regardless of any existing permissions that protect the file or folder.
Synchronize	The Synchronize permission allows or denies different threads to wait on the handle for the file or folder and synchronize with another thread that may signal it. This permission applies only to multithreaded, multiprocess programs.

File Permissions

File permissions include Full Control, Modify, Read & Execute, Read, and Write. Table 2.9 lists each file permission and specifies which special permissions are associated with that permission.

| TABLE 2.9 |

SPECIAL FILE PERMISSIONS

Special Permissions	*Full Control*	*Modify*	*Read & Execute*	*Read*	*Write*
Traverse Folder/ Execute File	x	x	x		
List Folder/ Read Data	x	x	x	x	
Read Attributes	x	x	x	x	
Read Extended Attributes	x	x	x	x	
Create Files/Write Data	x	x			x
Create Folders/ Append Data	x	x		x	

Special Permissions	Full Control	Modify	Read & Execute	Read	Write
Write Attributes	x	x			x
Write Extended Attributes	x	x			x
Delete Subfolders and Files	x				
Delete	x	x			
Read Permissions	x	x	x	x	x
Change Permissions	x				
Take Ownership	x				
Synchronize	x	x	x	x	x

Folder Permissions

Folder permissions include Full Control, Modify, Read & Execute, List Folder Contents, Read, and Write. Table 2.10 lists each folder permission and specifies which special permissions are associated with that permission.

TABLE 2.10

SPECIAL FOLDER PERMISSIONS

Special Permissions	Full Control	Modify	Read & Execute	List Folder Contents	Read	Write
Traverse Folder/ Execute File	x	x	x	x		
List Folder/ Read Data	x	x	x	x	x	
Read Attributes	x	x	x	x	x	
Read Extended Attributes	x	x	x	x	x	
Create Files/ Write Data	x	x				x
Create Folders/ Append Data	x	x				x

continues

| **TABLE 2.10** | *continued* |

SPECIAL FOLDER PERMISSIONS

Special Permissions	*Full Control*	*Modify*	*Read & Execute*	*List Folder Contents*	*Read*	*Write*
Write Attributes	x	x				x
Write Extended Attributes	x	x				x
Delete Subfolders and Files	x					
Delete	x	x				
Read Permissions	x	x	x	x	x	x
Change Permissions	x					
Take Ownership	x					
Synchronize	x	x	x	x	x	x

FIGURE 2.7
Special permissions configuration screen.

Special permission can be granted to users and groups from the Advanced button of the Security tab of a file or folder. The Permission Entry dialog box allows you to add, remove, and view/edit the special permissions assigned to users and groups. Figure 2.7 shows the special permissions assigned to the Everyone group on a folder (this dialog box is accessed by highlighting a user and group and clicking the View/Edit button).

File/Folder Ownership

The owner of a resource can manage the permissions associated with it. As the administrator of a system, you can always take ownership of a file or folder and manage its permissions. This is helpful in instances where a deleted user is the only account with access to a file or folder.

Step by Step 2.3 shows how to take ownership of a file or folder.

STEP BY STEP

2.3 Taking Ownership of a File or Folder

1. Open Explorer and locate the file or folder of which you want to take ownership.

2. Right-click the file or folder, click Properties, and then click the Security tab.

3. Click Advanced, and then click the Owner tab.

4. Click the new owner and then click OK.

Ownership can also be transferred in two ways:

◆ The current owner can grant the Take Ownership permission to others, allowing those users to take ownership at any time.

◆ An administrator can take ownership of any file on the computer. An owner cannot transfer ownership to others. This restriction keeps the administrator accountable when they've taken ownership of a file.

Copying and Moving Folders and Files

You might need to copy or move folders and files in your environment. You will find that copying and moving folders may affect the permissions that are assigned to them.

Copying Folders and Files

When you copy files or folders from one folder to another folder, or from one partition to another, permissions can change. The following lists the results you can expect from various copy operations:

◆ When you copy a folder or file within a single NTFS partition, the copy of the folder or file inherits the permissions of the destination folder.

◆ When you copy a folder or file between NTFS partitions, the copy of the folder or file inherits the permissions of the destination folder.

> **EXAM TIP**
>
> **Remember the Default NTFS Assignments**   Remember that when a new file is created, it inherits the permissions from its parent. A Copy operation creates a new version of the resource you are copying; therefore, the permissions of the parent are inherited.

◆ When you copy a folder or file to a non-NTFS partition, all permissions are lost (this is because non-NTFS partitions do not support NTFS permissions).

Moving Folders and Files

When you move files or folders from one folder to another folder, or from one partition to another, permissions may change. The following lists the results you can expect from various copy operations:

◆ When you move a folder or file within a single NTFS partition, the folder or file retains its original explicit permissions. Inherited permissions reflect the new location within the file tree.

◆ When you move a folder or file between NTFS partitions, the folder or file inherits the permissions of the destination folder. When you move a folder or file between partitions, you are creating a new version of the resource and therefore inherit permissions.

◆ When you move a folder or file to a non-NTFS partition, all permissions are lost (this is because non-NTFS partitions do not support NTFS permissions).

NTFS Permissions and Shared Folders

Shares represent the primary tool available for providing access to file resources over the network. In previous sections, we looked at shared folder permissions. Shared folder permissions provide very limited security; they protect resources only if they are accessed over the network. Shared folder permissions are also limited because they provide access to the entire directory structure from the share point down into the subdirectories. For these reasons, you will find that it is rare for shared folder permissions to be used in isolation from NTFS permissions. By combining both shared folder permission and NTFS permissions, you have the greatest level of control and security. To effectively use shared folder and NTFS permissions together, you must understand how they interact with each other.

Combining NTFS and Shared Folder Permissions

When users gain access to a shared folder on an NTFS partition, they need shared folder permissions and also the appropriate NTFS permission for each file and folder they access. This will require you to manage two sets of permissions for your environment.

Generally, you will use NTFS permissions to secure the resources in your file system. NTFS offers the greatest level of control and can be assigned to resources on an individual basis. You will then pick share points and create shares so users can access file resources over the network.

Users' effective permissions will be a combination of both the shared folder permissions and NTFS permissions. Unlike individual shared folder and NTFS permissions, however, the effective permissions will be the most restrictive permission of all permissions assigned to the user.

EXAM TIP

Permissions   Remember that shared folder permissions and NTFS permissions represent two different security systems within Windows XP.

NTFS on its own calculates effective permissions by adding all your permissions together (thereby granting you the least restrictive permission). Shared folder permissions are calculated the same way. You have two sets of permissions.

When the two security systems are used in combination, the most restrictive of your effective permissions (from each system) is applied.

Developing an Efficient Directory Structure

Network users will need resources on which to store their work. Where these resources are located is an important aspect of the planning process. Several decisions will need to be made before users actually start creating documents. The following sections detail user home directories, shared data folders, and application folders.

Shared Home Directories

One of the first things that must be completed is an assessment of the types of information that users will be storing. As an organization, you must also decide whether users are to have a private home directory that only they should have access to or a shared storage location the groups of users have access to. In most organizations, you will be required to plan for both private user directories and shared storage locations.

Home directories are generally considered a location where users can store their own documents. No one, including the administrator, should have access to these private directories. In contrast, shared directories are locations where groups of users can share information.

When planning the structure of users' home directories, you must decide whether those directories should be on the users' local machine or on the network. Both of these options can be good depending on your organization's needs.

Table 2.11 compares storing users' home directories on local machines versus network servers.

TABLE 2.11

SERVER-BASED HOME DIRECTORIES VERSUS LOCAL HOME DIRECTORIES

Server-Based Directories	*Local Home Directories*
Are centrally located so that a user can access them from any location on the network.	Available only on the local machine. Users cannot retrieve their data if they are away from their computers unless a share is set up.
Backups of user data are much easier and can be centrally managed.	Backups are much more difficult to manage. Generally, users are left to complete their own backups (something that cannot be counted on). This situation is dangerous; a crashed hard drive will cause all user data to be lost.
Computer policies can be set to limit the amount of space a user has occupied on a server.	If a user stores a lot of information on his local computer, the only person who will notice will be that user.
If the server is down, the users will not have access to their data.	The user has access to his file regardless of whether the network is up or down because his files are stored locally.
Some network bandwidth is consumed due to the over-the-network access of data or files.	No network traffic is generated by users accessing data as it is stored locally.

FIGURE 2.8
User home directory structure.

Generally, when you are creating home directories on the server, it is best to centralize the directories under one directory (typically called *USERS*). An example of such a structure is shown in Figure 2.8.

If your directory structure were on a non-NTFS–formatted partition, you would have to share out each and every user directory separately. This is required because share-level permissions are propagated to the lower-level directories. For example, if you shared at the USERS level and gave the Users group full control at the share, all users would be able to access anyone's user directories. For this reason, you would need to share each and every user directory separately.

If your directory structure were on an NTFS-formatted partition, you would share out the structure at the USERS level and ensure that the NTFS permissions be set to allow users into their home directories but no one else's.

Sharing Common-Access Folders

Like users' home directories, which need to have very restricted access controls placed on them, common access or shared data folders will need to be planned carefully. Shared data folders are required on the network so that users or groups of users can exchange data. In many instances, this data also needs to be centrally managed. One of the biggest challenges in planning for shared data folders is to determine who needs to share what and the level of access everyone needs to the information.

Figure 2.9 represents a sample directory structure for a set of common access folders. Note that a top-level directory called DEPARTMENTS was created to act as a share point to the data. Each department (SALES, ACCOUNTING, HUMAN_RESOURCES, and FINANCE) has a subdirectory in which to store department-specific data.

Sharing Application Folders

Another resource you will need to plan for is networked application folders. Shared application folders are typically used to give user access to applications that they will run from a network share point. Another option is to have users run applications locally from their own computer. Table 2.12 shows a comparison of these two options.

FIGURE 2.9
Shared departmental directory structure.

TABLE 2.12

NETWORKED APPLICATIONS VERSUS LOCALLY INSTALLED APPLICATIONS

Shared Network Applications	*Locally Installed Applications*
Take up less disk space	Uses more local disk space. on the local workstation.
Easier to upgrade/control.	Upgrades require that staff visit each computer (although this is becoming less of an issue as Group Policy objects and products such as Microsoft System Management Server can assist in the delivery of applications to the desktop).
More bandwidth is used.	Little network bandwidth is used as applications are stored locally.
If the server is down, users cannot run their applications.	Users can run applications regardless of server status.

As you can see, each method offers advantages depending on your environment.

When setting up shared application resources, consider the following:

◆ Different applications require that users have specific permissions to run over the network.

◆ Many applications require that users have a location available to store their personal preferences or application settings.

◆ Staff will be required to upgrade and maintain application directories.

Based on the preceding considerations, a common approach to application directories is to create a structure similar to the one shown in Figure 2.10.

In this example, you would share at the APPLICATIONS level and give users and administrators the appropriate permissions to the underlying applications. If you needed to restrict access to specific applications, you would share each application out separately, giving users share-level permissions to only the applications to which they require access.

FIGURE 2.10
Shared application directory structure.

OFFLINE FILES

Manage and troubleshoot access to and synchronization of offline files.

Network connections are becoming more common, and it is often assumed that your computer always has network access. However, if you are offline either because you are disconnected from the network or because you have undocked your laptop, you can still access files and folders to which you have configured offline access. Using Offline Files, you can navigate the shared folders and files as if you were connected to the network.

Offline Files and Mobile Users

If you travel frequently and use your laptop for most of your work, Offline Files provides a way to ensure that the network files you are working with are the most current versions and that changes you make when offline will be synchronized when you reconnect to the network.

When you undock your laptop, the shared network files that were configured as available offline remain just as they were when you were connected. You continue to work with them normally with the same access permission as the original network files. For example, a read-only document on a mapped network drive would remain read-only if you were disconnected from the network.

Selecting Items to Be Available Offline

The first step is to enable your Windows XP Professional computer to use offline files. Open My Computer from the start menu and select Folder Options from the Tools drop-down menu. Selecting the Offline Files tab will allow you to set synchronization events and enable offline file usage.

You must now indicate which folders or files are to be accessed when your computer is disconnected from the network. This flag is part of the menu list (right-click) for files and folders.

NOTE

Support for Offline Files   Any shared file or folder can be configured as offline. Any computer that supports Server and Message Block (SMB) File and Printer Sharing can be the source of offline files. Computers running Windows 95, Windows 98, and Windows NT 4.0 all support Offline Files. Offline Files is not supported for computers running Novell NetWare.

WARNING

Cache Setting   If you cache a lot of files, it is possible that you'll run out of space on your local hard drive for the cached files. This means that not all the files that you want to have available offline will be. By default, Windows XP sets the maximum amount of cached files to be 10% of the drive capacity. This might be too low a number for mobile users. To change the setting, go to My Computer, Tools, Folder Options, Offline Files and change the cache setting.

NOTE

Selecting Folders If you make a folder available offline, all the files within the folder are also available offline and the menu option for each of them is grayed out.

STEP BY STEP

2.4 Selecting a Folder for Offline Access

1. Select My Computer from the Start menu.

2. Select the network drive or folder by double-clicking until the appropriate folder appears in the folder view on the screen.

3. Right-click on the folder and select Make Available Offline. The Offline Files Wizard will appear.

4. Click the Next button to proceed past the welcome step.

5. Select the check box Automatically Synchronize the Offline Files When I Log On and Off My Computer, and click the Next button to proceed to the next step.

6. Click the Finish button to close the wizard, leaving reminders turned on.

7. Click the OK button when prompted whether you want to make subfolders available offline.

FIGURE 2.11
Setup options for synchronization.

Synchronizing

When you reconnect to the network (perhaps by docking your portable computer), changes that you have made to the offline files are synchronized back to their original network files. If someone else has made changes to the same file, you have the option of saving your version of the file, keeping the other version, or saving them both.

Synchronization can be started manually or by using the Synchronization Manager when you want to control what files are synchronized and when it occurs. Figure 2.11 shows the settings to synchronize a file when logging on or off a network.

STEP BY STEP

2.5 Using the Synchronization Manager

1. From the Start menu, select All Programs and then Accessories.

2. Select the Synchronize item to start the Synchronize Manager.

3. The display will list all the folders selected for offline availability. Double-click an entry to see the Offline Files folder.

4. Close the Offline Files folder display and return to the Items to Synchronize window. Click the Setup button.

5. You can select each item in the windows to be synchronized when you log on or log off, when the computer is idle, or at some scheduled time for each connection configured on your computer.

NOTE

Managing Your Workload   By choosing when to synchronize items, you can manage the workload placed on your computer and the network. For example, if you are connected to the network by modem, you can minimize synchronization time by clearing the automatic synchronization flags and manually synchronizing individual files.

When using **offline** files, you should always synchronize at logon. This will ensure that changes made on your computer are synchronized with changes made to the network files while you were disconnected.

File Conflicts

When you synchronize files, the files that you modified while disconnected from the network are compared to the versions saved on the network. If the network versions have not been changed by someone else, your changes will be copied to the network.

If someone else has updated the network versions of your offline files, you are given a choice of keeping your version, keeping the version currently on the network, or keeping both. To keep both versions, you have to give your version a different filename and then both files will appear on the network and in your offline files folder.

If you delete a network file on your computer while working offline but someone else on the network makes changes to that file, the file is deleted from your computer but not from the network.

If you change a network file while working offline but someone else on the network deletes that file, you can choose to save your version onto the network or delete it from your computer.

If you are disconnected from the network when a new file is added to a shared network folder that you have made available offline, that new file will be added to your computer when you reconnect and synchronize.

MANAGING FILE RESOURCES

Configure and manage file systems.

As the administrator of a Windows XP system, you will need to understand how to manage file resources. The following section provides an overview of the NTFS, FAT, and FAT32 file systems and details common management tasks.

NTFS, FAT32, or FAT

Before you decide which file system to use, you should understand the benefits and limitations of each file system. Changing a volume's existing file system can be time consuming, so choose the file system that best suits your long-term needs. If you decide to use a different file system, you must back up your data and then reformat the volume using the new file system. However, you can convert a FAT or FAT32 volume to an NTFS volume without formatting the volume (as with most disk operations; however, it is recommended that you back up your data before the conversion).

The following sections provide an overview of the differences among FAT, FAT32, and NTFS file systems.

FAT

File Allocation Table (FAT) is a file system that has been around for a very long time and is currently supported by most operating systems on the market.

The primary benefit of using FAT is that it is supported by Windows NT 3.5x/4.0, Windows 95/98, Windows 3.x, DOS, and many alternative operating systems. For this reason, FAT is an exceptional choice for systems that are required to dual-boot between Windows XP and one (or more) of the previously mentioned operating systems.

The version of FAT supported by Windows XP has a number of additional features that are not supported by systems running DOS. When used under Windows XP, the FAT file system supports the following additional features:

◆ Long filenames up to 255 characters

◆ Multiple spaces

◆ Multiple periods

◆ Filenames are not case sensitive but do preserve case

The FAT file system is a logical choice for systems where dual-boot capabilities are required. FAT is also a logical choice for small partitions (less than 200MB) because it has very low system overhead.

For all the benefits of FAT, it should be recognized that it has a number of major limitations that should make you stop and think before it becomes your file system of choice on your Windows XP system.

The primary limitations of FAT are as follows:

◆ FAT is inefficient for larger partitions. As files grow in size, they can become fragmented on the disk and cause slower access times. FAT also uses inefficient cluster sizes (a cluster is the smallest unit of storage on a partition). If the cluster size is too large, you can end up with lots of wasted space on the partition.

◆ The maximum size of a FAT partition is 4GB.

◆ No local security—the FAT file system does not support local security, so there is no way to prevent a user from accessing a file if the user can log in to the local operating system.

◆ FAT does not support compression, encryption, and disk quotas under Windows XP.

FAT32

The FAT32 file system is similar to FAT. FAT32 was introduced in the Microsoft product line with Windows 95 OSR 2. The primary difference between FAT and FAT32 is that FAT32 supports a smaller cluster size so it does not have as much wasted space associated with larger partitions.

Like FAT, FAT32 supports long filenames, multiple spaces, and multiple periods, and preserves case while not being case sensitive.

The primary limitations of FAT32 are as follows:

◆ No local security—FAT file system does not support local security, so there is no way to prevent a user from accessing a file if the user can log in to the local operating system.

◆ The maximum size of a FAT32 partition is 8TB (a 32GB limit is imposed by the Windows XP format utility if you create the partition on a Windows XP system).

◆ Does not support compression, encryption, and disk quotas under Windows XP.

◆ FAT32 is not supported by all versions of Windows 95 and is not supported by DOS and Windows NT, so you need to be careful when deciding to use it. (FAT32 is only supported on Windows 95 OSR2.) If you plan to dual-boot your system, ensure that all operating systems you are using support FAT32. If they do not, all FAT32 partitions will not be accessible.

NTFS

NTFS is the file system of choice on most systems running Windows XP. NTFS offers the following benefits:

◆ **Support for long filenames**—NTFS supports long filenames up to 255 characters.

◆ **Preservation of case**—NTFS is not case sensitive, but it does have the capability to preserve case for POSIX compliance.

◆ **Recoverability**—NTFS is a recoverable file system. It uses transaction logging to automatically log all files and directory updates so in the case of a system failure the operating system can redo failed operations.

◆ **Security**—NTFS provides folder- and file-level security for protecting files.

◆ **Compression**—NTFS supports compression of file and folders to help save disk space.

◆ **Encryption**—NTFS supports file-level encryption. This allows a user the ability to encrypt sensitive files so that no one else can read the files.

◆ **Disk quotas**—NTFS partitions support user-level disk quotas. This gives an administrator the ability to set an upper limit on the amount of space that a user can use on a partition. After the user reaches her limit, she is not allowed to store any more information on the partition.

◆ **Size**—NTFS partitions can support much larger partition sizes than FAT. NTFS can support partitions up to 16 exabytes in size (this is equal to 16 billion gigabytes).

Using NTFS gives you enhanced functionality and scalability when compared to FAT and FAT32.

The main limitation of NTFS is that other operating systems do not support it and it has high system overhead. If you need to dual-boot your system or have partitions less than 200MB in size, it is recommended that you format your partitions with FAT or FAT32.

File Compression

NTFS compression is used to make more efficient use of the hard drive space available on your system. If you need more space on your system, you will most likely want to add an additional hard drive. In an emergency, however, you can always compress your existing drives to free up space.

Compression is implemented at the folder or file level on NTFS-formatted partitions.

To compress a file or folder within Windows XP, you can complete the following steps.

> **WARNING**
>
> **NTFS 4.0 Versus NTFS 5.0** The version of NTFS used with Windows NT (NTFS 4.0) is different from the version used with Windows 2000 and Windows XP (NTFS 5.0). These two versions of NTFS are not compatible with each other, so you cannot dual-boot a Windows NT 4.0 and Windows XP system unless your installation of Windows NT 4.0 is running SP 4 or higher. This is very important if installing Windows XP on a system with an existing installation of Windows NT 4.0 because the installation process will automatically upgrade NTFS 4.0 partitions to NTFS 5.0.

STEP BY STEP

2.6 Compress a File

1. Right-click the file or folder you want to compress.

2. Choose the Properties option for the context menu.

3. Click the Advanced button from the General tab.

4. Check the Compress Contents to Save Disk Space check box from the Compress or Encrypt Attributes section of the Advanced Attributes dialog box.

You also can manage the compression attributes associated with files and folders on your system from the command prompt. The Compact utility enables you to compress files and folders as well as check the compression statistics.

The syntax for the compact utility is as follows:

```
COMPACT [/C | /U] [/S[:dir]] [/A] [/I] [/F] [/Q] [filename
[...]]
```

/C compresses the specified files. Directories will be marked so that files added afterward will be compressed.

/U uncompresses the specified files. Directories will be marked so those files added afterward will not be compressed.

/S performs the specified operation on files in the given directory and all subdirectories. Default "dir" is the current directory.

/A displays files with the hidden or system attributes. These files are omitted by default.

/I continues performing the specified operation even after errors have occurred. By default, COMPACT stops when an error is encountered.

/F forces the compress operation on all specified files, even those which are already compressed. Already-compressed files are skipped by default.

/Q reports only the most essential information.

Filename specifies a pattern, file, or directory.

You might want to use the compact utility instead of the Property tab of the files or folders because the compact command syntax can be included in batch files.

File Encryption

Encrypted File System (EFS) is a system service that allows the owner of a file system resource to encrypt it. The service is based on public/private key encryption technology and is managed by the Windows XP Public Key Infrastructure (PKI) services. Because EFS is an integrated service, it is very easy to manage, difficult to break into, and transparent to the user.

Windows XP manages the encryption process by associating certificates with a file before encrypting it. Users with full control can subsequently associate or dissociate other certificates with the file. Each certificate typically represents a user. When the file is encrypted by someone with full control access, the certificate corresponding to their user is automatically added to the list of users authorized to decrypt the information.

A user who has full control of a file system resource can either encrypt or decrypt the folder or file. If a user who does not own the resource attempts to access the resource, he will receive an access denied message.

The technology is based on a public key–based structure. Each user has a public and private key. The keys were created in such a way that anything encrypted using the private key can only be decrypted using the public key, and anything encrypted using the public key can only be decrypted using the private key. As the names suggest, the public key is made available to any resource that requests it. The private key is kept secret and never exposed.

When a file system resource encrypts the resource, a file encryption key is generated and used to encrypt the file. The file encryption keys are based on a fast symmetric key designed for bulk encryption. The file is encrypted in blocks with a different key for each block. All the file encryption keys are then stored with the file (as part of the header of the file), in the Data Decryption Field (DDF), and the Data Recovery Field (DRF). Before the file encryption keys are stored, they are encrypted using the public key of the owner, in the case of the DDF keys, and a recovery agent, in the case of the DRF

keys. Because the keys are stored with the file, the file can be moved
or renamed and it will not impact the recoverability of the file.

When a file is opened, EFS detects the access attempt and locates
the user's certificate, from the Windows XP PKI, and the user's associated private key. The private key is then used to decrypt the DDF
to retrieve the file encryption keys used to encrypt each block of the
file. The only keys in existence with the ability to decrypt the information are those of the associated users (through their certificate).
Access to the file is denied to anyone else, because they do not hold
the private key required for decrypting the file encryption keys.

If the private keys are not available for some reason (for example, the
user account was deleted), the recovery agent can open the file. The
recovery agent decrypts the DRF to unlock the list of file encryption
keys. The recovery agent must be configured as part of the security
policies of the local computer.

To encrypt a file or folder within Windows XP, you can complete
the following steps.

STEP BY STEP

2.7 Encrypting a File or Folder

1. Right-click the file or folder you want to compress.

2. Choose the Properties option from the context menu.

3. Click the Advanced button from the General tab.

4. Check the Encrypt Contents to Secure Data check box
   from the Compress or Encrypt Attributes section of the
   Advanced Attributes dialog box.

You can also manage the encryption attributes associated with files
and folders on your system from the command prompt. The Cipher
utility allows you to encrypt files and folders as well as check the
encryption statistics.

The syntax for the encryption utility is as follows:

```
CIPHER [/e| /d] [/s:dir] [/i] [/f] [/q] [filename [...]]
```

/e encrypts the specified files or folders. Files added to the folder afterward will be encrypted.

/d decrypts the specified files or folders. Files added to the folder afterward will not be encrypted.

/s: dir performs the specified operation on files in the given directory and all subdirectories.

/i continues performing the specified operation even after errors have occurred. By default, Cipher stops when an error is encountered.

/f forces the encryption or decryption of all specified files. By default, files that have already been encrypted or decrypted are skipped.

/q reports only the most essential information.

filename specifies a pattern, file, or directory.

> **NOTE**
>
> **Compression or Encryption** A file cannot be both compressed and encrypted. Windows XP will automatically uncompress a file that is encrypted.

> **WARNING**
>
> **Converting to NTFS Could Affect System Performance** Partitions and volumes that are converted from FAT/FAT32 to NTFS (rather than initially formatted with NTFS) may suffer from performance problems. There is a chance that the Master File Table (MFT) will be fragmented. It is best to run a defragmenter both before and after converting the volume.

Converting File Systems

In many instances, you might find that you need to change the format of your partitions. Your options are to reformat the partition or convert it. If you chose to reformat your partition, you will lose all data from the partition. Converting a partition allows you to change your file format without losing your data. You can only convert from FAT to NTFS or from FAT32 to NTFS; you cannot convert from NTFS to FAT or from NTFS to FAT32.

If convert cannot lock the drive, it will offer to convert it the next time the computer restarts. Locking the drive requires that the convert utility gain exclusive access to all files and folders on the drive. In other words, data cannot be in use by other applications or by the operating system. For this reason, you cannot convert the boot partition or any partition that contains any part of the paging file.

```
convert [drive:] /fs:ntfs [/v]
```

drive: specifies the drive to convert to NTFS.

/fs:ntfs specifies that the volume be converted to NTFS.

/v specifies verbose mode. All messages will be displayed during conversion.

PRINT RESOURCES

Connect to local and network print devices.

Printers are a common resource shared by users on the network. As a network administrator, you will need to be able to manage the print environment. Management tasks include setting up printer resources, securing print resources, managing print jobs, and connecting to shared printers over the network. This section reviews each of these management tasks.

The Print Environment

Four primary components make up the Windows XP print environment. As a network administrator, you should understand these components and how they interact with one another to create the print environment. The components are as follows:

◆ **Printer**—A printer is a software representation of a physical print device. You will find printers configured on computers so that print jobs can be sent to them. When a print job is sent to the printer, it is processed and forwarded to a physical print device (the process will vary depending on whether the physical print device is located on the network or attached directly to the computer generating the print job).

◆ **Print driver**—A print driver is used to convert print requests into a format understood by the physical print device being used in the environment.

◆ **Print server**—A print server is a computer that receives and processes documents from client computers for processing.

◆ **Print device**—A print device is the physical device that produces the printed output.

The following represents how a print job is processed:

1. A user on a computer generates a print job by issuing a print command from a software application.

2. The print job is sent to a printer configured on the local machine (remember that the printer is a software representation of a physical print device).

3. The printer defines where the printer job will go to reach the physical print device and how the job should be managed during the printing process.

4. From the printer, the print job is sent to a print server for processing.

5. The print server then uses a print driver to format the print job so that the physical print device can process it.

6. After the print driver has converted the print job into a specific printer language, it is forwarded to the physical print device.

7. When the physical print device receives the job, it is printed.

Windows XP supports print devices that are either local or networked. As the name implies, local print devices are connected to a local computer (the same machine as where the print job is generated). Network print devices are connected to a print server through the network.

Connecting to a Local Print Device

Installing printers in the Windows XP environment is accomplished with the aid of the Add Printer Wizard. The Add Printer Wizard is launched by double-clicking the Add Printer icon in the Printers folder of Control Panel. Step by Step 2.8 will walk you through the process of configuring a local printer.

STEP BY STEP

2.8 Installing a Local Printer

1. Double-click the Add Printer icon from the Printers folder of Control Panel.

2. At the Welcome to the Add Printer Wizard screen, click Next.

continues

continued

3. At the Local or Network Printer screen, click Local Printer. You also might want to uncheck the Automatically Detect and Install My Plug and Play Printer box. (Most likely, your Plug and Play–compatible printers would have been detected and installed at bootup.)

4. You will then need to select the port where the printer is installed. Generally, you will select LPT1 or LPT2 for your printer. Some specialized print devices might require a COM port. You also have the option of creating your own port. This option is used for printer redirection and will be discussed later. For now, select LPT1.

5. After you have indicated where the physical print device is located, you will need to indicate the print driver associated with your printer. You will find a large list of print drivers that ship with Windows XP. If your printer is not in the list, check with your printer's manufacturer; generally, they have drivers available. If you do have drivers for your printer, you can select the Have Disk button to indicate a path where the drivers can be found. Select an appropriate driver for the printer you are installing (if you don't have a printer to install, pick any driver).

6. You will now name your printer. This is the software representation of your physical print device. The name you choose should be descriptive, but it should be no more then 31 characters in length. You also will need to indicate whether the printer should be configured as the default Windows printer (if no other printers are currently installed on your computer, this option will not be presented). Enter the name `Test Printer` for your printer's name.

7. One of the last steps in configuring a printer is deciding whether you want the printer shared. If you do not share the printer, it will not be available to users on the network. If you want to share the printer, you can select the Share As: option and provide the share name you want to use to represent the printer on the network. Enter

`Test_Printer` as your share name. (Note: Because the share name is longer than 13 characters and has spaces in it, you will receive a warning that DOS-based workstations might not be able to access this resource. Keep the name short but descriptive and avoid spaces in the share name.)

8. You also will be prompted to enter descriptive information describing the location and any other comments you add about the printer. Enter **Lab** as the location and **Test Printer** in the comment box.

9. You are then asked whether you would like to print a test page. Indicating Yes will allow you to test your configuration. Select Yes to print a test page.

10. After you have entered all the required information, the Setup Wizard will provide a summary of the configuration you have requested. Click the Finish button to complete the installation.

You have now successfully installed a local printer.

Sharing a Local Printer

Sharing a local printer allows remote users to access it from across the network. This section describes how to share a local printer.

Creating a shared printer is very easy. It can be accomplished in one of two ways. The first method of creating a printer share was seen in Step by Step 2.8. During the installation of a local printer, the Printer Setup Wizard offers to automatically create a printer share for you. The other method involves viewing the properties of an existing printer object and selects the Sharing tab (you can access the property tab by right-clicking the printer object and selecting Properties from the menu). Figure 2.12 shows the Sharing property tab from a local printer object.

From this tab, you can configure the share name you would like to use (or turn sharing off). You also can configure the print drivers associated with the printer. By clicking the Additional Drivers button, you can install additional print drivers. Figure 2.13 shows the Additional Drivers screen.

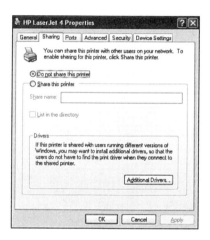

FIGURE 2.12
Sharing property tab for a local printer.

FIGURE 2.13
Additional Drivers screen of a shared printer.

If you select additional drivers to be installed, Windows will prompt you for the appropriate disk containing the drivers requested. After drivers are installed, additional types of workstation clients will be able to connect to the share and have the drivers made available to them without user intervention at the client side.

Printers Permissions

In many environments, printers are managed to ensure that only certain users (or groups of users) can access specific print devices. Access to the Windows XP print environment is managed through printer permissions.

Like file system shares, printer shares allow users to access print resources over the network. Printer shares have three different levels of access that can be granted. Each printer permission allows users to have a different level of access to the printer. For example, some users may have print access, which allows them to submit print jobs to the printer, whereas other users might have Manage Printers permissions allowing them to manage the print device.

Table 2.13 presents a listing of common tasks associated with the print environment and the permissions required to perform each task.

TABLE 2.13

PRINTER PERMISSIONS

Capabilities	Print Permission	Manage Documents Permission	Manage Printer Permission
Print documents	Yes	Yes	Yes
Pause, resume, restart, and cancel the user's own print jobs	Yes	Yes	Yes
Connect to the shared printer	Yes	Yes	Yes
Control job settings for all print jobs	No	Yes	Yes
Pause, resume, restart, and cancel all users' print jobs	No	Yes	Yes

Capabilities	Print Permission	Manage Documents Permission	Manage Printer Permission
Cancel all print jobs	No	Yes	Yes
Pause and resume a printer, and take a printer offline	No	No	Yes
Share a printer	No	No	Yes
Change printer properties	No	No	Yes
Delete a printer	No	No	Yes
Change printer permissions	No	No	Yes

FIGURE 2.14
Printer permissions.

You can allow or deny printer permissions. Denying permissions always takes precedence over all other permissions assigned to a user. Figure 2.14 shows the Printer Permission tab (Security tab) of printer properties. Right-click a printer object, select Properties from the context menu, and select the Security tab to access this screen.

Connecting to a Shared Printer

Connecting to a shared printer (or a network print server) allows a user to print to a remote printer over the network. Connecting to a remote printer can be done in a number of different ways. The following section will explore each of these methods.

One of the easiest ways to connect to a remote printer is to run the Add Printer Wizard. This can be run by double-clicking the Add Printer icon in the Printers folder of Control Panel. After the initial welcome screen, you will be prompted to install a local or network printer; select network printer. You will then be asked to provide the UNC name for the printer you would like to attach to (for example, the printer installed in Step by Step 2.4 would be called `\\WORKSTATION\Test_Printer`).

You also can access the printer using an HTTP (hypertext transport protocol) request. In this case, the path to the printer would be `HTTP://SERVER/printer_name`.

You also can connect to a printer by dragging the printer from the print server and dropping it into your Printers folder, or by simply right-clicking the icon and then clicking Connect from the context menu.

The last option you have for connecting to a printer involves the `net use` command. From the command prompt, you can issue the following command to map a local LTP port to a network printer:

```
Net Use LPT1 \\servername\printer name
```

After you have connected to a shared printer over the network, you can use it as if it were attached to your computer.

Managing Printers

After the print environment is set up, you will need to manage the printers. The Windows XP print environment is one of the easiest to use and manage. In the following sections, you will explore many common printer management tasks.

Assigning Forms to Paper Trays

Many printers support multiple paper trays and paper sizes. You can assign various paper types and sizes to the specific trays installed on your printer. After a form (or paper type/size) has been assigned to a specific tray, a user can select it from within her applications. When the user issues a print command, Windows XP automatically routes the print job to the paper tray with the correct form.

Figure 2.15 shows the device settings for an HP LaserJet printer. To assign forms to paper trays, complete the following:

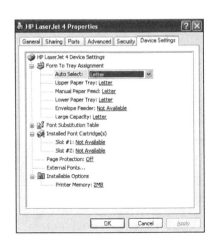

FIGURE 2.15
Device Settings tab of printer properties.

> **NOTE**
>
> **The Printer Properties Tabs Can Vary from Printer to Printer**   Different printers offer many different features and options. For this reason, you might find that the Properties tab for your printer will not be the same as shown in this book.

1. Open the Properties dialog box to the printer and click the Device Settings tab.

2. From the Form to Tray Assignment option, select a tray and assign a paper size to it (paper sizes are found in the drop-down lists).

Setting Separator Pages

Most printers are able to operate in many different modes (for example, PostScript or PCL [Printer Control Language]). Because different printers are configured to expect different print commands, you should be familiar with different types of separator pages and how they can be specified. A separator page is a file that contains the following commands:

◆ Identify each document that is being printed (also referred to as a banner page).

◆ Switch the print device between print modes (if supported by the physical printer). You could use a separator page to specify PostScript or PCL for a printer that is not able to automatically detect the type of print job it is processing.

Windows XP ships with four separator page files. They are located in the *systemroot\system32* directory. Table 2.14 presents the function of each file.

TABLE 2.14

SEPARATOR PAGE FILES

Separator File	Function
Pcl.sep	Prints a page after switching the printer to PCL printing.
Sysprint.sep	Prints a page after switching the printer to PostScript printing.
Pscript.sep	Does not print a page after switching the printer to PostScript printing.
Sysprtj.sep	A Japanese version of the Sysprint.sep file.

The separator page can be changed from the Advanced tab of a printer property sheet. From the Advanced tab, you can click the Separator Page button and you will be presented with a dialog box prompting you to enter the name and path to a separator file. After the file is specified, click OK.

Pausing and Restarting Printers

As the administrator of a printer, you might find situations where the printer needs to be taken out of service for a period of time. Printers can be paused (or resumed if currently paused), or all print jobs can be canceled. This can be accomplished by double-clicking a printer object from the Printers folder (found in the Control Panel).

NOTE **Restarting the Print Spooler Service**
In some rare instances, you might find that the Printer Spooler Service of your Windows XP system needs to be restarted to get printing to work properly. This service can be restarted from the Computer Management/Service/Print Spooler of the MMC Computer Manager snap-in.

A window will open showing all pending print jobs for the printer. From the Printer menu, you will find the Pause Printer and Cancel All Documents menu options.

Pausing a printer allows users to continue submitting print jobs to the printer even though the jobs will not print. This is useful in situations where you need to perform simple maintenance on the printer and do not want to disrupt the way users submit print jobs. After the printer is fixed, unpause the printer and print jobs will begin to print.

Canceling all documents allows you to quickly clear a print queue that has a large number of documents waiting to print.

Setting Print Priority and Printer Availability

In many environments, management of printers involves being a traffic cop regarding whose print jobs get printed first. For example, you might want to ensure that print jobs submitted by the president and her assistant print before all other jobs. To this end, you can install two printers (the software representations of a printer) on a machine and point them to the same physical print device. You would then assign a higher priority to the printer used by the president and her staff.

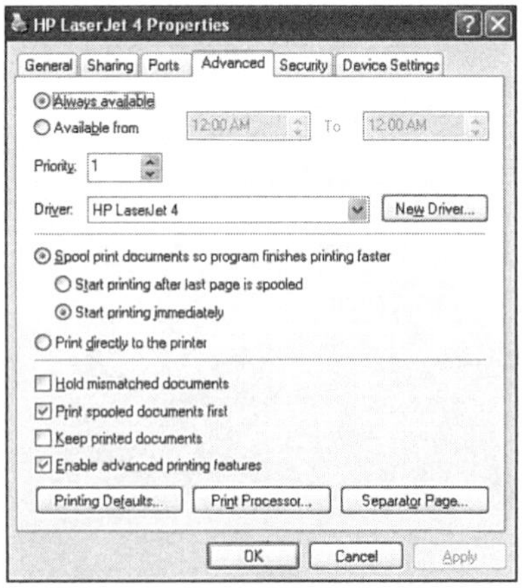

Figure 2.16 shows the Advanced tab of the Printer Properties page. This is where printer priorities can be set.

Table 2.15 presents the configuration options available from this page.

FIGURE 2.16
Printer Properties—Advanced tab.

TABLE 2.15

ADVANCED PRINTER SETTINGS

Option	Description
Availability	This option allows you to configure when this printer will print jobs that are submitted.
Priority	Set this printer's priority relative to other printers configured to print to the same physical print device. The range is from 99 to 1 (99 being the highest priority).

Option	*Description*
Spool Print Documents So Programs Finish Printing Faster	Spooling is the process of writing the print job to the hard disk before it is sent to the physical print device. The theory is that writing to the hard disk is significantly faster than sending a job to the physical printer. After the print job is written to disk, you can continue to work with the application and the spooler takes care of submitting the job to the physical printer in the background.
	Two options are associated with this configuration setting. The first, Start Printing After the Last Page Is Spooled, ensures that the entire print job has been completed before it is sent to the physical printer. This may require that the application participate in the print process longer because the entire job must be processed before it is printed.
	The second option, Start Printing Immediately, specifies that the print job be spooled and sent to the physical printer as soon as the spooler receives the job. This allows the print job to be processed faster.
Print Directly to the Printer	This option specifies that the print job should be sent directly to the printer and not spooled. This is a useful option if you are running low on disk space or if you have an application that requires a direct connection to the physical print device.
Hold Mismatched Documents	This option specifies that print jobs are checked to ensure the physical print device can print them (for example, the correct paper is loaded). Documents that cannot be printed are left in the spooler until the configuration of the printer is adjusted to accept the job. This setting allows mismatched jobs to sit in the spooler while other (nonmismatched) jobs print.
Print Spooled Documents First	When this option is enabled, the spooler chooses documents that have completed spooling to print first. This allows spooled documents to print first regardless of print priority.
Keep Printed Documents	This option instructs the print spooler not to delete jobs that have successfully printed. This allows jobs to be resubmitted if necessary.
Enable Advanced Printing Features	This option specifies whether the advanced printer features are enabled. When enabled, metafile spooling is turned on and options such as Page Order, Booklet Printing, and Pages Per Sheet are, as well.
Printing Defaults	Click this option to change the default document properties for all users of the selected printer. If you share your local printer, these settings will be the default document properties for each user.

continues

TABLE 2.15

ADVANCED PRINTER SETTINGS

Option	Description
Print Processor	Click this option to specify the data type used by this printer. In general, you should not need to change these settings. In some special instances, however, you might need to configure this setting for a few specialized programs.
Separator Page	As discussed previously, this option allows you to change the separator page used for this printer.

Printer Pooling

In very high-volume print environments, Windows XP offers a printer pooling option. Printer pooling allows a single printer to be directed to multiple physical printers (or in Microsoft lingo, *multiple print devices*).

Figure 2.17 shows the Ports tab of a Printer Property page.

By checking the Enable Printer Pooling box on the bottom of the page, you are able to select multiple ports from the ports list shown in the figure. As shown in Figure 2.17, this printer will print to LPT1, LPT2, and LPT3, depending on which printer is ready to accept a job when the spooler receives this job.

You will need to ensure that all physical print devices use the same printer driver (are of the same type). It is also recommended that all the printers be located in the same physical area (because users will not know which physical printer will be used to print their job).

Redirecting Printers

As the printer administrator in your environment, you might find it useful to redirect a printer. For example, if a printer fails and a large number of print jobs are currently spooled (and waiting to print), you can redirect the printer to another physical device so the jobs can print without needing to be resubmitted by the users who created them.

Step by Step 2.9 demonstrates the process of redirecting a printer. In this example, you will configure two local printers, pause the first

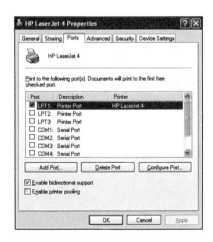

FIGURE 2.17
Printer Properties—Ports tab.

printer (to simulate a printer failure), and submit a few print jobs to the printer. You will then redirect printer 1 to printer 2 and resume printing on printer 1. Through redirection, you will see the print jobs transfer from printer 1 to printer 2. In the real world, the printers would not be on the same machine, but for demonstration purposes this works well.

STEP BY STEP

2.9 Configuring Printer Redirection

1. Create two local printers based on the information in Table 2.16 (if you need assistance, refer to Step by Step 2.8).

TABLE 2.16

PRINTER CONFIGURATION FOR STEP BY STEP 2.9

Configuration	Printer 1	Printer 2
Location	Local	Local
Port	LPT1	LPT2
Driver	HP LaserJet 5Si	HP LaserJet 5Si
Name	Printer1	Printer2
Share	HP1	HP2
Local/Comment	N/A	N/A

2. You should now have two printers configured on your local system. Pause Printer1 (right-click Printer1 and select Pause Printer from the context menu).

3. Set Printer1 as the Default Windows printer (right-click Printer1 and select Set As Default Printer). This step ensures that print jobs submitted are sent to printer1.

4. Launch Notepad and submit a number of printer jobs. Double-click Printer1; you should see the print jobs sitting in the printer queue.

continues

continued

5. Now configure Printer1 so that it redirects its print jobs to Printer2. From the Printer menu of Printer1's print queue display, select Properties. Select the Ports tab. Note that LPT1 is the current port for Printer1. Click the Add Port button. In the Printer Ports dialog box, click New Port. In the Port Name dialog box, enter `\\`**`computer`**`\`**`HP2`** (where *computer* is the name of your computer). Click OK. Click Close.

6. Notice that the new port you just created is now the port to which Printer1 will print.

7. Double-click Printer2 to display the print jobs in the print queue (it should be empty). Position the print queue windows for Printer1 and Printer2 so you can view them both on the screen.

8. Resume printing for Printer1. The jobs from Printer1 should start showing up in Printer2's print queue.

Managing Print Jobs

In addition to managing the physical printers in your environment, you will need to become proficient at the management of print jobs. By default, users have the ability to manage their own print jobs. Users with Manage Printers or Manage Documents permissions have the ability to manage all print jobs received at the printer. It is important that you plan for print job management in your environment; jobs will sometimes get stuck in a print queue and hold up printing for everyone.

The next section provides an overview of document management activities.

Pausing, Restarting, and Canceling Print Jobs

By double-clicking on a printer icon, you can view the print jobs currently sitting in the print queue. If you have the appropriate permissions, you can also manage print jobs.

You have the ability to pause, restart, or cancel jobs. Right-clicking on the job you would like to manage presents these options to you (see Figure 2.18).

By pausing the print job, you stop its printing. This will give you the opportunity to correct a problem with the job or allow other print jobs to print first. To resume the job, right-click the paused job and select Resume from the context menu.

Restarting a job allows you to restart a print job from the beginning. This is a useful option if a large job starts to print but is disrupted. It allows you to reprint the job without having to regenerate the job.

Canceling a print job causes the job to be removed from the print queue.

Setting Notifications and Priority Print Times

As a user with Manage Printer or Manage Documents permissions, you have the ability to set notification, priority, and printing time for individual print jobs (as the owner of a print job, you can also modify these settings, but only for the print jobs you own).

FIGURE 2.18
Print job management options.

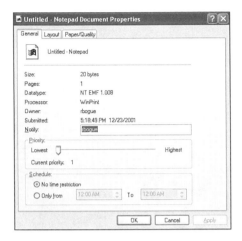

FIGURE 2.19
General tab of a print job.

Figure 2.19 shows the General tab of a print job (double-click a job to access this tab).

The Notify option allows you to specify a user who should receive a notification when the print job completes. This is a useful option for users who submit jobs but want their assistants to pick them up from the printer.

The Priority option allows a job to be given priority relative to other jobs currently in the print queue. The value can range from 99 to 1 (with 99 being the highest priority).

The Schedule option allows you to specify when a specific job will be printed.

Managing Printers Using a Web Browser

Windows XP enables you to manage printers from any computer running a Web browser. The computer acting as your print server must have Windows 2000 (or higher) and Internet Information Services (IIS) installed on it.

You can use your browser (you must be using Internet Explorer 4.0 or higher) to manage the printers installed on a remote machine by typing the following URL in the location box of your browser: `HTTP://printer_server_name/printers`. Figure 2.20 shows the resulting Web page that will be loaded.

FIGURE 2.20
Web-Based Printer Management screen.

By clicking the name of a printer, you can view the details of the print jobs in the queue for that printer. Figure 2.21 shows the details of a specific printer. Note that on the left side of the Web page, you have options that allow you to manage the printer and individual print jobs.

To manage a specific job, click the button beside the job you want to manage. You will find that the only limitation of this interface is that it does not allow you to manage advanced settings (such as notification, print time, or priority).

FIGURE 2.21
Web-Based Printer Details screen.

CASE STUDY: ABC COMPANY

ESSENCE OF THE CASE

Here are the essential elements in this case:

▶ File system security

▶ File system conversion

▶ Efficient directory structures

▶ Shared folder permissions

ABC Company is in the process of installing Windows XP Professional on all desktop computers in its organization. You want to ensure that you meet the following criteria with regard to the development of your file system and shared folder access plan:

· All resources must be secured.

· Only members of certain departments can gain access to department confidential data.

A large number of workstations and servers were installed six months earlier as part of the pilot rollout, and have been in operation since then. These workstations and servers were configured with FAT32 partitions when they were installed. You need to be sure that data from these machines is not lost.

ANALYSIS

This case revolves around four main issues. The first is that all computers will need to be configured with NTFS because NTFS is the only file system supported by Windows XP with folder- and file-level security. If security is a prime concern, NTFS is the only file system you can use to protect your equipment.

Second, for the workstations used during the pilot rollout of Windows XP, you will need to convert the FAT32 partitions to NTFS. It is important that the Convert utility be used to perform the operation, as it is the only utility that will change the file system and allow the data to be preserved.

CASE STUDY: ABC COMPANY

The last two issues revolve around NTFS/shared folder permissions and the directory structure used. It is important the directory structure make sense for the users of the company. To develop the structure, ABC Company will need to fully define all the different users that need to store information on the servers, determine who needs to access the data, and determine what level of access each user needs. The directory structure created should optimize the assignment of permissions so that permissions assigned high in the directory structure do not give too many permissions to users who do not require them.

CHAPTER SUMMARY

Companies install networks so that resources can be shared between users. The challenge facing a network administrator is to ensure that users are given access to the resources they need and nothing more. This chapter presented how to manage, configure, and troubleshoot two of the most heavily used network services (file and print).

In the discussions relating to NTFS permissions, you also looked at the basic skills required to manage an NTFS file system. Specifically, the chapter covered NTFS permissions, compression, encryption, Web folders, and conversion.

The print environment was also covered. In these sections, printer permissions, printer configuration, and print job management were covered.

KEY TERMS

- Folder share
- Offline Files
- Printer share
- NTFS permissions
- Printer permissions
- NTFS
- FAT
- FAT32
- Printer
- Print server
- Print driver
- Print device
- HyperText Transport Protocol (HTTP)

APPLY YOUR KNOWLEDGE

Exercises

2.1 Applying NTFS Permissions

In this exercise, you will assign permissions to a folder to test NTFS permissions. To test permissions, you will create a new folder on an NTFS partition and create a file in the folder. You will then create a new user account and assign the user account permission to the folder. You will then log on as the newly created user to test NTFS permissions.

Estimated Time: 10 minutes

1. Log on to your system as Administrator.

2. From the Users Accounts icon of Control Panel, Select the Advanced Tab, click the Advanced button, right-click Users, and select New User to create a new user called NTFSTest (create this user as a Standard User). Remember the password you assign to the user. (Note: These instructions assume that you are working on a Windows XP Professional computer that is part of a Workgroup. If your system is configured to be part of a Domain environment, you will need to use the Computer Manager snap-in to create and manage user accounts.)

3. Right-click the Start button (start Explorer).

4. Scroll to an NTFS partition on your system.

5. Create a new Folder called NTFSData on the partition.

6. Right-click the new folder and select Properties from the context menu.

7. Click the Security tab.

8. Click the Advanced button.

9. Uncheck the option "Inherit from parent the permission entries that apply to child objects. Include these with entries explicitly defined here," and click the Remove button when prompted.

10. Click the Add button, and then click the Locations button.

11. Select the first entry in the list, the local computer, and click OK.

12. Enter **NTFSTest** in the Enter the Object Name to Select box. Click OK.

13. Select the permissions of Read Permissions, List Folder, Read Data, and traverse Folder, Execute File. Click OK.

14. Click the Add button. Enter administrators in the box. Click OK. Select the Allow Full Control check box and click OK.

15. Click OK and OK again to close the open dialog boxes.

16. Create a new folder under the NTFSData folder called Sub1.

17. Verify the default permissions inherited by the Sub1 folder when it was created by right-clicking the folder, selecting Properties, and then selecting the Security tab. You should see the same permissions as assigned to NTFSData. The assignments will be grayed out to indicate that they are being inherited from the parent folders.

18. Assign the NTFSTest user Full Control permissions by selecting NTFSTest and clicking the Allow full control check box. Click OK to close the properties.

19. Log on as the NTFSTest User.

APPLY YOUR KNOWLEDGE

20. Use Explorer to locate the NTFSData folder. Try to create a new text file in the folder. You should not be able to complete the operation because you do not have the write permission.

21. Try to create a new text file called TESTDATA.TXT in the Sub1 folder. You should be able to create new files at this location.

2.2 Applying the Deny NTFS Permission

In this exercise, you will use the Deny permission to limit the ability of a user from accessing a resource. In Exercise 2.1, you gave a user named NTFSTest the ability to write to a folder named x:\NTFSData\Sub1. To demonstrate the Deny permission, you will be assigning the Users group Deny Write permission Sub1. This will block the NTFSTest user's ability to write to the Sub1 folder.

Estimated Time: 5 minutes

1. Log on as Administrator.

2. From the Security tab of the Sub1 folder, assign the Users group the Deny Write permission.

3. Log on as NTFSUser.

4. Attempt to create a new file in the Sub1 folder. You are not able to because you no longer have the Write permission. The Write permission is being denied because of your membership in the User group.

2.3 Taking Ownership of a File

In this exercise, you will delete the NTFSUser user account (this exercise assumes that you completed

Exercise 2.1). Because the NTFSUser created a file called TESTDATA.TXT in the Sub1 folder, you will need to manage the file. To do this, you must take ownership of the file and assign yourself permission to access it.

Estimated Time: 10 minutes

1. Log on to your system as Administrator.

2. From the Users and Password icon of Control Panel, delete the user called NTFSTest.

3. Using Windows Explorer, try to access the TESTDATA.TXT file in the Sub1 folder. You should be denied access.

4. Right-click the file and click the Security tab. Click the Advanced button, and then click the Ownership tab.

5. In the Change Owner To dialog box, select Administrator from the list and click OK. The administrator is now the owner of the file.

6. Click OK to close the Property box for the file.

7. Right-click the file and click the Security tab. Notice that the Add button is now available. Assign the Full Control permissions to the Administrator.

8. You can now manage the file.

2.4 Applying the Deny Shared Folder Permission

In this exercise, you will modify the Shared Folder permissions assigned in Exercise 2.4 so that the Users group will be denied access to the SharedData share. Because the ShareTest user is a member of this group, you will not be able to access the share.

Estimated Time: 10 minutes

APPLY YOUR KNOWLEDGE

1. Log on to your system as Administrator.

2. View the permissions on the SharedData share (right-click the SharedData folder, click the Sharing tab, and click the Permissions button). Click Add and add the Users group to the permission list with Deny Full Control.

3. Log on as the ShareTest user account.

4. Click Start, Run. In the Open dialog box, type *computername*\SHARETEST (where *computername* = the name of your system). You should not be able to attach to the shared directory.

2.5   Applying Shared Folder and NTFS Permissions

In this exercise, you will combine NTFS- and share-level permissions to secure a directory structure. In this exercise, you will give the user ShareTest full control permissions to a share and use NTFS permissions to limit the user's ability to write to the file system.

Estimated Time: 10 minutes

1. Log on to your system as Administrator.

2. View the permissions on the SharedData share (right-click the SharedData folder, click the Sharing tab, and click the Permissions button). Remove the Users group from the list of users with permissions to the resource. Add the ShareTest user to the resource with full control permissions.

3. Log on as the ShareTest user account.

4. Click Start, Run. In the Open dialog box. type *computername*\SHARETEST (where *computername* is the name of your system). You should be able to attach to the shared directory.

5. Create a new file in the directory. You should be able to create and access the file.

6. Log on as the Administrator.

7. Right-click the SharedData folder and click the Security tab. In the list of users with permissions, add the ShareTest user account with Deny Write permissions.

8. Log on as the ShareTest user account.

9. Click Start, Run. In the Open dialog box, type *computername*\SHARETEST (where *computername* is the name of your system). You should be able to attach to the shared directory.

10. Create a new file in the directory. You should not be able to create the file.

11. Try to edit the file you created in step 5. You should not be able to modify the file as you can no longer write to the directory.

Review Questions

1. How are effective NTFS permissions calculated for a user when he received those permissions from several groups?

2. A user leaves your company and her user account is deleted. You realize that company confidential data is still stored in that user's home directory. When you try to access the folder to retrieve the data (logged in as Administrator), you receive the message Access Denied. How can you fix this problem?

3. You move a file from a folder on one partition to a folder on another partition. What permissions will the file have after the move?

APPLY YOUR KNOWLEDGE

4. You move a file from one folder to another folder (on the same partition). What permissions will the file have after the move?

5. You are in a high-volume print environment. What feature of Windows XP will you use to help support the large number of print jobs submitted in your environment?

6. What feature of the Windows XP environment allows you to remotely manage shared folders?

7. Your printer supports multiple paper trays. When you print, your jobs are put on the incorrect paper. How can you fix this problem?

8. What is the significance of the Deny permission?

9. In NTFS permissions, which permissions take precedence: folder or file level?

Exam Questions

1. You are working as a help desk operator in a large corporate environment. Sally calls to complain that she is not able to access any of the data on the \\NT4_CORP\SALES share. You check the share permissions on the share and determine that Sally has Full Control shared folder permissions assigned to her user account. Sally is also able to ping the \\NT4_CORP server. What is your next course of action to help Sally?

   A. Verify Sally's membership in other groups to determine whether she is denied access to the share.

   B. Verify Sally's NTFS permissions to the file system.

   C. Verify that Sally can connect to the \\NT4_CORP server over the network.

   D. Verify Sally's shared folder permissions and NTFS permissions.

2. You are conducting a security audit on your company's servers to ensure that all confidential data is secure. A consultant has conducted a preliminary review and determined that many of your critical data partitions are unsecured and at risk of being accessed by unauthorized personnel. The consultant has based this conclusion on your shared folder strategy. Your servers are all configured with NTFS, and NTFS permissions have been assigned to groups to control access to the data. Shared folders have been created at the root of each partition and the Domain Users group has been assigned Full Control. Is the poor review from your consultant cause for concern? (Choose the two best answers.)

   A. No; NTFS permissions are being used to control access to data.

   B. Yes; where NTFS and share permissions combine, the least restrictive permission is granted and therefore security will be breached.

   C. Yes; assigning the Domain Users group Full Control to the share is a security breach.

   D. No; the consultant you hired is incompetent and should be fired, as he does not understand Windows XP share security.

3. As the manager of a high-volume order-processing center, you need to optimize the print environment for your users. A large number of order-entry staff is inputting a high volume of orders. A copy of each order must be printed

APPLY YOUR KNOWLEDGE

when the order is entered. All orders are collected in a central location to be filled. Problems arise when printers go offline, as the entire staff cannot print. You need a solution that can handle the high volume of print jobs and will allow users to continue printing even if a printer is offline. What should you suggest?

A. Configure a number of printers to use printer redirection to print to a very fast and reliable printer.

B. Buy a faster and more reliable printer.

C. Set up a large number of network printers and configure the users' workstations to point to a number of the printers.

D. Use printer pooling to create one printer with multiple physical devices.

4. You have configured your server with FAT partitions (the D: drive) and want to convert them to FAT32. You issue the following command, but find the system will not convert the drive.

```
Convert d: /fs:fat32
```

What is the cause of the problem? (Choose the two best answers.)

A. The syntax for the command is `Convert d: /fs:ntfs`.

B. You need to back up the FAT file system and reformat the drive as FAT32 and then restore from backup.

C. You should use the Format command to convert the drive.

D. You cannot convert from FAT to FAT32 in Windows XP.

5. As the support technician for a large company, you are called in to fix the president's PC. The president read in a magazine that Windows XP computers are secure only if they are configured with NTFS-formatted partitions. He then proceeded to convert his hard drive from FAT to NTFS using the format utility. He is now very concerned that his PC will not boot. What should you tell him?

A. The president should stop reading computer magazines.

B. You will have to reinstall Windows to access the newly formatted drive to recover the data.

C. The data is lost because the drive was formatted rather than converted.

D. The president should have used the correct command switches with the format utility.

6. As the network administrator of your company, you want to create a large number of user accounts with secure home directories. What is the most efficient way to secure these directories?

A. Create a shared folder named Users on a FAT or FAT32 partition and create subfolders for each user. You then share out the Users folders so all users can access it.

B. Create a shared folder named Users on an NTFS partition and create subfolders for each user (each user directory is secured so only one user can access it).

C. Create a folder named Users on an NTFS partition and create subfolders for each user. You then share each subfolder so only one user can access it.

D. Create a shared folder named Users on a FAT or FAT32 partition and create subfolders for each user. You then share out each subfolder so only one user can access it.

7. You are troubleshooting a resource access issue for a user on your network. Mikayla is not able to access data when accessing the shared data folder over the network. If Mikayla logs on locally at the computer where the shared data is stored, she can access the data directly from the file system. Where should you start troubleshooting her access problems?

A. Check the NTFS permissions assigned to Mikayla. She has been being assigned Deny— Full Control.

B. Check the NTFS permissions assigned to Mikayla. They are blocking her from accessing the resource when she attaches from the network.

C. Check the shared folder permissions assigned to Mikayla. She has been assigned Deny— Full Control.

D. Mikayla needs to be a member of the Authenticated User group to access resources from over the network.

8. As the network administrator for a large accounting firm, you are developing a strategy to secure a shared data folder for the executives in your company. You created a folder called EXECDATA on

a partition formatted with NTFS. Security is of prime concern, so you deny the Everyone group Full Control permissions to the folder. You then grant the Executives group Full Control permissions to the folder. To allow access to the resource over the network, you share the folder and grant Full Control access to the Executives group. Executives are not able to access the resource. What is the problem with your strategy?

A. The Administrators group must be granted Full Control so that the resource can be managed properly.

B. By denying full control to the Everyone group, all users are blocked from the resource regardless of group membership.

C. The executives should be accessing all resources locally so shared permissions should not be assigned.

D. Future investigation is required to determine whether this is an NTFS or a shared folder issue.

9. As the network administrator of a large company, you create a shared folder with the permissions presented in Table 2.17.

TABLE 2.17

SHARED FOLDER PERMISSIONS

User/Group	Shared Folder Permission
Mikayla	Allow Change
Sales	Deny Full Control
Executives	Allow Full Control

APPLY YOUR KNOWLEDGE

Mikayla is a member of the Sales group and the Executives Group. What are Mikayla's effective permissions on the shared folder?

A. Full Control.

B. Change.

C. Read.

D. No Access will be allowed.

E. Not enough information is presented to calculate permissions.

10. As the network administrator of a large company, you create a shared folder with the permissions presented in Table 2.18. The shared resource is located on a partition formatted as NTFS.

TABLE 2.18

SHARED FOLDER PERMISSIONS

User/Group	Shared Folder Permission	NTFS Permissions
Mikayla	Allow Read	Allow Read
Sales	Allow Read	
Executives	Allow Full Control	

Mikayla and John are members of the Sales group and the Executives group. What are Mikayla's and John's effective permissions on the resource?

A. Mikayla has Read; John has Read.

B. Mikayla has Read; John has no access.

C. Mikayla has no access; John has Read.

D. Mikayla has Full Control; John has Full Control.

E. Mikayla has Full Control; John has no access.

F. Mikayla has no access; John has Full Control.

G. Not enough information is presented to calculate permissions.

11. You are working the help desk late one night when a user calls to complain that when she moves a file from one network share to another, the permissions are getting messed up (the shared folders are on separate partitions). Table 2.19 presents the existing NTFS permissions on the file being moved. Table 2.20 presents the NTFS permissions on the target folder.

TABLE 2.19

SOURCE FILE NTFS PERMISSIONS

User/Group	NTFS Permission
Executives	Allow Full Control (inherited from the parent folder)
Sales	Deny Full Control

TABLE 2.20

TARGET FOLDER NTFS PERMISSIONS

User/Group	NTFS Permission
Sales	Allow Full Control

When the user moves the file to the target folder, what will the effective permissions be on the file?

A. Executives have Allow Full Control; Sales has Allow Full Control.

B. Executives have Deny Full Control; Sales has Deny Full Control.

APPLY YOUR KNOWLEDGE

C. Executives have Allow Full Control; Sales has Deny Full Control.

D. Executives have no permissions; Sales has Deny Full Control.

E. Executives have no permissions; Sales has Allow Full Control.

F. Executives have Deny Full Control; Sales has no permissions.

G. Executives have Allow Full Control; Sales has no permissions.

H. Not enough information is presented to calculate permissions.

12. You are working the help desk late one night when a user calls to complain that when she moves a file from one folder to another folder (on the same partition), the permissions are getting messed up. Table 2.21 presents the existing NTFS permissions on the file being moved. Table 2.22 presents the NTFS permissions on the target folder.

TABLE 2.21

SOURCE FILE NTFS PERMISSIONS

User/Group	NTFS Permission
Executives	Allow Full Control (inherited from the parent folder)
Sales	Deny Full Control

TABLE 2.22

TARGET FOLDER NTFS PERMISSIONS

User/Group	NTFS Permission
Sales	Allow Full Control

When the user moves the file to the target folder, what will the effective permissions be on the file?

A. Executives have Allow Full Control; Sales has Allow Full Control.

B. Executives have Deny Full Control; Sales has Deny Full Control.

C. Executives have Allow Full Control; Sales has Deny Full Control.

D. Executives have no permissions; Sales has Deny Full Control.

E. Executives have no permissions; Sales has Allow Full Control.

F. Executives have Deny Full Control; Sales has no permissions.

G. Executives have Allow Full Control; Sales has no permissions.

H. Not enough information is presented to calculate permissions.

13. You are the administrator of a large consulting organization. The consultants are all equipped with notebook computers. There is a set of template files that all consultants should have with them at all times. These templates change frequently. Which feature of Windows XP Professional should you use to keep these templates available to the consultants as they travel away from the network?

APPLY YOUR KNOWLEDGE

A. Use Group Policy Objects to force the templates to a directory on the consultant computers.

B. Have the logon scripts for each user copy the necessary files to each machine.

C. Use the Offline Folders feature to share a folder as Offline Enabled.

D. On each consultant computer select the share where the templates are and select Make Available Offline.

Answers to Review Questions

1. Effective NTFS permissions are calculated by adding permissions of the user and the permissions from the groups together, with the exception of deny permissions, which override individual permission. For additional information, see the section titled "Multiple NTFS Permissions."

2. Because the user account has been deleted, no users have access to the home folder. When a user account is deleted, all references to the user account's Security Identifier (SID) are deleted from the operating system. The Administrator is not given access to the directory because the Administrator account does not have permissions to the NTFS folder. To fix this situation, the Administrator will need to take ownership of the folder and give himself permission to access the folder. For additional information, see the section titled "Assigning Permissions."

3. The file will inherit the permissions from the parent folder into which it is being moved. When a file is moved between physical partitions, a new

copy of the file needs to be created on the target partition. The default NTFS permissions for a file are to inherit permissions from the parent. For additional information, see the section titled "Permission Inheritance."

4. The file will retain its existing permissions. Because you are moving a file within a partition, a new version of the file does not need to be created and therefore it can retain its permissions. This applies to all explicit permissions. Inherited permissions will change, as is appropriate, for the new location. For additional information, see the section titled "Copying and Moving Folders and Files."

5. The printer pool option would be best suited for this environment. Printer pooling allows all users in a high-volume print environment to print to the same printer. This printer is configured to send the print jobs to multiple print devices. For additional information, see the section titled "Printer Pooling."

6. The Microsoft Management Console with the Computer Management snap-in allows you to manage remote shares. For additional information, see the section titled "Creating Shared Folders."

7. You will need to see how the paper sources have been configured for the printer on your system. This can be accomplished from the Device Setting tab of Printer properties. For additional information, see the section titled "Managing Printers."

8. The Deny permission will always override permissions that have been granted. For example, a user receives Full Control permissions to a folder

from membership in Group1 and also receives Deny Full Control from membership in Group2. Because the user has been granted the Deny permission, she is not given access to the resource. For additional information, see the section titled "File Permissions."

9. File-level permissions take precedence over folder permissions. In most environments, however, you will want to make sure you are managing access to your resources at the folder level (the higher up in the folder structure, the better). For additional information, see the section titled "NTFS Permissions."

Answers to Exam Questions

1. **B.** Sally is able to connect to the share and access some of the data on it. Because of this, you can confirm that the shared folder is accessible. Remember that share permissions are assigned at the folder level and are then applied from that point in the directory structure down. The only reason why Sally would not be able to access all the data in the share has to do with NTFS permissions. When NTFS and share permissions are combined, the most restrictive permission applies. Answer A is incorrect, as Sally can access the share. Answer C is incorrect, as Sally can ping the server and can access some of the data from the share. Answer D is incorrect, as shared folder permissions are not the cause of Sally's difficulties. For additional information, see the section titled "NTFS Permissions and Shared Folders."

2. **A, D.** Answer A is correct; NTFS is being used to control access to resources. When NTFS and share permissions are combined, the most restrictive permission becomes the user's effective permissions. Answer D is also correct; the consultant you have hired is not qualified to conduct a security audit for your company. Answer B is incorrect, as NTFS and share permissions do not combine in the manner described. An argument could be made for answer C, but technically it is not correct if NTFS permissions are being managed properly in your environment. For additional information, see the section titled "NTFS Permissions and Shared Folders."

3. **D.** Answer D is the best answer for this scenario. Printer pooling allows one printer to point to multiple physical print devices. This allows workstations to be configured so they point to one network printer. If a printer fails, the pooling function will allow jobs to be routed to another printer. Answer A is not correct, as redirection forwards jobs from one printer to another printer. Answer B would help, but is not the best solution. Answer C is incorrect, as the users would need to change their printer configuration to print to a new printer if their current printer failed. For additional information, see the section titled "Managing Printers."

4. **B, D.** The convert command only allows you to convert FAT or FAT32 to NTFS. If you would like to change a FAT partition to FAT32, you need to back up your data, reformat the drive, and then restore the data. Answer A is incorrect, as this command will convert the drive to NTFS. Answer C is incorrect, as formatting a drive is not the same as converting a drive. During a format

APPLY YOUR KNOWLEDGE

all data is lost. Converting a drive will allow the data to be retained. For additional information, see the section titled "Converting File Systems."

5. **C.** Although answer A is tempting, it is not in your best interest to get the president upset. Technically, answer C is correct and the data is lost. Answers B and D are incorrect, as the format utility cannot be used to convert a drive under any circumstances. For additional information, see the section titled "Converting File Systems."

6. **B.** The key to this question is understanding the limitations of FAT and FAT32 partitions. Remember that FAT and FAT32 do not support folder and file level security. For this reason, they are not very efficient for creating user home directories (as these directories are typically secure). Answer A is incorrect, as the user folders would not be secure. Answer C is incorrect, as this requires a large effort (creating all the individual user shares). This effort is not required on NTFS partitions, where we can use file and folder security to secure the resource. To simplify the creating process, you can use the %Username% environment variable to create user home directories and assign NTFS permissions automatically when configuring the User home directory property of a user account. Answer D is incorrect, as this requires a large effort (creating all the individual user shares). Answer B represents the most efficient answer. See the section titled "Shared Home Directories" for more details.

7. **C.** You must remember how shared folder and NTFS permissions are applied when a user accesses a resource over the network. In this case, Mikayla can access a resource if she accesses the resource while logged on locally (she is accessing the resource directly from the file system) but cannot access the same resource from over the network. This situation points to a shared folder permission issue. When Mikayla is accessing the resource locally, shared folder permissions are not processed. You also know that Mikayla has NTFS permissions to the resource, as she can access it locally. For these reasons, C is correct. Answer A is incorrect, as Mikayla can access the resource if logged on locally. Answer B is incorrect, as NTFS permissions cannot be applied for network access versus local access. Answer D is incorrect, as membership in Authenticated Users cannot be changed (it is a built-in group). See the section titled "NTFS Permissions and Shared Folders" for details.

8. **B.** Expect a number of questions regarding troubleshooting permissions. The correct answer for this question revolves around the calculation of effective NTFS permissions. Remember that if a user is denied permission, it will override all other permissions granted to the user. In this case, denying Full Control to the Everyone group effectively denies access to all users on the network. Answer A is incorrect, as no such requirement exists in Windows XP (or any other version of Windows). Answer C is incorrect, as users need to be able to access resources from across the network. Answer D is incorrect, as the problem is an NTFS permission issue. See the section titled "NTFS Permissions and Shared Folders" for details.

9. **D.** Remember that shared folder permissions will combine unless a deny permission has been assigned. In this case, the Deny Full Control permission assigned to the Executives group will block Mikayla from this resource. Answers A, B,

and C are incorrect, as the effective permissions are Deny Full Control. Answer E is incorrect, as the permission table and group member is provided. This is all the information you need to calculate effective permissions. See the section titled "Multiple Share Permissions" for details.

10. **B.** When calculating effective permissions, you need to remember how both shared folder permissions and NTFS permissions work with each other. You also must remember that not being in the Access Control List of a resource is the same as not having permissions to a resource. In this question, Mikayla and John both have the same effective shared folder permissions (Full Control). This is true, as shared folder permissions add up to give you the effective permissions (unless the deny permission is assigned). The question, however, asks for Mikayla and John's effective permissions on the resource. To calculate the overall effective permissions, you also need to look at the NTFS permissions assigned to the users. Mikayla has Read permissions explicitly assigned to her user account. John does not have any NTFS permissions at all. The overall effective permissions is the most restrictive of the shared folder and NTFS permissions combined. For this reason, Mikayla receives Full Control shared folder permissions plus Read NTFS permissions for a total effective permission of Read. John receives Full Control shared folder permission plus no NTFS permissions for a total effective permission of no access (or no permissions assigned). See the section titled "NTFS Permissions and Shared Folders" for details.

11. **E.** Again, recall the rules when you move files on NTFS partitions:

- When you move a folder or file within a single NTFS partition, the folder or file retains its original permissions.

- When you move a folder or file between NTFS partitions, the folder or file inherits the permissions of the destination folder. When you move a folder or file between partitions, you are creating a new version of the resource and therefore inherit permissions.

- When you move a folder or file to a non-NTFS partition, all permissions are lost (this is because non-NTFS partitions do not support NTFS permissions).

In this question, we are moving a file between two different partitions, so the effective permissions on the target file are Sales Full Control. See the section titled "Copying and Moving Folders and Files" for details.

12. **D.** Again, remember the rules when you move files on NTFS partitions:

- When you move a folder or file within a single NTFS partition, the folder or file retains its original permissions.

- When you move a folder or file between NTFS partitions, the folder or file inherits the permissions of the destination folder. When you move a folder or file between partitions, you are creating a new version of the resource and therefore inherit permissions.

- When you move a folder or file to a non-NTFS partition, all permissions are lost (this is because non-NTFS partitions do not support NTFS permissions).

APPLY YOUR KNOWLEDGE

In this question, you are moving a file on the same partition, so the effective permissions on the target file are Sales Deny Full Control. In this case, you must also be aware of the fact that only explicitly assigned permissions carry over. See the section titled "Copying and Moving Folders and Files" for details.

13. **D.** Although you could use Group Policy Objects to force the templates to be copied to the local machine, the fact that they change frequently means that this will be resource intensive (and not the best option) for the administrator. Logon scripts can be used to copy the templates each time the user logs in; however, this will significantly delay the user's logon if the templates are very large. The question didn't specify the size of the templates. You can't share a folder as Offline Enabled. The client must request, or set, offline status for a share, or a folder underneath a remote share. See the section titled "Managing and Troubleshooting the Use and Synchronization of Offline Files" for details.

Suggested Readings and Resources

1. Deploying Microsoft Windows XP Professional, Microsoft Official Curriculum, Course 2520.

2. Implementing and Supporting Microsoft Windows XP Professional, Microsoft Official Curriculum Course 2272.

3. "Configuring Offline Files for Portable Computers," from the Windows XP Professional Resource Kit available at

   ```
   http://www.microsoft.com/technet/
   treeview/default.asp?url=/TechNet/
   prodtechnol/winxppro/reskit/
   prdc_mcc_pcdz.asp.
   ```

4. "File Systems," from the Windows XP Professional Resource Kit available at
   ```
   http://www.microsoft.com/technet/
   treeview/default.asp?url=/TechNet/
   prodtechnol/winxppro/reskit/
   prba_dwp_eqmn.asp.
   ```

5. *MCSE Training Kit—Microsoft Windows XP Professional, Microsoft Press, 2000.*

Implement, manage, and troubleshoot disk devices.

- **Install, configure, and manage DVD and CD-ROM devices.**

- **Monitor and configure disks.**

- **Monitor, configure, and troubleshoot volumes.**

- **Monitor and configure removable media, such as tape devices.**

▶ Disk technology is constantly evolving in capacity and available features. During the life of your computer, you probably will add new functionality to your storage or playback devices. Windows XP provides advanced support for new devices such as logical disk volumes, CD writing, and DVD playback.

Implement, manage, and troubleshoot display devices.

- **Configure multiple-display support.**

- **Install, configure, and troubleshoot a video adapter.**

▶ Windows XP provides support for a wide range of video adapters, as well as multiple monitors, simultaneously. With Windows XP, the desktop can extend over all the monitors attached to your system. Being able to use these features will extend what you can do with your system.

CHAPTER 3

Implementing, Managing, Monitoring, and Troubleshooting Hardware Devices and Drivers

Configure Advanced Configuration Power Interface (ACPI).

▶ Windows XP supports power management on all new systems; however, it is most useful in allowing you to preserve the limited resources available to mobile computers when running on battery. Being able to configure and use these features will impact what you can do with your mobile system.

Implement, manage, and troubleshoot input and output (I/O) devices.

- **Monitor, configure, and troubleshoot I/O devices, such as printers, scanners, multi-media devices, mouse, keyboard, and smart card reader.**

- **Monitor, configure, and troubleshoot multi-media hardware, such as cameras.**

- **Install, configure, and manage modems.**

- **Install, configure, and manage Infrared Data Association (IrDA) devices.**

- **Install, configure, and manage wireless devices.**

- **Install, configure, and manage USB devices.**

- **Install, configure, and manage handheld devices.**

- **Install, configure, and manage network adapters.**

▶ A Windows XP Professional computer system can have a variety of I/O devices connected to it, including printers, smart cards, cameras, and infrared devices. Being able to manage a wide range of devices is important to getting the most out of your computer system.

Manage and troubleshoot drivers and driver signing.

▶ Windows XP Professional allows you to automatically update drivers for a particular device either from a local source or over the Internet. You also can protect your system by specifying actions to take if the device driver has not been signed. A signed device driver has been thoroughly tested by Microsoft to run correctly with the Windows XP operating system. Being able to manage the device drivers on your system is important to getting the most out of your computer system while at the same time keeping it stable.

Monitor and configure multiprocessor computers.

▶ If your processing requirements grow as you increasingly use Windows XP Professional computer, there is the option of adding an additional processor. The capability to expand your computing power can have a significant impact on the workload your computer can manage.

OUTLINE

STUDY STRATEGIES

▶ Windows XP Professional supports more types of devices than any previous version of the operating system. In addition to the range of devices supported, configuration is made automatic because of Plug and Play. You can expect several questions related to installing and supporting newer hardware devices on your Windows XP Professional computer. Many of these questions will be presented as scenarios in which the capabilities of these devices are used to solve problems.

▶ You also should expect to see questions dealing with new disk capabilities to provide fault tolerance as well as more options in configuring disk storage.

▶ Greater disk storage capacity creates a need for offline storage capabilities. Expect to see questions on Removable Storage Management (RSM) and the configuration of robotic libraries and media pools.

▶ Some new devices that you can expect to see questions on are support for infrared (IrDA) and wireless support, plus support for Universal Serial Bus (USB) devices.

▶ Finally, Windows XP Professional can support an additional processor. You can expect to see some questions that focus on the impact of improving the CPU power of your Windows XP Professional computer and its impact on other resources available within your system.

▶ In short, by focusing on the previously mentioned major areas, you will be well prepared for this portion of the exam.

INTRODUCTION

This chapter is mainly concerned with the hardware devices that can tailor the generalized personal computer into a device that does what you want. The extra pieces of hardware, from DVD devices to additional monitors, can increase the functional value of the computer a great deal.

Understanding the configuration options available is key to arriving at solutions to problems likely to be presented in the exam. This chapter examines the disk configurations and removable storage options that can provide solutions to disk storage problems. We then will look at I/O devices such as multiple displays, wireless I/O, cameras, scanners and printers, and USB devices, to name a few. Plug and Play features are fully supported in Windows XP Professional, so we will be looking at that feature as well.

We will round out the chapter with a look at troubleshooting drivers and the multiple-CPU capability of Windows XP Professional.

INSTALLING HARDWARE

The Windows XP Professional operating system includes many enhancements to simplify device management. Some of these include Advanced Configuration and Power Interface (ACPI) and Plug and Play (PnP).

Plug and Play is a combination of hardware and software that enables a computer to recognize and modify its hardware configuration changes with minimal intervention from the user. To start with, your computer system must have a BIOS that supports Plug and Play. This will be the case for all new computer systems; however, some older models might not have an up-to-date BIOS installed.

The hardware device that you are installing must support the Plug and Play initiative to be automatically configured correctly. You will find that some older devices that predate Plug and Play will not be recognized.

NOTE

HAL and ACPI   Older laptops might not have a BIOS that is ACPI compliant. If you obtain an updated BIOS from your manufacturer and successfully install it, Windows XP Professional will not be able to start. ACPI is related to the HAL (Hardware Abstraction Layer) that is selected when you install Windows XP Professional. If you make a change that requires a new HAL, you will have to reinstall Windows XP Professional.

With Plug and Play, a user can add or remove a device dynamically without manual reconfiguration and without any intricate knowledge of the computer hardware. For example, you can have a laptop in a docking station that contains an Ethernet network connection and later use the same laptop connecting to the network using a different Ethernet adapter, without making any configuration changes.

With Plug and Play, you can make changes to the Windows XP Professional computer's configuration with the assurance that all devices will work and the computer will reboot correctly after the changes are made.

When you install a Plug and Play device, Windows XP Professional automatically configures the device to allow it to function properly with the other devices already installed in your computer. Windows XP Professional assigns system resources to the device including the following:

◆ Interrupt request (IRQ) number

◆ Direct memory access (DMA) channel

◆ Input/output (I/O) port address

◆ Memory address range

Each resource must be properly configured or the device will not function correctly.

If your new device is not automatically installed by Windows, the Found New Hardware Wizard will pop up and ask you to insert any media (such as compact or floppy disks) that were provided by the manufacturer.

When the device you are installing is not Plug and Play compatible, Windows XP Professional has no way of automatically configuring the device settings. You might have to manually configure the device driver or use the manufacturer-provided installation program.

You can configure devices using the Add Hardware applet in the Control Panel or by using the Device Manager, which is located in the Computer Management icon within the Administrative Tools folder in the Control Panel.

With most Plug and Play hardware, you simply connect the device to the computer and Windows XP Professional automatically configures the new settings. Plug and Play can be supported by devices and

> **WARNING**
>
> **Manually Adjusting Resources**
> The usual reason for adjusting device configuration is to support a legacy device (not Plug and Play) that requires either jumpers or a `config` utility to configure the device. These configuration parameters must then be configured in Windows XP Professional.
>
> If you must manually configure a non–Plug and Play device, the resources assigned become fixed. This reduces the flexibility that Windows XP Professional has for allocating resources to other devices. If too many resources are manually configured, Windows XP Professional might not be able to install new Plug and Play devices.
>
> Resource settings should be changed only if you are certain that the new settings do not conflict with any other hardware, or if the hardware manufacturer has supplied a specific set of resource settings with the device.

the drivers that control them. The possible combinations expand to four different support scenarios:

◆ Full Plug and Play support is provided when the hardware and the device driver fully support Plug and Play.

◆ If the hardware supports Plug and Play but the device driver does not, Windows XP Professional will not support Plug and Play and the device will be treated as a legacy NT 4.0 device.

◆ If the device driver supports Plug and Play but the hardware does not, Windows XP can provide partial Plug and Play support. In this case, Windows XP will not be able to automatically configure the device drivers, but Plug and Play will be able to manage resource allocations.

◆ Windows XP will not provide support for Plug and Play if neither the device driver nor the hardware supports Plug and Play.

For hardware that cannot be automatically identified, the Add Hardware applet provides a method of manually configuring the device resources. Occasionally, you might need to initiate automatic installation even for some Plug and Play hardware.

NOTE | **Administrator Rights** You must be an administrator to install device drivers on your computer if the device is not Plug and Play (you have to use the Add Hardware Wizard from the Control Panel), if the device is not digitally signed, if the device driver is new (not already installed on your system), or if your company has a domain policy that prevents you from installing new devices.

Using the Add Hardware Wizard

The Add Hardware Wizard started from the Control Panel is used to initiate automatic hardware installation of both Plug and Play and non–Plug and Play hardware devices. The following steps will initiate a search for new Plug and Play hardware or, in its absence, present you with a screen to add a new device or troubleshoot an existing device.

STEP BY STEP

3.1 Searching for New Plug and Play Hardware

1. Click Start, and then Control Panel.

2. Click Printers and Other Hardware.

continues

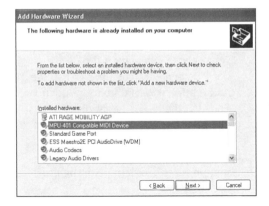

FIGURE 3.1
The Add Hardware Wizard lists all installed devices and lets you add new devices.

> 3. Click Add Hardware in the See Also pane.
>
> 4. Click Next to close the Welcome page and start the wizard.

Windows XP Professional will search for any new Plug and Play hardware and installs any it finds. If the wizard cannot detect any new hardware, it will ask whether the hardware has been installed already and then display a list of installed hardware for you to choose a device for troubleshooting (see Figure 3.1). Devices that have a question mark ("?") have been detected and could be Plug and Play devices that Windows XP Professional did not come with a driver for, or the Windows XP CD-ROM was not available when the device was detected. Devices that have an X have been disabled and are not in use. The last entry on the hardware list is Add a New Device to provide the option of installing a new device.

Confirming Hardware Installation

After you have installed new hardware, you can confirm that the device is installed and functioning properly by using the Device Manager.

To start the Device Manager, click Printers and Other Hardware in the Control Panel, and then click the System link in the See Also pane. Select the Hardware tab and click the Device Manager button. The result of this action is a display of a list of installed hardware, as shown in Figure 3.2.

Expanding a device type displays all the specific devices of that type installed on the computer. The device icon will indicate whether the device is functioning properly. You can use the information in Table 3.1 to determine the device status.

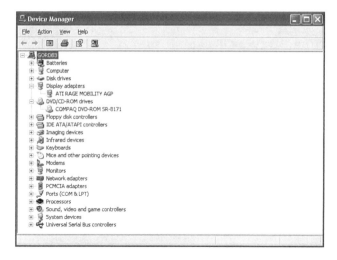

FIGURE 3.2
Installed devices listed by the Device Manager.

TABLE 3.1

DEVICE MANAGER HARDWARE STATUS

Device Icon	Device Status
Normal Icon	The device is functioning normally.
Stop Sign	Windows XP Professional has disabled the hardware because of resource conflicts. To correct this, right-click the device icon, click Properties, and set the resources manually according to what is available in the system.
Exclamation point	The device is not configured correctly or the device drivers are missing.

Determining Required Resources

When you are manually installing and configuring non–Plug and Play hardware, you need to understand the resources the hardware device expects to use. The manufacturer's product documentation will list the resources the device requires, and you will have to determine how to fit it into your existing system. Table 3.2 describes the resources available in a Windows XP Professional computer system that hardware devices use to communicate with the operating system.

NOTE

Finding the Device Manager   You can access the Device Manager from a number of directions. It can be started using the Device Manager button from the Hardware tab in the System applet from the Control Panel.

It also can be started from the Computer Management icon within the Administrative Tools folder in the Control Panel.

It can be started from Windows Explorer by selecting the properties of My Computer (right-click My Computer and select Properties), selecting the Hardware Tab, and clicking the Device Manager button.

Finally, it is available as a snap-in to the Microsoft Management Console (MMC). The MMC is a standard approach for creating consoles in Windows. You can see the basic environment by clicking Start, clicking Run, and entering the command MMC. To this environment you can add any number of supplied consoles, such as the Device Manager.

TABLE 3.2

HARDWARE DEVICE RESOURCES

Resources	Description
Interrupts	Hardware devices use interrupts to indicate to the processor that it needs attention. The processor uses this Interrupt Request (IRQ) as a way of determining which device is looking for service and what type of attention it needs. Windows XP provides interrupt numbers 0 through 15 to devices (IRQ 1 is always assigned to the keyboard).
Input/Output (I/O) port	I/O ports are areas of memory that the device uses to communicate with Windows XP Professional. When the processor sees an IRQ request, it checks the I/O port address to retrieve additional information about what the device wants.
Direct Memory Access (DMA)	DMAs are channels that allow the hardware device to access memory directly. This allows a device such as a disk drive or floppy drive to write information into memory without interrupting the processor. Windows XP Professional provides DMA channels 0 through 7. Devices that support DMA will transfer information more quickly than non-DMA devices. It is important, then, that disk controller cards and network adapters all support DMA.
Memory	Many hardware devices have onboard memory or can reserve system memory for their use. Any reserved memory is not available for any other device or for Windows XP Professional.

IN THE FIELD

SHARABLE RESOURCES

Some of the resources used by device drives are reserved for specific devices, and some can be shared between devices.

The Interrupt Request (IRQ) uses a Programmable Interrupt Controller (PIC) to request some service for the device. When a request is seen, the current operation is suspended and control is given to the device drive associated with the IRQ number (1–15).

This resource, therefore, cannot normally be shared between devices. Some PCI (peripheral component interconnect) devices can share IRQ numbers. PCI is a local bus structure that allows up to 10 PCI-compliant expansion cards to be connected to it.

The Input/Output (I/O) port is a memory block used by the device to communicate the service it is requesting. This is tied to the IRQ number and therefore is dedicated to a device.

The Direct Memory Access (DMA) is a direct channel between the device and the computer's memory. The DMA controller supports a number of channels (usually seven) and they are shared between devices (one at a time).

A device memory block is a portion of system memory mapped to the internal memory of the device (usually). This is dedicated to the device and cannot be used by any other process (including Windows XP Professional).

Determining Available Resources

After you determine what resources your device requires, you can use Device Manager to display the resources available on your computer. To view the available resources list, double-click Printers and Other Hardware in the Control Panel, click System in the See Also pane, and select the Hardware tab. Click the Device Manager button and select the Resources by Connection entry in the View menu. You also can use the program MSINFO32 (click Start, Run, and enter `MSINFO32` and click OK). Figure 3.3 shows the Hardware Resources (IRQs from MSINFO32).

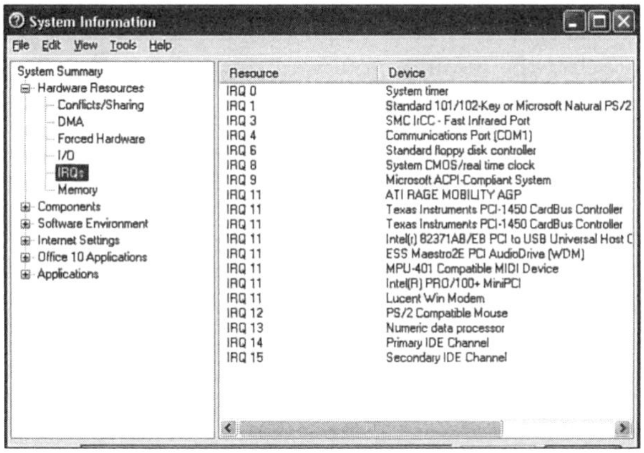

FIGURE 3.3
Hardware resources showing IRQs in use.

NOTE **Write It Down**   It's always a good idea to document the current and working configuration parameters before you make any modifications. Changing a resource configuration can leave a device in a nonfunctioning state.

NOTE **Changing Resources for Non–Plug and Play Devices**   Changing the resources assigned to a non–Plug and Play device will not actually change the resources the device uses. This only instructs the Windows XP Professional operating system as to what the device configuration is. You must consult the manufacturer's documentation on what jumpers or software switches to set on the device to conform to the resource assignment you have told Windows XP to expect. Some older non–plug-and-play devices can also require resource allocation at the BIOS level (usually done by interrupting the bootup process).

Changing Resource Assignments

You might encounter two devices that request the same resources that result in a conflict. To change a resource setting, use the Resources tab in the device's Properties information. The following procedure will allow you to modify a resource setting. A resource that is usually available to modify is the DMA address of the floppy disk controller device.

STEP BY STEP

3.2 Modifying a Device's Resource Configuration

1. Click Start, and then click Control Panel.
2. Click Printers and Other Hardware.
3. Click the System link in the See Also pane and select the Hardware tab.
4. Click the Device Manager button.
5. Expand the device type that you want to change.
6. Right-click the specific device you want to modify.
7. Click Properties and choose the Resources tab. If the Resources tab is not present, you will not be able to modify the device's resources.
8. Select the resource setting you will be modifying.
9. Clear the Automatic Settings box if it is checked. If this box is grayed out, you will not be able to modify the device's resources.
10. Select the resource you want to modify and click the Change Setting button.

At this point, you will be presented with a screen that will allow you to edit the value of the resource you have selected. Saving that new value will change what Windows XP Professional thinks the device will be using.

MEDIA DEVICES

Implement, manage, and troubleshoot disk devices.

The following sections address configuring and maintaining CD and DVD devices, fixed disks, volumes, and other media devices.

CD-ROM and DVD Devices

Current CD-ROM and DVD devices support Plug and Play and therefore should be automatically configured when you install the devices.

Support for the CD-ROM File System (CDFS) is maintained in Windows XP Professional for support of legacy applications and is used by RSM in storing CD-ROMs in removable storage libraries. CD-ROM devices support 650MB of storage per platter, and although this was once considered immense, it pales against the DVD standard, which currently can hold more than 26 times as much data (up to 17GB of information).

Windows XP Professional provides support for creating CD-R and CD-RW disks (providing your computer has a CD device that can create as well as read disks).

A CD-R or CD-RW disk can be created as a single session or a multisession disk. A session is defined as a lead-in, program data, and lead-out. The purpose of a multisession disk is to allow additional information to be added to a disk after the initial recording. The entire CD-R also has a lead-in and lead-out section that contains the table of contents and addresses for the various sessions recorded on the disk.

In addition, a disk can be written "Disk at Once," in which case the entire disk is written continuously without interruptions, or "Track at Once," in which case a session is made up of discrete tracks written to the disk; and, then, the disk is "finalized" and the session is closed off (by writing the lead-out).

Most pressed CD-ROMs are single-session, disk-at-a-time recordings. Most audio playback units can therefore play only the first session of a multisession CD-R.

N O T E **Recording Times** The two fundamental capacities of CD-R are 63 minutes and 74 minutes. These "time" capacities are translated to bytes of data by using the CD delivery rate of 75 blocks per second. Each block is 2,048 bytes, so a 74-minute CD-R disc contains 333,000 blocks and 681,984,000 bytes. This is often incorrectly translated as 680MB when it is really 650MB (after dividing by 1024×1024 to convert bytes into MB). Likewise, the 63-minute CD-R holds 283,500 blocks, or 580,608,000 bytes (580 million bytes), which is approximately 553MB. The MB-capacity rating of hard disk drives is customarily expressed in millions of bytes (the higher and incorrect number).

To create a CD-R with Windows XP Professional, you drag your data or audio files (for example) to your CD drive using Windows Explorer. A message bubble will pop up indicating that files are waiting to be copied to the CD. When, in Windows Explorer, you select to copy the files to the disk (right-click the CD device and select the menu option to create the disk), the copy process will ask for a disk name and then copy the files to the CD.

If the files are audio files (such as .MP3 files), Windows Media Player will start and allow you to adjust the order in which the MP3 files are written to the disk. When you have everything correct, select the Copy to CD button to have WMP convert the files, and then copy them to the CD.

Windows Media Player creates "Track at Once" CDs. There is a 50MB overhead (roughly) for each additional session. Disks created by Windows Media Player can be played by most consumer CD players provided that the disks are created as a single session.

DVD used to stand for *Digital Versatile Disk*. However, now it is recognized by the acronym alone. This line of devices is an enhancement of CD-ROM technology and is quickly replacing CD-ROMs as more multimedia technology is integrated into computer usage.

There are five primary types of DVD storage:

◆ **DVD-Video**—The actual technology usually referred to as *DVD*. This is a disk holding a video program, such as a feature film, that can be played back in either a DVD video player or a computer with a high-resolution display.

◆ **DVD-ROM**—The disk technology used to store computer data to be read by a DVD-ROM drive. All DVD devices should be able to read DVD disks, including double-sided, double-layered disks holding up to 17GB of data.

◆ **DVD-R**—A variation of DVD-ROM that supports one-time recording capabilities such as today's CD-R. Windows XP does not directly support the use of media that can be written to only once, such as WORM, CD-R, and DVD-R disks. If you want to use these, you must obtain additional software from the manufacturer.

◆ **DVD-RAM**—A variation of DVD-ROM supporting multisession recording capabilities similar to magneto-optical (MO) disks. DVD-RAM can support up to 9.4GB per disk with up to 100,000 rewrites.

◆ **DVD+RW**—This format is an extension of CD-R technology with the block size increased to support a greater capacity. This technology allows you to drag and drop files onto a DVD+RW drive for copying, similar to the way that CD-R works, while providing backward compatibility to existing DVD-ROM readers.

Support for DVD in Windows XP Professional includes the following:

◆ **DVD-ROM driver**—The DVD-ROM industry standard command set (known as Mt. Fuji) is supported by the new Windows Driver Model (WDM) DVD-ROM device driver. Windows XP, Windows 2000, and Windows 98 can read data sectors from a DVD-ROM drive.

◆ **UDF file system**—The Universal Disk Format (UDF) provides support for UDF-formatted DVD disks.

◆ **WDM streaming class driver**—A driver written to follow the new Windows Driver Model (WDM) support. This driver supports MPEG-2 and AC-3 hardware decoders providing full-motion video and surround-sound capability.

◆ **DirectShow**—DirectShow supports DVD video and audio streams.

◆ **DirectDraw**—The video streams created by DVD devices can overwhelm a PCI bus on a computer. The solution to this is the creation of a dedicated bus to transfer decoded video streams from an MPEG-2 decoder to the display card.

◆ **Copyright protection**—DVD provides copyright protection by encrypting key sectors on a disk and then decrypting them prior to decoding.

◆ **Regionalization**—As part of the copyright protection scheme used for DVD, six worldwide regions have been defined by the DVD Consortia. Disks are playable on DVD devices in some or all the regions, according to codes set by the creators of the content.

Monitoring CD-ROM and DVD Devices

The following procedure will allow you to view information about the device drivers controlling your CD-ROM and/or DVD devices.

STEP BY STEP

3.3 Displaying CD-ROM and DVD Device Information

1. Click Start, and then click Control Panel.

2. Click Printers and Other Hardware.

3. Click the System link in the See Also pane.

4. Select the Hardware tab and click Device Manager.

5. Expand the CD-ROM/DVD device type.

6. Right-click the specific device to view and select Properties.

A few properties can be manually adjusted, as shown in Figure 3.4.

Information on the name of the CD, the partition type, and recorded capacity, along with unused space, can be seen by selecting the Volume tab on the CD-ROM and DVD device properties.

Troubleshooting CD-ROM and DVD Devices

Most of these devices are now Plug and Play compatible and therefore not prone to configuration errors. The CD-ROM and DVD devices are not immune to installation problems, however. These errors would be indicated by the tray door not opening, the usage light not lit, or the device not showing up on your My Computer display. This type of problem (assuming the CD-ROM or DVD is not faulty) is probably caused by loose or improperly installed power or data cables. To confirm this, you must physically open the computer case and examine the device connections. You might need the manufacturer's operator's guide information to correctly identify the data connections.

If the device is installed correctly but does not function correctly, follow the troubleshooting steps for these devices summarized in Table 3.3.

FIGURE 3.4
CD-ROM and DVD device properties.

TABLE 3.3

TROUBLESHOOTING CD-ROM AND DVD DEVICES

Problem	Cause
The Device reads data but not audio.	The audio drivers are incorrect or missing. You must update the device drivers to the latest available from Microsoft (see "Maintaining Updated Drivers" later in this chapter) or the manufacturer.
The audio drivers are installed but no audio is heard.	Audio cables are installed incorrectly. To check this, you must open the computer case and examine the audio cables. With some devices, it is possible to have the cable ends reversed.
Audio is heard over headphones but not the computer speakers.	Audio drivers or adapters are missing from the computer or not configured correctly. You must install the latest available drivers from either Microsoft (see "Maintaining Updated Drivers" later in this chapter) or the manufacturer.
The computer plays audio but the CD cannot be read.	The CD-ROM is faulty.
The CD-ROM can't be read and will not play audio.	Windows XP Professional is having difficulty detecting the hardware. The device driver or the hardware might not be Plug and Play compatible. The next step would be to update the device drivers to the latest available.

Fixed Disks

Disk Management is a graphical tool used in Windows XP Professional to manage disks and volumes. Disk Management can be started from within Computer Management inside Administrative Tools in the Control Panel, and also can be configured as an MMC snap-in.

Disk Management was introduced in Windows 2000 and replaced the Disk Administrator in Windows NT in providing support for disk partitions, logical drives, and dynamic disks. Disk Management will perform most of its support tasks dynamically without requiring a reboot of your computer. Disk Management also allows you to select the computer you are configuring, either the local machine or one on the network. In any case, you must have administrative rights on the computer you are configuring.

After a new disk has been installed, Disk Management is used to rescan the drives. Normally, you have to power off your computer hardware to install a new disk drive unless your system has support for hot-pluggable disk drive bays. When you rescan your disks, Disk Management will scan all attached disks looking for configuration changes, removable media, CD-ROM drives, basic volumes, file systems, and drive letters. However, if the rescan does not detect your new disk drive, it might be necessary to reboot your computer anyway.

Disk storage is now configured as basic or dynamic (since the advent of Windows 2000). The terms *basic disk* and *dynamic disk* are not referring to a different type of disk, but rather the way the disk is configured. A disk can be configured as a basic disk and partitioned as you would have done in Windows NT 4.0 or configured as a dynamic disk and divided into volumes. When you first add a new disk to your Windows XP Professional computer, it will be configured as a basic disk.

Basic Disk Storage

Basic storage supports partition-oriented disk configurations. A disk initialized for basic storage is called a basic disk. A basic disk can contain primary partitions, extended partitions, and logical drives. Basic storage is supported by all versions of Microsoft Windows 3.x and Microsoft Windows 9x, the Microsoft Windows NT 4 platform, the Microsoft Windows 2000 platform, and the Microsoft Windows XP platform.

On a basic disk, a partition is a part of the disk that functions as a physically separate unit. A primary partition is reserved for use by an operating system. An active partition is a primary partition that contains the startup files for the operating system. Any disk can have up to four primary partitions (or three if there is an extended partition). An extended partition is created from free space and can be partitioned into logical drives. Only one extended partition is allowed per physical disk.

The following is a list of tasks that are supported on basic disks:

◆ The creation and deletion of primary and extended partitions and logical drives

◆ Marking a partition as active

◆ Upgrading basic disks to dynamic disks

◆ Upgrading basic partitions and volumes to dynamic volumes

Windows XP no longer supports the volume sets, mirror sets, stripe sets, or stripe sets with parity that were created with Windows NT 4.0 or earlier. If you have an NT 4.0 system with one of these disk configurations, you must back up the data and delete the volume before installing Windows XP Professional or moving the disks to a computer running Windows XP Professional. The following list of tasks are not supported on basic disks. These features are supported only on dynamic disks.

◆ Creating simple, spanned, striped, mirrored, and RAID-5 volumes

◆ Extending volumes and volume sets

◆ Adding a mirror to a simple volume

◆ Removing a mirror from a mirrored volume

> **NOTE**
>
> **Accessing NT 4.0 Volumes** If you have upgraded your computer to Windows XP Professional but neglected to back up and delete your NT 4.0 formatted fault-tolerant disks (mirrored, striped, and so on), you can still get access to the data using the FTOnline utility. The FTOnline utility can be installed using the Support Tools setup program located in the \support\tools folder on the Windows XP Professional CD. The disk will be mounted for the duration of the session so you can back up the data and re-create the disks as dynamic. FTonline is not intended to be used as perpetual access to legacy data volumes.

Dynamic Storage

Dynamic storage is designed for new volume-oriented disk configurations. A disk initialized for dynamic storage is called a *dynamic disk*. Dynamic disks are physical disks that contain dynamic volumes created using Disk Management. Storage is divided into volumes instead of partitions. A volume consists of a part or parts of one or more physical disks laid out as a simple, spanned, mirrored, striped, or RAID-5 structure. Dynamic disks cannot contain partitions or logical drives and can be accessed only by computers running Windows 2000 or Windows XP.

Dynamic disks can be reverted to basic disks using Disk Management; however, there is no automatic procedure to convert dynamic volumes back to partitions. This limitation requires you to remove the volumes contained on a dynamic disk before reverting it to a basic disk.

Whereas basic disks use the partition table located in the master boot record (MBR) to identify the starting and ending of partitions on the physical disk, dynamic disks do not follow the same format. A dynamic disk still has a partition table, but it has only one entry that encompasses the entire disk. This allows the system to see a valid partition table when it is booting. A dynamic disk configuration stores the volume information on the physical disk in a small, 1MB database at the end of the disk.

Each physical disk that has been initialized in a dynamic disk configuration contains a copy of this database replicated among each physical disk in the system. If one of the databases becomes corrupt, another copy is used and the corrupt one is refreshed with an uncorrupted copy.

Table 3.4 summarizes the major differences between basic disk configurations and dynamic disk configurations.

> **NOTE**
>
> **Converting Basic to Dynamic** For a basic disk to be upgraded to a dynamic configuration, enough space at the end of the disk must be available for this database. This space is automatically reserved when Disk Management creates partitions or volumes on a disk; however, a disk created by Windows NT 4.0 (for example) might not have the room available.

TABLE 3.4

DIFFERENCES BETWEEN BASIC AND DYNAMIC DISK CONFIGURATIONS

Basic Disks	*Dynamic Disks*
The configuration is stored in the partition table.	The configuration is stored in a 1MB database at the end of the disk
There can be four primary partitions, or three primary partitions and one extended partition.	There can be an unlimited number of volumes.
Free space in an extended partition can be used to create multiple logical drives.	Logical drives are not supported.

In addition, mirrored and RAID-5 configurations cannot be created on Windows XP Professional (or Home edition). However, Windows XP Professional can create these configurations on a remote Windows 2000 Server, Windows 2000 Advanced Server, or

Windows 2000 Datacenter Server. Also, dynamic disk configurations are not supported on portable computers. If you are using Disk Management on a laptop, you will find that the options for converting a basic disk to a dynamic disk are not present.

Disk Management

The Disk Management utility (see Figure 3.5) graphically displays disks and volumes and allows a user with administrative rights to configure disks and volumes.

One of the most basic commands is to rescan the hardware. This allows you to update any hardware information if a new disk has been installed that Disk Management has not detected automatically.

To set up new disks, Disk Management provides wizards to help with the following tasks:

◆ Add disks for basic or dynamic storage (either a new device or from another computer).

◆ Create primary or extended partitions and logical disk drives (on basic disks only).

◆ Create simple, spanned, striped, mirrored, or RAID-5 volumes (on dynamic disks only).

◆ Format volumes in File Allocation Table (FAT), FAT32, or Windows NT File System (NTFS) format.

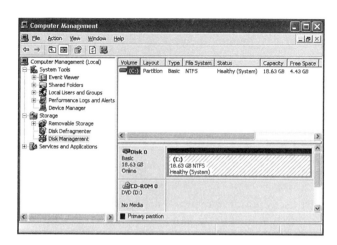

FIGURE 3.5
Disk management.

◆ Upgrade disks from basic to dynamic.

◆ Mount a local drive at any empty folder on an NTFS-formatted volume.

Disk Manager provides the means for moving a disk from one computer to another. In the case of basic disks, Windows XP Professional will automatically discover the new hardware. If it does not, you can have Device Manager scan for new hardware. In Disk Manager, rescanning the disks will make the new hardware available for use.

If the disk is dynamic, after you rescan the disks, Disk Manager will show the new drive as being foreign and provide an Import Foreign Disk Wizard to provide the steps for making the new disk available.

The capability to mount a local drive to a folder rather than using a drive letter is an interesting feature. For example, you might have an NTFS volume that is disk C: and a CD-ROM drive currently known as disk D:. If you create an empty folder at C:\CD-ROM (the name is not important here—just that it is empty and on an NTFS disk), Disk Manager can mount the CD-ROM drive at that folder. Now you can access the information on the CD-ROM from the C: drive and reuse the D: drive letter for other devices. You can extend this concept to include accessing several shared CD drives by linking them to empty folders under a single folder (subdirectory) in Windows Explorer.

Command-Line Utilities

You don't just have to use the graphical interfaces for everything. There are some command-line utilities available that you can incorporate into batch jobs (when doing large deployments of Windows XP Professional desktops). The following list of utilities is useful in batch or automated procedures:

◆ **CHKDSK**—Check and repair disk errors.

◆ **CONVERT**—Change FAT or FAT32 volumes into NTFS volumes.

◆ **DISKPART**—Extend basic or dynamic volumes, add or break mirrors, assign or remove a disk's drive letter, create or delete partitions and volumes, convert basic disks to dynamic disks, import disks, and bring offline disks and volumes online.

◆ **FORMAT**—Format a mounted drive with a file system.

◆ **FSUTIL**—Manage disk quotas, dismount a volume, or request volume information.

◆ **MOUNTVOL**—Mount or unmount a volume at an NTFS folder.

Upgrading Basic Disks to Dynamic Disks

When a basic disk has been converted to dynamic, all existing partitions become simple dynamic volumes. After you convert a basic disk to a dynamic disk, you cannot change the dynamic volumes back to partitions without deleting all the dynamic volumes (if you want to keep your data, you must first back it up or move it to another volume first).

Once upgraded, a dynamic disk cannot contain partitions or logical drives and cannot be accessed by MS-DOS or Windows operating systems other than Windows XP Professional or Windows 2000.

System and Boot Partitions

A basic disk that contains the system or active partition can be upgraded to a dynamic disk. These partitions become simple volumes that are active. An existing volume cannot be marked as active.

A basic disk that contains the boot partition can also be upgraded to a dynamic disk. The boot partition becomes a simple volume. A fresh installation of Windows XP Professional cannot be performed on an existing dynamic volume, but Windows XP can be upgraded on a dynamic boot volume. This limitation results from the Windows XP Professional setup program, which recognizes that only dynamic volumes contain partition tables. Partition tables occur only in basic volumes and dynamic volumes that were upgraded from basic volumes. If you create a new dynamic volume on a dynamic disk, the new volume will not contain a partition table.

Troubleshooting Disk Problems

If a disk or volume fails, you will naturally want to repair the problem as quickly as possible. Disk Management displays the status of disks or volumes in both the text and graphical view. The Disk Management display can be customized by selecting the View tab and then Top or Bottom. This allows you to set the top or bottom frames of the display to disk, volume, or graphical display.

One of the disk statuses shown in Table 3.5 will appear in the Status column of the Disk List view and in the Graphical view. If there is a problem with a disk, this will help you diagnose and correct the problem.

TABLE 3.5

DISK STATUS MEANINGS IN DISK MANAGEMENT

Disk Status	Meaning of Status
Online	The disk is accessible and has no detected problems.
Online (errors)	I/O errors have been detected. If the I/O errors are not permanent, you can reactivate the disk (using Reactivate Disk) to return it to Online status.
Offline	The disk is not accessible and may be powered down, disconnected, or corrupt.
Foreign	The disk has been moved to this computer from another Windows XP system. To set up this disk for use here, use the Import Foreign Disks task.
Unreadable	The disk cannot be accessed. It might have experienced hardware failure, corruption, or I/O errors. The 1MB database at the end of the physical disk also might be corrupted. Disks may be flagged as unreadable when they are spinning up or when Disk Management is rescanning all the disks in the system.
Unrecognized	The disk has a signature that Disk Management will not allow you to use. A disk from a Unix system displays the Unrecognized status.
No Media	No media is in the CD-ROM or removable drive. This disk status changes when you insert the appropriate media into the device.

Volume Sets

Dynamic volumes are new in Windows XP and provide new disk storage strategies. There are five types of dynamic volumes:

◆ Simple

◆ Spanned

◆ Mirrored

◆ Striped

◆ RAID-5

Mirrored and RAID-5 volumes can be created only on systems running Windows 2000 Server, Windows 2000 Advanced Server, or Windows 2000 Datacenter Server, and on .NET Servers. Because a system running Windows XP Professional can create mirrored and RAID-5 volumes remotely on servers, their definition is included in the following sections.

Simple Volumes

Simple volumes can be created only on dynamic disks. The number of volumes that can be created on a disk is limited only to the amount of free space available.

A simple volume can be extended to other regions on a disk or to other disks. When a simple volume extends to another disk, it becomes a spanned volume. No portion of a spanned volume can be deleted without deleting the entire spanned volume. Extended volumes cannot be striped or mirrored.

Spanned Volumes

A spanned volume is a mechanism for effectively using the free space on several disks. The disks used in a spanned volume can be dissimilar types, such as IDE and SCSI disk devices. Spanned volumes are created by combining the free space from 1 to 32 disks into one large volume. When the space on one disk is filled up, the system starts writing at the beginning of the next disk. This process continues in the same way up to a maximum of 32 disks.

Striped Volumes (RAID-0)

A striped volume is a mechanism for combining areas of free space from 2 to 32 disks into one logical volume. Data is divided into 64KB blocks and spread in a standard order among all the disks in the array. Windows XP Professional does not wait for each disk to finish its tasks before writing to the next disk in the stripe array, but rather assigns each disk the blocks of data to write and has all (or as many as necessary) disks write simultaneously.

NOTE

Extending Partitions The command-line utility DISKPART can be used to extend volumes into the next contiguous unallocated space. For basic volumes, the unallocated space must be on the same disk as the partition being extended and must follow the partition as well. A dynamic simple or spanned volume can be extended to any empty space on any dynamic disk.

If the partition (or logical drive) was previously formatted with the NTFS file system, the file system is automatically extended to occupy the larger partition without losing any data. This task will fail if the file system is not NTFS.

You cannot extend the current system or boot partitions.

NOTE

Performance Increases Using spanned volumes creates larger volumes and potentially improves system performance by spreading I/O across more drives, and it can reduce the number of drive letters used. Spanned volumes, however, are not fault tolerant.

E X A M   T I P
Extending Volumes   Expect questions on the exam about extending existing volumes that are not NTFS volumes. Existing spanned volumes formatted with NTFS can be extended by adding free space. Disk Management formats the new area without affecting the existing files on the original volume or the spanned volume. Spanned volumes formatted with FAT cannot be extended.

E X A M   T I P
Improved Performance   The exam will include questions on disk-management strategies and fault tolerance. Striped volumes offer the best performance of all the Windows XP Professional disk-management strategies but, as with spanned volumes, striped volumes are not fault tolerant. If a disk in a striped volume fails, the data in the entire volume is lost.

N O T E
Creating Mirrored Volumes   When creating a mirrored volume, it is best to use disks of the same size, model, and manufacturer to minimize disk geometry compatibility issues.

With striped volumes, Windows XP Professional writes data to multiple disks such as spanned disks; however, the data is spread across all disks at the same rate.

The I/O workload on a striped volume is spread evenly across all the disks with no space taken for fault tolerance. If your computer is doing 100 I/O operations per second (10% writes) and you have 4 disks at 40GB each and you configure them as a striped volume (RAID-0), the I/O load on each individual disk is

I/Os per disk = (Reads + Writes)/number of disks

In the preceding configuration, this would result in an I/O load at the disk level of 25 I/Os per second with a total of 160GB of disk available.

Striped volumes are almost never recommended for important file systems (such as databases) because they are not fault tolerant and will not protect your data against disk failure.

Mirrored Volumes (RAID-1)

A mirrored volume is a fault-tolerant volume that duplicates the data on two physical disks. It provides fault tolerance by using this copy to reduce the impact of a single disk failure. The mirror is always located on a different disk (locating it on the same disk is not only not fault tolerant, it takes away needed bandwidth). If one disk in the mirror fails, the system continues to operate using its copy.

A mirrored volume has good overall I/O performance when compared to a RAID-5 volume (slower on reads than a RAID-5 configuration but slightly faster on writes). There is also no performance loss when a member disk in a volume fails. Mirrored volumes are more expensive because you are using half the number of disks in your RAID-1 array for fault tolerance.

For example, a mirrored disk structure made of four disks actually has eight disks configured, each disk having its partner on the opposite side of the mirror. If, for example, disk3 fails on one side of the mirror, its counterpart will continue to function normally. If the remaining disk3 fails, the volume is unavailable until the hardware is repaired. In this way, up to half the disks can go offline before the mirror fails. On the other hand, if both sides of a mirror fail, the disk array is offline with only two disk failures.

Mirrored drives perform write functions faster than RAID-5 and therefore might be considered for write-intensive functions (such as database transaction logs).

The I/O workload on a mirrored volume is duplicated between the two disks in the mirror with each half of the mirror maintaining a copy of the other half. If your computer is doing 100 I/O operations per second (10% writes) and you have 4 disks at 40GB each and you configure them as a mirrored volume (RAID-1), the I/O load on each individual disk is

I/Os per disk = (Reads + (2 * Writes))/2

In the preceding configuration, that would result in an I/O load at the disk level of 55 I/Os per second (there would be two RAID-1 structures so the I/O could be as low as 27 I/Os per second total) with a total of 80GB of disk available.

Mirroring (RAID-1) provides a high degree of fault tolerance and good performance. You might use RAID-1 arrays in which all the data fits onto one disk (such as the operating system), or a database transaction log (that only does sequential writes). The cost of creating a RAID-1 disk array means it will not usually be used for large disk arrays; however, it can be important when used strategically.

RAID-5 Volumes

A RAID-5 volume is fault tolerant with data and parity information striped intermittently across 3 to 32 disks. If a portion of a physical disk fails, the RAID-5 structure allows the hardware to re-create the lost data using the remaining parity information. RAID-5 is a good fault-tolerant solution in which the application mainly reads data. The RAID-5 configuration requires the equivalent of an additional disk to store parity information. In small configurations (three disks), this consumes 33% of the disk space (two drives going to the volume and one drive used for parity information). However, as the number of physical drives in the RAID-5 structure increases, it become more efficient (a 10-drive RAID-5 structure has nine disks going to the volume and one being used for parity information).

When a member disk of a RAID-5 volume has failed, the read performance is degraded by the need to recover the data using only the parity information. RAID-5 was designed to protect against physical disk failure and therefore protects only against a single device failing in the volume. If a second device fails before the first is repaired, the volume goes offline and the data is lost.

The I/O workload on a RAID-5 volume is spread evenly across all the disks with the equivalent space of one disk taken for fault tolerance. If your computer is doing 100 I/O operations per second (10% writes) and you have 4 disks at 40GB each and you configure them as a RAID-5 volume, the I/O load on each individual disk is

I/Os per disk = (Reads + (4 * Writes))/number of disks

In the preceding configuration, that would result in an I/O load at the disk level of 32 I/Os per second with a total of 120GB of disk available.

RAID-5 volumes are usually recommended for read-intensive applications. A disk volume that does more than 10% writes is not a good candidate for RAID-5. Disk caching can improve the write performance of a RAID-5 volume; however, you must be sure the cache is backed up by a battery.

RAID-5 arrays use only one disk for parity. When this is used in a three-disk array, the resulting volume is only 66% of the total disk capacity. When this is used in a 10-disk array, the resulting volume is 90% of the total disk capacity. RAID-5 therefore is a very economical way of providing fault tolerance to a large disk structure. However, with each disk added to a structure, the chance of a hardware failure increases. It is not good practice to expand a RAID-5 volume past the point where protection of fault tolerance is overwhelmed by the likelihood of a hardware failure.

The three RAID levels covered in this section can be summarized in Table 3.6.

TABLE 3.6

SUMMARY OF RAID CHARACTERISTICS

RAID Level	Performance	Fault Tolerance	Cost
RAID-0	Best	None	Most economical
RAID-1	Good	Good	Most expensive
RAID-5	Good Reads Slow Writes	OK	Most economical with fault tolerance

These volumes can be provided in software or by external disk controllers. In the case of the external disk controllers, the fault tolerance provided and the disk structure being used is transparent to Windows XP Professional. This is usually the recommend approach because it has the highest performance possible.

Troubleshooting Volume Problems

If a disk or volume fails, it is important to repair the problem as quickly as possible. Disk Management displays the status of disks or volumes in both the list and graphical view. The Disk Management display can be customized by selecting the View tab and then Top or Bottom. This allows you to set the top or bottom frames of the display to disk, volume, or graphical display.

One of the disk statuses shown in Table 3.7 will appear in the Status column of the Volume List view and in the Graphical view. If there is a problem with a volume, this will help you diagnose and correct the problem.

TABLE 3.7

VOLUME STATUS DESCRIPTION IN DISK MANAGEMENT

Disk Status	*Meaning of Status*
Healthy	The volume is readable with no detected problems.
Healthy (At Risk)	The volume is currently readable, but I/O errors have been detected on one of the volume's physical disks. The disk view will show a disk that is Online (Errors). Use Reactivate Disk to return the disk to Online status, which will return the volume to Healthy status.
Initializing	The volume is being initialized. Only dynamic volumes display the Initializing status.
Resynching	The volume's mirrors are being resynchronized to contain identical data.
Regenerating	Data and parity are being regenerated for a RAID-5 volume. The RAID-5 volume can be accessed while regeneration is in progress.
Failed	The volume cannot be started automatically.

continues

TABLE 3.7	*continued*

VOLUME STATUS DESCRIPTION IN DISK MANAGEMENT

Disk Status	*Meaning of Status*
Failed Redundancy	The data on the volume is no longer fault tolerant because one of the underlying physical disks is not online.
Failed Redundancy (At Risk)	The data on the volume is no longer protected by a fault-tolerant configuration, and I/O errors have been detected on the physical disk. The disk view will show a physical disk with Online (Errors) as the status. Returning the disk to Online status (using Reactivate Disk) will return the volume to Failed Redundancy status.

If the underlying disk is not online, but is successfully reactivated (using Reactivate Disk), the volume should automatically repair itself. A mirrored volume repairs itself by resynchronizing the data (sometimes called *resilvering*). A RAID-5 volume repairs itself by regenerating its parity and data.

If the disk returns to Online status but the volume does not, reactivate the volume manually using Reactivate Volume.

If the underlying disk will not reactivate, there is probably something wrong with the disk. Replace the disk and rebuild any mirror by using the Remove Mirror and Add Mirror commands. A RAID-5 volume can be rebuilt using the Repair Volume command.

Removable Media

Removable Storage Management (RSM) is the interface in Windows XP Professional for accessing removable media, including automated devices such as changers, jukeboxes, and libraries. RSM is installed by default to control most types of removable media including CD-ROM, DVD-ROM, magneto-optical (MO) Jaz, and Zip drives in both standalone and library configurations. RSM cannot manage the A: and B: drives.

RSM considers all device changes as a subset of an ideal standard. A given minidriver tells RSM what functionality the actual changer implements, allowing RSM to treat it appropriately. This model is similar to the way Windows XP Professional treats network adapters and printers, each one having a slightly different way of doing common tasks with an intermediate driver allowing client applications to access services in standard ways.

Client programs such as backup applications and Hierarchical Storage Management (HSM) systems use RSM to access their media. After the media is available, the client applications use standard Windows XP API calls to read and write data.

This model provides the following benefits:

◆ **A common driver model**—The driver model allows a tape library to be used with any RSM-compatible application. An application written to use RSM can work with any device changer where the manufacturer has provided an RSM minidriver.

◆ **Library sharing**—Multiple applications can now share a common library. Previously, if you wanted to use both a backup application and an HSM application supplied from two different vendors, you required two device changers. When using RSM, both applications can use the same changer.

◆ **Offline media**—A backup application does not need to know where the media is. It simply requests the media and RSM loads it, or it asks the operator to mount it as required.

◆ **Media tracking**—RSM tracks all media that it recognizes in an internal database. Applications can register with RSM, allowing it to recognize its own media. Applications can also use RSM to search the database and load a particular type of media.

◆ **A common interface**—Backup applications that are RSM compatible work the same with a changer or with a standalone drive.

Windows XP Professional uses RSM to manage ATAPI CD-ROM changers and to mount and dismount all removable media. This includes disks contained in ATAPI CD-ROM changers that hold several CD-ROMs. This type of device receives only a single letter in Windows XP.

NOTE

Legacy Applications RSM will interfere with legacy applications because it controls all media changers on the system exclusively. This breaks applications that expect to access these changers directly. These applications must now access the changers via RSM.

The Windows XP Professional backup utility uses RSM for tape media but not for media with file systems (such as Zip or Jaz drives).

Media Pools

RSM organizes removable media into media pools. RSM can then reassign media to different media pools to provide the amount of storage different data management applications need.

A media pool is a logical collection of similar media with similar properties. All RSM media belong to a media pool, and each media pool holds either tape or disk (but not both). Applications use media pools to gain access to specific types of media from a library.

RSM supports two classes of media pools:

◆ System, including unrecognized, import, and free.

◆ Application, created for data management applications. Several application media pools can be created. Media reserved for an application (allocated) cannot be moved between media pools.

Unrecognized Media Pools

Unrecognized media pools contain new (blank) media. This should be immediately moved from the unrecognized media pool to the free media pool so it can be used by applications.

Import Media Pools

Import media pools contain media the RSM recognizes but has not catalogued in the RSM database. Media can be moved from import media pools to free or application media pools for reuse.

Free Media Pools

Free media pools contain media that are not currently allocated by an application and contain no current data. Media pools should be configured to draw from the free media pool when there is nothing available for a particular application.

Application Media Pools

Application media pools are created and used by data-management applications. Media in an application pool are controlled by the management application or by the administrator. An application can use more than one media pool and more than one application can share a media pool.

Library Types

Each medium in RSM belongs to a library and there are two types of libraries, as described in the following sections.

Robotic Libraries

Robotic libraries are automated units (such as jukeboxes) that hold multiple tapes or disks and can have multiple drives.

Standalone Libraries

Standalone libraries are single-slot CD-ROM or tape devices that hold a single piece of media.

RSM can also track offline media that are catalogued but not currently in a library. This media can be physically located elsewhere (for offsite storage supporting disaster recovery plans).

Media Resources

Before RSM can be set up and used, there must be removable media resources to manage. There are three types of removable media supported by RSM. They are described in the following sections.

Tape

The two major tape technologies in use today are Digital Audio Tape (DAT) and Digital Linear Tape (DLT).

Read-Only Optical Disk

Read-only optical media includes CD-ROM and DVD-ROM disks. These are written by the manufacturer and cannot be overwritten or erased. This type of media is most useful as reference material (such as online catalogues or documentation) or licensed software programs (such as applications and games).

Writable Optical Disk

Writable optical media includes magneto-optical (MO) devices, Phase Change (PC), Write Once Read Many (WORM), CD-Recordable (CD-R) and CD-RW, and DVD-Recordable (DVD-R, DVD-RAM, and DVD+RW) disks. MO and PC media can be erased and overwritten, whereas WORM, CD-R, and DVD-R disk can be written to only once.

Operator Requests

An operator request is a message that requests a specific task. Operator requests are generated when offline media have been requested, or an application has requested media and none is available. An operator request will also be generated if a fault occurs in one of the libraries or a drive needs cleaning and no cleaner cartridges are available.

Troubleshooting RSM

Problems can occur when using RSM in either standalone configurations or with robotic libraries. To prevent problems, follow the guidelines in this list:

◆ Verify that the library is supported by Windows XP. A good place to check is the Hardware Compatibility list (HCL) on the Microsoft Web site (www.microsoft.com/hcl).

◆ Verify that the library is properly connected. If the library uses a SCSI connection, be sure there are no SCSI ID conflicts with other devices in the computer, such as with hard drives or CD-ROMs. In addition, verify that all cables are installed and terminated properly and do not exceed the maximum length allowed.

◆ Use Device Manager to ensure that Windows XP has recognized the library and associated drives and has configured the device drivers correctly.

◆ If Removable Storage still cannot automatically configure the library correctly, it will need to be manually configured.

◆ If the library is configured correctly but begins malfunctioning, look at the Windows XP system event log. Many problems can be caused by device errors.

R E V I E W   B R E A K

▶ Devices support Plug and Play to make their installation and configuration automatic and dynamic (without a reboot).

▶ The Device Manager can display the resources a device is using and allow you to edit and change any (not all will be available).

▶ Disk Management is the MMC snap-in GUI interface into managing disks, partitions, volumes, logical drives, and other configurations.

▶ Disks are either basic disks or dynamic disks.

▶ Basic disk configurations are stored in the partition table on each disk.

▶ Basic disks may have up to four primary partitions, or three primary partitions and one extended partition.

▶ Basic disk extended partitions can be divided into logical drives.

▶ Dynamic disk configurations are stored in a 1MB database at the end of the physical disk.

▶ Dynamic disks use volumes rather than partitions.

▶ Spanned, mirrored, striped, and RAID-5 configurations can be created on dynamic disks.

▶ Only Windows XP and Windows 2000 can access dynamic disks.

▶ Removable Storage manages access to standalone and robotic libraries and allows you to group disks and tapes into media pools.

▶ RSM keeps track of all catalogued media, even if it is currently not in a library device. Requesting the media will find the media or generate an operator message requesting the media be placed in a library.

DISPLAY DEVICES

Implement, manage, and troubleshoot display devices.

Windows XP Professional adds support for up to nine display adapters. This allows the desktop to extend to nine monitors supporting large graphical drawings (such as those produced by CAD systems). There are some important things to take into consideration if you are setting up a multiple-display system.

Multiple-Display Support

All the video adapters used with multiple-display units must be Peripheral Component Interconnect (PCI) or Accelerated Graphics Port (AGP) devices.

The hardware requirements for the primary video adapter (that drives the first screen of the multiple displays) are different from the requirements for the secondary video adapters. If the video adapter built into the motherboard is to be used as a secondary screen in a multiple display, it must be compatible with those requirements.

If you are using a video adapter built into the motherboard for a multiple display, you must first completely install Windows XP Professional before adding any other adapters. The Windows XP Professional setup program will disable an onboard video adapter if it sees an additional one. The BIOS in some systems will also shut down the onboard video adapter if an additional one is seen. If you can't defeat this detection, the built-in video adapter cannot be used in a multiple display.

One last consideration to remember is that the primary video adapter cannot be turned off. Because the multiple-display configuration uses the primary as the "anchor point" of the extended desktop, any system that shuts down the primary video adapter will not support multiple displays. Laptops that are placed in docking stations usually do just that and therefore will not function correctly in this configuration.

The Virtual Desktop

Windows XP Professional creates a virtual desktop when configuring multiple displays and uses this to determine the relationship of the displays to one another. The virtual desktop sets the coordinates of the top-left corner of the primary screen at (0,0). Additional screens are configured to exactly touch each other on the virtual desktop, allowing the mouse to move seamlessly from screen to screen; there are no spots not covered by a display.

The position of the displays on the virtual desktop can be viewed by clicking the Display icon in the Control Panel. Select the Settings tab in the Control Panel to show the screen layout. Display positions are changed by dragging the icon representing the screen to its new location. There is also a check box to indicate which screen (and therefore video adapter) is going to be the primary monitor.

Configuring Multiple-Display Adapters

After the secondary adapter(s) are installed, the virtual desktop must be configured.

The following procedure outlines the configuration of a two-monitor system.

STEP BY STEP

3.4 Configuring Two Displays

1. Click Start and then Control Panel.

2. Click Appearance and Themes and click the Display link.

3. Select the Settings tab. The numbers in the monitor representations indicate the displays. The primary display is 1, and 2 through 9 are the secondary displays.

4. Select the primary display and click Use This Device as the Primary Monitor check box.

5. Select the video adapter for the primary display.

6. In the Colors box, select the color depth desired.

7. Move the screen area slider to select the resolution.

8. Select display number 2.

9. Select the Extend My Windows Desktop onto This Monitor check box.

10. Select the color depth desired.

11. Move the Screen Area slider to select the resolution.

This procedure is similar to the one you would follow when configuring your display. In the case of multiple monitors, you must first choose the monitor you are configuring and then provide the same configuration for all the monitors in the system.

Troubleshooting Multiple Displays

Problems with multiple displays usually relate to the video adapter not initializing properly or not being supported as a secondary display. Table 3.8 presents some typical symptoms and their solutions.

TABLE 3.8

PROBLEMS WITH MULTIPLE DISPLAYS

Symptom	Solution
There is no output on a secondary display.	Confirm that the device is activated in the Display Properties dialog box.
	Confirm that the correct video driver is installed.
	Confirm that the secondary display was initialized when the computer restarted. You can do this by checking Device Manager for the status of the video adapter.
	Physically switch the order of the adapters in the PCI slots. (This may require that the primary adapter also qualify as a secondary adapter.)
The Extend My Windows Desktop onto This Monitor check box is unavailable.	Confirm that the secondary display is highlighted in the Display Properties dialog box.
	Confirm that the secondary display adapter is supported.
	Confirm that the secondary display is detected.
There are problems displaying an application on a multiple-display configuration.	Run the application on the primary display rather than on a secondary display, or on a window that spans more than one screen.
	Run the application on a full screen rather than on a window.
	Disable the secondary display and rerun the application to see whether the problem is specific to multiple-display support.

Video Adapters

Most computers are designed with a video adapter built into the motherboard, and generally this device will work best with most applications. With some new games or high-end multimedia applications, however, additional hardware acceleration is needed to power the effects.

Video adapters now support the Plug and Play standard and will be detected and installed by Windows XP Professional either during setup or when you reboot your computer after installing the device.

In the event that Plug and Play cannot detect the card directly, you can use the following procedure to install the new device.

STEP BY STEP

3.5 Installing a New Video Adapter

1. Click Start and then Control Panel.

2. Click Printers and Other Hardware and click the Add Hardware link in the See Also pane.

3. Click Next to close the Welcome page.

4. If you have already installed the new video adapter, select the Yes button and click Next. (Selecting No will abort the wizard and you will be asked to power off the computer and add the new device.)

5. The wizard will display a list of devices already installed. Highlight the new video device and click Next.

6. Click Finish to complete the installation.

FIGURE 3.6
Display settings.

After the new video adapter is installed, you can change the characteristics of your screen using the Display applet in the Control Panel. Figure 3.6 shows the Settings screen from the Display applet in Control Panel. From this point, you can vary the color depth and the screen resolution.

Table 3.9 lists the settings and advanced options for configuring your display.

TABLE 3.9

ADVANCED DISPLAY OPTIONS

Option	Description
Color Quality	Lists the color quality options for the display adapter. (Settings)
Screen Resolution	Configures the screen resolution (pixels high by pixels wide) of the display. (Settings)
Font Size	Allows selection of small or large font size. (Appearance)
Display	Allows selection of the monitor type that the display adapter is using. (Settings)
Screen Refresh Frequency	Allows selection of the refresh frequency the display adapter will use with the monitor. (Settings/Advanced/Monitor)
Hardware Acceleration	Allows setting of the amount of hardware acceleration and performance supplied by the graphics hardware. (Settings/Advanced/Troubleshooting)
DPI Setting	Changes the screen resolution (Dots per inch) to make viewing small objects easier.

POWER MANAGEMENT

Configure Advanced Configuration Power Interface (ACPI).

Being mobile with your computer is becoming the rule rather than the exception. Within corporations, a significant number of desktop systems are laptops in docking stations. Support for these devices requires special considerations compared to stationary desktop systems. Chief among these is Power Management.

Advanced Power Management

Advanced Power Management (APM) is the legacy power management scheme based on a BIOS approach that was first supported in Windows 95. Most of the interesting features of APM are in the BIOS, which is hidden from the Windows XP Professional operating system.

APM has been superseded by the Advanced Configuration and Power Interface (ACPI) standard. This is a more robust scheme for power management and system configuration supported in Windows 98 and Windows XP Professional.

Many laptop computers will have both ACPI and APM support, but some will have only APM support. Support for APM in Windows XP is mainly intended for laptops with limited support on desktop computers.

APM in Windows XP Professional is designed to support battery status, suspend and resume functions, and auto-off for hibernate. Functions such as wake on timed event, wake on LAN, and wake on ring are not supported.

Advanced Configuration Power Interface

Advanced Configuration and Power Interface (ACPI) is an industry specification that allows the integration of power management into both application programs and the operating system. This integration allows Windows XP Professional to handle all the power management resources for the computer and its peripherals. Almost all new desktops and laptops include support for ACPI.

ACPI is configured for your Windows XP Professional computer during setup only if all the peripherals present support power management. That will not always be true if you are using any older peripherals. Some components do not support power management and may prevent ACPI from being installed, and may cause erratic behavior even with the older Advanced Power Management (APM) system.

Power Options and the Airlines
Commercial airlines usually request that you turn off any portable computers and refrain from using cell phones while the plane is in flight. Placing your computer into standby does not comply with this request; you must turn off your computer completely. In Standby, your computer is still running but in a low-power state, and it could come back to life for any number of reasons.

If you configure Hibernation and place the computer into this mode, the computer is turned off and your state is saved to disk.

If your portable computer is equipped with a cellular modem, you must also ensure that it is completely turned off.

Plug and Play with ACPI

To take full advantage of Plug and Play, ACPI must be installed and running. This allows Windows XP Professional rather than the hardware to configure and monitor the computer.

Under ACPI, Windows XP Professional controls the computer's resources and configuration, which allows you to add a new peripheral and Windows XP Professional to load the drivers and enable the new device without restarting the system.

Windows XP Professional also tracks which programs are active and can direct power to devices as they need it, thereby preventing unnecessary power demands.

Configuring ACPI

ACPI is configured by the Power Options applet in the Control Panel. The first thing to consider when configuring Power management on your computer is the way that you want to use it. For example, you might be traveling and want to maximize your battery life, or you could be giving a presentation while on battery and want to always keep the monitor on, while powering off other peripherals. There are two ways to configure this—by selecting a predefined power scheme or by defining your own configuration and saving it for later use. The following procedure will enable you to select different power schemes and view their configuration.

STEP BY STEP

3.6 Selecting a Power Scheme

1. Click Start, and then click Control Panel.

2. Click Performance and Maintenance.

3. Click the Power Options link. The Power Options Properties page will display.

4. Click the down arrow to display the drop-down list of Power Schemes defined for your computer. Note the current one and select various others. The values for the Turn off Monitor, Turn off Hard Disk(s), and System Standby settings for both the plugged-in and on-battery states will change.

5. Change some of the timer values (for example, the timer on when hard drives spin down while on battery to 15 minutes) and click Save As and name it MyTest.

6. Click the down arrow to display the drop-down list of Power Schemes and select MyTest. The configuration you previously created and saved will now be selected.

7. Click Cancel to return to the current power scheme or Apply to apply the new configuration to the computer.

Windows XP Professional also provides an alarm feature to alert you when the battery in your laptop is low or critically low. The alarm page of the Power Options applet allows you to set the level of remaining battery power to trigger an alarm and to allow you to define what happens when the alarm goes off.

Configuring Standby and Hibernation

On a portable computer, there are usually two buttons to power on or off the computer. One is usually recognized as the power button and one as a sleep or standby button. Windows XP Professional allows you to define what happens when you press the sleep button or the power button or when you close the laptop completely.

On the Advanced page of the Power Options applet, there are three drop-down lists that define the available options for each of the three events previously listed. The two most often used options are standby and hibernate.

Standby

When your computer switches to standby mode, it goes into a low-power state where devices, such as monitors and disk drives, are turned off and your computer uses less power. By pressing standby again, the computer powers up quickly and your desktop is restored exactly as before. Standby is particularly useful for conserving battery life when you plan on being away from your computer for short periods of time. Standby does not save any information to disk, so a power failure (letting the batteries run out) will cause you to lose unsaved information.

N O T E

Using Standby and Hibernate in a Domain Your computer can be configured to go into Standby mode or to Hibernate when it is inactive for a defined period of time. If your computer is part of a Windows 2000 domain, certain domain policies can interfere with this. Group policies are refreshed on each computer every 90 minutes (the default) plus or minus 30 minutes (to prevent every computer from updating simultaneously). If the group policy refresh timer is similar to the standby or hibernate timer, your laptop may never be idle long enough for this to happen.

Hibernation

Hibernation is an option that will save everything in memory to disk, turn off your monitor and disk drive, and power down your computer. When you restart your computer, your desktop is restored exactly as you left it. This takes longer because it must reboot your computer and then reinitialize your desktop. However, it is a quick way to save your environment when you are going to be away from your computer for a long time.

For hibernation to be available as an option when pressing the power buttons, it must be configured. The Hibernate tab on the Power Options applet will allow you to configure Hibernation and also show the amount of disk space the option will take. When Hibernation is enabled, it will show up as an option on the advanced drop-down lists.

INPUT AND OUTPUT DEVICES

Implement, manage, and troubleshoot input and output (I/O) devices.

Since their introduction, personal computers have always been generalized in design. Additional functionality and personalizing features were provided by manufacturers of add-on cards and adapters. However, with many different manufacturers all providing different approaches to installing and configuring their devices, using PC add-ons was often confusing and contradictory.

Windows XP Professional supports the Plug and Play standard, and most new devices use this to standardize their installation steps.

Configuring Input and Output Devices

Devices such as printers, image-capturing devices, multimedia, pointing and input devices, and now smart cards form a class of device that works more at the human-machine interface than other devices (such as display adapters or network cards). This means that there are more features combined into these devices, making them more than a single-purpose device. The installation and configuration of these devices are therefore discussed separately.

Printers

The printing system is modular and works hand in hand with other systems to provide printing services. When a printer is a local printer and a print job is specified by an application, data is sent to the Graphics Device Interface (GDI). The GDI calls the printer driver for print device information useful in rendering the print job into the printer language of the print device. The GDI is therefore the main interface between the application and the printing system. The print job is passed to the spooler and is written to disk as a temporary file so it can survive a power outage or system shutdown. Print jobs can be spooled in either the RAW or Enhanced Meta File (EMF) spool format. Figure 3.7 shows the layout of the components of the Windows XP Professional printing subsystem.

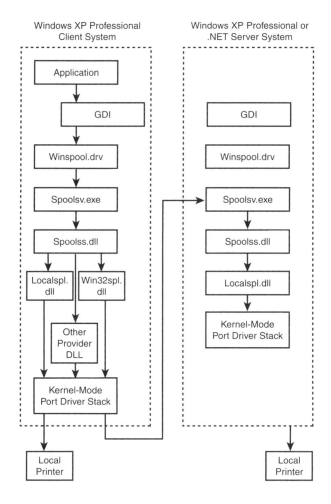

FIGURE 3.7
Components of the Windows printing subsystem.

The client side of the print spooler is `winspool.drv`, and that driver makes an RPC call to the `spoolsv.exe` server side of the spooler. This split in functionality is what allows print devices to be local to your computer or remotely installed on a print server and still function the same. Clients for `spoolsv.exe` include `winspool.drv` for handling locally created print jobs and `win32spl.dll` for print jobs created on remote machines.

If the printer is located on a different Windows XP or Windows 2000 server or Windows NT server, the network provider `win32spl.dll` is used. This module uses RPC calls to redirect the print jobs from the client's computer to the server's `spoolsv.exe` process. There, the server's local print provider will handle the print job.

You generally install printers using the Add Printer Wizard that you find in the Printers folder in Control Panel. After you step through the wizard, you will have created a local printer with the name you provided. You can create any number of local printers that print to the same physical printer but are configured to print differently, have different security schemes, or provide different access times. You can manipulate printers by performing the following actions:

◆ Double-click the printer to see any spooled jobs, provided you have the privilege to do so.

◆ Right-click the printer to view a shortcut menu that provides several options. You can delete a printer that no longer exists or use the Default Printer command to set this printer as the default one for your Windows XP Professional computer.

◆ Right-click a printer and select the Properties command from the shortcut menu to access the Printer Properties and control any number of settings.

Using a Basic Error Checklist

Any number of things can go wrong when you attempt to print to a printer. In many cases, Windows XP Professional alerts you to an error and in some cases will actually tell you what the error type is.

Here is a standard checklist of the most common solutions to print problems. If your print job spools but does not print, try the following:

◆ Check that the printer is turned on and all the connections are secure.

◆ Check that the paper tray is full and no paper is jammed inside the printer.

◆ Verify that the printer is operational. If the printer is a shared resource and other users can print, the problem is not with the printer or the print server.

◆ Verify that the printer does not have any outstanding error conditions set.

◆ If there is a job currently printing that is hung up (looking for paper that is not loaded on the printer, for example), you can delete it by pausing the printer and deleting the stopped print job. Restarting the printer will allow other spooled jobs to complete.

The preceding problems are so simple that it is easy to waste time and overlook them. A large percentage of printer problems will disappear when you restart your printer. If that fails, restart your Windows XP computer.

If none of these solutions seems to work, try the following:

◆ Verify that the printer is using the correct printer driver. If the printer is a shared resource and other users have operating systems other than Windows XP Professional, be sure you install all the drivers necessary.

◆ Verify that the printer you attempted to print to is either the default printer for your system or the printer you selected from your application.

◆ Verify that you can access the printer you are attempting to use. Select the Printers item from the Setting submenu on the Start menu. Right-click the printer icon and select Open. If the printer control panel does not open correctly and the status persists at Opening or Unable to Connect, there could be a permissions problem.

◆ Print a test page from the printer's Properties page.

◆ Verify that there is enough hard disk space to create the temporary spool file.

◆ Try printing a smaller page of text from Notepad. This will often confirm that the print problem is application specific.

◆ Print to a file and copy the file to the printer port being used either locally or on the printer server. If you can print in this manner, there could be a spooler or data-transmission error.

IN THE FIELD

UPDATE YOUR PRINT DRIVERS

At the very worst, you can try reinstalling the printer and supplying a new or updated printer driver.

There are a number of places to find updated printer drivers, including the following:

· The Windows XP Professional distribution disks.

· The setup disks that come with the printer.

· The printer manufacturer's Web site.

· The Microsoft Web site. Use the Search button to search for the particular model of printer.

Scanners

Scanners are added by using the Scanners and Cameras Wizard found in the Control Panel.

After installing the scanner and connecting any cables required to your Windows XP Professional computer, you can use the procedure in Step by Step 3.7 to install a scanner.

STEP BY STEP

3.7 Installing a Scanner

1. Click Start and click Control Panel.

2. Click Printers and Other Hardware, and click the Scanners and Cameras link.

3. Click the Add button to start the Scanners and Cameras Installation Wizard.

4. Click Add an Imaging Device in the Imaging Task window.

5. Click Next to close the Scanner and Camera Installation Wizard welcome page.

6. Select the manufacturer and device model that you are installing, and click Next.

7. Select the port on which you have installed your scanner or select automatic port selection and click Next.

8. Provide a name for the device and click Next.

9. Click Finish to complete the installation.

> **NOTE**
>
> **Administrator Privileges** You must be logged on with a user ID that has administrator privileges to complete the procedure for installing a scanner. If your scanner supports Plug and Play, Windows XP Professional will detect it and install the correct drivers automatically.

Keyboards

Keyboards can be built in, connected with a specific device port, or operate as a USB device connected directly or via a USB hub.

Windows XP Professional will detect a new keyboard if it is Plug and Play compatible. If it is not, you will have to use the Add Hardware Wizard and use the manufacturer's setup disks to install the device manually. Figure 3.8 shows the hardware properties of a typical keyboard.

After the keyboard is installed, you can change the characteristics of the device to meet your personal requirements. The Repeat Delay sets the amount of time the system delays before repeating the key you are holding down. The Repeat Rate is the speed at which the repeated key is added. Figure 3.9 shows the Speed tab on the Keyboard Properties page.

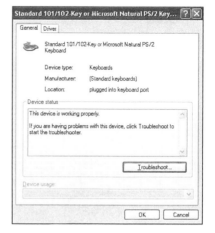

FIGURE 3.8
General information on a working keyboard.

FIGURE 3.9
Adjusting speed characteristics of a keyboard.

Keyboard Customizations

The Accessibility Options applet in the Control Panel also provides a number of ways to customize how your keyboard functions. The following features allow you to customize your keyboard functions:

◆ **StickyKeys**—This option allows you to press a modifier key, such as Ctrl, Alt, Shift, or the Windows Logo key, and have it remain in effect until a nonmodifier key is pressed.

◆ **FilterKeys**—This option allows you to ignore brief or repeated keystrokes. FilterKeys are turned on by holding down the right Shift key for eight seconds.

◆ **ToggleKeys**—This option emits a sound when locking keys are pressed.

To enable any of these functions, double-click the Accessibility applet in the Control Panel and select the Keyboard tab.

Shortcut Key Combinations

For those who are keyboard wizards and like to use shortcuts rather than the mouse to find and select certain options, Windows XP Professional provides shortcuts to well-known tasks (see Table 3.10). You should note that if you are in an application (such as Word or Excel), some of these shortcuts will take on application-specific meanings (for example, F4 in Word will repeat the last text you entered).

TABLE 3.10

WINDOWS XP PROFESSIONAL KEYBOARD SHORTCUTS

Shortcut	Function
Ctrl+C	Copy
Ctrl+X	Cut
Ctrl+V	Paste
Ctrl+Z	Undo
Delete	Delete
Shift+Delete	Delete selected item permanently without placing the item in the Recycle Bin
Ctrl while dragging an item	Copy selected item

Shortcut	*Function*
Ctrl+Shift while dragging an item	Create shortcut to selected item
F2	Rename selected item
Ctrl+right arrow	Move the insertion point to the beginning of the next word
Ctrl+left arrow	Move the insertion point to the beginning of the previous word
Ctrl+down arrow	Move the insertion point to the beginning of the next paragraph
Ctrl+up arrow	Move the insertion point to the beginning of the previous paragraph
Ctrl+Shift with any of the arrow keys	Highlight a block of text
Shift with any of the arrow keys	Select more than one item in a window or on the desktop, or select text within a document
Ctrl+A	Select all
F3	Search for a file or folder
Ctrl+O	Open an item
Alt+Enter	View properties for the selected item
Alt+F4	Close the active item, or quit the active program
Ctrl+F4	Close the active document in programs that allow you to have multiple documents open simultaneously
Alt+Tab key	Switch between open items
Alt+Esc	Cycle through items in the order in which they were opened
F6	Cycle through screen elements in a window or on the desktop
F4	Display the Address bar list in My Computer or Windows Explorer
Shift+F10	Display the shortcut menu for the selected item
Alt+spacebar	Display the System menu for the active window
Ctrl+Esc	Display the Start menu
Alt+underlined letter in a menu name	Display the corresponding menu

continues

TABLE 3.10 *continued*	
WINDOWS XP PROFESSIONAL KEYBOARD SHORTCUTS	
Shortcut	*Function*
Underlined letter in a command name on an open menu	Carry out the corresponding command
F10	Activate the menu bar in the active program
Right arrow	Open the next menu to the right, or open a sub-menu
Left arrow	Open the next menu to the left, or close a submenu
F5	Refresh the active window
Backspace	View the folder one level up in My Computer or Windows Explorer
Esc	Cancel the current task
Shift when you insert a CD into the CD-ROM drive	Prevent the CD from automatically playing

FIGURE 3.10
Setting mouse properties.

Mouse

Like keyboards, the mouse can be directly connected to a mouse port, built into the keyboard as a piezoelectric control, or connected to the serial port or device on a USB port or hub.

After the mouse has been installed, you can adjust the characteristics of its action by changing the configuration on the Properties page of the Mouse applet in the Control Panel. Figure 3.10 shows a typical Mouse Properties page.

Using the Mouse applet, you can select the mouse to be left-handed or right-handed, select double- or single-click to select objects, and set the speed at which a double-click is recognized.

You also can have the mouse pointer jump to the default dialog box or button, thereby requiring fewer mouse movements to make a selection. You can configure the mouse pointer to accelerate if you move the mouse faster. This results in the mouse pointer moving a longer distance with a quicker mouse movement than it would if you moved the mouse over the same distance but at a slower rate.

Windows XP Professional fully supports the IntelliMouse wheel without any additional software. Windows XP Professional also natively supports the positioning wheel found in many mouse devices. Figure 3.11 shows the Wheel configuration screen from the Mouse applet in Control Panel, showing the detection of a positioning wheel.

Multimedia

Categories of multimedia devices in Windows XP Professional include audio, video, and MIDI. In addition, the Microsoft Media Player can use the Web to access music files and radio stations that broadcast programming. The CD Player can be used to control the playback of music CDs from the system CD-ROM drive.

Figure 3.12 shows the Sounds configuration page from the Sounds and Audio Devices folder in the Control Panel.

This provides a mechanism to control the sounds used for specific events within Windows XP and many of its installed services (such as NetMeeting, MSN Messaging, or Active Sync). You also can customize the sounds used for these events and save the configuration as a sound scheme.

The Speaker tab also allows you to specify the type of speaker system you have attached to your Windows XP Professional computer. This can vary from the simple to a five-speaker surround-sound setup (see Figure 3.13).

Smart Cards

Smart cards are programmable computing devices that are usually credit-card size. Applications and data can be downloaded onto these cards for a variety of uses, including authentication, certificate storage, record keeping, and so on.

Although the processor included in the card can give it great capability, a smart card is not a standalone computer. It must be connected to other computers to be useful. Smart cards today contain an 8-bit microcontroller with 16KB or more of memory.

FIGURE 3.11
Advanced mouse properties.

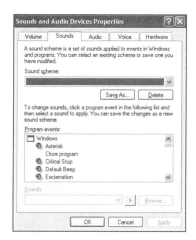

FIGURE 3.12
Sound configuration options in Sounds and Audio Devices.

FIGURE 3.13
A complex speaker system setup.

In the Windows XP operating system, smart cards and certificate-based logons are fully supported. In this architecture, the smart card contains the certificate and associated private key. When you are logging on to your Windows XP Professional computer, a challenge is sent to the smart card. The smart card signs the challenge with the private key and the result, along with the certificate, is submitted to the authentication service. The authentication service verifies the signature and permits or denies the logon request.

To communicate with its host computer, a smart card must be placed in a smart card reader. The Step by Step 3.8 describes how to connect a smart card reader to your Windows XP Professional computer.

STEP BY STEP

3.8 Installing a Smart Card Reader

1. Shut down and turn off your computer.

2. Attach the smart card reader to an available serial port or insert it into an available PCMCIA slot.

3. If you are installing a serial reader and it has a supplemental cable, attach your keyboard or mouse connector to it, and then connect the smart card reader to your keyboard or mouse port. Newer smart card readers use power from the keyboard or mouse port.

4. Boot your machine and log on.

5. If your smart card reader is a Plug and Play–compliant device, Windows XP Professional will automatically detect it and install the correct device drivers.

6. If your device is not Plug and Play compliant, you will require a setup disk from the manufacturer and possibly the Windows XP Professional CDs to load the correct device drivers.

7. Click Start and click Control Panel.

8. Double-click Administrative Tools.

9. Double-click Computer Management.

10. Expand Services and Applications and click Services.

11. Right-click Smart Cards, select Properties, and choose Automatic from the Startup Option.

12. Click Start to start the Smart Card and click OK.

Cameras

Cameras are added by using the Scanners and Cameras Wizard found in the Control Panel. After installing the camera and connecting any cables required to your Windows XP Professional computer, you can use Step by Step 3.9 to install a camera.

STEP BY STEP

3.9 Installing a Camera

1. Click Start, and then click Control Panel.

2. Double-click the Scanners and Cameras icon.

3. Click the Add button to start the Scanners and Cameras Installation Wizard.

4. Click Add an Imaging Device from the Imaging Task Windows and click Next.

5. Click Next to close the Scanner and Camera Installation Wizard Welcome screen.

6. Select the manufacturer and device model you are installing, and click Next.

7. Select the port on which you have installed your camera, and click Next.

8. Provide a name for the device and click Next.

9. Click Finish to complete the installation.

> **NOTE**
>
> **Administrator Privileges**   You must be logged on with a user ID that has administrator privileges to complete the camera installation. If your camera supports Plug and Play, Windows XP Professional will detect it and install the correct drivers automatically.

Modems

Windows XP Professional supports many different brands of modems. To check whether the modem you are installing is supported, you can review the Hardware Compatibility List (HCL) on the Microsoft Web site (www.microsoft.com/hcl).

Modems are most commonly used to dial up remote systems or Internet service providers using speeds up to 56Kb over analog phone lines. Modems from different manufacturers achieve high-speed transmission by using a variety of techniques (some of which are proprietary to that company). Compatibility problems between these different methods can cause your modem to drop to a lower speed in search of a compatible transmission technique. Line speed can also be reduced due to lower baud rates being available in remote areas. Static on the line can also lower the available line speed.

Installing Modems

Step by Step 3.10 will allow you to install a new modem into your Windows XP Professional computer.

STEP BY STEP

3.10 Installing a Modem

1. Click Start, and then click Control Panel.

2. Click the Printers and Other Hardware link, click the Phone and Modem Options link, and select the Modems tab.

3. Click Add to start the Add Hardware Wizard.

4. If your modem supports Plug and Play, click Next to allow Windows XP Professional to detect any new hardware.

5. If your modem is not detected automatically, click Don't Detect My Modem and click Next.

6. Select the manufacturer and model of modem you have installed and click Next.

7. Select the port you have installed your modem on and click Next to start the modem installation.

8. Click Finish to complete the modem setup.

Troubleshooting Modem Installations

The following are some troubleshooting suggestions when you run into problems while installing a new modem:

◆ **Turn on external modems**—Plug and Play–compliant devices might not be detected correctly if they are not powered on.

◆ **Check the manufacturer's Web site**—The modem manufacturer might have new installation files (INF files) available online.

◆ **Use diagnostics**—By selecting your new modem (after installation and setup), clicking Properties, and selecting the Diagnostics tab, you can query the modem and view log files.

◆ **Check hardware settings**—Typical settings for a modem are 8 data bits, no parity, and 1 stop bit. An alternative (and older) configuration is 7 bits, even parity, and 1 stop bit.

◆ **Use the Add Hardware Wizard**—If you install an internal modem card or PCMCIA modem card that is not Plug and Play compatible, you might need to configure its internal COM port using the Add Hardware Wizard in the Control Panel.

◆ **Use Modem Properties**—The Diagnostics tab found in the Modem Properties page allows you to execute a standard query to the modem that will list its characteristics. If the modem needs to have a specific initialization string, this can be entered by selecting the Advanced tab. Finally, the size of the input and output buffers can be set by the Advanced Port Settings button on the Advanced tab page of modem properties.

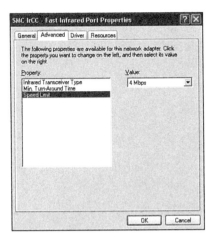

FIGURE 3.14
The Infrared device property page.

Infrared Data Association (IrDA) Devices

Windows XP Professional supports the IrDA protocols enabling data transfer over infrared connections. The Windows XP Professional Plug and Play architecture will automatically detect and install the IrDA components for computers with built-in IrDA hardware (most laptops, for example, will have an infrared port somewhere). For computers that do not have built-in infrared ports, you can attach a serial IrDA device to a COM port or connect one using a USB port or hub.

Most laptops now ship with IrDA ports that provide either 115Kbps or 4Mbps transmission speeds. Figure 3.14 shows the properties page of the IrDA port where the maximum speed of the port is configured.

The most common implementation of the infrared ports on portable computers is the Serial IrDA (SIR) standard. This is a half-duplex system with a maximum transmission speed of 115Kbps and will adjust to accommodate lower speed devices. This standard provides short-range infrared asynchronous serial connections with eight bits of data, no parity, and one stop bit.

There is a high-speed extension (FIR) that supports half-duplex connections at 4Mbps. This standard is commonly installed on new devices and can communicate with existing lower-speed devices. In a device that is half duplex, communications cannot go in both directions at once. Access to the line is signaled and control of the communications link will flip back and forth between one device and the other. This turnaround does take some time to happen, so if many small messages are being sent, full duplex (even at a slower speed) might be more efficient. The high-speed half-duplex connections are best for devices that are transmitting data in bulk (such as cameras or scanners).

Installing Infrared Devices

Most internal IrDA devices will be installed automatically by Windows XP Professional setup or when you reboot your computer after adding an IrDA device.

The following procedure shows you how to install a new infrared serial transceiver.

STEP BY STEP

3.11 Installing an Infrared Device

1. Click Start and click the Printers and Other Hardware link.

2. Click the Add Hardware link in the See Also pane.

3. Click Next to close the Add Hardware Wizard Welcome page.

4. After the Add Hardware Wizard searches for installed devices, select the Yes button indicating the new device has been installed. Click Next to continue.

5. If the new device is in the list provided, select it and click Next to complete the installation.

6. If the device is not in the list, select Add a New Hardware Device at the bottom of the list and click Next.

7. Select the Install the Hardware That I Manually Select from a List button and click Next.

8. Select Infrared Device and click Next.

9. Select the Manufacturer and Infrared device that matches your hardware. If you have a manufacturer-supplied installation disk, click Have Disk to copy them. Click Next to continue.

10. Click Next to start the device installation.

11. Click Finish to complete the installation.

NOTE

Configuring IrDA Devices You can change the infrared device properties by using Device Manager. Select the General tab to determine whether the device is working correctly. The Advanced tab will display other properties, including maximum transmission speed, that you can view or change.

Wireless Devices

The Wireless Link file transfer program, infrared printing functions, and image transfer capability are installed by default with your

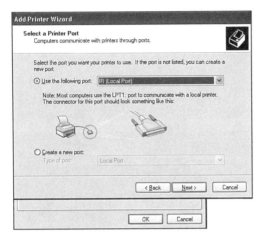

FIGURE 3.15
The infrared port is available for printing.

Windows XP Professional operating system. In addition, IrDA supports Winsock API calls to support programs created by other software and hardware manufacturers. The Winsock API calls can be used to provide infrared connections to printers, modems, pagers, PDAs, electronic cameras, cell phones, and handheld computers.

In addition to sending or printing files, you also can set up network connections between two computers using the infrared port. This capability can be used to set up shared drives and work with files and folders from your laptop to a host computer.

If your computer comes with an infrared port or you have installed an infrared transceiver, Windows XP Professional will include an infrared port as a local port in the Add Printers Wizard dialog box. If you associate a printer with this port, Windows XP Professional will use the IrDA port (using a protocol called *IrLPT*) to transmit output to the printer. Figure 3.15 shows the point in the Add Printer Wizard dialog box where the infrared printer port can be selected.

Linking Infrared Devices

Infrared links are established between two infrared devices. In any link, one device is considered to be primary and one secondary. This role is determined dynamically when the link is established and continues until the link is broken. Normally, any station can assume any role, so data transfer can be initiated from either side.

When communications are first established, the commanding station sends out a connection request at 9600bps. The responding station assumes the secondary role and returns information listing its capabilities. Both the primary and secondary stations then change the connection rate and link parameters to the common set established by this initial negotiation. With the connection established, data transfer is put under the control of the primary device.

A single IrDA device cannot link to more than one other IrDA device at a time. You can, however, install multiple IrDA devices to COM ports or USB hubs to provide simultaneous links to multiple remote devices. For example, you can have a desktop computer connect to a notebook and a digital camera simultaneously using two IrDA transceivers.

The Winsock API does support multiple simultaneous connections over a single IrDA device. This allows different programs to use the infrared device to perform many tasks with the remote device. For example, your laptop can connect to a desktop device, share files, synchronize offline folders, and send and receive mail. Each task is controlled by a different program on the laptop; however, they all use the single connection over an IrDA device.

Printing to an Infrared Printer

Printing to an infrared-connected printer is much the same as printing to a locally connected printer. After you establish an infrared connection to the printer, Windows XP Professional automatically installs the printer onto your system. You may need to install the printer manually using the Add Printer Wizard if Plug and Play does not detect or install the new printer, or if you have installed the infrared transceiver to the COM port.

> **NOTE**
>
> **Establish a Connection** Before printing to the infrared attached printer, you must always establish a connection first. You do that by aligning the IR "eyes" until the Infrared connection icon appears in the taskbar.

Infrared Network Connections

If your computer has a built-in infrared port or you have installed an infrared transceiver, you can create a direct connection to another computer using the infrared port. When Windows XP Professional detects an infrared port, it includes that information as an available connection using Network and Dial-Up Connections. This enables you to map shared drives on your network (through a host computer) to your laptop.

To connect two computers using the infrared port, you must first create an infrared network connection on both computers. When you use the Network and Dial-Up Connections Wizard to create a network connection, you specify a local connection using the infrared port.

The following procedure can be used to create an infrared network connection.

STEP BY STEP

3.12 Creating an Infrared Network Connection

1. Click Start and click Control Panel.

2. Double-click Network and Internet Connections.

3. Click the Network Connection link and click Create a New Connection in the Network Tasks window.

4. Select the button for Set Up an Advanced Connection and click Next.

5. Select Connect Directly to Another Computer and click Next.

6. Select Host (to host the data guests will access) and click Next.

7. Select the infrared port on your computer from the Devices for This Connection drop-down list and click Next.

8. Check those users who are allowed to access your computer through the infrared port (and optionally add additional users) and click Next.

9. Click Finish to complete the connection setup.

Universal Serial Bus Devices

The Universal Serial Bus (USB) is an external polled serial bus deployed in a Star topology that allows you to connect high-speed, low-latency devices to your computer. The USB protocol runs at 1 to 12Mb/sec, and supports Plug and Play and power management. USB devices are hot-pluggable to allow you to add or change devices without restarting your Windows XP Professional computer. The higher speed and polling rate at which USB performs provides better support for games, and the higher bandwidth provides better support for multimedia devices.

USB is a token-based protocol that Windows XP Professional polls to detect changes to the number and type of devices connected. A computer equipped with a USB port can support up to 127 devices attached simultaneously. This means you can have a scanner, printer, camera, mouse, keyboard, game controller, and speakers running simultaneously. Connecting this many devices to the USB port is accomplished using a USB hub (or set of USB hubs).

Hubs can be self-powered with an external power source or they can be bus-powered and get their power from the bus itself. The USB definition allows for a total of five tiers (that is, hubs attached to hubs) in a USB network. With the Windows XP Professional computer acting as the USB host, that leaves a total of four tiers (or network segments) for actual devices.

Figure 3.16 is a representation of the way that USB connections are depicted.

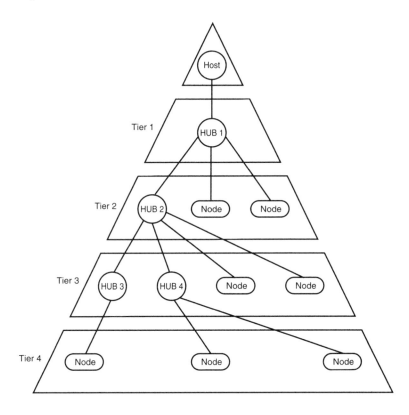

FIGURE 3.16
USB architecture.

Following are a few restrictions on using a multitiered architecture:

◆ Bus-powered hubs cannot be plugged into bus-powered hubs if a device is connected after the second hub that uses the full bandwidth of 12Mb/sec.

◆ Bus-powered hubs cannot have more than four downstream ports.

◆ Bus-powered hubs cannot support bus-powered devices that use more than 100 milliamps. Bus-powered hubs will, however, support self-powered devices.

◆ The hub cascade depth, including the host computer, cannot exceed five tiers.

Handheld Devices

Install, configure, and manage handheld devices.

Handheld devices used to be relegated to being simple organizers and calendars. Today's devices have much more power and therefore can act as an extension to your desktop or laptop computer. Windows XP Professional will connect to handheld devices through a number of means, including infrared port, serial cables, and USB connection.

Getting Connected

Handheld devices (such as Compaq's IPaq) all have infrared ports. When you place a handheld infrared port within range of the infrared port on your laptop, Windows XP Professional will announce that another machine is within range and provide a link to the file transfer screen. From this screen, you can select files on your laptop and send them to folders on your handheld device. Figure 3.17 shows a file selected to be sent to a handheld that is linked by Infrared.

Handheld devices often come with previously prepared folders in which business or personal files can be kept. The following process can be used to transfer a small spreadsheet file (such as a phone list) to the business folder on your handheld device.

FIGURE 3.17
Sending a file to your handheld device.

STEP BY STEP

3.13 Transferring a File to Your Handheld Device

1. Align your handheld device with the infrared port on your Windows XP Professional computer (or laptop).

2. The Infrared Port indicator on the taskbar should animate, showing a constant transfer between two ports.

3. Click the Infrared Port icon on the taskbar. This will open up the Wireless Link page showing files and folders you can send to the handheld device.

4. Select a small file created by Excel and click Send.

5. A Sending Files screen will pop up showing the connection to your handheld device and the progress of the file transfer. Quite often, this is accompanied by squeaks, pops, and whistles as every device now needs to sound like R2D2.

6. Click Close to shut the Wireless Link Page. Your file is now on your handheld device.

You can look at the contents of your handheld device when it is connected to your desktop or laptop by expanding the Mobile Device icon from Windows Explorer. Figure 3.18 shows the file that was sent to the handheld device now residing in its new folder.

After a file is on the handheld device, you can take it with you when you are away from your desktop or laptop computer and hopefully the information on it will be useful. Because handhelds are used often for making schedule changes, preparing e-mail to send, or taking notes at meetings, there will be new information to merge with your desktop or laptop the next time you connect to it.

The following process can be used to copy files from your handheld back to your Windows XP Professional desktop or laptop computer.

STEP BY STEP

3.14 Copying a File from Your Handheld Device

1. Click Start, and then click My Computer.

2. Double-click Mobile Device, and wait for it to refresh the display. The Mobile Device page should show any folders or files on the handheld device.

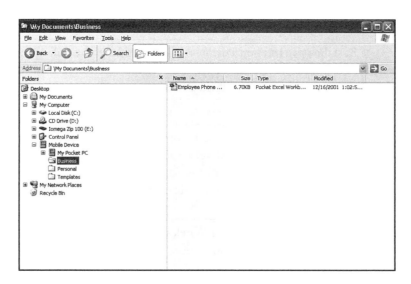

FIGURE 3.18
Files copied to your mobile device.

3. Double-click the folder you previously placed your Excel document in.

4. Click the file you would like to return to your desktop or laptop. The Folder Task pane will expand to show all the tasks you can do with this file.

5. Click Copy this Item from the Folder Task pane. A Copy Items page will open showing the folders on your desktop or laptop that can receive the handheld device file. Select a location and click Copy to initiate the file copy. A message screen will pop up showing the progression of this task.

6. Close the Mobile Device page.

Getting Mobile

If you want to integrate your handheld device into your daily work, you will need to do more than just copy files back and forth.

Microsoft provides a synchronization program called *ActiveSync* that will do just that. ActiveSync will synchronize files between your Windows XP Professional desktop or laptop and your handheld device, and it will also synchronize selected items from e-mail and Outlook as well. ActiveSync is available on the www.microsoft.com Web site and can be found by following the "more download" link.

When you are installing Microsoft ActiveSync, you are prompted to create a partnership between your Windows XP Professional desktop or laptop and your handheld device. At this time you select synchronization options and file conversion settings.

Your desktop computer can set up partnerships with many different handheld devices, but a handheld device can have partnerships with only two computers.

Figure 3.19 shows the synchronization options available through Microsoft ActiveSync.

As with any device that can go offline and then return with updated information, conflicts can arise. With Microsoft ActiveSync, you can

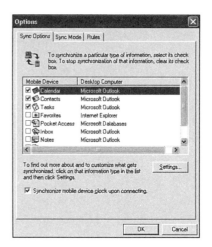

FIGURE 3.19
Synchronizing options through ActiveSync.

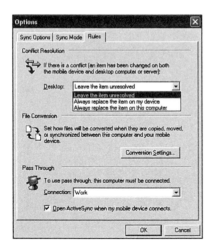

FIGURE 3.20
Conflict resolution rules in ActiveSync.

choose to leave conflicts unresolved, in which case you must manually fix the problem, or you can make the handheld device or the desktop or laptop computer take priority and overwrite the other.

Figure 3.20 shows the options available through Microsoft ActiveSync for resolving synchronization conflicts.

Troubleshooting

If you find that you cannot link your desktop or laptop to your handheld device, there are several areas in which problems can arise.

If you are trying to connect via infrared but the Infrared icon on the taskbar does not animate, there might be something wrong with your infrared device driver. Look at the infrared device statistics from Device Manager for problems in this area.

If ActiveSync will not connect to the handheld device, there could be a problem with the partnership information or the connection is being connected over a device that is unexpected. For example, ActiveSync can connect over infrared or serial using various ports, or it can connect via USB port. If the one you are attempting to connect through is disabled, it will attempt but never succeed. ActiveSync will not cycle thorough different ports after one has been chosen.

If the partnership information is the problem, your only choice is to delete the partnership and re-create it. This is not a long process and no information is lost. However, it can be done only over USB or serial cable. Infrared cannot be used to create partnerships.

Network Adapters

If you install a new network adapter in your computer, a new local area connection icon appears in the Network and Dial-Up Connections folder the next time you start Windows XP Professional. Plug and Play functionality finds the network adapter and creates a local area connection for it. By default, the local area connection is always activated. If your computer has more than one network adapter, a local area connection icon is displayed for each adapter in the Network and Dial-Up Connections folder.

The new network adapter is linked into the operating system by using bindings. Windows XP Professional divides networks into several layers, each acting independently of the other. The bottom layer is the network adapter card and driver.

A *binding* is the process that links the network components on different layers. A component in a layer can be linked to multiple components in the layer just above or below it. When configuring a network card, you assign protocols to it. The order in which these protocols are assigned can significantly improve the response you get from your network. If you have NWLink and TCP/IP traffic on your network, but your computer usually uses TCP/IP, moving that binding to the top of the list will provide better response overall. If you are connecting to a server, the server does not need to have the protocols ordered, just the Windows 2000 Professional workstation.

Installing a Network Adapter

In addition to checking the connection to the operating system, you also can view and change the characteristics of a network card itself from the Device Manager screen.

The following procedure allows you to view and modify Network Adapter options.

STEP BY STEP

3.15 Modifying Network Adapter Options

1. Click Start, Control Panel, and then click Performance and Maintenance.

2. Click System.

3. Select the Hardware tab and click the Device Manager button.

4. Expand the Network Adapters entry and select a specific network adapter.

5. Right-click the network adapter and select Properties.

6. Select the Advanced tab to display the options available for your network adapter.

If you disconnect your local area connection, the connection will not be automatically activated. Because your hardware profile saves this setting, it can accommodate your requirement for different devices at different locations. For example, if you travel to a remote sales office and use a separate hardware profile for that location which does not enable your local area connection, you do not waste time waiting for your network adapter to time out. The network adapter does not even try to connect.

By selecting the Advanced tab in Network and Dial-Up Connections and clicking Advanced Settings, you can modify the order in which adapters are used by a connection, along with the associated clients, services, and protocols for the adapter.

Managing Network Adapters

Windows 2000 Professional creates a local area connection in the Network and Dial-Up Connections folder for each network adapter installed on your computer. You can eliminate possible confusion by renaming each local area connection to reflect the network to which it is connected.

You must enable the network clients, services, and protocols that are required for your local area connections. When you do so, the client, service, or protocol is enabled automatically in all other network and dial-up connections.

You can create multiple dial-up, VPN, or direct connections by creating new ones with the wizard or by copying them in the Network and Dial-Up Connections folder. After you copy the connections, you can rename them and modify the connection settings.

DRIVERS AND DRIVER SIGNING

Manage and troubleshoot drivers and driver signing.

The device drivers that are delivered with your Windows XP Professional CD have been extensively tested with the operating system to ensure they function correctly in all circumstances. As time passes, however, these drivers will become out of date and might not support devices that did not exist when they were written. At some point, you will want to add new devices and updated drivers to your system.

Updating Drivers

Windows XP Professional provides a mechanism to automatically update device drives on your computer. The following procedure can be used to update a single device driver.

STEP BY STEP

3.16 Updating a Device Driver

1. Click Start, and then click Control Panel.

2. Click the Printers and Other Hardware link and select the System link in the See Also pane.

3. Select the Hardware tab and click the Device Manager button to display the list of devices by type.

4. Expand a device type to show the specific devices installed.

5. Right-click a specific device and select Properties.

6. Select the Driver tab and click the Update Driver button.

7. Click Next to close the Welcome page of the Update Device Driver Wizard.

8. Select Install the Software Automatically and click Next to start the search for a more updated driver.

9. Click Finish to complete the installation.

> **NOTE**
> **Administrative Privileges Are Required to Update Drivers** You must be logged on with a user ID that has administrative privileges to update device drivers. The permissions that your user ID requires will allow you to load and unload a driver, copy files into the system32\drivers directory, and write settings to the Registry.

Instead of individually addressing each device on your computer, Windows XP Professional provides an additional mechanism for updating all device drivers and software at once.

When using Windows Update, the hardware IDs for the devices installed are compared to what the Microsoft Web site offers. If an exact match is made, the new driver is downloaded and installed. If an update to an existing driver is found, the new software components will be listed in the Web site and a download button will load the updated drivers onto your Windows XP Professional computer into a temporary directory for installation.

The following procedure will update all the device drivers on your computer.

N O T E

Administrative Privileges Are Required to Use Windows Update You must be logged in with a user ID that has administrative privileges. Your computer also must be connected to a network with access to the Internet. The first time you visit the Product Updates page, you might be required to install additional software or controls.

STEP BY STEP

3.17 Using Windows Update

1. Click Start and select Windows Update.

2. Click Products Updates on the Microsoft Windows Update Web page.

3. Select the components to download and click the Download icon.

If you find that the new driver with which you have updated your system works worse than the replaced one, you can have Windows XP Professional roll the device driver back to the previous one.

By expanding the device in question in Device Manager and looking at the Driver tab in the device's properties page, you will see a button labeled Roll Back Driver. This will reload the previous driver for this device and you should have a working (although not perfectly) device again.

Managing Driver Signing

Windows XP Professional includes a mechanism called *Driver Signing*. All Windows operating system files and device drivers are digitally signed to ensure their quality. A digital signature on a driver indicates that the file has passed a volley of tests to assure the file works well in the Windows XP Professional environment. The digital signature is also used to guarantee the file has not been overwritten by another program's installation process.

Driver signing uses the existing digital-signature technology. A hash of the driver binary and other relevant information is stored in a catalog file (CAT file), and the CAT file is signed with the Microsoft digital signature. A CAT file is created for each signed driver but the driver binary itself is not touched. The link between the driver binary and the CAT file is maintained in the driver's INF file.

You can configure Windows XP Professional to ignore digital signatures and install the software anyway; issue a warning whenever a driver is being installed without a digital signature; or block the installation of any unsigned driver.

The impact of allowing unsigned drivers onto your system can range from no problems at all to a blue screen. That is the problem with unsigned drivers; they are unpredictable. Many corporations are introducing "signed drivers only" policies to reduce problems introduced by untested device drivers.

Figure 3.21 shows the options available for driver signing.

FIGURE 3.21
Driver signing options.

Dealing with Windows File Protection

In Windows NT and earlier, installing software might have involved overwriting some shared system files, dynamic-link libraries (.dll files) or executable files (.exe files). When this happened, the performance of the computer would become erratic and unpredictable.

The introduction of Windows File Protection (WFP) in Windows 2000 prevents the replacement of system files. WFP runs in the background and protects all files installed by the Windows Setup program.

Windows File Protection checks the file's digital signature to determine whether the new file has the correct version. If that check fails, the file is replaced by its backup (stored in the Dllcache folder) or from the Windows XP Professional CD. If Windows XP Professional can't locate the correct file, it will prompt you to mount the correct media. If you are not an administrator, you will not see any prompts as Windows File Protection runs under a SYSTEM account and will interact only with administrators.

File Signature Verification

You can view a list of unsigned files on your computer by running the utility program sigverif. The following process will run the File Signature Verification program.

NOTE

Administrative Privileges Are Required to Manage Driver Signing
You must be logged in with a user ID that has administrative privileges to modify the actions taken with unsigned drivers and make it the system default. The Driver Signing Options page has a check box that administrators can select to make the configured action the system default. When you log on, you can select a different setting for your own use.

STEP BY STEP

3.18 Running File Signature Verification

1. Click Start and select Run.

2. Enter **Sigverif** and click OK.

3. Click Start to create the list of unsigned files.

MULTIPLE-PROCESSOR MACHINES

Monitor and configure multiprocessor computers.

Windows XP Professional is designed to run uniformly on uniprocessors and symmetric multiprocessor platforms.

Windows XP Professional supports the addition of a second CPU. Support for multiprocessors has the following conditions:

◆ Both CPUs are identical and either have identical coprocessors or no coprocessors.

◆ Both CPUs can share memory and have uniform access to memory.

◆ Both CPUs can access memory, process interrupts, and access I/O devices.

Although the Windows XP Professional operating system has been designed for both uniprocessor and multiprocessor operations, if you originally installed Windows XP Professional on a computer with a single CPU, the Hardware Abstraction Layer (HAL) must be updated to use the additional CPU.

The following procedure will install support for multiple CPUs.

STEP BY STEP

3.19 Supporting Multiple CPUs

1. Click Start, and then click Control Panel.

2. Click Printers and Other Hardware and select the System link in the See Also pane.

3. Select the Hardware tab and click the Device Manager button.

4. Expand the Computer item. Make note of the current CPU support.

5. Double-click the computer type listed, and select the Drivers table.

6. Click the Update Driver button, and then click Next to close the Welcome screen of the Update Driver Wizard.

7. Select Display a List of Known Drivers for This Device and click Show All Hardware of This Device Class.

8. Click Next, and then click Finish.

Monitoring Multiple CPUs

Scaling is the process of adding processors to your system to achieve greater throughput. CPU-intensive applications such as database servers, Web servers, and file and print servers will benefit from multiple CPUs. Applications such as scientific, financial, or CAD systems may also demand the power of multiple CPUs.

You can monitor the activity of your multiprocessor system by using the Performance Monitor counters and charts. The following factors are important when looking at the performance of multiple CPUs:

◆ **Processor utilization and queue length**—Your workload may be structured such that one CPU is overloaded.

◆ **Processor data**—Context switches and interrupts, for example, can provide information on the workload your system is handling.

◆ **Resource utilization information**—Disk, memory, and network components, for example, may indicate that your system requires an increase in the capacity of these resources.

Impact on Resources

Increasing the performance power of your computer will place additional strain on system resources. For example, sharing resources will increase memory latency. A multiprocessor system needs to lock out shared data to ensure data integrity, and locked-shared data may result in contention for shared data structures. The synchronization mechanism used to lock shared structures increases the processor code path. As a rule of thumb, it is necessary to increase other resources when adding additional processor resources.

Memory

It is recommended that you scale the amount of memory with the number of CPUs. For example, if your uniprocessor system required 64MB of memory, a dual-processor system will require 128MB of memory.

Disk and Networking

When adding processors to your system, it is generally necessary to increase the disk capacity and network capacity. This can mean replacing your disks with disks of higher rotational speed or by striping or mirroring some data disks. Networking components can be upgraded to intelligent interrupt pooling adapters that reduce the processor workload. Table 3.11 contains the Performance Monitor objects that are most useful in monitoring a system with multiple CPUs.

TABLE 3.11

PERFORMANCE MONITOR COUNTERS FOR MULTIPLE-
CPU SYSTEMS

Counter	Description
Process: Thread Counter	Shows the instantaneous value, not the average. You need to monitor this counter at various times to get an accurate picture of activity.
Processor: % DPC Time	Determines how much time the processor is spending processing Deferred Procedure Calls (DPCs). DPCs originate when the processor performs tasks requiring immediate attention (such as answering an interrupt request), and then defers the remainder of the task to be handled at lower priority. DPCs represent further processing of client requests.
Processor: % Interrupt Time	Determines how much time the processor is spending processing interrupts.
	If processor time is more than 90 percent and this value is greater than 15 percent, the processor is probably overloaded with interrupts.
Processor: DPCs Queued/Sec	Monitors the rate at which DPCs are queued on a particular processor.
Processor: Interrupts/Sec	Reflects the rate at which the processor is handling interrupts.
System: Context Switches/Sec	Indicates that the kernel has switched the thread it is running on a processor. A context switch occurs each time a new thread runs or takes over from another. A large number of threads is likely to increase the number of context switches. Context switches allow multiple threads to share time slices on the processors, but they also interrupt the processor and might reduce overall system performance, especially on a multiprocessor. You should also observe the level of context switching over time.
System: System Calls/Sec	Monitors the frequency of calls to Windows XP Professional system service routines. These are the services exported to applications from the kernel.
Processor: % Processor Time	Monitors processor time usage for each processor on the system.

CASE STUDY: THE AMARANTH ENGINEERING COMPANY

ESSENCE OF THE CASE

The following points summarize the essence of the case study:

- The back-end database has all the important files on one disk.

- The disk failed with no recent backup.

- Recovery to the previous night required the next day's data to be reentered.

SCENARIO

Although you work at an engineering company, your responsibility is to oversee the computer systems that support the company's works. In this case, you are analyzing the recent events of the company's accounting system. The company uses a commercial accounting system that uses a single server for a back-end database. This was installed more than a year ago and has been working well. However, the database was installed with all the default settings and a single large database file holding indexes, and data was created. The transaction log files are also held on this main disk and full backups are done each night. The incident you are reviewing involves a disk failure on the database disk late one afternoon last week. The disk was replaced but the database needed to be recovered from the previous backup. No transaction logs are available to apply and the entire day's work needs to be reentered. Your task is to prevent this from happening again.

ANALYSIS

This situation is quite common. An application system (in this case, an accounting application) uses a back-end database to store data and produce invoices and reports. After all this is set up, there is a tendency to not revisit the initial configuration again until there is a problem.

Having the database tables and indexes on one disk is generally considered a potential disk performance bottleneck; however, the real problem comes when the previous night's backup is restored to disk. There are no transaction logs left to apply to the database in order to bring it

CASE STUDY: THE AMARANTH ENGINEERING COMPANY

up to the current time. With the database recovered to the previous night, all the day's transactions are lost.

The solution to this problem lies in using the disk-management features of Windows XP Professional to create a fault-tolerant disk structure on the Windows 2000 Server that houses the database and transaction logs. First, transaction logs should always be separated from the database tables because they are written sequentially and the database is accessed randomly. Because the transaction logs are usually only written and not read, they are best on mirrored volumes that are not striped. Striping divides the data across multiple spindles so that reading can proceed in a parallel fashion. If you are only writing to a file, this is not important.

The database tables, however, are read and written randomly. In an accounting application, it may

seem that you are entering a great deal of data, but almost every field must be validated against existing data (customer name, address, existing invoice number, and so on); therefore, the database is read from much more than it is written to. Because of this, the database tables should be configured as a RAID-5 structure to provide redundancy and better read performance. If the database is maintained on a Windows XP Professional computer then an external RAID-5 device can be used to house the database because Windows XP Professional will see it as a simple NTFS volume.

The combination of separating the transaction logs onto a mirrored set of disks, and the database files to a RAID-5 structure reduces your system's vulnerability to single-device failures in the future.

CHAPTER SUMMARY

KEY TERMS

- Plug and Play
- Dynamic disks
- Simple volumes
- Spanned
- Striped
- RAID-5
- Mirrored
- Media pools
- Libraries
- Advanced Power Management (APM)
- Advanced Configuration and Power Interface (ACPI)
- IrDA devices
- USB devices

This chapter focused on devices and drivers that you can add to your computer to customize it for your needs.

First, the Windows XP Professional implementation of Plug and Play was discussed along with resources available in Windows XP Professional and ways of assigning them to devices. The new dynamic disk structures available were discussed along with CD-ROM technology and removable storage.

Second, the new Windows XP Professional feature allowing multiple video displays was discussed, along with the procedures for configuring your virtual desktop.

Third, to support mobile computing and APM/ACPI, features of Windows XP Professional were discussed along with problems associated with these devices.

Fourth, the general I/O devices available for both the desktop and laptop computer were discussed. This included keyboards, the mouse, printers, scanners, handheld devices, and cameras.

Fifth, the procedures for automatically updating device drivers and setting driver-signing options were discussed.

Finally, the procedure for installing multiple CPUs into your computer and the performance characteristics you should measure when you do were covered.

Exercises

3.1 Upgrading a Basic Disk to Dynamic

This exercise will go through the steps necessary to convert a basic disk with enough free space to support the dynamic volume database, to a simple volume on a dynamic disk.

Estimated Time: 10 minutes

1. Open Disk Management by clicking Start, Control Panel and Performance and Maintenance.

2. Click Administrative Tools, double-click Computer Management, and double-click Disk Management.

3. Right-click the disk you want to convert to dynamic and select the Upgrade to Dynamic Disk menu option (see Figure 3.22).

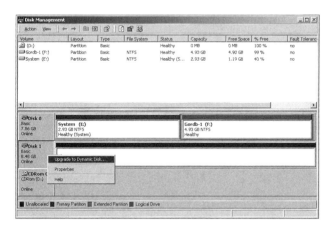

FIGURE 3.22
Selecting a basic disk for upgrade to dynamic.

4. Select the disk drive to upgrade and click OK.

5. Right-click the unallocated space on the new dynamic disk and select Create Volume.

6. Click Next to close the Welcome screen of the Create Volume Wizard.

7. Select the Simple Volume button and click Next.

8. Set the size of the volume to approximately one half of the available space on the dynamic disk and click next.

9. Select Don't Assign a Drive Letter or Drive Path and click Next.

10. Check off Perform a Quick Format (for brevity) and click Next.

11. Click Finish to start the volume creation process.

3.2 Extending a Volume

This exercise will extend the volume created in the previous exercise to use the remaining disk space on the dynamic disk.

Estimated Time: 10 minutes

1. Open Disk Management by clicking Start, Control Panel, and Performance and Maintenance.

2. Click Administrative Tools, Computer Management, and Disk Management.

3. Right-click the disk volume you want to expand and select Extend Volume.

4. Click Next to close the Welcome screen on the Extend Volume Wizard.

5. Select the amount of disk to use in extending the existing volume and click Next.

6. Click Finish to start the extension process.

APPLY YOUR KNOWLEDGE

3.3 Placing a Volume Under a Folder

This exercise will create an empty folder and then mount the volume created in the preceding exercises under that folder.

Estimated Time: 10 minutes

1. Open Windows Explorer and create an empty folder under the system drive (C:).

2. Open Disk Management by clicking Start, Control Panel, and Performance and Maintenance.

3. Click Administrative Tools, Computer Management, and Disk Management.

4. Right-click the volume to mount under the empty folder and select Change Drive Letter and Path.

5. Click the Add button and choose the Mount in the NTFS Folder button.

6. Enter the path of the empty folder created in step 1 (or use Browse to locate it) and click Next.

7. Return to the Windows Explorer screen to see the new folder is now associated with a disk icon.

3.4 Enabling Hibernation

This exercise will enable your system to go into hibernation depending on conditions within your computer. This lab assumes you are setting up hibernation on a portable computer.

Estimated Time: 5 minutes

1. Open Power Options in Control Panel by clicking Start, Control Panel, and Performance and Monitoring.

2. Click Power Options and select the Hibernate tab.

3. Select the Enable Hibernate Support check box.

4. Click Apply to set up Hibernation. (If Enable Hibernate is not available, your system does not support hibernation or there is not enough disk space available to support the process.)

5. Selecting the Power Schemes tab will allow you to set the time delays for blanking the monitor, spinning down hard drives, and putting the system on standby when under battery power.

6. Select the Advanced tab. Under the Power Button section select Hibernate from the drop-down list under When I Close the Lid of My Portable Computer.

7. Click OK to close the Power option menu.

8. Open Notepad and enter some text onto the page.

9. Close the lid of your laptop.

10. Wait for the computer to go into hibernation and power off. The more memory you have installed in your laptop, the longer this will take.

11. Open the lid of the portable computer and press the power button.

12. Wait for the system to restart. The desktop will resume in a locked state; you will have to unlock it by entering your user ID and password. Notepad should be opened on the desktop with the text you entered.

APPLY YOUR KNOWLEDGE

3.5 Installing a USB Device and Measuring Power Used

This exercise will go through the steps to install a bus-powered USB device and then cover how to measure the power consumed. This lab uses a Microsoft IntelliMouse Optical but any USB device that is recognized by Windows XP Professional will work.

Estimated Time: 10 minutes

1. Unplug any existing mouse currently connected to your Windows XP Professional computer.

2. Plug the Microsoft IntelliMouse Optical mouse into a USB port on your computer.

3. Wait until the Found New Hardware window closes (it should find a Microsoft IntelliMouse Optical and a USB Human Interface Device). The new optical mouse should now function.

4. Click Start, Control Panel and Performance and Maintenance.

5. Click Administrative Tools and double-click Computer Management, and then click Device Manager.

6. In the right window, expand the Universal Serial Bus Controllers item.

7. Right-click USB Root Hub and select Properties.

8. Select the Power tab and you should see a device on the hub identified as an HID-compliant mouse using a total of 100mA. This will vary depending on the type of USB device you have installed for this lab.

3.6 Transferring Files Using Wireless Connection

This exercise will walk through the steps necessary to set up a connection and transfer files between computers using a wireless (IrDA) connection. This lab will require you to have two devices (computers or a computer and a handheld device) with IrDA capabilities.

Estimated Time: 10 minutes

1. Click Start, Control panel, Printers and Other Hardware, and double-click Wireless Link.

2. Select the File Transfer tab and check the Display an Icon on the Taskbar Indicating Infrared Activity check box.

3. Click OK to close the Wireless Link window.

4. Reposition the two infrared transceiver windows until the Infrared icon appears on the taskbar.

5. Click the Infrared icon on the taskbar.

6. In the Wireless Link dialog box, select the files you want to send and click Send.

7. You can also send files using the IRFTP program started from Start/Run or any command prompt.

Review Questions

1. You change the resources your non-Plug and Play video adapter uses in Device Manager, but now the system will not boot correctly. What is wrong?

APPLY YOUR KNOWLEDGE

2. Your application currently uses logical drives on which to store some of its data. The application needs to reference these logical devices using drive letters. You have converted your system to use dynamic disks and would like to organize these files into subdirectories rather than on separate devices. Will your application be able to read its data? Why or why not?

3. What devices does RSM manage on a typical desktop computer?

4. You have a laptop that you have configured with multiple display adapters while it is in its docking bay. When you boot your laptop, the multiple displays do not work correctly. What is the reason?

5. You have a device that is not working perfectly. You install an updated driver from the manufacturer's site and find that the device doesn't work at all now. What do you do?

6. You install a new high-speed modem that the salesman said would run at 56Kb. When you dial up to your Internet service provider (ISP), you find you can't get as much speed as you expected. What is the reason?

7. You have just purchased a new desktop computer that has Windows XP Professional already installed on it. You want to ensure that the latest device drivers available are installed and the drivers are all signed. What is your most efficient course of action?

8. You are using Performance Monitoring to display how busy your computer is. You note that the CPU is at 100% utilization for extended periods of time. What other performance variable should you chart to help you decide whether adding another CPU would help the throughput of your system?

Exam Questions

1. You have a home computer that originally had Windows NT 4.0 installed. You configured the two disks you had installed on the system as a stripe set. Later, you upgraded your machine to Windows 2000 Professional. Now you want to upgrade the machine to Windows XP Professional. What do you have to do first?

   A. Upgrade the computer to Windows XP Professional and run `Diskpart` to convert the stripe to a striped volume.

   B. Upgrade the computer to Windows XP Professional and run `FTOnline` to mount the stripe set and copy the data to a backup device.

   C. Back up the information from the stripe set, delete the stripe sets, and re-create the disk as dynamic with a simple volume, and reload the data.

   D. Convert the disk to dynamic and continue with the upgrade.

2. You own a laptop that you use when you are on the road visiting customers. You would like to be able to put your machine into hibernation while your plane takes off and lands. You look at the power options but do not see a hibernation tab. You determine that your laptop is not ACPI compliant. You visit the manufacturer's Web site and download the latest BIOS which is ACPI compliant. After installing it, Windows XP Professional will not start. What do you do?

   A. Enable ACPI support in the BIOS.

   B. Boot the computer with the Last Known Good Configuration option.

C. Reinstall Windows XP Professional.

D. Reload Windows XP Professional from your last backup.

3. You are responsible for maintaining online copies of graphical images used by an application program. These images need to be available all the time; however, you have no idea how much storage space will be needed. How should you configure storage on your computer?

   A. Connect a tape drive to your computer and save the image files to tape when your disk fills.

   B. Add additional disks to your computer when storage space runs low and use Disk Management to create a spanned volume.

   C. Compress the images and place them in Zip files.

   D. Create a RAID-5 disk structure on a Windows 2000 Server and store the images there.

4. You are the applications expert at an engineering firm.

   You are attempting to install multiple display adapters to your Windows XP Professional workstation to enhance your CAD application.

   You are at the point in the process when you are about to extend the virtual desktop to the new display, but Windows XP Professional has grayed out the check box, indicating that it cannot use the device.

What should be your first debugging step?

   A. Run the application Full Screen.

   B. Confirm that the video adapter is supported as a secondary display.

   C. Confirm that the secondary display is detected.

   D. Run the application on the Primary screen.

5. You have an application that performs an analysis of statistical data captured by your engineering firm. To do this analysis, your application reads and writes large amounts of temporary files to disk. You want to provide the best throughput possible for this temporary information, but you do not need to provide any fault tolerance. What should you do?

   A. Create a spanned volume across two or more disks.

   B. Create a striped volume across two or more disks.

   C. Create a RAID-5 structure on a Windows 2000 Server and store the temporary files there.

   D. Create a single large volume named \TEMP and direct your application to store its temporary files there.

6. You routinely visit your company's branch offices where you use your laptop for doing presentations and making reports. Occasionally, when you are using your laptop intermittently, you find that your battery has gone dead. You have configured your machine to turn off your disk and monitor after 20 minutes but this is apparently not enough. What other configuration changes should you make?

APPLY YOUR KNOWLEDGE

A. Increase the timeout period for the disk and monitor.

B. Configure the computer to hibernate when you press the Sleep button.

C. Have an alarm sound when the battery gets critically low.

D. Configure the machine to go into standby mode when inactive for 30 minutes.

7. You are visiting one of your company's remote customer offices and need to transfer some files from your laptop to a local machine. For security reasons, you do not want to join your customer's domain, but you still need to transfer the files. What should you do?

A. Create a null modem cable and transfer the files via FTP.

B. Create a crossover network cable and copy the files via command line or Windows Explorer drag and drop.

C. Align the machines' IrDA ports and copy the files using the wireless link.

D. Connect to your ISP host and copy the files to the customer's Web site using FTP.

8. You administer your company's Active Directory. The desktops that your users have range from NT 4.0, Windows 2000 Professional, and a few that are Windows XP Professional. You have installed a new shared printer in your company's domain. The printer is attached to a Windows XP Professional workstation on your network.

The users with NT 4.0 workstations report that every time they try to print to the new shared printer, they are asked for a manufacturer's disk. You try to use the shared printer from your

Windows XP Professional workstation and find no problem.

Which of the following actions should you take to correct this problem with the minimum of effort?

A. Correct the share permissions for this printer on each workstation.

B. Install the NT 4.0 print driver on each NT 4.0 computer in your network.

C. Assign separate permissions for this printer to the NT 4.0 computers.

D. Install the NT 4.0 print driver for this printer onto the Windows XP Professional print server.

9. As the system administrator, you set the policy on the configuration of new computer hardware purchased for the company. You decide that, for flexibility, you will have all the disk storage devices for new Windows XP Professional computers configured as simple volumes. When you configure this on a new laptop, you find that the option to do the conversion from basic to dynamic disks is not present. What is your course of action?

A. Make sure you purchase disk drives that support being dynamic disks.

B. Amend your policy to allow laptops to remain configured with basic disks.

C. Manually fix the DMA, I/O, and IRQ resources used by the disk drive rather than letting Plug and Play choose them.

D. The disk drives cannot be made dynamic until a small partition is created at the end of the device.

APPLY YOUR KNOWLEDGE

10. You are setting up a computer system to be used in displaying CAD output in a lecture theater. You have already set up the nine display devices and are now ready to install the computer system to drive them. What is your course of action?

    A. Install Windows XP Professional and then install the display adapters.

    B. Install the display adapters and then install Windows XP Professional.

    C. Disable the built-in AGP-compliant video adapter.

    D. Turn off the built-in video adapter after the system is set up.

11. You are working on the helpdesk when a user calls in complaining about the RAS line dropping. The user is working from home and dialing into the corporate network using the built-in 56Kb modem on his laptop. The user can get connected and logged in but after that it's only a matter of time until the line drops and the connection is lost. What should you do to resolve this user's problem?

    A. Set the dial-in connection speed of your company's RRAS (Routing and RAS Server) to something lower than 56Kb.

    B. Have the user reduce the modem speed on his computer to something lower than 56Kb.

    C. Have the user reduce the connection speed between his laptop and the modem to 57,600 baud.

    D. Have the user configure Personal Firewall on the dial-up connection he is using to connect to the corporate network.

12. You have a Windows XP Professional laptop for which you have purchased a new network card. When you take your laptop home or when you are traveling, you would like to have the card turned off to preserve battery life.

    What action should you take?

    A. Configure the system to power down the network card in Power Options.

    B. Remove the card when you are traveling.

    C. Disable the driver when you are out of the office.

    D. Create a new profile and disable the device in the new profile.

13. You are in charge of the desktop deployments at a large telco. The company policy is to evergreen the user's desktop every three years. That means that you can expect a steady stream of new systems to be coming to you to be configured. You already have a standard image to apply to new machines, but you would also like to convert the disks to Dynamic before sending them to users' offices. You would like to have an automatic way to do this during the imaging or Sysprep phase of the installation.

    What action should you take?

    A. You create a script that runs `FSUTIL` with the `/Dynamic` switch and run it after Sysprep.

    B. You create a script with `Diskpart` to convert the disks after Sysprep.

APPLY YOUR KNOWLEDGE

C. You create a script that calls Convert with a [Dynamic] modifier after the drive letter and run this script after Sysprep.

D. You include a script that will reformat the new drive. All new drives in Windows XP Professional are Dynamic disks with simple volumes.

14. You have installed a new device driver for your video card and the instructions say to now reboot your machine. When you do, the system shows a blue screen after the text-only (non-GUI) part of the startup. You reboot your machine but it does the same thing. What action should you take to get your machine to boot up correctly?

A. Insert your latest Automatic System Recovery disk and reboot your machine.

B. Press F8 during the startup and select the boot option "Last Known Good Configuration."

C. Reinstall the device driver from within Device Manager.

D. Boot up with the recovery console and disable the device driver.

15. You are helping to troubleshoot a system for an end user at your company. The mouse has stopped working but the user has been working on a lengthy document that must be saved before the machine can be rebooted to restart the mouse driver. Unfortunately, the application is not in focus and therefore you cannot use the Alt+keys to access its menus. What key sequence can you use to focus this application?

A. Alt+Esc to go through each application.

B. Alt+Tab to go to the application specifically.

C. Ctrl+Esc to bring up the Start Menu and select the application.

D. Alt+Space to display the system menu allowing you to shut down the application.

E. F6 to cycle through the screen elements on the open Desktop.

Answers to Review Questions

1. Non–Plug and Play devices may appear in Device Manager's list but their requirements as far as the Device Manager is concerned are unknown. By manually configuring the resources used, you have told Windows XP Professional which resources to reserve for your device. You now need to reconfigure the device by using the manufacturer-supplied configuration program or by manually selecting onboard switches or jumpers. See "Implementing, Managing, and Troubleshooting Hardware Devices and Drivers."

2. Dynamic disks can be accessed using an assigned drive letter as well as using a path. If, however, you are going to reorganize your files into subdirectories, your only access is via the path. Your application that expects to use drive letters will not be able to access its data. See "Fixed Disks."

3. Removable Storage Manager (RSM) manages all devices that can be removed or replaced with other media. This includes tape drives, CD-ROM and DVD-ROM drives, and Jaz and Zip drives. RSM can handle any removable device except A: and B:. See "Removable Media."

APPLY YOUR KNOWLEDGE

4. One of the rules for using multiple displays on your Windows XP Professional computer is that the primary display cannot be turned off. When you insert a laptop into its docking station, the display is usually disabled. This prevents the multiple-display system from functioning. See "Troubleshooting Multiple Displays."

5. There is an option in Device Manager that will allow you to roll back the driver to an earlier version. Although the earlier version did not work perfectly, it at least ran better than on the new driver. You can find this option by expanding the device in question and examining the driver tab under its properties. See "Updating Drivers."

6. Modems get their speed from various compression techniques. The faster the modem, the more elaborate the compression techniques. Unfortunately, these methods are not always compatible and, when connecting to an ISP, your system has negotiated a lower speed to where both devices agree on the compression methods being used. See "Modems."

7. The most efficient way to ensure that you have the latest device drivers installed on your system and that these drivers have been signed is to use the Windows Update option directly from the Start menu. This will canvass the Microsoft Web site for the latest signed version of drivers for your system and allow you to download them for installation. See "Maintaining Updated Drivers."

8. The other variable to chart would be the Processor Queue Length. A busy processor may be handling the workload very efficiently, or it could be overwhelmed by the workload. In that case, the backlog of work waiting to be done by the CPU would be building. This situation is identified by the processor queue length, or the number of tasks that are ready to execute if there are enough CPU resources available. See "Monitoring Multiple CPUs."

Answers to Exam Questions

1. **D**. A stripe set was available in NT 4.0 on basic disks, and maintained for backward compatibility in Windows 2000. Because you upgraded your machine from NT 4 to Windows 2000, you were able to continue to use the stripe set. In Windows XP Professional, stripe sets on basic disks are not supported. You must upgrade the disks to dynamic disks, which will make the stripe set a striped volume before you can continue with the operating system upgrade.

   You cannot run Diskpart because the upgrade to Windows XP Professional will not continue with the stripe set configured. FTOnline was created to allow temporary access to legacy disk volumes; however, you will not be able to run FTOnline until the operating system upgrade completes. You can certainly back up your data, delete and re-create the disk volume, and then restore your data but a procedure this complicated is not necessary. See "Disk Management."

2. **C**. ACPI is the new standard that combines power management with Plug and Play technology. If the BIOS is ACPI compliant, Windows XP Professional automatically adds support for it by installing the appropriate HAL (Hardware Abstraction Layer) during the installation. If you upgrade your computer to be ACPI compliant, you're going to need a new HAL. That can be done only by reinstalling Windows XP Professional.

APPLY YOUR KNOWLEDGE

Typically, there is not way to enable ACPI in an ACPI-compatible BIOS. Rebooting your system using the last-known-good configuration will not touch the BIOS changes you have made. It is specifically designed to recover from the installation of a bad device driver when you can't log onto the system. Reloading the operating system (OS) from your last backup would not fix the incompatibility between the HAL and your new BIOS (if you could actually log onto the system). See "Installing Hardware."

3. **B**. The solution calls for online storage but there is no performance requirement mentioned. The application that uses the image files will not be able to find them if the images are rolled out to tape. Although this solution provides for all the images to be available, manual intervention would be required to load needed images back to disk. Likewise, most applications would not be able to extract a file from a Zip library and creating a RAID-5 structure provides more fault tolerance and input/output (I/O) performance than is requested. The most efficient solution would be to create a dynamic disk with a simple volume and span that volume to additional disk devices when space runs low. This allows the images to appear to be available from one location even though that may span several disks. See "Spanned Volumes."

4. **B**. The first thing to check is whether the device to which you are trying to extend is actually supported as a secondary display. You can assume that if the display adapter is listed in Device Manager, it has been detected successfully. Running the application in full-screen mode or on the primary display are steps that you would take if you were having problems running the

application on multiple screens. In this case, you have not gone that far in the process yet. See "Multiple Display Support."

5. **B**. The problem requires better throughput on disk for data that is not going to be stored. There is no requirement for a fault-redundant RAID-5 configuration. Likewise, providing a single large volume or a spanned volume would not give the same performance as a striped volume. A striped volume will write 64KB blocks to each disk in rotation. This will have the effect of spreading the I/O load across all drives evenly. See "Striped Volumes."

6. **D**. If your laptop runs out of power while you are away from it, change the power options configuration to have the machine go into standby mode after 30 minutes of inactivity. Standby is a low–power usage state that will preserve your data until you return. It is more effective than just turning off the monitor and disk drive.

   Increasing the timeout times for the disk and monitor will only use your battery faster. Configuring the system to hibernate when you press the Sleep button will not help you save your battery when you are not around. Likewise, sounding a low-battery alarm is helpful only when someone is there to hear it. See "Power Management."

7. **C**. The easiest solution uses the built-in capabilities of Windows XP Professional. The built-in IrDA ports can transfer data at a rate up to 4Mb per second. This would be far faster and easier than using the COM port or built-in modem. See "Infrared Network Connections."

8. **D.** When you configure a Windows XP Professional system as a print server, you will normally get only the Windows XP–compatible print drives installed. The simplest approach here is to install Windows NT 4.0 print drivers on the Windows XP print server as well. When those running NT 4.0 systems then attempt to use the printer, they will not be asked for the manufacturer's disk or CD to install the drivers locally.

You could install the NT 4.0 drivers on each NT 4.0 machine but that is not the most efficient way to handle this situation. Changing the permissions to the printer or creating a special group will not help the fact that you are missing the correct print drivers. See "Printers."

9. **B.** Windows XP does not support dynamic disks on laptops, so your policy must be changed to reflect that. Neither Plug and Play nor the type of disk defines whether it can be dynamic. The "dynamic" part of dynamic disks refers to the storage structures created on the device, not the device itself. Finally, the Disk Management application will automatically reserve space at the end of the disk for its database when converting a basic disk to dynamic. See "Upgrading Basic Disks to Dynamic Disks."

10. **A.** Windows XP Professional must be completely installed before adding any more devices for a virtual desktop. There would be no reason to disable a built-in adapter that is AGP compliant because that is one of the accepted standards for multiple displays on Windows XP Professional. After the virtual desktop has been established, you cannot turn off the first adapter because it forms the anchor point for the displays. See "Multiple Display Support."

11. **B.** The speed of your system's modem can be thought of as the maximum possible connect speed negotiated by the two modems (yours and the remote system's). The actual throughput will vary because of a number of factors, including the condition of the phone lines and static. If the user can connect and log in, there is nothing wrong with the connection. If the connection drops, the line cannot maintain the speed and you should instruct the user to reduce the speed of his modem.

Setting the speed of the RRAS server would not impact the speed of incoming dial-in connections. Changing the transfer speed between the laptop and the modem would not impact the outgoing speed of the modem's connection. The personal firewall is there only to protect your system from outside intrusion and does not impact the speed of the connection. See "Troubleshooting Modem Installations."

12. **D.** Hardware profiles contain unique configuration information. You can create different hardware profiles to match the different configurations you need. In this case, you do not want to have the card using power if you don't need it. The best approach is to create a new hardware profile by copying your existing one and disabling the card in the new profile. If you delete the card, Windows XP Professional will just reinstall it.

There is no option under ACPI to manage devices such as PCMCIA cards. You could remove the card, but then it can be either damaged or lost. Disabling the card each time you are out of the office is a more complicated procedure than necessary. See "Creating a New Hardware Profile" (Chapter 4).

APPLY YOUR KNOWLEDGE

13. **B.** Diskpart is a command-line utility that allows administrators to perform many disk-management tasks. You can create a script that uses Diskpart to convert the basic disks in a new system to dynamic. That script can be run automatically during the post-Sysprep stage of an image installation (the GUIRUNONCE section of Sysprep.inf).

    The FSUtil utility will mount, dismount or extend file systems and not convert basic disks to dynamic. In addition, there is no /Dynamic switch on FSUtil. Convert is used to convert FAT or FAT32 to NTFS but not to convert basic disks to dynamic. In addition, there is no [Dynamic] modifier in Convert. Format will still create only a basic disk. See "Disk Management."

14. **B.** This is a situation in which you have changed a driver on your system and you cannot complete the boot process. The driver is not yet considered to be permanent until the boot process completes. Until that time, you can revert to the previous driver by selecting the boot option Last Known Good Configuration. That will cause Windows XP Professional to load the previous version of the video driver during the boot process.

    The ASR disk is used to rebuild a damaged Windows XP Professional system and is not a bootable device. You can't get the system to boot so you will not be able to access Device Manager. You could boot up with the recovery console if you have installed it and if you know all the device driver files to delete (by hand) and where to get the correct ones. This is too complicated a procedure for this situation. See "Advanced Boot Options" (Chapter 4).

15. **A, B.** Alt+Esc will cycle through the applications that are open, bringing each one into focus. Alt+Tab will display a dialog box with a list of icons representing each open application. Using the arrow keys, you can select the application you need to access. By pressing Enter, you will jump to the selected application. See "Shortcut Key Combinations."

Suggested Readings and Resources

1. *Microsoft Windows XP Inside Out* (Microsoft Press)

2. *Microsoft Windows 2000 Performance Tuning Technical Reference* (Microsoft Press)

3. *Microsoft SQL Server 2000 Performance Tuning Technical Reference* (Microsoft Press)

This chapter helps you prepare for the MCSE Windows XP Professional exam by covering the following objectives:

Monitor, optimize, and troubleshoot performance of the Windows XP Professional desktop.

- **Optimize and troubleshoot memory performance.**

- **Optimize and troubleshoot processor utilization.**

- **Optimize and troubleshoot disk performance.**

- **Optimize and troubleshoot application performance.**

- **Configure, manage, and troubleshoot Schedule Tasks.**

▶ The performance monitoring subsystem in Windows XP provides a comprehensive array of indicators from within various areas of the operating system. Monitoring disk performance, memory usage, application-assigned resources, and network activity can give you the information you need to enhance the performance of your system. The Task Scheduler can be used to periodically run maintenance tasks to help improve your system's stability.

Manage, monitor, and optimize system performance for mobile users.

▶ The proliferation of laptops brings with it some special considerations when it comes to getting the most out of your mobile system. You can configure and invoke various hardware configurations to help optimize your system.

CHAPTER 4

Monitoring and Optimizing System Performance and Reliability

Restore and back up the operating system, system state data, and user data.

- **Recover system state data and user data by using Windows Backup.**

- **Troubleshoot system restoration by using safe mode.**

- **Recover systems state data and user data by using the Recovery Console.**

▶ The ultimate goal of backing up your system and data files is the recovery of all your data in the event of a hardware or software failure. Your system may contain either company-specific information and/or personal information. In either case, the data might not be reproducible without a good backup/restore procedure. Being able to recover your system, regardless of the type and extent of the failure, will significantly improve the reliability of your computer.

▶ You can expect a number of questions related to maintaining or increasing the performance of the disk and memory subsystems of your Windows XP Professional computer. Many of these will be in scenario format, in which the causes of a performance problem will be related to more than one factor. The author's suggestion is to first understand the important counters maintained within the Performance Monitoring system and be able to relate changes in those counters to events happening in the computer. After you have a solid understanding of the theory presented here, you should work with your Windows XP Professional system to see firsthand the impact of varying the availability of resources on system response. Look to the resource kits to provide tools to strain the resources of your computer at various points (high memory consumption, memory leaks, high CPU usage, and excessive network activity) that will allow you to gain some practical experience with reading performance data.

▶ You also should expect scenario questions on both recovering a system using some options from the safe boot menu (Recovery Console and using the last known good configuration) and saving and restoring data using backup. In the latter, you can expect questions where the backup method is not wisely chosen and can be optimized to better suit the users' needs. Understanding the options available and the impact that one style of backup over another would have on the availability of your computer system in the event of a failure will allow you to address this type of exam question well.

▶ In short, by focusing on the preceding two major areas, you will be well prepared for this portion of the exam.

INTRODUCTION

This chapter is mainly concerned with the performance and reliability of your computer. The techniques available in Windows XP range from digital signing of device drivers and operating system files to running a command-based Recovery Console in the event the system will not even boot.

To make the most of the hardware you have available, you need to take steps to optimize its use and to prevent the operating system from being modified without your consent. Finally, you must be able to recover the system in the case of a catastrophic failure.

OPTIMIZING AND TROUBLESHOOTING PERFORMANCE OF THE WINDOWS XP PROFESSIONAL DESKTOP

Monitor, optimize, and troubleshoot performance of the Windows XP Professional desktop.

In general, performance monitoring addresses how the operating system and any applications or services use the resources of the system, including disks, memory, processors, and network components. The statistics measured are usually throughput, queues, and response times that represent resource usage.

Windows XP Professional defines performance data in terms of objects, counters, and instances. An object is any resource, application, or service that you can measure.

Table 4.1 is a partial list of the objects on which Performance Monitor can display statistics.

TABLE 4.1

SOME OBJECTS ON WHICH PERFORMANCE MONITOR CAN DISPLAY STATISTICS

Object	Description
Cache	Reports activity for the file system cache
IP	Reports activity on the Internet Protocol (IP) traffic
Network Interface	Reports rates at which bytes and packets are sent or received over a network connection
Paging File	Reports activity to the paging file used to back up virtual memory allocations
Physical Disk	Reports activity to the disks
Process	Reports resources used by individual processes
Processor	Reports on how resources are being divided up for each processor
System	Reports statistics for systemwide counters that reflect file operations and processor usage
Memory	Reports statistics for memory requests and usage as well as paging file activity

In addition to the previously listed objects, there are usually more objects added with some applications. For example, adding SQL Server to your system will include 17 additional objects ranging from internal cache usage to locks and latches statistics. Other software developers will also add performance objects and counters to allow you to track the software performance over time (for example, virus-checking programs).

Each object has counters that are used to measure various aspects of performance such as transfer rates for disks, packet transmit rates for networks, or memory and processor time consumed by applications or services.

Each object will have at least one counter, although most have many different counters available. Each counter reflects data captured systemwide (as in the Memory counter) or it can display information collected for different instances. An instance can vary widely from counter to counter. For example, the Physical Disk counter collects statistics for different disks, Network Interface collects statistics for different network adapters, and SQLServer Databases collects statistics on different databases accessed on your system.

The tool used to display performance statistics is the Performance Monitor. The Performance Monitor provides a graphical interface to the counters maintained by the operating system in the Registry or using Windows Management Interface (WMI) and provides ways to capture or log the output or to display it graphically on the screen.

To view the Performance Monitor system, click Start, Control Panel and select the Performance and Maintenance item. Click Administrative Tools, and then double-click the Performance applet. Maximize the display and click the plus sign on the chart menu bar. The Add Counters display has a window called Performance Object. This drop-down list will show all the areas in the operating system about which performance counters are kept.

Optimizing and Troubleshooting Memory Performance

Memory availability is one of the most important factors in managing the performance of your Windows XP Professional computer. Knowing the amount of memory you have configured and understanding how Windows XP will use that memory is one of the first steps to take in understanding your system's performance.

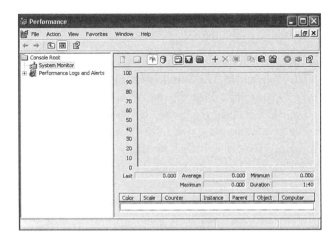

FIGURE 4.1
The main screen of the Performance Monitor system.

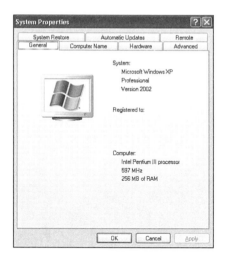

FIGURE 4.2
Determining physical memory.

Determining the Physical Memory Available

You can identify the amount of physical memory configured by running the System applet from the Control Panel and selecting the General tab. The physical memory available is under the Computer section of the display. Figure 4.2 shows the General display of the System applet.

The Windows XP Professional operating system distinguishes memory usage depending on whether it is part of the paged pool or the nonpaged pool. The paged pool contains memory that can be paged to disk; memory in the nonpaged pool cannot. The size of each pool is based on the amount of physical memory available.

The paging file (also called the *swap file* by old Unix types) is a file on the hard disk that serves as a temporary virtual memory space. By utilizing the paging file, Windows XP Professional can allocate virtual memory space that exceeds the amount of physical memory available. Two important measurements of the paging file are the amount of space allocated to a process and the amount of available space that is not in use by any processes. The memory that is allocated to open processes is called the *working set.*

File System Cache

A portion of memory in your Windows XP Professional system is reserved as a file system cache. This is memory that contains recently used information for quick access. The size of the file system cache depends on the amount of physical memory installed and the amount of memory required for applications.

Memory that is not used for the working sets of processes is available for the file system cache. The Windows XP Professional operating system will dynamically adjust the size of cache as needed. It is more appropriate, when monitoring cache, to measure its effectiveness (hit ratio) rather than its absolute size. When data is found in the cache, the performance system registers a hit. If the cache size is too small and data is not found, the performance system registers a miss. This could also indicate that your applications are reading a large number of different files. If you understand the type of work your system is doing, you can use this counter to indicate a low physical memory situation.

You can determine the amount of cache being used by starting the Task Manager and selecting the Performance tab. The value for System Cache reflects only the currently mapped pages but does not reflect any cache pages currently swapped to the paging file. Figure 4.3 shows the System Cache information available from the Task Manager. Don't forget you can start the Task Manager by pressing Ctrl+Alt+Del and selecting Task Manager from the available options. An alternative way to start the Task Manager is to move your mouse to a blank area on the taskbar, right-click the mouse to display the menu, and select Task Manager.

The Paging File

During setup, Windows XP creates one paging file (Pagefile.sys) on the partition containing the operating system installed. The default size is 1.5 times the amount of physical memory. If the paging file is too small, you will exhaust the amount of virtual memory available for applications. If the amount of physical memory is too low, it will generate excessive activity on the paging file disk, slowing response time for the system.

Setting the paging file's initial size and maximum size to the same value increases efficiency because the operating system does not need to expand the file during processing. Setting different values for initial and maximum size can contribute to disk fragmentation. Care must be taken not to consume all the free space on the system disk. The Windows XP Professional operating system requires a minimum of 5MB free space to operate.

Expanding the initial size of the paging file can increase performance if applications are consuming virtual memory and the full capacity of the existing file is being used.

Creating a large paging file on a disk that is very active or has limited space will impact system performance. Changing the file size gradually will allow you to optimize the size of the paging file without consuming too much free space.

If disk space is limited or the system disk is very active, you can improve the performance of your system by moving the paging file to another physical disk. Moving the paging file to a different volume on the same disk will not provide any benefit.

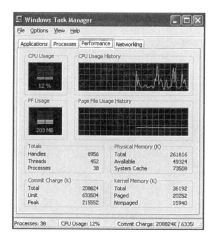

FIGURE 4.3
Determining system cache size.

> **NOTE**
>
> **Sizing the Paging File**   You can use two counters from the Memory object in the Performance Monitor application to determine the best size of the paging file.
>
> To determine how large your paging file should be based on your system workload, monitor the Process (_Total)/Page File Bytes counter. This indicates, in bytes, how much of the paging file is being used.
>
> You also can determine the appropriate size of a paging file by multiplying the Paging File/% Usage Peak counter value by the size of Pagefile.sys. The % Usage Peak counter indicates how much of the paging file is being used.

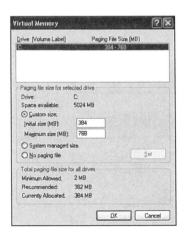

FIGURE 4.4
Virtual Memory properties.

NOTE

Ram Versus Paging File   If your computer is short on memory, a better solution would be to add physical RAM rather than just provide more virtual memory. Performing input/output (I/O) operations to a disk is a thousand times slower than memory operations. In addition, the extra memory required to manage the increased virtual memory will actually make your memory problem worse.

Figure 4.4 shows the current and maximum size of the paging file on the Virtual Memory screen that is used to make changes in the Paging file configuration. The Navigation route to this page is described in the following Step by Step 4.1.

The system requires a 2MB file on the system disk to write events to the system log, automatically restart the system after a system failure, or to send an administrative alert.

If you want to be able to write debugging information to a file, the system requires a file that is equal to the size of RAM plus 12MB on the system root directory. If performance is more critical than recoverability, you can put the paging file on a physical disk separate from the operating system.

Although Windows XP limits the size of each paging file to 4GB, you can supply more virtual memory to applications by spreading paging files across multiple disks. Creating multiple paging files on a single physical disk will provide more space but not improve performance. The following procedure can be used to change the amount and location of the paging files:

STEP BY STEP

4.1 Changing or Adding a Paging File

1. Click Start, right-click My Computer, and then select Properties.

2. Select the Advanced tab and click the Settings button in the Performance window.

3. Select the Advanced tab on the Performance Options page and click the Change button in the Virtual Memory section.

4. This will display the Performance Options page. Clicking the Change button will display the Virtual Memory page.

5. This screen displays the minimum, maximum, and recommended amount of virtual memory to configure, plus it shows you where your paging files are currently.

There are two other controls on the advanced Performance Options page in the preceding Step by Step 4.1.

The first option impacts processor scheduling. Selecting the Programs option will result in faster response time for foreground tasks. If you are running a background task (such as Backup) and you want it to run faster, you should select the Background Services option.

The second option impacts memory usage. If you use your computer primarily as a workstation, you can have more memory dedicated to running your programs by selecting the Programs option. Your programs will run faster and your system cache size will be the default. If your computer is used primarily as a file server, you can specify that more memory be dedicated to a large system cache by selecting the System Cache option. You also can select this if your programs require a large file system cache.

Memory Shortages

Your Windows XP Professional computer can develop memory shortages if processes demand much more memory than what is available or the applications you are running leak memory. To identify a memory shortage situation, you can watch the counters displayed in Table 4.2.

TABLE 4.2

IMPORTANT MEMORY COUNTERS

Counter	Description
Available Bytes	The amount of physical memory available to processes. Indicates the amount of physical memory that remains after the working sets of running processes and the cache have been served.
Cache Bytes	The number of bytes currently being used for the file system cache.
Commit Limit	The amount of virtual memory that can be committed without expanding the paging file.
Committed Bytes	The amount of committed virtual memory.

continues

TABLE 4.2   *continued*

IMPORTANT MEMORY COUNTERS

Counter	Description
Page Faults/Sec	The overall rate of page faults per second including hard page faults (the page is on disk) and soft page faults (the page is elsewhere in memory).
Pages/Sec	The number of pages read from or written to disk to resolve hard page faults.
Pool Nonpaged Bytes	The amount of space in the nonpaged pool of memory. These pages must remain in physical memory.
Pool Paged Bytes	The amount of space in the paged memory pool. These pages can be written to disk when they are not being used.

Available Bytes in the Memory object indicates the amount of physical memory remaining after all the processes and cache requirements are met.

Working Set in the Process Area indicates the amount of memory used by one or more processes when there is abundant memory. When memory is in short supply, the working sets of some processes are reduced to allow other processes to expand. This results in an increase in page faults.

Pages per Second in the Memory Object indicates the number of pages that were not immediately available in memory and had to be read in from disk, or were in memory and had to be written to disk to make way for other information. This value will be high if there are too many hard page faults.

Disk Activity to the Paging File

Memory shortages can lead to paging activity that results in a disk bottleneck. If hard page faults are occurring, it is important to understand how the disk is performing during this paging.

Acceptable rates for the Memory counter Pages per second range from 40 per second on older computers to 150 per second for the newest disk systems. When looking at paging activity, it is appropriate to have the scan rate as low as once every second because paging will appear as a burst of activity. A scan rate that is too long will show only the average usage and not activity spikes. The scan rate of the Performance Monitor can be adjusted by opening the properties page. The properties page can be opened by clicking the icon that looks like a hand pointing to a page from the selection just above the chart (it's next to the red stop symbol), or you can just press Ctrl+Q. On the properties page, select the General tab and change the value in the Sample Automatically Every: box to the number of seconds between samples.

The Memory object Pages Input per Second and Pages Output per Second indicate the rate at which pages were read from disk or written to disk to provide room in physical memory for other pages. A high value here can indicate low physical memory. Figure 4.5 shows the effect of low physical memory on the paging rate.

The other Memory object, Pages Output per Second, indicates the rate at which pages were written back to the disk. This activity does not generate hard page faults but can indicate a memory shortage and does result in additional disk activity. Pages are written back to disk when the Virtual Memory Manager needs to reduce pages from a working set of a process and it finds that some data pages contain changes. The changed data must be written back to the paging file rather than just being discarded, and this generates disk activity.

To understand what impact paging is having on your system, you must first ascertain whether paging is dominating your disks' workload.

NOTE

Some Paging Is Normal Page faults and page reads happen any time you require something in RAM. Even if you have a lot of available RAM, if you launch Word you will get page faults. The system looks for Word in RAM, but it is not there (because it is not running) and that will trigger a series of page faults as Word is loaded into RAM. Only excessive paging is cause for concern.

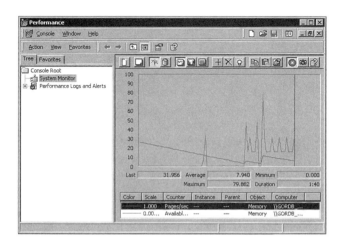

FIGURE 4.5
The effect of low memory on paging rate.

The Memory counter Page Reads per Second indicates the number of read operations required to retrieve pages referenced by page faults. If you compare this number to the number of pages faulted, you will be able to determine how many pages are retrieved per read. A high ratio means a large number of faulted pages are not found in physical memory and must be retrieved from disk. This will create a disk bottleneck. Figure 4.6 shows the effects of a high paging rate on disk activity.

Although the effect of this paging rate is on disk activity, it also might indicate that the physical memory available is not large enough to hold the working set for the active applications. Adding more physical memory can alleviate this constraint.

To determine what portion of your disk's work this paging activity occupies, you can compare the page reads versus disk reads. These are found in the Memory counter Page Reads per Second and the PhysicalDisk counter Disk Reads per Second. If there is a correlation between these two counters, it is likely that paging activity makes up most of your disk activity and you could have a disk bottleneck and memory constraint.

Another way of looking at this is to compare the PhysicalDisk counter Average Disk Read Bytes per Second to the Memory counter Page Reads per Second. The Disk Read Bytes per Second indicates the rate at which the disk is transferring data during reads (don't forget to convert bytes to pages by dividing by 4,096).

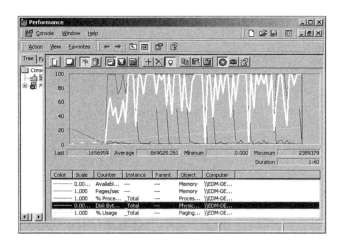

FIGURE 4.6
Disk I/O caused by paging.

If the result is about equal to the Memory counter Page Reads per Second, the majority of the disk activity is caused by paging and any memory shortage that results in a high paging rate will result in a disk bottleneck. The exact extent of a disk bottleneck will depend on the disk and the number of I/O transactions per second it will be able to sustain.

Monitoring the Cache

The Windows XP file system cache is an area of memory into which the I/O system keeps a copy of recently used data from disk. If a process needs to read from or write to disk and the I/O Manager has the data still in cache, the data can be copied much quicker than if it must be retrieved from disk.

The file system cache can't be a bottleneck because it is just a part of physical memory. However, if there is not enough memory to make an effective cache area, the result is increased disk activity and perhaps a disk bottleneck. Table 4.3 shows important file cache counters.

NOTE

Don't Get Bogged Down   The problem with performance monitoring is the huge number of counters to look at and the fact that important ones are not grouped together. If you reduce your problem to a simple statement—high disk activity, low available memory, and high page faults—you can see that the problem is not a disk bottleneck—it's a memory bottleneck. The performance counter will support this assumption if it is true.

TABLE 4.3

IMPORTANT FILE CACHE COUNTERS

Counter	Description
Copy Read Hits %	A value over 80% indicates that the cache is very efficient.
Copy Reads/Sec	The rate at which the file system attempts to find data in cache.
Data Flush Pages/Sec	The rate at which cached pages are changed and written back to disk.
Data Flush Pages/Sec	The rate at which applications are changing cached pages and the pages are written back to disk.
Data Flushes/Sec	The rate at which cache data is written to disk.
Data Maps/Sec	The rate at which file data pages are copied into cache.
Fast Reads/Sec	The rate at which the data is found in cache rather than on disk.
Lazy Write Flushes/Sec	The rate at which applications change data, causing the cache to write back to disk.

continues

TABLE 4.3	*continued*

IMPORTANT FILE CACHE COUNTERS

Counter	*Description*
Lazy Write Pages/Sec	The rate at which pages are changed by applications and written back to disk.
Read Aheads/Sec	The rate at which the Cache Manager detects a file being read sequentially.
Cache Bytes (Memory object)	This counter indicates the growth or shrinking of the cache.
Cache Faults/Sec (Memory object)	The rate at which cache pages were sought but not found and had to be retrieved from disk.

Resolving Memory Bottlenecks

Adding memory to a computer is an easy solution but not always cost effective. Prior to purchasing more memory, you can try some of the following:

◆ Correct any applications that might have memory leaks.

◆ Check for available space on the disk with the paging file(s). Low disk space can manifest itself as memory problems.

◆ Avoid using some display and sound features. Features that consume memory are animated cursors, desktop icons, large bitmap wallpaper, and some screensaver programs.

◆ Remove unused protocols and drivers. Idle protocols still use space from both paged and nonpaged memory.

◆ Remove unneeded background services (the icons in your system tray). Investigate moving services to other computers.

◆ As a last resort, increase the size of the paging file. Generally, the bigger file you can make, the better performance will be. You also can make multiple files on different disks to increase performance. Striped volumes can also be used to spread the work of accessing the paging file over many disks. This solution will actually reduce the amount of available RAM (it takes memory to manage the paging file) but it will allow programs to run (although slowly) in a memory-strapped system.

Optimizing and Troubleshooting Processor Performance

After memory consumption, processor activity is the most important thing to monitor in your system. A busy processor might be efficiently handling all the work on your computer, or it might be overwhelmed. The following factors provide an indication as to the workload on your Windows XP Professional computer:

◆ The processor queue length and processor utilization together indicate the overall processor usage.

◆ Interrupt activity and context switches are activities that can significantly add to the processor workload.

◆ Individual processes can monopolize the available CPU resources.

◆ Threads within the active processes can sometimes have their priorities changed to improve performance. This cannot be done from the operating system but can be done by making system calls within the program. This option is best used with applications developed by your own company.

Processor Counters

The System, Processor, Process, and Thread objects contain counters that provide useful information about the work of your processor. Examine the thread counters shown in Table 4.4 for details about computer processes.

TABLE 4.4

IMPORTANT COUNTERS FOR PROCESSOR ACTIVITY

Counter	*Description*
System: Context Switches/Sec	The average rate per second at which context switches among threads on the computer. High activity rates can indicate inefficient hardware or poorly designed applications.
Processor: Interrupts/Sec	The average rate per second at which the processor handles interrupts.

continues

TABLE 4.4	*continued*

IMPORTANT COUNTERS FOR PROCESSOR ACTIVITY

Counter	*Description*
System: Processor Queue Length	The number of threads that are in the processor queue.
Processor: % Processor Time	The percentage of time the processor was busy during the sampling interval.
Process: % Privileged Time	The percentage of time a process was running in privileged mode. Privileged or kernel mode is the processing mode that allows code to have direct access to all hardware and memory in the system.
Process: % Processor Time	The percentage of time the processor was busy servicing a specific process.
Process: % User Time	The percentage of time a process was running in user mode.
Thread: Context Switches/Sec	The average rate per second at which the processor switches context among threads. A high rate can indicate that many threads are contending for processor time.
Thread: % Privileged Time	The percentage of time a thread was running in privileged mode.
Thread: % User Time	The percentage of time a thread was running in user mode. User mode is the processing mode in which applications run.

Because System Monitor samples processor time, the values for processor time counters reported by the Processor, Process, and Thread objects might underestimate or overestimate activity on your system that occurs before or after collection of the sample.

Processor Bottlenecks

A processor bottleneck will occur when the processor is so busy that it cannot respond to an application that is requesting time. High activity can indicate that a processor is either handling the work adequately or is a bottleneck and slowing down the system. Looking for a sustained processor queue is a better indicator of a bottlenecked processor. The following counters can help in identifying processor bottlenecks:

◆ The % Processor Time counter in the Processor object, with its value often exceeding 80%

◆ The Processor Queue Length in the System object, with its value often greater than 2, in a single-CPU system

◆ Unusually high values for context switches/sec or interrupt switches/sec

Processor Time Counter

The Processor object counter % Processor Time determines the percentage of time the processor is busy. It does this by measuring the amount of time the Idle process is running and subtracting that from 100 percent.

What would appear as high values (70% or greater) on this counter might not in fact indicate a problem. High processor time situations will always occur when a process is starting up, although this is not usually a concern. Values that exceed 70% for extended periods of time, however, might indicate a problem and additional counters can be monitored to provide more information.

If the Processor Time counter is consistently high, you need to determine whether a processor queue is causing a bottleneck and preventing important work from being done.

Processor Queue Length

A collection of threads that are ready to run, but which are not able to because of an active thread currently using the processor, is a *processor queue*. A sustained queue of more than two threads is a sign of a processor bottleneck. Although queues are most often seen when the processor is very busy, they can develop with any utilization rate.

If the Processor Queue Length counter shows that many threads are ready to use the processor, you can identify which threads are using processor time by displaying the processes that appear in the Instance windows on the % Processor Time counter in the Process object.

Figure 4.7 shows the effects of a busy processor on the Processor Queue Length counter.

> **NOTE**
>
> **Normal Workloads** Some normal activities within Windows XP Professional will generate interrupts. For example, the processor's timer ticks occur every 15 milliseconds (or about 66 ticks per second), at which point the processor hardware timer is updated. Interrupt rates are also affected by hardware—faster hardware can handle more interrupts per second.

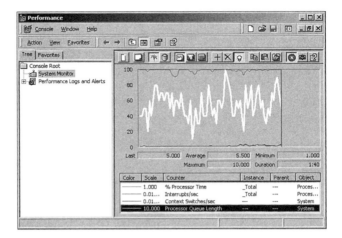

FIGURE 4.7
Processor queue length on a busy system.

Interrupts

The Interrupts/Sec counter in the Processor object reports the number of interrupts the processor is servicing from applications or hardware devices. The value of this counter could be 100 per second, or more (depending on the capacity of your computer), for computers running Windows XP Professional.

If you are connected to a network, you might want to upgrade your Windows XP Professional computer to include a driver that supports Interrupt moderation or avoidance. Interrupt moderation allows for several interrupts to be grouped into one hardware interrupt. This provides for greater efficiency in servicing the interrupt. Interrupt avoidance allows the processor to continue processing interrupts without new ones being queued until pending interrupts are complete. High values for % Processor Time for threads of the system process can also indicate a problem with a device driver.

Context Switches

When the kernel switches the processor from running one thread to another (for example, a thread with a higher priority), a context switch occurs. The Context Switches/Sec counter can indicate that a thread is monopolizing the processor. If the rate of context switches is low, the processor is spending all its time with one process. If the rate of context switches is high, the processor is being shared among many processes all at the same priority. A rate of 150 context switches per second is moderate but a rate of 500 or more context switches per second is high and might indicate a problem.

Context switches can be displayed using the Context Switches/Sec counter in the System object.

Processes Causing a Bottleneck

If you have decided that your processor is overloaded and that it is the cause of your computer's performance problem, the next step is to investigate whether there is a single process that is monopolizing your CPU, or whether it is being consumed by running many processes. You can display the percentage of the processor time that each process is consuming by using the following procedure.

STEP BY STEP

4.2 Process Usage of the CPU

1. Start the Performance Monitor program.

2. Click the plus sign to add some counters.

3. Select the Process object.

4. Select the % Processor Time counter.

5. Select each process instance. You can do this quickly by selecting the first counter (after the _Total instance) and then selecting the last counter while holding down the Shift key.

6. Click Add and then Close to display the counters.

NOTE

Avoiding Processor Bottlenecks Some device drivers' problems can cause high % Processor Time values for the System process. Additionally, if you are using a screensaver, particularly one that uses OpenGL, you will find that it can consume large amounts of processor time. If possible, change to a screensaver that uses less processor time.

If a single process is monopolizing the processor, the chart for that process will be higher than all the rest. If the cause of your processor performance problems is a specific application, your options include moving it to a different computer (perhaps running it on a larger server with a more powerful processor) or running it at times when you are not trying to use the Windows XP Professional computer at the same time.

Eliminating a Processor Bottleneck

If you determine that you do have a processor bottleneck, some of the following steps might shorten the processor queue and reduce the burden on your processor:

◆ Delete memory bottlenecks that might be consuming the processor. Memory bottlenecks are far more common than processor bottlenecks and severely degrade processor performance.

◆ Upgrade your network or disk adapters to intelligent, network adapters. Intelligent adapters provide better overall system performance because they allow interrupts to be processed on the adapter itself and provide additional accelerations such as Fast Forwarding Path Support.

◆ Try to obtain adapters that have optimization features such as interrupt moderation, and features for networking such as card-based TCP/IP checksum support.

◆ Upgrade to a faster processor. A faster processor improves response time and throughput for any type of workload.

◆ Add another processor. If the process you are running has multiple, active threads that are processor intensive, it is a prime candidate for a multiprocessor computer.

◆ Move some processes running on your computer to another machine. For example, if your application requires SQLServer, you can usually move the database to another, more powerful server with a simple application configuration change.

Examining and Tuning Disk Performance

The disk system handles the storage of programs and data as well as the movement of these between disk and memory. Because disk transfers run many hundreds of times slower than memory transfers, the overall influence of disk problems on your system will be great.

Disk Monitoring Concepts

There are many factors that you need to consider in determining whether the disk system is impacting the performance of your Windows XP Professional computer. The level of utilization, the rate of throughput, and the development of a queue are all important factors. Other types of activity may arise from disk operations, such as interrupts and paging activity.

Many of these factors are interrelated. For example, if disk utilization is high, an I/O queue may form. If, at this time, memory utilization also peaks and paging increases, the overall performance of the computer will suffer.

Enabling Disk Counters

Windows XP Professional includes counters that monitor the activity of physical disks. The PhysicalDisk object provides counters that report both physical disk activity and logical disk activity mapped to the physical disk drivers; the LogicalDisk object provides counters that report statistics for logical disks and storage volumes. Both objects measure disk throughput, queue length usage, and other data but from different points of view.

The usefulness of the LogicalDisk object and diskperf is in remote monitoring of older servers. In that case, you still might have to enable the LogicalDisk counters on the remote machine using the following command:

```
diskperf –yv
```

After the next reboot of the remote computer, the LogicalDisk object counters will be available to your Performance Monitor.

Diskperf has several command-line switches that are used to modify the availability of performance-monitoring counters on Windows 2000 systems:

◆ -y will enable both physical and logical disk performance counters.

◆ -yd will enable physical disk performance counters.

◆ -yv will enable logical disk performance counters.

◆ -n will disable all disk performance counters.

NOTE

Changes to LogicalDisk Counters

In Windows XP, the LogicalDisk object counters have been combined with the PhysicalDisk object counters. The system now maps physical drives to logical drives using the same instance name. If you have, for example, a dynamic volume that spans several physical disks, the counter instances in the PhysicalDisk object might appear as "Disk 0 C:", "Disk 1 C:", "Disk 2 D:". In this example, C: is made up of two physical disk drives. In the reverse case where you have two logical partitions on a single physical disk, the PhysicalDisk object might appear as "Disk 0 C: D:".

Both sets of counters are available in Windows XP by default. This also means that the diskperf command is no longer needed for your local machine but is still used for those times you are managing the performance counter of Windows 2000 or Windows NT servers remotely.

The LogicalDisk counters are still used for those times you want to look at logical disks separately from the physical mapping or you are looking at % Free Space and Free Megabytes. These counters are not available in the PhysicalDisk object.

◆ `-nd` will disable physical disk performance counters.

◆ `-nv` will disable logical disk performance counters.

Windows NT supports only the `-y` and `-n` switches to enable or disable all disk counters.

Any change in the availability of performance-monitoring counters set by `diskperf` will be made when the system is restarted.

When you are looking at logical volumes, remember that they might share a physical disk and the performance might represent contention between the logical volumes trying to share a single resource. Similarly, spanned, striped, or mirrored volumes supported by disk controllers that provide a hardware-enabled support for these types of volumes might represent several physical disks within a single logical disk. If you have a RAID array that is supported by software, the counters will report data for each physical disk separately. Table 4.5 lists important physical disk performance counters.

TABLE 4.5

IMPORTANT PHYSICAL DISK PERFORMANCE COUNTERS

Counter	Description
Avg. Disk Bytes/ Transfer	This counter measures the size of I/O operations. If disk accesses are efficient, larger amounts of data will be transferred.
Avg. Disk/Sec Transfer	This counter measures the average time for each transfer regardless of the size. A high rate for this counter might mean the system is retrying requests because of disk queuing.
Avg. Disk Queue Length	The total number of requests waiting as well as the requests in service. If more than two requests are continually waiting, the disk might be a bottleneck.
Current Disk Queue Length	This counter reports the number of I/O requests waiting as well as those being serviced. This is an instantaneous snapshot of the disk queue rather than an average.
Disk Bytes/Sec	The rate at which data is being transferred to the disk. This is the primary measure of disk throughput.

Counter	*Description*
Disk Transfers/Sec	The number of reads and writes completed per second, regardless of the amount of data involved. This is the primary measure of disk utilization.
Split IO/Sec	The rate at which the operating system divides I/O requests into multiple requests. This might indicate a fragmented disk.
% Disk Time	The percentage of time the selected disk drive is busy reading or writing. This counter can span more than one sample period and therefore overstate the disk utilization. Compare this against % Idle Time for a more accurate picture.
% Disk Write Time	The percentage of time the selected drive was busy servicing write requests.
% Disk Read Time	The percentage of time the selected drive was busy servicing read requests.
% Idle Time	The percentage of time the disk subsystem was not processing requests and no I/O requests were queued.

> **NOTE**
>
> **Watch for Exaggerated Rates**   The % Disk Read Time and % Disk Write Time counters can exaggerate disk time. They report busy time based on the duration of the I/O request, which includes time spent on activities not actually reading or writing to the disk. All the busy times are summed and divided by the duration of the sample interval. If multiple requests are in process, this can result in a number greater than 100%.
>
> If your Windows XP Professional computer has more than one disk installed, the _Total instance for % Disk Time, for example, reports the value totaled for all disks but does not divide by the number of disks sampled. Therefore, a system with one idle disk and one busy disk appears to have all disks busy.

Monitoring Disk Space

It is important to monitor the amount of available storage space on your disks because a shortage of disk space can adversely affect the paging file and as the disk space diminishes, disk fragmentation usually increases.

The % Free Space and Free Megabytes counters in the LogicalDisk object allow you to monitor the amount of available disk space. If the amount of available space is becoming low, you might want to move some files to other disks if available, compress the disk, and remove temporary files to free up some disk space.

Disk fragmentation can slow the transfer rate and increase the seek time of your disk system. On a single disk system, the Split IO/Sec counter in the Physical Disk object will indicate the degree of fragmentation. If this counter increases, run the Disk Defragmenter to help keep disk storage organized for the best performance.

> **NOTE**
>
> **Free Space on DFS Volumes**   Free space on a Distributed File System (DFS) share will change as you move from one directory to another. Do not assume that the amount of free space you see at the root of the DFS share is the actual space available throughout the entire tree. DFS volumes may be partially or completely replicated from one site to another and span many computers. A number that represents the total free space would not be very meaningful.

Investigating Disk Performance Problems

Several factors must exist simultaneously for your Windows XP Professional computer to have a disk bottleneck. These factors include a high and sustained rate of disk activity, disk queues longer than two for extended periods of time, and an absence of significant amounts of paging. Without these conditions, it is unlikely that you have a disk bottleneck. Figure 4.8 shows the effects of a high I/O load on Disk Queue Length.

If these conditions do exist and you think there is a disk bottleneck, the following counters will be useful during analysis of the problem:

◆ Paging counters (found in the Memory object): Pages/Sec, Page Reads/Sec, Page Writes/Sec

◆ Usage counters: % Disk Time, % Disk Read Time, % Disk Write Time, % Idle Time, Disk Reads/Sec, Disk Writes/Sec, Disk Transfers/Sec

◆ Queue-length counters: Avg. Disk Queue Length, Avg. Disk Read Queue Length, Avg. Disk Write Queue Length, Current Disk Queue Length

◆ Throughput counters: Disk Bytes/Sec, Disk Read Bytes/Sec, Disk Write Bytes/Sec

NOTE

Processors Can Be Impacted by Disk Hardware   The rate of interrupts generated by your disk hardware can have a performance impact. If a significant number of interrupts is generated, the result will be a slowed processor. Although this is not strictly a disk bottleneck, it is a processor bottleneck caused by the disk system.

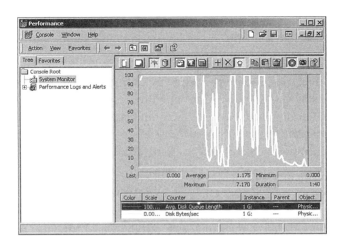

FIGURE 4.8
Disk queue length on an I/O-bottlenecked system.

Paging

The symptoms of a memory shortage are similar to a disk bottleneck. When physical memory is scarce, the system starts writing to the paging file and reading smaller blocks more frequently. The less physical memory available, the more disk space used and the greater the load on the disk system.

It is important, therefore, to monitor memory counters along with disk counters when you suspect a performance problem with your disk system.

Usage

A high-performance disk is capable of at least 50 random I/O operations per second. Some newer disks with faster rotation speeds can handle 100 or more I/O operations per second. The actual capacity of the disk is decided by factors other than the actual disk components, including bus speed and I/O request size.

Sustained values at 70% to 85% of the maximum capacity of the disk are a definite cause for concern. If a queue is developing at lower usage rates, it may indicate that the disk might be unable to handle the load.

Queue Length

To determine whether there is a queue developing for service on your disk system, examine the value of the Avg. Disk Queue Length. If it exceeds twice the number of physical disks configured in your system, you probably have a disk bottleneck.

Resolving Disk Bottlenecks

A disk bottleneck can cause the entire system to slow. If you have determined that disk availability or capacity is responsible for your performance problem, you should consider taking one or more of the following actions:

◆ Add another disk if you can move some files to it, if you can create a stripe set, or if you are out of space. For disk space problems only, you can consider compressing the disk if your processor has enough power to handle the compression activity.

NOTE

When to Defragment Your Disk   If you see high physical disk I/O and disk queuing whenever your applications are accessing a disk, it might be time to defragment your disk. This is an often-overlooked performance improvement technique. Disk files will get fragmented over time as they are updated. If there is no room, Windows XP will move part of the file elsewhere on the disk. The file is still logically in order, but physically spread out. Accessing the various pieces takes time and can slow down your system.

◆ Add memory if the disk activity you have measured is related to the paging file.

◆ Defragment the disk.

◆ Use stripe sets to spread the I/O requests across several disks simultaneously. If your applications are read intensive and require fault tolerance, consider a hardware-level RAID-5 volume. Use mirrored volumes for fault tolerance and good overall I/O performance. If you can live without fault tolerance, a stripe set will provide fast reading and writing and, usually, higher storage capacity.

◆ If there is no throughput improvement seen with additional disk capacity or the addition of a stripe set, the bottleneck could be caused by contention between disks for the disk adapter. You should consider adding an adapter to distribute the load.

◆ Distribute the workload across multiple drives. For example, a database application may have the transaction logs on separate disks from the data. Writing to a transaction log is sequential and performs better on a physical disk than the random operations against the data, which perform better on striped volumes.

◆ Limit the use of file compression or encryption. These features add overhead to disk I/O and should be used only if performance is not critical.

◆ When purchasing disk systems, use the most intelligent and efficient components available. Upgrading to faster controllers with wider bandwidth access will generally improve throughput.

Optimizing and Troubleshooting Application Performance

Applications are not developed in a vacuum. They are driven by a business case and have requirements they must meet to be considered successful. One requirement is achieving the necessary performance. Other equally or even more important factors include ease of development and maintenance, time to develop, availability of good programming tools, and developer expertise. Very few applications require high performance as a top priority. One example would be real-time data collection or a transaction system with a potentially unlimited load (such as the stock market).

For everyone else, it becomes important to define what the required performance level is and to determine a way to measure it.

Application performance can be described from three points of view:

◆ **The real performance**—This is how fast the application actually performs its work.

◆ **The perceived performance**—This is how fast the application looks and feels to the user. This is often related to real performance. However, if there is a long initial startup sequence or heavy network traffic at some point in the processing, the user might consider the application to be slow despite its actual level of performance.

◆ **The consistency of the application's response**—This aspect of performance can be characterized in terms of the stability, scalability, and availability of the application. As the workload increases, the application will scale gracefully and still continue to perform well.

The application that satisfies all three views will always be considered successful.

If you are the application developer, there are usually tools available within the development environment to aid in understanding the performance of your application as it scales up. For example, if you are developing within Visual Studio, you can use the Application Performance Explorer to create runtime scenarios to stress the application infrastructure. APE is configurable to show the performance implications of client loads, network bandwidth, machine boundaries, transfer methods, and other factors that impact performance in the real world.

After the application has been deployed, an important step is to define a baseline of expected performance. This involves stressing the application to real load and measuring how it responds and what resources it consumes. You first have to realize that in any system there will always be bottlenecks. There is no point in looking for them before you have a performance problem to solve.

If the performance "out of the box" is not acceptable or if over time the performance of the application, as compared to the baseline performance, degrades, the performance-monitoring tools can be used to pinpoint the bottleneck.

CPU Scheduling Priorities

All applications are started with Normal scheduling priority. Processes can be scheduled at one of six scheduling levels. These are Realtime, High, Above Normal, Normal, Below Normal, and Low. If you have an application that is monopolizing the CPU and causing other applications to run slower, you can lower its chances of getting CPU time by starting it with a /Belownormal or /Low switch. The command would look like the following:

```
Start /Belownormal application
```

This would lower all the threads with the application relative to others concurrently running on your computer and speed up the other tasks on your system.

Memory Bottlenecks

Application consumption of memory can create a bottleneck on your Windows XP Professional computer when it is added to an existing workload. For example, if an application accesses a database and opens a large client-side cursor with the intent to speed later processing, it will do so by consuming memory (and network bandwidth). If physical memory is scarce, this may cause an increase in paging and appear outwardly to be a disk-system bottleneck.

Because of that, it is important to view several performance counters in comparison to one another.

The Process object in Performance Monitor supplies statistics about active processes. Important Application counters are listed in Table 4.6.

TABLE 4.6

IMPORTANT APPLICATION COUNTERS

Resource	Counter
Memory	Pool Paged Bytes, Pool Nonpaged Bytes, Working Set, Working Set Peak
Processor	% Privilege Time, % User Time, % Processor Time
I/O	Read Bytes/Sec, Read Operations/Sec, Write Bytes/Sec, Write Operation/Sec

In conjunction with the Process counters, the Network Interface counters for Bytes Read, Bytes Sent, Output Queue Length, and the System counter Process Queue Length are useful in assessing impact on other parts of your Windows XP Professional computer.

Application Disk Space

Even if you are not currently short on disk space, you need to be aware of the storage requirements for applications you are running. To evaluate whether the existing capacity of your computer's disk system is enough for your application requirements, estimate the expected disk usage as indicated in the following steps:

1. For best results, start with 1GB even though the minimum disk size required by the operating system might be lower.

2. Add the total size of all applications.

3. Add the size of the paging file (this depends on the amount of memory; this size should be at least twice that of system memory).

4. Add the amount of disk space budgeted per user (if a multi-user system).

5. Multiply by the number of users.

6. Multiply by 110% to allow room for expansion (this percentage can vary based on your expected growth).

The result is the size of disk you need.

Disk Usage by Applications

How an application uses the disk will often have a major impact on the performance seen by the end user.

Applications can access data sequentially or randomly. Sequential access is faster than random access because of the way in which disk hardware works. The seek operation that must occur when the disk head is repositioned takes more time than any other part of the I/O operation. Because random I/O involves several seeks, the overall throughput of data to and from the disk will be lower. The same is true for random writes. If you find that disk activity is predominantly random, you might consider positioning the application's disk files on a stripe set. This allows the I/O access to be spread over many spindles providing some parallel access.

For any type of input/output, the best solution involves using drives with the fastest rotational speeds and the fastest seek times for random I/O.

If your application has a high I/O rate, a stripe set will improve performance because the increased number of disk spindles provide for concurrent access. Hardware-enabled RAID sets provide better performance than stripe sets enabled by software.

For workloads of either random or sequential I/O, use drives with faster rotational speeds. For workloads that are predominantly random I/O, you should use a drive with a faster seek time.

Working with 16-Bit Applications

Windows XP Professional still maintains the capability to run 16-bit Windows applications. However, they run separately from the 32-bit applications in a separate virtual DOS machine (NTVDM). All the 16-bit applications are run within this one process and therefore share memory and are scheduled as a unit. Windows XP Professional uses preemptive multitasking in its scheduling and the CPU can take control from a process. Within the NTVDM, the processes must surrender control before another can be scheduled. The XP scheduler does not schedule within the NTVDM; however, the NTVDM is scheduled preemptively with other 32-bit applications. If you have several 16-bit applications and they are running slowly, they might be creating scheduling conflicts within the NTVDM. If you assign each 16-bit application its own memory space, each

NOTE

Fragmentation Can Impact Performance   Even if an application reads and writes data sequentially, if the file is fragmented the I/O will not be sequential. If the disk transfer rate deteriorates over time in comparison to the baseline performance, you should run Disk Defragmenter.

application will have its own NTVDM. This way, all your 16-bit applications can be scheduled in the same manner as your 32-bit applications.

Working with the Task Scheduler

Earlier versions of Windows provided the AT command to schedule programs or scripts to run at specific times. Windows 2000 introduced (and Windows XP still includes) a graphical utility called the Task Scheduler that enhances this scheduling capability.

The Task Scheduler is not the same as the AT command. However, they share many common characteristics. When a task is scheduled by AT, an entry for it appears in the Task Scheduler task window.

With the Task Scheduler, you can specify the user account to run a task (even if scheduled with the AT command). Whenever you use Task Scheduler to modify an AT task, you can no longer use AT to modify any characteristics of the job.

Creating a Scheduled Task

When you open the Scheduled Tasks folder from the Control Panel and double-click the Add Scheduled Task, you start a wizard that will create the job file that represents the task to run (see Figure 4.9). The file contains user ID and password information to allow the job to be copied from one machine to another.

The wizard allows you to customize the information shown in Table 4.7.

EXAM TIP	
	16-Bit Memory Space Microsoft loves to ask questions about compatibility and is sure to include problems to which moving your 16-bit applications into their own memory space will be the answer.

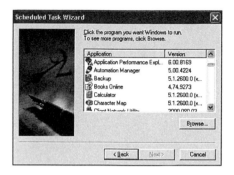

FIGURE 4.9
Selecting programs to run with the Scheduled Task Wizard.

TABLE 4.7

SCHEDULED TASK WIZARD OPTIONS

Option	Description
Program to Run	The application to schedule. This can be an entry from the supplied list or a batch file or other program selected using the Browse command.
Task Name	A local name for the scheduled task.

continues

| TABLE 4.7 | *continued* |

SCHEDULED TASK WIZARD OPTIONS

Option	Description
Frequency	How often the task will be executed. You can select daily, weekly, monthly, once only, when the computer starts, or when you log in.
Time and Date	The start time and date the task file executes on. Depending on the frequency, you also can specify the month and/or the day of the week to run the job.
User Name and Password	You can specify the user ID that is used to execute this job. If your user ID does not have the security rights required by the scheduled task, you can specify a different user ID.
Advanced Properties	This check box will cause the properties page for the scheduled task to display after the Finish button is clicked. Advanced properties include editing the command line to run, the starting directory, and the user ID and password to execute the task with. You also can modify the jobs schedule and some system environmental factors such as not running the job if the computer is on battery power.

STEP BY STEP

4.3 Creating a Scheduled Task

1. Click Start, and then click All Programs.

2. Select Accessories, System Tools and double-click Scheduled Tasks.

3. Double-click the Add Scheduled Task icon.

4. Click Next to continue the Add Scheduled Task Wizard.

5. Click Browse to start a task not on the default list.

6. Enter the string `c:\Windows\system32\notepad.exe` in the File windows and click Open.

7. Provide a name for the scheduled task, select the Daily option, and click Next.

8. Choose a time and date for the job to run and click Next.

9. Enter the password to your account in both the Password and Confirm windows and click Next.

10. Click Finish to complete the task creation.

There will now be a file in the Windows\Tasks folder that represents the task you just created. Right-clicking the task icon and selecting the Properties menu item will display the parameters used to run this job. Figure 4.10 shows the properties sheet.

FIGURE 4.10
Properties of a sample job in Scheduled Tasks.

Managing and Optimizing Performance for Mobile Computers

Manage, monitor, and optimize system performance for mobile users.

Laptops pose special problems when you are trying to optimize their performance or manage them remotely. The fact that mobile computers are not always connected to a network means there must be a variety of configurations used to define devices that might or might not be available when the system is started. If the network is not available, additional services must be configured to provide access to information when the system is offline and a means to merge changed data back when the system is online again. The small footprint size of laptops also dictates a constraint on resources. Power conservation is of primary importance to laptop users.

Managing Hardware Profiles

Hardware profiles tell your Windows XP Professional computer which devices to start and what setting to use for each device.

When you first install Windows XP Professional, a hardware profile called *Profile 1* (or for laptops, *Docked Profile* or *Undocked Profile*) is created. By default, this profile contains every device that is installed on your computer at the time you install Windows XP Professional.

Hardware profiles are useful if you have a portable computer and use it in a variety of locations. Most people who have laptops use them in locations other than where the docking station is (at home or in the office). Because of that, network adapters, CD-ROM devices, and perhaps floppy disk drives that are part of the docking station are usually not available when you are staying in a hotel, for example. You might want to use a modem and a portable printer when you are away that you would not use when in the office. Hardware profiles allow you to maintain different configurations of available peripherals.

Creating a New Hardware Profile

You create hardware profiles from the System applet in the Performance and Maintenance screen in the Control Panel. If there is more than one hardware profile, you can designate one as the default that will be loaded when you start your Windows XP Professional computer (assuming you don't make a choice manually). After you create a hardware profile, you can use Device Manager to enable or disable devices in the profile. When you disable a device while a hardware profile is selected, that device will no longer be available and will not be loaded the next time you start your computer. Figure 4.11 shows the making of a new hardware profile by copying the original.

FIGURE 4.11
Making a new hardware profile from the original.

STEP BY STEP

4.4 Creating a Hardware Profile

1. Click Start, and then click Control Panel.

2. Click Performance and Maintenance, and then click System.

3. Select the Hardware tab and click Hardware Profiles.

4. Under Available Hardware Profiles, click Profile 1 (or Docked Profile if it is the default).

5. Click Copy and then OK.

After a profile has been created, reboot your computer and select it during the boot process. After the computer boot has completed and you have logged in as an administrator, you can modify the devices available when using this profile.

> **N O T E**   **Administrator Rights**   You must be logged on as the administrator to copy or create hardware profiles.

STEP BY STEP

4.5 Changing Devices in a Profile

1. Click Start, and then click Control Panel.

2. Click Performance and Maintenance, and then click System.

3. Select the Hardware tab and click Device Manager.

4. To disable a specific device driver, expand the section that pertains to that device. For example, to disable a network card, expand Network Adapters.

5. Highlight the driver to disable and right-click. Select the Disable menu item and close the window.

When you next reboot the system and select the hardware profile you have modified, the driver you disabled will not be loaded.

Using the Briefcase to Synchronize Files

A Briefcase is a mechanism of sharing files between two computers that are directly connected (for example, via a direct cable). The Briefcase functions just like its namesake; when you leave one computer, you put files onto your laptop for editing or other work, and replace them when you return. You can also create a Briefcase on a floppy or removable disk drive (for example, a Zip drive).

A Briefcase will automatically update the file on your main computer to the modified version. You don't have to move the modified version from the Briefcase or delete the existing copies on your main system.

A Briefcase also allows you to view the status of the files you have offline. They can either be linked to an original file or be orphaned. You can organize your offline files by having multiple Briefcases, or have multiple folders in a single Briefcase.

Windows XP Professional has more than one method of managing offline files. Offline Files are discussed in detail in Chapter 2. You can choose between using a Briefcase and Offline folders by considering the following:

◆ A Briefcase is the best tool if you frequently transfer files between your laptop and your server computers using a direct connection or between your computer and a removable storage device. Using Briefcase, you can synchronize the files you modified on another computer with their counterparts on your main computer. You can keep your files organized by creating multiple Briefcases.

◆ Offline Files is the best tool if you work with shared files on a network. With Offline Files, you can make changes to the shared files while disconnected from your LAN and have them automatically synchronize when you next log in.

Of course, you can copy network share files and folders to a Briefcase and return them when you are online again. However, Offline Files was designed with that situation in mind.

Creating a Briefcase

You can create a Briefcase in any folder by opening the folder in Windows Explorer and right-clicking anywhere in the folder. Then select New and select Briefcase.

Likewise, you can create a Briefcase on your desktop by right-clicking your mouse anywhere on the desktop screen. By selecting New and Briefcase, a Briefcase icon will be added.

The two methods, however, place the Briefcase in different places. If you create a Briefcase on your desktop, Windows Explorer shows that particular Briefcase at the bottom of its folder list (usually after My Network Places) and there is an icon on your desktop. If you create a Briefcase within a folder, there is no desktop icon created and the Briefcase stays in the folder where it was created.

Adding Files to Your Briefcase

To add files to your Briefcase, use Windows Explorer to drag files with which you would like to work offline to your Briefcase. Select the Make Sync Copy option in the dialog box that is displayed. Windows XP Professional will then copy the selected file to your Briefcase and create a synchronization link back to the original.

STEP BY STEP

4.6 Creating a Briefcase for Offline Files

1. Display the Windows XP desktop and right-click anywhere on the desktop to display the menu. Select New and click Briefcase to create a Briefcase Icon.

2. Use Windows Explorer to display a file on a network share.

3. Left-click the file and drag it to the Briefcase.

4. Select the Make Sync Copy option.

5. Double-click the Briefcase icon to display the contents of the Briefcase. The status should be Up-to-Date.

Synchronizing

When you reconnect with your main computer, network share, or removable storage device, the changes that you have made to the file in the Briefcase can be synchronized back to their originals.

The philosophy behind synchronization is to make the two files the same. If no changes were made to either file, they are still synchronized. If the Briefcase file was updated, the original file is replaced with the Briefcase version. If the original was updated, the Briefcase version is refreshed. If both files were updated, you will have to decide which file to keep. If one file was deleted, Briefcase will suggest that the other should be deleted as well.

Figure 4.12 shows files in the Briefcase have been modified and the originals need updating.

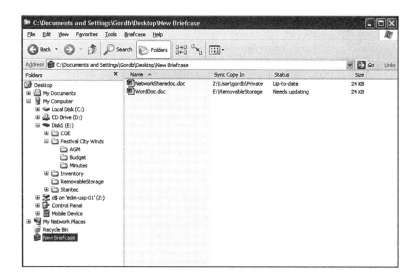

FIGURE 4.12
Briefcase files that need updating.

The following process can be used to synchronize the updated files back to their original copies.

STEP BY STEP

4.7 Synchronizing Files from a Briefcase

1. Open Windows Explorer and right-click the Briefcase.

2. Select the Update All menu item.

3. If Windows XP Professional cannot find the original share, removable disk, or desktop computer, a dialog box will pop up and you will have to cancel the synchronization until the link is available.

4. When Windows XP Professional locates the original file, an Update page is displayed with options to allow you to choose which is the more recent file. Figure 4.13 shows the option page for updating the Briefcase file. Click Update to overwrite the original file with the copy in the Briefcase.

5. The status of the file in the Briefcase will return to Up-to-Date. Close Windows Explorer.

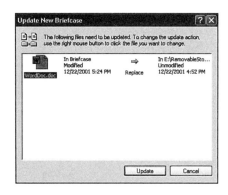

FIGURE 4.13
Updating Briefcase files.

Breaking the Links

You also can separate the files in your Briefcase from their originals. By right-clicking a file in your Briefcase and selecting Properties and then selecting the Update Status tab, you are shown more detailed update status. By clicking Split from Original, you will sever the link from your file in the Briefcase to its original copy. Any status information on the file will now show it to be an Orphan file. This allows you to keep the original file while also saving the changes you have made to a different version of the file.

Power Options for Mobile Systems

The nature of laptops means that some time will be spent running on battery power only. Controlling the rate of power usage on your laptop is an important issue in optimizing the performance you get.

The Power Options applet in Control Panel was discussed at length in Chapter 3, "Implementing, Managing, Monitoring, and Troubleshooting Hardware Devices and Drivers," and will be covered only in summary here.

The Power Options applet can help you manage power consumption in a number of ways.

The Power Schemes tab allows you to select the amount of time your laptop is idle before turning off the monitor, hard disk, going into standby, or hibernating. You have options for times you have power and times you are on battery power. You can create your own scheme specific to your needs, or you can select from a series of preconfigured power schemes.

The Alarms tab provides a place to define the battery levels that will trigger alarms and/or take corrective actions (such as going into standby).

The Power Meter tab displays the status of the current power source (plugged in or on batteries) and the amount of battery power left.

The Advanced tab provides a place for you to define the action that occurs when you close the portable computer lid, press the power button, or press the sleep button on your laptop. Options include prompt for action, do nothing, go into standby, hibernate, or shut down.

FIGURE 4.14
Typical portable Power Scheme options.

The Hibernate tab allows you to enable hibernation and shows the amount of disk space hibernation will use.

Figure 4.14 shows the typical power scheme settings for a laptop.

RECOVERING SYSTEM AND USER DATA

Restore and back up the operating system, system state data, and user data.

This section addresses the recovery of system and user data through the use of System Restore, Windows Backup, Safe Mode, and the Recovery Console.

Recovering a System Using System Restore

System Restore is a new feature in Windows XP Professional that you can use to recover your computer to a previous state without losing your data. System Restore monitors changes to the system (and some application files) and creates restore points. These restore points allow you to revert your system to an earlier state. Restore points are created daily and whenever the system changes (with a new driver installation). You also can create and name your own restore points.

This doesn't mean that you don't have to back up your data. You still should have a regular schedule for backing up important data files. The important point to remember is that System Restore will not lose any data files when it reverts the system to an earlier state. If you did a full backup and restore, everything—including your data—would be reverted to the time that the backup was taken.

How Does System Restore Work?

By default, System Restore monitors and restores all partitions and drives on your computer. It also monitors all installations of applications or drivers that you may do yourself, or that SMS or IntelliMirror may do for you.

System Restore immediately creates a restore point if it detects that you are installing an unsigned driver to your computer. If the installation of the driver makes undesirable changes to your computer, you can select this restore point to undo the changes and restore your computer to the state that existed before you installed the driver. This allows you to roll back a driver installation after you have successfully booted your computer, which complements the Restore Last Known Good Configuration option in the boot sequence (and which will roll back a driver installation if you have not successfully booted your computer).

When you perform a recovery using the Backup utility, System Restore immediately creates a restore point before the process starts. If the recover process puts your computer in a state that you don't like or can't work with, you can select this recovery point and restore the system to its state just before the recovery.

Each time you perform a restoration, it is a change made to your computer. System Restore creates restore operation restore points to track the change and the restoration. You can select these restore points, in essence, to undo the restoration.

Items Preserved Through a System Restore

System Restore does not cause you to lose your personal files or password. Items such as documents, e-mail messages, browsing history, and the last specified password are saved when you revert to an earlier state with System Restore.

System Restore protects your personal files by not restoring any files in the My Documents folder. It also does not restore any files that use common data filename extensions, such as .doc or .xls. If you're not sure whether your personal files use common data filename extensions, and you do not want the data files to be affected by System Restore, save them in the My Documents folder.

If a program was installed after the restore point to which you are restoring was created, the program might be uninstalled as part of the restoration process. Data files that are created with the program are not lost. However, to use them with the application, you will have to reinstall the software.

The actual number of saved restore points depends on how much activity there has been on your computer, the size of your hard disk

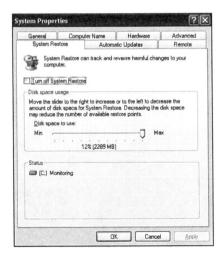

FIGURE 4.15
System Restore Properties shows the amount
of disk used for System Restore points.

(or the partition that contains your Windows XP Professional folder), and how much disk space has been allocated on your computer to store System Restore information. Figure 4.15 shows the System Restore Properties page.

Step by Step 4.8 can be used to create a restore point.

STEP BY STEP

4.8 Creating a Restore Point

1. Click Start; select Control Panel.

2. Select Help and Support and click Undo Changes to Your Computer with System Restore.

3. Select Create a Restore Point on the Welcome screen and click Next (see Figure 4.16).

4. Name the restore point to be created and click Create (see Figure 4.17).

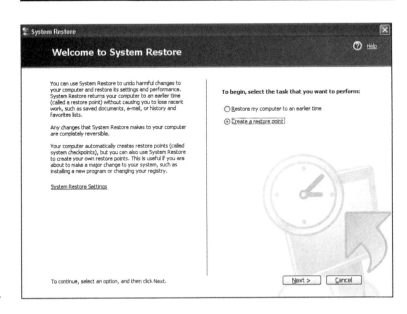

FIGURE 4.16
Welcome screen of the System Restore Wizard.

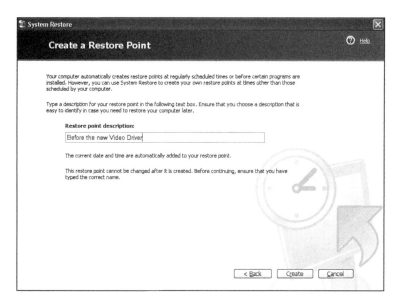

FIGURE 4.17
Naming the new restore point.

Step by Step 4.9 can be used to recover your system to a restore point.

STEP BY STEP

4.9 Restoring Your System to a Restore Point

1. Select Start, and then click Control Panel.

2. Select Help and Support and click Undo Changes to Your Computer with System Restore.

3. Select Restore My Computer to an Earlier Time and click Next.

4. The Select a Restore Point screen will be displayed (see Figure 4.18). This screen allows you to select a date (the numbers on the calendar are bold when there are system restore points available for those dates) and the restore points within the date. Click Next to continue.

continues

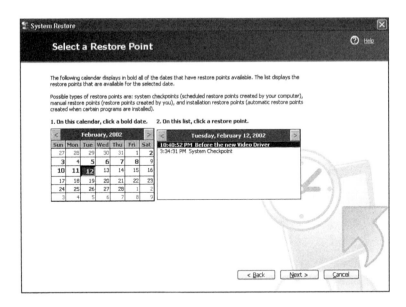

FIGURE 4.18
Selecting a restore point for recovery.

continued

5. The Confirm Restore Point Selection screen allows you a last chance to change your restore point selection. When you confirm by clicking Next, the system will start the restore point. During this procedure, the system will be returned to its previous state, Windows will shut down, and the system will restart. It will then return to the login screen.

Recovering System and User Data by Using Windows Backup

Information is the most important resource on your computer. Programs and services can often be easily reinstalled in the event of a hardware problem. However, the data is often irreplaceable. The best mechanism to back up your Windows XP Professional computer is to copy important data to a tape drive attached directly to your computer.

Backing up your computer to tape is safer than making copies to disk (and it's cheaper), and it allows you to keep versions of your data over time. The capability to keep backup copies for an extended period of time (for example, a 12-week rotation of tapes) can be used to provide protection against virus infections (you can retrieve a file from an earlier time) or from problems that may occur but not be fatal until later (for example, from a corrupted file).

The default backup mode in Windows XP Professional is a volume shadow copy. This mode allows you to create shadow copy backups of volumes and exact point-in-time copies of files, including all open files. Prior to Windows XP, open files (for example, database files or data files from a long running program) might have been skipped by the backup process. With volume shadow copy, these files are backed up correctly, even though they might be open and exclusively assigned. Volume shadow copy backup ensures

◆ Applications continue to write data to the volume during a backup.

◆ Files that are open are no longer omitted during a backup.

◆ Backups can be performed at any time, without locking out users.

A tested backup and recovery procedure is one of the most important administrative tasks to perform. When you are creating your backup policy, you must consider the following issues:

◆ How often should a backup be done?

◆ What type of backup is the most appropriate?

◆ How long should backup tapes be stored?

◆ How long will the recovery of lost data take?

Naturally, as you use your Windows XP Professional computer over time, the location and importance of the data you back up will vary. An occasional reassessment of risk will help to keep your backup policy relevant and minimize your exposure to loss.

Backup Types

Five types of backups are available through the Windows XP Backup utility:

◆ A normal backup copies all selected files and marks each as being backed up. With normal backups, you can restore files quickly because the files on tape are the most current.

◆ A copy backup copies all the selected files but does not mark them as backed up. This is useful if you want to make a backup copy of some of your files between scheduled backups without altering your backup operations.

◆ An incremental backup copies only those files created or changed since the last normal or incremental backup. It marks the files as having been backed up. If you use a combination of normal and incremental backups, a system restore would require a restore of the last normal backup and then all the incremental backups done since.

◆ A differential backup copies those files created or changed since the last normal backup. It does not mark the files as having been backed up. If you are using a combination of normal and differential backups, a system restore would require a restore of the last normal backup and then the last differential backup.

◆ A daily backup copies those files that have been modified the day the daily backup is performed. The files are not marked as backed up. This is useful if you are about to make a change to your system and need to back up any files modified since your last backup. That way, you can modify your disk configuration and still be able to recover all your data files if you decide it is not what you want to do.

Each type of backup has its advantages and disadvantages when it comes to recovering data from your backup tape set. Table 4.8 lists the advantages and disadvantages of each type.

TABLE 4.8

ADVANTAGES AND DISADVANTAGES OF BACKUP TYPES

Backup Type	Advantages	Disadvantages
Normal	Files are easy to find because they are always on the current backup tape. Recovery requires only one set of tapes.	This is the most time-consuming backup process. If your files do not change frequently, the backups are redundant.
Incremental	This uses the least amount of tape storage and the backups take the least amount of time.	Files are more difficult to find because they are on several tapes. Restores take longer.
Differential	This is less time-consuming than a normal backup.	The Restore operation uses only two sets of tapes, the normal backup and the last differential. However, if most of your backed-up files change every day, this begins to resemble a normal backup.

Although it is best to have at least three copies of your data, the frequency at which you create these backups depends on how often your data changes and its value to you. It is not likely that any one type of backup will be the only one used by you. A combination of backup types can provide the most effective recovery. For example, a weekly full backup and daily differential will mean a full system recovery has to read only two tapes.

Backing Up Your Data

Windows XP Professional provides two ways to create backup jobs using the Windows Backup utility: a wizard to walk you through the steps involved and a graphical interface to allow you to define the backup job manually. Figure 4.19 shows the Backup Wizard screen for selecting files to back up.

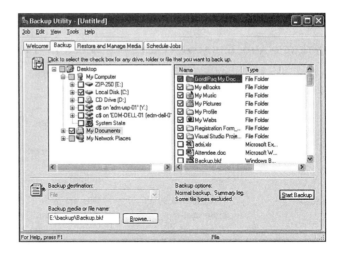

FIGURE 4.19
Selecting files to back up.

To define the files to back up and the tape drive to write to, use the procedure in Step by Step 4.10.

STEP BY STEP

4.10 Creating a Sample Backup Job

1. Click Start and select All Programs, Accessories, System Tools, Backup.

2. In the Backup or Restore Wizard window, click Advanced Mode.

3. Click the Backup tab to display the Backup Utility screen.

4. From the Job menu on the menu bar, click New.

5. Check the box next to any folder you want to back up, or click the folder to show the files within the folder. Check the box next to any file you want to back up.

6. In Backup Destination, select either File (the default) if you are backing up to a single file or select a tape device if backing up to a tape.

7. If you are backing up to a file, enter the path and filename of the backup file.

8. If you are backing up to a tape, click the tape you want to use.

9. Select Tools from the menu bar and click Options.

10. Select the Backup Type tab and choose the type of backup to do.

11. Select the Backup Log tab and choose the type of log information to keep.

12. Click OK to close the Options window.

13. Click Start Backup to start the backup and display the Backup Job Information screen.

14. Click the Advanced button to select data verification and backup of Remote Storage and to disable Volume Shadow copy if desired.

15. Click Schedule. You will be prompted to save the selections to a script file. Enter a pathname and filename in which to save your backup file selections.

16. The Set Account Information window will prompt you for a domain user ID and password to run the scheduled job. Enter a valid user ID and password.

17. The Schedule Job Options window will prompt you for a name to save the job as, which will be the name that the Task Scheduler will use to reference this job.

18. Click Start Backup to start the backup operation.

19. Review the log when the job is finished and click Close to return to the Backup Utility Screen.

When you finish creating this job, you will find that the Microsoft Backup utility has created a job that you can now review using the Task Scheduler.

Saving System State

System State information is composed of those files that are necessary for the correct running of your Windows XP Professional computer, but are unavailable to back up through normal means. In Windows XP Professional, System State files are defined as the

Registry, COM+ Class Registration database, files under Windows File Protection, and boot files.

Starting in Windows 2000, system state also includes the Certificate Services database if the system is a certificate server. If the system is a domain controller, the Active Directory and the SYSVOL directory are also considered to be System State information.

If you are running Domain Name Services (DNS) on a domain control, the System State information also contains DNS database files or Active Directory–integrated DNS zone data.

If the Windows server is also running the Cluster service, the System State information will include resource Registry checkpoints and the quorum resource recovery log.

Backing Up System State Data

When you are backing up System State data, it's an all-or-nothing thing. You do not get to choose to back up or restore individual components of the System State. There are many dependencies among the various components of the System State data, so it must be considered a single item.

Creating an Automated System Recovery (ASR) Disk

The Windows XP Professional backup program (ntbackup) provides a mechanism of last resort to recover your system from a total system failure. This would be the equivalent of replacing the disk and using ASR to return it to its state at the last backup.

The ASR Wizard backs up the system state, system services, and all disks associated with the operating system. It also creates a floppy disk containing information about the backup and the disk configurations (basic and dynamic) and how to accomplish a restore.

Creating an Automated System Recovery disk should be made a part of the regular backup cycle for your Windows XP Professional computer. With programs such as Windows Update that can be used to maintain currency of your configuration and manual changes to drivers and system configuration that are needed from time to time, any single copy of the ASR system state will become obsolete quickly.

Restoring a system using Automated System Recovery is like rein-stalling Windows XP Professional to a new disk. You reboot your computer from the CD and press F2 during the text portion of the setup. The setup routine then asks you to load the ASR disk into drive A: to complete the recovery.

Restoring Your Data

Windows XP Professional provides two ways to restore files using the Windows Backup utility: a wizard to walk you through the steps involved and a graphical interface that allows you to define the restore job manually.

When you want to recover some or all the files stored during a back-up job, you must select the backup set to restore from and then the specific files (or all files) to restore. The backup catalogs are stored by the name of the media (see Figure 4.20). You also can restore the files to their original location or to an alternative location if you want to copy the recovered files by hand.

Step by Step 4.11 is an example of restoring some selected files from a previous backup.

> **N O T E** **Don't Forget Your Data** ASR does not back up any user data. This process backs up the system state, disk configuration, and operating system files necessary to return the system to its former operating config-uration. You should always have a cur-rent backup available to recover your data.

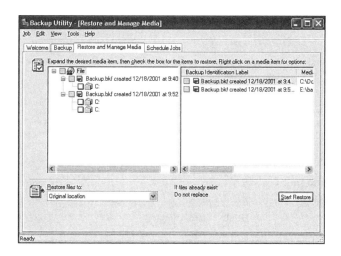

FIGURE 4.20
Backup catalogs are stored by media name.

STEP BY STEP

4.11 Restoring Files from a Normal Backup

1. Click Start and select All Programs, Accessories, System Tools, Backup.

2. Open the Backup or Restore Wizard window and click Advanced Mode.

3. Select the Restore and Manage Media tab.

4. In the left frame, select the backup set you would like to restore from and expand the file listings.

5. Use the Restore Files to: drop-down menu to select either the original location or an alternative.

6. Click Start Restore.

7. From the Confirm Restore window, click Advanced.

8. Set any options regarding removable storage or security and click OK.

9. Click OK to start the restore.

10. Enter the path of the backup set if it has changed (been moved) and click OK.

11. When the restore is complete, the Restore Progress window will allow you to view a report of the restore's actions or close the utility.

Troubleshooting the System Boot Process

If at some point when you reboot your Windows XP Professional computer it fails before Windows XP is started, you could have a problem somewhere in the boot process. The key to solving this type of problem is to understand the sequence of events that occurs in the computer as it is starting up. Windows XP shows you various boot sequence errors, the meaning of which should help you diagnose the problem with your system. You also can diagnose problems in the boot.ini file, apply your Automated System Recovery to fix to your system, and have Windows XP automatically attempt to repair the process.

A boot error is a very obvious problem. When you can't start your computer system, you know you have a problem. It's also the kind of problem that forces you to stop what you are doing and fix it before you go on.

The Boot Process

The boot process occurs in stages. The first stage is preboot, in which the system is checked and the boot information located.

Preboot

The computer runs a Power On Self Test (POST) to determine the amount of memory and what hardware components are present. The hardware devices are enumerated and configured during preboot. The system may display a series of messages indicating that the mouse is detected, that certain IDE or SCSI adapters are detected, responses from devices on the SCSI chain, and so forth. Failure at this stage represents a hardware concern and is not really a boot sequence error.

If all the hardware components are present and working, the computer BIOS locates the boot device and loads the Master Boot Record (MBR) into memory and executes it. The MBR scans the partition table to locate the active partition and loads the boot sector from the active partition into memory and executes it.

The computer finds and loads the file NTLDR from the active partition. NTLDR is a hidden system file located in the root folder of your system partition.

Initial Boot Phase

After NTLDR is executing, it does the following:

◆ Switches the processor from real mode into a 32-bit flat memory mode that NTLDR requires to complete its function.

◆ Starts the appropriate minifile system drivers, which are built into NTLDR to find and load Windows NT from different file system formats, File Allocation Table (FAT or FAT32), or Windows NT File System (NTFS).

NOTE
When `boot.ini` Is Missing   If the `boot.ini` file is not present, NTLDR attempts to load Windows XP from `\Windows` on the first partition of the first disk. The `boot.ini` file is hard to find anyway, as it is a hidden file.

NOTE
On Dual-Boot Systems   If you select another operating system such as Microsoft Windows 98, NTLDR loads and executes `BOOTSECT.DOS`. This is a copy of the boot sector that was on the system partition at the time that Windows XP Professional was installed and executing it begins the boot process for the selected operating system.

NOTE
Automatically Choosing the Default Profile   If you do not press the spacebar, or if there is only a single hardware profile, NTLDR will load Windows XP Professional using the default hardware profile configuration.

◆ Displays the Boot Loader Operating System Selection menu from the `boot.ini` file. This provides you with a selection of operating systems to use. If you do not select an entry before the timer reaches zero, NTLDR will load the operating system specified by the default parameter in `boot.ini`. The default parameter is the most recent operating system installed. If there is only one operating system to load, this option does not appear.

◆ After you select the operating system, a hardware-detection routine is initiated. For Windows XP, this is `NTDETECT.COM` and `NTOSKRNL.EXE`.

`NTDETECT.COM` collects a list of the hardware components currently installed and returns this list to NTLDR for inclusion in the Registry under `HKEY_LOCAL_MACHINE/HARDWARE`.

`NTDETECT.COM` will detect the following components:

◆ Computer ID

◆ Keyboard

◆ Communications ports

◆ Mouse/pointing devices

◆ Floating-point coprocessor

◆ Floppy disks

◆ Bus/adapter type

◆ Parallel ports

◆ Small Computer System Interface (SCSI) adapters

◆ Video adapters

Configuration Selection

After NTLDR starts loading Windows XP and collects hardware information, OS Loader will look at hardware profiles. If more than one is available, it will present you with the option of selecting a hardware profile to use. Profiles that a laptop normally has (docked and undocked) will be chosen automatically.

Kernel Load Phase

After the configuration has been selected, the Windows kernel (NTOSKRNL.EXE) loads and initializes. NTOSKRNL.EXE also loads and initializes device drivers and services. During this phase of the boot procedure, the screen clears and a bar graph appears at the bottom of the screen.

During the kernel load phase, NTLDR performs the following:

◆ Loads NTOSKRNL.EXE but does not initialize it.

◆ Loads the hardware abstraction layer file (Hal.dll).

◆ Loads the HKEY_LOCAL_MACHINE\SYSTEM Registry key from %systemroot%\System32\Config\System.

◆ Selects a configuration. The first hardware profile is highlighted by default. If you have created other hardware profiles, use the down-arrow key to select the one that you want to use.

◆ Selects the control set it will use to initialize the computer.

◆ Loads the low-level hardware device drivers (for example, hard disk device drivers).

NTLDR now initializes the kernel and passes control to it. The kernel uses the data collected during hardware detection to create the HKEY_LOCAL_MACHINE\HARDWARE key. This key contains information about the hardware components and interrupts used.

When the kernel load phase is complete, the kernel initializes, and then NTLDR passes control to the kernel. At this point, the system displays a graphical screen with a status bar indicating load status.

The kernel initializes the low-level device drivers that were loaded during the kernel load phase. If an error occurs while loading or initializing a device driver, the boot process may do any of the following:

◆ Ignore the error and proceed without issuing an error message.

◆ Display an error message and proceed.

◆ Restart using the Last Known Good control set or ignore the error if the Last Known Good control set is causing the error. This option can be picked from the menu that is displayed after pressing F8 during the initial boot process. The Last

---

NOTE **Debugging the Boot Process**   By entering the /SOS switch in the boot.ini file, Windows XP Professional will list the driver's name on the screen as the system starts up.

NOTE **Loading the Device Drivers**   A *control set* contains configuration data used to control the system, such as a list of the device drivers and services to load and start.

NOTE **Specifying Driver Order**   The value of the LIST entry specified in the HKEY_LOCAL_MACHINE\SYSTEM\ CurrentControlSet\Control\ ServiceGroupOrder subkey defines the order in which NTLDR loads the device drivers.

Known Good control set represents the Registry configuration that was used the last time the computer was successfully logged onto. This configuration will not be replaced until the next successful logon.

◆ Restart using the Last Known Good control set or halt if the Last Known Good control set is causing the error.

Advanced Boot Options

Pressing F8 during the operating system selection phase displays a screen with advanced options for booting Windows XP. Table 4.9 lists the Windows XP advanced boot options and their functions.

TABLE 4.9

ADVANCED BOOT OPTIONS

Option	Function
Safe Mode	Loads only the basic devices and drivers required to start the system. This includes the mouse, keyboard, mass storage, base video, and the default set of system services.
Safe Mode with Networking	This performs a Safe Load with the drivers and services necessary for networking.
Safe Mode with Command Prompt	This performs a Safe Load but launches a command prompt rather than Windows Explorer.
Enable Boot Logging	Logs the loading and initialization of drivers and services.
Enable VGA Mode	Restricts the startup to use only the base video.
Last Known Good Configuration	Uses the Last Known Good Configuration to boot the system.
Directory Services Restore Mode	Allows the restoration of the Active Directory (on Domain Controllers only).
Debugging Mode	Turns on debugging.

When logging is enabled, the boot process writes the log information to `\%systemroot%\NTBTLOG.TXT`.

When you use one of the Safe Boot options, an environmental variable is created, `Safeboot_Option`, which is set to either Network or Minimal.

Understanding the `boot.ini` File

The `boot.ini` file includes two sections, [boot loader] and [operating systems], that contain information that `NTLDR` uses to create the Boot Loader Operating System Selection menu.

The contents of the `boot.ini` file can be viewed with the `bootcfg` utility. This utility is part of Windows XP Professional and can be run from any command prompt.

The following is a typical `boot.ini` configuration showing both Windows XP Professional and the Recovery console installed.

```
Boot Loader Settings

-------------------
timeout: 5
default: multi(0)disk(0)rdisk(0)partition(1)\WINDOWS

Boot Entries
------------
Boot entry ID:  1
Friendly Name:  "Microsoft Windows XP Professional"
Path:       multi(0)disk(0)rdisk(0)partition(1)\WINDOWS
OS Load Options: /fastdetect

Boot entry ID:  2
Friendly Name:  "Microsoft Windows Recovery Console"
Path:       C:\CMDCONS\BOOTSECT.DAT
OS Load Options: /cmdcons
```

The following process can be used to make changes to the `boot.ini` configuration.

STEP BY STEP

4.12 Modifying `boot.ini`

1. Click Start and then right-click My Computer and select Properties.

2. Select the Advanced tab.

3. Click the Settings button in the Startup and Recovery section.

4. The Startup and Recovery window allows you to select the default operating system to boot, the countdown timer before the automatic system is loaded, and actions to take in the event of errors. The Edit button will bring the `boot.ini` configuration up in Notepad for manual edits.

5. Click OK to close the window.

During installation, Windows NT generates the `boot.ini` configuration, which contains ARC (Advanced RISC Computing) paths pointing to the computer's boot partition. The following is an example of an ARC path:

```
multi(0)disk(0)rdisk(1)partition(2)
```

Table 4.10 describes the naming conventions for ARC paths.

TABLE 4.10

ARC FIELD DEFINITIONS

Convention	Description
Multi (*x*) or scsi (*x*)	The adapter/disk controller. Use scsi to indicate a SCSI controller on which SCSI BIOS is *not* enabled. For all other adapter/disk controllers, use multi, including SCSI disk controllers with the BIOS enabled.
	The *x* field represents a number that indicates the load order of the hardware adapter. For example, if you have two SCSI adapters in a computer, the first to load and initialize receives number 0, and the next SCSI adapter, number 1.

Convention	Description
Disk(*y*)	The SCSI ID. For multi, this value is always 0.
Rdisk(*z*)	A number that identifies the disk. This is not used with SCSI controllers.
Partition(*a*)	A number that identifies the partition.

In both multi and scsi conventions, multi, scsi, disk, and rdisk numbers are assigned starting with (0). Partition numbers start with (1). All Primary partitions are assigned numbers first, followed by logical drives in extended partitions.

You can add a variety of switches to the entries in the [operating systems] section of the `boot.ini` file to provide additional functionality. Table 4.11 describes optional switches that you can use for entries in the `boot.ini` file.

TABLE 4.11

`boot.ini` SWITCHES

Switch	Description
/basevideo	Boots the computer using the standard VGA video driver. If a new video driver is not working properly, this switch will allow Windows XP to load.
/baudrate=*n*	Uses a baud rate different from the default (19200).
/crashdebug	Sends debug information only on a fatal system error.
/debug	Always sends debug information.
/debugport=com*x*	Uses serial port *x* instead of the default.
/maxmem:n	Specifies the amount of RAM that Windows XP uses. This switch is used if you suspect a memory chip is bad.
/nodebug	Does not send debug information.
/noserialmice=com*x*	Disables the serial mouse connected on port *x*.
/sos	Displays the device driver names as they are loaded. This switch is used when startup fails while loading drivers.

The following is an example of the output produced when the /sos switch is included in the boot.ini file on an Intel processor. The multi(0)disk(0)rdisk(0)partition(1) refers to the system disk. This is followed by the path (usually \Windows\System32) and then the file, dll, or system driver that is being loaded.

```
multi(0)disk(0)rdisk(0)partition(1)\Windows\System32\
ntoskrnl.exe
multi(0)disk(0)rdisk(0)partition(1)\Windows\System32\
hal.dll
multi(0)disk(0)rdisk(0)partition(1)\Windows\System32\
KDCom.dll
multi(0)disk(0)rdisk(0)partition(1)\Windows\System32\
BOOTVID.DLL
multi(0)disk(0)rdisk(0)partition(1)\Windows\System32\
config\system
multi(0)disk(0)rdisk(0)partition(1)\Windows\System32\
c_1252.nls
multi(0)disk(0)rdisk(0)partition(1)\Windows\System32\
c_850.nls
multi(0)disk(0)rdisk(0)partition(1)\Windows\System32\
l-intl.nls
multi(0)disk(0)rdisk(0)partition(1)\Windows\FONTS\
vgaoem.fon
multi(0)disk(0)rdisk(0)partition(1)\Windows\APPACH\
dvmain.sdb
multi(0)disk(0)rdisk(0)partition(1)\Windows\System32\
DRIVERS\ACPI.sys
multi(0)disk(0)rdisk(0)partition(1)\Windows\System32\
DRIVERS\WMILIB.sys
multi(0)disk(0)rdisk(0)partition(1)\Windows\System32\
DRIVERS\pci.sys
multi(0)disk(0)rdisk(0)partition(1)\Windows\System32\
DRIVERS\isapnp.sys
multi(0)disk(0)rdisk(0)partition(1)\Windows\System32\
DRIVERS\compbatt.sys
multi(0)disk(0)rdisk(0)partition(1)\Windows\System32\
DRIVERS\battc.sys
multi(0)disk(0)rdisk(0)partition(1)\Windows\System32\
DRIVERS\intelide.sys
multi(0)disk(0)rdisk(0)partition(1)\Windows\System32\
DRIVERS\PCIIDEX.SYS
multi(0)disk(0)rdisk(0)partition(1)\Windows\System32\
DRIVERS\pcmcia.sys
multi(0)disk(0)rdisk(0)partition(1)\Windows\System32\
DRIVERS\MountMgr.sys
multi(0)disk(0)rdisk(0)partition(1)\Windows\System32\
DRIVERS\ftdisk.sys
multi(0)disk(0)rdisk(0)partition(1)\Windows\System32\
DRIVERS\partmgr.sys
multi(0)disk(0)rdisk(0)partition(1)\Windows\System32\
DRIVERS\volsnap.sys
multi(0)disk(0)rdisk(0)partition(1)\Windows\System32\
DRIVERS\atapi.sys
```

```
multi(0)disk(0)rdisk(0)partition(1)\Windows\System32\
DRIVERS\disk.sys
multi(0)disk(0)rdisk(0)partition(1)\Windows\System32\
DRIVERS\classpnp.sys
multi(0)disk(0)rdisk(0)partition(1)\Windows\System32\
DRIVERS\ino_flpy.sys
multi(0)disk(0)rdisk(0)partition(1)\Windows\System32\
DRIVERS\KSecDD.sys
multi(0)disk(0)rdisk(0)partition(1)\Windows\System32\
DRIVERS\NTFS.sys
multi(0)disk(0)rdisk(0)partition(1)\Windows\System32\
DRIVERS\Mup.sys
multi(0)disk(0)rdisk(0)partition(1)\Windows\System32\
DRIVERS\agp440.sys
```

You can modify the timeout and default parameter values in the boot.ini file by using System Properties in the Control Panel. In addition, you can edit these and other parameter values in the boot.ini file manually. You might want to modify the boot.ini file to add more descriptive entries for the Boot Loader Operating System Selection menu or to include various switches to aid in troubleshooting the boot process.

Last Known Good Configuration

Configuration information in Windows XP Professional is kept in a control set subkey. A typical Windows XP installation would have subkeys such as ControlSet001, ControlSet002, and CurrentControlSet. The CurrentControlSet is a pointer to one of the ControlSetxxx subkeys. There is another control set named *Clone* that is used to initialize the computer (either the Default or LastKnownGood). It is re-created by the kernel initialization process each time the computer starts.

The key HKEY_LOCAL_MACHINE\SYSTEM\Select contains subkeys named *Current*, *Default*, *Failed*, and *LastKnownGood*, which are described in the following list:

◆ **Current**—This value identifies which control set is the CurrentControlSet.

◆ **Default**—This value identifies the control set to use the next time Windows XP starts (unless you choose Last Known Good Configuration during the boot process).

◆ **Failed**—This value identifies the control set that was the cause of a boot failure the last time the computer started.

◆ **LastKnownGood**—This value identifies the control set that was used the last time Windows XP was started successfully. After a successful logon, the Clone control set is copied to the LastKnownGood control set.

When you log on to a Windows XP Professional computer and modify its configuration by adding or removing drivers, the changes are saved in the Current control set. The next time the computer is booted, the kernel copies the information in the Current control set to the Clone control set. After the next successful logon to Windows XP, the information in the Clone control set is copied to LastKnownGood.

If you experience problems starting the computer that you think might be related to the Windows XP configuration changes you just made, restart the computer with logging on and press F8 during the initial boot phase. Selecting the Last Known Good Configuration will restore the system configuration to the last one that Windows XP used to start successfully.

Using the Last Known Good Configuration does not help in the following situations:

◆ If the problem is not related to the Windows XP configuration, such as problems with a user profile or with file permissions.

◆ If you complete the boot process and log on to the Windows XP system, the information in the LastKnownGood control set is updated.

◆ If the startup problem is related to hardware failures or missing or corrupted files.

System Recovery Using Safe Mode

If booting your system with Last Known Good Configuration will not repair the problem with your system, the next step to try is booting in Safe Mode. By restarting your computer and pressing F8 during the initial boot sequence, a menu of boot options is displayed. If you select Safe Mode, the system will boot with the minimum number of devices possible (mouse, monitor, keyboard, mass storage, base video, default system services, and no network connections).

You also can choose an option that is Safe Mode with Network Connections if you think you might need to retrieve drivers from the manufacturer's Web site.

Choosing the option Safe Mode with Command Prompt will load the system with the minimum device drivers but rather than presenting you with a graphical interface, the system starts with a command prompt.

You can use Safe Mode to help you diagnose problems. If a symptom does not reappear when you start in Safe Mode, you can eliminate the default settings and minimum device drivers as possible causes. If a newly added device or a changed driver is causing problems, you can use Safe Mode to remove the device or reverse the change.

System Restore in Safe Mode

You can use System Restore to restore your computer to any restore point while in Safe Mode. If you cannot start the computer in standard mode, you can use System Restore to restore to a time when you could start the computer without errors.

While the computer is in Safe Mode, System Restore does not create any restore points. Therefore, you cannot undo a restoration that you performed when the computer was in Safe Mode.

Using the Windows XP Recovery Console

If your computer will not start because of a corrupted or missing file, and the Last Known Good Configuration and Safe Mode boot options will not fix the problem, you can use the Windows XP Recovery Console to gain access to the disk without starting Windows XP. This will provide you with a command prompt from which you can perform limited administrative tasks. The following is a list of some of the tasks you can perform from the Recovery Console:

- ◆ Enable or disable services.
- ◆ Copy data from a floppy disk or a CD.
- ◆ Read or write data on a local drive.

◆ Format a disk drive.

◆ Repair the boot sector or boot record.

If you get an error message when booting your computer that indicates that a system file is missing, you can use the Recovery Console to start the system and copy a new version of the file from the CD to the system drive.

The Recovery Console does have some limitations, however:

◆ You cannot copy files from the hard drive to a floppy disk.

◆ You can view only the `%windir%` directory (usually `C:\Windows`) and its subdirectories.

◆ If you are going to remove a driver, you need to know the files that are part of the driver in order to delete them.

◆ You need to identify yourself by logging in as the Administrator. If the Security Accounts Manager (SAM) hive is corrupt or missing, you will not be able to use the Recovery Console.

Configuring the Windows XP Recovery Console

To use the Recovery Console, you must first install it from the Windows XP CD. The Installation Wizard will create all the files necessary and modify `boot.ini` to provide an additional boot menu item that will allow you to select the Recovery Console while starting your system. In the event that your machine won't boot, and you have not installed the Recovery Console, you can run it directly from the CD. When you boot from CD, the text portion of the setup sequence will allow you a chance to repair an existing installation by selecting the Repair or Recover option (R). If you have more than one operating system loaded, you will have to choose the one that needs repairing. The Recovery Console will then prompt you for the Administrator password.

Installing the Recovery Console

The Recovery Console Wizard is started with the following command:

```
Path_to_executable\WinNT32 /cmdcons
```

path_to_executable refers to the \I386 subdirectory on the Windows XP CD. For example, if you have two hard drives and your CD-ROM drive is E:, the command to start the Recovery Console Installation Wizard would look like the following:

```
E:\I386\WinNT32 /cmdcons
```

Using the Recovery Console

The following procedure can be used to start your computer with the Windows XP Recovery Console.

STEP BY STEP

4.13 Starting the Windows XP Recovery Console

1. Start your computer and select the Windows XP Recovery Console boot menu item.

2. Enter the number of the Windows XP installation you want to log on to (there may be more than one if there are multiple operating systems loaded on your computer).

3. Enter the administrator password when prompted.

4. Make any required changes to the system.

5. Type **Exit** to restart your computer.

The Windows XP Recovery Console gives you a command prompt in %windir% directory, usually c:\Windows.

Table 4.12 lists the commands available to you when running the Windows XP Recovery Console.

TABLE 4.12

WINDOWS XP RECOVERY CONSOLE COMMANDS

Command	*Description*
Disable servicename	Disables a service or driver.
Enable servicename	Enables a service or driver.
DiskPart [/add|/delete] [*device*|*drive*|*partition*] If the partition is being added, [*size*]	Adds or deletes a disk partition. *size* specifies the size of the new partition.
FixBoot [*driveletter*]	Replaces the Windows XP boot sector in the system partition or on the disk specified by *driveletter* (if specified).
FixMBR devicename	Repairs the master boot record (MBR) of the boot partition. This is used if the MBR has become corrupted and Windows XP cannot start.
ListSVC	Lists the services and whether they are automatically or manually started.
Logon	Lists the available system to log on to, requests the administrative password, and then logs you on to a Windows XP installation.
Map arc	Lists all connected drives. The *arc* command will list them in ARC paths instead of drive letters. ARC paths are used in the boot.ini file to specify the local drives to boot from.
SystemRoot	Sets the current directory to systemroot.
ChkDsk	Checks the status of a disk.

The Windows XP Recovery Console also supports a number of commands, such as Attrib, Cd, Cls, Copy, Delete, Dir, Extract, Format, Md, More, Rd, Rename, and Type. These are similar to the familiar DOS commands but are more restrictive in use of wildcards and options.

Removing the Recovery Console

If you would like to remove the Recovery Console, there are a number of manual tasks to perform.

The first is to remove the folder \CmdCons. This is a hidden folder in your root directory. You can use the following procedure to view hidden files.

STEP BY STEP

4.14 Viewing Hidden Files

1. Click Start and then click My Computer.

2. Double-click the disk containing the Recovery Console.

3. Select the Tools menu and click Folder Options.

4. Select the View tab.

5. Select the check box for Show Hidden Files and Folders and clear the check box for Hide Protected Operating System Files.

6. Click OK.

The next task is to delete the file CMDLDR (no extension) that is also in the root directory.

The last step is to edit the boot.ini file and remove the line about the recovery console. It will resemble the following:

```
C:\cmdcons\bootsect.dat="Microsoft Windows Recovery
Console" /cmdcons
```

Save the boot.ini file. The next time you reboot, the recovery console will not be available.

Troubleshooting Stop Errors

If a Stop error screen appears, it could be a transient problem that will not reoccur if you restart, or it could signify a more serious or permanent error occurring in your computer. If the Stop screen reoccurs, use the following steps to identify the problem:

1. Verify that any recently installed hardware or software is properly installed.

2. Disable or remove any newly installed hardware (such as RAM, network adapters, or modems), drivers, or software.

3. If you can start Windows XP, check the Event Viewer for additional error messages that might help identify the cause of your problem. To open the Event Viewer, click Start, point to Settings, click Control Panel, double-click Administrative Tools, double-click Event Viewer, and click System Log.

4. If you cannot start Windows XP, try to start the computer in Safe Mode. From here, you should be able to disable or remove any added drivers or programs. To start your computer in Safe Mode, press F8 during the initial boot screen and select Safe Mode.

5. Verify that you have the latest drivers for any hardware devices and that you have the most recent system BIOS. Check with your hardware manufacturer for this information (often available free over the Internet).

6. Disable any BIOS memory options such as caching or shadowing.

7. Check for viruses on your computer, using a current version of your virus-protection software.

8. Verify that all the hardware and drivers installed in your computer are on the Microsoft Hardware Compatibility list for Windows XP Professional.

9. Run any system diagnostic programs that were included when you purchased the computer. Especially important will be any memory checks.

10. Revert to the Last Known Good Configuration.

With NT 4.0, Microsoft found that at least 18% of the errors reported to them were directly related to driver errors. It is for this reason the driver-signing option was created—to reduce the occurrences of device-driver errors.

CASE STUDY: PERFORMANCE PROBLEMS WITH A NEW PROCESS

ESSENCE OF THE CASE

The following points summarize the essence of the case study:

- The system has just had a new application installed.

- The application runs continually as a service to local and remote users.

- After a number of days of continual running, the system performance degrades.

- Rebooting the system temporarily resolves the problem. However, it eventually returns.

- Available memory is consumed and paging activity increases.

SCENARIO

You have installed a new locally developed service program. This service runs in the background continually. You and a number of remote users who are accessing data on your system use it. When you first install it, you run the Performance Monitor on your system to establish a baseline of performance during normal working conditions. A few days later, your system becomes sluggish and noticeably slower in all functions. You reboot your system and it appears to be working normally again. A few days later, the same performance problems occur again. You run the Performance Monitor and discover that the amount of available memory has dropped to almost zero and the paging file is active.

ANALYSIS

When dealing with performance problems, it is important to remember that almost everything is interrelated with everything else. Memory problems can cause disk activity, which can manifest itself as a processor bottleneck. In this case, because the problem was apparently solved when the system was restarted, the problem is likely related to consumption of a resource rather than an elevated rate of activity. When the problem occurred again days later, the Performance Monitor showed a higher-than-expected paging activity and almost no available memory. That combination would normally indicate a system that is underconfigured in memory for the process running. Because this situation did not exist when the new application was brought

continues

CASE STUDY: PERFORMANCE PROBLEMS WITH A NEW PROCESS

continued

online, the conclusion is that the new background service leaks memory. In this situation, memory acquired by the service during normal processing is not returned to the system. Over time, the amount of working memory assigned to the service would exceed the amount available and the Windows XP Professional operating system would begin to page to meet the needs of its normal workload. The recommendation would be to send the new service back to the developers for analysis.

CHAPTER SUMMARY

KEY TERMS

- Performance Monitor
- Hardware profiles
- Task Scheduler
- Briefcase
- Synchronization
- Performance Counter
- LastKnownGood Configuration
- Recovery Console

This chapter focused on actions you can take and procedures you can use to increase the reliability and performance of your Windows XP Professional computer system. Knowing how your system functions and the workload under which you normally expect to see it perform is vital to being able to recover your data in the event that something catastrophic occurs. Planning how to recover your system is not a task that can occur after the problem happens.

The processes built into Windows XP Professional to assist in protecting your currently well-running system from being corrupted by the addition of an incompatible driver or a driver not certified as working with Windows XP Professional were covered first.

Next, additional built-in processes to assist in running daily or routine tasks using the Task Scheduler were discussed. Additionally, the capabilities of the Briefcase were shown to allow mobile users to function off the network as well as they could when on the network and to allow them to reintegrate changes made when reconnected.

The third topic of performance monitoring was discussed from the point of view of memory usage, processor resource utilization, and network and disk activity, as well as how all those factors combine to influence how user applications run.

Finally, this chapter addressed the topics of backup and restore, booting options available when problems arise during startup, and the added functionality of the Recovery Console.

APPLY YOUR KNOWLEDGE

Exercises

4.1 Scheduling a Task

This exercise will help you explore the Task Scheduler by having it schedule a batch job. An important part of managing your Windows XP Professional computer is having it automatically run jobs that you create.

Estimated Time: 10 minutes

1. Open a command window and create a BAT file with a `net send` command. You can use the following command to create the file.

   ```
   Echo net send machine-name Hi There >
   C:\HI.BAT
   ```

   You should substitute your computer name for *machine-name* in the command.

2. Click Start and then Control Panel.

3. Double-click Scheduled Tasks.

4. Double-click Add a Scheduled Task.

5. In the Scheduled Task Wizard, click Next.

6. Click Browse.

7. Highlight the test `HI.BAT` file created for this exercise and click Open.

8. Select the option One Time Only and click Next.

9. Select a time one or two minutes into the future and click Next.

10. Enter the user ID and password under which the job should run and click Next.

11. Click Finish to create the job. At the time selected, a pop-up window should appear with the message `Hi There`.

4.2 Watch Memory Usage Using Performance Manager

This exercise explores using the Performance Manager to watch typical memory counters on your Windows XP Professional system. The techniques used here are applicable to all the other performance objects available through the Performance Manager. Performance Manager is an important tool in understanding the workload on your system.

Estimated Time: 15 minutes

1. Click Start; click Control Panel.

2. Click Performance and Maintenance and then click Administrative Tools.

3. Click Performance.

4. Expand the Performance Monitor to full screen size and click the plus (+) button.

5. In the Performance Object drop-down list, select the Memory entry.

6. Select and add the counters Available Bytes, Cache Bytes, Pages/Sec, Nonpaged Bytes, and Paged Bytes.

7. Select the performance object Cache.

8. Select and add the counter Copy Read Hits %.

9. Close the Add Counters window.

10. Observe the counter's behavior as your computer performs its background tasks. Try giving your machine additional tasks to do and observe the impact on these counters.

11. Close the Performance window to exit.

APPLY YOUR KNOWLEDGE

4.3 Create a New Hardware Profile

This exercise explores creating a new hardware profile and modifying it to disable drivers not used in the new profile. This is a method the Windows XP Professional provides to allow mobile users to have hardware configurations other than the complete configuration usually available at the docking station.

Estimated time: 10 minutes

1. Click Start and click Control Panel.

2. Click Performance and Maintenance and then click System.

3. Select the Hardware tab.

4. Click Hardware Profiles.

5. Select a profile to copy (either Profile 1 or Docked Profile).

6. Click Copy.

7. Name the new profile and click OK.

8. Click OK twice and close the Control Panel.

9. Restart your computer and select the new profile when prompted.

10. After the system restarts, click Start.

11. Select Settings and click Control Panel.

12. Double-click System.

13. Select the Hardware tab.

14. Click Device Driver.

15. Select the devices to disable when using this profile by expanding a device type (such as Network Adapters), right-clicking a device, and selecting Disable.

16. Click OK to close the system applet and close the Control Panel.

17. Restart your computer selecting the new profile. Check the device manager to ensure your changes have been made.

18. Return to the hardware profile screen and remove the new profile.

4.4 Install the Recovery Console

This exercise explores the steps to install and then run the Recovery Console. This feature of Windows XP Professional provides an additional mechanism for repairing your system in the event of a problem at boot time.

Estimated time: 15 minutes

1. Insert the Windows XP Professional disc in the CD-ROM device.

2. Open a command window and change drives to the CD-ROM.

3. Change to the I386 subdirectory.

4. Enter the command Winnt32 /cmdcons.

5. Answer Yes at the installation window. (Note that installation of the Recovery Console takes about 7MB of disk space.)

6. Wait until the necessary files are copied to disk and answer OK to finish when prompted.

7. Restart your Windows XP Professional computer.

8. Select the Recovery Console boot option when prompted.

9. Wait for the installation process to complete.

APPLY YOUR KNOWLEDGE

10. Select the Windows installation to log in to (choose your normal boot system).

11. Enter the Administrator password when prompted.

12. At the command prompt, enter a **DIR** command. You should be in the C:\WINDOWS directory.

13. Enter **HELP** to see the commands available.

14. Enter **EXIT** to exit the Recovery Console and automatically reboot your computer.

4.5 Backing Up Files

This exercise selects and backs up a single file. The backup file is saved into a temporary folder for later recovery.

Estimated time: 15 minutes

1. Click Start.

2. Select All Programs, Accessories, System and click Backup.

3. Click Next to close the Welcome screen.

4. Select Backup Files and Settings and click Next.

5. Select Let Me Choose What to Back Up and click Next.

6. In the Items to Back Up window, select My Computer, select Local Disk, and expand one of the folders shown (select one arbitrarily for the lab).

7. Check off a single file to include in the backup and click Next.

8. Use the Browse button to create a new folder under C:\ called Temp Backup.

9. Click Next and then Finish to start the backup.

10. When the backup has completed, you can click the Report button to review the log and then click Close to exit.

4.6 Recovering Files to an Alternative Location

This exercise uses a set of previously backed-up files to explore reloading to an alternative location. This technique is very useful in restoring either data or programs without impacting other information contained in the folder.

Estimated time: 15 minutes

1. Click Start.

2. Select All Programs, Accessories, System and click Backup.

3. Click Next to close the Welcome screen.

4. Select Restore files and Settings and click Next.

5. The catalog of files to restore is sorted by the media name given during the backup procedure. Expand a media entry for Test Backup.bkf and select the folder or files to restore.

6. Click Next and then click the Advanced button to change the location of the restore.

7. In the Restore File To drop-down window, select Alternate Location and use the Browse feature to select the Temp Backup folder.

8. Select how you want to restore the files (do not overwrite, overwrite only older files, always overwrite) and click Next.

9. Ensure that security is restored and click Next.

10. Click Finish to start the process.

APPLY YOUR KNOWLEDGE

11. Enter the path of the media file to restore from and click OK.

12. Click Close when the process is complete and close the Backup window.

13. Use Windows Explorer to open the Temp Backup folder to ensure that the file selected was restored to this location.

14. Delete the Temp Backup folder when finished.

4.7 Create a Briefcase and Synchronize Files

This exercise explores using the Briefcase to copy files to your computer for offline access. This technique is very useful if you need to copy files from a machine, removable storage device, or another directly connected computer.

Estimated Time: 10 minutes

1. Click the Desktop icon in the taskbar.

2. Right-click the desktop, select New, and click Briefcase.

3. Open Windows Explorer and expand a network share.

4. Create a text file on a network share.

5. Right-click the file and drag it to the Briefcase Icon at the bottom of the Windows Explorer folder list.

6. Select the Make Sync Copy option.

7. Double-click the file in the Briefcase folder and update it.

8. Double-click the file in the original network share folder and update it.

9. Right-click the Briefcase Icon in Windows Explorer and select Update All.

10. Select the Briefcase file or the Network share file to be updated and click Update.

4.8 Identify the Behavior of a Memory Leak

This exercise explores using the Performance Manager to watch typical memory counters on your Windows XP Professional system that has an application that leaks memory. A memory leak is caused by a program that asks for memory but, because of a programming error, does not return the memory after it is finished with it. Performance Manager is an important tool in understanding the workload on your system.

Estimated Time: 10 minutes

1. Search for and obtain the application program LeakyApp.exe. This can be found on the Microsoft Web page in a resource kit available online.

2. Click Start, and then click Control Panel.

3. Double-click Administrative Tools.

4. Double-click Performance.

5. Clear the windows if any performance counters are being charted.

6. Select the Paging File Object and add % Usage to the chart.

7. Select the Memory object and add the Cache Byte, % Committed, Available KB, and Pages/Sec counter to the chart.

8. Open a command window and start five copies of Leakyapp (it can take some time for one application to consume all the virtual memory your computer may have).

9. Start each one leaking and return to the Performance chart.

10. As the available virtual memory is consumed, note how the cache bytes chart becomes unstable, how the % usage of the paging file continually increases, and how the memory pages/sec counter suddenly jumps.

11. When all memory is consumed, stop each Leakyapp from leaking memory.

12. Note that the paging rate remains elevated.

13. Exit each of the Leakyapp programs one at a time.

14. Note that the amount of virtual memory returns as a block.

15. Note when the paging rate drops back to zero (almost).

16. Exit all Leakyapp applications and shut down the Performance Monitor.

Review Questions

1. What performance counters would you chart to tell whether paging was dominating I/O to your system disk?

2. How do you run a job under administrative rights with Task Scheduler?

3. If memory is in short supply, what does the Windows XP Professional operating system rely on?

4. What is the best indicator to look at when judging a processor to be overloaded?

5. How do you disable logical disk counters?

6. If you have copied Profile 1 to a new hardware profile, how do you disable devices you don't want to load?

7. If you want to reload some files by using only two sets of backup tapes, what backup method should you have used?

8. If you load a new device driver and your Windows XP Professional computer will not boot, what safe boot option should you use to recover?

Exam Questions

1. You are a user with administrative rights on your Windows XP Professional computer. You download a new driver for your video card over the Internet and update your system to include it. When you restart your computer, you find that it halts partway through the boot sequence. What action should you take first to diagnose the problem?

   A. Reboot your computer, start the Recovery Console, and remove the new driver from your system.

   B. Use the Automated System Recovery feature to restore the system.

   C. Use the Recovery Console to start a restore of the system from your last backup.

   D. Reboot using the LastKnownGood option and enable driver signing as soon as possible.

APPLY YOUR KNOWLEDGE

2. You are in charge of reviewing new software for your IT department. You install a new device on your Windows XP Professional computer. You successfully log on but after a short while your system stops responding. You suspect the driver for the new device is the problem. What should you do to correct the problem?

   A. Restart your computer, press F8, and choose Last Known Good Configuration.

   B. Restart your computer, press F8, and choose Safe Mode and disable the device.

   C. Restart your computer and roll the device driver back using the Device Manager.

   D. Use System Restore to return your system to an earlier state.

3. Your company is installing Windows XP on everyone's desktop but still maintains some older 16-bit applications. As your users run these, they complain that those applications run slower than the new applications on your system. What should you do to make the 16-bit applications run faster?

   A. Configure each 16-bit application to run in its own memory space.

   B. Make sure the 16-bit applications do not have CPU affinity assigned.

   C. Upgrade your system CPUs.

   D. Lower the scheduling priority of your 32-bit applications.

4. You use a high-end graphic package as part of your job in a graphics design shop. You have other tasks running on your Windows XP Professional computer but when you are running your graphic program, the other tasks seem to run slowly. What should you do to improve their performance?

   A. Restart the graphics program with a /Belownormal switch.

   B. Upgrade your CPU.

   C. Increase the priority of your background applications.

   D. Assign your graphics package to run on one CPU only.

5. You work on the Helpdesk of a large mining company. You usually have several Windows Office applications open at any time plus a third-party Trouble Ticket application that you use to track incidents. You notice that with all your applications open, your computer runs slower than you expected. You would like to quickly obtain information on what the applications are doing. What should you do to find CPU-utilization information quickly?

   A. Use the Task Manager to show you information about CPU, memory, and network usage.

   B. Run the performance monitor, select the appropriate CPU and memory counters, and wait for the system to complete a graph cycle.

   C. Run the same applications on a Windows XP Professional machine with a more powerful CPU and compare the results.

   D. Increase the scheduling priority of the Windows Office applications.

APPLY YOUR KNOWLEDGE

6. You are in charge of a Windows XP Professional system that has suffered from hardware failures in the past. You are worried that you might lose data if the problems persist. You want to not lose any more than one day's activity and minimize the number of tapes it takes to reload your system. What type of backup scheme should you implement?

   A. A Normal backup each week and an Incremental backup each day.

   B. A Normal backup each week and a Differential each day.

   C. A Normal backup each month, an Incremental backup each week, and a Daily backup each day.

   D. A Normal backup each week and a Copy backup each day.

7. You have just installed a new Contact Management application on your Windows XP Professional computer. Some time later, your system begins to run noticeably slower. You decide to remove the application but it doesn't complete correctly and the system is still running slow. You want to get your old performance back but not lose any data you may have added since you installed the Contact Management application. What is your best approach?

   A. Restore your computer system from your last backup tape(s).

   B. Use System Restore to restore your system to yesterday's checkpoint.

   C. Manually remove the Registry entries for the application.

   D. Retry the Application Uninstall procedure.

8. You are a business leader in a user department in a large telco. As a business leader, you are the local IT expert to whom your users go first for advice. Your company has just upgraded the network in your department so you decide to try a larger bandwidth adapter in your computer to see what difference the network changes make. You add a faster network adapter but find that your computer seems a little sluggish. You check the Performance Monitor and see that the CPU is very busy, interrupts are way up, and there is a little paging.

   What change should you make to your system to compensate?

   A. Get a faster processor.

   B. Replace the network adapter with one that supports interrupt avoidance or moderation.

   C. Balance the disk activity to reduce the overall interrupt activity.

   D. Add memory to reduce the paging activity.

9. You have just installed a new device in your Windows XP Professional computer. You restart your system after the device driver has been installed but the system halts almost immediately. You suspect the new device driver is causing the problem. You can obtain another one from the manufacturer over the Internet but you need your computer to do that. What action should you take to get your computer running again?

   A. Restart your computer, press F8, and select Safe Mode from the boot options.

   B. Restart and select the Recovery Console as the system to start. Disable the device driver using the command line and then restart your system.

APPLY YOUR KNOWLEDGE

C. Use System Restore to return your system to an earlier revision.

D. Use Device manager to disable the device driver.

10. You work in a company that has a Windows 2000 domain. You are required to back up your Windows XP Professional desktop machine so that in the case of a hardware failure, you can return your machine to the network with its computer account and system settings intact. What task would you have Backup do to ensure this?

A. Direct Backup to save System State as well.

B. Perform incremental backups each day.

C. Backup the Registry each day.

D. Ensure that all user profiles are backed up.

11. You are a database specialist working for a software company. You are building an application that uses a COM object to extract employee changes from your company's financial system and saves them in a database that is referenced by the company's internal home page as an employee directory listing. Your company has recently merged with another of about the same size and has reorganized, which has resulted in a large number of changes daily. You notice that retrieving data takes longer now than you expect, even after examining the indexes on the database. You examine your system and find that memory is not in short supply and the paging activity is normal. The disk subsystem the database is on is performing only about 15 I/O operations per second and the CPU is not busy. You suspect the database has been configured to grow its datafiles in too small an increment, resulting in disk fragmentation.

You need to return the performance to its previous levels. What should you do? Choose the most correct answer.

A. Defragment the disk the database data files are on.

B. Resize the database, defragment the disk, save and reload the database, and rebuild the indexes.

C. Replace the disk holding the database with one with a higher rotational speed.

D. Replace the disk holding the database with a hardware-enabled RAID-5 structure.

12. You run a very large spreadsheet model on your Windows XP Professional computer. When the spreadsheet is running, you notice that the CPU is at 100%. You check the performance counters as the spreadsheet is running and notice that paging is high as well. When the spreadsheet is closed, the CPU returns to normal but the paging rate remains high. What should you do to increase the performance of your machine?

A. Upgrade your machine's CPU.

B. Use a better network adapter card that interrupts the CPU at a low rate.

C. Add more RAM.

D. Increase the size of the Paging file.

13. You have two hard disks on your Windows XP professional computer. All the system files are on C: and your application programs are on D:. Both C and D are volumes on the same physical

APPLY YOUR KNOWLEDGE

disk. Your databases and other files are all kept on E:, which is the other disk. When you run several applications at the same time, you notice that the paging rate is up and your applications slow down. What should you do to improve your system's performance?

A. Defragment your C: and D: drives.

B. Move the paging file to E:.

C. Increase the paging file size.

D. Increase the priority of your important applications.

14. You are a database analyst in a small engineering firm. You are running a SQL Server database from a Windows XP Professional desktop and providing access to this database to others in your workgroup. Your co-workers complain that after a few minutes, response on the database drops off. You open up the performance monitoring system on the desktop and notice that CPU usage and disk activity appears normal. During this time, the performance of the database also appears normal. When you close the screen, the problem returns after a delay. You suspect that some task is consuming all the available CPU but you can't identify it.

You need to have the system respond better with greater predictability. What should you do? Pick the most correct answer.

A. Remove any scheduled tasks that are executing in the background.

B. Remove any screensaver being used on the desktop.

C. Increase the amount of physical memory available to SQL Server.

D. Increase the performance of the disks on which the database resides.

15. You have Windows XP Professional on your computer at work. Over the past few months, you have noticed a gradual slowing of the performance of your machine and now there is a noticeable delay when you are opening a file. You look at some performance counters and find that the physical disk I/O is high as is the disk queues but memory is not in short supply. What should you do to improve the performance of your machine?

A. Defragment your disk.

B. Convert your disk to FAT32.

C. Convert your disk to NTFS.

D. Increase the size of the paging file.

Answers to Review Questions

1. To answer this question, you need to compare disk I/O to the paging file to the amount of paging the system reports it is doing. The counters would be Disk Reads/Sec to the disk holding the paging file from the PHYSICALDISK Object and Page Reads/Sec from the Memory object. Comparing these two counters and seeing them track together would indicate the majority of your disk I/O to the disk the paging file is on. The counter could also be I/O transfers or Writes/Sec but Reads/Sec should track closer as information on the pagefile could be transferred

APPLY YOUR KNOWLEDGE

into memory and then dropped without actually writing the information back to the pagefile. See "Optimizing and Troubleshooting Memory Performance."

2. Part of the information required by the Task Scheduler's Add a New Task Wizard is the inclusion of a domain/user ID and password under which to run the job. This allows the user to schedule a job with a user ID that has privileges other than the one currently logged in. See "Configuring, Managing, and Troubleshooting the Task Scheduler."

3. The Windows XP Professional operating system uses the paging file as the extension to physical memory. It is used as a backup to allocated virtual memory and to provide a place to contain memory dumps of the system in case of a failure. The paging file is normally 1.5 times larger than physical memory, but that can vary depending on the processes run on the system. The paging file can be moved, added to, or split across a number of disks and controllers to increase performance. See "Optimizing and Troubleshooting Memory Performance."

4. The best indicators are those that show that a queue is forming to access the resource. This is true for other resources (such as disk and network interfaces) as well. If there is a process-bound task running, the Windows XP Professional operating system will allocate all of it to that task. The CPU will appear to be 100% busy. However, it is not a bottleneck until some other task needs it, but the processor is not available because it is being monopolized or is busy doing other administrative tasks such as paging or seeking disk sectors. See "Optimizing and Troubleshooting Processor Performance."

5. Windows XP Professional enables both the physical disk counters and logical disk counters when it starts. This can be verified by running the DISKPERF command, which will show the status of both physical and logical disk counters. To disable the logical disk counters, the command is DISKPERF -NV. After the system is restarted, the logical counters will be unavailable. See "Optimizing and Troubleshooting Disk Performance."

6. The process to modify a hardware profile is to reboot the system under that hardware profile and then, by using an account with administrative privileges on the local computer, start the System application from the Control Panel, access the Device Manager, and disable those devices that are not needed. By copying the original hardware profile, you will be starting with all the devices you have configured on your computer. See "Managing Hardware Profiles."

7. The best approach is a normal backup weekly with daily differential backups. Planning your backup strategy is important and, of course, dependent on how you want to perform any recover actions. In this case, the normal backup will capture all files and the differential backups will capture those that have been modified since the last normal backup. The timing between normal backups will depend on how long you want to maintain those tapes and also how much the system is changing. If the number of files chosen by the differential backup become a significant portion of the normal backup, the differential backup becomes wasteful of both time and tape resources. See "Recovering System State and User Data by Using Windows Backup."

8. The best option is to reboot your computer and press F8 during the boot process to access the Last Known Good Configuration. When a change is made to the Registry to include a new driver, that change is not made permanent until after a successful logon. If you are having problems getting past that point, you still have the last working copy of the Registry to fall back to. Rebooting with the Last Known Good option will throw the changes away and revert to a working environment. See "Troubleshooting System Restoration Using Safe Mode."

Answers to Exam Questions

1. **D**. The new device driver has been installed in the system but the changes are not permanent until a successful boot has completed. No matter how many times you try to get through a boot, if it fails, the last changes made can still be rolled back. The way to recover the last working configuration is to reboot the computer and press F8 to access the Safe Boot menu and select the LastKnownGood configuration option. This will load the working copy of the Registry and the system will restart with the old video driver in place. Using the Recovery Console is primarily for repairing disk damage and file corruption and is not appropriate for reloading the system or manually configuring device drivers. The ERD contains the configuration of the system at the point the ERD was created, and although this would work, it would also wipe out any changes made since that time. See "Troubleshooting System Restoration Using Safe Mode."

2. **B**. Safe Mode starts Windows with a graphical interface and the minimum of device drivers necessary. If the system starts correctly and runs afterward, the drivers for the keyboard, mouse, network, and video adapter are not your problem. From this point, you can disable the new device driver and restart your system normally. You cannot use the Last Known Good Configuration boot option because you have successfully logged on. The new device driver would not be rolled back. The device manager cannot roll the driver back to an earlier version because this is a new device and there is no earlier version. If the system were unstable, you would have to boot using Safe Mode to get access to the System Restore functions. See "Troubleshooting System Restoration Using Safe Mode."

3. **A**. Windows XP runs all 16-bit applications within a single DOS virtual machine (NTVDM). Windows XP does not schedule with the NTVDM, only between the other 32-bit applications. The 16-bit applications must surrender CPU control before another thread within the NTVDM can be scheduled. To put them more on par with the 32-bit applications, you need to assign the 16-bit applications to their own memory space. That will create an NTVDM for each 16-bit application. Upgrading the CPU will not help because the basic problem is scheduling, not CPU power. Any CPU affinity assignments would impact the 32-bit applications and not just the 16-bit applications. Lowering the 32-bit applications' scheduling priority will not keep the 16-bit applications from interfering with one another. See "Working with 16-Bit Applications."

APPLY YOUR KNOWLEDGE

4. **A**. The most appropriate answer is to lower the scheduling priority of your graphics program. By reducing its priority, you will make it more likely for the Windows XP scheduler to choose one of the other concurrently running programs. Upgrading the CPU will not affect performance because it is a scheduling problem and not shortage of CPU power. You could increase the priority of all your other programs but lowering one is more likely to succeed. Changing the affinity would help only if you had more than one CPU. See "CPU Scheduling Priorities."

5. **A**. Task Manager can be used to quickly look at CPU, memory usage, and network activity. If you have some situation that is occurring on your computer, you may not have time to start up Performance monitoring, select counters, and review the scans. Running the application on a more powerful Windows XP machine will tell you whether it needs additional CPU but that requires a lengthy install process. Changing the scheduling priority of your tasks may improve their performance but it will not tell you whether your CPU is fully utilized. See "File System Cache."

6. **B**. The criteria to meet is to recover the data with no more than a day's interruption and with the minimum number of tape swaps. The best way to do this is to perform a regular Normal backup (that backs up all files) and a daily Differential (that backs up all files changed since the last Normal). Daily Incremental backups will also capture all the data files but will require each day's tape to be mounted and scanned to completely restore the system. The Copy backup will copy only the data files selected, which is not guaranteed to be everything you need. The

monthly Normal with an Incremental each week and Daily each day will also back up all your files but will require many more tapes to be mounted and scanned in the event of a reload. See "Backup Types."

7. **B**. System Restore automatically checkpoints your system state every day or when new devices are added or system reloads from backup are performed. In this case, you can pick the checkpoint from yesterday (or the day before) and reset the system to that point. If this is before you installed your application, the Registry will not have any traces of it left. Because this does not reload any files, you will not lose any data files. If, however, you have installed some other applications after the time of the checkpoint, you may have to reinstall them. Reloading the system from your latest backup will also reload your data files and you will probably lose data. Editing the Registry by hand is not recommended as it can cause permanent damage to your installation. After you try an uninstall process, retrying it will either not be possible or not work any better. See "Recovering a System Using System Restore."

8. **B**. This is a case of a problem manifesting itself in many areas of the system. The new network adapter provides greater bandwidth and therefore a larger workload to the processor. The amount of memory it reserves from the nonpaged pool will be greater (because of the faster packet I/O rate) and the increased memory has triggered an increase in paging. These events combine to slow the system down. Adding a faster processor can address some of the symptoms but does not attack the bottleneck directly. Likewise, working with the disks to even out the interrupt rate does not deal with the problem directly. Adding

APPLY YOUR KNOWLEDGE

memory is always a good idea, but the real solution is to replace the network adapter with one that does not interrupt the system as much. See "Monitoring Network Performance."

9. **B**. Your system halts almost immediately in the boot sequence. The only approach you have is to select the Recovery Console as the system to start and disable the device driver. The command to do this (after you log in as administrator) is `disable device-driver`. At that point, you can restart your system normally. You cannot boot up in Safe Mode because the system stops almost immediately and you would not have a chance to select a boot option before the system halted. Similarly, you have to log in to use the device manager to uninstall a device or to use System Restore to return your computer to an earlier state. See "Recovering a System Using System Restore."

10. **A**. Saving the System State on a Windows XP Professional computer includes all boot files, all files protected by Windows File Protection (WFP), the Registry entries, and the COM+ class registrations. When you repair your hardware problem and restore your data files, the system state will allow you to rejoin the domain as if nothing had failed. Just saving the Registry will not be enough to allow you to return your system to full use. The profiles are where users can save their personal configuration settings and will not help return your computer to full use. Running Incremental backups each day will save your data files but will not touch your computer's system settings. See "Saving System State."

11. **B**. The problem here is the incremental growth the database would experience because the workload has changed in the way described. As an expert analyzing the impact an application has on the use of system resources, you must take into account the behavior of the application as well. A database system uses disk space at two levels. The first is as a normal application writing to a system file. The second is as a database system using that system file space as its own complicated storage mechanism that it allocates to tables, indexes, and logs. Both these structures can fragment when many small increments are made over time. Just defragmenting the disk space at the system file level will not gain you the performance you want. Reloading the data will allow you to load the data back into the database tables contiguously for best performance. Replacing the disk drive with a faster rotating one will help reads because a database does its I/O randomly, and reducing the seek time will make the system faster; however, it does not address the root problem, which is a fragmented database structure. Similarly, adding a hardware-enabled RAID-5 disk system for the database will provide multiple disk drives for each read request, which will speed up response, but does not address the root problem. See "Examining and Tuning Disk Performance."

12. **C**. Adding RAM to your system will improve its performance. Your system is constantly paging even a normal workload. When you add your spreadsheet model, the CPU becomes 100% utilized. The load from your spreadsheet model plus the paging workload is consuming all the CPU available. When you shut down your spreadsheet, the CPU usage drops, but the paging rate continues to be high. This indicates your system is short on memory. Increasing the paging file size will actually consume memory (to manage the paging file) and make your situation worse. Changing your network adapter to a more intelligent one

APPLY YOUR KNOWLEDGE

might address interrupts, but not paging. Upgrading your CPU would make everything run better but does not address the primary problem of being short on memory. See "Memory Bottlenecks."

13. **B**. Moving the paging file to E: would improve the performance of this system. When you are running several applications at once, there are four types of I/O being done. The first is to the operating system for system tasks, the second is to the application to run programs, the third is to the application data files for information, and the last is to the paging file to swap memory pages. Even if there is lots of available memory, the system will need to access the paging file to reserve virtual space. In this scenario, three of the four types of I/O are being done on one physical disk. You can't move the operating system or the applications to the E: drive without having to reinstall them. The disk might need defragmenting but that is not the primary problem here. There is no indication that CPU is being used excessively by any application and increasing the paging file is warranted only if the system reports itself low on virtual memory. See "Disk Activity to the Paging File."

14. **B**. The key to the solution here is the timing of the performance problems. In this case, the database performance is unacceptable when the system is running by itself. When you begin to examine performance counters on the display, the performance returns to acceptable levels. The correct answer lies in removing a screensaver that is starting up a length of time after the keyboard and mouse go inactive, and is probably building a complex screen (such as Pipes) and consuming too much CPU in the execution. See "Optimizing and Troubleshooting Processor Performance."

15. **A**. The disk performance counters indicate that the machine is doing a lot of physical I/O without memory being low. This indicates that the disk is fragmented and needs some repair. Changing the format of the drive to either FAT32 or NTFS will not impact where XP has had to place the files. Only a defragmentation will help. The memory counters indicate that memory is not slow, so the I/O is not going to the paging file. There is therefore no reason to resize it. See "Enabling Disk Counters."

Suggested Readings and Resources

1. Bott, Ed and Siechert, Carl. *Microsoft Windows XP Inside Out*. Microsoft Press, 2001.

2. Chaudhry, Irfan and Mueller, John Paul. *Microsoft Windows 2000 Performance Tuning Technical Reference*. Microsoft Press, 2000.

3. Whalen, Edward (Editor), *Microsoft SQL Server 2000 Performance Tuning Technical Reference*. Microsoft Press, 2001.

This chapter will help you prepare for the "Configuring and Troubleshooting the Desktop Environment" section of the exam.

Configure and manage user profiles and desktop settings.

▶ All users logging on to a local computer running Windows XP on a Windows 2000 domain receive a user profile. There are two types of user profiles, local and roaming. As the administrator, you can specify the type of user profile that the user receives and whether the user is able to make changes to the profile that persist after the user logs off.

Configure support for multiple languages or multiple locations.

- **Enable multiple-language support.**
- **Configure multiple-language support for users.**
- **Configure local settings.**
- **Configure Windows XP Professional for multiple locations.**

▶ In multinational organizations, it is common to see the use of different versions (linguistically) of the Windows XP operating system in different countries. To accommodate users who travel between countries, it might be necessary to enable and configure different regional settings that allow a user to easily switch between languages. We will look at how to configure regional options and explain input locales.

CHAPTER 5

Configuring and Troubleshooting the Desktop Environment

Manage applications by using Windows Installer packages.

▶ The Windows Installer service is a component of the IntelliMirror Management Technologies. IntelliMirror can be broken into three core areas: User Data Management, User Settings Management, and Software Installation and Maintenance. The Windows Installer service falls within the Software Installation and Maintenance component of IntelliMirror. Two goals of IntelliMirror and, subsequently, the Windows Installer Service, are to reduce total cost of ownership and provide all users with a truly roaming desktop wherein a user's desktop area and applications are always available. It achieves this lofty goal through a new file type known as an *.msi file* that allows applications to be rolled out to users and computers through application packages. The cost reduction is achieved through rollout benefits and through application of self-repair features that we will examine. By providing a more stable desktop environment to your users for a longer period of time and reducing the time it takes to correct desktop problems, the cost of ownership can be reduced.

▶ The concept of local and roaming profiles has not changed from Windows NT 4.0 Workstation to Windows XP Professional. You need to understand how to configure both local and roaming profiles as well as personal and mandatory profiles.

▶ Know how to analyze and configure a local security policy through the Security Configuration and Analysis snap-in.

▶ Know how to set up and configure a local group policy and the order in which multiple policies get applied.

▶ Be sure you are comfortable with the theory and application of the Windows Installer service in Windows XP Professional and the available options for software installation.

▶ Know the available Internet Explorer options that allow you to configure your Internet settings in Windows XP Professional.

INTRODUCTION

In this chapter, we will explore how to configure and troubleshoot the Windows XP desktop environment. Knowing how to configure the Windows XP desktop environment is critical for systems administrators; this skill will be a key component of their management responsibilities. We will cover creation and configuration of local and roaming profiles, use of Windows Installer, and configuration of desktop and Internet options.

CONFIGURING USER PROFILES

Configure and manage user profiles and desktop settings.

User profiles define a specific user's desktop settings, printer and drive mappings, background color, wallpaper, and display options. A user's personal profile defines his own unique settings on the computer. Your personal local user profile could be compared to your office or cubicle in your department (assuming you are not working in an "open concept" environment). You hang your own pictures on the wall and put your family photos on the desk. Every day, you come in to work and your office is the same as you left it the day before. The way in which you set up your office could be correlated to your profile. It is "local" in the sense that if you went to another geographical location where your company had offices, your office would not be there. Your office does not roam or travel with you. In the context of user profiles, this means that your local user profile is stored on one computer, the computer that it was originally created on by you as a user logging on to that computer. The path to this profile is `C:\Documents and Settings\`*Username*, where *username* is the user's logon name.

User profiles contain all the user-specific settings and are saved in the user's profile directory. If the only location of this directory is the local hard disk in the path `C:\Documents and Settings`, the profile is known as a *local user profile*. In this directory, there are a series of subdirectories, as shown in Figure 5.1, for the user rbogue. As you can see in the figure, some of the subdirectories appear shaded, which denotes a hidden directory. To see these directories, you must change your view settings in Windows Explorer to Show All Files. In addition to the directories in each user's profile folder is a file called NTUSER.DAT. When a user logs on, his configuration settings in his profile directory and the settings in the NTUSER.DAT file are loaded. The user's profile settings found within the user's directory are used to make changes to the desktop and the contents of the NTUSER.DAT are loaded into the HKEY_CURRENT_USER portion of the Registry of the local computer. It is the NTUSER.DAT file that is used to maintain the users' environment preferences during their logon sessions. The settings that combine to make up the NTUSER.DAT file are outlined in Table 5.1. Table 5.2 defines the settings that are included in the user's profile directory.

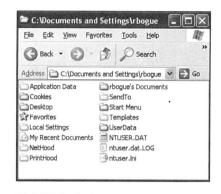

FIGURE 5.1
Local profile directory structure.

TABLE 5.1

NTUSER.DAT SETTINGS

Setting	Definition
Windows Explorer	Any persistent connections and user-defined Windows Explorer settings.
Taskbar	Taskbar settings, personal program groups and associated settings, and program items and associated properties.
Printer Settings	All the user's network printer settings.
Control Panel	Any user settings made in Control Panel.
Accessories	All Windows XP application settings for applications such as Notepad, Paint, Calculator, Clock, and Hyperterminal.
Help Favorites	Any user-defined Help favorites.

TABLE 5.2

USER PROFILE COMPONENTS

Component	Contents
Application Data	Application-specific data. The contents of the data stored in this directory are determined by the software vendor.
Cookies	User preferences and information, most commonly used on the Web to track site visits and areas of interest.

continues

Other Directories   You also might
have a few other directories under the
profile. These directories are not currently documented by Microsoft and
will not be on the exam.

NOTE

TABLE 5.2 | *continued*

USER PROFILE COMPONENTS

Component	*Contents*
Desktop	The desktop layout and content including program shortcuts, files, and folders.
Favorites	Shortcuts to your favorite sites on the Internet or intranet.
Local Settings	Application data, temporary files, and your history of sites on the Web you have visited recently.
My Documents	The default location where you store your data.
My Pictures	A subdirectory of My Documents created to save your personal pictures.
NetHood	Shortcuts to My Network Places.
PrintHood	Printer shortcuts.
Recent	Shortcuts to your most recently accessed documents.
SendTo	Configuration of the SendTo menu. Applications or storage locations to which to send a document (such as Notepad, 3 1/2-inch Floppy, Mail Recipient, and so on).
Start Menu	User's personal Start menu configuration. All common Start Menu shortcuts are found in the All Users profile directory in C:\Documents and Settings\All Users.
Templates	User templates.

User Profile Types

Going back to the example we discussed earlier, if you wanted to have your office environment travel with you between geographical locations, a great deal of work would be involved. Having your user profile travel with you is not as much work. To have your user profile travel with you, it must be changed from a local user profile to a roaming user profile. This would not change your user profile settings; only the location of your user profile would be changed. The user profile would have to be moved to a network share where it could be accessed from anywhere in the network.

This brings us to the two types of profiles that exist in Windows XP: local and roaming. Roaming profiles can be further divided into two subtypes, known as either personal or mandatory. In other words, a roaming profile could be either a roaming personal profile that allows a user to make changes, or a roaming mandatory profile that does not allow a user's changes to be saved. Likewise, a roaming personal profile allows a user to make changes to her profile that travels or roams with her. A mandatory roaming user profile does not allow a user to make changes that persist, but it does roam or travel with the user.

Local User Profiles

A local user profile is created automatically when a user logs on to a computer running Windows XP and is stored locally on that machine. This makes the local user profile available to the user only when logging on to the same machine. A local user profile is configurable by the user, and the changes made to that profile get saved when the user logs off the computer.

Every user who logs on locally to a computer running Windows XP Professional receives a local user profile. Two default profile folders are used in the creation of all new local user profiles and are installed with Windows XP. These two default profile folders are known as the Default User profile and the All Users profile.

The Default Users profile acts as a template for all local user profiles. The contents of the Default User profile are copied to a folder named after the username of the user logging on. Every user's initial local profile begins as a simple copy of the Default User profile. This copy gets stored on the local machine in the path `C:\Documents and Settings\User_name`. This local storage location means that this profile is available only on the machine on which it is stored; therefore, it is a local user profile.

The All Users profile contains settings that apply to every user logging on locally to the computer. These settings are appended to the user's own profile settings. An example of the types of settings contained in the All Users profile are program shortcuts that appear on every user's Start menu. This is different from the Default User profile in that when changes are made to the default user profile after a

> **NOTE**
>
> **Location of Local Profiles** The local profiles location can vary depending on how Windows XP was installed. If you upgraded to Windows XP from Windows NT Workstation 4.0, local profiles will still be located in their NT 4.0 location (`%windir%\profiles\user_name`, where *user_name* represents the user's logon name). If a clean installation of Windows XP Professional or an upgrade from Windows 2000 Professional was performed, the local profiles will be stored in the path `C:\Documents and Settings\user_name`.

user's profile has been created, they won't change the user's profile. However, the All Users profile is merged into the user's profile each time the user logs in so changes made to the All Users profile will be seen by everyone logging into the system.

Step by Step 5.1 demonstrates the automatic creation of a local user profile.

STEP BY STEP

5.1 Creating a Local Profile

1. Log on to a computer running Windows XP Professional as the Administrator. Select Control Panel from the Start menu, then Administrative Tools, and then Computer Management. If Administrative Tools doesn't appear, click the Classic View link on the left side of the Control Panel.

2. Under System Tools, expand Local Users and Groups and right-click the Users folder.

3. Select New User from the context menu. Figure 5.2 shows the New User dialog box.

4. In the User Name box, enter **user1** and remove the check mark from the box titled User Must Change Password at Next Logon. Click Create and click Close. Close Computer Management. User1 is the user account that you will use to log on locally and for which a local user profile will be created automatically.

5. To verify that user1 does not have a local user profile, double-click My Computer, and then double-click the drive that contains the Windows XP Professional system files. Double-click the Documents and Settings folder and verify that no folder for User1 exists. Also confirm that there are folders named Administrator, All Users, and Default User.

6. Close My Computer and log off as Administrator.

FIGURE 5.2
Creating a new local user account in Computer Management.

7. Log on as User1.

8. To see the newly created local user profile, in the Start menu click My Computer, double-click the drive that contains the Windows XP Professional system files, and double-click the Documents and Settings folder. A folder named user1 should now appear. This is the folder that contains the local user profile for user1.

> **NOTE**
>
> **Changing Your View Settings in Windows Explorer** If you do not see the Default User folder, you might have to change your view. The Default User folder is a hidden folder and cannot be seen with the default view settings. Select Tools from the menu bar followed by Folder Options. Select the View tab and select Show Hidden Files and Folders. Click OK, and the Default User folder should appear. If the folder still does not appear, select View on the menu followed by Refresh.

Now we know how local user profiles are created and where they are stored when a user logs on locally to a computer running Windows XP Professional. Unfortunately, having a local profile on one computer doesn't help us if we want to log on to another computer. To solve this dilemma, we need to configure the second type of user profile: a roaming profile.

Roaming User Profiles

A roaming user profile is stored on a network share and can be accessed from any computer across the network. Like local user profiles, roaming user profiles can be either personal or mandatory. We will start our discussion by looking at the concept of a roaming profile and then looking at the difference in both personal and mandatory profiles.

A roaming user profile is very similar to a local user profile; the difference is that a roaming user profile can be accessed from any computer on the network. If changes to the profile are permitted, they are saved to a network location as opposed to the local hard disk when the user logs off, and are applied again when the user logs back on by accessing the network location.

To configure a roaming user profile, we must edit the user's properties and enter the path to the network share that contains the user's profile. Step by Step 5.2 demonstrates how to enable a roaming user profile.

STEP BY STEP

5.2 Creating a Roaming User Profile

1. Log on as Administrator to the local machine.

2. To enable access to a roaming profile, a network share must exist in which to store the profiles. To create a network share, from the Start menu click My Computer, and double-click the C: drive. From the menu bar, select File, New Folder. Enter Profiles as the name of the new folder and press Enter. Right-click the Profiles folder and select Sharing. Select Share This Folder and in the Share Name box, Profiles will appear. Click OK to create the network share. Close My Computer.

3. From the Start menu, click Control Panel. Double-click Administrative Tools and double-click Computer Management. If Administrative Tools doesn't appear, click the Classic view link on the left side of the window.

4. Expand System Tools and Expand Local Users and Groups. Right-click the Users folder and select New User. In the User Name box, enter **user1**. Clear the check mark in the box titled User Must Change Password at Next Logon, and click Create, followed by Close.

5. Click the Users folder. In the list of users on the right side, double-click user1. The user1 Properties dialog box appears. Select the Profile tab, as shown in Figure 5.3. In the Profile Path box, type the Universal Naming Convention (UNC) path to the profiles share on your computer. Enter *computer_name**profiles**%username%* (where *computer_name* is the name of your computer, *profiles* is the name of the network share you created in step 2, and *%username%* is a variable that will be replaced with the user's logon name). Click OK and close Computer Management.

IN THE FIELD

USING ENVIRONMENT VARIABLES

The variable *%username%* is an environment variable that tells the operating system to replace that variable with the user account ID of a particular user. Using the variable in this situation will create a subdirectory in the profiles network share named user1 (the user's logon name) and store user1's roaming profile within that folder. An alternative would be to enter **computer_name\profiles\user1** but this is more likely to result in spelling or typing mistakes.

This environment variable can be especially useful when creating multiple-user accounts. A template account can be created by the administrator that is configured with all the settings required by all the users in a particular department, perhaps Sales, and named #SalesTemplate. The reason for the "#" symbol is that it will be listed at the top of your list of users, making it easier to find in Active Directory Users and Computers. This template account can then be set to use the profile path \\computername\profiles\%username%. When the template account is copied, the variable is renamed to that of the username and a roaming profile is automatically configured. One restriction to be aware of is that you can copy only in Active Directory Users and Computers, so this applies only to domain user accounts.

FIGURE 5.3
The user1 Properties dialog box.

6. Log off as administrator and log on as user1.

7. From the start menu, click My Computer, double-click the drive that contains the Profiles network share, and double-click the Profiles shared folder. You should see a folder named user1. This folder will contain user1's roaming personal profile. If you double-click the user1 folder, it will currently be empty. The reason for that is that user1 must log off before the profile is saved to the network share. To prove this, log off user1.

8. Log on again as user1. From the Start menu, click My Computer, double-click the drive containing the Profiles shared folder, and double-click the Profiles shared folder. Double-click the user1 folder. The user2 folder now contains the contents of user1's roaming profile. This roaming profile gets updated with the changes user1 makes during his current session when he logs off.

Personal User Profiles

Roaming personal user profiles can be configured on a number of individual Windows XP Professional computers and set to direct the user to a network share, but this would be a very tedious and highly inefficient process. The recommended approach would be to configure a domain environment and create user accounts in the domain. Then, configure the profile path of each user account to point to the shared network location. Step by Step 5.3 walks through an alternative method of changing a user's profile from local to roaming that involves using the User Profiles tab in the System applet in Control Panel.

STEP BY STEP

5.3 Changing a Local User Profile to a Roaming User Profile Through the System Applet in Control Panel

We will start this step by step by creating a local user account and local profile by logging on as the newly created user.

1. Log on as Administrator.

2. From the Start menu, select Control Panel, then Administrative Tools, and finally Computer Management. If you don't see Administrative Tools, click the Classic view link on the left side. Expand Local Users and Computers and right-click the Users folder.

3. Select New User from the Context menu and enter the username Bill. Clear the check mark next to User Must Change Password at Next Logon and click Create, followed by Close.

4. Close Computer Management and log off.

5. Log on as Bill with a blank password. This will create the local user profile for the user Bill.

6. Log off and log back on as Administrator.

7. Open Control Panel and double-click the System applet. Select the advanced tab, click the Settings button in the User Profiles section, and select the user Bill.

8. With the user Bill selected, click the Copy To button in the bottom-right corner of the dialog box.

9. In the Copy To dialog box, enter the path to the network location where your roaming profiles are to be stored. Sticking with the location we used in Step by Step 5.2, enter `\\`*`computername`*`\profiles\`*`%username%`* in the Copy Profile To box.

10. In the Permitted to Use section of the Copy To dialog box, be sure that the user Bill is listed. The Change button allows you to change the user or group of users permitted to use this profile. In this case, we want only Bill to use it, so we will leave it as is. Changing who could use the profile will change the NTFS permissions on the directory to which we have selected to copy this profile if the directory is located on an NTFS volume or partition.

11. At this point, we have changed the location of the local user profile from `C:\Documents and Settings\Bill` to the shared network path of `\\computername\profiles\Bill` but the profile is still not a roaming profile. To configure it as a roaming profile, we must complete the remaining steps.

12. Open Computer Management and expand Local Users and Computers. Click the Users folder, and then double-click the Bill user.

13. The Bill Properties dialog box appears. Select the Profile tab and in the Profile Path box enter the path to the network share where the profile has been copied to (`\\computername\profiles\Bill`) and click OK.

14. Close Computer Management. Log off as Administrator. Log on as Bill. This will force the change from a local user profile to a roaming user profile to occur. Log off as Bill.

continues

continued

15. Log on as Administrator to confirm the change has taken place.

16. In Control Panel, double-click the System applet and select the User Profiles Tab. The Bill profile should now appear under the Type column as Roaming, not Local any longer.

Mandatory User Profiles

A roaming mandatory user profile travels with the user regardless of the computer the user is logging on to. Any changes that the user makes during their logon session do not get saved when they log off. Mandatory roaming user profiles are useful in environments where you want a group of users to always have the same profile regardless of the computer they log on to. An example of this might be for bank tellers. Suppose a bank has 14 different teller windows, each equipped with a computer, and you would like every teller to get the same settings regardless of at which teller window they are working. To accomplish this, you could create a mandatory roaming user profile and configure each of your teller accounts to use that profile.

Think of a mandatory profile as a hotel room. While you are checked into the hotel, you can hang your own pictures on the wall and change the layout of the room, but when you check out, the staff will change everything back to the way it was when you originally checked in. In this case, the changes you made do not persist after you check out, or log off, in the case of a mandatory profile.

Creating a roaming mandatory user profile is not very different from creating a roaming personal user profile except we must ensure that any changes the user makes to the profile are not saved. The key to not allowing the user to maintain changes is to rename the NTUSER.DAT file to NTUSER.MAN. The NTUSER.DAT file can be found in the user's profile folder on the server and renamed from there.

Step by Step 5.4 walks you through the process of changing user2's roaming personal profile to a roaming mandatory profile.

STEP BY STEP

5.4 Changing a Roaming Personal User Profile to a Roaming Mandatory User Profile

1. Log on as Administrator. From the Start menu, click My Computer, and double-click the drive on which the Profiles shared folder is located. Double-click the profiles shared folder and double-click the user2 folder.

2. Rename the file NTUSER.DAT to NTUSER.MAN and close My Computer.

3. Log off as Administrator and log on as user2. Right-click the desktop and select Properties from the context menu. On the Appearance tab, click the Advanced button. Select Black in the Color 1 drop-down, as shown in Figure 5.4, and click OK.

4. Log off and log back on as user2.

5. When you log back on, the desktop color is the default, teal, rather than black, confirming that you have configured a roaming mandatory user profile for user2.

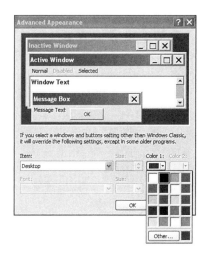

FIGURE 5.4
Advanced Appearance dialog box.

Before we move on, we should discuss one of the potential troubleshooting issues with mandatory profiles that might arise. When configuring a roaming mandatory profile, the user's properties must be changed to indicate the network share in which the profile is located. This folder should not include an extension (such as *computername**profiles*\Bill.man) because this will prevent the user from logging on. Be careful with mandatory profiles and do not name folders with extensions.

In this section, we have learned about the two types of user profiles: local and roaming. We discussed the process that the operating system uses to create a local user profile from the Default User and All Users profiles. We have also learned the two types of roaming profiles—personal and mandatory—and walked through how to create all types. In the next section, we will look at what is involved in configuring your desktop environment.

The facts on profiles can be summarized as follows:

▶ The two types of profiles are local and roaming. Only the roaming profile can be mandatory.

▶ Changes made during a logon session to a mandatory profile are not saved.

▶ Changes made during a logon session to a personal profile are saved.

▶ Local profiles are available only on the computer on which they are stored.

▶ Roaming profiles are stored on a shared network location, making them available from anywhere across the network.

CONFIGURING THE DESKTOP ENVIRONMENT

Configure and manage user profiles and desktop settings.

Understanding that not all users are the same is the first step in configuring the desktop environment. Some of the users that we as administrators are responsible for supporting have special needs. The Windows XP operating system offers us a number of options to address the needs of our users.

In this section, we will look at the available regional and accessibility options in Windows XP Professional.

Video Settings

One of the critical desktop settings is the video display size and number of colors. It's critical not only because of its impact on the users' experience but also because of the potential damage that can be done by incorrect configuration.

Monitors are designed so that they can accept a specific set of frequencies and can be driven at a specific set of resolutions. Video cards typically have a much broader range of settings that they can reproduce. Failing to select a video resolution and refresh rate that your monitor can handle can eventually damage the monitor.

To protect against this, Windows XP performs a confirmation prompt after making a change to either resolution or refresh rate to ensure that you can still read the display. If you accidentally set a video resolution or refresh rate that your monitor does not support and your display becomes garbled, or the monitor makes a high-pitched screeching sound, you should turn the monitor off immediately and press the Escape key. Turning the monitor off helps prevent damage and pressing the Escape key signals Windows XP that you need to return to the previous configuration. You can turn the monitor back on after 20 seconds or so.

The timeout on the window asking to confirm the settings is 15 seconds, so even if you don't get the Escape key pressed, the video settings should have returned to their previous settings. However, if the monitor starts screeching again, you should turn the monitor off, physically power the computer down, and then reboot, selecting Last Known Good Configuration from the boot options menu.

Let's walk through the process of changing a video resolution.

STEP BY STEP

5.5 Changing the Video Display Properties

1. Right mouse-click the desktop and select Properties.

2. Click the setting tab. You should now see a dialog box similar to Figure 5.5.

3. Select the new screen resolution that you want to try.

4. Click the Apply button. You should (hopefully) see a dialog box such as the one shown in Figure 5.6 asking you to confirm your settings. Respond Yes to keep the new settings.

continues

FIGURE 5.5
Video Settings look straightforward.

FIGURE 5.6
Windows XP always confirms a resolution setting.

continued

5. Change the color quality to something other than its current setting (for example, 256 colors) and click the Apply button again. You should again see a dialog box similar to the one shown in Figure 5.6.

6. Click the Advanced button.

7. Click the Monitor tab.

8. Select a new screen refresh rate. Click the Apply button.

9. Answer Yes to accept the new setting if you can see the confirmation dialog box as shown in Figure 5.6, or press the Escape key if you cannot see the confirmation dialog box.

10. Click OK to exit the monitor and video card properties dialog box.

11. Click OK to exit the Display properties dialog box.

Changing the video display settings isn't complicated, but it's important that you make sure you can read the confirmation dialog box.

Configuring Regional Options

Configure support for multiple languages or multiple locations.

With the globalization of the world economy, the requirements for business travel and language diversity are also increasing. More than ever before, we need to be able to access documents in multiple languages. Windows XP offers users the ability to switch between various regional settings to change the display format of numerical data or the keyboard layout.

The Regional Options applet in Control Panel allows you to switch between units of measurement, or the way the time, date, currency amounts, and numbers with decimals or fractions are displayed to the user. It also allows you to add in the support for multiple input locals so that a user visiting a United States office from your Paris office could switch to the French keyboard layout from the current default U.S. keyboard layout. Step by Step 5.6 walks you through the setup of multiple input locales in the Regional Options utility.

STEP BY STEP

5.6 Configuring Multiple Input Locales

1. Log on as Administrator.

2. From the Start menu, select Control Panel. From the Control Panel, double-click the Regional and Language Options icon. If you don't see the Regional and Languages Options icon, click the Classic view on the left side of the Control Panel.

3. Click the Languages tab to select it.

4. Click the Details button to open the Text Services and Input Languages dialog box.

5. Click the Add button in the Installed Input Locales section of the dialog box. From the Input Locale drop-down list, select the locale you would like to add and the keyboard layout and click OK. Repeat this step until you have added all the input locales that you require.

6. Select one of the input locales to be the default by selecting it in the drop-down list as shown in Figure 5.7. Click the OK button to return to the Regional and Language options and OK again to close the Regional and Language options.

7. From the Start menu, select All Programs, Accessories, and finally Wordpad. Type the sentence **My dog is fast.** and press Enter to start a new line of text. Hold down the left Alt key on the keyboard and press Shift, and then type the same sentence again.

You should notice that the text is different. This is because you have switched between the two input locales with the Alt+Shift key sequence. Switching between input locales changes the keyboard layout to the format associated with that language.

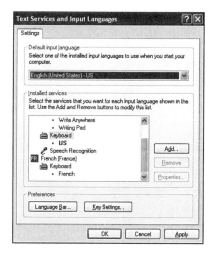

FIGURE 5.7
Establishing a default locale.

This exercise was meant to demonstrate to you how easy it is within the Windows XP desktop to switch between two different input locales in the very same document.

Another component of the Windows XP desktop environment is the support for accessibility options, which we will explore next.

Configuring Accessibility Options

Accessibility options can be configured within Windows XP to assist users with special needs or disabilities and help those users to more effectively interact with the operating system. Table 5.3 outlines the accessibility options available in Windows XP.

TABLE 5.3

ACCESSIBILITY OPTIONS

Tool	*Function*
StickyKeys	Allows you to press key sequences such as Ctrl, Alt+Del individually in sequential order instead of all at once for users with limited hand dexterity.
FilterKeys	Alerts Windows XP to ignore brief or repeated keystrokes.
ToggleKeys	Allows you to configure sounds for certain locking keys such as Caps Lock, Num Lock, and Scroll Lock.
SoundSentry	Provides visual warnings when your system makes a sound for the hearing impaired.
ShowSounds	Displays captions for speech and sound made by your applications.
High Contrast	Configures Windows XP to use colors and fonts designed for easier reading.
MouseKeys	Allows the mouse pointer to be controlled by the numeric keypad.
SerialKey Devices	Allows support for serial key devices.

Step by Step 5.7 walks through how to configure and enable FilterKeys.

STEP BY STEP

5.7 Configuring and Enabling FilterKeys Options

1. From the Start menu, click Control Panel. From the Control Panel, double-click Accessibility Options.

2. To enable FilterKeys, place a check mark in the box to the left of Use FilterKeys. Click Apply. You should notice the FilterKeys icon appear in the bottom-right corner of the screen in the System Tray.

3. To change the settings of the FilterKeys, click the Settings button in the FilterKeys section of the dialog box. Make your changes and click OK when you are finished.

In addition to the accessibility options enabled through Control Panel, Windows XP also ships with accessibility programs. The accessibility programs can be found in the Accessories area on the Start menu. These programs are described in Table 5.4.

TABLE 5.4

ACCESSIBILITY PROGRAMS

Program	Function
Accessibility Wizard	A wizard that walks you through setting Accessibility options.
Magnifier	Allows a portion of the screen to be magnified for easier viewing.
Narrator	Reads the contents of the screen aloud, assisting people with limited vision or vision impairment.
On-Screen Keyboard	Allows users the ability to type onscreen with a pointing device.
Utility Manager	Enables administrative users to define the startup properties of accessibility programs and to start and stop individual accessibility programs.

The accessibility options included with Windows XP are not all-encompassing; many users with special needs will require additional applications that address their special requirements. To find out more about available accessibility programs, visit the Microsoft Accessibility section of the Microsoft Web site at `http://www.microsoft.com/enable`. Microsoft also has a catalog of accessibility aids that can be used with the Windows operating system available by phone at 1-800-426-9400, via fax-back at 1-800-727-3351, or by writing Microsoft Sales Information Center, One Microsoft Way, Redmond, Washington 98052-6393.

Now that we have examined how to configure and optimize the Windows XP desktop to meet our regional and accessibility requirements, we will explore the management and configuration of applications. The Windows XP operating system will rarely be configured without applications. Normally, users will require that multiple applications be installed on the computer to allow them to do their work. In the next section, we will look at the options available to install and configure applications on Windows XP Professional.

Program Compatibility Options

New to Windows XP is a feature that attempts to allow even misbehaved programs to function without problems in Windows XP. Icons in the Start menu can have a set of compatibility options applied to them, which allow programs to operate in ways that are similar to earlier versions of Windows.

If you have a program that is not responding correctly, open the Start menu and right-click the icon of the errant application. This will display the properties for the application icon. Select the Compatibility tab to display the Windows compatibility options.

The first option is to run the application in a specific compatibility mode. Modes are available for Windows 95, Windows 98/Me, Windows NT 4.0 (Service Pack 5), and Windows 2000. These settings are designed to closely emulate the operating environment of each of these operating systems.

Additionally, you can set display compatibility options that limit the appearance of the display in ways that may help the application run better. You have options for restricting the colors to 256, forcing a 640×480 screen size, or perhaps more helpfully, disabling visual themes.

If you don't want to set these options manually, you can run the Program Compatibility Wizard. It can be found in the Start menu under All Programs, Accessories.

INSTALLING AND CONFIGURING APPLICATIONS

Manage applications by using Windows Installer packages.

The ongoing management and administration involved with desktop applications is generally one of the highest contributors to the cost of ownership of desktop computers. Microsoft has realized this and integrated technologies into the Windows XP operating system to reduce these associated costs.

The Windows XP operating system offers a number of options to install and configure applications on computers running Windows XP Professional. One of the options available to install applications is the Add/Remove Programs utility in Control Panel. This utility is not new to Windows operating systems and exists in many of Microsoft's previous GUI-based operating systems. Another option that was new to Windows 2000 is the Windows Installer service. The Windows Installer service allows application packages to be assigned or published to users or computers running Windows 2000 or Windows XP and offers some additional features that help reduce total cost of ownership.

There are essentially two approaches to installing programs. The first is to use the Add/Remove Programs applet in the Control Panel. The second is to use the installation program included with the application.

Add or Remove Programs

The Add or Remove Programs utility found in the Control Panel in Windows XP uses the Windows Installer service to simplify the installation, removal, configuration, and repair of applications.

Step by Step 5.8 walks through the process of removing an installed application.

STEP BY STEP

5.8 Removing an Installed Application Through Add/Remove Programs

1. From the Start menu, click Control Panel.

2. Double-click the Add or Remove Programs icon.

3. Select the program that you would like to remove. Examine the Size and Last Used On properties of the application.

4. Click the Remove button.

5. Respond to any application-specific questions pertaining to the removal.

Add or Remove Programs has been enhanced in Windows XP and now includes three sections, as shown in Figure 5.8.

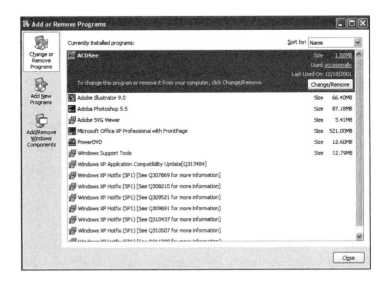

FIGURE 5.8
The Add or Remove Programs applet.

The Change or Remove Programs section lists all of your currently installed programs, listed by name, and indicates their respective size. By clicking one of the installed applications, as shown in Figure 5.6, you receive more information about the application and are able to change or remove it. Other very useful information from an administrative perspective includes the date when the application was last used. This can be helpful when deciding on an application to remove if disk space is filling up. If you ask a user which applications he would like removed, he might say, "Not that one—I use it all the time." This is a great way of seeing whether that statement is entirely true.

Additionally, if you would like to sort the installed applications by size or last used, you can use the Sort By option at the top-left corner of the Add/Remove Programs dialog box.

The second section is Add New Programs, which allows you to install an application from floppy disk, CD, the hard drive, or across the network. It also allows you to activate a Windows Update.

Windows Update is a Web extension to the operating system that allows you to connect to the Microsoft Web site and download critical or optional updates, fixes, and device drivers. Clicking the Windows Update button launches Internet Explorer and takes you to `http://windowsupdate.microsoft.com`. Step by Step 5.9 demonstrates how to perform a Windows Update.

This step-by-step tutorial will require Internet access in order to work.

STEP BY STEP

5.9 Performing a Windows Update

1. From the Start menu, click Control Panel.

2. Double-click the Add or Remove Programs applet and select Add New Programs, and then click the Windows Update button.

3. Internet Explorer will launch and take you to the Windows Update site at Microsoft.

4. Click the Scan for Updates link. Select the update(s) that are of interest to you and proceed by clicking the Download link at the top of the right frame.

> **NOTE**
> **Links** Microsoft periodically changes the appearance of all its Web sites. The name or location of the correct link might change by the time you read this.

N O T E

Disabling Windows Update   As the network or systems administrator in a corporate setting, you might not want your users to have the ability to access Windows Update. It is possible to disable access to the Windows Update for all users. To do this, at the Run command type `mmc`, and from the Console menu select Add/Remove Snap-In. Click Add, and choose Group Policy from the list of available snap-ins. Click Add again, followed by Finish, Close, and OK. Expand the Local Computer Policy, then expand User Configuration, Administrative Tools, and select the Start Menu & Taskbar folder. Double-click the Disable and Remove Links to Windows Update and select the Enabled option. Click OK, and close the mmc. Select No to save the console settings when prompted. The preceding outlined steps may differ slightly depending on the operating system that you are working with (for example, Server or Professional).

It is also possible to disable the use of Windows Update for users in a domain by configuring a Group Policy with Active Directory Users and Computers.

FIGURE 5.9
Context menu of an .msi (Windows Installer) file.

The third section to Add/Remove Programs is Add/Remove Windows Components. This is where new or additional services and accessories such as games are added or removed. Previously, in Windows NT 4.0, services were added and removed through the Network icon in Control Panel and Accessories were added or removed through Add/Remove Programs.

Windows Installer

The Windows Installer service does not exist in isolation. With the introduction of the Windows Installer service comes Windows Installer files, which end with the extensions .msi and .mst. All applications and service packs released from Microsoft will now be released with Windows Installer files.

An example of a Windows Installer file can be found in the Windows\System32 directory and is called *webfldrs.msi*. This Windows Installer file gets added to the system32 directory during the installation of Windows XP Professional and is used to install/reinstall the Web folders' functionality. Some of the functionality provided by Windows Installer files can be seen by right-clicking the file to bring up the context menu seen in Figure 5.9.

The context menu includes a number of choices, including Install, Repair, and Uninstall. These options do not require a great deal of additional explanation except to note that total cost of ownership can be greatly reduced by their use. This is particularly true of the Repair option. The Repair option is designed to eliminate the need for a technical support call at the user's desktop. If a user accidentally or intentionally deletes a system file or executable associated with an application and then tries to launch that application, with any previous Windows operating system, the application will fail. Now in Windows XP, by right-clicking the .msi file that was used to install the application and selecting Repair, the required system files are reinstalled and the application can launch without error.

Support for the Windows Installer service and Windows Installer files can also be incorporated into Windows 9x and Windows NT 4.0 by downloading and installing the Platform SDK or the Core SDK and the Windows Installer SDK available at `http://www.microsoft.com/msdownload/platformsdk/sdkupdate`.

In a corporate environment with an Active Directory domain structure, it is possible to roll out software through Windows Installer packages to either users or computers. Windows Installer packages can be either assigned or published. The configuration of Group Policy is broken into two different configurations much like System Policy in Windows NT 4.0: User Configuration and Computer Configuration. The creation of the Windows Installer packages, although important, will not be a focus of this exam, but an understanding of how the packages could affect the Windows XP Professional desktop environment is important, so that is where we will focus our attention.

Assigning Windows Installer Packages

A Windows Installer package file can be assigned to either a user or a computer. When a package is assigned to a user, the application's shortcuts will be created on the Start menu and desktop the next time the user logs on. The application is not installed at logon—only the shortcuts are created and the file associations made within the Registry. The application is installed the first time the user starts the application via the shortcuts or by double-clicking a file with an extension associated with the assigned application. This allows a user's applications to roam with the user in the same way a user's profile can roam with the user. This gives the user access to the applications they require regardless of the computer running Windows 2000 that they log on to, but installs the application only if the user needs to work with it.

A Windows Installer package can also be assigned to a computer. Assigning a package to a computer launches the installation of the application the next time the computer is turned on. This is a useful approach if all users of that computer require the assigned application. This ensures that the application is available to all users of the computer and is not tied to a specific user.

The assignment of applications through Windows Installer packages has an additional benefit: resilience through self-repair. If a system file or executable is accidentally or maliciously deleted but was originally assigned to either a user or computer, it will repair itself the next time it is started. The application will use the Windows Installer service to reconnect to the original distribution point and copy the required files back to the computer running Windows XP Professional and reinstall them. Following that, the application will launch and a technical support call can be averted.

Publishing Windows Installer Packages

Windows Installer packages can also be published, but the publishing support is limited to users only. Publishing a Windows Installer package to a user makes that application available through Add or Remove Programs the next time the user logs on. The application can be installed one of two ways when it is published to a user. The first way involves the user installing the application through Add or Remove Programs. The second way is through document invocation. By double-clicking a file with an extension that is associated with the published application, the installation will begin.

Windows Installer packages cannot be published to a computer. The reason for this is that a computer will never invoke an application nor will a computer ever know to install an application through Add or Remove Programs.

> **WARNING**
>
> **Planning and Testing When Using Windows Installer** Caution and testing should be the rule of thumb with Windows Installer files and the Windows Installer service. Although it is not well documented, Windows Installer files that were installed manually have been known to be resilient in some cases. It appears that the MSI installs remember the original installation location and try to go back to that location for self-repair. Often, the location will no longer contain the installation files, particularly in the case of a CD drive where the CD has been removed, but the point is that it does seem to try. Planning and testing the use of Windows Installer files are highly recommended. It is also recommended that you install from a fault-tolerant Distributed File System (DFS) share when possible so you don't need to worry about providing media.

Publishing ZAP Files

An alternative to publishing Windows Installer files is to use .zap files. A .zap file is a text file that can be read and used to execute software installation. These files come with some restrictions and offer a lot less functionality than Windows Installer files, so it should be stressed that the use of Windows Installer files is recommended whenever possible.

The limitations of .zap files include the following:

◆ .zap files can only be published. They cannot be assigned to users or computers.

◆ .zap files offer no resiliency and do not attempt to repair themselves if files are deleted or become corrupted.

◆ The majority of .zap files will require user intervention during the installation.

◆ .zap files do not have the capability to install with elevated privileges, which means that users must have the ability to install software on their local computers.

Any text editor can be used to create a .zap file. Each file has two primary sections: the Application section and the File Extensions section.

The Application section includes information that will be displayed to users in Add or Remove Programs and must include two tags: FriendlyName and SetupCommand. The Application section is mandatory.

The FriendlyName tag is the name that will be used in Add or Remove Programs.

The SetupCommand tag is the name of the executable or command to install the application. The path to this command should be relative to the .zap file itself, meaning that if the setup command is in the same folder as the .zap file, only the name of the setup file needs to be entered.

The second section of the .zap file is the File Extensions section. This section is used to associate the application with file extensions saved in Active Directory. This section is optional. A sample .zap file looks something like the following:

```
[Application]
FriendlyName = Microsoft Office 2000
SetupCommand = setup.exe /unattend
[Ext]
DOC=
DOT=
```

CHAPTER SUMMARY

KEY TERMS

- Accessibility options
- Group policy
- Local profile
- Roaming profile
- Mandatory profile
- Windows Installer
- IP Security

Summarized briefly, this chapter covered the following main points:

◆ **Understanding Profiles**—This section defined the two types of profiles (local and roaming) and the differences between personal and mandatory profiles.

◆ **Understanding the Windows Installer Service**—This new service in Windows 2000 helps to reduce the total cost of ownership through both application self-repair and making applications available to users from any Windows 2000 computer they log on to.

◆ **Configuring the Desktop**—We broke this section into local security policy and local group policy and examined the similarities and differences between the two. We also discussed the application of local policy and the order in which it is applied—first.

◆ **Configuring Internet Options**—This section looked at the options available to us in Internet Explorer and how to configure the home page, proxy settings, temporary Internet file size and location, and the setting of security zones.

APPLY YOUR KNOWLEDGE

Exercises

5.1 Remove a Program

In this exercise, you've run out of disk space. To recover some space until your request for a new hard drive is approved, you've decided to remove your least-used programs.

Estimated Time: 10 minutes

1. From the Start menu, select Control Panel.

2. Double-click the Add or Remove Programs applet.

3. Click each program in the installed programs list looking at Used and Last Used On, as well as the size of the application to determine which application is the least used and the largest in size.

4. Press the Change/Remove button.

5. Follow the program-specific instructions for removing the program.

5.2 Set Windows 95 Compatibility for a Program

In this exercise, you have an application that does not run well with Windows XP. It worked fine on Windows 95. It is your job to try to get the application to run on Windows XP. You've contacted the vendor who's sending you an updated application, but it won't arrive until next week.

Estimated Time: 10 minutes

1. From the Start menu, right-click the program that is having trouble. (You can select any non–Windows XP–included program.)

2. Click the Compatibility tab.

3. Check the Run This Program in Compatibility Mode For check box and select Windows 95 from the drop-down list.

4. Click the check box to Disable Visual Themes.

5. Click the OK button to save the compatibility changes.

Review Questions

1. What are the two different types of user profiles?

2. What feature allows Windows Installer to dynamically install applications?

3. What are the two sections of a .zap file?

4. What is the purpose of accessibility options?

Exam Questions

1. Which solution is best suited to an environment where you need to control the changes that are made to a profile?

   A. Mandatory profiles

   B. Group policies

   C. Accessibility options

   D. Mandatory profiles and group policies

2. You need to develop a standard desktop operating environment for your data entry staff. They all do the same data entry into the same system. There is no need for them to be able to change their environment. In fact, the company doesn't want them to change their environment at all. What should you use?

A. Mandatory profiles

B. Group policies

C. Accessibility options

D. Mandatory profiles and group policies

3. Your environment has three general-purpose workstations that are shared among 200 employees and used as kiosk computers for customizing employee health benefits. Each employee needs access to a workstation for only a short period of time, and doesn't necessarily always use the same one. Which setup is best?

   A. Local user profiles on each machine

   B. Roaming profiles on the network

   C. Mandatory profiles on the network

   D. Group policies and roaming profiles on the network

4. The display of numbers, dates, and times is strange. You notice that commas and periods are transposed, and that other punctuation appears to be transposed. What is the most likely cause?

   A. Your display font is corrupted; restart the computer.

   B. Your display font is corrupted; reinstall the font.

   C. Your regional options are not correct.

   D. You have the wrong time zone set in the Time/Date applet.

5. You're running out of hard disk space and need to generate space quickly. What should you do?

A. Delete old Word documents that you don't need anymore.

B. Go write a purchase order to get a new, larger, hard drive.

C. Remove unneeded applications by using the Add/Remove Programs applet.

D. Clear the event logs.

6. You need to remove a program that you installed. The application uses the Windows Installer technology. What is the best way to remove the program?

   A. Delete the directory in which the program was installed.

   B. Reinstall Windows XP Professional.

   C. Run the Add or Remove Programs applet.

   D. Run the third-party uninstallation program.

7. You tried changing the resolution and color depth of your display and now your monitor is making a very nasty screech. What should you do?

   A. Reboot the PC immediately.

   B. Reinstall Windows XP Professional.

   C. Turn off the monitor and wait 20 seconds.

   D. Press Ctrl+Alt+Del.

8. Your accounting department is running an old version of their accounting software that has not been tested for use with Windows XP. It was running fine with Windows 98 on their workstations before. They are reporting that they sometimes have some screen corruption (garbage) when running the application. You've requested an updated

APPLY YOUR KNOWLEDGE

version of the software from the vendor. What else should you do?

A. Uninstall Windows XP and wait for the updated version of the program.

B. Create a Microsoft Installer (MSI) package for the file and reinstall it to all the Windows XP workstations.

C. Use the compatibility options to run the program in Windows 98 compatibility mode.

D. Use the compatibility options to run the program in 256 colors.

9. Your company has just hired a new employee whose vision is impaired to the point where he is legally blind even with glasses. You've given him a 20-inch monitor but he is still having trouble reading the company's documents on the computer screen. What should you do?

A. Buy a serial input device and enable serial input from Accessibility Options.

B. Turn on the narrator service.

C. Turn on the magnifier service.

D. Turn on the onscreen keyboard.

10. You have a user who logs in to several computers. However, changes that he makes on these computers don't seem to stick. What is the most likely reason for this?

A. The user has a local profile.

B. The user has a mandatory profile.

C. The group policies are set to disallow changes.

D. The user has selected the Don't Save Changes at Exit check box.

11. Joe, the president of your company, normally uses his notebook to log on to the network, but occasionally he logs in from the plant floor. He keeps complaining that his desktop isn't the same on the plant floor as it is on his notebook. What is the most likely cause?

A. The machine on the plant floor is configured for local profiles.

B. The machine on the plant floor is configured for roaming profiles.

C. Joe is configured for local profiles.

D. Joe is configured for roaming profiles.

12. Your shop floor is very noisy but your primary software vendor has provided software that rings a bell when there's a problem. However, there's no visual identification that there's a problem from the main screen that the employees use. What action should you take to improve the chances that they will notice the bell?

A. Install louder speakers.

B. Turn the volume control all the way up in the Sounds and Multimedia applet.

C. Turn on Sound Sentry.

D. Turn on Show Sounds.

13. You need to have the ability to enter documents in multiple languages but there's no locale item on the language bar. What are the potential causes? (Choose two.)

A. The program you're using to enter the information doesn't support input locales.

B. The input locales feature isn't installed.

C. There is only one input locale installed.

D. Display of the icon isn't enabled.

APPLY YOUR KNOWLEDGE

Answers to Review Questions

1. The two different types of user profiles are local and roaming. Roaming profiles can be further divided into either personal (which allow the users' changes to be saved) or mandatory (which do not save the users' changes). See the section "User Profile Types."

2. Advertising an application allows it to be installed automatically and with elevated privileges by the Windows Installer Service. An application can be assigned to either a user or a computer. Assigning an application to a user creates the program shortcuts and file associations in the Registry but does not install the application until it is invoked. Assigning an application to a computer forces the install to take place at the next reboot. See the section "Assigning Windows Installer Packages."

3. The two sections of a .zap file are the Application section and the File Extensions sections. The Application section is mandatory within a .zap file but the File Extensions section is not. See the section "Publishing ZAP Files."

4. The purpose of accessibility options is to make Windows XP Professional usable to a wider audience. In addition to the accessibility features included with the operating system, there are a number of additional add-on programs and products to assist people with disabilities. See the section "Configuring Accessibility Options."

Answers to Exam Questions

1. **B**. The solution best suited to an environment in which you need to control the changes that are made to a profile is a group policy. Group policy would allow you to enforce the level of control you require. Mandatory profiles allow control of an environment, but only absolute control, and only prevent changes from being saved. Accessibility options are methods for improving a user's ability to use the operating system and are not a valid option in this case. The use of mandatory profiles in conjunction with group policies is also not an option; you don't want to prevent profile changes—only limit them. See the sections "Mandatory User Profiles" and "Implementing Local Group Policy."

2. **D**. The correct answer in this case is the use of both group policies and mandatory user profiles. This way, you can govern what the users have access to and not allow them to make changes to their profiles that get saved. Mandatory profiles could be used in this case by multiple users, and would prevent changes from being saved, but group policies will further restrict the user of the desktop. Accessibility options don't solve the problem and group policies alone are not enough. See the sections "Mandatory User Profiles" and "Implementing Local Group Policy."

3. **D**. Group policies and roaming user profiles on the network is the correct answer. Group policies can be used to restrict access to the three machines and allow users limited access to only the Human Resource information they require. Roaming profiles could be used as well to ensure that all 200 users still get their unique profiles when logging on to the kiosk computers. See the sections "Roaming User Profiles" and "Implementing Local Group Policy."

4. **C**. Regional options control the display of dates, times, and numbers. Many other locales use punctuation for these types of information

APPLY YOUR KNOWLEDGE

differently than we do in the United States. Although it's possible that a display font was corrupted, it's unlikely as the effect is only on the punctuation. An incorrect time zone won't cause the punctuation of a time or date to change. See the section "Configuring Regional Options."

5. **C.** The key here is to free up space quickly. The fastest way to accomplish this is to remove large applications that have not been used for a period of time. Space can be recouped by deleting Word documents but they are generally so small that it will have little impact. Writing a request for a new hard drive is a good solution but not an immediate one in most cases. Lastly, cleaning out the event logs will have little or no effect on the amount of disk space in use. See the section "Add/Remove Programs."

6. **C.** Running the Add/Remove Programs applet ensures that all the components of the application that were installed will be removed. Deleting the application directory is the wrong way to remove an application; this action won't remove any shared files or Registry settings. Reinstalling Windows XP isn't practical and could be very time consuming. The third-party installation program may or may not get all the changes unapplied, depending upon its ability to effectively monitor all changes. See the section "Add/Remove Programs."

7. **C.** When you change your display settings, Windows XP Professional tests those settings for 15 seconds. If you don't confirm the change, Windows will revert to the old settings. Rebooting the PC is an option but will take a long time. Reinstalling Windows XP is an even longer process. Finally pressing Ctrl+Alt+Del isn't a bad answer, other than it presumes that the

monitor can handle the input it's getting from the video card. It's important to not expose the monitor to the incorrect settings and, if it does happen, you want to make sure it is for as little time as possible. See the section "Configuring the Desktop Environment."

8. **C.** Uninstalling Windows XP is an option—but not a good one. It is quite time consuming. Creating an installer file for the application will not have any impact on its capability to run on Windows XP. Running the program in Windows 98 compatibility mode has the greatest chance of success because the application ran under Windows 98. Because the application is not a graphic application (it's for the accounting department), it's unlikely that the number of colors on the display is the problem. See the section "Program Compatibility Options."

9. **C.** Because the person is legally blind, a new input device wouldn't be of much use, but the magnifier service might help. Many legally blind individuals are able to read if the print is large enough. Turning on the narrator service may seem, at first glance, to be the perfect solution but the narrator service reads only dialog boxes and controls; it may not read the text in the application itself. See the section "Configuring Accessibility Options."

10. **B.** If changes do not persist, it could be that the user has been assigned a mandatory profile. Mandatory profiles prevent changes made by a user during their logon session from being saved. If the user had a local profile, it should persist. A group policy would prevent the change from occurring, not discard the change after logoff. There is no Don't Save Changes at Exit check

APPLY YOUR KNOWLEDGE

box in Windows 2000. See the section "Mandatory User Profiles."

11. **C**. The most likely cause is that Joe's user account is configured for local profiles. Machines cannot be configured for profiles—only users—so both answers A and B are incorrect. If Joe's user account were configured with a roaming profile, the problem wouldn't occur, thus eliminating that answer. See the section "Local User Profiles."

12. **C**. The best solution here would be to enable Sound Sentry, which would indicate on the screen that a sound has occurred. Turning up the volume or installing new, louder speakers might help, but would probably just lead to the generation of more noise. Show Sounds might also

work, but it depends on support from the software vendor, which isn't very likely at this time. See the section "Configuring Accessibility Options."

13. **C, D**. If no input locales are installed, the icon certainly will not be there. Even when additional input locales are installed, the icon must still be enabled to be seen. Input locales are not an optional part of the operating system, making this an invalid option. Applications do need to support the use of input locales but this would not prevent the icon from appearing—only the application from using them. See the section "Configuring Regional Options."

Suggested Readings and Resources

1. Web sites:

   - http://www.microsoft.com/windows2000/professional/

   - http://www.microsoft.com/train_cert/

   - http://www.labmice.net/

   - http://activewin.com/win2000/

   - http://www.microsoft.com/enable (Accessibility section)

   - http://www.microsoft.com/windows2000/library/planning/management/groupsteps.asp (Group Policy Whitepaper)

   - http://www.microsoft.com/windows/professional/deploy/compatible/default.asp (Hardware and Software Compatibility List)

   - http://windowsupdate.microsoft.com/ (Windows Update)

   - http://www.ietf.org/rfc/rfc2401.txt

2. MOC 1560B *Updating Support Skills from Microsoft Windows NT to Microsoft Windows 2000.*

3. MOC 2152A *Supporting Microsoft Windows XP Professional.*

4. *Windows 2000 Group Policy Technical Paper,* Version 2.0 (May 1999).

5. *Microsoft Windows XP Professional Support and Management Improvements* white paper.

6. *Microsoft Windows NT Server Guide to Microsoft Windows NT Profiles and Policies* white paper.

This chapter helps you prepare for the MCSE 70-270 Windows XP Professional exam by covering the following objectives:

Configure and troubleshoot the TCP/IP protocol.

▶ The de facto standard for networking on the Internet is TCP/IP. It also is a very common protocol found in many business networks and has been adapted to support many different kinds of media. To effectively access network resources, you must understand how to install and configure the TCP/IP client and use the services available on TCP/IP networks.

Connect to computers by using dial-up networking.

- **Connect to computers by using a virtual private network (VPN) connection.**

- **Create a dial-up connection to connect to a remote access server.**

- **Connect to the Internet by using dial-up networking.**

- **Configure and troubleshoot Internet Connection Sharing.**

▶ Connectivity between LANs where a persistent connection is not needed can be provided by dial-up network connections. To accomplish this, you must be able to install and configure dial-up components in various configurations. ICS provides a mechanism to share a single network connection with the machines on a small locally managed network segment.

C H A P T E R **6**

Implementing, Managing, and Troubleshooting Network Protocols and Services

Connect to resources using Internet Explorer.

▶ The proliferation of services available through either your own intranet or the Internet means that more resources can be accessed through the browser alone rather than having to run several separate programs to accomplish the same thing. This includes locating printers, publishing files to the Web or to your own local machine, and securely transferring files between computers.

Configure, manage, and implement Internet Information Services (IIS).

▶ The Web is quickly becoming a common form of communication between individuals, workgroups, project teams, and even families. To accomplish this, you must be able to install and configure Internet Information Services to provide a base for your own Web creations.

Configure, manage, and troubleshoot remote desktop and remote assistance.

▶ A new feature in Windows XP Professional is remote assistance. This is a feature that allows you to ask for help or be of assistance to someone in your circle of friends. The ability to take control of another computer and render assistance while the other person watches is far superior to trying to explain a complex operation over the phone.

Configure, manage, and troubleshoot an Internet connection firewall.

▶ If you work in a large enterprise, chances are you are protected by a firewall. If you then take your laptop home and connect to the Internet, your only protection is the security configuration you have implemented on your machine. Most people do not lock down their computers, so their protection is minimal. Internet Connection Firewall is a personal firewall you can enable when you need it.

STUDY STRATEGIES

▶ Exam questions on TCP/IP and networking will focus on several separate areas. The first is the configuration of network components and where they fit within the Windows XP Professional architecture. You should also expect exam questions to focus on the configuration of the TCP/IP components, including addressing, subnet masking, and gateway addressing. This is an area that is fundamental to understanding how TCP/IP functions in finding resources on the network and responds to requests from other computers.

You should expect to find scenario questions on the exam that will require you to know addressing, subnet masking, and routing to troubleshoot a problem. The exam also will have scenario questions that will test your understanding of how DCHP works and how DNS is used for name resolution.

▶ An important part of Windows XP Professional, and an area the exam will cover, is dial-up connection configurations and troubleshooting. It's important to understand how PPTP and VPN services work, as well as Internet Connection sharing. You also should expect scenario questions that address finding and connecting to resources on the network both by browsing and by using the Net commands.

▶ The exam also will address your knowledge of using Internet Explorer to connect to resources (such as printers and Web folders) on your intranet or the Internet.

▶ The exam will also test your understanding of managing IIS (with MMC) and how to configure it to meet your requirements.

▶ A new feature in Windows XP Professional, and one sure to be addressed during the exam, is remote assistance. Exam questions will focus on setting up remote assistance and resolving problems you typically might encounter.

▶ Finally, you should expect scenario questions that focus on the installation and use of another new feature in Windows XP Professional— Internet Connection Firewall.

If you focus on the areas mentioned previously, you will be well prepared for this portion of the exam.

INTRODUCTION

A *local area network (LAN)* is a collection of computers in a specific area that are connected by a communications network. This can range from just two computers to hundreds or thousands. LANs are considered to be computers that all share high-speed network access. LANs in geographically separate areas can be connected into a *wide area network (WAN)*. Generally, the speed at which computers connect within a LAN is greater than what is available between LANs (across the WAN). It is also common for computer networks, even if primarily composed of Windows XP Professional and .NET Server computers, to include diverse operating systems such as Unix and Novell NetWare. Interoperability between these systems is important. Connectivity with the Internet is also important, and its availability can be a part of the design of distributed applications. For Windows XP Professional to participate as a desktop or Network Operating System (NOS) in various LAN and WAN configurations, you must be able to properly configure its network components.

THE WINDOWS XP PROFESSIONAL NETWORKING MODEL

Before reviewing how to configure the networking components of Windows XP Professional, it's important to examine the underlying components that make up the network architecture. These components are put together as layers, from interfacing with an application program down to interfacing with the physical connection to the network. Each layer interacts only with the layers directly above and directly below it through a well-defined interface. Knowledge of how the different layers interact is important in understanding how the Windows XP network architecture enables computers in a network to communicate.

All the networking components in Windows XP Professional are built into the operating system, although some of them are not automatically installed. Any Windows XP computer can participate as the following:

◆ A client or a server in a distributed application environment

◆ A client in a peer-to-peer networking environment

To participate with distributed applications or peer-to-peer network applications, you must ensure that the proper client software is installed on your Windows XP Professional computer.

The built-in networking components allow Windows XP Professional systems to share printers, files, and applications with other networked computers (including other computers not based on Windows NT, Windows 2000, or Windows XP).

> **NOTE**
>
> **Peer-to-Peer Networking** A peer-to-peer network enables any computer to connect to shares and direct output to printers on any other computer in the network (not just to a specialized server).

WINDOWS XP NETWORKING VERSUS THE OSI REFERENCE MODEL

The Open Systems Interconnection (OSI) model is one system that can help you understand the networking architecture used in Windows XP Professional. The OSI model was developed by the International Standardization Organization (ISO) and is a layered model that standardizes how computers participating in a network should communicate and how the network data is exchanged between layers from the application to the network media.

The OSI model divides the network protocol stack into seven layers to which software systems must adhere to communicate over the network. In the case of Windows XP, the system does not implement each layer separately; however, the end result complies with the overall OSI model.

The advantage of this modular design is the increase in flexibility and reliability. Each layer communicates only with the layers directly above and below it, with clearly defined interfaces between each layer. It's much easier to test and change a module of code rather than the entire block of network software. With each layer interfacing only with its neighbor, new capabilities can be added much more easily. Figure 6.1 compares the Windows XP network architecture with the OSI network model.

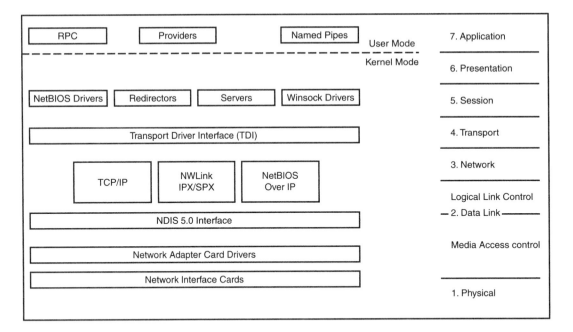

FIGURE 6.1
Windows XP networking architecture versus the OSI model.

NDIS-Compatible Network Adapter Card Drivers

The bottom layers of the Windows XP network architecture include the network adapter card driver and the network interface card (NIC). These must be 32-bit and compliant with the Network Device Interface Specification (NDIS) 3.0, 4.0, or 5.0. NDIS supports both connection-oriented protocols, such as ATM and ISDN, and the traditional connectionless protocols, such as Ethernet, Token Ring, and Fiber Distributed Data Interface (FDDI). The mechanism that NDIS uses to bridge these two layers is the miniport driver specification. The miniport drivers directly access the network adapters while providing common code where possible. Hardware vendors, therefore, do not have to write complete Media Access Control (MAC) drivers, and protocols can be substituted without changing network adapter card drivers.

NDIS 5.0

NDIS 5.0 extends the previous versions of NDIS that define the interaction of network protocols and network card adapters.

The initial connection made between each protocol being used and the network card driver is referred to as a *network binding*. The actual set of network components is called a *protocol stack*. If you have more than one network adapter in your computer, each adapter card's protocol stack can be configured individually. The only limit on the number of network adapter cards you can install is the capacity of your computer hardware.

The NDIS 5.0 specification adds the following features to networking:

◆ **Power management and network wake-up**—NDIS power management can power down network adapters at the request of the user or the system. For example, the user might want to put the system in sleep mode, or the system might request this based on the keyboard/mouse inactivity. A power-down request can also be caused by disconnecting the network cable (if supported by the NIC). The system can also be awakened from a lower power state based on network events. A wake-up signal can be caused by the detection of a change in the network link state (for example, cable reconnect), receipt of a network wake-up frame, or a Magic Packet (16 contiguous copies of the receiving system's Ethernet address).

◆ **NDIS Plug and Play**—Installs, loads, and binds miniports when a new adapter card is introduced.

◆ **Task Offload**—Available if the network adapter card has the capability to support check-summing and forwarding for performance enhancements. Newer adapter cards have onboard processing power and can take over the tasks of certain processes that would otherwise have to be performed by the central CPU. Examples of these are performing check-summing activities and forwarding packets from one port to another without using the CPU. This would be a common task if your Windows XP Professional computer were acting as a router.

◆ **Support for Quality of Service (QoS) and connection-oriented media such as ATM and ISDN**—These improvements extend the functionality of Windows XP Professional even further.

Network Protocols

The network protocols referred to earlier in Figure 6.1 control the communications among computers on the network. Different network protocols provide varying communications services and capabilities.

In this section, we will examine two major protocols, TCP/IP and IPX/SPX. In Windows Professional XP, support for the NetBEUI protocol has been discontinued. NetBEUI (NetBIOS Extended User Interface) was a protocol used mainly for small departmental networks. The NetBIOS application programming interface (API) is still supported. NetBIOS API calls are used by programs to send datagrams between nodes on the network and to manage names and sessions.

TCP/IP

Transmission Control Protocol/Internet Protocol (TCP/IP) is the default protocol for Windows XP Professional and is an industry-standard suite of protocols available for wide area networks (WAN) and the Internet. The TCP/IP suite for Windows XP is designed to make it easy to integrate Microsoft systems into large-scale networks and to provide the ability to operate over those networks in a secure manner.

Microsoft's implementation of TCP/IP provides several standard features, including the following:

◆ Ability to bind to multiple network adapters with different media types

◆ Logical and physical multihoming

◆ Internal IP routing capability

◆ Internet Group Management Protocol (IGMP) version 2 (IP Multicasting)

◆ Duplicate IP address detection

◆ Multiple default gateways

◆ Dead gateway detection

◆ Automatic Path Maximum Transmission Unit (PMTU) discovery

◆ IP Security (IPSec)

◆ Quality of Service (QoS)

◆ Virtual Private Networks (VPNs)

In addition, Windows XP includes the following performance enhancements:

◆ **Internet Router Discovery Protocol (IRDP)**—Windows XP performs router discovery through an improved method of configuring and detecting default gateways. Instead of manually configuring default gateways or using DHCP to set them, hosts can dynamically discover routers on their subnet and can automatically switch to a backup router if the primary router fails or the network administrators change router preferences.

◆ **TCP scalable window sizes**—The TCP receive window size is the amount of receive data (in bytes) that can be buffered at one time on a connection. The sending host can send only that amount of data before waiting for an acknowledgment and window update from the receiving host. The Windows XP TCP/IP stack will tune itself and use a larger default window size than earlier versions. Rather than using a hard-coded default receive window size, TCP adjusts in even increments of the maximum segment size (MSS).

◆ **Selective acknowledgments (SACK)**—Windows XP supports an important performance feature known as *Selective Acknowledgment* (SACK). SACK is especially important for connections using large TCP window sizes. With SACK enabled, the receiver continues to use the ACK number to acknowledge the left edge of the receive window, but it also can acknowledge other blocks of received data individually.

◆ **TCP Fast Retransmit**—There are some circumstances under which TCP retransmits data before the time that the retransmission timer expires. The most common of these occurs due to a feature known as *fast retransmit*. When a receiver that supports fast retransmit receives data with a sequence number beyond the current expected one, it's likely that some data was dropped. To help make the sender aware of this event, the receiver immediately sends an ACK, with the ACK number set to the sequence number that it was expecting. The receiver continues to do this for each additional TCP segment that arrives containing data after the missing data. When the sender starts to receive a stream of ACKs that are acknowledging the same sequence number, and that sequence number is earlier than the current sequence number being sent, the sender infers that a segment (or more) must have been dropped and immediately resends the segment that the receiver is expecting in order to fill in the gap in the data.

Windows XP Professional TCP/IP also provides a number of services, including the following:

◆ Dynamic Host Configuration Protocol (DHCP) client

◆ Windows Internet Name Service (WINS), a NetBIOS name-resolution client

◆ Domain Name System client (DNS)

◆ Dial-up (PPP/SLIP client) support

◆ Point-to-Point Tunneling Protocol (PPTP), used for virtual private remote networks

◆ TCP/IP network printing (lpr/lpd)

◆ SNMP agent

◆ NetBIOS interface

◆ Windows Sockets version 2 (Winsock2) interface

◆ Remote Procedure Call (RPC) support

◆ Network Dynamic Data Exchange (NetDDE)

◆ Wide Area Network (WAN) browsing support

NWLink IPX/SPX-Compatible Transport

NWLink is an NDIS-compliant, native 32-bit implementation of Novell's IPX/SPX protocol. NWLink supports two networking Application Programming Interfaces (APIs): NetBIOS and Windows Sockets. These APIs allow communication among computers running Windows XP and between computers running Windows XP and NetWare servers.

The NWLink transport driver is an implementation of the lower-level NetWare protocols, which include InterNetwork Packet Exchange (IPX), Sequenced Packet Exchange (SPX), Routing Information Protocol over IPX (RIPX), and NetBIOS over IPX (NBIPX). IPX controls addressing and routing of packets of data within and between networks. SPX provides reliable delivery through sequencing and acknowledgments. NWLink provides NetBIOS compatibility with NetBIOS layers over IPX.

When used in conjunction with a redirector such as Client Service for NetWare (CNSW), NWLink allows a computer running Windows XP to access files or printers shared on a NetWare server. Non-NetWare computers on a network that are not running NWLink or another IPX/SPX transport can access NetWare files and print resources through a computer running Windows .NET Server that has been configured with Gateway Services for NetWare and NWLink. For a NetWare client to access print and file services on a computer running Windows XP, File and Print Services for NetWare and NWLink must be installed on the Windows XP system.

TABLE 6.1

WINDOWS XP INTEROPERABILITY WITH NETWARE

Platform	Running	Can Connect To
Windows XP	NWLink	Client/server application running on a NetWare server
Windows XP	NWLink and Client Services for NWLink	NetWare servers for file and print services
NetWare Client	IPX with NetBIOS, Named Pipes, or Windows Sockets	Computers running Windows XP (with NWLink) running IPX-aware applications
NetWare Client	IPX	Computers running Windows XP Server (with NWLink and File and Print services for NetWare) for file and print services

NWLink can be used if there are NetWare client/server applications running that use Sockets or NetBIOS over the IPX/SPX protocol. The client component of the application can be run on a Windows XP Professional system to access the server portion on a NetWare server, and vice versa. The NWLink component is used to format NetBIOS-level requests and pass them to the NWLink component for transmission on the network.

Transport Driver Interface

The Transport Driver Interface (TDI) is a common interface for drivers (such as the Windows XP redirector and server) to use to communicate with the various network transport protocols, allowing services to remain independent of transport protocols. Unlike NDIS, there is no driver for TDI, which is just a specification for passing messages between two layers in the network architecture.

TDI provides greater flexibility and functionality than existing interfaces (such as Winsock and NetBIOS), and all Windows XP transport providers directly interface with the Transport Driver Interface. The TDI specification describes the set of functions and call mechanisms by which transport drivers and TDI clients communicate.

Network Application Programming Interfaces

An Application Programming Interface (API) is a set of routines that an application program uses to request and carry out lower-level services performed by the operating system. Windows XP network APIs include those outlined in the following sections.

Winsock API

The Winsock API allows Windows-based applications to access the transport protocols. Winsock in Windows XP is a protocol-independent implementation of the widely used Sockets API and is the standard for accessing datagram and session services over TCP/IP and NetBIOS. Applications written to the Winsock interface include File Transfer Protocol (FTP) and Simple Network Management Protocol (SNMP).

NetBIOS API

NetBIOS is a standard application programming interface used for developing client/server applications. NetBIOS has been used as an *interprocess communication* (IPC) mechanism since its introduction and is included with Windows XP to support legacy applications.

Telephony API

Telephony is a technology that integrates computers with telephone networks. Telephony API (TAPI) supports both speech and data transmission and allows for a variety of terminals.

The TAPI allows programmers to develop applications that provide support for call management, call conferencing, call waiting, and voicemail.

Messaging API

The *Messaging Application Programming Interface* (MAPI) API allows developers to write messaging applications and back-end services that can be connected in a distributed computing environment. MAPI is part of WOSA (Windows Open Services Architecture) and includes a *messaging subsystem* that provides various services, such as common UI for messaging applications, message stores, and address books.

WNet API

WNet APIs provide Windows networking (WNet) capabilities that extend networking functionality to applications. This set of APIs is also known as the Win32 APIs and allows applications to access networking functions while remaining independent of the network over which they communicate.

Network services are one of many categories of services that the Win32 APIs can provide. Requests for network services are provided by the Multiple Provider Router (MPR), which after receiving the network command determines the appropriate redirector and passes the command to it. The Multiple Provider Router then routes the requests for network service to the appropriate provider for transmission over the network.

Interprocess Communication

Interprocess communication (IPC) allows bidirectional communication between clients and multiuser servers working on different computer systems. IPCs can also be used as an intertask communication system on a local computer as well as between a local and a remote computer.

Applications that split processing between networked computers are referred to as *distributed* applications. The two or more portions of a distributed application can be located on the same machine or on separate machines. A client/server application uses *distributed processing*, in which processing is divided between a workstation (the client) and a more powerful server. The client portion is sometimes referred to as the *front end* and the server portion is referred to as the *back end*. The client portion of a client/server application can consist of just the user interface to the application. However, there are no hard and fast rules, and the application can actually be split at various places with the client end handling only the screen drawings, keyboard entry, and movement of the mouse.

Multitier applications (often called *three-tier*) are an extension of the basic client/server model with an additional application-specific component between the client and the back-end server. It's common for this type of application to be split between a user interface on the client, the application code or business rules in the middle tier, and data services interacting with a large shared database server on the back end.

There are a number of ways in which the Windows XP operating system implements IPC mechanisms.

Distributed Component Object Model

Windows XP supports the distributed component object model (DCOM). DCOM allows components to be efficiently invoked on multiple computers so that the application can take advantage of optimal resources on the network. Processing occurs transparently to the user because DCOM handles the function of locating the called component.

Remote Procedure Call

Remote Procedure Call is another mechanism that allows client and server software to communicate. The Microsoft RPC facility is compatible with the Open Group's Distributed Computing Environment (DCE) specification for remote procedure calls and is interoperable with other DCE-based RPC systems, such as those for HP-UX and IBM AIX Unix-based operating systems.

The Microsoft RPC mechanism uses other IPC mechanisms, such as named pipes, NetBIOS, or Winsock to establish communications between the client and the server with the program logic and related procedure code existing on different computers.

Named Pipes

Named pipes provide connection-oriented messaging by using a portion of memory called a pipe. A *pipe* connects two processes such that the output of one process is used as the input to the other. The processes being connected can either be local on the same machine or remote.

Common Internet File System

The *Common Internet File System* (CIFS) is the standard way in which computer users share files across corporate intranets and the Internet. It's an enhancement to the cross-platform Server Message Block (SMB) protocol that defines a series of commands used to pass information between networked computers. The CIFS messages can be broadly classified as follows:

- ◆ Connection establishment messages that start and end a redirector connection to a shared resource

- ◆ Namespace and file manipulation messages used by the redirector to gain access to files

- ◆ Printer messages used by the redirector to retrieve information and send data to a print queue

- ◆ Miscellaneous messages used by the redirector to write to mailslots and named pipes

CIFS supports most common operating systems, such as Windows or Windows 9x through Windows XP, Unix, and VMS.

CIFS complements Hypertext Transfer Protocol (HTTP) while providing more sophisticated file sharing and file transfer than older protocols, such as FTP. CIFS works at the application level of the Windows XP network architecture and services user requests, selecting the correct redirector and protocol for transport. For NetBIOS requests, NetBIOS is encapsulated in the IP protocol and transported over the network to the appropriate server. The request is passed up to the server, which sends data back to satisfy the request.

Basic Network Services

Network services support application programs and provide the components and APIs necessary to access files on networked computers. Both the server service and the workstation service also assist in accessing input/output (I/O) requests.

Server Service

The *server service* is located above the TDI and is implemented as a file system driver. The CIFS server service interacts directly with other file-system drivers to satisfy I/O requests, such as reading or writing to a file. The server service supplies the connection requested by client-side redirectors and provides them with access to the resources they request.

When the server service receives a request from a remote computer asking to read a file that resides on the local hard drive, the following steps occur:

1. The low-level network drivers receive the request and pass it to the server driver.

2. The server service passes the request to the appropriate local file-system driver.

3. The local file-system driver calls lower-level, disk-device drivers to access the file.

4. The data is passed back to the local file-system driver.

5. The local file-system driver passes the data back to the server service.

6. The server service passes the data to the lower-level network drivers for transmission back to the remote computer.

Workstation Service

All user requests from the *Multiple Uniform Naming Convention Provider* (Multi-UNC Provider) go through the *workstation service*. This service consists of two components: the user interface and the redirector, which is a file-system driver that interacts with the lower-level network drivers by means of the TDI interface.

The workstation service receives the user request and passes it to the kernel redirector.

Windows XP Redirectors

The *redirector* is a component that resides above TDI and is the mechanism through which one computer gains access to another computer. The Windows XP operating system redirector allows connection to Windows 9x, Windows for Workgroups, LAN Manager, LAN Server, and other CIFS servers. The redirector communicates to the protocols using the TDI specifications.

The redirector is implemented as a Windows XP file system driver. This provides several benefits:

◆ It allows applications to call a single API (the Windows XP I/O API) to access files on local and remote computers. From the I/O manager perspective, there is no difference between accessing files stored on a remote computer on the network and accessing those stored locally on a hard disk.

◆ It runs in kernel mode and can directly call other drivers and other kernel-mode components, such as cache manager. This improves the performance of the redirector.

◆ It can be dynamically loaded and unloaded, like any other file-system driver.

◆ It can easily coexist with other redirectors.

Interoperating with Other Networks

Besides allowing connections to Windows 9x, peer-to-peer networks, LAN Manager, LAN Server, and MS-Net servers, the Windows XP redirector can coexist with redirectors for other networks, such as Novell NetWare and Unix networks.

Providers and the Provider-Interface Layer

For each additional type of network, such as NetWare or Unix, you must install a provider. The provider is the component that allows a computer running Windows XP Professional to communicate with the lower levels of the network. Client Services for NetWare is an example of such a provider.

Client Services for NetWare is included with Windows XP Professional and allows the computer to connect as a client to the NetWare network.

When a process on a Windows XP computer tries to open a file that resides on a remote computer, the following steps occur:

1. The process calls the I/O manager to request that the file be opened.

2. The I/O manager recognizes that the request is for a file on a remote computer, and passes the request to the redirector file-system driver.

3. The redirector passes the request to lower-level network drivers that transmit it to the remote server for processing.

Network Resource Access

Applications have a unified interface for accessing network resources, independent of any redirectors installed on the system. Access to resources is provided through the *Multiple Uniform Naming Convention Provider* (Multi-UNC Provider) and the Multi-Provider Router (MPR).

Multiple Uniform Naming Convention Provider

When applications make I/O calls containing *Uniform Naming Convention* (UNC) names, these requests are passed to the Multiple UNC (Multi-UNC) Provider. The Multi-UNC Provider is implemented as a driver, unlike the TDI, which is only a specification defining the way one network layer talks to another.

The Multi-UNC Provider allows multiple redirectors to coexist in the computer. However, if multiple redirectors are present, there must be a means of deciding which one to use. One of the Multi-UNC Provider's functions, then, is to act as an arbitrator to decide the most appropriate redirector to use.

Universal Naming Convention Names

UNC is a naming convention for describing network servers and the share points on those servers. UNC names start with two backslashes followed by the server name. All other fields in the name are separated by a single backslash. A typical UNC name appears as follows:

```
\\server\share\subdirectory\filename.ext
```

Not all the components of the UNC name need to be present with each command; only the server and share components are required. For example, the following command can be used to obtain a directory of the root of a specified share:

```
dir \\server_name\share_name
```

I/O requests from applications that contain UNC names are received by the I/O manager, which passes the requests to the Multi-UNC Provider. If the Multi-UNC Provider has not seen the UNC name during the previous 15 minutes (approximately), the Multi-UNC Provider sends the name to each of the UNC providers registered with it.

When the Multi-UNC Provider receives a request containing a UNC name, it checks with each redirector to find out which one can process the request. It then looks for the redirector with the highest registered-priority response that claims it can establish a connection to the UNC. This connection remains as long as there is activity. If there has been no request for approximately 15 minutes on the UNC name, the Multi-UNC Provider negotiates to find another appropriate redirector.

Multi-Provider Router

Not all programs use UNC names in their I/O requests. Some applications use WNet APIs, which are the Win32 network APIs. The Multi-Provider Router (MPR) supports these applications.

MPR is similar to Multi-UNC Provider. MPR receives WNet commands, determines the appropriate redirector, and passes the command to that redirector.

> **NOTE**
>
> **MPR Versus MPR**   The abbreviation MPR is also used for the Multi-Protocol Router, a series of routing components supplied with Windows NT 4. In Windows XP, the Multi-Protocol Router has been replaced with Bridging Services.

ADDING AND CONFIGURING THE NETWORK COMPONENTS OF WINDOWS XP

You can configure all your network components when you first install Windows XP Professional. If you want to examine how your network components are configured or make changes to your network identification, click Start, right-click My Computer, select Properties from the menu, and select the Computer Name tab (see Figure 6.2).

FIGURE 6.2
The Computer Name tab in the System applet.

Identification Options

Use the Network Identification option in the System applet to view your computer name and your workgroup or domain information. Click the Network ID button to start the Network Identification Wizard, which will walk you through the process to join a workgroup or domain. Windows XP can support both Active Directory and the NT 4 domain structures. If you are joining an NT 4 domain, the domain name you enter must be 15 characters or fewer. If the domain you are joining is a Windows 2000 domain, the domain structure will resemble an Internet domain address (such as ntdev.microsoft.com).

Figure 6.3 shows a computer being moved from one domain to another.

The Windows XP security system requires that all Windows XP Professional computers joining a domain first have a machine account. If a domain administrator has not previously created a machine account, Windows XP Professional will attempt to create one for you. Only domain administrators or people who have been delegated the right to create user and machine accounts can create computer accounts.

To join a domain, you must be a local administrator on your computer. If the user ID that you logged on with does not have administrative privileges, the Network ID and Change buttons will be grayed out.

Clicking the Network ID button will start the Network Identification Wizard. You will need to provide your domain user ID and password and know the account domain you are joining. If a computer account is already set up in the domain by a domain administrator, you will be able to join the domain directly. If the computer account has not been set up, you will be asked to enter in a domain admin user ID and password that will be used to create the account for you. The computer will need to be rebooted to complete the process of joining the domain.

To view or modify the protocols, services, and clients available to your computer, click Start and right-click My Network Places and select Properties from the menu. In that display, right-click the local area network connection for the adapter you want to view or modify, and select the Properties entry. The Properties window will display all the clients, services, and protocols currently configured for that adapter. Selecting an entry in the components window and clicking the Uninstall button will remove that component.

Protocol Options

To configure Protocols, click the Install button. This will bring up the Select Network Component Type button. Highlight the Protocol entry and click the Add button. This will show the protocols that are available to install on your computer (see Figure 6.4).

FIGURE 6.3
Joining a new domain.

NOTE

Joining a Domain   To join a domain, you must have already established network connectivity to a domain controller in the domain that you want to join. It's important when joining a Windows domain with an Active Directory that the machine's DNS configuration be correct. The login procedure depends on accessing information in the Active Directory, so pointing to the correct DNS servers is very important.

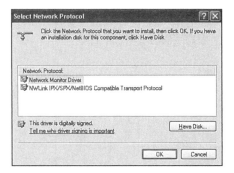

FIGURE 6.4
Protocols available to install.

FIGURE 6.5
Services available to install.

FIGURE 6.6
Clients available to install.

◆ **Network Monitor Driver**—This driver allows the Network Monitoring system (NetMon) to acquire packets from the network.

◆ **NWLink IPX/SPX/NetBIOS Compatible Transport Protocol**—This driver will install the IPX/SPX protocol to allow your computer to send and receive packets from Novell Networks.

Service Options

Clicking the Install button and selecting a service to add will display all the available services not currently installed (see Figure 6.5). The QoS Packet Scheduler implements quality-assurance standards for network transmissions. Service Advertising Protocol (SAP) is used in IPX/SPX networks to advertise every service your computer has or knows about.

Client Options

Selecting the Client entry and clicking the Add button will show the clients available to install on your computer (see Figure 6.6).

CONFIGURING THE TCP/IP PROTOCOL

Configure and troubleshoot the TCP/IP protocol.

TCP/IP is the default protocol for Windows XP Professional and is supported by most common operating systems. TCP/IP is a suite of protocols used to provide connectivity within an enterprise network (LAN) in addition to providing connectivity to the Internet. When you manually configure a computer with a TCP/IP network adapter, you must enter the appropriate settings for connectivity with your network.

This section concentrates on configuration issues. The section "Troubleshooting TCP/IP Connections" that appears later in the chapter covers troubleshooting issues.

IP Addressing

Before delving into IP addressing schemes, it's appropriate to review binary-to-decimal conversions. IP addresses are 32-bit integers that are usually depicted as four 8-bit numbers. This can be thought of as a series of 1s or 0s, with eight taken together to be a number. Each position in the 8 bits (from right to left) is twice the value of the field before it (in decimal notation, the same rule would state that each column is worth 10 times the value of the previous column—100s versus 10s versus 1s). The smallest integer number that can be represented with 8 bits then is 0 0 0 0 0 0 0 0 (2^0-1), or 0. The largest integer that can be represented by 8 bits is 1 1 1 1 1 1 1 1 (2^8-1), or 255. Because of this, you will always see IP addresses as four numbers ranging from 0 to 255.

Each TCP/IP connection must be identified by an address. The address is a 32-bit number that is used to uniquely identify a host on a network. The TCP/IP address has no dependence on the Data-Link layer address, such as the MAC address of a Network adapter.

Although the IP address is 32 bits, it's customary to break it into four 8-bit numbers expressed in decimal and separated by dots. This can be referred to in dotted decimal format and is expressed as *w.x.y.z.* The value to breaking down this address into four 8-bit values can be seen in the following example. Suppose you have an address that is 192.168.8.4. If you had to remember that as a binary 32-bit number, it would be 11000000101010000000100000000100 or, converted to a decimal number, it would be the sum of $2^3+2^{12}+2^{20}+2^{22}+2^{24}+2^{31}+2^{32}$, which is

2^3	8
2^{12}	4,096
2^{20}	1,048,576
2^{22}	4,194,304
2^{24}	16,777,216
2^{31}	2,147,483,648
2^{32}	4,294,967,296
Totals	6,464,475,144.

192.168.8.4 is definitely easier to remember.

This addressing scheme is again broken down into two halves: a Network ID (also known as the network address) and the Host ID (also known as the host address). The Network ID must be unique in the Internet or intranet, and the Host ID must be unique to the Network ID. The network portion of the *w.x.y.z* notation is separated from the host through the use of the subnet mask. See the section titled "Subnet Mask" later in this chapter.

The Internet community was originally divided into five address classes. Microsoft TCP/IP supports classes A, B, and C addresses assigned to hosts.

The class of addresses defines which bits are used for the Network ID and which bits are used for the Host ID. It also defines the possible number of networks and the number of hosts per network. Here is a rundown of the five classes:

◆ **Class A Addresses**—The high-order bit is always binary 0 and the next seven bits complete the Network ID. The next three octets define the Host ID. This represents 126 networks with 16,777,214 hosts per network.

◆ **Class B Addresses**—The top two bits in a class B address are always set to binary 1 0. The next 14 bits complete the Network ID. The remaining two octets define the Host ID. This represents 16,384 networks with 65,534 hosts per network.

◆ **Class C Addresses**—The top three bits in a class C address are always set to binary 1 1 0. The next 21 bits define the Network ID. The remaining octet defines the Host ID. This represents 2,097,152 networks with 254 hosts per network.

◆ **Class D Addresses**—Class D addresses are used for multicasting to several hosts. Packets are passed to a selected subset of hosts on a network. Only those hosts registered for the multicast address accept the packet. The four high-order bits in a class D address are always set to binary 1 1 1 0. The remaining bits are for the address that interested hosts will recognize.

◆ **Class E Addresses**—Class E is an experimental address that's reserved for future use. The high-order bits in a class E address are set to 1 1 1 1.

Table 6.2 indicates how the three classes supported by Microsoft TCP/IP divide up Network IDs and Host IDs.

TABLE 6.2

CLASS ADDRESS RANGES

Class	Network ID	Network Portion	Host Portion	Number of Networks	Number of Hosts
A	1-126	w.	x.y.z	126	16,777,214
B	128-191	w.x	y.z	16,384	65,534
C	192-223	w.x.y	z	2,097,152	254

Subnet Mask

After an IP address from a particular class has been decided upon, it's possible to divide it into smaller segments to better utilize the addresses available. Each segment is bounded by an IP router and assigned a new subnetted Network ID that is a subset of the original class-based Network ID.

A subnet mask (also known as an *address* mask) is defined as a 32-bit value that is used to distinguish the Network ID from the Host ID in an IP address. The bits of the subnet mask are defined as follows:

◆ All bits that correspond to the Network ID are set to 1.

◆ All bits that correspond to the Host ID are set to 0.

The subnet mask is broken down to four 8-bit octets in the same fashion as the class addresses.

Table 6.3 lists the default subnet masks using dotted decimal notation.

NOTE **Hosts Need a Subnet Mask** Each host on a TCP/IP network requires a subnet mask even if it is on a single-segment network. Although the subnet mask is expressed in dotted decimal notation, a subnet mask is not an IP address.

TABLE 6.3

DEFAULT SUBNET MASKS

Address Class	Bits for Subnet Mask	Subnet Mask
Class A	11111111 00000000 00000000 00000000	255.0.0.0
Class B	11111111 11111111 00000000 00000000	255.255.0.0
Class C	11111111 11111111 11111111 00000000	255.255.255.0

Table 6.3 shows the default subnet mask of a class C address to be 255.255.255.0. An example of a class C address might be 192.168.40.55. A computer with this address and the default subnet mask would be host 55 on the subnet. The last 8 bits would be used to define the host on the subnet and the first 24 bits would be used to define the network. If the subnet mask used is not the default, but rather 255.255.255.224, that means only 5 bits are used to define the host on the subnet (the number 224 is derived by setting the top 3 bits to 1). The largest number that fits into just 5 bits is 32 (2^5). This means that every 32 hosts, we switch from one subnet to the next and two computers with addresses of 192.168.40.55 and 192.168.40.75 would be in different subnets. Table 6.4 shows the address ranges for a class C address and a subnet mask of 255.255.255.224.

TABLE 6.4

A SUBNETTED CLASS C NETWORK

Subnet	Host Address Range
0	192.168.40.33—192.168.40.62
1	192.168.40.65—192.168.40.94
2	192.168.40.97—192.168.40.126
3	192.168.40.129—192.168.40.158
4	192.168.40.161—192.168.40.190
5	192.168.40.193—192.168.40.222

This example follows the convention of not using any subnet address in which the host address can be all zeros or ones (that is, the top and bottom subnet). There are always two host addresses between each subnet—the first is the broadcast address for the lower subnet and the second is the network address for the next subnet. Looking at subnet 0 in Table 6.4, the address 192.168.40.63 is the broadcast address for subnet 0 and 192.168.40.64 is the network address for subnet 1.

Default Gateway (Router)

This optional setting is the IP address of the router for this subnet segment. Each subnet segment is bounded by a router that will direct packets destined for segments outside the local one to the correct segment or to another router that can complete the connection. Routers, therefore, have connections to more than one network segment, and this address points to the router's network adapter on the same segment as your computer. If this address is left blank, this computer will be able to communicate only with other computers on the same network segment.

Figure 6.7 shows a hypothetical network that's using a subnet mask of 255.255.255.224. This provides for a maximum of six subnets of 32 hosts each; however, in this example, only three connections are being used. The hosts on the subnet 192.168.40.32 would each have the default gateway address set to the address of the router port connecting that subnet, 192.168.40.33. The IP address of each router connection is local to the subnet it serves, allowing the hosts on that subnet to communicate with it directly.

Windows Internet Name Service

Computers can use IP addresses to identify one another, but users generally prefer to use computer names. Windows XP Professional allows Windows 9x and Windows NT 4 clients to use NetBIOS names to communicate, and therefore requires a means to resolve NetBIOS names to IP addresses. The Windows Internet Name Service is an enhanced NetBIOS name server that registers NetBIOS computer names and resolves them to IP addresses. WINS provides

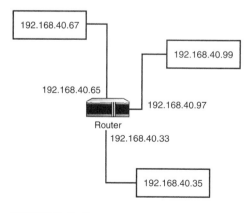

FIGURE 6.7

Default gateways on a subnetted network.

NOTE

The Dynamic Nature of WINS   WINS eliminates the need for an LMHOSTS file, which is a static alternative to WINS. Maintaining an LMHOSTS file requires much more administrative overhead than using WINS.

EXAM TIP

NetBIOS Name Resolution
NetBIOS name resolution follows a sequence: NetBIOS cache, WINS, broadcasting, and using an LMHOSTS file. Most routers do not pass broadcast messages, and having an incorrect WINS address in your TCP/IP configuration will not generate an error.

NOTE

Name Resolution   Name resolution is the process of translating fully qualified domain names (FQDN) to IP addresses. The resolution of a fully qualified domain name follows a sequence: the local hostname, an entry in the HOSTS file, the local DNS cache, and finally a DNS server.

WARNING

TCP/IP Setting   If the settings for the TCP/IP protocol are incorrectly specified, you will experience problems that might keep your computer from establishing communications with other TCP/IP hosts in your network. In extreme cases, communications on your entire subnet can be disrupted.

a dynamic database that maintains mappings of computer names to IP addresses. Windows XP Professional allows you to configure up to 12 WINS server addresses.

Domain Network Systems Server Address

DNS is an industry-standard distributed database that provides name resolution and a hierarchical naming system for identifying TCP/IP hosts on Internets and private networks. A DNS address must be specified to enable connectivity with the Internet or with Unix TCP/IP hosts. You can specify more than one DNS address and the search order in which they should be used.

The IPCONFIG command can be used to display information recently obtained from the DNS service.

The IPCONFIG /DISPLAYDNS command displays the contents of the DNS client resolver cache, which includes entries preloaded from the local HOSTS file, as well as any recently obtained resource records for name queries recently resolved by the system. This is used by the DNS Client service to quickly resolve frequently queried names.

The resolver cache can also support negative caching of unresolved or invalid DNS names. These entries are added by the DNS Client service when it receives a negative answer from a DNS server for a queried name. The negative result is then cached for a brief period of time so that this name is not queried again repeatedly by the system.

The IPCONFIG /FLUSHDNS command will flush and reset the DNS resolver cache. After this option is used, the computer must query DNS servers again for any names previously used on the computer.

Windows.Net Server contains a dynamically updated DNS service. This service is updated with records obtained from either a DHCP server or the DHCP client service on a Windows XP Professional workstation. Normally, this is done when the DHCP address is assigned to the Windows XP Professional workstation. The IPCONFIG /REGISTERDNS command provides a mechanism to manually initiate dynamic registration for the DNS names and IP addresses configured at a computer. This option would normally be used only in troubleshooting DNS name-resolution problems.

By default, the IPCONFIG /REGISTERDNS command refreshes all DHCP address leases and registers all related DNS names configured and used by the client computer.

You can specify all the settings for the TCP/IP protocol manually, or they can be automatically configured through a network service called *Dynamic Host Configuration Protocol (DHCP)*.

Understanding DHCP

One way to avoid the possible problems of administrative overhead and incorrect settings for the TCP/IP protocol (which are usually caused by manual configurations) is to set up your network so that all your clients receive their TCP/IP configuration information automatically through DCHP. DHCP centralizes and manages the allocation of the TCP/IP settings required for proper network functionality for computers that have been configured as DHCP clients. One major advantage of DHCP is that most of the configuration of your network settings need to happen only once, at the DHCP server. Also, the TCP/IP settings that the DHCP client receives from the DHCP server are only leased, and must be periodically renewed. This lease and renewal sequence enables a network administrator to change client TCP/IP settings, if needed. Some of the settings the network administrator can control are DNS and WINS addresses and the gateway router for your subnet.

Using DHCP

To configure a computer as a DHCP client, all you must do is specify an IP address automatically in the TCP/IP Properties box (see Figure 6.8). Exercise 6.2 at the end of the chapter contains complete instructions.

When you configure your Windows XP Professional computer to use DHCP, an additional tab is added to the TCP/IP Properties page. This allows you to define an alternative configuration that will be used if a DHCP server cannot be found. Figure 6.9 shows the Alternate Configuration screen.

EXAM TIP

Server Addresses   A common error at some sites, and one that might be addressed in the exam, is having your server obtain its addresses through DHCP (dynamically, without using reservations). Normally, this causes no problem; however, if a server is rebooted, it might obtain a different address. The DNS cache in Windows XP Professional then would not be able to find the server without issuing an IPCONFIG /FLUSHDNS command.

NOTE

Dynamic DNS Only   The REGISTERDNS option on IPCONFIG will function correctly only if the DNS allows the client to register directly (it's configurable by the network administrator) or if the DNS can accept configuration records. This is true only with the Microsoft DNS service and recent versions of BIND.

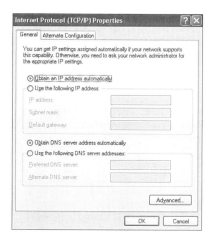

FIGURE 6.8
Specifying that TCP/IP configuration comes from a DHCP server.

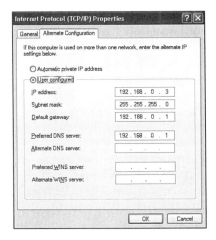

FIGURE 6.9
Alternate Configuration if a DHCP host is not found.

EXAM TIP

Automatic Private IP Addressing
If a DHCP server is not reached after 60 seconds or the lease on the IP address expires, Windows XP Professional will either use the setting defined in the Alternate Configuration or use APIPA to automatically generate a unique IP address in the range 169.254.0.1 through 169.254.255.254 (with a subnet mask of 255.255.0.0). This range of IP addresses is reserved by the Internet Assigned Number Authority (IANA) and they are not used on the Internet. If your IPCONFIG output shows an IP address in this range, your DHCP lease has expired or not been obtained and you have just dropped off your network.

Testing DHCP

To determine the network settings that a DHCP server has leased to your computer, type the following command at a command prompt:

```
IPCONFIG /all
```

The following is a sample output from the IPCONFIG command:

```
Windows IP Configuration
    Host Name . . . . . . . . . . . . : gordb3
    Primary Dns Suffix  . . . . . . . : barknet.ads
    Node Type . . . . . . . . . . . . : Mixed
    IP Routing Enabled. . . . . . . . : No
    WINS Proxy Enabled. . . . . . . . : No
    DNS Suffix Search List. . . . . . : barknet.ads

Ethernet adapter Local Area Connection:

    Media State . . . . . . . . . . . : Media disconnected
    Description . . . . . . . . . . . : Intel(R) PRO/100+
MiniPCI
    Physical Address. . . . . . . . . : 00-D0-59-10-FC-F4

Ethernet adapter Wireless Network Connection:

    Connection-specific DNS Suffix  . : Barknet.ads
    Description . . . . . . . . . . . : ORiNOCO Wireless
LAN PC Card (5 volt)
    Physical Address. . . . . . . . . : 00-02-2D-1D-4C-6B
    Dhcp Enabled. . . . . . . . . . . : Yes
    Autoconfiguration Enabled . . . . : Yes
    IP Address. . . . . . . . . . . . : 192.168.0.6
    Subnet Mask . . . . . . . . . . . : 255.255.255.0
    Default Gateway . . . . . . . . . : 192.168.0.1
    DHCP Server . . . . . . . . . . . : 192.168.0.1
    DNS Servers . . . . . . . . . . . : 192.168.0.1
    Lease Obtained. . . . . . . . . . : Wednesday, December
26, 2001 9:17:36 PM
    Lease Expires . . . . . . . . . . : Thursday, January
03, 2002 9:17:36 PM
```

The IPCONFIG command will show you the current address and configurations supplied by a DHCP server if your addresses are obtained dynamically. If you look at the network configuration in the control panel, you will see only that the address will be obtained from a DHCP server, and not what the current address is. The IPCONFIG command also gives you full details on the duration of your current lease. You can verify whether a DHCP client has connectivity to a DHCP server by releasing the IP address and requesting a new lease. You can conduct this test by typing the following commands in a command window:

```
IPCONFIG /release
IPCONFIG /renew
```

Manually Configuring TCP/IP

You can manually configure your TCP/IP settings by entering the required values into the TCP/IP Properties sheet (see Figure 6.10). For complete details, see Exercise 6.1 at the end of the chapter.

Name Resolution with TCP/IP

DNS and WINS are not the only name-resolution methods available for Windows XP TCP/IP hosts. Microsoft also provides two different lookup files: LMHOSTS and HOSTS. You can find samples of these files in the *winnt_root*\SYSTEM32\DRIVERS\ETC folder. Read the contents of each sample file for instructions on how to use them.

Advanced TCP/IP Configuration

As the complexity of networks grows, the requirement for more sophisticated access and control of information flowing over the networks grows as well. Two recent additions to the TCP/IP configuration options in Windows XP are Virtual Private Networks (VPN) and IP Security (IPSec). These automatic methods encrypt the information flowing between two computer systems even if it is using the public Internet network.

Virtual Private Networks

A *Virtual Private Network (VPN)* allows the computers in one network to connect to the computers in another network by the use of a tunnel through the Internet or other public network. The VPN provides the same security and features formerly available only in private networks.

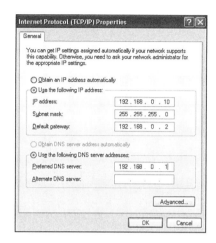

FIGURE 6.10
Manual configuration of a TCP/IP host.

> **NOTE**
>
> **LMHOSTS File**   Although the sample LMHOSTS file in the *winnt_root*\SYSTEM32\DRIVERS\ETC folder is named LMHOSTS.SAM, it must be renamed to LMHOSTS with no file extension. Otherwise, it will not be used for name resolution. The LMHOSTS.SAM file does contain full instructions on how to use the file.

A VPN connection allows you to connect to a server on your corporate network from home or when traveling using the routing facilities of the Internet. The connection appears to be a private point-to-point network connection between your computer and the corporate server.

Additionally, VPNs can be used to connect remote office LANs to the corporate LAN or to other remote LANs to share resources and information using direct connection of dial-up access.

The following are the basic functions managed by VPNs:

 ◆ **User Authentication**—Verify the user's identity and restrict VPN access to authorized users only.

 ◆ **Address Management**—Assign the client's address on the private Net and ensure that private addresses are kept private.

 ◆ **Data Encryption**—Data carried on the public network must be unreadable to unauthorized clients on the network.

 ◆ **Key Management**—Encryption keys must be refreshed for both the client and the server.

 ◆ **Multiprotocol Support**—The most common protocols used in the public network are supported.

A VPN is not a protocol in itself, but rather the encapsulation of existing protocols and the encryption of the data being transmitted.

Windows XP Professional provides two protocols to encapsulate and encrypt the actual information being sent over the VPN connection.

Point-to-Point Tunneling Protocol (PPTP)

This protocol enables the secure transfer of data from your computer to a remote computer on TCP/IP networks. PPTP tunnels, or encapsulates, IP inside PPP datagrams. PPTP can work over dedicated Internet connections or over dial-up connections; however, it does require IP connectivity between your computer and the server to which it is authenticating before the tunnel can be established.

In Point-to-Point Tunneling, a PPP frame (containing an IP datagram) is wrapped with a Generic Routing Encapsulation (GRE) header and an IP header. In the IP header is the source and destination IP address that corresponds to the VPN client and VPN server.

Figure 6.11 shows the PPTP encapsulation of a PPP payload.

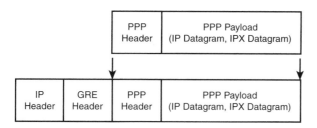

FIGURE 6.11
PPTP encapsulation of an encrypted datagram.

PPTP Encryption

The PPP frame is encrypted with Microsoft Point-to-Point Encryption (MPPE) by using encryption keys generated from the MS-CHAP V2 or EAP authentication process. Virtual private networking clients must use either the MS-CHAP V2 or EAP authentication protocol to encrypt PPP payloads. PPTP does not provide encryption services. PPTP encapsulates a previously encrypted PPP frame.

Layer 2 Tunneling Protocol (L2TP)

L2TP is an Internet tunneling protocol that has been adopted industrywide. L2TP has roughly the same functionality as PPTP using the industry-standard IPSec to encrypt the payload rather than MPPE. The Windows XP implementation of L2TP is designed to run natively over IP networks.

Encapsulation for L2TP consists of two separate layers:

◆ A PPP frame (containing an IP datagram) is wrapped with an L2TP header and a UDP header.

◆ The resulting L2TP message is then wrapped with an IPSec Encapsulating Security Payload (ESP) header and trailer, an IPSec Authentication trailer that provides message integrity and authentication, and a final IP header. In the IP header are the source and destination IP addresses that correspond to the VPN client and VPN server.

Figure 6.12 shows the L2TP encapsulation of a PPP payload.

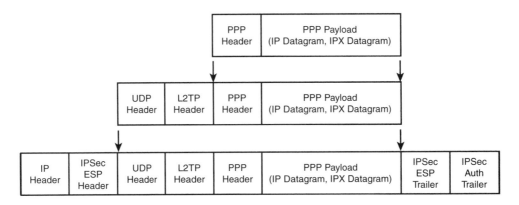

FIGURE 6.12
L2TP encapsulation of an encrypted PPP pay-load.

Encryption

The L2TP message is encrypted with IPSec encryption mechanisms by using encryption keys generated from the IPSec authentication process. The portion of the packet from the UDP header to the IPSec ESP Trailer inclusive is encrypted by IPSec.

Installing VPN Connections

A VPN connection is configured running the New Connection Wizard (Create a New Connection) in the Network Connections applet in the Control Panel. A VPN is created by selecting the option Connect to the Network at My Workplace. The connection can be configured to dial to an Internet service provider (ISP) or to connect directly to a VPN server if your computer is directly con-nected to the Internet.

The type of connection (PPTP or L2TP) is defined by the server to which you are connecting. In any case, the connection and security are negotiated automatically.

CONNECTING TO COMPUTERS BY USING DIAL-UP NETWORKING

Connect to computers by using dial-up networking.

Dial-Up Networking enables you to extend your network to unlim-ited locations. A dial-up connection connects your computer to a private network or the Internet (through an Internet service provider), or to a private network through the public Internet using a secure Virtual Private Network (VPN) connection.

The dial-up connection can be made by a modem over the public switched network (also known as the Plain Old Telephone System, or POTS), or through a cable modem, xDSL service, an X.25 interface, or high-speed ISDN line. The incoming connections can also be made by Point-to-Point (PPP) or Serial Line Internet Protocol (SLIP) to support dial-up connections to SLIP servers.

After clients connect to a Remote Access Server (RAS), it's registered into the local network and can take advantage of the same network services and data that they could if they were actually connected to the local network. The only difference that clients would notice is that WAN connections are much slower than direct physical connections to their LAN.

Line Protocols

The network transport protocols (TCP/IP and NWLink) were designed for the characteristics of LANs and are not suitable for use in phone-based connections. To make the network transport protocols function properly over phone-based connections, it's necessary to encapsulate them in a line protocol. Windows XP Professional supports two different line protocols: SLIP and PPP.

Serial Line Internet Protocol

SLIP is an industry-standard line protocol that supports TCP/IP connections made over serial lines. SLIP is a very simple protocol designed when networks were simpler. Because of this, SLIP implementations have several limitations:

◆ SLIP supports TCP/IP only. It does not include support for IPX, and because there is no mechanism in the SLIP definition to identify other protocols, TCP/IP is assumed.

◆ SLIP requires that both computers understand the other's IP address for routing purposes. It provides no mechanism for hosts to communicate addressing information over a SLIP connection, and there is no support for DHCP.

N O T E

Limits on SLIP Support   Windows XP Professional supports only SLIP client functionality. A Windows XP computer can't act as a SLIP server.

N O T E

Multilink Connections   PPP includes support for multilink dialing. This feature enables you to combine multiple physical links into one logical connection. A client with multiple ISDN, X.25, and modem lines can establish a multilink connection that transmits data at a rate equal to the sum of the physical connections. For example, if a computer has two phone lines at 28.8Kb, a PPP multilink connection over these two physical connections would result in logical connections of 56Kb.

Multiple links can also be allocated only as they are required, thereby eliminating excess bandwidth.

◆ SLIP has no error detection, so noisy phone lines will corrupt packets in transit. When SLIP was created, phone line speeds were quite low (remember 2400 baud?) and network applications usually detect a checksum error in the encapsulated TCP/IP packet. Some applications, such as NFS, however, usually ignore checksums.

◆ SLIP does not support any encryption and therefore passwords are sent as clear text.

◆ To log on to a SLIP server, it's usually necessary to include some scripting or manual intervention to complete the connection.

Point-to-Point Protocol

The limitations of SLIP prompted the development of a newer industry-standard protocol: Point-to-Point Protocol (PPP). Some of the advantages of PPP include the following:

◆ Supports TCP/IP, IPX, and other protocols

◆ Supports both static IP addresses and DHCP

◆ Supports encryption for authentication

◆ Scripting and other manual interventions not required to complete the logon process

Point-to-Point Tunneling Protocol

Point-to-Point Tunneling Protocol (PPTP) is an extension to PPP. PPTP can be used to create secure connections (VPNs) on LAN connections and it can be used with dial-up networking. In this configuration, a dial-up connection is established with an RAS server (through an Internet access provider or an RAS server in a private network). PPTP will use this connection to establish a secure tunnel from your computer to the remote network to which you are connecting.

Installing a Dial-Up Networking Connection

The wizard for installing a dial-up networking connection is started when you double-click the Create a New Connection icon in the Network Connections Control Panel applet. The wizard automatically creates outgoing connections to other networks or incoming connections from remote computers.

The wizard allows the creation of three types of connections (see Figure 6.13). These are discussed in the following sections.

Connect to the Internet

This option is used to connect to an Internet service provider (ISP). You can choose to pick an ISP from a list or use a wizard to find one for you, or you can use a CD provided by your ISP. The third way of connecting to the Internet is to manually enter the configuration values. The configuration options include the following:

◆ Naming the provider

◆ Entering the phone number

◆ Providing the logon user ID and password (usually provided by the ISP)

◆ Configuring the personal firewall

Security is a major consideration when connecting to a public network. You can configure security on a VPN connection by clicking Start, right-clicking My Network Places, and selecting Properties. In the Network Connections pane, click your VPN connection and select Change Settings of This Connection in the Network Tasks pane. Select the Security tab in the Properties page that is displayed, click the Advanced radio button, and click Settings. As shown in Figure 6.14, you can choose from several different security settings, including the following:

◆ **Password Authentication Protocol (PAP)**—PAP sends the username and password as unencrypted text. As you can imagine, it would be fairly simple to sniff the network watching for PPP packets with plain-text user IDs and passwords in them.

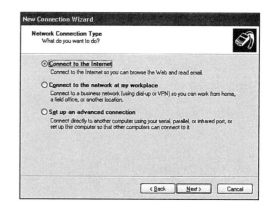

FIGURE 6.13
Dial-up connection types available.

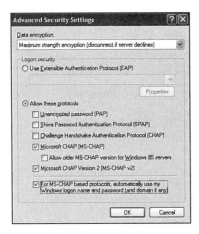

FIGURE 6.14
Encrypted authentication options.

PAP is typically seen only in older Unix-based remote access servers rather than in any modern authentication protocols. You cannot use MPPE data encryption when PAP is used as the authentication mechanism.

◆ **Challenge Handshake Authentication Protocol (CHAP)**—This uses a secure encryption authentication technique based on the Message Digest 5 (MD5) hashing algorithm. CHAP uses challenge-response with one-way MD5 hashing on the response. In this way, you can prove to the server that you know your password without actually sending the password over the network. By supporting CHAP and MD5, Network Connections is able to securely connect to almost all third-party PPP servers. When you connect to a remote server, however, it might negotiate clear-text authentication if it does not support MD5 hashing. You cannot use Microsoft Point-to-Point Encryption (MPPE) data encryption when CHAP is used as the authentication mechanism.

◆ **Shiva Password Authentication Protocol (SPAP)**—SPAP is a simple encrypted password-authentication protocol supported by Shiva remote access servers. When authenticating with SPAP, the client sends an encrypted password to the remote server. The remote access server decrypts the password and uses the plain-text form to authenticate the remote access client. SPAP is a two-way encryption algorithm, unlike MS-CHAP or MS-CHAP V2. You cannot MPPE data encryption when SPAP is used as the authentication mechanism.

◆ **Microsoft Challenge Handshake Authentication Protocol (MS-CHAP)**—MS-CHAP is a variation on CHAP that uses Message Digest 4 (MD4) hashing algorithm and the Data Encryption Standard (DES) encryption algorithm to generate the challenge-response. In this way, you can prove to the server that you know your password without actually sending the password over the network. During the MS-CHAP authentication process, shared secret encryption keys for MPPE are generated.

◆ **Microsoft Challenge Handshake Authentication Protocol Version 2 (MS-CHAP V2)**—Windows XP Professional supports MS-CHAP V2. MS-CHAP V2 provides mutual authentication in which both the client and the server prove that they have knowledge of the user's password without actually sending the password. MS-CHAP V2 also creates stronger initial data-encryption keys for Microsoft Point-to-Point Encryption (MPPE), and different encryption keys for sent and received data. Because it is more secure than MS-CHAP, MS-CHAP V2 will be offered before MS-CHAP for every connection.

◆ **Extensible Authentication Protocol (EAP)**—This is an extension to PPP that allows arbitrary authentication methods using credential and information exchanges of arbitrary lengths, such as smartcards and certificates. EAP provides greater security against attacks, such as password guessing or dictionary attacks, than other methods, such as CHAP. Figure 6.15 shows the configuration options for EAP with smart-card properties.

Connect to the Network at My Workplace

This option provides for a secure virtual private network connection over the public Internet. This type of network connection allows you to select a dial-up connection to establish first; or, if you already have a persistent connection to the Internet through a LAN connection (for example, a cable modem), the VPN can be established using the local connection. The remote VPN server computer's name or IP address is added to complete the configuration.

Set Up an Advanced Connection

This option allows you to configure your Windows XP computer to accept incoming calls or to set up a direct connection to another computer. The configuration options for accepting incoming calls, or for directly connecting to another computer where your Windows XP Professional computer is acting as the host, include the following:

◆ Select the device to make the connection.

◆ Select the Users allowed to make the connection.

◆ Select the networking software to make available to the incoming connection.

FIGURE 6.15
EAP configuration options with smart-card properties.

EXAM TIP

Password and Data Encryption
It's important to understand the authentication schemes that will allow password encryption and data encryption (MS-CHAP V2 and CHAP) and how to force strong authentication with smart cards (EAP options). Understand the various combinations that might be used in dial-up scenarios.

If you are acting as a guest in a direct connection to another computer, you need only to define the name of the other computer and select the device with which the connection will be made.

Internet Connection Sharing

With the Internet connection-sharing feature of Network Connections, you can use Windows XP to connect your home network or small office network to the Internet. If you have a home network and connect to the Internet using a dial-up connection, xDSL, or a cable modem, by enabling connection sharing you provide network address translation, addressing, and name resolution for all the other computers on your home network.

The Internet connection-sharing feature is intended for use in a small office or home office in which network configuration and the Internet connection are managed by the computer running Windows XP where the shared connection resides. It's assumed that on its network, this computer is the only Internet connection, is the only gateway to the Internet, and sets up all internal network addresses.

A computer with Internet connection sharing needs two connections: one to the internal LAN and one to the Internet. Internet connection sharing is enabled on the Internet connection. This shared connection will allow your internal network to receive its addresses using DHCP, provide a DNS service to resolve names, and provide a gateway service to access computer systems outside your home network. The Network Address Translation (NAT) service allows your home network to use any addressing scheme you want because the internal addresses are not visible from the Internet.

Network Address Translation is transparent to both the client and the server. The client appears to be talking directly with the external server and the external server believes the NAT is the end client. To the client, the NAT will be its default gateway.

When the NAT is doing address and port translation, all internal addresses will be mapped to the single IP address of the NAT's external network card or dial-up interface. Ports will be mapped so that they remain unique. For example, if two Windows XP Professional computers on the internal network are running an application that uses TCP port 1025 as a source, after translation, the clients will have the same IP address but will need unique ports to identify their applications.

When the NAT receives an outbound packet, it checks its internal tables to see whether there is already a mapping. If there is a mapping, it will be used; if not, a new one is created.

◆ In an outgoing packet, the NAT modifies the source IP address and port number. For example, the source of 10.0.0.2, TCP port 1025 may become 157.55.1.10, TCP port 2000.

◆ In an incoming packet, the NAT modifies destination IP address and port number.

The computer on which Internet connection sharing is enabled becomes a DHCP allocator for the home network. DHCP dynamically distributes TCP/IP addresses to users as they start up.

You cannot modify the default configuration created by enabling Internet connection sharing. This includes items such as disabling the DHCP allocator or modifying the range of private IP addresses that are handed out, disabling the DNS proxy, configuring a range of public IP addresses, or configuring inbound mappings. If you want to modify any of these items, you must use network address translation.

Internet connection sharing supports the use of VPN tunnels from corporate servers on the Internet back to your home network. The VPN connection is authenticated and secure, and creating the tunneled connection allocates proper IP addresses, DNS server addresses, and WINS server addresses for the corporate network.

Internet Connection Sharing Settings

When you enable Internet connection sharing, certain protocols, services, interfaces, and routes are configured automatically. Table 6.5 describes the settings used when Internet connection sharing is enabled.

NOTE **Persistence of Information** By default, an idle TCP session will remain in the NAT table for 24 hours and a UDP mapping will remain for one minute.

WARNING **Internal Versus External Connection Sharing** Enabling Internet connection sharing on the internal network connection rather than the external one can cause DHCP to grant TCP/IP addresses to users outside your home network, causing network problems on their computers.

NOTE **Roles** You must be a member of the Administrators group to configure Internet connection sharing.

If you are using Internet connection sharing, it should be on a network with no other Windows XP domain controllers, DNS servers, gateways, DHCP servers, or computers using static IP addressing. The server that's sharing the Internet connection assumes the role of gateway and DHCP allocator. The DHCP allocator provides IP addresses and gateway configurations to all computers on the local network that require an Internet connection. Problems will arise if there are other servers providing the same service.

TABLE 6.5

INTERNET CONNECTION SHARING SETTINGS

Configured Item	*Action*
IP address 192.168.0.1	Configured with a subnet mask of 255.255.255.0 on the LAN adapter that's connected to the small office or home office network
AutoDial feature	Enabled
Static default IP route	Created when the dial-up connection is established
Internet connection sharing service	Started
DHCP allocator	Enabled with the default range of 192.168.0.2 to 192.168.0.254 and a subnet mask of 255.255.255.0
DNS proxy	Enabled

Internet Connection Sharing for Applications

If you have applications that interact with services on the Internet (usually games), you will need to configure the application in the Internet connection sharing service. In addition, if you want to provide services to users on the Internet (for example, you are hosting a Web site), you must configure the Web server service.

STEP BY STEP

6.1 Configure Internet Connection Sharing for Applications and Services

1. Click Start, and then right-click My Network Places.

2. Right-click the shared connection and select Properties.

3. Select the Advanced tab and verify that Allow Other Network Users to Connect Through This Computer to the Internet is selected, and then click Settings.

4. To configure a service to provide to remote users, select the Settings tab and check the boxes next to the services your computer should provide.

5. To add new services to the list, click Add and enter the name of the service and the port number (TCP and/or UDP) that it will be listening on.

CONNECTING TO RESOURCES USING INTERNET EXPLORER

Connect to resources using Internet Explorer.

The Web has become so pervasive that Internet Explorer and Outlook (or Outlook Express) can be the most used applications on your computer. You should therefore be able to find almost any resource you need by using the browser.

Accessing Files Using Internet Explorer

You can use Internet Explorer to access files on your computer, or on a remote computer on your Internet by using the address format `File://drive:/filepath/filename.ext`.

For example, you might want to look at a text file `example.txt` that is located in a subdirectory named `FTP` on your local machine.

The address you would provide to Internet Explorer would be `File://C:/FTP/example.txt`.

Internet Explorer would display that file in Notepad (probably) because of the affinity of Notepad to the `.txt` extension.

If the file were on a share on some other server in your network, the command format would be `File://server/share/filename.ext`.

In the preceding example, the command `File://gordb3/FTP/example.txt` would also display the file in Notepad (provided that the FTP subdirectory is a share).

Finding and Installing Printers from Internet Explorer

Occasionally, you might need to find a printer while you are inside Internet Explorer. Normally, you would search for a printer using the Add a Printer command inside Printers and Faxes in the Control Panel. You also can install printers on your local system from within Internet Explorer.

If you know the name of your local print server, you can retrieve a list of the printers that are located on the server.

The command

```
http://printserver/printers
```

will display a list of printers defined on the server named *printserver*. Figure 6.16 shows the status of a printer through Internet Explorer. By clicking the Connect link, you will install the correct printer drivers on your computer and create a new entry for the printer in Printers and Faxes in Control Panel.

Accessing Web Sites

The first thing that everyone using Internet Explorer learns to do is access Web sites. The usual form of a Web site address is

```
http://webname/page
```

FIGURE 6.16
Status of a printer in Internet Explorer.

In this example, *webname* is the fully qualified domain name of the Web site. An example might be www.microsoft.com. In the DNS entries at Microsoft, there is an entry named WWW that resolves to an IP address (or virtual IP address if the Web site is load balanced). You can specify a page or leave it blank (stop a *webname*) and get the default page for that site.

How Web pages are displayed by Internet Explorer depends on the options set on your Windows XP Professional computer. By looking in the Tools menu tab and selecting Internet Options, you can see a list of options available to change the way Internet Explorer functions. For example, in the Multimedia section of the list there is a box named Show Pictures. Unchecking this box will cause all images displayed by Internet Explorer to be replaced with an image symbol but no image. If Internet Explorer is not displaying Web pages correctly, this is the place to check. Clicking Restore Defaults often will repair any problem.

Another configuration parameter that might impact your Web site surfing is Security and Security Zones.

Security and Security Zones

When you are downloading a program (or a program downloads as part of a Web site), you need to know that it's coming from a reliable source. Internet Explorer uses Microsoft's Authenticode technology to verify that the program has a valid certificate and the software publisher's identity matches the certificate. You can always block programs from sources you do not trust.

> **NOTE**
>
> **Any Guarantees** The use of certificates does not prevent a software author from downloading software that just doesn't run well, but it reduces the chance of someone downloading malicious software onto your computer.

Internet Explorer divides the Internet into four zones. You can assign a Web site to a zone with a suitable security level.

For example, you might consider your local intranet to be safe and therefore set the security settings for Local to be low. This will reduce the amount of prompts you need to answer when using the browser on your corporate network, but it also will relax security.

A different site outside your corporate net might be considered unsafe and placed in the Restricted Zone with a much higher security setting.

The particular zone you are in is displayed on the status bar in the lower-right corner of the Internet Explorer screen.

Table 6.6 shows the four zones and typical security settings.

TABLE 6.6

INTERNET EXPLORER SECURITY ZONES

Zone	Security Description
Internet	This zone contains anything not in any other zone. The default setting is Medium. You cannot add sites to this zone.
Local Intranet	This zone is usually made up of sites that don't require a proxy server and are local intranet sites or network paths. The default security setting is Medium-Low, and Internet Explorer will allow cookies to be saved on your machine. You can add sites to this zone.
Trusted Sites	This zone contains sites that you can trust. The default security setting for this zone is Low, and Internet Explorer will allow cookies to be saved on your machine. You can add sites to this zone.
Restricted Sites	This zone contains sites that you don't trust. The default security setting for this zone is High, and Internet Explorer will block all cookies. You can add sites to this zone.

Dealing with Proxy Servers

Most corporations now run proxy servers to connect the corporate LAN to the Internet without compromising security and to provide some additional performance. Internet Explorer allows you to configure proxy settings for each type of network connection you may configure. For example, if you are dialing into an Internet service provider (ISP) to access Hotmail and the Internet, you would not use a proxy server; however, your LAN connection when you are in the office might have a proxy defined and a list of addresses for which to bypass the proxy.

These options are available by selecting Tools, Internet Options and selecting the Connections tab.

Defining a proxy service can be accomplished companywide by defining it in a Group Policy, so you might not be aware of the proxy setting for your computer. This occasionally becomes an issue when you connect into another company's network and need to access the Internet. If the proxy setting is incorrect, you will not have access to anything. If the network you are connecting to has a proxy, you can select an option to automatically detect proxy servers and override your settings. Selecting this option will allow you to connect to another network and still access the Internet.

CONFIGURING, MANAGING, AND IMPLEMENTING INTERNET INFORMATION SERVICES

Configure, manage, and implement Internet Information Services (IIS).

When Web sites were first gaining acceptance, they were always run on dedicated servers. Now, Web sites are ubiquitous and are used to store files (in Web folders), or to access information (from SQL databases) and display data (through Visual InterDev and ASP Pages) and static content (using FrontPage).

Windows XP Professional allows you to configure one Web site on your computer. Each Web site can, of course, have many virtual directories to access other information.

Installing IIS on Your Computer

IIS is installed as a Windows Component and will automatically install MMC snap-ins as well as help files and other common components.

The following process can be used to install IIS on your Windows XP Professional computer.

STEP BY STEP

6.2 Installing IIS

1. Click Start, and then click Control Panel.

2. Click Add or Remove Programs.

3. Click Add/Remove Windows Components to display the Windows Components Wizard.

4. Check the Internet Information Services box and click Details.

5. Ensure that all optional subcomponents are selected and click OK.

The Default Web Site

Windows XP Professional allows you to create one Web site in IIS. This Web site (called, naturally, the Default Web) can be managed through the Internet Information Services snap-in for the Microsoft Management Console (MMC).

The following process can be used to see the status of the default Web site.

STEP BY STEP

6.3 IIS Snap-In in the MMC

1. Click Start, and then click Run.

2. Enter MMC in the Open: Windows and click OK.

3. Click File and select Add/Remove Snap-In.

4. Click Add in the Add/Remove Snap-In window.

5. Double-click Internet Information Services in the Add Standalone Snap-In window.

6. Click Close and then OK to return to the main MMC Console screen.

7. Expand the tree below Console Root to display the Default Web site.

8. Right-click the Default Web site and select Properties.

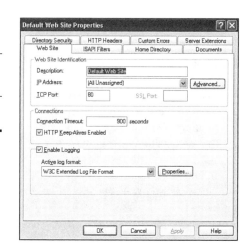

FIGURE 6.17
Default Web site Property page.

Figure 6.17 shows the property page of a typical default Web site.

Host Headers and Web Site Names

The default Web site name is also the name of your Windows XP Professional computer. If you want to name the Web site something other than that, you must use Host Headers. You can still create only one Web site on your Windows XP Professional computer, but you can name it what you like. To have this Web site available to others on your intranet, for example, you would have to have your network administrator make an entry in the corporation's DNS service linking the Web site name in your Host Header to your Windows XP Professional's IP address. Using any other name to resolve to your IP address will not connect you to the Web site. This is an important step to remember when troubleshooting Web site connectivity problems.

The following process can be used to configure a Host Header name in IIS.

STEP BY STEP

6.4 Configuring a Host Header Name

1. Click Start, and then click All Programs.

2. Select Administrative Tools and click IIS.MSC.

3. Expand the Console Root tree to display the Default Web site.

4. Right-click the Default Web site and select Properties.

continues

continued

<table>
<tr><td>

EXAM TIP

Name Resolution   If you use Host Headers, you must also provide some mechanisms to resolve the name of the Web site back to your Windows XP Professional computer. That necessitates either making a manual entry into DNS or creating an entry in a valid HOSTS file. Otherwise, the Web site will not be found.

</td></tr>
</table>

5. Select the IP address that the site will use and click Advanced.

6. In the Multiple Identities for This Web Site window, select the IP address to configure and click Edit.

7. Add the Host Header name for this site.

8. Click OK to apply the changes.

9. Register the Host Header name in your DNS or HOSTS file.

10. Internet Explorer should now open the correct Web page with the Host Header name for an address.

Virtual Directories

Virtual directories provide a mechanism to include content on your Web site that is stored in a directory structure under root. For example, if you have a computer called *TestWeb1* and you create a virtual directory called *WebProject1* under the default Web site, the default page (if you create one) would be addressed as http://TestWeb1/WebProject1/default.htm. Similarly, a second virtual directory called *SQLProject* would have its default Web page addressed as http://TestWeb1/SQLProject/default.htm. In this way, it appears that you have more than one Web site running on your computer when in fact you are addressing different contents in different virtual folders.

You create virtual directories in the IIS snap-in by right-clicking the Default Web site and selecting New. The Virtual Directory Creation Wizard guides you through selecting an alias for this directory and where to put the physical files. Normally, the alias is what you want to address the Web page as and the physical files are placed in a subdirectory under InetPub/wwwroot.

<table>
<tr><td>

EXAM TIP

Only One Web Site   Windows XP Professional supports only one Web site. If you start or stop the default Web site, all the virtual directories under the default Web site will not be available. Windows XP Professional is considered a development environment for Web projects and can support only 10 simultaneous client connections.

</td></tr>
</table>

The Web page then becomes available under the address http://machinename/alias, where machinename is the name of your Windows XP Professional computer and alias is the name chosen for the Web page.

Configuring, Managing, and Troubleshooting Remote Desktop and Remote Assistance

Configure, manage, and troubleshoot remote desktop and remote assistance.

Remote Desktop and Remote Assistance both use Terminal Services technology to allow you to access remote computers. Remote Desktop allows you to access your computer when you are at a different computer. Remote Assistance allows you to request a friend to assist you with a problem on your Windows XP Professional computer. Your friend can view your desktop to watch what you are doing, or take control of your desktop to show you the solution.

Configuring Remote Desktop

Remote Desktop is configured in the System Applet in Control Panel. The Remote tab will display a Remote Desktop window. Ensure the check box labeled Allow Users to Connect Remotely to This Computer is checked to enable Remote Desktop.

By default, your domain user IDis enabled for Remote Desktop. This means you can remotely use your computer when you are at a different computer. By default as well, any user who is also in the administrators group has administrative access to your computer.

You can use the Select Remote Users button to add additional users who will have remote access to your machine.

Running an Application Remotely

The following process can be used to start up and shut down a remote desktop session.

Drive Mappings   The Remote Desktop connection also maps the drives from the calling computer onto the remote computer. This will allow you to use the CPU in a much more powerful computer while still accessing data from your calling machine (or network shares from your calling machine). It is therefore important that you trust the computer you are calling.

STEP BY STEP

6.5 Starting and Stopping a Remote Desktop Session

1. Click Start, and then click All Programs.

2. Select Accessories, then Communications, and click Remote Desktop Connection.

3. Enter the name of the computer to which you want to connect, and click Connect.

4. The system will display the login screen from the remote computer.

5. Enter your user ID and password to log in.

6. Start up Windows Explorer and note the drive mappings.

7. Click Start and select Logout to shut down the Remote Desktop session.

When you initiate a remote desktop session, the screen is automatically locked out, preventing anyone from accessing the console while you are logged in.

Configure Remote Assistance

Remote Assistance is configured in the System applet in Control Panel. The Remote tab will display a Remote Assistance window. Ensure the check box labeled Allow Remote Assistance Invitations to Be Sent from This Computer is checked to enable Remote Assistance. Select the Advanced button to view the Remote Assistance Setting screen. Ensure the check box labeled Allow This Computer to Be Controlled Remotely is checked. Remote Assistance requires that both parties have Windows XP Professional on their computers and the MSN Instant Messenger service configured and running.

Requests for Assistance and Offering Help

There are two ways that a friend can assist you in solving your problem—you can email an invitation or your friend can offer remote assistance.

A request for assistance can be done through two mechanisms. The first is the help system (Help and Support). The main screen is Help, and Support has a link under Ask for Assistance that is labeled Invite a Friend to Connect to Your Computer with Remote Assistance. This link will take you to a screen to request Remote Assistance and to monitor outstanding invitations. Figure 6.18 shows the help screen to request Remote Assistance.

Taking the link to request Remote Assistance will display a screen with your current Instant Messenger contact list to which to send a Remote Assistance request. The screen also has a place to send an email–based request.

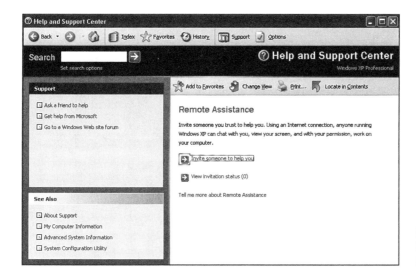

FIGURE 6.18
Screen to make and review Remote Assistance initiations.

> **NOTE**
>
> **Connected with Email** Both you and your friend must be using either Instant Messenger (MSN Messenger can also be used because it relies on IM) or a MAPI-compliant email system such as Outlook or Outlook Express.
>
> Both you and your friend must be connected to the Internet. If the person asking for assistance disconnects and then reconnects, the invitation must be resent.
>
> If you are behind a firewall, you must ask the administrator to open up the port necessary for Remote Assistance (Port 3389 TCP/IP).

The second way of sending a Remote Assistance request is to start Instant Messenger directly and select Ask for Remote Assistance from the Tool drop-down menu. This path takes you to basically the same place as the Help and Support Center.

The link to offer Remote Assistance is harder to find. If you open the Help and Support Center and search for Offer Remote Assistance, you will get one search item returned. That link is to the screen to offer remote assistance to a computer name or IP address.

Both the request for Remote Assistance and the offer of Remote Assistance can be added to the Help and Support Center favorites list for easy retrieval.

Figure 6.19 shows the screen for offering Remote Assistance.

If you are at a help desk and use remote assistance to solve problems, you should also consider compiling a FAQ (Frequently Asked Questions) list and send that file along with every desktop visit you make. You will lower the number of calls you get if users can solve common problems themselves.

FIGURE 6.19
Offering Remote Assistance.

CONFIGURING, MANAGING, AND TROUBLESHOOTING AN INTERNET CONNECTION FIREWALL

Configure, manage, and troubleshoot an Internet connection firewall.

A *firewall* is a service that intercepts network traffic and applies a set of rules to decide whether the packets should be allowed or denied passage. The information used to make this determination comes from the packet header and includes source and destination address, ports, and other information.

A Stateful Packet Filter

Internet Connection Firewall is more than just a static packet filter that decides to drop or pass a packet solely on its addressing information. ICF bases its decision in context with an established session. This allows the rules to be more comprehensive than those in a static filter.

State, for a connection-oriented protocol such as TCP, is the equivalent of the protocol's definition of a session, where the connection is opened and closed. For a connectionless protocol such as UDP, state is maintained as long as information flows between two endpoints without interruption for a given period of time.

This concept of state allows three primary rules to be defined:

◆ Any packet that matches an established connection is forwarded.

◆ Any packet sent that does not match an established connection will create a new entry in the state table, and the packet is forwarded.

◆ Any packet received that does not match an established connection is dropped.

This policy allows for normal client Internet access and prevents packets that are not expected (or desired) from accessing the network.

ICF also performs additional duties, such as dropping packets that have contradictory flags and enforcing the TCP three-way handshake for open ports. This reduces the effectiveness of some scanning techniques and denial of service attacks that rely on sending large numbers of random packets.

ICF supports the standard Internet protocols, such as FTP, H.323 (Telephony Service), LDAP (Lightweight Directory Access Protocol), T.120 (Multipoint Control Service for Conferencing), and PPTP.

Certain Microsoft products have been written to work seamlessly with ICF. These include Windows Messenger and Remote Assistance as well as any games that use DirectPlay. Other Windows services, such as the Help and Support Center, Windows Time, and Windows Update, use protocols that work through firewalls without special modification.

NOTE

Administrator You must be in the Administrators group on your local Windows XP Professional computer to be able to configure ICF.

Configuring ICF (Internet Connection Firewall)

There are four places where you can configure Internet Connection Firewall on your Windows XP Professional computer:

- ◆ **Welcome to Windows**—During the installation of Windows XP Professional, you are given the option to connect to the Internet for activation of your copy of Windows XP, to create user accounts, and to enable ICF if you have a single network connection to be used for Internet access.

- ◆ **Network Setup**—If you run the Network Setup Wizard, you are asked how your computer is connected to the Internet. If you are directly connected to the Internet, NSW will enable ICF on the connection.

◆ **New Connection**—If you run the New Connection Wizard and select the connection to be directly to the Internet, ICF will be enabled on the connection.

◆ **Network Connections**—You can always select the Advanced tab in the Properties page of an existing connection and enable the ICF check box. Figure 6.20 shows the configuration screen to enable ICF on an existing network connection.

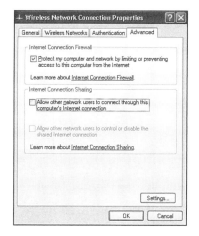

FIGURE 6.20
Configuring a network connection for ICF.

What to Filter and What to Allow

By default, all unexpected inbound packets are dropped by ICF. This would be a problem if you were running a Web site. If port 80 were not open, the Web site would never see any requests. You can allow certain types of packets to flow past ICF by creating a port mapping. Creating a port mapping for port 80, for example, allows incoming HTTP requests to arrive at IIS for service by your Web site.

Some applications (such as streaming media and chat programs) are designed to have responses return on different ports from that on which the outgoing request was made. You can use Port Mappings to allow response traffic to handle this situation.

Internet Connection Firewall (ICF) opens and closes ports dynamically, depending on the services you are accessing; however, there are a few exceptions.

Windows Messenger versions 4.0 and 4.5 both include the capability to transfer files. By default, ICF blocks file transfer and you will need to open a port for Messenger to accomplish this. The process is similar if you require additional ports to support multiple simultaneous file transfers (ports 6891-6900).

The following process can be used to open a port for Messenger File Transfer.

NOTE

Supported Connections ICF can be enabled on a LAN connection (including wireless), RAS connections such as PPPoE, dial-up connections, and VPN connections.

If a machine configured with two network cards has ICS configured, ICF can be enabled on the public Internet connection but not on the internal private network connection.

ICF should also not be configured on a network connection that is part of a network bridge, or on any incoming connections.

NOTE

ICF and ICS When you have ICF and ICS configured on the same connection, a port mapping made by one service is automatically picked up by the other. The two services share the same mapping table.

FIGURE 6.21
Defining a new port.

STEP BY STEP

6.6 Opening a Single File Transfer Port

1. Click Start, right-click My Network Places, and click Properties.

2. Right-click the network connection on which you want to enable the ports and select Properties.

3. Select the Advanced tab, ensure the Internet Connection Firewall box is checked, and click Settings.

4. On the Advanced Setting page, click the Services tab and click the Add button.

5. Name the service Messenger File Transfer, hosted on your Windows XP Professional machine, using TCP port 6891. Figure 6.21 shows the Messenger File Transfer port being created.

6. Click OK to complete the configuration.

In addition, TCP and UDP ports 6901 are used for incoming computer-to-computer voice calls and UDP ports 6801, 6901 and 2001-2120 for computer-to-phone voice calls.

Looking at the Logs

No firewall would be complete without comprehensive logging to help you track attacks on your computer and to decide whether additional ports need to be filtered.

The logs created by Internet Connection Firewall conform to the W3C Extended Log File format. These ASCII text files can be imported into other programs for analysis.

There are four basic options to select to enable logging. Logging is disabled by default.

◆ **Log All Dropped Packets**—This option logs all dropped packets for both inbound and outbound connections.

◆ **Log Successful Connections**—This option will log all successful outbound and inbound connections.

◆ **Log File Name and Location**—This is where the log file is kept. The default is `%windir%\pfirewall.log`.

◆ **Log File Size**—The default size of the ICF log is 4MB. The maximum is 32MB.

The fields in the log file are defined in Table 6.7.

TABLE 6.7

DATA STORED IN THE ICF LOGS

Field	Description
Date	Specifies the year, month, and day the recorded transactions occurred.
Time	Specifies the hour, minute, and seconds at which the recorded transaction occurred.
Action	Specifies which operation was observed by the firewall. The options available to the firewall are OPEN, CLOSE, DROP, and INFO-EVENTS-LOST.
Protocol	Specifies which protocol was used for the communication.
Source IP	Specifies the source IP address (the IP address of the computer attempting to establish communications).
Destination IP	Specifies the destination IP address (the IP address of the destination of a communication attempt).
Source Port	Specifies the source port number of the sending computer.
Destination Port	Specifies the port of the destination computer.
Size	Specifies the packet size in bytes.
TCP Flags	Specifies the TCP control flags found in the TCP: Ack—Acknowledgment Fin—No more data from sender Psh—Push function Rst—Reset the connection Syn—Synchronize sequence numbers Urg—Urgent point field

continues

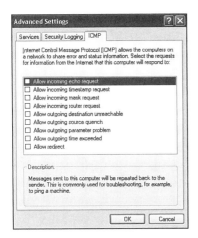

FIGURE 6.22
ICMP Filter Options.

> **Can't Ping**   If you are on the phone to the help desk and they are trying to debug a network problem between your machine and the corporate resource you are trying to use, one of the first debugging steps is to ping your machine. If you have ICF enabled with the default settings, it will filter out the ICMP echo request (which is what a ping uses) and the help desk will not know whether the network has an error.
>
> — EXAM TIP

TABLE 6.7   *continued*

DATA STORED IN THE ICF LOGS

Field	Description
TCP Sequence Number	Specifies the TCP sequence number in the packet.
TCP Ack Number	Specifies the TCP acknowledgment number.
TCP Window Size	Specifies the TCP window size.
ICMP Type	Specifies a number that represents the Type field.
ICMP Code	Specifies a number that represents the Code field.
Info	Specifies an information entry.

Internet Control Message Protocol (ICMP) is used by PCs and routers to report errors and to send control commands to each other. These can be used in hacking and Denial of Services (DoS) attacks and are therefore filtered out by default. Figure 6.22 shows the list of ICMP messages on which ICF filters.

ICF and Policies

Although Active Directory group policies are generally out of sight to a Windows XP Professional user, there is one situation in which a group policy should be understood.

ICF comes with a group policy that allows domain administrators to shut down ICF running in their domain. ICF can be configured to run when the PC is not on the network, but this policy disables it when the PC is connected to the network.

This means that you can have ICF enabled all the time, but your domain administrators disable it when you are connected to the corporate LAN. If, for example, you go to a conference that is running an Internet Café or Wireless hotspot, ICF will recognize that it is not on the corporate LAN anymore and it will be enabled. When you return to work and reconnect to the corporate LAN, ICF will shut down again.

TROUBLESHOOTING TCP/IP CONNECTIONS

Configure and troubleshoot the TCP/IP protocol.

A large number of network troubleshooting tools are available for TCP/IP and the Windows XP platform. Some of these are included in the Windows XP release, and some are part of the resource kits and SMS (NetMon). However, the best approach for troubleshooting network connections is to work from the bottom up, eliminating configuration issues first before checking basic connectivity, and then advancing to higher functions and services.

Configuration Errors

The first thing to check when troubleshooting TCP/IP networking connections is the local TCP/IP configuration.

The IPCONFIG /all command is used to get a detailed listing of the host computer configuration information, including the IP Address, subnet mask, and the default gateway.

Typical problems found in the configuration are duplicate IP addresses with other computers on the network, or a subnet mask of 0.0.0.0.

The following example is the result of an IPCONFIG /all command on a computer system that is configured to have DHCP supply the TCP/IP configuration values, including the IP address and WINS, and the DNS name resolution server addresses:

```
Windows IP Configuration

    Host Name . . . . . . . . . . . . : gordb3
    Primary Dns Suffix  . . . . . . . : barknet.ads
    Node Type . . . . . . . . . . . . : Mixed
    IP Routing Enabled. . . . . . . . : No
    WINS Proxy Enabled. . . . . . . . : No
    DNS Suffix Search List. . . . . . : barknet.ads

Ethernet adapter Local Area Connection:
```

```
      Media State . . . . . . . . . . . : Media disconnected
      Description . . . . . . . . . . . : Intel(R) PRO/100+
MiniPCI
      Physical Address. . . . . . . . . : 00-D0-59-10-FC-F4

Ethernet adapter Wireless Network Connection:

      Connection-specific DNS Suffix  . : Barknet.ads
      Description . . . . . . . . . . . : ORiNOCO Wireless
LAN PC Card (5 volt)
      Physical Address. . . . . . . . . : 00-02-2D-1D-4C-6B
      Dhcp Enabled. . . . . . . . . . . : Yes
      Autoconfiguration Enabled . . . . : Yes
      IP Address. . . . . . . . . . . . : 192.168.0.6
      Subnet Mask . . . . . . . . . . . : 255.255.255.0
      Default Gateway . . . . . . . . . : 192.168.0.1
      DHCP Server . . . . . . . . . . . : 192.168.0.1
      DNS Servers . . . . . . . . . . . : 192.168.0.1
      Lease Obtained. . . . . . . . . . : Wednesday, December
26, 2001 9:17:36 PM
      Lease Expires . . . . . . . . . . : Thursday, January
03, 2002 9:17:36 PM
```

If your local address is returned as 169.254.y.z, you have been assigned an IP address by the Automatic Private IP Addressing (APIA) feature of Windows XP. This means that the local DHCP server is not configured properly or cannot be reached from your computer, and an IP address has been assigned automatically with a subnet mask of 255.255.0.0.

If your local address is returned as 0.0.0.0, the Microsoft MediaSense software detects that the network adapter is not connected to a network. If the connection is solid and the problem persists, you might have to update the network adapter drivers to the latest revision.

Checking Basic Connectivity

If the computer system appears to be configured correctly, the next step is to try to connect to other hosts on the TCP/IP network.

Using PING

PING is a tool that will help to verify connectivity at the IP level. The PING command will send out an ICMP Echo request to the target hostname or IP address. Although this does not always work because some servers will not respond to echo requests as a security measure, you will find that most workstations automatically enable echo requests.

The best process to follow when using PING to detect network problems is to use IP addresses only (so as not to confuse name-resolution errors with network errors) and to ping progressively more remote computers.

The first interface to check is the loopback address. The following command will verify that TCP/IP is installed correctly:

```
Ping 127.0.0.1
```

If this fails, the TCP/IP drivers are corrupted, the network adapter is not working, or some other service is interfering with TCP/IP.

Next, ping the IP address of the local computer using the following command:

```
Ping <ip address of local host>
```

If the routing table is correct, this will simply be forwarded to the loopback address.

Next, ping the default gateway:

```
Ping <ip address of gateway>
```

This command will determine that the default gateway is functioning and that you can communicate with a local host on the local network.

Next, ping a remote host to verify that you can access a remote network through a router:

```
ping <IP address of remote host>
```

PING uses hostname resolution (via HOSTS file, WINS, and then DNS). If you can access a remote system using its IP address but not its hostname, the problem is in name resolution, not network connectivity.

Using Tracert

The Tracert diagnostic utility determines the route taken to a destination by sending Internet Control Message Protocol (ICMP) echo packets with varying IP Time-to-Live (TTL) values to the destination. Each router along the path is required to decrement the TTL on a packet by at least 1 before forwarding it. When the TTL on a

> **NOTE**
>
> **Try Remote Addresses First** In all the troubleshooting examples used with PING, the IP address is used rather than the hostname. This way, you will not confuse a DNS problem with a network connectivity problem. When you are sure your network connections are working properly, try pinging the remote host by name. If that works, both network access and DNS name resolution are working properly and your trouble lies elsewhere.

packet reaches 0, the router should send an ICMP Time Exceeded message back to the source computer.

Tracert determines the route by sending the first echo packet with a TTL of 1 and incrementing the TTL by 1 on each subsequent transmission until the target responds or the maximum TTL is reached. The route is determined by examining the ICMP Time Exceeded messages sent back by intermediate routers. Some routers silently drop packets with expired TTLs and are invisible to the Tracert utility.

Tracert cannot record the path the packet takes in returning. However, it will show whether the destination was reachable. If this is not the case, the remote computer might be off the network, behind a firewall, or behind a router that filters ICMP packets.

The following is a sample output from a tracert to www.yahoo.com. In doing a tracert, occasionally you will see echo times replaced by an asterisk (*). This indicates a timeout in getting a response from an intermediate router.

```
Tracing route to www.yahoo.akadns.net [64.58.76.228]


over a maximum of 30 hops:

  1     3 ms     4 ms     3 ms  [192.168.0.1]
  2    37 ms    43 ms    59 ms  [24.79.156.1]
  3    78 ms    21 ms    22 ms  [24.64.127.7]
  4    83 ms    27 ms    88 ms  [66.163.76.2]
  5    53 ms    93 ms    31 ms  [66.163.76.65]
  6   139 ms    89 ms    92 ms  [66.163.76.42]
  7   206 ms    84 ms   212 ms  [204.209.212.46]
  8   107 ms   127 ms   135 ms  [216.64.194.18]
  9   188 ms    98 ms   137 ms  [206.79.9.129]
 10   177 ms   117 ms   109 ms  [206.79.9.134]
 11   161 ms   295 ms   135 ms  [206.79.9.165]
 12   237 ms   118 ms   135 ms  [64.15.224.17]
 13   143 ms   128 ms   119 ms  [206.79.9.102]
 14   181 ms   156 ms   146 ms  [216.33.96.146]
 15   135 ms   153 ms   175 ms  [216.33.98.26]
 16   284 ms   195 ms   131 ms  [216.35.210.126]
 17   141 ms   116 ms   120 ms  [64.58.76.228]

Trace complete.
```

Using ARP

Windows XP TCP/IP will communicate with remote computers over a network using an IP address, a NetBIOS name, or a hostname.

Regardless of what naming convention is used, eventually the address must be resolved to a MAC address (for shared access media such as Ethernet and Token Ring).

Troubleshooting the ARP cache is one of the more difficult tasks because the problems are often intermittent.

For example, if two computers are using the same IP address on a network, you might see an intermittent problem in accessing the correct one because the most recent ARP table entry is always the one from the host that responded more quickly to any ARP request.

You can add static addresses to the ARP table using the ARP command-line utility. This can cause some problems if network-adapter cards are changed because the link between static IP address and MAC address would change. Dynamic entries in the cache age and are deleted when the site is no longer referenced. ARP entries are refreshed roughly every two minutes.

IP addresses assigned by DHCP do not cause duplicate IP conflicts (unless, of course, DHCP is configured with overlapping ranges), so most conflicts are because of static IP addresses. Examining a list of static IP addresses and their corresponding MAC address will help you track down the problem.

If you do not have a record of all IP and MAC address pairs on your network, you can still get some information from the manufacturer bytes of the MAC addresses for inconsistencies. These three-byte numbers are called Organizationally Unique Identifiers (OUIs) and are assigned by the Institute of Electrical and Electronics Engineers (IEEE). The first three bytes of each MAC address identify the card's manufacturer. Knowing what equipment you installed and comparing that with the values returned by ARP might allow you to determine which static address was entered in error.

The following is an example of the ARP -a command that is used to display current cache of IP addresses and the MAC addresses associated with them.

```
Arp -a
Interface: 157.57.18.16 on Interface 0x1000003
  Internet Address      Physical Address      Type
    157.57.18.1         00-d0-ba-09-9c-d6     dynamic
    157.57.18.26        00-a0-c9-96-03-7f     dynamic
```

This output indicates that the current IP address is 157.57.18.16 and that two addresses have been recently used: 157.57.18.1 and

157.57.18.26. Check the output of the `ipconfig` command to see whether either or both of the addresses are part of the IP configuration (such as the default gateway) or use `tracert <ip address>` to resolve the name.

If the problem still persists and no obvious error is apparent, check the Event Viewer for additional clues. For example, DHCP might have detected a duplicate card on the network and denied the computer's request to join.

Verify Server Services

Sometimes, a system configured as a remote gateway or router is not functioning as a router. To confirm that the remote computer you want to contact is set up to forward packets, you can either examine it with a remote administration tool (assuming that it's a computer you administer) or you can attempt to contact the person who maintains the computer.

Resolving Hostnames in TCP/IP

The process for two computers to communicate using TCP/IP involves four distinct steps:

1. Resolve the hostname or NetBIOS name to an IP address. Hostname resolution follows the somewhat tortuous route described in the following list:

    - Is the name to resolve your own hostname?

    - Check DNS cache.

    - Check the HOSTS file for a static entry.

    - Request name resolution from a DNS server.

   NetBIOS name resolution follows a similar route described in the following list.

    - Is the name in the local NetBIOS name cache?

    - Check a WINS server.

    - Broadcast (depending on your node type).

    - Check the LMHOSTS file for a static entry.

If that does not resolve the name, NetBIOS name resolution continues and follows the hostname resolution path.

2. Use the IP address and the routing table to determine the interface to use and the forwarding IP address.

3. Use ARP to resolve the forwarding IP address to a MAC address.

4. Use the MAC address to send the IP datagram.

If the computer to be reached is a hostname or a NetBIOS name, the name must be resolved to an IP address before any data can be sent. Hostnames and NetBIOS names are resolved in different ways.

Resolve a NetBIOS Name to an IP Address

Resolving a NetBIOS name means successfully mapping a 16-byte NetBIOS name to an IP address. When your computer starts up, it registers a unique NetBIOS name (padded to 15 characters) and appends a service indicator as the 16th character. Depending on what services your machine provides, a number of names can be registered. The following list shows the output from an NBTSTAT -n command that lists all the NetBIOS names registered:

```
Local Area Connection:
Node IpAddress: [0.0.0.0] Scope Id: []


    No names in cache


Wireless Network Connection:
Node IpAddress: [192.168.0.3] Scope Id: []


          NetBIOS Local Name Table


    Name                Type        Status
    ---------------------------------------------

    GORDB3         <00>  UNIQUE      Registered

    NORTHAMERICA   <00>  GROUP       Registered

    GORDB3         <03>  UNIQUE      Registered
```

GORDB3	<20>	UNIQUE	Registered
NORTHAMERICA	<1E>	GROUP	Registered
NORTHAMERICA	<1D>	UNIQUE	Registered
.._MSBROWSE_.<01>		GROUP	Registered
GORDB	<03>	UNIQUE	Registered

The service indicator is the hex number contained within the <> brackets. This number can be between 0 and 255 (decimal) or 00 and FF Hex. This number is usually displayed as a hex number because many of them translate into unprintable characters.

For example, the File and Printer Sharing for Microsoft Networks service in Windows XP Professional uses NetBIOS name resolution. When your computer starts up, this service registers a unique NetBIOS name based on the name of your computer (padded out to 15 characters if it is shorter than that) with 0x20 as the 16th character.

Table 6.8 contains a partial list of the NetBIOS service codes. Some of these are in the preceding sample printout. In this table, the Type column indicates whether the service is unique or a group service.

TABLE 6.8

NetBIOS Service Codes

Name	Number	Type	Description
<computername>	00	U	Workstation Service
<computername>	01	U	Messenger Service
\\--_MSBROWSE>_	01	G	Master Browser
<computername>	03	U	Messenger Service
<computername>	06	U	RAS Server Service
<computername>	1F	U	NetDDE Service
<computername>	20	U	File Server Service
<computername>	21	U	RAS Client Service
<computername>	22	U	Microsoft Exchange Interchange (MSMail Connector)
<computername>	23	U	Microsoft Exchange Store

Name	*Number*	*Type*	*Description*
`<computername>`	24	U	Microsoft Exchange Directory
`<computername>`	30	U	Modem Sharing Server Service
`<computername>`	31	U	Modem Sharing Client Service
`<computername>`	43	U	SMS Clients Remote Control
`<computername>`	44	U	SMS Administrators Remote Control Tool
`<computername>`	45	U	SMS Clients Remote Chat
`<computername>`	46	U	SMS Clients Remote Transfer
`<computername>`	4C	U	DEC Pathworks TCPIP service on Windows NT
`<computername>`	42	U	McAfee VirusScan
`<computername>`	52	U	DEC Pathworks TCPIP service on Windows NT
`<computername>`	87	U	Microsoft Exchange MTA
`<computername>`	6A	U	Microsoft Exchange IMC
`<computername>`	BE	U	Network Monitor Agent
`<computername>`	BF	U	Network Monitor Application
`<username>`	03	U	Messenger Service
`<domain>`	00	G	Domain Name
`<domain>`	1B	U	Domain Master Browser
`<domain>`	1C	G	Domain Controllers
`<domain>`	1D	U	Master Browser
`<domain>`	1E	G	Browser Service Elections
`<INet~Services>`	1C	G	IIS
`<IS~computer name>`	00	U	IIS

When you attempt to make a file-sharing connection to a computer running Windows XP by name, the File and Printer Sharing for

Part I EXAM PREPARATION

Microsoft Networks service on the file server you specify corresponds to a specific NetBIOS name. For example, when you attempt to connect to a computer called COMMONSERVER, the NetBIOS name corresponding to the File and Printer Sharing for Microsoft Networks service on that computer is as follows:

```
COMMONSERVER   [20]
```

Note that the name of the server is padded out to 15 characters.

To actually use the file server, its IP address must be established.

The exact mechanism by which NetBIOS names are resolved to IP addresses depends on the NetBIOS node type that's configured for the node. Table 6.9 covers the various node types and the associated resolution mechanism.

NODE TYPES AND RESOLUTION MECHANISMS

Node Type	Description
B-node (broadcast)	B-node uses broadcast NetBIOS name queries for name registration and resolution. B-node has two major problems: Broadcasts disturb every node on the network, and routers typically do not forward broadcasts, so only NetBIOS names on the local network can be resolved.
P-node (peer-peer)	P-node uses a NetBIOS name server (NBNS), such as a WINS server, to resolve NetBIOS names. P-node does not use broadcasts; instead, it queries the name server directly. A problem that can occur with this configuration is two computer systems on the same network segment but using two different WINS servers might not be able to connect to each other if the WINS servers do not replicate to each other.
M-node (mixed)	M-node is a combination of B-node and P-node. By default, an M-node functions as a B-node. If an M-node is unable to resolve a name by broadcast, it queries an NBNS using P-node.
H-node (hybrid)	H-node is a combination of P-node and B-node. By default, an H-node functions as a P-node. If an H-node is unable to resolve a name through the NBNS, it uses a broadcast to resolve the name.

NOTE

NetBIOS Nodes Computers running Windows XP are B-node by default and become H-node when they are configured with a WINS server.

Windows XP can also use a local database file called LMHOSTS to resolve remote NetBIOS names. The LMHOSTS file is stored in the *systemroot*\System32\Drivers\Etc folder.

NetBIOS names are resolved to an IP address by the NetBIOS session service through the following sequence:

◆ Is the name in the local NetBIOS name cache?

◆ Check a WINS server.

◆ Broadcast (depending on your node type).

◆ Check the LMHOSTS file for a static entry.

The NetBIOS cache is always checked first. The next step taken in resolving a name depends on the node type.

A B-node will broadcast locally only. A P-node will query the WINS server to resolve the name only. An M-node will broadcast locally first and then query the WINS server to resolve the name. The default node (H-node) will query the WINS server and then broadcast locally to resolve the name.

If these methods fail, the following methods are attempted:

◆ Query the HOSTS file.

◆ Query the DNS server if it is configured.

The Nbtstat utility and the NET USE command can be used to diagnose NetBIOS name-resolution problems.

Resolve a Host or Domain Name to an IP Address

Hostnames are resolved by using the HOSTS file or by querying a DNS server. Problems in the HOSTS file usually involve spelling errors and duplicate entries.

The Nslookup utility can be used to diagnose hostname resolution problems.

Nslookup.exe is a command-line tool that will resolve names to IP addresses and vice versa. Nslookup can be an excellent tool for testing and troubleshooting DNS servers, and it can be run in both interactive and noninteractive modes. Noninteractive mode is useful when only a single piece of data needs to be returned. The syntax for noninteractive mode is as follows:

```
nslookup [-option] [hostname] [server]
```

> **NOTE**
>
> **NetBIOS Name-Resolution Problem**
> If the problem accessing the remote computer is related to the NetBIOS name resolution, the computer can still be reached by using the IP address.

To start `Nslookup.exe` in interactive mode, simply type **nslookup** at the command prompt:

```
C:\> nslookup
Default Server:  nameserver1.domain.com
Address:  10.0.0.1
>
```

Typing **help** or **?** at the command prompt will generate a list of available commands. Anything typed at the command prompt that is not recognized as a valid command is assumed to be a hostname and an attempt is made to resolve it using the default server. To interrupt interactive commands, press Ctrl+C. To exit interactive mode and return to the command prompt, type **exit** at the command prompt.

What follows is the help output. It contains the complete list of options. The general syntax is given first.

Commands (identifiers are shown in uppercase; [ ] means optional) :

```
NAME            - print info about the host/domain NAME
using default server
NAME1 NAME2     - as above, but use NAME2 as server
help or ?       - print info on common commands
set OPTION      - set an option
    all             - print options, current server and
host
    [no]debug       - print debugging information
    [no]d2          - print exhaustive debugging
information
    [no]defname     - append domain name to each query
    [no]recurse     - ask for recursive answer to query
    [no]search      - use domain search list
    [no]vc          - always use a virtual circuit
    domain=NAME     - set default domain name to NAME
    srchlist=N1[/N2/.../N6] - set domain to N1 and search
list to N1,N2, etc.
    root=NAME       - set root server to NAME
    retry=X         - set number of retries to X
    timeout=X       - set initial time-out interval to
X seconds
    type=X          - set query type (ex.
A,ANY,CNAME,MX,NS,PTR,SOA,SRV)
    querytype=X     - same as type
    class=X         - set query class (ex. IN
(Internet), ANY)
    [no]msxfr       - use MS fast zone transfer
    ixfrver=X       - current version to use in IXFR
transfer request
server NAME     - set default server to NAME, using current
default server
```

```
lserver NAME      - set default server to NAME, using initial
server
finger [USER]     - finger the optional NAME at the current
default host
root              - set current default server to the root
ls [opt] DOMAIN [> FILE] - list addresses in DOMAIN
(optional: output to FILE)
    -a            -  list canonical names and aliases
    -d            -  list all records
    -t TYPE       -  list records of the given type (e.g.
A,CNAME,MX,NS,PTR etc.)
view FILE             - sort an 'ls' output file and view it
with pg
exit              - exit the program
```

Determine Whether the Address Is Local

The subnet mask, along with the IP address, is used to determine whether the IP address is local or on a remote subnet. An ill-configured subnet mask can result in the system's inability to access any other system on the local subnet while still being able to communicate with remote systems. If the IP address is local, ARP is used to identify the destination MAC address.

Problems at this point are usually related to an invalid ARP cache (such as a duplicate address) or an invalid subnet mask. The utilities ARP and IPCONFIG can be used to solve local address-resolution problems.

Determine the Correct Gateway

If the IP address is remote from the local subnet, the gateway used to reach the remote address must be determined. If the network has a single router, this problem is straightforward. In a network with more than one router connected, additional steps must be taken.

To solve this problem, the system uses the routing table. The entries in the routing table enable IP to determine through which gateway to send outgoing traffic. The routing table has many entries for individual routes, each one consisting of a destination, network mask, gateway interface, and hop count (metric).

The Route utility can be used to diagnose problems with accessing the gateway.

The Route program is a utility that is called from the command line to manipulate network routing tables. Most of the routing information that your system uses is maintained automatically by Windows XP Professional. However, in the event that you need to add a static route from your system to a remote network, the key to remember is to route to the network you cannot see by using the nearest gateway that you can see. Because that gateway is also a router (by definition), it will be able to access networks to which you have no direct access.

The structure of the command line is as follows:

```
ROUTE [-F] [-P] [COMMAND [destination] [MASK subnetmask]
[gateway] [METRIC costmetric]]
```

The -F parameter clears the routing tables of all gateway entries. If this is used in conjunction with one of the commands, the tables are cleared before running the command.

The -P parameter, when used with the add command, makes a route persistent across boots of the system. By default, routes are not preserved when the system is restarted. When used with the print command, -P displays the list of registered persistent routes. It's ignored for all other commands, which always affect the appropriate persistent routes.

The following is the definition of the command-line arguments for ROUTE:

◆ COMMAND—Specifies one of the following commands:

PRINT	Prints a route
ADD	Adds a route
DELETE	Deletes a route
CHANGE	Modifies an existing route

◆ destination—Specifies the computer to which to send the command.

◆ MASK subnetmask—Specifies a subnet mask to be associated with this route entry. If not specified, 255.255.255.255 is used.

◆ gateway—Specifies gateway.

◆ METRIC costmetric—Assigns an integer cost metric (ranging from 1 to 9999) to be used in calculating the fastest, most reliable, and/or least expensive routes.

The following is an example of the output derived from the `print` command in the route utility:

```
===========================================================================
Interface List
0x1 ........................ MS TCP Loopback interface
0x1000003 ...00 80 c7 ba df 9e ...... Xircom Ethernet 10/100 PC Card
===========================================================================
Active Routes:
Network Destination        Netmask          Gateway       Interface  Metric
        0.0.0.0          0.0.0.0       157.57.18.1    157.57.18.16   1
      127.0.0.0        255.0.0.0       127.0.0.1       127.0.0.1   1
    157.57.18.0  255.255.255.192     157.57.18.16    157.57.18.16   1
   157.57.18.16  255.255.255.255      127.0.0.1       127.0.0.1   1
  157.57.255.255 255.255.255.255     157.57.18.16    157.57.18.16   1
      224.0.0.0        224.0.0.0     157.57.18.16    157.57.18.16   1
255.255.255.255 255.255.255.255     157.57.18.16    157.57.18.16   1
Default Gateway:       157.57.18.1
===========================================================================
Persistent Routes:
  None
```

The IP routing table for this Windows XP computer contains the following routes:

◆ **Default route**—The route with the network destination of 0.0.0.0 and the netmask of 0.0.0.0 is the default route. Any destination IP address ANDed with 0.0.0.0 results in 0.0.0.0. Therefore, for any IP address, the default route produces a match. If the default route is chosen because no better routes are found, the IP datagram is forwarded to the IP address in the Gateway column using the interface corresponding to the IP address in the Interface column.

◆ **Loopback network**—The route with the network destination of 127.0.0.0 and the netmask of 255.0.0.0 is a route designed to take any IP address of the form 127.*x.y.z* and forward it to the special loopback address of 127.0.0.1.

◆ **Directly attached network**—The route with the network destination of 157.57.18.0 and the netmask of 255.255.255.192 is a route for the directly attached network. IP packets destined for the directly attached network are not forwarded to a router but sent directly to the destination. Note that the gateway address and interface are the IP address of the node. This indicates that the packet is sent from the network adapter corresponding to the node's IP address.

◆ **Local host**—The route with the network destination of 157.57.18.16 and the netmask of 255.255.255.255 is a host route corresponding to the IP address of the host. All IP datagrams to the IP address of the host are forwarded to the loopback address.

◆ **All-subnets directed broadcast**—The route with the network destination of 157.57.255.255 and the netmask of 255.255.255.255 is a host route for the all-subnets directed broadcast address for the class B Network ID 157.57.0.0. The all-subnets directed broadcast address is designed to reach all subnets of class-based Network ID. Packets addressed to the all-subnets directed broadcast are sent out of the network adapter corresponding to the node's IP address. A host route for the all-subnets directed broadcast is present only for network IDs that are subnets of a class-based network ID.

◆ **Multicast address**—The route with the network destination of 224.0.0.0 and the netmask of 240.0.0.0 is a route for all class D multicast addresses. An IP datagram matching this route is sent from the network adapter corresponding to the node's IP address.

◆ **Limited broadcast**—The route with the network destination of 255.255.255.255 and the netmask of 255.255.255.255 is a host route for the limited broadcast address. Packets addressed to the limited broadcast are sent out of the network adapter corresponding to the node's IP address.

For example, when the Windows XP computer sends traffic to 157.57.18.60, the route determination process matches two routes—the default route and the directly attached network route. The directly attached network route is the closest matching route. Because the gateway address and the interface address for the directly attached network route are the same, the forwarding IP address is set to the destination address 157.57.18.60. The interface on which to forward the IP datagram is identified by the IP address in the Interface column. In this case, the interface is the Xircom Ethernet 10/100 PC Card, which is assigned the IP address 157.57.18.16.

When the Windows XP computer sends traffic to 204.71.200.68, the route determination process matches the default route (the default route will always match with the destination IP address). Because the gateway address and the interface address for the directly attached network route are different, the forwarding IP address is set to the IP address in the Gateway column (157.57.18.1). The interface on which to forward the IP datagram is identified by the IP address in the Interface column. In this case, the interface is the Xircom Ethernet 10/100 PC Card, which is assigned the IP address 157.57.18.16.

Determine the Gateway Address

By definition, the gateway address is local to the computer system. The ARP process is used to determine its MAC address in the same manner in which a local address is found. The IP datagram can then be sent to the gateway for further routing.

Identifying Name-Resolution Problems

To determine why a remote hostname cannot be resolved, you must first distinguish whether the remote computer is being addressed using NetBIOS or Sockets. If the application uses the NET commands or is an NT 4.0 version administrator tool, it is a NetBIOS problem. If the application uses WinSock such as Telnet, FTP, and the Web browsers, the problem will lie with DNS or the HOSTS file.

Net View Errors

If the Net View utility returns an Error 53 message, the problem is most commonly a NetBIOS name-resolution error or an error in establishing a NetBIOS session. The distinction between these two situations can be determined by entering the following command, where <hostname> is a remote computer you are sure is active:

```
net view * \\<hostname>
```

If this works, name resolution is not the source of the problem. To confirm this, check the status of the temporary session that NetBIOS creates for the NET VIEW command by entering the following command, where *<ip address>* is the same remote computer used in the previous procedure:

```
net view  \\<ip address>
```

If this also fails, the problem is in establishing a session.

If the NET VIEW command fails with a System Error 53 Has Occurred message, the computer running Windows XP is not running the File and Printer Sharing for Microsoft Networks service.

Socket Connection Errors

If the problem is not NetBIOS, the name-resolution problem is related to either a HOSTS file or a DNS configuration error.

If you can ping the remote IP address but not the hostname, there is a problem in the HOSTS file or the DNS entries in the TCP/IP configuration on the computer.

STEP BY STEP

6.7 Check the Hostname Resolution Configuration

1. In the Control Panel, right-click My Network Places and click Properties.

2. Right-click Local Area Connections, and then select Properties.

3. Click Internet Protocol (TCP/IP), and then click Properties.

4. Click the Advanced button in the Microsoft TCP/IP Properties dialog box.

5. Click the DNS tab.

6. Confirm that DNS is configured properly. If the DNS server IP address is missing, add it to the list of DNS server addresses.

Check the HOSTS File

If you are having trouble connecting to a remote system using a hostname and are using a HOSTS file for name resolution, the problem might be with the contents of that file. Be sure the name of the remote computer is spelled correctly in the HOSTS file and by the application using it.

The HOSTS file or a DNS server is used to resolve hostnames to IP addresses whenever you use TCP/IP utilities such as PING. You can find the HOSTS file in the following directory:

```
\\%systemroot%\system32\drivers\etc
```

This file is not dynamic, so all entries must be made manually. Hostname resolution will check the HOSTS file before checking a DNS server, so if an incorrect entry is in the HOSTS file, your system will not check the DNS server for an address.

Hostname Resolution Using DNS

The DNS system is a worldwide distributed database that replaces the HOSTS file with a hierarchical domain name system that maps names to IP addresses.

If you were trying to contact a computer with the name testcomp.microsoft.com, for example, the following steps would be performed in using DNS to resolve this:

1. The client contacts the DNS name server with a recursive query for testcomp.microsoft.com. The server must now return the answer or an error message.

2. The DNS name server checks its cache and zone files for the answer but doesn't find it. It contacts a server at the root of the Internet (a root DNS server) with an iterative query for testcomp.microsoft.com.

> **NOTE**
>
> **DNS Configuration**   If the IP addresses are supplied by DHCP, there will not be any DNS entries; these entries are supplied when the IP address is obtained. You can see your current IP address and the DNS systems you are using by using the IPCONFIG command. Check the DNS configuration for your subnet with the system administrator.

3. The root server doesn't know the answer, so it responds with a referral to an authoritative server in the .com domain.

4. The DNS name server contacts a server in the .com domain with an iterative query for `testcomp.microsoft.com`.

5. The server in the .com domain does not know the exact answer, so it responds with a referral to an authoritative server in the `Microsoft.com` domain.

6. The DNS name server contacts the server in the `microsoft.com` domain with an iterative query for `testcomp.microsoft.com`.

7. The server in the `microsoft.com` domain does know the answer. It responds with the correct IP address to the preferred client's DNS server.

8. The DNS name server responds to the client query with the IP address for `testcomp.microsoft.com`.

In the Step by Step, a number of references were made to iterative queries and recursive queries. In an iterative query, the client asks for a name resolution and, if the DNS server does not know the answer, receives a list of other servers to query for the answer. In a recursive query, if the DNS server does not know the answer, it will query other systems on your behalf and relay the answer back to you. In addition, a recursive query will store the answer in a local cache, which will speed up subsequent queries for the same address.

DNS Error Messages

Errors in name resolution can occur if the entries in a DNS server or client are not configured correctly, if the DNS server is not running, or if there is a problem with network connectivity. To determine the cause of any name-resolution problem, you can use the Nslookup utility.

Queries that cannot be answered will fail with several different error messages depending on the actual problem encountered. For example, Nslookup replies that a name cannot be found if the name can't be resolved, or with a timeout message if the DNS server doesn't reply within the expected time. The actual problem could be that the server is down or the network access to the server is interrupted somewhere.

LMHOSTS File Errors

The LMHOSTS file is scanned from the top down. If there is more than one address listed for the same hostname, TCP/IP uses the first value it encounters.

Long Connect Times Using LMHOSTS

To determine the cause of long connect times after adding an entry to LMHOSTS, take a look at the order of the entries in the LMHOSTS file. Delays in resolving names when using an LMHOSTS file can be minimized by using the #PRE tag to preload an entry and placing often-used entries at the top of the file. These entries are preloaded into the NetBIOS Name Cache, which is always checked first when doing a NetBIOS name resolution.

WINS Configuration Errors

To examine your computer's WINS configuration, take the following steps:

STEP BY STEP

6.8 Examine Your WINS Configuration

1. In the Control Panel, right-click My Network Places and click Properties.

2. Right-click the Local Area connection and select Properties.

3. Select the Internet Protocol (TCP/IP) and select Properties.

4. Click Advanced and select the WINS tab.

The WINS server IP address should be listed in the Configuration box unless the address is obtained from a DHCP server. This is also the place that LMHOSTS lookup is enabled and NetBIOS over TCP/IP is selected as well.

Table 6.10 lists most of the main tools used in troubleshooting communications problems. Some of these tools have been discussed in detail in this chapter. For those that have not been covered or were not covered in great detail, you might want to review the Help and Support pages for these tools to become familiar with each utility.

TABLE 6.10

TCP/IP DIAGNOSTIC UTILITIES

Utility	Function
ARP	View the ARP (Address Resolution Protocol) cache on the interface of the local computer to detect invalid entries.
Hostname	Display the hostname of the computer.
Ipconfig	Display current TCP/IP network configuration values, and update or release Dynamic Host Configuration Protocol (DHCP) allocated leases, and display, register, or flush Domain Name System (DNS) names.
Nbtstat	Check the state of current NetBIOS over TCP/IP connections, update the NetBIOS name cache, and determine the registered names and scope ID.
Netstat	Display statistics for current TCP/IP connections.
Netdiag	Check all aspects of the network connection.
Nslookup	Check records, domain host aliases, domain host services, and operating system information by querying Internet domain name servers.
Pathping	Trace a path to a remote system and report packet losses at each router along the way.
Ping	Send ICMP Echo Requests to verify that TCP/IP is configured correctly and that a remote TCP/IP system is available.
Route	Display the IP routing table, and add or delete IP routes.
Tracert	Trace a path to a remote system.

There are also some Windows XP tools that can be used to aid in TCP/IP network troubleshooting that have not been covered in this chapter.

◆ Microsoft SNMP service provides statistical information to SNMP management systems.

◆ Event Viewer tracks errors and events.

◆ Microsoft Network Monitor performs in-depth network traces. The full version is part of the Systems Management Server (SMS) product, and a limited version is included with Windows XP Server.

◆ Performance Monitor analyzes TCP/IP network performance.

◆ Registry editors `Regedit.exe` and `Regedt32.exe` allow viewing and editing of Registry parameters.

CASE STUDY: HOME OFFICE

ESSENCE OF THE CASE

- There is an internal TCP/IP network.
- There is a Windows XP Server sharing a connection with the Internet.
- There is a VPN connection to a corporate server.
- Access to hosts on the Internet is failing.

SCENARIO

Like everyone else, you work too much and have set up an office in your home. There is a TCP/IP network internal to your house that connects all the PCs and laptops you have together as one network. You are running Windows .NET Server on one of the systems that acts as a gateway and it is sharing a connection to the Internet through a local cable company. Your laptop is running Windows XP Professional with TCP/IP configured by DHCP. You normally connect to your company VPN server via the cable modem and from there, the Internet in general. Today, you find that you cannot access your favorite search engine Web page.

ANALYSIS

Several network interfaces are being used in this case study. The first is the TCP/IP configuration of the Windows XP Professional computer that's trying to access the search engine home page. The TCP/IP configuration for this computer will be DHCP enabled and point to the internal domain hosted by the Windows XP Server system. The `IPCONFIG /ALL` display should show a

continues

CASE STUDY: HOME OFFICE

continued

DHCP-enabled connection with the IP address in the range 192.168.0.x (the default address assigned by the server) with a gateway address that points to the Windows XP server computer. In addition, the domain name should be the domain that was set up when the Windows XP server was installed. If any of these values is missing or incorrect, the following command will refresh the configuration:

```
Ipconfig /release
Ipconfig /renew
```

The second network interface is on the Windows XP server. This system will have two network adapters: one on the inside network and one on the outside. When this system was installed, that distinction was made and connection sharing was enabled on the outside connection. The IPCONFIG /ALL display should show two connections: an inside connection that has a static IP address (usually 192.168.0.1) and an outside address that is usually configured as DHCP supplied. The local cable company normally would supply the outside address when the cable modem became active on their network. As with the Windows XP Professional system, the following commands will refresh the configuration provided by the cable company:

```
Ipconfig /release
Ipconfig /renew
```

The third network interface is the VPN connection between the Windows XP Professional computer and the VPN server in your corporation. That connection is established on the Windows XP Professional machine through the gateway server (the gateway server does not need a connection itself). This will appear as a new network entry on your Windows XP Professional computer with an IP address from your corporate network. In addition, DNS and WINS entries will be assigned from your corporate network and they should be displayed by the IPCONFIG /ALL command.

The first thing to try after reviewing all the configurations is to ping your gateway. From the Windows XP Professional computer, that would be the Windows XP server system. If that works, try to ping an outside host (such as your search engine home page) from the Windows XP Server. If that works, but it does not work from the Windows XP Professional computer, the problem is in the connection-sharing setup. Unconfiguring it and reinstalling it on the server will correct any problem.

The next thing to try is to trace the route that packets take to a known outside host (the search engine home page again). From the Windows XP Professional computer, enter the following command, where *<host name>* is the search engine hostname:

```
Tracert <host name>
```

Tracert will trace the hops (routers) that a packet must take to get to the destination. If it gets to the destination, your problems are solved. If it can't display a router name and shows only IP addresses, the problem is in the DNS servers provided by your cable company. If you get to your corporate network routers (as identified by the IP address ranges) but you don't get from there to the destination, the problem is in your corporate DNS servers or gateway, or the configuration provided when you logged in to the VPN server. Logging out and logging back in will refresh this configuration and solve the problem. If the problem persists, the error is likely on your corporate network and a call to tech support is in order.

CHAPTER SUMMARY

This chapter discussed the main topics of implementing, managing, and troubleshooting network protocols and services. The essence of these topics is to understand the components of networking with emphasis on TCP/IP and the role that each component plays in successfully connecting to a network.

Also covered were the various configurations available for accessing outside networks, including ISDN multilink, access to private RAS servers, connections to the Internet, and VPN connections through the Internet to secure servers on your corporate network.

KEY TERMS

- TCP/IP
- DNS
- WINS
- DHCP
- VPN
- IPSec
- UNC
- ICF and ICS
- RAS, MS-CHAP, and EAP
- IIS and IE

APPLY YOUR KNOWLEDGE

Exercises

6.1 Install Internet Connection Firewall on a Network Connection

This exercise shows you how to install ICF onto the network connection that attaches to the Internet.

Estimated Time: 10 minutes

1. Click Start, right-click My Network Places, and click Properties.

2. Right-click a network connection attached to the Internet.

3. Select Properties and then the Advanced Tab.

4. Check the Internet Connection Firewall box and click Settings.

5. Select any services you want the Internet user to be able to access.

6. Select the ICMP tab and enable any control message you want ICF to pass.

7. Select the Logging tab and define the logging you want ICF to do. Select a location and size of the log file.

8. Test your firewall by connecting to a testing facility such as Gibson Research (grc.com) and using a tool such as ShieldsUP! to review how good your firewall is. Don't forget that if your system is behind another firewall, it is that firewall that will be tested.

6.2 Change the TCP/IP Properties to Use DHCP

This exercise shows you how to change the properties of the TCP/IP protocol from a static IP to that of a DHCP client.

Estimated Time: 10 minutes

1. Save your current configuration using the command `ipconfig /all > c:\ipconfig.txt`.

2. Click Start, right-click My Network Places, and click Properties.

3. Right-click the connection for which you want to modify TCP/IP and select Properties.

4. Select Obtain an IP Address Automatically and click OK.

5. Click OK to close the Properties page.

6. Open a command window and enter the command **IPCONFIG /RELEASE** and then **IPCONFIG /RENEW**.

7. To verify that DHCP is supplying your computer with configuration information enter the command **IPCONFIG /ALL**.

8. If you don't see a valid IP address with lease information, verify that the DHCP server is functioning and attempt another renew.

9. Return your configuration to the original settings stored in `c:\ipconfig.txt`.

6.3 Install a Dial-Up Connection to the Internet

This exercise shows you how to set up your computer to access the Internet by dialing your ISP.

Estimated Time: 10 minutes

1. Click Start, and then click Control Panel.

2. Right-click My Network Places and click Properties.

APPLY YOUR KNOWLEDGE

3. Click the Create a New Connection icon in the Network Tasks pane.

4. Click Next to close the Welcome page.

5. Select Connect to the Internet and click Next.

6. Select Set Up My Connection Manually and click Next.

7. Select Connect Using a Dial-Up Modem and click Next.

8. Give the connection a name and click Next.

9. Enter the phone number **555-5555** and click Next.

10. In the connection availability screen, select Anyone's Use and click Next.

11. Enter your ISP user ID and password and select whether ICF should be used on this connection.

12. Click Finish to complete the Connection setup.

6.4 Install a VPN Connection to Your Office

This exercise shows you how to set up your computer to access your Corporate Network using a VPN server.

Estimated Time: 10 minutes

1. Click Start, right-click My Network Places, and click Properties.

2. Click the Create a New Connection link in the Network Tasks pane.

3. Click Next to close the Welcome screen.

4. Select Connect to the Network at My Workplace and click Next.

5. On the New Connection Wizard screen, select Virtual Private Network connection and click Next.

6. Provide a name for this Connection and click Next.

7. On the Public Network screen, select the Do Not Dial the Initial Connection button and click Next.

8. Enter the name of the VPN server at your office or alternatively provide its public IP address.

9. On the Connection Availability screen, select Anyone's Use and click Next.

10. Click Finish to complete the configuration.

6.5 Connect to Your Corporate Network Using RAS

This exercise shows you how to connect your computer to an RAS server at your office and configure it for encryption.

Estimated Time: 10 minutes

1. Click Start, right-click My Network Places, and click Properties.

2. Double-click the Create a New Connection link in the Network Tasks pane.

3. Click Next to close the Welcome screen.

4. Select Connect to the Network at My Workplace and click Next.

5. Select Dial-Up Connection and click Next.

6. Provide a name for the connection and click Next.

7. Enter the phone number for your company RAS server or **555-5555** as an example.

8. On the Connection Availability screen, select Anyone's Use and click Next.

APPLY YOUR KNOWLEDGE

9. Click Finish to complete the setup.

10. Return to the Network Connections screen and right-click the new dial-up connection.

11. Select Properties and select the Security Tab.

12. Select Advanced and click Settings.

13. In the Data Encryption drop-down list, select Maximum Strength Encryption (disconnect if server declines).

14. Select Use These Protocols and select MS-CHAP, MS-CHAP Version 2.

15. Click OK to accept the changes.

6.6 Configure a Connection to Use Connection Sharing

This exercise shows you how to take an existing connection and reconfigure it to share the connection with other computers on your private TCP/IP network.

Estimated Time: 10 minutes

1. Click Start, right-click My Network Places, and click Properties.

2. Highlight the connection to share. This connection should be on the Internet or some external private network.

3. Right-click the connection icon and select Properties.

4. Select the Advanced tab.

5. Select the Enable Internet Connection Sharing box.

6. Click Settings.

7. Add any service that you are providing to external users. This could be a Web service.

8. Click OK to accept the changes.

6.7 Request Assistance in Solving a Problem

This exercise shows you how to request a friend to view or take over your desktop to solve a problem. Both parties must be connected through the Internet using Windows Messenger. Both computer systems must be running Windows XP Professional.

Estimated Time: 10 minutes

1. Click Start, and then Help and Support.

2. Under Ask for Assistance, click the link Invite a Friend to Connect to Your Computer with Remote Assistance.

3. In the Remote Assistance frame, click the link Invite Someone to Help You.

4. The Remote Assistance frame will show your current online Windows Messenger contacts plus an e-mail line.

5. Select a contact from your Windows Messenger list and click Invite This Person.

6. That will send a Windows Messenger message to your friend who will be asked to Accept or Reject the request for assistance.

7. If that person chooses to accept the invitation, a dialog box opens on your screen to confirm the request.

8. You can chat, send files, and so on over this link.

9. To have your friend take control of your machine, he must click Take Control on the menu bar.

10. This will open up a dialog box on your machine confirming that you want your friend to take control of your machine.

11. After your friend has solved the problem, he can select Release Control or Disconnect from the menu bar to return control to you.

6.8 Running Remote Desktop

This exercise will show you how to log in remotely to your desktop at work while accessing your local drives. To do this lab, you will need two computers on your home network. The Home version of Windows XP does not support the Remote Desktop connection feature.

Estimated Time: 10 minutes

1. Click Start and select All Programs.

2. Select Accessories and then Communications.

3. Click Remote Desktop Connection.

4. Enter the name of the machine you want to access. If this is within your Corporate Network, you will have to VPN or RAS into it first to find the machine name.

5. Note the tab at the top of the screen indicating you are viewing a Remote machine. Log into your remote Desktop using your domain user ID and Password.

6. Start up Windows Explorer and note that there is a series of drive mappings that reflect your C:, D:, and perhaps E: drives on your local machine.

7. Click the drive mapping that refers to your CD-ROM and see that your local CD drive spins up.

8. Click Start and then Log-Off to log off and terminate the connection.

Review Questions

1. You know that your network has a WINS server on a remote segment but your program cannot locate its server using NetBIOS. What is the most likely problem?

2. You have just installed ICS on a dual-homed machine in your home office. From your workstation, you find that you cannot access the Internet yet. Where is the first place you should look?

3. You are working at home dialed up to the office and have a problem with your machine. You call the corporate help desk but they say they cannot ping your machine. What is blocking that?

4. You have manually configured a TCP/IP connection with a subnet mask of 255.255.255.252 but find that you can't connect to any other computers on your network. What is the problem?

5. What do you have to do to configure smartcard access for a remote dial-up connection?

6. You have a machine that requests its network configuration via DHCP. You find that everything appears correct but you cannot access any servers on your network. What's the most probable cause of this difficulty?

7. You need to have contractors access your corporate network through RAS. You want them to use the strongest encryption. What configuration changes do you make to their machines?

8. You have your servers all obtain their network addresses through DHCP. When a server is rebooted for routine maintenance, users complain that they can no longer see it. What should you tell them to do to fix this problem?

APPLY YOUR KNOWLEDGE

Exam Questions

1. You are the network administrator for a small but rapidly growing company. When first installed, your network consisted of only 10 computers running Windows XP Professional and one computer running Windows 2000 Server. Since then, the number of computers on your network has grown considerably and your old method of using manually assigned IP numbers is becoming clumsy. You wonder whether there is a better way to do this.

   What plan should you implement on your network?

   A. Create a common HOSTS file and copy it to each computer.

   B. Configure each machine to use DHCP but allow them to find their own addresses using APIPA.

   C. Configure a DHCP server and have it distribute network IP addresses.

   D. Continue using fixed addresses because that is the most efficient mechanism possible.

2. You have set up a home office that connects to a cable modem. You want the other computers in your household to be able to access the Internet through this single connection.

   You add a new network card to your gateway computer and attach it to your home network. On the external connection, you enable ICS.

   One computer cannot find any Web sites on the Internet. You examine its network settings and find the following when you look at IPCONFIG:

   Ethernet adapter Wireless Network Connection:

   ```
   Connection-specific DNS Suffix  . :
   Barknet.ads
   IP Address. . . . . . . . . . . :
   192.168.1.6
   Subnet Mask . . . . . . . . . . :
   255.255.224.0
   Default Gateway . . . . . . . . :
   192.168.1.10
   ```

   What should you do to fix the problem and allow the computer access to the Internet?

   A. Disable ICF from the connection that attaches to the Internet.

   B. Disable all TCP/IP filters in the Options part of the ICS gateway Network Configuration.

   C. Set the computer up for DHCP because it does not have the correct subnet mask and does not point to the ICS gateway.

   D. Reset the subnet mask to 255.255.255.0.

3. You are a Web developer within a department in the government. You need to create a new Web site named HRINFO on one of your existing Web servers. The server is running Windows XP Professional as the operating system.

   There are already a number of virtual directories on the Web server that you do not want to move. The HR department wants to link to the Web site by using http://HRinfo.

   How will you configure the Web site and what will it be called?

   A. Create a Web site, specify that it be called HRInfo in its host headers, and reference it as http://hrinfo.

   B. Obtain a new IP address, define it as HRINFO in the DNS, create a new Web site, and reference it as http://hrinfo.

C. Obtain a new IP address, create a new Web site, and reference it as `http://IP address`.

D. Create a new virtual directory below the default Web site and refer to it as `http://machinename/HRInfo`.

4. You are doing help-desk duty when a user sends you an e-mail request for assistance to change a configuration parameter.

   You accept the connection but find that you can only view the desktop and not take control.

   What should you instruct the user to do?

   A. Go to the Remote tab in the System applet and enable the box that's labeled Allow This Computer to Be Controlled Remotely.

   B. Instruct the user to reissue the request for assistance and you reaccept it.

   C. Go to the Offer Assistance link from the Help and Support Center and connect to the user's computer from that point.

   D. Start a Remote Desktop session to take control of the remote computer.

5. You have installed Windows XP Professional on your home computer. You use this machine to access the Internet as well as keep some home account information. You are concerned about being hacked, so you enable ICF and ICS on the Internet Network Connection.

   Later, you check the logs and find that a remote system is opening and closing port 80.

   What should you do to protect your system?

   A. Disable the ICS service.

   B. Block the SMTP service from within ICF.

C. Block the Web server (HTTP) service.

D. Define a new Web service that uses port 80 and then block it.

6. You are doing help-desk duty when a user who is working at home sends you an e-mail request for assistance to change a configuration parameter. The user disconnects from RAS and calls you for more information on how to do Remote Assistance.

   You explain the process to the user and accept the connection but find that you can't connect.

   What should you instruct the user to do?

   A. Go to the Remote tab in the System applet and enable the box that's labeled Allow This Computer to Be Controlled Remotely.

   B. Instruct the user to reissue the request for assistance and you reaccept it.

   C. Go to the Offer Assistance link from the Help and Support Center and connect to the user's computer from that point.

   D. Start a Remote Desktop session to take control of the remote computer.

7. You are in charge of a financial model at the manufacturing plant where you work. You find that the model has been getting bigger and bigger as it evolves, and now it's at the point where it still runs on your desktop machine but is too big for your laptop. You'd like to be able to work from home on this model instead of always going into work, and your laptop does have an internal modem.

APPLY YOUR KNOWLEDGE

What actions should you take to make this program run faster?

A. Configure your desktop computer to be remotely controlled (from the Remote tab inside the System applet).

B. Log into the Office RAS connection and open a Remote Desktop Connection to your desktop machine.

C. Set up Offline Files on your desktop machine and synchronize the appropriate files with your laptop.

D. Create the necessary shortcuts to the application and place them on your desktop.

8. You have just taken a new position at a manufacturing company that requires you to travel frequently. The company provides a high-speed cable-modem connection to your home and also has RAS servers to allow you to dial in from hotels. You must use a virtual private network because of security concerns.

You create a VPN network configuration but when you try to connect to the corporate VPN server, you get a message box that says Error 781—No Valid Certificate Was Found.

What should you do to configure the connection correctly?

A. Open port 443 on your ICF configuration.

B. Configure the connection to use PPTP VPN.

C. Configure the connection to use L2TP IPSec VPN.

D. Configure the connection to use a secure password but not encryption.

9. You have just taken a new position at a manufacturing company that requires you to travel frequently. The company provides a high-speed cable-modem connection to your home and also has RAS servers to allow you to dial in from hotels. You must use a virtual private network because of security concerns.

You are making a presentation at a customer site and need to access your corporate Web site to find some information for the customer.

You plug into the customer's network but find that you cannot access anything on the Internet from your browser.

What should you do to enable your laptop to access your Corporate LAN?

A. Configure your default gateway address to be 192.168.0.1.

B. Issue an IPCONFIG /RENEW command to get the latest IP address from the customer's network.

C. Enable Detect Proxy Settings in Internet Explorer.

D. Have the customer's Network group allow VPN access to your Corporate Network.

10. You are doing help-desk duty when a user from your HR department working at home dials in via RAS and sends you an e-mail request for assistance to change a configuration parameter.

You accept the connection but find that you can't connect to the desktop. You verify that the user is online and is using ICF to protect the RAS connection.

APPLY YOUR KNOWLEDGE

What should you instruct the user to do?

A. Go to the Remote tab in the System applet and enable the box that's labeled Allow This Computer to Be Controlled Remotely.

B. Instruct the user to reissue the request for assistance and you reaccept it.

C. Go to the Offer Assistance link from the Help and Support Center and connect to the user's computer from that point.

D. Instruct the user to open up port 3389 (Remote Desktop service) in ICF.

11. You are the network administrator at a software design company. Occasionally, you use contractors to work on specific parts of code you are developing for your customers. For security reasons, you insist on using the strongest data encryption possible for all RAS sessions. What do you instruct your contractors to configure their RAS connections to use?

A. PAP

B. CHAP

C. MS-CHAP v2

D. SPAP

12. Murray works on the help desk for the transportation department of the city. The building in which he works occupies three floors, with one subnet for each floor. For the network layout, refer to Figure 6.23.

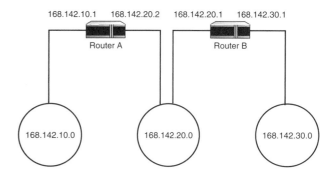

FIGURE 6.23
The Transportation department network map.

A user who is on a Windows XP Professional workstation with an IP address of 168.142.10.12 reports that she cannot reach a server that you identify as having an IP address of 168.142.30.15. She also reports that she is having no problem assigning a drive letter to a server that you identify as being on the same subnet as she is.

You have tried to ping the server directly but you receive a timeout error from PING.

What address should you attempt to reach next?

A. 127.0.0.1

B. 168.142.20.2

C. 168.142.20.1

D. 168.142.30.1

13. Darrell is a member of the network group at a large company. The network uses TCP/IP exclusively and is made up of several subnets, each of

APPLY YOUR KNOWLEDGE

which has servers used by the users in that subnet. He receives a report from a user who says he cannot reach any servers in his local group. Using the NetMon utility, Darrell notices that every time the user tries to connect to a server, his workstation sends out an ARP request for the address of the local gateway.

Which of the following should Darrell identify as most likely the problem?

A. The DNS information is not configured properly.

B. The WINS addresses are missing.

C. The subnet mask is incorrect.

D. The IP address is a duplicate of one on the local subnet.

14. Kevin is part of the networking group at a large metropolitan utility. He has been part of a project that involves moving several computers from one subnet to another. The next day, a user complains that he can connect to local servers but cannot connect to any remote server. Other users on the same subnet do not have this problem. The IPCONFIG output from the user's computer contains the following information:

IP Address: 168.142.66.31

Subnet Mask: 255.255.224.0

Default Gateway: 168.142.32.1

What should Kevin identify as the most likely cause of the problem?

A. The IP address is incorrect.

B. The subnet mask is incorrect.

C. The default gateway address is incorrect.

D. There is a problem in the user's network connection.

15. You are the manager of a network that is made up of several subnets. You have a mixture of computers running Windows XP Professional and Windows 2000 Server in your pool of domain controllers. A user whose computer is running Windows XP Professional on one subnet reports that she can browse servers on her local network but nothing remote. You try to map a drive to the server but you are not successful.

What is most likely the problem?

A. The default gateway on the client's computer is incorrect.

B. The DNS server is not available.

C. The router for this subnet is not functioning.

D. WINS is unavailable.

Review Answers

1. Check that the address of your network connection has been configured for WINS. If the WINS address is not correct, your NetBIOS-based program will not be able to translate server names into IP addresses. This configuration error will not show any dialog boxes or error messages. The backup to using WINS is broadcasting; however, most routers do not pass broadcast messages. See "Windows Internet Name Services."

2. When you configure ICS, the setup process creates a single-range DHCP service as well as a

APPLY YOUR KNOWLEDGE

DNS proxy to your ISP (usually the cable company or telecommunications company). You should configure all machines in your private network to use DHCP for network configuration. Either the Gateway address or the DNS address is not pointing to 192.168.0.1. You might just need to do an IPCONFIG /RENEW to refresh your DHCP info. See "Internet Connection Sharing."

3. Two common situations will cause this. If you have a laptop that moves from the corporate LAN to a dial-up network connection, you might find that ICF is configured to run when you are not on the corporate LAN. If that's the case, you must manually configure it to allow ECHO messages in the ICMP filter of ICF. This is not on by default. See "What to Filter and What to Allow."

4. The subnet specified has only two nodes on it. With such a restricted subnet, every address other than the one remaining address on your subnet would be considered remote. The other local address must therefore be a router if you are to communicate with any remote systems at all. This configuration is usually used for router connections; however, it's not very useful when connecting computers. See "Subnet Mask."

5. Smartcard access is configured in the Security section of a dial-up network connections property page. By selecting Advanced and then clicking Settings, you are shown the Advanced Security Settings page. Here, you can choose Use Extensible Authentication Protocol, which includes smartcards as one of its supported authentication schemes. See "Virtual Private Networks."

6. The DHCP server did not respond to your request because it was busy or offline. Your machine then chose an IP address from the Automatic IP Private Addressing (APIPA) subnet with addresses in 169.254.*.*. You need to investigate why the DHCP server did not respond in time and reattempt the configurations by issuing an IPCONFIG /RENEW command. See "Testing DHCP."

7. You should go to the Properties page of the network connection used to access your Corporate RAS server. In the Security tab, you can select the Typical settings and select Require Secured Password from the drop-down list and also select the Require Data Encryption option. Alternatively, you can use the Advanced settings to select only MS-CHAP or MS-CHAP V2 authentication options. See "Virtual Private Networks."

8. When your server returned to the network, it received a different DHCP address than it had originally. The information kept in the users' Windows XP Professional computers would still be pointing to the old address. They would have to issue an IPCONFIG /FLUSHDNS command to delete all their cached DNS entries. When they access the server again, DNS will retrieve the latest addresses assigned by DHCP. See "Windows Internet Naming Service."

Answers to Exam Questions

1. **C.** The correct answer is to set up a DHCP service on an existing server and use it to automatically manage and distribute IP addresses to computers on your network. You could create a common HOSTS file and distribute it to each

APPLY YOUR KNOWLEDGE

machine; however, that does not make your system any easier to maintain. Allowing the APIPA mechanism doesn't provide a mechanism for you to see what machine is at what address because there is no central database of mappings. Continuing with your current mechanisms of fixed addresses might be slightly faster at bootup, but it's not the most efficient way to manage a large network address space in that it requires manual reconfiguring whenever a change in the network topology is made. See "Using DHCP."

2. **C**. The computer is not using DHCP. The IP addresses leased by the DHCP service set up as part of ICS range from 192.168.0.2 to 192.168.0.254 with a subnet mask of 255.255.255.0. The second clue is the Default Gateway address, which is always 192.168.0.1 for an ICS gateway. ICF never blocks outgoing Web traffic and the IP filters are used to enable certain TCP, UDP, or protocols from reaching your system (you would have to enable everything but port 80 for your system to function correctly on your network). Just setting the subnet mask to the correct value will not provide access to the Internet because of the incorrect gateway address. See "Understanding DHCP."

3. **D**. Windows XP Professional will support only one Web site. Normally, that's the default Web site access by the name of your machine, with virtual directories beneath the machinename address. There are already existing Web sites on this machine, so introducing Host Headers will make them unreachable. See "The Default Web Site."

4. **A**. The Remote Assistance service allows a friend or helper to take control of your machine to help solve some problem. You can configure Remote

Assistance to just view the desktop or to take control. The latter is controlled through an option found in the System applet (in Control Panel) under the Remote tab. With this option in place, the help desk should be able to control the user's desktop. Offering Assistance is an alternative path to the same end result and will still require the option to remotely control the machine to be set. Remote Desktop will lock the screen and log you onto a different session. This can't be used to help a user solve a problem if the user can't see or use the desktop. See "Configuring Remote Assistance."

5. **C**. If you do not have a Web site on your system, you should not allow anyone to attempt to access the service. What you are seeing is a remote user attempting to open up a Web site on your machine. Blocking port 80 will halt this. The ICS service is used to share a single port with a small network of computers and is not used to block network attacks. The SMTP service will block or pass port 25 traffic. There is no need to define a new service for port 80 because it's a common port already described in ICF. See "Configuring ICF (Internet Connection Firewall)."

6. **B**. When the user disconnected from their ISP service, the link between their invitation and their session was broken. The user must reconnect to the Internet through their ISP service and reissue the invitation for remote assistance. The option to control the computer remotely might be incorrectly set; however, you can't even connect yet so that is not the primary problem. The Offer Assistance link is an alternative way to connect to the user's machine; however, the problem is in how the user requested Remote Assistance.

APPLY YOUR KNOWLEDGE

The Remote Desktop would lock the user's screen and require you to log on to the remote machine with your own user ID. See "Configuring Remote Assistance."

7. **B**. The Remote Desktop service is designed to have you logged into a remote machine, but have the keyboard and mouse input and screen I/O be local. That way, you can use the power of another machine while using your less-powerful machine as a console. Using Remote Assistance is designed to provide momentary assistance for a friend who needs help in solving a problem. The mechanism of taking control involves someone answering questions during the setup. That would not work if you were at home and no one was sitting at your desktop console at work. The offline files would not help because the data for running your model is already on your desktop and if that is where you want to run the program there is no need to copy it elsewhere. Likewise, application shortcuts on your desktop don't add any value. See "Configuring Remote Desktop."

8. **B**. If you see a request for a certificate during a VPN connection setup, the connection has been configured to use IPSec under L2TP. IPSec uses certificates to establish machine identity. PPTP does not use certificates and therefore does not issue this error message. The problem is not related to encryption because under PPTP the keys for MPPE encryption are set up automatically. Port 443 is used in Internet Explorer for SSL connections (HTTPS). See "Layer 2 Tunneling Protocol (L2TP)."

9. **C**. Many corporations use a proxy server to provide network security and performance enhancements to Web access on the Internet. There are

Group Policies that would automatically download that information to your machine if you formally joined their network and had your machine added to an Organizational Unit (OU) that had that GP applied. Just plugging into their network would not be enough and your current proxy setting (if you have one at all) would probably prevent you from getting any access to your Corporate Internet. Setting your IE browser to detect proxy servers and to download their setting information will allow you to get access to the customer's proxy gateway. Resetting your default gateway address is relevant only on ICS networks, which a large corporation would not have. Neither would asking for a new IP address lease obtain the needed information. You could VPN out of the Customers network into your Corporate network and then use your existing configuration to access your Internet Web site, but that is certainly taking the long way around. See "Dealing with Proxy Servers."

10. **D**. Remote Assistance and Remote Desktop both use Terminal Services technology and both use port 3389 for access. If the user is using RAS to access the Corporate Network and ICF is configured on that connection, the most likely problem is that the Remote Desktop service has not been enabled in ICF. The Remote Control option in the System applet controls the degree to which a desktop can be controlled but does not allow or block it. That is set at the network connection. The Offer Assistance approach to desktop assistance is a different path to the same conclusion and still relies on port 3389. See "Configure Remote Assistance."

11. **C**. Only MS-CHAP V2 will provide data encryption as well as secure password authentication.

APPLY YOUR KNOWLEDGE

MS-CHAP V2 will automatically set up data-encryption keys while authenticating your contractor's user ID and passwords. PAP does not encrypt passwords. SPAP will encrypt passwords while connecting to a Shiva LAN Rover. CHAP will also encrypt passwords; however, none of the protocols other than MS-CHAP V2 will encrypt data. See "PPTP Encryption."

12. **B**. The problem with using PING as a diagnostic tool is that the problem in reaching an IP address could be caused at any node along the way. The problem is to determine by the most direct method where on the network the problem occurs. The first address to check is 127.0.0.1 (the loopback address) and then your IP address. A reply from both of these tests will indicate that the network adapter is working and configured correctly. The next step would be to ping the far side of the server acting as Router A. The next step would be to ping the near side of the server acting as Router B and then the far side of the same system. See "Using PING."

13. **C**. IP must first resolve the MAC address of the destination IP. At this point, WINS, DNS, and any static files (HOSTS and LMHOSTS) are not used. IP compares its IP address with its subnet mask and then inspects the destination address. If the destination address is remote (on a different subnet), IP will use the local gateway to help determine the destination MAC address. If the address is local (on the same subnet as defined by IP current address and the subnet mask), IP will use ARP to return the MAC address directly. If the subnet mask is incorrect, local addresses could appear remote and remote addresses appear as if they are local. If the IP address is duplicated, TCP/IP notifies the user with a dialog box repeatedly until the problem is fixed. See "Using ARP."

14. **C**. The default gateway for a computer must be in the same subnet. The gateway is used by IP on the local computer to help determine the MAC address of the destination IP address. If the default gateway is already remote, it can't be used to locate remote addresses. The class B address 168.142.0.0 with a subnet mask of 255.255.224.0 divides into six usable subnets with the following addresses:

168.142.32.1	168.142.63.254
168.142.64.1	168.142.95.254
168.142.96.1	168.142.127.254
168.142.128.1	168.142.159.254
168.142.160.1	168.142.191.254
168.142.192.1	168.142.223.254

Note that the first and last subnets are not included as they may not have valid addresses for older TCP/IP implementations.

The IP of the computer is on the second subnet; however, the gateway address is on the first subnet and therefore cannot be reached to help resolve remote addresses. If the host address were incorrect and the gateway address were correct, no local addresses would be reachable. See "Default Gateway (Router)."

15. **D**. If the WINS servers are not available, your computer will not be able to translate NetBIOS names to IP Addresses for remote segments. For the local segment, broadcasting can be used to resolve names; however, routers do not forward broadcasts so remote subnets will not be detected. See "Windows Internet Name Service (WINS)."

APPLY YOUR KNOWLEDGE

Suggested Readings and Resources

1. *Microsoft Windows XP Inside Out* (Microsoft Press).

2. *Microsoft Windows 2000 Performance Tuning Technical Reference* (Microsoft Press).

3. *Microsoft Windows 2000 Administrator's Pocket Consultant* (Microsoft Press).

4. *Microsoft Windows 2000 TCP/IP Protocol and Services* (Microsoft Press).

5. *Optimize Network Traffic (Notes from the Field)* (Microsoft Press).

This chapter covers topics associated with Windows XP security. It helps you prepare for the exam by addressing the following exam objectives:

Configure, manage, and troubleshoot Encrypting File System (EFS).

◆ Encrypting File System is a service supported in the Windows XP environment. It's important that network administrators understand how EFS can be used to secure file resources. It also is important that administrators understand how encrypted files can be recovered if a user is not available to decrypt the file.

Configure, manage, and troubleshoot a security configuration and local security policy.

◆ Tools that have been significantly enhanced in the Windows XP environment are security templates. Administrators will find that security templates are even more powerful than they were in Windows 2000 and can make the overall administration of computers in their environment easier.

Local security policy is a very powerful tool built into Windows XP. Local security policy gives an administrator the ability to secure a computer's local settings.

Configure, manage, and troubleshoot local user and group accounts.

• **Configure, manage, and troubleshoot auditing.**

• **Configure, manage, and troubleshoot account settings.**

• **Configure, manage, and troubleshoot account policy.**

CHAPTER 7

Implementing, Monitoring, and Troubleshooting Security

- **Configure and troubleshoot local users and groups.**

- **Configure, manage, and troubleshoot user and group rights.**

- **Troubleshoot cache credentials**

◆ The efficient management of user accounts is critical to the overall management of a network. Administrators must understand the tools that are available to them to manage user accounts in the Windows XP environment.

Configure, manage, and troubleshoot a security configuration.

◆ A tool that has been significantly enhanced in the Windows XP environment is security templates. Administrators will find that security templates are even more powerful than they were in Windows 2000 and can make the overall administration of computers in their environment easier.

Configure, manage, and troubleshoot Internet Explorer security settings.

◆ With more and more malicious code running around both on Web sites and through email viruses, it's important to properly configure Windows XP's Internet Explorer settings to protect the Windows XP machine from unintentional damage.

STUDY STRATEGIES

◆ This chapter presents several concepts related to securing your environment. It's important for you to remember that securing your environment is a process of setting many different features and services. Each feature or service works in conjunction with the others to provide a secure environment. If one security feature fails, the remaining features will present a new line of defense.

◆ As you review the material in this chapter always try to distinguish whether the topic is related to the workgroup or to the domain environment.

INTRODUCTION

This chapter provides an overview of Windows XP security and presents several different topics that relate to securing your environment. We start with a discussion of the workgroup and domain models and user/group management. Effectively managing your users and groups will make or break the security plans for your organization. During this discussion, we specifically look at creating and managing users and groups in both the workgroup and domain environments and the type of groups supported by Windows XP. We also look at the account settings at our disposal to assist in the management of the accounts.

Other security technologies also are covered in this chapter. We look at the use of local policies for securing the local desktop environment and for managing passwords. The last three topics in this chapter look at the use of Encrypted File System, audit policies, and security templates to assist in securing your environment.

USER AND GROUP MANAGEMENT

Configure, manage, and troubleshoot local user and group accounts.

User accounts are used to represent people in your networked environment. A user account contains information about a person who can gain access to your network. Information stored in a user account includes the user's name and password, as well as other information that describes the configuration of the user. Accounts enable users to identify themselves when they log on to the local computer or domain. Users accounts also are used to grant or deny access to resources. Through user accounts, you can control how a user gains access to a resource.

User accounts are stored in a protected database on Windows XP systems. When a user logs on to a system, the Security Accounts Manager (SAM) will compare the user's name and password against the data stored in the database. If these credentials are correct, the user can gain access to the computer or network. If the credentials are incorrect, the user is denied access to the system or network.

Windows XP supports two user account models: the workgroup model and the domain model. The following sections provide a brief overview of these models.

The Workgroup Model

In the workgroup model, each computer in your environment is responsible for the management of its own local account database. Local user accounts contain information that defines users for the local computer. With a local user account, a user can log on to the local computer and gain access to local resources. To gain access to resources on another computer, a user must use an account on the other computer.

The workgroup model is meant for small environments. This model has a very high administrative cost because user accounts must be managed on each computer in your environment. For example, if you have five computers on your network and you require access to resources on each computer, you must create user accounts on every computer. If you change the password on one computer, you also must change the password on the remaining four computers. However, the workgroup model is very simple to implement and does not require specialized computers to manage a shared account database.

The workgroup model is also useful for temporary environments. If, for example, a team of people needs to share resources for a short period of time, the workgroup model makes sense. For longer projects, however, the team would most likely benefit from the centralized database of account information provided by the domain model.

The Domain Model

Under the domain model, a centralized database of user accounts is managed for a grouping (or domain) of computers. Domain user accounts contain information that defines users within the domain.

All user account information for the domain is stored in the Active Directory database. Active Directory is stored on special computers called *domain controllers*. With a single domain user account, a user can log on to the network and gain access to resources on any computer in the Active Directory environment (referred to as an *Active Directory tree*, or *forest*) provided they have the correct permissions. The primary benefit of the domain model is that account management is simplified, as each user in your environment will have only one user account defined. This model, however, can be much more complex to set up, design, and configure.

Although a detailed discussion of Active Directory is beyond the scope of this course, it is useful to note the following features of Active Directory:

◆ Active Directory stores network resource information as objects in a centralized database. Objects represent resources and clients (that is, users, printers, shared folders, and so on).

◆ Each object contains several attributes. Attributes contain values. Attributes are used to store information about objects (for example, a user's name, password, and so on).

◆ Users and administrators can search Active Directory to locate objects. Searches are based on the attributes of objects.

◆ All object information is stored centrally. Administrators can centrally organize, manage, and control access to network resources through the directory.

◆ Administrators can delegate authority to users to administer portions of Active Directory. This enables the administrative activities to be distributed to select users.

The basic building blocks of Active Directory are domains. Active Directory organizes domains into a hierarchical structure, based on Domain Name Service (DNS) naming conventions.

The primary characteristic of an Active Directory tree is that the domain names used fall within a contiguous DNS name space (that is, a parent/child relationship is created between domains, based on a contiguous namespace). Figure 7.1 shows a sample of an Active Directory tree.

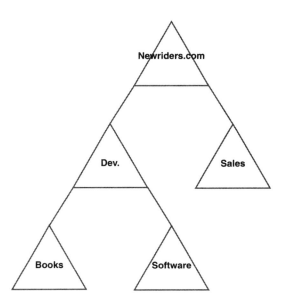

FIGURE 7.1
Sample Active Directory tree.

Active Directory also enables the creation of *forests*. A forest is a collection of domains that do not share a common DNS name space. Figure 7.2 shows a sample of an Active Directory forest.

All domains within an Active Directory tree or forest have the following three things in common:

◆ **Common database schema**—The database schema defines the database objects and the attributes that can be stored about each object.

◆ **Two-way transitive trust relationships**—Two-way transitive trusts enable users from any domain to access resources in any other domain (if they have the appropriate permissions).

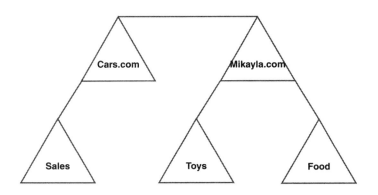

FIGURE 7.2
Sample Active Directory forest.

◆ **A Global Catalog (GC)**—The GC is a service that runs on selected domain controls within the Active Directory forest. The GC contains data about every object in the forest but only a select number of attributes about each object. This limits the total amount of data that needs to be replicated and stored on the GC servers.

Active Directory is a very powerful tool that can be used to manage your environment. Active Directory is designed to support very large environments. The directory database in Active Directory also can be modified to support new objects and attributes. We are seeing new Active Directory–aware applications that can access the data stored in Active Directory. Microsoft Exchange 2000 is an example of an Active Directory–aware application. It stores most of its information in Active Directory. The benefits of this environment are significant because all data is stored in one secure and manageable location.

Accounts and Security Identifiers

Every account with Windows XP that can be assigned permission to a resource is considered a security principal within Windows XP. A unique security identifier, or SID, identifies security principals on the network. This is a very important concept because a SID is unique to each security principal and will never be modified for the life of the account (unless it is migrated to another domain). In addition, SIDs are never reused when new objects are created.

Renaming a user account enables an account to receive a new name and retain its security assignments and group membership (because the SID is not changed). This is a very useful option if a user leaves the company and is replaced. Instead of creating a new user account for the new staff member, you can rename the old staff member's account so that the new staff member can use it.

NOTE

Windows NT Versus Windows XP— Can They Play with Each Other? You can add a Windows XP–based computer to a Windows NT 4.0 domain and receive all the benefits of centralized user accounts.

You also can add a Windows NT–based computer to a Windows 2000 domain. In this case, however, you will find that not all the functionality of Active Directory is available to the Windows NT–based computer.

User Accounts

As a network administrator in the Windows XP environment, you need to learn the skills required to manage users and groups. The following sections demonstrate how to manage and create users in both the workgroup and domain environments.

Windows 2000 and XP automatically create two user accounts, called *built-in accounts*, when they are installed. The Administrator account is the account used to manage the configuration of the computer and users stored on the computer. The Administrator account is capable of managing all aspects of the computer, so access to this account must be protected. You can rename the Administrator account, but it cannot be deleted. Guest is the second built-in account created when Windows XP is installed. The Guest account can be used to grant occasional, anonymous users access to resources. The Guest account is disabled by default.

Additionally, Windows XP creates at least two other accounts: HelpAssistant and SUPPORT. The HelpAssistant account is used to allow others to provide remote assistance with your Windows XP Professional machine. The SUPPORT account will have the name of SUPPORT followed by an underscore and a hexadecimal number. For example, the Windows XP Professional system that I'm using to write this chapter has a support account named SUPPORT_388945a0. This account is used exclusively for Microsoft support.

Finally, both Windows 2000 and Windows XP professional will create an `IUSR_%COMPUTERNAME%` and `IWAM_%COMPUTERNAME%` account if Internet Information Services are installed. These accounts are used for anonymous access and for IIS to launch processes, respectively. These accounts will not be created unless IIS is installed.

Regardless of whether you are managing a workgroup or a domain environment, you need to plan for user accounts. Details that you should consider are listed in Table 7.1.

TABLE 7.1

USER ACCOUNT PLANNING CONSIDERATIONS

Planning Consideration	Topic	Details
Naming Conventions	User logon name and full names must be unique	Domain user accounts must be unique to the domain. Local user accounts must be unique to the local machine.
		User logon names can contain up to 20 uppercase or lowercase characters. The field will allow for additional characters, but Windows XP uses only the first 20 entered.
	User logon name can contain up to 20 characters	Logon names can contain up to 20 characters of uppercase or lowercase characters. Windows recognizes any alphanumeric character except for "/\[];:ll=.+*?<>.
	Naming convention must accommodate duplicate employee names	You should develop a naming convention that will accommodate duplicate employee names—for example, two users named Sally Smith. Your naming convention should accommodate both users.
Secure Passwords	Assign passwords to administrator accounts	The administrator (and all accounts with administrator privileges) should have a password assigned. Access to the Administrator account must be closely guarded or you will not be able to secure your systems.
	Password management	You should determine whether the administrator or the users will control passwords. You can assign passwords for the users' accounts and prevent users from changing them, or you can allow users to enter their own passwords and manage them afterward.

Planning Consideration	*Topic*	*Details*
	User education	Users need to understand that passwords are there to protect them (and you, as administrator). If a user uses an obvious password, it can compromise network security. Generally, users should avoid passwords such as family names or a pet's name; use long passwords (passwords can be up to 128 characters long); passwords are case sensitive; a mix of upper- and lowercase can help secure passwords.

Creating Local User Accounts

Local user accounts typically are associated with the workgroup model previously discussed. Local user accounts can be used to access the computer on which the account physically resides and resources on the local machine. Local user accounts are limited to local resources.

Local user accounts are managed from the Computer Management Microsoft Management Console (MMC) snap-in. The Computer Management snap-in can be accessed by clicking the Start, Programs, Administrative Tools, Computer Management menu options. Alternatively, you can add the Computer Management snap-in to the MMC. Step by Step 7.1 demonstrates how to view the Computer Management snap-in from a custom MMC and how to create a new local user account.

NOTE **Users and Passwords Applet**   If you are working with Windows XP Professional systems configured as part of a workgroup, you also can use the User Accounts applet to create user accounts. The applet is found under Control Panel.

STEP BY STEP

7.1 Creating Local User Accounts by Using the Computer Management Snap-In

This Step by Step assumes that your computer is running Windows XP Professional.

1. From the Start Menu, select Control Panel. From the Control Panel, select Administrative Tools and then Computer Management.

2. Click the plus sign to the left of the Local Users and Groups node (underneath System Tools).

3. Click the Users folder (underneath Local Users and Groups). Figure 7.3 shows what the Computer Management window should look like now.

4. To create a new Local User, right-click the Users folder. From the context menu, select New User. This action will launch the New User dialog box (see Figure 7.4).

5. You need to enter the information for the user account. Table 7.2 defines the information required and the values used for this walkthrough.

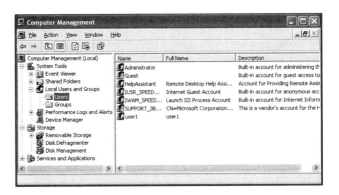

FIGURE 7.3
Computer Management snap-in Local Users and Groups node.

TABLE 7.2

NEW USER CONFIGURATION OPTIONS

Configuration Setting	Description	Value for This Walkthrough
Username	The user's unique logon name.	RLBogue
Full name	The user's full name.	Robert L. Bogue
Description	This option is for information purposes and gives you the option to describe the purpose of the account.	Local Backup/ Maintenance Account
Password/Confirm Password	To ensure that you type the password correctly, you must enter the password in the Password and Confirm Password fields. Be careful typing; passwords are case sensitive.	AlexanderNathaniel
User Must Change Password at Next Logon	Select this check box if you want the user to change his password the first time he logs on. This ensures that the user is the only person who knows the password. Note: This option is disabled if the user cannot change password or the Password Never Expires options are checked.	Checked
User Cannot Change Password	Select this check box if you never want the password to be changed for this user. This is a great option if multiple users use this account to access the system (and you don't want one of them to change the password so the rest can't log on). Note: This option is disabled if you select the User Must Changethe Password at Next Logon option.	N/A

FIGURE 7.4
Create a new user in the New User dialog box.

continues

TABLE 7.2	*continued*	

NEW USER CONFIGURATION OPTIONS

Configuration Setting	*Description*	*Value for This Walkthrough*
Password Never Expires	Select this check box if you never want the password to change. This setting will override policies that indicate passwords must be changed. Note: This option is disabled if you select the User Must Change the Password at Next Logon option.	Unchecked
Account Is Disabled	Select this check box to prevent use of this user account.	Unchecked

6. After you have entered the user configuration, click Create. The user will be created, and the dialog box will be cleared so that you can create additional users. After you have created all the user accounts that you want, click Close to return to the MMC.

7. Log off your workstation and log on as the RLBogue account. Note that you will be required to enter a new password (and confirm it) when you log on—you have verified that the account is operational. Log off the RLBogue account and log on as your Administrator account (or an account with Administrative privileges).

Every user in your environment should have his or her own user account. For security reasons and auditing, users should not share user accounts. If each user is assigned his own unique account, it's his responsibility to keep his password secure. When individual accounts are assigned, it's assumed that the person to whom the account was issued is the person who actually logs on. System administrators rely on passwords to ensure that user accounts are not used inappropriately (that is, by someone other than the appropriate user). If system administrators cannot rely on users to protect their passwords, many audit and security functions on the network are defeated.

In some special instances, groups of users might share user accounts. For example, your company might have a semipublic application for use by authorized personnel, but for which there is no need to track access. One example might be a set of blueprints while an addition to the building is being constructed. You might want the builders to have access to the electronic drawings, but wouldn't normally want this information widely available. Because the builders are likely to rotate on and off the project—and because they are not members of your company—you might not want to create separate accounts for them. If more than one user shares the same account, you should ensure that the User Cannot Change Password option is set for the account. This will prevent anyone from changing the password and locking out all the other users.

Network administrators also will want to ensure that users change their passwords often. This can be accomplished through group and local policies. Again, it's important for users to understand the importance of their passwords. You might have noticed that administrators have the ability to set a user account so that passwords never expire. This option is useful for system and service accounts. If this option is not set for system and service accounts, you might find that the services relying on the accounts stop operating correctly if their password expires.

After the user account is created, you might need to manage the account. Common management tasks are as follows:

- ◆ Resetting passwords
- ◆ Deleting accounts
- ◆ Renaming accounts
- ◆ Enabling accounts
- ◆ Unlocking accounts

FIGURE 7.5
TestUser Properties page—General tab.

FIGURE 7.6
TestUser Properties page—Member Of tab.

◆ Changing group membership

◆ Modifying profile paths

◆ Modifying user home directory paths

All these tasks are completed from the Computer Management snap-in of the MMC. The first task, resetting passwords, can be performed for a user account by right-clicking the user account and selecting Set Password from the context menu. You also will find the Rename Account and Delete Account options from the user account context menu.

The second task, deleting an account, can be accomplished by right-clicking the user and selecting Delete. Deleting a user account will permanently remove the account from the system. In general, it's a bad idea to delete user accounts. It's a better idea to disable the accounts in case the user comes back to work for the company, or if audit logs need to be reviewed.

The third task, renaming an account, can be accomplished by right-clicking on the user and selecting Rename.

Double-clicking the user account (or right-clicking the account and selecting Properties from the context menu) can access the remaining configuration options.

Figure 7.5 shows the TestUser Properties page. From this page, you can modify the full name and description of the account. You also have the ability to configure how passwords should be managed for the user and disable the account (as discussed in Step by Step 7.1).

Groups are used to simplify resource access (groups are discussed in greater detail later in this chapter). The Member Of tab enables you to manage the group membership of a user account. From this tab, you can click the Add or Remove buttons to modify group membership (see Figure 7.6).

The Profile tab enables you to configure the User profile (profile path and logon script) and home folder location (see Figure 7.7).

Groups

Groups are used to simplify the overall management of accounts in your environment. In most environments, users can be grouped into categories of user account (accountants, salespeople, and so on). These categories of user account generally define common access needs for groups of users in your environment. To assist in the management of access needs for these users, Windows XP supports the creation of groups within its account database. Group objects can then be granted access to resources. Being a member of a group automatically grants you the same rights as the group object. If you have memberships in multiple groups, the rights associated with each group will be combined (how your effective rights are calculated depends on the type of rights being combined). Depending on the type of group, you also can make groups members of other groups.

FIGURE 7.7
TestUser Properties page—Profile tab.

Creating Local Groups

Local groups are managed from the Computer Management Microsoft Management Console (MMC) snap-in. You've seen in the previous section how to open the Computer Management snap-in. Step by Step 7.2 demonstrates how to create a new local group.

STEP BY STEP

7.2 Creating Local Groups by Using the Computer Management Snap-In

1. From the Start menu, select Control Panel. Double-click Administrative Tools, and then double-click Computer Management.

2. Open the Local Users and Groups node of the Computer Management snap-in by clicking the plus sign to the left of it. Click the Groups folder underneath Local. From this location, you can create and manage groups on your system. Figure 7.8 shows the appropriate MMC screen.

continues

NOTE **%username%**   When setting up a user's home directory, you can use the following syntax to reference the location of his or her folder:

\\servername\sharename\%username%

Using this syntax, the system will automatically substitute the user's username in place of the variable %username%.

NOTE The discussion of groups here is limited to Windows XP Professional's definition of groups—this is all you'll need to know for the exam. However, you should know that there are several different types and categories of groups in an Active Directory (Domain) environment.

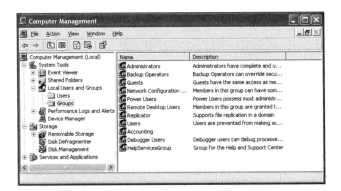

continued

FIGURE 7.8
Computer Management snap-in—Local Users and Groups.

3. To create a new Local group, right-click the Groups folder in the Local Users and Groups node. From the context menu, select New Group. This action launches the New Group dialog box (see Figure 7.9).

4. Enter the name of the group (call the group TEST for the purposes of this walkthrough); enter a brief description.

5. Click the Add button to add users to the group. In the Select Users or Groups dialog box, select the Administrator user account and click Add. Then, select the Authenticated Users group and click Add. This will add the Administrator user account and Authenticated Users group to the membership list of the new group. Click Cancel to close the Select Users or Groups dialog box.

6. After you enter the group configuration, click Create. The New Group dialog box will reappear so you can create another group. Click Close to close the dialog box.

To add additional members, you can right-click the group and select Add to Group from the context menu.

You can rename and delete a group by right-clicking it and selecting the appropriate option from the context menu. If you rename a group, the name of the group is changed and the security assignments (that is, permissions assigned to it) will be retained. If you

FIGURE 7.9
The New Group dialog box.

delete a group, all references to it will be deleted and its security assignments will be lost (the objects that represent the members of the group will not be deleted).

Built-In Groups

Windows XP systems have a number of built-in groups associated with them. These groups provide a powerful tool for the management of resources on the local system or domain. Membership in one (or more) of these groups gives users rights to access (and manage) the local operating system, depending on the group. Each group is, by default, assigned a useful collection of rights and privileges.

User rights are rules that determine the actions a user can perform on a computer (user rights are discussed in detail in later sections). In addition, user rights control whether a user can log on to a computer directly (locally) or over the network, add users to local groups, delete users, and so on. Built-in groups have sets of user rights already assigned. Administrators usually assign user rights by adding a user account to one of the built-in groups or by creating a new group and assigning specific user rights to that group. Users who are subsequently added to a group are automatically granted all user rights assigned to the group account. User rights are managed by using Group Policy.

To gain an understanding of how groups and user rights relate, the following section provides a review of the privileges that have been assigned to each built-in group. We will then look at where the built-in groups receive their default configuration.

Built-In Local Groups

Built-in local groups are used to manage Windows XP Professional workstations. The built-in Local groups added during installation are as follows:

- ◆ Administrators
- ◆ Backup Operators
- ◆ Guests
- ◆ HelpServicesGroup

◆ Network Configuration Operators

◆ Power Users

◆ Remote Desktop Users

◆ Replicator

◆ Users

The following sections describe each of the built-in local groups.

Administrators Group

Membership in the Administrators group enables a user to manage all aspects of the local operating system. Members of this group have the ability to manage user accounts, load and unload system drivers, and perform backups and restores of file systems.

Users with administrative authority have a great deal of privilege on a system. Membership does not, however, give the user automatic access to all resources on the system. If a user with administrative rights tries to access a resource that he or she does not have permission to use, he or she will receive an access denied message. The administrative user, however, does have the ability to take ownership of any resource, if the need arises. After the user owns a resource, he or she can change the permissions on the resource to allow access.

Membership in the Administrators groups should be managed very closely. Administrator access to the system should be limited to individuals who perform the following types of tasks:

◆ Install the operating system and components (such as hardware drivers, system services, and so on)

◆ Install service packs and Windows packs

◆ Upgrade the operating system

◆ Repair the operating system

◆ Configure critical operating system parameters (such as password policy, access control, audit policy, kernel mode driver configuration, and so on)

> **NOTE**
>
> **Administrative Access to EFS** Files encrypted with Windows XP's Encrypting File System (EFS) are a special case where the administrator might or might not be able to open the file depending on the way in which EFS was set up.

> **NOTE**
>
> **The Administrator User Account and the Administrators Group** The administrator user account is automatically made a member of the Administrators group. The Administrator user account cannot be removed from this group.
>
> Internally, the administrator account is indistinguishable from the Administrators group. There are certain immutable properties for this user and this group.

Backup Operators Group

Regular users have the ability to back up and restore files that they have permission to access without being part of this group. In most environments, however, backups are managed centrally so that they can be completed at set intervals with a high degree of reliability.

Membership in the Backup Operators group enables a user to back up and restore file systems regardless of permissions, ownership, encryption settings, or audit settings. Membership in this group enables you to assign users the authority to back up file systems without having to assign the users specific permissions to access the resources.

Guests

The Guests group is used to give someone limited access to resources on the system. The Guest account is automatically added to this group. The Guest account can be removed from the Guests group if you want.

Two additional Guest accounts are added if you have installed the Internet Information Server (IIS) on your system (`ISUR_computername` and `IWAM_computername`). These accounts are used to support anonymous access to the IIS content.

Guest access is typically used when it is impractical to create user accounts for every user who might conceivably want to use resources on the local system. The most popular example of this is a printer. You might want to share your local printer and allow anyone to use it if they need it.

HelpServicesGroup

The HelpServicesGroup has only one member by default—the `SUPPORT_` account that was created to facilitate support from Microsoft. Other than this account, no other users are added by default, and no user rights are assigned specifically to these users.

Network Configuration Operators

The Network Configuration Operators group is designed to allow the users permission to change the network configuration but not make the complete spectrum of operations that a power user is able to change. It might be appropriate to add users to this group when

> **NOTE**
>
> **Encrypted Files and Backups**
> Encrypted files are always backed up in their encrypted state. Being a member of the Backup Operators group (or the Administrators group) just allows the user to copy the file to a removable medium such as a tape.

they need to change from network to network and manually change their configurations but you don't want them to be able to install applications.

Power Users Group

Members of the Power Users group have more permission than members of the Users group and less permission than members of the Administrators group. Power Users can perform most operating-system tasks.

Members of the Power Users group can perform the following tasks:

◆ Install and remove applications that can be run by all users (except for the software that can be removed only by an administrator).

◆ Customize systemwide resources including printers, date/time, power options, and other Control Panel resources.

◆ Share resources on the local system.

Members of the Power Users group do not have permission to add themselves to the Administrators group, and they do not have access to the data of other users on an NTFS volume.

In addition, members of the Power Users group have the ability to create and administer user accounts and groups. Power Users are limited to managing the accounts they have created and, therefore, cannot manage the Administrators group or Administrator user account. Power Users can, however, manage membership of the Power Users group.

Remote Desktop Users

The Report Desktop Users group has the ability to log into the Windows XP Professional machine using Terminal Services, or, in other words, remote desktop. This group will be able to remotely control the operation of the computer.

Replicator

The Replicator group is used by the Windows XP Directory Replication Service to replicate content between domain controllers. It can be used to replicate content from a domain controller to a Windows XP Professional workstation but is rarely used for this purpose.

NOTE **Legacy Applications and the Power Users Group** Power Users might not be able to install some applications written for previous versions of Windows because these applications do not use the Windows XP installer service and, therefore, do not operate from within its security context.

Users

By default, all users (with the exception of the built-in Administrator and Guest accounts) created on the local system are made members of the Users group. The Users group provides the user with all the necessary rights to run the computer as an end user.

Ideally, all users will be able to run applications that have been installed on the local system by the administrator or by the members of the Power Users group. Users will not be able to run applications that have been installed on the local system by other users.

In addition, on volumes formatted with NTFS, members of the Users group are able to access only files that they have permission to use. For this reason, users are not able to see one another's files and folders. The default security configuration of Windows XP limits the ability of a user to modify operating system files (that is, a user cannot modify system-critical files and configuration settings).

NOTE

Legacy Application Support Users will not be able to run some applications written for previous versions of Windows because most of these applications were not designed with knowledge of Windows XP security. Members of the Power Users group should be able to run applications written for previous versions of Windows.

Special Groups

Windows XP supports several built-in groups that can be used for a variety of purposes. You cannot change the membership of these groups; the assignment happens as an internal part of Windows XP.

Everyone

The Everyone group includes all current network users, including guests and users. Whenever a user logs on to the network, Windows XP automatically adds the user to the Everyone group.

Authenticated Users

The Authenticated Users group includes all users with valid user accounts on the computer or in a trusted Active Directory. Use the Authenticated User group instead of the Everyone group to prevent anonymous access to a resource. In other words, Authenticated Users does not include guests.

Creator Owner

The Creator Owner group includes the user account for the user who created or took ownership of a resource. This group is used most often to grant permissions to users who print. Each print job inherits the Creator Owner permission allowing the user special abilities such as the ability to delete their own print job. If a member of

WARNING

Use Authenticated Users When Granting Permissions The default permissions used in Windows XP are that the Everyone group is given full control to resources. This assignment should be changed to the Authenticated Users group as soon as resources are created.

the Administrators group creates a resource, the Administrators group is the owner of the resource.

Interactive

The Interactive group includes all users currently logged on to a particular computer. Whenever a user logs on to a system, they are automatically added to the Interactive group.

Network

The Network group includes users currently accessing a given resource over the network (as opposed to users who access a resource by logging on locally to the computer on which the resource resides). Whenever users access a given resource over the network, Windows XP automatically adds them to the Network group. This group is frequently used to prevent network access to a file. By setting the deny permission on the network group, you can prevent access of a resource from the network.

User Rights

In the previous section, you read about the rights that each of the built-in groups has on a Windows XP Professional computer. These groups receive their rights from a set of local user rights. Local user rights can be modified, if needed.

You can view the current configuration of your system's local user rights from the Local Computer Policy snap-in.

Step by Step 7.3 provides details on how to view the Local Computer Policy settings.

STEP BY STEP

7.3 Viewing the Local Computer Policy Settings

1. From the Start menu, select Control Panel. From the Control Panel, select Administrative Tools. From Administrative Tools, select Local Policy.

2. Click the plus sign on the Local Policies object.

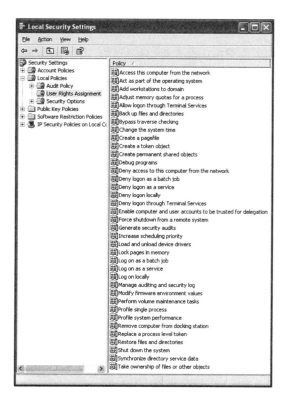

FIGURE 7.10
The Local Computer Policy.

You can now view the individual local user rights currently configured on your system in the right window of the console. To see the rights assignments for each policy, double-click the policy. Figure 7.11 shows the users granted the right to log on locally. Table 7.3 provides a description of the default user rights assigned to the built-in Windows XP groups on Windows XP Professional (this is not a complete listing of all user rights, just the most commonly used).

FIGURE 7.11
Viewing the users and groups authorized for a specific user right.

TABLE 7.3

WINDOWS XP PROFESSIONAL USER RIGHTS

User Right	Description	Granted To
Access this computer from the network	Having this user right enables you to access resources from the computer over the network (for example, attach to a network share being hosted from a computer). Having this right does not give you the ability to access resources that your user account has not been given permission to use.	Everyone, User, Power Users, Backup Operators, Administrators
Back up files and directories	This user right enables users to back up file system resources regardless of permissions held by the user. Most users can only back up files they have permission to use or own. This does not lend itself to the centralized management of backups.	Backup Operators, Administrator
Bypass traverse checking	This right enables a user to access a file resource deep in a directory structure even if the user does not have permission to the file's parent directory.	Everyone, User, Power Users, Backup Operators, Administrators
Change the system time	This user right enables a user to change system time.	Power Users, Administrators

User Right	*Description*	*Granted To*
Create a pagefile	This user right enables a user to configure the virtual memory management of a system.	Administrators
Deny access to this computer from the network	This user right (or the lack of a right, as the case might be) restricts a user from accessing this computer over the network regardless of group membership. For example, the Joe user account has been granted the right to access this computer from the network through his membership in the Users group. If we wanted to override Joe's ability to access this computer from the network, we could explicitly restrict Joe from doing so by granting him this user right. This is a very powerful right for system and service accounts. Typically, you do not want people using these accounts to access your systems over the network.	
Deny logon locally	This user right explicitly restricts a user from logging on to a system from the local console.	

continues

TABLE 7.3

WINDOWS XP PROFESSIONAL USER RIGHTS

User Right	*Description*	*Granted To*
Force shutdown from a remote system	This user right enables a user to remotely shut down a system by using a remote shutdown utility (you can find the shutdown utility in the Windows 2000 Resource Kit).	Administrators
Increase quotas	This user right enables users to modify quota settings for NTFS-formatted partitions.	Administrators
Increase scheduling priority	This user right enables you to reschedule jobs that have been submitted to the scheduling service.	Administrators
Load and unload drivers	This user right enables you to load and unload device drivers.	Administrators
Log on locally	This user right enables you to log on at the computer from the local computer console.	Guest, Users, Power Users, Backup Operators, Administrators
Manage auditing and security	This user right enables a user to specify what type of resource access will be audited.	Administrators

User Right	Description	Granted To
Remove computer from docking station	This user right enables a user to undock a laptop from its docking station.	Users, Power Users, Administrators
Restore files and directories	This user right enables users to restore a backup of a file system of permissions held by the user.	Backup Operators, Administrators
Shut down the system	This user right enables a user to shut down the local system.	Users, Power Users, Backup Operators, Administrators
Take ownership of files of other objects	This user right enables a user to take ownership of files, directories, printers, and other objects on the computer. This right supersedes permissions protecting objects.	Administrators

When determining what group to add a particular user account to, remember the default assignments. If a group exists that has the rights required by a user, add them to that group. If a group does not exist with the appropriate privileges, create a new one. Be careful when assigning group membership: Do not use groups with too many rights; give users only the rights they need to get the job done (no more, no less).

It's helpful to remember the default rights assignments found in the built-in groups. Default rights assignments for Windows XP Professional are summarized in Table 7.4.

TABLE 7.4

WINDOWS XP PROFESSIONAL DEFAULT RIGHTS ASSIGNMENTS

Right	Admin	Power Users	Users	Guests	Everyone	Backup Operators
Access this computer from the network	x	x	x		x	x
Back up files and directories	x					x
Bypass traverse checking	x	x	x		x	x
Change the system time	x	x				
Create a pagefile	x					
Deny access to this computer from the network						
Deny logon locally						
Force shutdown from a remote system	x					
Load and unload drivers	x					
Log on locally	x	x	x	x	x	X
Manage auditing and security	x					
Remove computer from docking station	x					
Restore files and directories	x					x
Shut down the system	x	x	x			x
Take ownership of files of other objects	x					

In addition to the default rights listed in Table 7.4, Windows XP also has built-in user capabilities. You cannot modify these built-in rights. The only way to give a user one of these rights is to put that user in a group that has the capability. If you want to give a user rights to create and manage user accounts, for example, you must put that user into either the Power Users or Administrators groups.

Table 7.5 lists the built-in capabilities on a Windows XP Professional computer.

TABLE 7.5

WINDOWS XP BUILT-IN USER CAPABILITIES

Right	Admin	Power Users	Users	Guests	Everyone	Backup Operators
Create and manage user accounts	x	x				
Create and manage local groups	x	x				
Lock the workstation	X	X	X	X	X	x
Override the lock of a workstation	x					
Format a hard drive	x					
Share and stop sharing directories	x	x				
Share and stop sharing printers	X	x				

LOCAL GROUP POLICY

Configure, manage, and troubleshoot a security configuration and local security policy.

Securing a Windows XP environment involves many steps. In previous sections of this chapter, we looked at the management of users and groups and how they can be used to control access to the network. User and group management is a very important aspect of network management. If not managed correctly, network resources are impossible to secure.

After you develop an effective user and group management strategy, you must consider the management of the computers in your environment. Specifically, we are concerned with how a user (or group of users) can interact with the computer (that is, reconfigure the computer).

Group Policy is a new set of technologies included with the Windows XP products. Group Policy is primarily used to manage the user and computer environment through the Active Directory database. A complete discussion of Group Policy is beyond the scope of this book, but we will look at local Group Policy and how it relates to Windows XP Professional.

Each computer running Windows XP has a local Group Policy object associated with it. Using this object, Group Policy settings can be stored on individual computers whether or not they are part of an Active Directory environment or a networked environment.

Local Group Policy objects enable you to control the following components:

◆ **Administrative templates**—Registry-based settings that control access to various system settings.

◆ **Software settings**—Enables software to be assigned to users and computers so that it's available to users when they need it.

◆ **Security settings**—Security settings for computers and users.

◆ **Scripts**—User Logon/Logoff, Computer Startup/Shutdown scripts.

◆ **Folder redirection**—Enables data directories (usually part of a user's profile) to be placed on networked drives instead of on the local computer.

NOTE

Local Policy Versus Domain-Level Group Policy Because a Group Policy object associated with sites, domains, or organizational units can override its settings, the local Group Policy object is the least influential one in an Active Directory environment. In a non-networked environment (or in a networked environment lacking a Windows 2000 or .NET domain controller), the local Group Policy object's settings are more important because they are not overridden by other Group Policy objects.

LOCAL ACCOUNT POLICY

Configure, manage, and troubleshoot local user and group accounts.

Account policies give administrators the ability to control how user passwords and lockouts are configured.

The following section provides details on password policy settings and account lockout policy settings.

Password Policies

Table 7.6 shows the Windows XP password policies. These policies enable you to manage the properties of a user's password (that is, length or complexity).

TABLE 7.6

PASSWORD POLICY SETTINGS

Policy Setting	Description
Enforce Password History	This setting tells the system to remember a user password so that it cannot be reused. This setting requires the administrator to input a value for the history length. Windows XP can track the history for your previous 24 passwords.
Maximum Password Age	This setting specifies the maximum age of a user password. Users are forced to change their passwords when the maximum age is met. The maximum value you can enter is 999 days.
Minimum Password Age	This setting specifies the minimum age of a user password. Users are not allowed to change their passwords unless the minimum password age has passed.
Minimum Password Length	This setting specifies the minimum length of the password (the value can be set between 0 and 14).

continues

TABLE 7.6	*continued*

PASSWORD POLICY SETTINGS

Policy Setting	*Description*
Password Must Meet Complexity Requirements	This setting implements the following password policy:
	Passwords must be at least six characters long.
	Passwords must contain characters from at least three of the following four classes:
	English uppercase letters (A, B, C, ... Z)
	English lowercase letters (a, b, c, ... z)
	Westernized Arabic numerals (0, 1, 2, ... 9)
	Nonalphanumeric ("special characters") such as punctuation symbols.
	Passwords may not contain your username or any part of your full name.
	These requirements are hard-coded in the Passfilt.dll file and cannot be changed through the user interface or Registry.
Store Password Using Reversible Encryption	This setting stores user passwords in encrypted, clear-text format. It's useful when pass-through authentication is required.
User Must Log On to Change Password	This setting specifies that users must be logged on to the system to change their passwords. If users let their passwords expire, they will not be able to log on and will need the assistance of an administrator to reset their passwords.

Account Lockout Policy

Table 7.7 shows the Windows XP account lockout policy configuration settings.

TABLE 7.7	

ACCOUNT LOCKOUT POLICY SETTINGS

Policy Setting	Description
Account Lockout Duration	If your account is locked out, this setting specifies the duration (can be set between 1 and 99,999 minutes).
Account Lockout Threshold	Specifies the number of times you can use an incorrect password before your account lockout is triggered. If this option were set to five, you could type your password incorrectly five times within the Reset Account Lockout Counter time period. This setting can be configured between 1 and 999 invalid logon attempts.
Reset Account Lockout Counter After	Specifies the number of minutes between resets of the account lockout counter (can be set between 1 and 99,999 minutes).

You should ensure that you use Account Lockout policy settings appropriately for your environment. You should ensure that you are using the auditing functions of Windows XP to detect invalid logon attempts. Account lockouts will go unnoticed in many environments in which the user account is enabled after the account lockout duration has passed.

MONITORING SECURITY EVENTS

As a network administrator, you might find that monitoring the activities of users, Windows XP system events, and application events is a powerful method of ensuring that your systems are secure and running properly. Windows XP enables you to monitor most events on a system. Events are user actions that are recorded, based on an audit policy, other significant occurrences in Windows XP, or an application running on the system. Administrators need to monitor these events to track security, system performance, and application errors.

Events are recorded in event logs. You can view and analyze event logs to determine whether security breaches are occurring or system services are failing, or to determine the nature of application errors. This section provides an overview of the Event Viewer, audit policies, the security log, categories of security events, object access events, and analyzing security events.

Event Logs and the Event Viewer

The Event Viewer is a tool that enables you to view three different logs that are stored by Windows XP. The Event Viewer can be used to view the following logs:

◆ **System log**—The system log contains events logged by the Windows XP system components, such as drivers or other system components that failed to load during startup. Windows XP predetermines the event types logged by system components.

◆ **Application log**—The application log contains events logged by applications or programs. For example, a database program might record a file error in the application log. The program developer decides which events to record. Many Windows XP services (that is, DHCP, DNS, File Replication Services, and so on) use the application log.

◆ **Security log**—The security log, if configured to do so, records security events, such as valid and invalid logon attempts. Events that are related to resource use, such as creating, opening, or deleting files also can be logged. An administrator can specify what events are recorded in the security log policy.

The Event Viewer can be accessed through the Microsoft Management Console (MMC). By selecting the log type in the node pane (that is, left pane) of the MMC, the corresponding log data is displayed in the results pane (that is, the right pane). Figure 7.12 shows the system log being displayed.

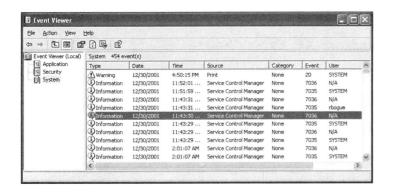

FIGURE 7.12
The Microsoft Windows XP Event Viewer.

The data being displayed can be sorted by selecting a column heading. You also have the ability to filter the results log entries being presented. To accomplish this, select Filter from the View menu. Figure 7.13 shows the options available when setting a filter.

You also can set the columns of data being presented by selecting Choose Columns from the View menu. Table 7.8 provides details regarding the column options.

TABLE 7.8

WINDOWS XP EVENT VIEWER

Name	*Definition*
Type	The Event Viewer tracks five basic types of events:
	Error—A significant problem, such as loss of data or loss of functionality. For example, if a service fails to load during startup, an error will be logged.
	Warning—An event that is not necessarily significant but might indicate a possible future problem. For example, when disk space is low, a warning will be logged.
	Information—An event that describes the successful operation of an application, driver, or service. For example, when a network driver loads successfully, an Information event will be logged.

continues

FIGURE 7.13
Microsoft Windows XP Event Viewer filter options.

TABLE 7.8	*continued*

WINDOWS XP EVENT VIEWER

Name	*Definition*
	Success Audit (security logs only)—An audited security event in which a user's attempt to access a resource succeeds. For example, a user's successful attempt to log on to the system will be logged as a Success audit event.
	Failed Audit (security logs only)—An audited security event in which a user's attempt to access a resource fails. For example, if a user tries to access a network drive and fails, the attempt will be logged as a Failure audit event.
Date	The date of the event.
Time	The time at which the event occurred.
Source	The source (typically, a service or process) that reported the event to the Event Viewer.
Category	The category of the event. In many cases, the category relates to the subsystem that reported the event. For example, when disk quotas are initialized, the Event Viewer application log has an entry stating that the operation has completed. The category of the event would be "Disk."
Event	The name of the event that was reported.
User	The user account associated with the event (this is not always applicable).
Computer	The computer on which the event occurred.

NOTE

Event ID The Event ID is a numeric code that can be used to obtain information from Microsoft regarding the event being logged. You can search Microsoft's Web site for the Event ID or Microsoft TechNet for details on each code.

Audit Policies

An audit policy defines the categories of user activities that Windows XP records in the security logs on each computer. Audit policies are set up to track authorized and unauthorized access to resources.

By default, auditing is not enabled. Before your organization enables auditing, you must define exactly what needs to be audited and why you want it to be audited. Auditing can slow down system performance.

Categories of Security Events

Security events are divided into categories. This enables the system administrator to configure audit policies to specific categories of events (based on your organization's auditing and security plan). When viewing the event logs, you can search for specific categories of events. Table 7.9 presents security event categories.

TABLE 7.9

CATEGORIES OF SECURITY EVENTS

Category	Description
Account logon	Logs an event each time a user attempts to log on. For example, specific events logged include logon failures for unknown user accounts; time restriction violations; user account has expired; user does not have the right to log on locally; account password has expired; account is locked out.
	Successful logons also can be tracked through events.
Logon events	Logs an event for logon events that are occurring over the network or generated by service startup (for example, an interactive logon or service such as SQL starting).
Account management	Logs an event each time an account is managed. This is a useful function if you are concerned about changes being made to user accounts in your environment.
Directory service	Logs an event each time an event occurs within the Active Directory services—for example, successful or failed replication events.
Policy change	Logs an event each time a policy is successfully or unsuccessfully changed in your environment.
Process tracking	Logs an event for each program or process that a user launches while accessing a system. Administrators can use this information to track the details of a user's activities while accessing a system.
	Note that the event specifically tracks the creation of new processes and the exiting of processes.
Object access	Logs an event each time a user attempts to access a resource (that is, printer, shared folder, and so on). These events provide a very effective way of monitoring access to sensitive data on your network.

continues

TABLE 7.9	*continued*

CATEGORIES OF SECURITY EVENTS

Category	*Description*
Privilege use	Logs an event each time a user attempts, successfully or unsuccessfully, to use special privileges, such as changing system time. These events enable you to closely monitor the activities of the administrators in your environment.
System event	Logs a designated system event. Windows XP may log system events when a user restarts or shuts down a computer. These events provide a great deal of information about system services.

Auditing can be enabled for either success or failure of specific events. You must decide what you want to use your log information for to determine whether logging successes or failures is most appropriate. For example, if you decide to audit account logons, you must look at what the information will be used for. Your network Security group will most likely be interested in logging failed logon events (that is, it can provide signs that someone is trying to log on with an account for which he or she does not have a correct password). This same Security group also might be interested in logging successful logons to determine whether users are accessing workstations in areas of the network that they should not be using.

Audit policies can be defined through Group Policy (either at the domain or computer level). Enabling auditing for Account Logon, Privilege Use, or System Events will automatically enable auditing of those events. Auditing of Object Access requires levels of configuration. The following section reviews the configuration of Object Access audit policies.

Object Access Events

An audit policy can be configured to monitor access to objects such as files and folders, printers, and other objects. The audit policy defines what events will be entered in the event log. Table 7.10 presents a listing of the objects that can be audited and the type of events that can be audited for each.

TABLE 7.10	

AUDITING OBJECT ACCESS

Object	*Activities That Can Be Audited*
File and Folders (files and folders can be audited only in an NTFS partition)	Displaying the contents of a file or folder.
	Changing the contents of a file or folder.
	Adding data to a file.
	Deleting a file or folder in a folder.
	Changing permissions for a file or folder.
Printers	Changing printer settings, pausing a printer, sharing a printer, or removing a printer.
	Changing job settings; pausing, restarting, or deleting documents.
	Changing printer properties.
Objects in Active Directory	Viewing audited objects.
	Creating objects within an audited container.
	Deleting objects within an audited container (or an audited object).
	Changing the permissions for the audited object.

Setting Up Auditing

Setting up auditing is a two-step process. Step 1 involves enabling Auditing for the local policy of the computer (or domain). Step 2 requires you to configure auditing for each resource that you want to monitor.

To enable auditing for the local security policy, you need to access the computer's local policy. Step by Step 7.4 provides details on enabling object auditing. In this Step by Step, we will enable object auditing and account logon events in the local policy and then set up auditing on a folder. As you complete this Step by Step, notice that setting up auditing on an object is a two-step process.

NOTE

GrpConsole.MSC You may also use the GrpConsole.MSC that we created in Chapter 5 instead of loading the snap-in manually as shown here. If you use the GrpConsole file we created in Chapter 5, you can skip ahead to step 7.

STEP BY STEP

7.4 Enabling Auditing for a Computer

1. Click Start and Run; in the Open dialog box, type **MMC** and click OK.

2. From the File menu, select Add/Remove Snap-In.

3. In the Add/Remove Snap-In dialog box, click Add.

4. In the Add Standalone Snap-In dialog box, scroll down until you find the Group Policy snap-in and click Add.

5. You will be prompted to select the local computer or a remote machine. If you wanted to manage a remote system, you would provide the name here. In this case, however, select the local computer.

6. After the required snap-in has been added to your MMC, close the Add Standalone Snap-In dialog box and the Add/Remove Snap-In dialog box.

7. We will now enable auditing. Auditing is configured through Group Policy. From the Group Policy snap-in, click Computer Configuration, Windows Settings, Security Settings, Local Policies, Audit Policies. This will expose the various types of auditing that are supported by Windows XP. By double-clicking one of the audit types, you can enable auditing for successful events or failure events.

8. Enable auditing for Account Logon events by double-clicking the Audit account logon events object. In the Local Security Policy Setting dialog box, check the Success and Failure check boxes to enable account logon auditing.

9. Enable auditing for a file system share by double-clicking the Audit object access. In the Local Security Policy Setting dialog box, check the Success and Failure check boxes to enable object access auditing.

10. Auditing is now enabled. To apply the policy, close the MMC.

11. We will now configure Auditing on a folder. Select a folder on an NTFS partition. Right-click the folder and select Properties from the context menu. Select the Security tab. Click the Advanced button on the bottom of the Securities tab to view the Access Control Settings dialog box for the folder. Select the Auditing tab. Figure 7.14 shows the Auditing tab of the Access Control Settings for a folder.

12. When you select the Auditing tab, you are presented with a list of all users who are currently being audited for this resource. (In the case of Figure 7.14, there are none.) Click the Add button and add the Everyone group to the list. Then, select the specific events that you want to audit for this group of users (as shown in Figure 7.15). Notice that you can audit both successful and failed access. Select all the check boxes.

13. Close the dialog boxes.

14. Create a new file in the folder.

15. By accessing the folder, an audit event will be generated. From the Start menu, select Control Panel, then Administrative Tools, and then Event Viewer.

continues

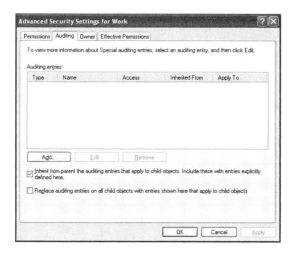

FIGURE 7.14
The Auditing tab of the Access Control Settings for a folder.

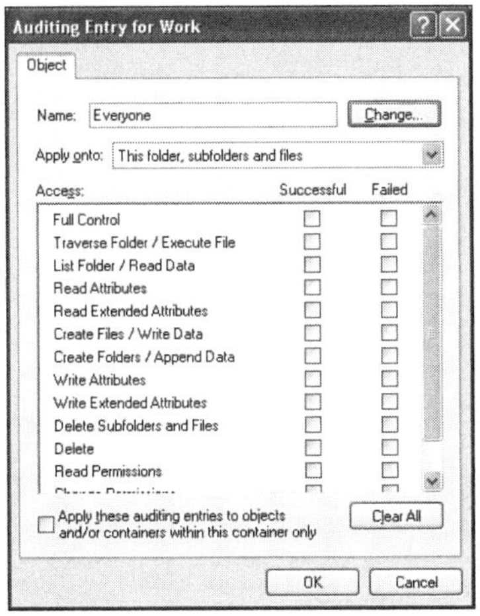

FIGURE 7.15
Select specific events in the Auditing Entry dialog box.

continued

16. Access the security log. You should see several entries, indicating a successful audit entry.

17. Log off of and on to your system. Check the security event to see the events that were generated.

WINDOWS XP SECURITY CONFIGURATIONS

Configure, manage, and troubleshoot a security configuration and local security policy.

Windows XP supports the management of computers through security templates. Security templates are provided for common security scenarios. These can be assigned directly to a computer as is or modified to suit unique security requirements.

The predefined security templates are as follows:

◆ Compatible workstation (`compatws.inf`)

◆ Secure workstation or server (`securews.inf`)

◆ Secure domain controller (`securedc.inf`)

◆ Highly secure workstation or server (`hisecws.inf`)

◆ Highly secure domain controller (`hisecdc.inf`)

◆ Root File System Security (`rootsec.inf`)

◆ Setup Security (`setup security.inf`)

By default, these templates are stored in the *\systemroot*\security\templates folder.

By default, Windows XP applies security templates to new installations of Windows XP. The default templates are used to secure Windows.

WARNING

Security Templates and the Upgrade Process Windows XP default security settings are not applied to upgrade installations of Windows XP.

If Windows XP is installed on a computer with FAT or FAT32 partitions, you should be aware that security configuration templates cannot be applied.

Security Templates

The basic configuration (`basicwk.inf`, `basicsv.inf`, `basicdc.inf`) templates are provided to assist you if you apply an inappropriate security configuration to your system. The basic configuration applies the Windows XP default security settings to all security areas except for sections covering user rights. User rights are not modified in the basic templates because application setup programs commonly modify user rights.

Compatible (`compatws.inf`)

Windows XP and Windows NT use different security settings to support applications running on them. Under Windows NT, applications were allowed a great deal of leeway regarding where they stored their configuration settings and Registry entries. In many instances, users needed elevated privileges to install applications. Windows XP has changed this model and provided a more structured environment for the installation of applications. Windows XP applications (that is, applications that use the Windows Installer service to install) are fully managed during installation, and users do not require elevated privileges because the application is installed in the security context of the installer service.

If you require compatibility with non-Windows XP applications in your environment, you might need to apply the compatible template. Under this template, all users who are authenticated by Windows XP are automatically elevated to have the permissions associated with the Power Users group. This enables applications to access system files and Registry keys that are required to operate properly.

Secure (`secure*.inf`)

The secure template is the middle ground between the compatibility template, which opens up security so applications can run, and the highly secure template, which will almost certainly cause problems with all applications except those written for Windows 2000 or Windows XP.

Highly Secure (`hisec*.inf`)

The highly secure templates define a secure network communications environment for Windows XP. The security areas are set to protect network traffic and protocols used between computers running Windows XP. Computers configured with this template can communicate only with other Windows XP machines. This limits their capability to communicate with Windows NT and Windows 9x systems.

Root Security (`rootsec.inf`)

The root security template contains only a few basic pieces of security information. Essentially, it defines the default security settings for NTFS volumes at the root. It will not reset permissions on folders on the drive.

Setup Security

The setup security template contains the security settings that are applied by the setup program. You can use this template if you want to return your system to the way it was after setup was run.

Configure System Security

The Security Templates snap-in enables you to manage security templates from the Microsoft Management Console (MMC). You can create or modify security templates by using this utility.

Step by Step 7.5 provides details on how a security template can be created.

STEP BY STEP

7.5 Creating Security Templates

1. Launch the Microsoft Management Console (MMC) by clicking the Start menu and selecting Run. In the Open dialog box, type **MMC**. Click OK. The MMC will launch.

2. Add the Security Templates snap-in to the MMC by clicking the Console/Add and Remove Snap-in menu. In the Add and Remove Snap-In dialog box, click Add. In the Add Standalone Snap-In dialog box, click Security Templates. Click Add, and then click Close. Close the remaining windows to view the MMC with the snap-in added, as shown in Figure 7.16.

3. Open the compatws template in the left pane of the MMC. Opening the template exposes the settings that can be configured through the template.

4. If you were creating a new template, you would now edit the template and save the changes. You can save your changes from the Action menu.

After you create a security template for your environment, you need to apply it to your computer. When you apply a template to existing security settings, the settings in the template are merged into the computer's security settings. Step by Step 7.6 demonstrates how to apply a security template to a Windows XP Professional system.

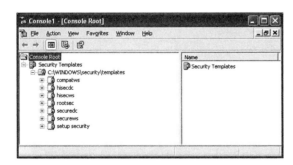

FIGURE 7.16
The Security Template MMC snap-in.

STEP BY STEP

7.6 Applying Security Templates

1. Launch the Microsoft Management Console (MMC) by clicking the Start menu and selecting Run. In the Open dialog box, type **MMC**. Click OK. The MMC will launch.

2. Add the Group Policy snap-in to the MMC by clicking the Console/Add and Remove Snap-In menu. In the Add and Remove Snap-In dialog box, click Add. In the Add Standalone Snap-In dialog box, click Group Policy. Click Add. You will be prompted to select the Group Policy object that you want to manage. Select the Local Computer and click Finish. Close the remaining windows to view the MMC with the snap-in added, as shown in Figure 7.17.

3. To import a new security template, open the Computer Configuration/Windows Settings options on the left side of the MMC. Right-click the Security Settings and select Import Policy from the context menu.

4. You will be prompted to select the template file that you want to import into your environment.

From the Group Policy snap-in, you are also able to export the security template for your system. Procedures to accomplish this are detailed in Step by Step 7.7.

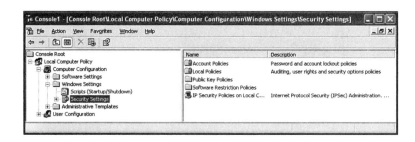

FIGURE 7.17
The Local Computer Policy MMC snap-in.

STEP BY STEP

7.7 Exporting Security Templates

1. Launch the Microsoft Management Console (MMC) by clicking the Start menu and selecting Run. In the Open dialog box, type MMC. Click OK. The MMC will launch.

2. Add the Group Policy snap-in to the MMC by clicking the Console/Add and Remove Snap-In menu.

3. In the Add and Remove Snap-In dialog box, click Add. In the Add Standalone Snap-In dialog box, click Group Policy. Click Add.

4. You will be prompted to select the Group Policy object that you want to manage. Select the Local Computer and click Finish. Close the remaining windows to view the MMC with the snap-in added.

5. To export the existing security configuration for your system to a security template, open the Computer Configuration/Windows Settings options on the left of the MMC. Right-click the Security Settings and select Export Policy from the context menu.

6. The following are the two export options present:

   • Export the local policy from your system. This will be the complete local policy regardless of whether or not it is currently effective for your system (policies need to be processed before they become effective).

   • Export the effective policy from your local system. This will be the policy currently being applied by your system.

7. You will be prompted to select the name under which you want to store your template file.

Validating a Security Configuration

The state of the operating system and applications on a computer is dynamic. For example, security levels might be required to change temporarily to enable immediate resolution of an administration or network issue; this change can often remain. This means that a computer might not meet the requirements for enterprise security any longer.

Regular analysis enables an administrator to track and ensure an adequate level of security on each computer. Analysis is provided at a micro level; information about all system aspects related to security is provided in the results. This enables an administrator to tune the security levels and, most importantly, to detect any security flaws that might open up in the system over time.

Security configuration and analysis enables quick review of security analysis results: Recommendations are presented alongside current system settings, and icons or remarks are used to highlight any areas where the current settings do not match the proposed level of security. Security configuration and analysis also offer the ability to resolve any discrepancies revealed by an analysis.

If frequent analyses of a large number of computers are required, as in a domain-based infrastructure, the `secedit.exe` command-line tool may be used as a method of batch analysis. Analysis results still must be viewed, however, with security configuration and analysis.

Step by Step 7.8 provides details on how to use the Security Configuration and Analysis tool to compare the security configuration of a computer against a security template.

N O T E

Secedit Help For more information on Secedit, type `secedit.exe /help` at the command prompt.

STEP BY STEP

7.8 Security Configuration and Analysis

1. Add the Security Configuration and Analysis snap-in to an MMC console (see Step by Step 7.1 for details on adding a snap-in).

2. Right-click Security Configuration and Analysis, and then click Open Database.

3. Select an existing database file or type a new name to create a new database, and then click Open.

4. If you open an existing database, it will already contain information about the template to which you are comparing your configuration. If you are creating a new database, you will need to import the security template to which you want to compare your system configuration.

5. Right-click Security Configuration and Analysis, and then click Analyze Computer Now.

6. In the Perform Analysis dialog box, choose a location for the analysis log, and then click OK.

7. Windows XP will then compare the effective security configuration of your local computer against the security template. Any differences in your configuration will appear with a red x.

After completing the analysis, you can perform several tasks, including the following:

◆ Eliminate discrepancies by configuring the settings in the database to match the current computer settings. To configure the database settings, double-click the setting in the detail pane of the MMC.

◆ Import another template file. This enables you to add additional security templates to the analysis.

◆ Export the current database setting to a template file. To export the template file, right-click Security Configuration and Analysis, and then click Export Template.

ENCRYPTING FILE SYSTEM (EFS)

Configure, manage, and troubleshoot Encrypting File System (EFS).

Encrypting File System (EFS) is a system service that enables a user to encrypt files to which they have the access (you need a minimum of modify permissions). The service is based on public/private encryption technology and is managed by the Windows XP Public Key Infrastructure (PKI) services. Because EFS is an integrated service, it is very easy to manage, difficult to break into, and transparent to the user.

After a file is encrypted, only the user who encrypted it (and a special account called *recovery agent*) can decrypt the file. If a user other than the user who encrypted the file or the recovery agent tries to use the resource, he or she will receive an access denied message.

The technology is based on a public-key–based structure. Each user has a public and private key. The keys were created in such a way that anything encrypted with the private key can be decrypted only by using the public key and anything encrypted with the public key can be decrypted only by using the private key. As the names suggest, the public key is made available to any resource that requests it. The private key is kept secret and never exposed to unauthorized resources.

When the owner of a file encrypts a file, a file encryption key is generated and used to encrypt the file. The file-encryption keys are based on a fast symmetric key designed for bulk encryption. The file is encrypted in blocks with a different key for each block. All the file encryption keys are then stored with the file (as an extended attribute). Before the file encryption keys are stored, they are encrypted by using the public key of the owner, in the case of the data decryption field (DDF) keys; and the recovery agents, in the case of the data recovery field (DRF) keys. Because the keys are stored with the file, the file can be moved or renamed without impacting the recoverability of the file.

When a file is accessed, EFS detects the access attempt and locates the user's certificate from the Windows XP PKI and the user's associated private key. The private key is then used to decrypt the DDF to retrieve the file encryption keys used to encrypt each block of the file. The only key in existence with the capability to decrypt the information is the user who encrypted the file. Access to the file is denied to everyone else because they do not hold the private key required for decrypting the file encryption keys.

If the owner's private key is not available for some reason (for example, the user account was deleted), the recovery agent can open the file. The recovery agent decrypts the DRF to unlock the list of file encryption keys. The recovery agent must be configured as part of the security policies of the local computer.

Step by Step 7.9 provides details for encrypting a file or folder within Windows XP.

STEP BY STEP

7.9 Encrypting Files and Folders

1. Right-click the file or folder that you want to encrypt.

2. Choose the Properties option from the context menu.

3. Click the Advanced button from the General tab.

4. Check the Encrypt Contents to Secure the Data check box from the Compress or Encrypt attributes section of the Advanced Attributes dialog box.

> **WARNING**
>
> **Manage the Recovery Agent Properly** The recovery agent can be configured through local policies (or Group Policy objects in the domain environment). If you change the recovery agent, you might not be able to recover encrypted files that were encrypted before the change (as the keys used to encrypt the file bulk encryption keys in the recovery agent field were encrypted by using the old agent's key).

You also can manage the encryption attributes associated with files and folders on your system from the command prompt. The Cipher utility enables you to encrypt files and folders as well as check the compression statistics.

The syntax for the encryption utility is as follows:

```
CIPHER [/e| /d] [/s:dir] [/i] [/f] [/q] [filename [...]]
```

where

- ◆ /e encrypts the specified files or folders. Files added to the folder afterward will be encrypted.

- ◆ /d decrypts the specified files or folders. Files added to the folder afterward will not be encrypted.

- ◆ /s: dir performs the specified operation on files in the given directory and all subdirectories.

- ◆ /i continues performing the specified operation even after errors have occurred. By default, cipher stops when an error is encountered.

◆ /f forces the encryption or decryption of all specified files. By default, files that have already been encrypted or decrypted are skipped. This option forces files to be reencrypted, even if they are currently encrypted. This would be important if a new recovery agent had been configured for your system because the files would be reencrypted with a new key.

◆ /q reports only the most essential information.

◆ *Filename* specifies a pattern, file, or directory.

Step by Step 7.10 demonstrates how to use EFS.

STEP BY STEP

7.10 Using EFS

1. Create two new user accounts named EFSUser and Hacker on your computer.

2. Log on as user EFSUser.

3. Create a simple text file on an NTFS-formatted partition. Open the text file with Notepad. Enter a message in the file, save the file, and exit Notepad.

4. Right-click the file you just created and select Properties from the context menu. Click Advanced.

5. Check the Encrypt Contents to Secure the Data option box.

6. Log off the system and log on as the Hacker account you created in step 1.

7. Try to open the file that you created in step 3. You will not be allowed access to the file.

8. Log off and log on as the Administrator account.

9. We will now verify that the recovery agent can access the file. Access the Local Computer Policy and view the Encrypted Data Recovery Agents list (found under Computer Configuration, Windows Settings, Security

Settings, Public Key Policies, Encrypted Data Recovery Agents). The default configuration has the local Administrator account in the list. This means that the administrator can access encrypted files.

10. Try to access the file you created in step 3. You should be able to recover the file.

CONFIGURING INTERNET OPTIONS

Configure, manage, and troubleshoot Internet Explorer security settings.

The configuration of Internet options is becoming increasingly important as more and more companies have integrated Internet access into their network architectures. We will look at some of the settings that can be configured for Internet Explorer that can simplify administration and streamline Internet access.

One of the most basic of choices that we can configure for individual users is the default home page. The default home page is defined in the properties of Internet Explorer but can also be assigned through a group policy. Step by Step 7.11 walks through the steps of setting up the default home page individually.

STEP BY STEP

7.11 Setting the Default Home Page

1. Right-click Internet Explorer in the Start menu and select Internet Properties.

2. On the General tab, in the Address box of the Home Page section, type the URL of the Internet or intranet site that you would like to have as your default home page.

The location and size of temporary Internet files is also an important setting to govern, particularly if the amount of available disk space on a client computer is limited. Step by Step 7.12 walks through how to set the size and location of temporary Internet files.

STEP BY STEP

7.12 Setting the Size and Location of Temporary Internet Files

1. Right-click Internet Explorer in the Start menu and select Internet Properties.

2. On the General tab, click the Settings button in the Temporary Internet files section.

3. Select a setting from the list at the top of the dialog box that will determine when newer versions of stored pages are checked for.

4. In the Temporary Internet Files Folder section, use the slide rule or the size box to allocate how much disk space is reserved for temporary Internet files.

5. To move the temporary Internet files folder's location, click the Move Folder button and browse the directory structure to indicate where you would like the temporary Internet files to be stored.

Proxy settings can also be set within the properties of Internet Explorer for users that access the Internet through a proxy server. Internet Explorer can be set up to automatically detect settings, use an automatic configuration script, or use a static proxy server address. The benefit of the automatic configuration script is that a number of settings can be provided through the automatic-configuration script as opposed to a simple proxy address. The automatic-configuration script also centralizes administration by allowing the administrator to create one script for all users; by directing users to that script, all users are identically configured.

Step by Step 7.13 addresses the process of configuring proxy settings.

STEP BY STEP

7.13 Configuring Proxy Settings

1. Right-click Internet Explorer in the Start menu and select Internet Properties.

2. Select the Connections tab and the LAN Settings button.

3. To configure your client for automatic configuration, select one of the automatic configuration settings. To specify a single, static proxy server, enable the Use a Proxy Server box and enter an address and port number for the proxy server.

4. To enable the Bypass Proxy Server for Local Addresses option, select that box.

Many companies have or are beginning to establish a set of Internet User guidelines that restricts users to viewing only certain material or surfing only to specific sites using the corporation's Internet access. These types of restrictive options are available within Internet Explorer but are by no means all-encompassing. Third-party products are generally used in most corporate environments where there is interest in filtering or blocking access to certain Internet sites. We will examine the options available to us in Internet Explorer.

Internet Explorer offers the capability to control security through Authenticode publishers, security zones, and content ratings.

Security zones enable you to assign specific Web sites to specific security zones, of which there are four defaults from which to choose. The four different zones are explained in Table 7.11.

TABLE 7.11

INTERNET EXPLORER SECURITY ZONES

Zone	Description
Internet	Contains all Internet sites
Local Intranet	Used for computers connected to the local intranet
Trusted Sites	Allows for the assignment of sites you trust
Restricted Sites	Allows for the assignment of sites you do *not* trust

Adding sites to which you are interested in preventing access can be accomplished by adding those particular sites to the Restricted Sites zone. Step by Step 7.14 details the process of adding sites to the Restricted Sites zone.

STEP BY STEP

7.14 Configuring a Restricted Zone

1. Right-click Internet Explorer in the Start menu and select Internet Properties.

2. Select the Security tab and in the list of zones at the top, select the Restricted Sites zone.

3. Click the Sites button and add one or more URLs of sites that you want to define as restricted. Click OK.

4. Again on the Security tab, select the security level for the restricted zone using the slide rule or click the Custom Level button to define your own security settings for the zone.

In this section, we looked at how to configure several different Internet Explorer settings for a Windows XP Professional client. These settings are useful in defining a common Internet environment for many clients. Although setting the properties locally is not the most efficient way to define these settings, it is an available option when only a few computers need configuring. Alternatively, these settings could be applied through a group policy to all computers or users within a site, domain, or organizational unit.

CASE STUDY: ABC COMPANY

ESSENCE OF THE CASE

Here are the essential elements in this case:

- Account policies
- Security template development
- Audit policies
- Company policies for EFS

ABC Company is in the process of developing a network design for its Canadian operation. ABC Company has nine offices spread across Canada and employs 5,000 staff. It is currently running a mix of Novell and Windows NT 3.51/4.0. The company is very concerned with the rising cost of managing its networked resources. The company has decided on a multiple-domain design based on the legal organization of its company (that is, one division in the company partners with a company in Europe and, therefore, requires lower levels of encrypting technology). Your job is to develop a complete security strategy plan for this company.

ANALYSIS

ABC Company is undertaking a major reworking of its network. This case focuses on security. To secure your environment, you need to manage your account policies, security templates, and audit policies correctly.

First, you should evaluate password policies. Does your company require complex passwords? What is the minimum length of passwords? How long can a user use a password before he or she must change it?

Now that the user accounts are protected, you will want to develop a strategy for securing individual systems. One of the most effective ways of doing this is through a security template and by auditing access to resources.

Remember that each of the preceding features of Windows XP work together to secure your environment. Think of them as lines of defense. If one line fails, another is there to protect your resources.

CHAPTER SUMMARY

KEY TERMS

- Workgroup
- Domain
- Active Directory
- User Account
- Group
- Security groups
- Distribution groups
- Local groups
- Built-in group
- Local Group policy
- Account policy
- Auditing
- Event logs
- Security template
- Encrypting File System

In Chapter 7, we explored the tools built into Windows XP to secure the networked environment. The chapter started with an overview of the user account. User accounts are a very important aspect of network security because they are your first line of defense against intruders. If your user accounts are not managed properly, it's impossible to secure the network. In the discussion of user accounts, we also reviewed the differences between a workgroup and a domain environment. Next, groups were covered in detail. Groups are a very powerful tool that can ease management and, if used properly, make implementing a secure environment easier. With a full understanding of users and groups, we then looked at local policies and account policies. Policies are tools that we can use to secure user accounts and computers.

Monitoring security events was also described, as well as the process of defining an audit policy. Security templates and the Encrypting File System were discussed, as well.

APPLY YOUR KNOWLEDGE

Exercises

7.1 Creating Local Users and Groups

In this exercise, you create a new local user account and group. You will then make the new user a member of the group.

Estimated Time: 10 minutes

1. From the Start menu, select Control Panel, Administrative Tools, Computer Management.

2. Open the System Tools node of the Computer Management snap-in by clicking the plus sign beside the node.

3. Open the Local Users and Groups node of the Computer Management snap-in. From this location, you can create and manage users on the system.

4. To create a new local user, right-click the Users folder in the Local Users and Groups node. From the context menu, select New User. This action launches the New User dialog box.

5. Use the following information to create the account:

   - Username = Joe

   - Full name = Joe Smith

   - Description = Test User for Exercise 7.1

   - Password = password

   - Uncheck the User must change password on first logon box

   - Leave all other boxes unchecked

6. After you have entered the user configuration, click Create. Click Close to return to the MMC.

7. To create a new Local group, right-click the Groups folder in the Local Users and Groups node. From the context menu, select New Group. This action launches the New Group dialog box.

8. Enter the name of the group as `Exercise 7.1 Test Group` and enter `Test group` as the description.

9. After you have entered the group configuration, click Create. The New Group dialog box will reappear so you can create another group. Click Close to close the dialog box.

10. To add the user Joe to the membership of the group you just created, double-click the group. Click the Add button. In the Select Users or Groups dialog box, find Joe, click the Add button, and click OK.

11. Click OK to close the properties box for the group. Close the MMC. When prompted to save the changes, say No.

7.2 Using Local Group Policy

In this exercise, you will configure the local Group Policy to remove the Run option from the Start menu of your computer.

Estimated Time: 15 minutes

1. Click Start/Run. In the Open dialog box, type `MMC` and click OK.

2. From the Console menu, click the Add/Remove Snap-In menu.

3. In the Add/Remove Snap-in window, click Add.

4. In the Add Standalone Snap-In window, highlight the Group Policy snap-in, and click Add.

APPLY YOUR KNOWLEDGE

5. In the Select Group Policy Object window, select the local computer. Click Finish in the Computer Management window.

6. Close the Add Standalone Snap-In and Add/Remove Snap-In windows by clicking OK.

7. Open the Local Computer Policy snap-in by clicking the plus sign beside the snap-in.

8. Open the User Configuration node of the Local Policy snap-in by clicking the plus sign beside the node.

9. Open the Administrative Templates node by clicking the plus sign beside the node.

10. Select the Start Menu & Taskbar folder in the scope pane. You should now see the individual policy settings in the results pane (that is, the right window).

11. Double-click the Remove Run menu from Start menu and select Enable. Click OK.

12. Exit the MMC.

13. Log off the system and log on again.

14. Check to see whether the Run menu exists. It should be gone.

15. Launch the MMC and disable this policy setting.

7.3 Using Local Account Policies

In this exercise, you will configure the local account policy so the users can use incorrect passwords only three times within a 10-minute period. If users get their passwords incorrect three times within this period, their accounts are locked out for 30 minutes.

Estimated Time: 15 minutes

1. Click Start/Run. In the Open dialog box, type **MMC** and click OK.

2. From the Console menu, click the Add/Remove Snap-In menu.

3. In the Add/Remove Snap-In window, click Add.

4. In the Add Standalone Snap-In window, highlight the Group Policy snap-in and click Add.

5. In the Select Group Policy Object window, select the local computer. Click Finish in the Computer Management window.

6. Close the Add Standalone Snap-In and Add/Remove Snap-In Windows by clicking OK.

7. Open the Local Computer Policy snap-in by clicking the plus sign beside the snap-in.

8. Open the Computer Configuration node of the Local Policy snap-in by clicking the plus sign beside the node.

9. Open the Windows Settings node by clicking the plus sign beside the node.

10. Open the Security Settings node by clicking the plus sign beside the node.

11. Open the Account Policies node by clicking the plus sign beside the node.

12. In the scope pane, highlight Account Lockout Policy. You should now see the individual account lockout policies in the results pane.

13. Double-click the account lockout duration policy in the results pane. Enter 30 minutes as the account lockout duration. Click OK to close the policy.

14. The system will provide you with a list of suggested values for the other related account lockout policies. Click OK to accept them.

APPLY YOUR KNOWLEDGE

15. Change the values associated with the account lockout threshold (three bad logon attempts) and reset account lockout counter after values (10 minutes).

16. Log off your system and try to log on as Joe. Type your password incorrectly and try to log on. Note the error message states that you provided an incorrect username or password.

17. Continue to try to log on to the system with the incorrect password. After the third attempt, the system should issue a new error message stating that you are unable to log on because your account has been locked out.

7.4 Unlocking an Account

In this exercise, you will unlock the user account from Exercise 7.3.

Estimated Time: 5 minutes

1. Log on as Administrator (or a user with administrative permissions).

2. Click Start/Run. In the Open dialog box, type **MMC** and click OK.

3. From the Console menu, click the Add/Remove Snap-In menu.

4. In the Add/Remove Snap-In window, click Add.

5. In the Add Standalone Snap-In window, highlight the Computer Management snap-in and click Add.

6. In the Computer Management window, select the local computer. Click Finish in the Computer Management window.

7. Close the Add Standalone snap-in and Add/Remove Snap-In windows by clicking OK.

8. Open the Computer Management snap-in by clicking the plus sign beside the snap-in.

9. Open the System Tools node of the Computer Management snap-in by clicking the plus sign beside the node.

10. Open the Local Users and Groups node of the Computer Management snap-in.

11. Double-click the Joe user account. Uncheck the Account is locked out box to unlock Joe's account.

12. Click OK to close the Joe Property dialog box.

13. Log off as Administrator and log back on as Joe (this time with the correct password).

Review Questions

1. What utilities are used to create users and groups in a workgroup environment?

2. What are the differences between a workgroup and a domain environment?

3. You want to stop hackers from trying to guess passwords in your environment; what feature of Windows XP should you use?

4. How does the Encrypting File System work and why would you want to use it?

5. What are local policies used for?

6. What is the `secedit.exe` utility used for?

7. What are user rights and how do they relate to built-in groups?

8. What types of events can be audited?

APPLY YOUR KNOWLEDGE

Exam Questions

1. You are working as a consultant for a small firm in Toronto, Canada. Your client wants to implement a Windows XP network but cannot decide whether the workgroup or domain model is best suited for their environment. Which statements are true of the workgroup and domain models? (Select all that apply.)

   A. The workgroup model is best suited for large environments with centralized administration.

   B. The domain model is best suited for large environments with centralized administration.

   C. The workgroup model offers much tighter security and control over user accounts than the domain model does.

   D. The domain model offers much tighter security and control over user accounts than the workgroup model does.

   E. Generally, the workgroup model is limited to small environments with no centralized administration.

2. You are working as a help desk operator and receive a call from a user who cannot log on. The user explains that she just finished changing her password before lunch. The system accepted the password change. The user logged off her workstation at lunchtime (as all good users do). When she returned from lunch, the system indicated that the password she provided was incorrect. What is the most likely cause of the problem? (Choose the best answer.)

   A. The password change has not replicated to the domain controllers yet.

   B. The user has forgotten that passwords are case sensitive and is not using the correct case.

   C. The user account has been disabled, as the user is not a member of the Account Operators group, which is required to change the password.

   D. The user is not allowed to log on from the workstation from which she attempted to log on because of computer restrictions.

3. As the network administrator of your company's network, you are very concerned about security. Your predecessor was fired because users managed to hack their way into the Human Resources database. You don't want to have the same thing happen to you.

   To help catch the hackers, you configure auditing. You set auditing so that the activities of the domain users group are monitored in the directories that contain the Human Resources database. Somehow hackers still manage to get in. Why didn't auditing help in this situation? (Choose three from the following.)

   A. Configuration of auditing is a two-step process. You didn't set the local policy to include auditing.

   B. You audited the wrong group. If you are auditing to determine unauthorized users who are accessing a resource, you should audit the Everyone group to ensure that all users (including those not authenticated to the network) are audited.

C. You cannot use auditing alone to secure resources.

D. Auditing cannot be set to track users who are accessing directories and files.

4. You are the administrator of a small network. The manager of the accounting department approaches you because one of her staff has encrypted all of their data in a shared folder. The user is sick and will not be back to work for an extended period. You are asked to decrypt the data. What is your best option?

   A. Take ownership of the files and change the permissions on them so that you own them. Then decrypt the files.

   B. Call the sick user and ask for her password. Log on as the user and decrypt the files.

   C. Log on as the administrator and decrypt the files.

   D. Log on as the recovery agent and decrypt the files.

5. As the network administrator of a large accounting firm, you configure all Windows 2000 Servers in your environment to use the highly secure template. You receive a number of complaints from users that they are not able to connect to the servers from Windows 95/98 and Windows NT workstations. The workstations are able to connect to one another. How can the problem be corrected? (Choose two from the following.)

   A. Add the highly secure template to the Windows 95/98 and Windows NT workstations.

B. Upgrade the Windows 95/98 and Windows NT workstations to Windows XP Professional.

C. All users must have Power Users– (or Administrator–) level access to attach to the servers configured with the highly secure template.

D. Remove the highly secure template from the Windows 2000 Servers by reapplying the setup security template.

6. You are working as a support tech for a small manufacturing company in Toronto, Canada. You are servicing one server that starts without problems, but the IIS server will not start. The IIS server was running fine until the last day or so. As far as you know, no configuration changes have been made to the server. What should be your first course of action in solving this problem?

   A. Check to see whether the server is running in the Services node of Computer Manager.

   B. Reboot the server.

   C. Check the Event Viewer to see whether any error message has been logged.

   D. Check the audit logs to see whether anyone has reconfigured the server.

7. As the system support specialist for the accounting department of your company, you have been asked to encrypt a large number of files and folders on a number of NTFS partitions on your servers. You spend an entire weekend encrypting the approximately 1,000 folders and 100,000 files. On Monday morning, users can no longer

APPLY YOUR KNOWLEDGE

access the files that they need to do their jobs. You realize that because you used your account to encrypt the files, accounting staff will not be able to access the information unless they log on as your user account. For security reasons, you don't want regular users logged on as an administrator.

Your boss does not care about these technical problems and tells you to decrypt the files fast. What is the fastest way to decrypt the files? (Remember that they are spread over multiple NTFS drives—it took you two days to encrypt the files by using Explorer.)

A. Have everyone log on to the system as the recovery agent (Administrator) and access the files.

B. Create a batch file with the following commands and execute it at the root of all NTFS volumes containing encrypted files:
   `CIPHER /e /s`

C. Create a batch file with the following commands and execute it at the root of all NTFS volumes containing encrypted files:
   `CIPHER /d`

D. Create a batch file with the following commands and execute it at the root of all NTFS volumes containing encrypted files:
   `CIPHER /d /s /i`

8. As the server administrator at your company, you install a new accounting package on your server. The software has a number of components that run as a service and require user accounts to operate. Your company has a policy in place that requires users to change their passwords every 30 days. Every 30 days, your accounting package fails to start because the logon account it uses

must change its password. What should you do to correct the problem?

A. Set up the application so that it uses the Administrator account, as this account does not require password changes.

B. Write a script that will change the account password in both the account database and for the application every 30 days.

C. Configure the account so that its password does not expire.

D. Be sure that someone resets the password on the account each month.

9. You're creating a new share on an NTFS-formatted volume. The share will be used to hold case studies for the consulting company for which you work. Each case study should be able to be modified only by the consultant who created it. How should you set the permissions in this directory?

A. Allow the Everyone group the modify privilege.

B. Allow the Users group the modify privilege.

C. Allow the Creator Owner group the modify privilege.

D. Allow the Network group the modify privilege.

10. Your network extends to the front lobby where marketing representatives can plug in and download marketing information. There are quite a number of marketing representatives and they don't need anything else from the network. Which solutions can you use to allow marketing representatives to attach to the network in the lobby and get the marketing materials?

A. Create a user MarketingRep with a password of MyMktRep. Uncheck the option for Change Password at Next Logon. Check Password Never Expires and check User Cannot Change Password.

B. On the computer that hosts the share that contains the marketing materials: Enable the guest account, and add the read permission to the Everyone group on the folder that hosts the share and the share itself.

C. Create a group MarketingRep. Give the group read access to the marketing folder.

D. Create a user for each marketing representative and give each user access to the appropriate folder and share.

11. Your users are complaining that they can't download ActiveX controls from Web sites on the Internet; however, they can download other ActiveX controls from the intranet. What is the most likely cause?

A. They can't download ActiveX controls from either location—you've previously downloaded the ActiveX controls to their systems for them.

B. The ActiveX controls on the Internet are different from the ones used on the intranet.

C. The security for the different zones are set differently. In the intranet zone, you have Internet Explorer set to allow ActiveX controls; and, in the trusted zone, you have Internet Explorer set to not download ActiveX controls.

D. ActiveX controls must be authorized individually.

12. Your users are complaining that on some, but not all, Web sites on the Internet Java applets aren't working. What is the most likely cause?

A. Some of the Web sites, the ones where the Java applets aren't working, are set up in the Trusted Zone.

B. Some of the Web sites, the ones where the Java applets aren't working, are set up in the Restricted Zone.

C. Some of the Web sites, the ones where the Java applets aren't working, are set up in the intranet Zone.

D. Some of the Web sites, the ones where the Java applets aren't working, are set up in the Internet Zone.

13. You've recently read a news report about a Web site that runs Java code that downloads user information from the computers that log on. You want to prevent users from going to this site and having their information stolen. You don't have a proxy server or firewall capable of blocking specific addresses. What should you do?

A. Add the site to the trusted sites zone.

B. Add the site to the Restricted Zone.

C. Add the site to the intranet Zone.

D. Do nothing—you cannot prevent this from happening without a proxy server or firewall capable of blocking specific addresses.

14. One of your users needs to install a new application on their hard drive but there is not enough room. They've deleted unnecessary programs and emptied their recycle bin. What can be done to Internet Explorer to free up a significant amount of space?

APPLY YOUR KNOWLEDGE

A. Uninstall optional components.

B. Clear the browser History.

C. Clear the temporary files.

D. Remove Cookies.

15. You decide to audit access to the list of Employee home addresses in your small company because you're concerned that employees may be accessing this for purposes other than those that are company sanctioned. You turn on auditing on the file but don't see any audit events showing up in the security log. Why not?

   A. You must turn on auditing on the server.

   B. You must specify which users to audit.

   C. The file isn't on an NTFS partition.

   D. The file was accessed from the network. Network accesses are not audited.

Answers to Review Questions

1. The Computer Management snap-in is used to manage users and groups in a workgroup environment—in the Computer Management snap-in, there is a node called Local Users and Groups. For additional information, see the section "Creating Local User Accounts."

2. Under the workgroup model, each computer in your environment is responsible for the management of its own local account database. The workgroup model is meant for small environments. This model has a very high administrative cost, as user accounts must be managed on each computer in your environment. The workgroup model is very simple to implement and does not require that specialized computers manage a shared account database.

Under the domain model, a centralized database of user accounts is managed for a grouping (or domain) of computers. Domain user accounts contain information that defines users within the domain. In Windows XP, all user account information for the domain is stored in the Active Directory database. Active Directory is stored on a special computer called a *domain controller*. With a single domain user account, a user can log on to the domain and gain access to resources on any computer in the domain. The primary benefit of the domain model is that account management is simplified, as each user in your environment will have only a single user account defined. This model, however, is much more complex to set up, design, and configure. For additional information, see the sections "The Domain Model" and "The Workgroup Model."

3. The local policy of a computer contains settings related to account policies. Under account policies you can configure an account lockout policy. These settings enable you to specify the total number of bad password attempts a user can have within a given period of time. If the number of bad password attempts is exceeded, the user account is locked. You also should consider auditing failed logins. For additional information, see the sections "Local Group Policy" and "Audit Policies."

4. The Encrypting File System (EFS) enables a user to encrypt the contents of a file so that only that user (and a recovery agent) can access the file. This is helpful in environments in which users work with very sensitive data.

APPLY YOUR KNOWLEDGE

When a user encrypts a file, a session key is generated. This session key is used to encrypt the file. The file bulk data encryption key is then encrypted by using the user's public key. The encrypted session key is then saved with the file. A version of the key encrypted by a recovery agent is also saved with the file so that it can be recovered if the user account (and corresponding private key required to retrieve the session key) is unavailable. For additional information, see the section "Encrypting File System."

When a user attempts to open the file, the system will detect that it is encrypted and use the user's private key to decrypt the session key stored with the file. The session key is then used to decrypt the file.

5. Local Group Policy objects enable you to control the following components:

- **Administrative templates**—Registry-based setting that controls access to various system settings.

- **Software settings**—Enables software to be assigned to users and computers so that it is available to users when they need it.

- **Security settings**—Security settings for computers and users.

- **Scripts**—User Logon/Logoff, Computer Startup/Shutdown scripts.

- **Folder redirection**—Enables data directories (usually part of a user's profile) to be placed on networked drives instead of the local computer.

For additional information, see the section "Local Group Policy."

6. The secedit.exe command-line tool, when called from a batch file or automatic task scheduler, can be used to automatically create and apply templates and analyze system security. It can also be run dynamically from a command line.

This tool is useful when you have multiple computers on which security must be analyzed or configured and need to perform these tasks during off-hours. For additional information, see the section "Windows XP Security Configurations."

7. User rights are specific permissions that can be assigned to users and groups. These permissions give users or groups the ability to manage various aspects of a system. Built-in groups relate to user rights because built-in groups get their rights from being assigned, by default, useful combinations of user rights. For additional information, see the section "User Rights."

8. The following events can be audited:

- **Account logon**—Logs an event each time a user attempts to log on.

- **Logon events**—Logs an event for logon events that are occurring over the network or generated by service startup (for example, an interactive logon or a service such as SQL starting).

- **Account management**—Logs an event each time an account is managed. This is a useful function if you are concerned about changes being made to user accounts in your environment.

APPLY YOUR KNOWLEDGE

- **Directory service**—Logs an event each time an event occurs within the Active Directory services (for example, successful or failed replication events).

- **Policy change**—Logs an event each time a policy is successfully or unsuccessfully changed in your environment.

- **Process tracking**—Logs an event for each program or process that a user launches while accessing a system. This information can be used by administrators to track the details of a user's activities while accessing a system.

- **Object access**—Logs an event each time a user attempts to access a resource (that is, printer, shared folder, and so on).

- **Privilege use**—Logs an event each time a user attempts, successfully or unsuccessfully, to use special privileges such as changing system time.

- **System event**—Logs designated system events. Windows XP may log system events when a user restarts or shuts down a computer.

Answers to Exam Questions

1. **B, D, E**. The key to this question is remembering where user accounts are stored under each model. Under the Workgroup model, user accounts are stored and managed at the local machine. This model does not fit into environments with centralized Information System management. Under the domain model, user accounts stored in centralized locations are accessible throughout the domain. Generally, accounts stored and managed from a central location offer easier administration and better security. Answer A is not correct, as the workgroup model is not appropriate in large environments with centralized administration. Answer B is correct, as the domain model does work well in large environments with centralized administration. Answer C is not correct; the workgroup model does not offer better security. Answer D is correct; the domain model does offer better security. Answer E is also correct, as the workgroup model is limited to smaller environments. For additional information, see the sections "The Workgroup Model" and "The Domain Model."

2. **B**. Most likely, the user reset her password with the CAPS lock on. Answer A is not correct, as passwords are considered priority changes and are replicated immediately. Answer C is not correct, as users do not need to be a member of the account operators group to change their passwords. Answer D is incorrect, as no mention was made that a workstation restriction was put in place. For additional information, see the section "User Accounts."

3. **A, B, C**. Remember that audit policies are configured in two places. You must enable auditing through a policy and then configure the resources that you want to be audited. When you configure the resource level, it is in your best interest to audit the Everyone group. The Everyone group includes all users (even users who are not authenticated to the network). You also should realize that auditing alone does not protect your resources. You generally use auditing to confirm that your security configuration is working properly. In this case, the network administrator should have reviewed the SQL database security,

APPLY YOUR KNOWLEDGE

NFTS permissions, share permissions, and user password policies to ensure that the network is secure. Answer D is incorrect, as auditing can be used to track users accessing directories. For additional information, see the section "Audit Policies."

4. **D**. The Encrypting File System supports a recovery agent account to assist, if encrypted files need to be decrypted and the user is unavailable. Answer C is correct under the default installation of Windows XP. The Administrator account is, by default, the recovery agent. Being the administrator, however, does not guarantee that you are also the recovery agent, if the default configuration has been changed. Answer A is incorrect because if you take ownership of the files, the encryption keys required to decrypt the file are not available to you. Answer B would work but is not an acceptable practice for network administrators. For additional information, see the section "Encrypting File System."

5. **B, D**. You will need to remember the purpose of the security templates for the exam. The highly secure template configures secure network communications between Windows 2000 or Windows XP based. For this reason, answers B and D are correct. Answer B suggests upgrading the workstation so they have the ability to communicate with the servers. Answer D is less desirable but would work. In this case, we are going to apply the default security template to reset the servers to their default configuration, which does support communications with Windows 95/98 and Windows NT systems. Answer A is incorrect, as Windows 95/98 and Windows NT do not support security template configurations. Answer C is incorrect, as the user that is logged on does not impact the secure communication channel required between client and server under the highly secure template. For additional information, see the section "Windows XP Security Configurations."

6. **C**. In this question, you must be able to sort out the logical first place to look when troubleshooting a problem. Generally, the first place you will look for troubleshooting information is the Event Viewer. Remember that the Event Viewer shows information about services running on your servers. If the service is failing, some of the reasons should appear in the event log. Answer A is another potentially correct answer. The Services node of Computer Manager, however, does not show any troubleshooting information (it shows only whether the service is running or not). Answer B is incorrect, as rebooting the server is generally considered a last resort when troubleshooting a problem (it also does not provide information as to the nature of the problem, if it does fix the problem). Answer D is incorrect, as the audit process will audit information about processes only if you configured the server to audit for these events. For additional information, see the section "Event Viewer."

7. **D**. This question requires that you understand how EFS works. Remember that the user who encrypts a file is the only user who can access the file (except for the recovery agent). In this scenario, we need a quick solution. The absolutely fastest method we have available is to allow the users to log on as Administrator (that is, the recovery agent). This solution would compromise network security and is totally inappropriate (therefore, answer A is incorrect). The next best solution is to write a batch file that runs the

APPLY YOUR KNOWLEDGE

CIPHER command to decrypt the files. This involves mapping a drive to the root of each NTFS drive containing encrypted files and running the file. The only trick is getting the command syntax correct. Answer B is incorrect, as it uses the /e switch, which instructs CIPHER to encrypt files. Answer C is incorrect, as it does not include the /s switch, which tells CIPHER to decrypt files and subfolders. Answer D is correct, as CIPHER is configured to decrypt files (/d), including subfolders (/s), and not stop on errors (/i). The /i option is important because when the command runs, you might try to decrypt files you did not encrypt (that is, files encrypted by other users). By default, CIPHER stops if it encounters an error. For additional information, see the section "Encrypting File System."

8. **C**. This question requires that you put on your administrator's hat. Most administrators want things to be as simple as possible. In this scenario, you are having problems because the account policies in your environment require you to change your password every 30 days. This setting causes your service accounts to fail when their passwords expire. The simplest solution is C: Set the service account so its password does not expire. Answer A is incorrect, as the Administrator also needs to reset passwords based on account policies. Answers B and D would work but would require more effort than necessary. For additional information, see the section "Account Settings."

9. **C**. The special built-in group Creator Owner always contains the owner of the document. By allowing the modify permission to only the Creator Owner group, consultants will be able to modify their own documents but no one else's

documents. Granting modify to the Everyone group will allow all users (including guests) to modify any case study. Granting the modify privilege to the Users group will, by default, allow any user who has successfully logged in to modify the case studies. For additional information, see the section "Groups."

10. **A, B**. One approach to this problem is to create a shared user account which the receptionist could give to the marketing reps when they come in. This is an acceptable solution but not optimal because the marketing rep's computer will need to be able to log on to your network with this account—something that can be difficult from Windows 9x workstations. The second approach is to make the share available to everyone on the network—including those users who have not been authenticated. This would allow them to use the resource without having to log on at all. Answer C is incorrect because just creating a group would not give users who don't have accounts on the local network access. Answer D is incorrect because this is a very time-consuming process—something the question specifically indicates is not an option. For additional information, see the section "Groups."

11. **C**. The different security zones within Internet Explorer allow and disallow different things, including the downloading and running of ActiveX controls. The intranet zone is configured to allow ActiveX controls to download and run. For additional information, see the section "Configuring Internet Options."

12. **B**. The different security zones within Internet Explorer allow and disallow different things, including the running of Java applets. The restricted zone typically allows fewer things to

APPLY YOUR KNOWLEDGE

run. It's not possible to set up Internet sites within the intranet zone, nor is it possible to explicitly set up any site within the Internet zone. For additional information, see the section "Configuring Internet Options."

13. **B.** Adding a site to the restricted zones will turn off the ability to execute most code, including the kinds of code necessary to fetch user information. For additional information, see the section "Configuring Internet Options."

14. **C.** Internet Explorer caches some of the pages that you visit in order to show them to you more quickly when you revisit them. This cache is controlled by Internet Options and can be quite large. Clearing the history file or the cookies will

free up some space but the amount of space freed is relatively immaterial because both cookies and history shortcuts are very small. Additionally, uninstalling Internet Explorer options is not directly supported. For additional information, see the section "Configuring Internet Options."

15. **B.** Auditing is a two-step process. You must specify the resource to audit—and whom to audit. Answer A is incorrect because you don't turn on auditing at a server level. Answer C is incorrect because you would not have been able to turn on auditing on the file in the first place if it weren't on an NTFS partition. Answer D is incorrect because network accesses are audited. For additional information, see the section "Audit Policies."

Suggested Readings and Resources

1. *Active Directory Overview*, White Paper. Microsoft Corporation, 2000. Available from www.microsoft.com.

FINAL REVIEW

Fast Facts

Study and Exam Prep Tips

Practice Exam

The seven chapters of this book cover the objectives for the Windows XP Professional exam. After reading all of that, what are the important points that you really need to know? What should you review in that last hour before walking into the testing center to write your first (or next) Microsoft certification exam?

The following sections cover the most significant points of the previous seven chapters. They also provide some insight into the information that makes particularly good exam material. There's no substitute for real-world, hands-on experience. There's no substitute for reading the rest of this book. However, this material is the perfect review before heading into the testing center. Knowing what to expect on the exam will go a long way toward getting a passing score. The information that follows provides the material that you must know to pass the exam. Don't memorize the concepts given; attempt to understand the reasons why they are so, and you will have no difficulty passing the exam.

Fast Facts

Exam 70-270

INSTALLING WINDOWS XP PROFESSIONAL

Planning for and installing Windows XP Professional, naturally, is the first step to successfully using the product. The first consideration is the hardware requirements of the operating system and the application you plan to run.

Windows XP Professional requires a Pentium 133MHz or higher with 64MB of memory, a system disk of at least 2GB with 650MB free space, a network adapter, VGA resolution graphics adapter or higher, a CD-ROM drive, and finally, a keyboard and mouse.

System Configuration

The next task to installing Windows XP Professional is deciding on the disk layout. Windows XP Professional supports both basic disks and dynamic disks. Basic disks use partitions (up to four per disk) and extended partitions with logical drives. Dynamic disks are broken up into logical volumes, with the disk configuration information being kept on the disk rather than in the Windows Registry. Windows 9x and Windows NT 4.0 do not support dynamic disks—an important fact if you plan to implement a dual-boot system.

After you decide the layout, you need to choose the file system type. There are three types:

- ◆ FAT
- ◆ FAT32
- ◆ NTFS

File Allocation Table (FAT) supports the greatest number of operating systems and, therefore, is a good choice for dual-boot systems. It supports long filenames with spaces and additional periods, but it does not support encryption, disk quotas, or local security and is inefficient for large partitions.

FAT32 was introduced to have a smaller cluster size to therefore support larger disk partitions. Otherwise, it suffers the same problems as FAT without the wide support. FAT32 does not support all versions of Windows 95, DOS, or Windows NT.

NTFS is the file system of choice for systems running Windows XP. NTFS supports compression, encryption, quotas, and file- and folder-level security, and it uses transaction logging to support recoverability. NTFS supports sparse files that use only the space used in the file, but they are preallocated for more space and very large partitions (16 exabytes).

During the installation, you will be asked to select the network security group to install. The choices are workgroup and domain. The workgroup approach maintains a security database on each local machine in a grouping. This is naturally restricted to small groups of machines. The domain approach maintains a central database of security information. To join a domain, there must be a DNS name resolution system and a domain controller on your network.

Installation Methods

Manual (or automatic) installation of Windows XP Professional is completed in four steps. The first is to boot the computer from the CD. The installation enters the text phase. In this phase, you can select any third-party RAID/SCSI drivers, a boot partition, and file system type. The setup process copies files to the hard drive and reboots into graphical mode. In the graphical phase, you are prompted for configuration information, such as the local administrator's password and regional settings. The installation then configures the network adapters and selects a workgroup or domain to join. The final phase applies the configuration settings, cleans up any temporary files, and reboots the system.

If you want to start the installation procedure from a running system, you would choose to run `WINNT.EXE` from DOS or `WINNT32.EXE` from Windows 95/98 or Windows NT.

Unattended Installation

Installation of Windows XP Professional can also be done without user intervention.

Two different files are used during unattended installation: the unattended text file (or answer file) and the uniqueness definition file (UDF). The first represents all the standard things in an installation and the second represents the unique settings found in each machine. The unattended text file is used to configure all the standard options for each machine (one file for each type of hardware platform in your environment); the UDF file is used to configure the unique aspects of each individual computer (such as computer name, domain to join, and network configuration).

There is a tool in the Windows XP resource kit (`Setupmgr.exe`) that will create both the answer file and the UDF file, as well as a batch file that will correctly apply the command switches to `WINNT32.EXE` to perform the unattended installation.

Remote Installation Services

Another way to install Windows XP Professional is by using Remote Installation Services (RIS). RIS runs on a server (domain controller or member server) and contains one or more operating system images that can be downloaded over the network. RIS requires Active Directory, DNS, and DHCP to be in use. The Remote Image Preparation utility (Riprep) is used to remove all SID, computer name, and Registry information.

An RIS client uses the Pre-Boot Execution Environment (PXE) BIOS to obtain an address from DHCP and query DNS about the availability of RIS servers. You are prompted to log on and a list of RIS images to download is displayed.

A final way to install Windows XP Professional is by reimaging a computer's hard drive with Sysprep and third-party disk imaging software.

Migrating User Environments

Windows XP offers two tools that can be used to migrate user settings and files from older workstations to Windows XP Professional. The first method is the File and Settings Transfer (FAST) Wizard. This interactive tool can transfer information via removable media (that is, floppy disks), over a network or over a direct cable connection. The FAST Wizard is run interactively in a window.

The other set of utilities is the User State Migration Tool (USMT). This set of utilities enables you to fetch and put the user settings just as the FAST tool does but also offers the flexibility of including additional files or settings that the FAST tool does not support. The `SCANSTATE.EXE` utility is used to fetch the information from a computer and store it in directory structure. The `LOADSTATE.EXE` utility is used to take the information gathered by `SCANSTATE.EXE` and put it on a computer. The USMT utilities can be run in a batch file or logon script without user intervention.

IMPLEMENTING AND CONDUCTING ADMINISTRATION OF RESOURCES

This section deals with allowing and controlling access to network resources. The most often used and also the most complex network resource is that of file system access.

When a file is "shared" on the network, the owner is granting Read, Change, and Full Control permissions to users and groups. Read allows the user to read the contents of files and subfolders within the share and also to execute programs held there. Change provides all the Read permissions as well as the ability to add files and subfolders to the share and append and delete from files already existing on the share. Full Control allows the user Read and Change privileges plus the ability to take ownership of the resource. It's also an option to deny access to the resource by a group.

Permissions are always cumulative with the exception of Deny, which overrides all others.

After a share has been created and access provided for, the user can connect to it in one of four ways. The first is by using the command-line `net use x:\\computer\share` to link a drive letter to a shared resource. The same drive letter mapping can be done using the Windows Explorer under the Tools menu. Shares can also be accessed by using My Network Places and entering `\\computer\share` into the Windows Run menu. Finally, files and directories can be accessed using Web folders through Internet Explorer.

Some default shares are automatically created when installing Windows XP Professional. These include *driveletter*$ (that is, C$ or D$), which allows administrative personnel to attach to the root directory of a drive; ADMIN$ (used during remote administration), which is linked to the \WINNT subdirectory on the system drive; and IPC$, which is used as a communications link between programs.

Shared folder permissions provide very limited security; they protect resources only if they are accessed over the network. Shared folder permissions are also limited because they provide access to the entire directory structure from the share point down into the subdirectories. For these reasons, you will find that it's rare for

shared folder permissions to be used in isolation, without NTFS permissions.

To secure folders and files on an NTFS partition, we assign NTFS permissions for each user or group that requires it. If a user does not have any permissions assigned to his user account, or does not belong to a group with permissions assigned, the user does not have access to the file or folder. The NTFS folder permissions available to set for users or groups are shown in the following list:

- **Read**—See the files and subfolders and view folder attributes, ownership, and permissions.

- **Write**—Create new files and subfolders, change folder attributes, and view folder ownership and permissions.

- **List Folder Contents**—See the names of files and subfolders in the folder.

- **Read and Execute**—The combination of the Read permission and the List Folder Contents permission and the ability to traverse folders. The right to traverse folders allows you to reach files and folders located in subdirectories even if the user does not have permission to access portions of the directory path.

- **Modify**—The combination of Read and Write permissions plus the ability to delete the folder.

- **Full Control**—Change permissions, take ownership, delete subfolders and files, and perform the actions granted by all other permissions.

The NTFS file permissions available to set for users or groups appear in the following list:

- **Read**—Read a file and view file attributes, ownership, and permissions.

- **Write**—Overwrite a file, change file attributes, and view file ownership and permissions.

◆ **Read and Execute**—The combination of Read plus rights required to run applications.

◆ **Modify**—The combination of the Read and Execute permissions, plus the ability to modify and delete a file.

◆ **Full Control**—Change permissions, take ownership, delete subfolders and files, and perform the actions granted by all other permissions.

File and folder permissions are cumulative exactly as described for file shares, and permissions can be inherited from the folder above. When you view the permissions of a file or folder, inherited permissions appear grayed out. Inheritance can also be blocked and inherited permissions removed from a file or folder. This would leave only the explicitly assigned permissions. Permissions applied to the file level override permissions inherited from the folder level.

When you copy files or folders from one folder to another or from one partition to another, permissions might change. The following lists the results you can expect from various copy operations:

◆ When you move a folder or file within a single NTFS partition, the folder or file retains its original explicit permissions and inherits the permissions of the destination folder if the file or folder is set to allow inheritable permissions to propagate.

◆ When you move a folder or file between NTFS partitions, the folder or file inherits the permissions of the destination folder.

◆ When you move a folder or file between partitions, you are creating a new version of the resource and therefore inherit permissions.

◆ When you move a folder or file to a non-NTFS partition, all permissions are lost (because non-NTFS partitions do not support NTFS permissions).

Best Practices

Users will access network resources for a variety of purposes (home directories, shared files, or applications). Home directories, for example, are usually seen as the place where users keep their own documents. If this is on a server (as a shared resource), there are usually automatic backup and restore services provided. A user's files are also available even if the user is not at his normal workstation. Local home directories are available when the network is down or unavailable, but backups are left to the user (and that usually is not done regularly) so the information is at risk of disk failure.

Common files usually are shared at the top of the directory structure to provide a single starting point for all users. Access to individual files and folders is handled at the NTFS level to allow or deny access to individuals or groups.

Application shares allow common programs to be kept in one spot on the network. This allows for better control over versions and software upgrades and makes the application available, even if the user is not at his normal workstation.

NTFS volumes also enable you to compress the data held on them to increase the amount of space available. This naturally increases the amount of time to access the file and uses some CPU power. However, in an emergency, it can quickly provide some needed space. Compression can be enabled from Windows Explorer from the Properties page of the volume. It also can be done using the COMPACT program from a command window.

One further step that you might want to take to secure information held locally on your computer is to encrypt the file or folder using the Encrypting File system provided by Windows XP Professional. Details on this feature are found in Chapter 7, "Implementing, Monitoring, and Troubleshooting Security."

Sharing Printer Resources

The four components that make up the Windows XP print environment appear in the following list:

❖ **Printer**—A printer is a logical or software representation of a physical print device. You will find printers configured on computers so that print jobs can be sent to them.

❖ **Print driver**—A print driver is used to convert print requests into a format understood by the physical print device being used in the environment.

❖ **Print server**—A print server is a computer that receives and processes documents from client computers for processing.

❖ **Print device**—A print device is the physical device that produces the printed output.

Printers can be either local or network based. If you are installing a local printer, you are given the option of automatically creating a network share that will allow other users access to it. Access to shared printers is managed in the same fashion as shared files. In the case of printers, there are three types of permissions that you can assign to users or groups:

❖ Print

❖ Manage Documents

❖ Manage Printers

The various tasks you might want to perform with printers or print jobs will require different permissions. Table 1 outlines the permissions required to manage the printing environment.

TABLE 1
PERMISSIONS FOR THE PRINT ENVIRONMENT

Capabilities Permission	Print Permission	Manage Documents Permission	Manage Printer
Print documents	Yes	Yes	Yes
Pause, resume, restart, and cancel the user's own print jobs	Yes	Yes	Yes
Connect to the shared printer	Yes	Yes	Yes
Control job settings for all print jobs	No	Yes	Yes
Pause, resume, restart, and cancel all users' print jobs	No	Yes	Yes
Cancel all print jobs	No	Yes	Yes
Pause and resume a printer, and take a printer offline	No	No	Yes
Share a printer	No	No	Yes
Change printer properties	No	No	Yes
Delete a printer	No	No	Yes
Change printer permissions	No	No	Yes

Managing a printer environment can also include providing higher priority to some print jobs and providing greater capacity for some printers. Priority can be set by installing an additional printer pointing to the same physical printer as an existing printer, but with a higher priority.

Windows XP Professional enables you to create a printer pointing to several devices (print pooling), thereby providing a higher capacity than any one physical print device alone.

Using and Synchronizing Offline Files

If you travel frequently and use your laptop for most of your work, offline files provide a way to ensure that the network files you are working with are the most current versions and that changes you make when offline will be synchronized when you reconnect to the network.

When you reconnect to the network (perhaps docking your portable computer), changes that you have made to the offline files are synchronized back to their original network files. If someone else has made changes to the same file, you have the option of saving your version of the file, keeping the other version, or saving them both.

IMPLEMENTING, MANAGING, MONITORING, AND TROUBLESHOOTING HARDWARE DEVICES AND DRIVERS

Windows XP Professional supports Plug and Play (PnP), allowing you to add new hardware (or remove hardware) without making configuration changes. PnP will detect a new device both dynamically (adding a PCMCIA card) and at boot time (detecting a new video adapter).

Devices that are not Plug and Play compliant will have to be manually configured. Device drivers usually need configuration information on the following topics:

◆ **Interrupts**—An Interrupt Request (IRQ) is a way of determining which device is looking for service and what type of attention it needs. Windows XP provides interrupt numbers 0 through 15 to devices (IRQ 1 is always assigned to the keyboard).

◆ **Input/Output (I/O) ports**—I/O ports are areas of memory that the device uses to communicate with Windows XP Professional.

◆ **Direct Memory Access (DMA)**—DMAs are channels that allow the hardware device to access memory directly. Windows XP Professional provides DMA channels 0 through 7.

◆ **Memory**—Many hardware devices have onboard memory or can reserve system memory for their use.

The Resource by Device display from the Device Manager shows the availability of resources in your computer system.

CD-ROM and DVD Devices

Current DVD and CD-ROM devices all support Plug and Play and should install automatically without intervention.

Hard Disk Devices

Disk storage is now configured as basic or dynamic. The terms *basic disk* and *dynamic disk* are not referring to a different type of disk, but rather the way the disk is configured. A disk can be configured as a basic disk and partitioned as you would have done in Windows NT 4.0 or configured as a dynamic disk and divided into volumes.

Dynamic storage is designed for new volume-oriented disk configurations. A disk initialized for dynamic storage is called a dynamic disk. Dynamic disks are physical disks that contain dynamic volumes created using Disk Management. Storage is divided into volumes instead of partitions. A volume consists of a part or parts of one or more physical disks laid out as a simple, spanned, mirrored, striped, or RAID-5 structure.

Dynamic disks cannot contain partitions or logical drives and can be accessed only by computers running Windows XP.

In addition, mirrored and RAID-5 configurations are not supported on Windows XP Professional; however, Windows XP Professional can create these configurations on a remote Server Windows 2000 Server, Windows 2000 Advanced Server or Windows 2000 Datacenter Server. Dynamic disk configurations are not supported on portable computers. If you are using Disk Management on a laptop, you will find that the options for converting a basic disk to a dynamic disk are not present.

Removable Storage

Windows XP Professional supports Removable Storage Management (RSM) as the interface for accessing removable media, including automated devices such as changers, jukeboxes, and libraries. RSM is installed by default to control most types of removable media including CD-ROM, DVD-ROM, magneto-optical (MO), and Jaz and Zip drives in both standalone and library configurations. RSM can be used to manage anything except the A: and B: drives.

Multiple Displays

Windows XP Professional adds support for up to 10 display adapters. This allows the desktop to extend to 10 monitors supporting large graphical drawings (such as CAD displays) or topographical maps.

Power Management

Advanced Power Management (APM) is the legacy power management scheme based on a BIOS approach that was first supported in Windows 95. Most of the interesting features of APM are in a machine-specific BIOS that is hidden from the Windows XP Professional operating system.

APM has been superseded by the Advanced Configuration and Power Interface (ACPI) standard. This is a more robust scheme for power management and system configuration supported in Windows 98 and Windows XP Professional.

Standby

When your computer switches to standby mode, it goes into a low-power state where devices such as monitors and disk drives are turned off and your computer uses less power. By pressing standby again, the computer powers up quickly and your desktop is restored exactly as before. Standby is particularly useful for conserving battery life when you plan on being away from your computer for short periods of time. Standby does not save any information to disk, so a power failure (letting the batteries run out) will cause you to lose unsaved information.

Hibernation

Hibernation is an option that will save everything in memory to disk, turn off your monitor and disk drive, and power down your computer. When you restart your computer, your desktop is restored exactly as you left it. This takes longer because it has to reboot your computer and then reinitialize your desktop; however, it's a quick way to save your environment when you are going to be away from your computer for a long time.

For hibernation to be available as an option when pressing the power buttons, it must be configured. The Hibernate tab on the Power Options applet will allow you to configure Hibernation and also show the amount of disk space the option will take. When Hibernation is enabled, it will show up as an option on the advanced drop-down lists.

Input/Output Devices

Windows XP Professional supports the Plug and Play standard, and most new devices use this to standardize their installation steps.

Printers

The printing subsystem is modular and works hand in hand with other subsystems to provide printing services. When a printer is local and a print job is specified by an application, data is sent to the Graphics Device Interface (GDI) for rendering into a print job in the printer language of the print device. The GDI is the interface between the application and the printing subsystem. The print job is passed to the spooler and is written to disk as a temporary file so it can survive a power outage or system shutdown. Print jobs can be spooled in either the RAW or EMF printer language.

The spooling process is logically divided into two halves. The division between the client side and the server side allows the process to be on two different computers, allowing for the print process to use either a local or remote printer.

Keyboards

Keyboards can be built in, connected with a specific device port, or operate as a USB device connected directly via a USB hub.

Keyboard Customizations

The Accessibility Options applet in the Control Panel also provides several ways to customize how your keyboard functions:

- ◆ **StickyKeys**—This option allows you to press a modifier key such as Ctrl, Alt, Shift, or the Windows Logo key and have it remain in effect until a nonmodifier key is pressed.

- ◆ **FilterKeys**—This option allows you to ignore brief or repeated keystrokes.

- ◆ **ToggleKeys**—This option emits a sound when locking keys are pressed.

- ◆ **SerialKeys**—This option allows you to use an alternative input device instead of a keyboard and mouse.

Mouse

Like keyboards, mice can be directly connected to a mouse port, built into the keyboard as a piezoelectric control, connected to the serial port or to a device on a USB port or USB hub. After the mouse has been installed, you can adjust the characteristics of its action by using the Mouse applet in the Control Panel.

Multimedia

Categories of multimedia devices in Windows XP Professional include audio, video, and MIDI. In addition, the Microsoft Media Player can use the Web to access music files and radio stations that broadcast programming. The CD Player can be used to control the playback of music CDs from the system CD-ROM drive.

Smart Cards

Smart cards are credit card–size programmable computing devices. Applications and data can be downloaded onto a card for a variety of uses, including authentication, certificate storage, record keeping, and so on.

Although the processor included in the card can give it great capability, a smart card is not a standalone computer. It must be connected to other computers to be of much use. Smart cards today contain an 8-bit microcontroller with 16KB or more of memory.

In the Windows XP operating system, smart cards and certificate-based logons are fully supported. In this architecture, the smart card contains the certificate and associated private key. When you are logging on to your Windows XP Professional computer, a challenge is sent to the smart card. The smart card signs the challenge with the private key and the result, along with the certificate, is submitted to the authentication service. The authentication service verifies the signature and permits or denies the logon request.

Modems

Modems are most commonly used to dial up remote systems or Internet service providers using speeds up to 56Kb over analog phone lines. Modems from different manufacturers can achieve high speeds in different ways, causing compatibility problems for error correction and data compression. You might find that a high-speed modem will drop back to run at a lower speed because of compatibility differences with the modem at the other end of the phone line.

Infrared Devices

Windows XP Professional supports IrDA protocols that enable data transfer over infrared connections. The Windows XP Professional Plug and Play architecture will automatically detect and install the IrDA components for computers with built-in IrDA hardware.

Most laptops now ship with IrDA ports that provide either 115Kbps or 4Mbps transmission speeds.

Wireless Devices

The Wireless Link file transfer program, infrared printing functions, and image transfer capability are installed by default with your Windows XP Professional operating system. In addition, IrDA supports Winsock API calls to support programs created by other software and hardware manufacturers. The Winsock API calls can be used to provide infrared connections to printers, modems, pagers, PDAs, electronic cameras, cell phones, and handheld computers.

Linking Infrared Devices

When communications are first established, the commanding station sends out a connection request at 9600Kbps. The responding station assumes the secondary role and returns information listing its capabilities. Both the primary and secondary stations then change the connection rate and link parameters to the common set established by this initial negotiation. With the connection established, data transfer is put under the control of the primary device.

A single IrDA device cannot link to more than one other IrDA device at a time. You can install multiple IrDA devices to provide simultaneous links to multiple remote devices. For example, you can have a desktop computer connect to a notebook and a digital camera simultaneously using two IrDA transceivers.

USB Devices

The Universal Serial Bus (USB) is a serial protocol that runs at up to 12Mb/sec, supporting Plug and Play and power management. USB is a token-based protocol that Windows XP Professional polls to detect changes to the devices connected.

Hubs can be self powered with an external power source or can be bus powered and get their power from the bus itself. The USB definition allows for a total of five tiers (such as hubs attached to hubs) in a USB network. With the Windows XP Professional computer acting as the USB host, that leaves a total of four tiers (or network segments) for actual devices.

Managing Network Adapters

Windows 2000 Professional creates a local area connection in the Network and Dial-Up Connections folder for each network adapter installed in your computer. You can eliminate possible confusion by renaming each local area connection to reflect the network to which it is connected.

You must enable the network clients, services, and protocols that are required for your local area connections. When you do so, the client, service, or protocol is enabled automatically in all other network and dial-up connections.

You can create multiple dial-up, VPN, or direct connections by creating new ones with the wizard or by copying them in the Network and Dial-Up Connections folder. After you copy the connections, you can rename them and modify the connection settings.

Updating Drivers

When using Windows Update, the hardware IDs for the devices installed are compared to what the Microsoft Web site has to offer. If an exact match is made, the new driver is downloaded and installed. If an update to an existing driver is found, the new software components will be listed on the Web site and a download button will load the updated drivers onto your Windows XP Professional computer into a temporary directory for installation.

Windows XP Professional includes a mechanism called *Driver Signing.* All Windows operating system files and device drivers are digitally signed to ensure their quality. A digital signature on a driver indicates that the file has passed a volley of tests to assure the file works well in the Windows XP Professional environment. The digital signature is also used to guarantee the file has not been overwritten by another program's installation process.

Driver signing uses the existing digital-signature technology. A hash of the driver binary and other relevant information is stored in a catalog file (CAT file), and the CAT file is signed with the Microsoft digital signature. A CAT file is created for each signed driver but the driver binary itself is not touched. The link between the driver binary and the CAT file is maintained in the driver's INF file.

You can configure Windows XP Professional to ignore digital signatures and install the software anyway; issue a warning whenever a driver is being installed without a digital signature; or block the installation of any unsigned driver.

The impact of allowing unsigned drivers onto your system can range from no problems at all to a blue screen. That's the problem with unsigned drivers; they are unpredictable. Many corporations are introducing "signed drivers only" policies to reduce problems introduced by untested device drivers.

Multiple Processing Units

Windows XP Professional is designed to run uniformly on a uniprocessor and symmetric multiprocessor platforms.

Windows XP Professional supports the addition of a CPU under the following conditions:

◆ Both CPUs are identical and either have identical coprocessors or no coprocessors.

◆ Both CPUs can share memory and have uniform access to memory.

◆ In symmetric multiprocessor platforms, both CPUs can access memory, process interrupts, and access I/O control registers.

MONITORING AND OPTIMIZING SYSTEM PERFORMANCE AND RELIABILITY

This section is concerned with the performance and reliability of your computer.

Performance Monitoring

Windows XP Professional defines performance data in terms of objects, counters, and instances. An object is any resource, application, or service that you can measure. Each object has counters that are used to measure various aspects of performance, such as transfer rates for disks, packet transmit rates for networks, or memory and processor time consumed by applications or services.

Each object will have at least one counter, although most have many different counters available. Each counter will have at least one instance (usually Total or Average), although some objects (such as Process) will have an instance for each process currently active on the computer.

Memory Performance

Memory usage in Windows XP Professional is divided into paged (can be written out to disk) or nonpaged (must reside in memory). The paging file provides a place for memory in the paged pool to reside when not in use and extends the amount of virtual memory available. Memory not in use by processes is allocated to the file cache. This holds recently read or written data for quick access if required. The size of the file cache depends on the amount of physical memory available and the number of processes being run. You can find the current value for your computer by looking in the Performance tab in Task Manager.

The size of the paging file is set to the amount of physical memory plus 12MB, but its use and size will be different on every system. If you configure your paging file too small, Windows XP Professional will spend more time looking for space and therefore will run slower. You could also exhaust the amount of virtual memory available and generate errors when running applications. A best practice would be to move the paging file to a disk other than the one holding the system files and to set its minimum and maximum size to the same amount to prevent disk fragmentation.

Because memory performance is tied to the paging file (and therefore disk performance), the most important counters to watch are Available Bytes (the amount of memory available) and Pages In and Pages Out (pages being written to and from the paging file).

The file system cache can't itself be a bottleneck. However, if there is not enough memory to make an effective cache area, the result is increased disk activity and perhaps a disk bottleneck. An important counter to watch is Copy Read Hits %, which should be 80% or greater to be optimal. If your system is consistently below this value for long periods of time, you might have a memory shortage.

Processor Performance

The System, Processor, Process, and Thread objects contain counters that provide useful information about the work of your processor.

A processor bottleneck occurs when the processor is so busy that it cannot respond to an application that is requesting time. High activity might indicate that a processor is either handling the work adequately or is a bottleneck and slowing down the system. The Processor Queue Length counter from the System object and the % Processor Time counter from the Processor object will indicate whether your processor is just busy or is overwhelmed by requests. The processor queue length should be less than 2 as an average. The % Processor Time should be less than 80% as an average.

If you determine that you do have a processor bottleneck, some of the following actions might shorten the processor queue and reduce the burden on your processor:

◆ Remove memory bottlenecks that might be consuming the processor. This can include stopping unnecessary services, adding physical memory, or moving processing jobs to other computers.

◆ Upgrade your network or disk adapters to intelligent, 32-bit adapters.

◆ Try to obtain adapters that have optimization features.

◆ Upgrade to a faster processor.

◆ Add another processor.

Disk Performance

Disk performance counters can reflect both physical disk activity and logical disk and volume activity.

Following are some important disk counters:

◆ **Avg. Disk Bytes/Transfer**—This counter measures the size of I/O operations.

◆ **Avg. Disk/Sec Transfer**—This counter measures the average time for each transfer regardless of the size.

◆ **Avg. Disk Queue Length**—This is the total number of requests waiting as well as the requests in service. If more than two requests are continually waiting, the disk might be a bottleneck.

◆ **Current Disk Queue Length**—This counter reports the number of I/O requests waiting as well as those being serviced.

◆ **Disk Bytes/Sec**—This is the rate at which data is being transferred to the disk. This is the primary measure of disk throughput.

◆ **Disk Transfers/Sec**—This is the number of reads and writes completed per second, regardless of the amount of data involved. This is the primary measure of disk utilization.

◆ **% Idle Time**—The percentage of time the disk subsystem was not processing requests and no I/O requests were queued.

It's important to monitor the amount of available storage space on your disks because a shortage of disk space can adversely affect the paging file and as the disk space diminishes, disk fragmentation usually increases.

The % Free Space and Free Megabytes counters in the `LogicalDisk` object allow you to monitor the amount of available disk space. If the amount of available space is becoming low, you might want to move some files to other disks if available and compress the disk and remove temporary files to free up some disk space. The Disk Cleanup program (under Accessories and then System Tools) will search your hard drive for temporary files, Internet cache files, and unnecessary program files in an attempt to salvage disk space.

If you think there is a disk bottleneck in your computer, the following counters will be useful during analysis of the problem:

◆ **Paging counters (found in the Memory object)**—Pages/Sec, Page Reads/Sec, Page Writes/Sec

◆ **Usage counters**—% Disk Time, % Disk Read Time, % Disk Write Time, % Idle Time, Disk Reads/Sec, Disk Writes/Sec, Disk Transfers/Sec

◆ **Queue-length counters**—Avg. Disk Queue Length, Avg. Disk Read Queue Length, Avg. Disk Write Queue Length, Current Disk Queue Length

◆ **Throughput counters**—Disk Bytes/Sec, Disk Read Bytes/Sec, Disk Write Bytes/Sec

Application Performance

Only a very few applications require the high performance of a real-time data collection or a transaction system. Therefore, it's important to define what the required performance level is and to determine a way to measure it.

Application performance can be described from three points of view:

◆ **The real performance**—This is how fast the application actually performs its work.

◆ **The perceived performance**—This is how fast the application looks and feels to the user.

◆ **The consistency of the application's response**—This aspect of performance can be characterized as in terms of the stability, scalability, and availability of the application.

The application that satisfies all three views will always be considered successful.

Here are some important counters for measuring application performance. These are found in the Process object:

◆ **Memory**—Pool Paged Bytes, Pool Non-Paged, Non-Paged Bytes, Working Set, Working Set Peak

◆ **Processor**—% Privilege Time, % User Time, % Processor Time

◆ **I/O**—Read Bytes/Sec, Read Operations/Sec, Write Bytes/Sec, Write Operations/Sec

Working with the Task Scheduler

Earlier versions of Windows provided the AT command to schedule programs or scripts to run at specific times. Windows XP includes a graphical utility called the *Task Scheduler* that enhances this scheduling capability.

The Task Scheduler is not the same as the AT command; however, they share many common characteristics. When a task is scheduled by AT, an entry for it appears in the Task Scheduler task window.

With the Task Scheduler, you can specify the user account to run a task (even if scheduled with the AT command). Whenever you use Task Scheduler to modify an AT task, you can no longer use AT to modify any characteristics of the job.

Hardware Profiles

Hardware profiles tell your Windows XP Professional computer which devices to start and what setting to use for each device.

You create hardware profiles from the System applet in the Control Panel. If there is more than one hardware profile, you can designate one as the default that will be loaded when you start your Windows XP Professional computer (assuming you don't make a choice manually). After you create a hardware profile, you can use Device Manager to enable or disable devices in the profile. When you disable a device while a hardware profile is selected, that device will no longer be available and will not be loaded the next time you start your computer.

Using the Briefcase to Synchronize Files

A Briefcase is a mechanism of sharing files between two computers that are directly connected (for example, through a direct cable). The Briefcase functions just like its namesake; when you leave one computer, you put files onto your laptop for editing or other work and replace them when you return. You also can create a Briefcase on a floppy or removable disk drive (that is, a Zip drive).

A Briefcase will automatically update the file on your main computer to the modified version. You don't have to move the modified version from the Briefcase or delete the existing copies on your main system.

A Briefcase also allows you to view the status of the files you have offline. They can either be linked to an original file or be orphaned. You can organize your offline files by having multiple Briefcases.

Recovering System and User Data Using Backup

A tested backup and recovery procedure is one of the most important administrative tasks to perform. When you are creating your backup policy, you must consider the following issues:

- ◆ How often should a backup be done?
- ◆ What type of backup is the most appropriate?

- ◆ How long should backup tapes be stored?
- ◆ How long will the recovery of lost data take?

Five types of backups are available through the Windows XP Backup utility:

- ◆ **Normal backup**—Copies all selected files and marks each as being backed up. With normal backups, you can restore files quickly because the files on tape are the most current.
- ◆ **Copy backup**—Copies all the selected files but does not mark them as backed up.
- ◆ **Incremental backup**—Copies only those files created or changed since the last normal or incremental backup. A system restore would require a restore of the last normal backup and then all the incremental backups done since.
- ◆ **Differential backup**—Copies those files created or changed since the last normal backup. It does not mark the files as having been backed up.
- ◆ **Daily backup**—Copies those files that have been modified the day the daily backup is performed. The files are not marked as backed up.

Restoring Your Data

Windows XP Professional provides two ways to restore files using the Windows Backup utility: a wizard to walk you through the steps involved and a graphical interface to allow you to define the restore job manually.

When you want to recover some or all the files stored during a backup job, you must select the backup set to restore from and then the specific files (or all files) to restore. You can also restore the files to their original location or to an alternative location if you want to copy the recovered files by hand.

Booting Your Computer Using Safe Mode

Press F8 during the operating system selection phase to display a screen with advanced options for booting Windows XP. The following list describes the functions available from the advanced boot menu:

◆ **Safe Mode**—Loads only the basic devices and drivers required to start the system. This includes the mouse, keyboard, mass storage, base video, and the default set of system services.

◆ **Safe Mode with Networking**—Performs a Safe Load with the drivers and services necessary for networking.

◆ **Safe Mode with Command Prompt**—Performs a Safe Load but launches a command prompt rather than Windows Explorer.

◆ **Enable Boot Logging**—Logs the loading and initialization of drivers and services.

◆ **Enable VGA Mode**—Restricts the startup to use only the base video.

◆ **Last Known Good Configuration**—Uses the Last Known Good configuration to boot the system.

◆ **Directory Services Restore Mode**—Allows the restoration of the Active Directory (on domain controllers only).

◆ **Debugging Mode**—Turns on debugging.

When logging is enabled, the boot process writes the log information to `\%systemroot%\NTBTLOG.TXT`.

Last Known Good Configuration

Configuration information in Windows XP Professional is kept in a control set subkey. A typical Windows XP installation would have subkeys such as `ControlSet001`, `ControlSet002`, and `CurrentControlSet`. The `CurrentControlSet` is a pointer to one of the `ControlSetxxx` subkeys. Another control set named Clone is used to initialize the computer (either the Default or LastKnownGood). It is re-created by the kernel initialization process each time the computer successfully starts.

The key `HKEY_LOCAL_MACHINE\SYSTEM\Select` contains subkeys named Current, Default, Failed, and LastKnownGood, which are described in the following list:

◆ **Current**—This value identifies which control set is the `CurrentControlSet`.

◆ **Default**—This value identifies the control set to use the next time Windows XP starts (unless you choose Last Known Good configuration during the boot process).

◆ **Failed**—This value identifies the control set that was the cause of a boot failure the last time the computer started.

◆ **LastKnownGood**—This value identifies the control set that was used the last time Windows XP was started successfully. After a successful logon, the Clone control set is copied to the LastKnownGood control set.

When you log on to a Windows XP Professional computer and modify its configuration by adding or removing drivers, the changes are saved in the Current control set. The next time the computer is booted, the kernel copies the information in the Current control set to the Clone control set. After the next successful logon to Windows XP, the information in the Clone control set is copied to LastKnownGood.

If, when starting the computer, you experience problems that you think might be related to Windows XP configuration changes that you just made, restart the computer without logging on and press F8 during the initial boot phase. Selecting the Last Known Good configuration will restore the system configuration to the last one that Windows XP used to start successfully.

Configuring the Windows XP Recovery Console

To use the recovery console, you must first install it from the Windows XP CD. The Installation Wizard will create all the files necessary and modify `boot.ini` to provide an additional boot menu item that will allow you to select the recovery console while starting your system. In the event that your machine won't boot, and you have not installed the Recovery Console, you can run it directly from the CD. When you boot from CD, the text portion of the setup sequence will give you a chance to repair an existing installation by selecting the "repair or recover option (R)." If you have more than one operating system loaded, you will have to choose the one that needs repairing. The Recovery Console then will prompt you for the Administrator password.

Installing the Recovery Console

The Recovery Console Wizard is started with the command

```
\I386\WINNT32 /cmdcons
```

in which the `\I386` is a subdirectory on the Windows XP CD.

Recovering a System Using System Restore

System Restore is a new feature in Windows XP Professional that you can use to recover your computer to a previous state without losing your data. System Restore monitors changes to the system (and some application files) and creates restore points. These restore points allow you to revert your system to an earlier state. Restore points are created daily and whenever the system changes (with a new driver installation). You also can create and name your own restore points.

How Does System Restore Work?

By default, System Restore monitors and restores all partitions and drives on your computer. It also monitors all installations of applications or drivers that you may do yourself, or that SMS or IntelliMirror may do for you.

System Restore immediately creates a restore point if it detects that you are installing an unsigned driver to your computer. If the installation of the driver makes undesirable changes to your computer, you can select this restore point to undo the changes and restore your computer to the state that existed before you installed the driver. This allows you to roll back a driver installation after you have successfully booted your computer, which complements the "restore last good configuration" option in the boot sequence which will roll back a driver installation if you have not successfully booted your computer.

When you perform a recovery using the Backup utility, System Restore immediately creates a restore point before the process starts. If the recovery process puts your computer in a state that you don't like or can't work with, you can select this recovery point and restore the system to its state just before the recovery.

Each time you perform a restoration, it is a change made to your computer. System Restore creates restore operation restore points to track the change and the restoration. You can select these restore points to, in essence, undo the restoration.

Items Preserved Through a System Restore

System Restore does not cause you to lose your personal files or password. Items such as documents, email messages, browsing history, and the last specified password are saved when you revert to an earlier state with System Restore.

System Restore protects your personal files by not restoring any files in the My Documents folder. It also does not restore any files that use common data filename extensions, such as .doc or .xls. If you're not sure whether your personal files use common data filename extensions, and you do not want the data files to be affected by System Restore, save them in the My Documents folder.

If a program was installed after the restore point to which you are restoring was created, the program might be uninstalled as part of the restoration process. Data files that are created with the program are not lost. However, to use them with the application, you will have to reinstall the software.

The actual number of saved restore points depends on how much activity there has been on your computer, the size of your hard disk (or the partition that contains your Windows XP Professional folder), and how much disk space has been allocated on your computer to store System Restore information.

CONFIGURING AND TROUBLESHOOTING THE DESKTOP ENVIRONMENT

This section reviews configuring and troubleshooting the desktop environment.

User Profiles

Windows XP is a multiuser operating system, meaning that the expectation is there will be more than one user who uses the system. Windows XP Professional supports this through user profiles. There are three different types of profiles:

◆ **Local profiles**—These profiles are stored on the local workstation and will not follow a user to another computer if they should log on to one.

◆ **Roaming profiles**—Roaming profiles are defined as a profile that's stored on a Windows 2000 Server. This allows the profile to follow the user when logging on to a different computer.

◆ **Mandatory profiles**—This is a special variation of a roaming profile that will not save configuration changes made by the user.

Configuring Support for Multiple Languages

The starting point for multiple languages is the Regional Options applet of the Control Panel. This allows you to configure the appearance of numbers and date fields displayed by Windows XP Professional. In addition to being able to change the appearance of numbers, dates, and times, you can change the default input locale for a document. This allows you to enter letters and documents in a language other than the one your prompts and dialog boxes are in.

Windows Installer

Microsoft's Windows Installer technology is designed to address the limitations of software distribution:

◆ **On-demand installation of applications**—
When an application is needed by the user, the
operating system automatically installs the application from a network share, or by requesting the
user insert the appropriate media.

◆ **On-the-fly installation of application components**—The Windows Installer technology allows
applications to dynamically launch an installation
to install additional components not initially
installed on the computer.

◆ **Automatic application repair**—Windows applications are sometimes corrupted by users deleting
some required files, or by errant installations of
other software. The Windows installer can automatically repair damaged programs, making your
application more resilient.

Automatic installation is sometimes called Install on
First Use. Some of the different options allowed when
installing software by Windows Installer are as follows:

◆ **Run from My Computer**—This is the traditional installation method that loads the application
onto the local hard drive.

◆ **Run from CD**—Run the component without
installing any software on the local computer.
This will cause the component to run slower, but
will allow the component to be run when space is
at a premium.

◆ **Install on First Use**—The component will be
installed on its first use; in other words, if you
never use a component, it won't be installed.

◆ **Not Available**—The component isn't installed.
This option is useful when you don't want users
to be able to install a feature on their own.

Configuring Desktop Settings

Windows XP Professional allows great latitude of
choices and tastes when customizing the look of the
desktop, including toolbars, shortcuts, wallpaper, desktop, and screen savers.

By effectively managing elements such as favorites,
shortcuts, network connections, and desktop items, you
can ensure that the most relevant and current information is easily accessible.

Setting a desktop standard within your company or
workgroup can reduce support and training costs by
eliminating the need to learn about the changes to each
user's desktop. Windows XP allows you to create a
unique standard operating environment, including user
interface (UI) standards, based on the needs of your
organization.

Windows XP Professional in the Windows 2000 Server Network

When Windows XP Professional is part of a Windows
2000 Server network running Active Directory, powerful administrative functions such as Group Policy and
Change and Configuration Management are available
to customize and control the desktop.

Group Policy can be used to set and enforce policies on
multiple workstations from a central location. There are
more than 550 policies, including policies that help
prevent users from making potentially counterproduc-
tive changes to their computers. You can optimize the
desktop for the specific needs of each workgroup or
department in your organization.

Comparing Standalone and Active Directory–Based Management Features

All the Group Policy snap-ins that can be used on a local computer can also be used when Group Policy is focused on an Active Directory container.

However, the following activities require Windows .NET or Windows 2000 Server, an Active Directory infrastructure, and a client running Windows XP:

◆ Centrally managed software installation and maintenance for groups of users and computers

◆ User data and settings management, including folder redirection, which allows special folders to be redirected to the network

◆ Remote operating system installation

Using Group Policy on Standalone Computers

You will sometimes need to implement a group policy on a standalone computer. On a standalone computer running Windows XP Professional, local Group Policy objects are located at `\%SystemRoot%\System32\GroupPolicy`. The following settings are available on a local computer:

◆ **Security settings**—You can define security settings for only the local computer, not for a domain or network.

◆ **Administrative templates**—These allow you to set more than 400 operating system behaviors.

◆ **Scripts**—You can use scripts to automate computer startup and shutdown, as well as how the user logs on and off.

The following are examples of business rules that you might enforce through local group policy:

◆ The users cannot access the Run command.

◆ An antivirus program runs every time the computer is restarted.

◆ Common program groups are hidden in the Start menu.

To manage Group Policy on local computers, you need administrative rights to those computers.

Desktop Control Through Local Group Policies

There are a few simple rules to remember about the effects of group policies on user settings:

◆ The group policy always takes precedence. If it is set, the users covered by the policy will all have the setting specified.

◆ If the group policy doesn't have a value for a particular setting, or if there is no group policy, the user has the freedom to change the setting to whatever she would like.

◆ If a group policy is added to the system after the user has set up her environment, the group policy will take priority and override any user settings.

Remember that when setting up group policies, you may disable the user's ability to change something, but you may or may not disable the part of the user interface where changes to the setting are made. This sometimes causes confusion because the change just doesn't appear to have taken effect. See Chapter 5, "Configuring and Troubleshooting the Desktop Environment."

Accessibility Services

Several built-in technologies and Windows Explorer options are available for administrators and users to configure their computers with the accessibility features they need. Many of these features have added functionality beyond Microsoft Windows, including Magnifier, Narrator, On-Screen Keyboard, Utility Manager, high-visibility mouse pointers, and high-contrast color schemes. Again, see Chapter 5 for details on using the Accessibility Wizard to configure these services.

Program Compatibility Options

Because Windows XP is intended as a replacement for the Windows 9x series of operating systems, it includes a set of features designed to help applications run, even if they were not initially intended to run on Windows XP. In short, Program compatibility options allow you to

◆ Emulate a different operating system.

◆ Limit the display to 640×480.

◆ Limit the display to 256 colors.

IMPLEMENTING, MANAGING, AND TROUBLESHOOTING NETWORK PROTOCOLS AND SERVICES

The bottom layers of the Windows XP network architecture include the network adapter card driver and the network interface card (NIC). NDIS supports both connection-oriented protocols such as ATM and ISDN

and the traditional connectionless protocols such as Ethernet, Token Ring, and Fiber Distributed Data Interface (FDDI). The mechanism that NDIS uses to bridge these two layers is the miniport driver specification. The miniport drivers directly access the network adapters while providing common code where possible. Hardware vendors, therefore, do not have to write complete Media Access Control (MAC) drivers, and protocols can be substituted without changing network adapter card drivers.

NDIS 5.0 is the current level supported by Windows XP Professional and adds new functionality to networking. The following list describes of some of the new features of NDIS 5.0:

◆ **Power management and network wake-up**— NDIS power management can power down network adapters at the request of the user or the system. The system can also be awakened from a lower power state based on network events such as a cable reconnect or the receipt of a network wakeup frame or a Magic Packet packet (16 contiguous copies of the receiving system's Ethernet address).

◆ **NDIS Plug and Play**—Installs, loads, and binds miniports when a new adapter card is introduced.

◆ **Task Offload**—Available if the network adapter card has the capability to support check-summing and forwarding for performance enhancements.

◆ **Support for Quality of Service (QoS) and connection-oriented media such as ATM and ISDN**—QoS allows for bandwidth to be reserved for uses such as video conferencing. Protocols such as ATM do not support features such as broadcasts used by TCP/IP (broadcasts for a DHCP server). This must be emulated in connection-oriented media.

TCP/IP

Transmission Control Protocol/Internet Protocol (TCP/IP) is the default protocol for Windows XP Professional and is an industry-standard suite of protocols available for wide area networks (WAN) and the Internet.

NWLink IPX/SPX–Compatible Transport

NWLink is an NDIS-compliant, native 32-bit implementation of Novell's IPX/SPX protocol.

Adding and Configuring Network Components

You can configure all your network components when you first install Windows XP Professional. If you want to examine how your network components are configured or make changes to your network identification, double-click the System applet in the Control Panel and select the Network Identification tab.

Identification Options

Use the Network Identification option in the System applet to view your computer name and your workgroup or domain information.

To configure network options, open the Network Connections applet in Control Panel, right-click a connection, and select Properties.

Protocol Options

To configure Protocols, click the Install button. This brings up the Select Network Component Type button.

Service Options

Click the Install button and select a service to add to display all the available services not currently installed.

Client Options

Select the Client entry and click the Add button to show the clients available to install on your computer.

IP Addressing

Each TCP/IP connection must be identified by an address. The address is a 32-bit number used to uniquely identify a host on a network. The TCP/IP address has no dependence on the Data-Link layer address, such as the MAC address of a Network adapter. Although the IP address is 32 bits, it's customary to break it into four 8-bit numbers expressed in decimal and separated by dots. This can be referred to in dotted-decimal format and is expressed as *w.x.y.z.*

This addressing scheme is again broken down into two halves: a network ID (also known as the *network address*) and the host ID (also known as the *host address*). The network ID must be unique in the Internet or intranet, and the host ID must be unique to the network ID. The network portion of the *w.x.y.z* notation is separated from the host through the use of the subnet mask.

The Internet community was originally divided into five address classes. Microsoft TCP/IP supports class A, B, and C addresses assigned to hosts.

The class of address defines which bits are used for the network ID and which bits are used for the host ID. It also defines the possible number of networks and the number of hosts per network. Here is a rundown of the five classes:

◆ **Class A addresses**—The high-order bit is always binary 0 and the next seven bits complete the network ID. The next three octets define the host ID. This represents 126 networks with 16,777,214 hosts per network.

◆ **Class B addresses**—The top two bits in a class B address are always set to binary 1 0. The next 14 bits complete the network ID. The remaining two octets define the host ID. This represents 16,384 networks with 65,534 hosts per network.

◆ **Class C addresses**—The top three bits in a class C address are always set to binary 1 1 0. The next 21 bits define the network ID. The remaining octet defines the host ID. This represents 2,097,152 networks with 254 hosts per network.

◆ **Class D addresses**—Class D addresses are used for multicasting to several hosts. Packets are passed to a selected subset of hosts on a network. Only those hosts registered for the multicast address accept the packet. The four high-order bits in a class D address are always set to binary 1 1 1 0. The remaining bits are for the address that interested hosts will recognize.

◆ **Class E addresses**—Class E is an experimental address reserved for future use. The high-order bits in a class E address are set to 1 1 1 1.

Table 2 shows the most common address classes and the number of networks and hosts supported by them.

TABLE 2
ADDRESS CLASSES, NETWORKS, AND HOSTS

Class	Network ID	Network Portion	Host Portion	Number of Networks	Number of Hosts
A	1-126	w.	x.y.z	126	16,777,214
B	128-191	w.x	y.z	16,384	65,534
C	192-223	w.x.y	z	2,097,152	254

Subnet Mask

After an IP address from a particular class has been decided upon, it's possible to divide it into smaller segments to better use the addresses available. Each segment is bounded by an IP router and assigned a new subnetted network ID that is a subset of the original class-based network ID.

A subnet mask (also known as an *address mask*) is defined as a 32-bit value that is used to distinguish the network ID from the host ID in an IP address. The bits of the subnet mask are defined as follows:

◆ All bits that correspond to the network ID are set to 1.

◆ All bits that correspond to the host ID are set to 0.

The subnet mask is broken down to four 8-bit octets in the same fashion as the class addresses.

Table 3 shows the default subnet mask and the dotted notation used to describe them to Windows XP Professional.

TABLE 3
DEFAULT SUBNET MASK AND DOTTED NOTATION EQUIVALENT

Address Class	Bits for Subnet Mask	Subnet Mask
Class A	11111111 00000000 00000000 00000000	255.0.0.0
Class B	11111111 11111111 00000000 00000000	255.255.0.0
Class C	11111111 11111111 11111111 00000000	255.255.255.0

Default Gateway (Router)

This optional setting is the IP address of the router for this subnet segment. Each subnet segment is bounded by a router that will direct packets destined for segments outside the local one to the correct segment or to another router that can complete the connection. If this address is left blank, this computer will be able to communicate only with other computers on the same network segment.

Windows Internet Name Service

Computers may use IP addresses to identify one another, but users generally prefer to use computer names. Windows XP Professional allows Windows 9x and Windows NT 4 clients to use NetBIOS names to communicate and therefore requires a means to resolve NetBIOS names to IP addresses. Windows Internet Name Service (WINS) provides a dynamic database that replaces the static LMHOST file and maintains mappings of computer names to IP addresses.

Domain Name Systems Server Address

Domain Name Systems (DNS) is an industry-standard distributed database that provides name resolution and a hierarchical naming system (Fully Qualified Domain Name) for identifying TCP/IP hosts on Internets and private networks that replaces the static HOST file.

Understanding DHCP

One way to avoid the possible problems of administrative overhead and incorrect settings for the TCP/IP protocol (which are usually caused by manual configurations) is to use DCHP. DHCP centralizes and manages the allocation of the TCP/IP settings required for proper network functionality for computers that have been configured as DHCP clients.

Virtual Private Networks

A Virtual Private Network (VPN) allows the computers in one network to connect to the computers in another network by the use of a tunnel through the Internet or other public network. The VPN provides the same security and features formerly available only in private networks.

A VPN connection allows you to connect to a server on your corporate network from home or when traveling using the routing facilities of the Internet. The connection appears to be a private point-to-point network connection between your computer and the corporate server.

Additionally, VPNs can be used to connect remote office LANs to the corporate LAN or to other remote LANs to share resources and information using direct connect or dial-up access.

The basic functions managed by VPNs are the following:

❖ **User authentication**—Verify the user's identity and restrict VPN access to authorized users only.

❖ **Address management**—Assign the client's address on the private net and ensure that private addresses are kept private.

❖ **Data encryption**—Data carried on the public network must be unreadable to unauthorized clients on the network.

❖ **Key management**—Encryption keys must be refreshed for both the client and the server.

❖ **Multiprotocol support**—The most common protocols used in the public network are supported.

A VPN is not a protocol in itself, but rather the encapsulation of existing protocols and the encryption of the data being transmitted.

Windows XP Professional provides two encapsulation methods for VPN connections: Point-to-Point Tunneling Protocol (PPTP) and Layer 2 Tunneling Protocol (L2TP).

Point-to-Point Tunneling Protocol

This protocol enables the secure transfer of data from your computer to a remote computer on TCP/IP networks. PPTP tunnels, or encapsulates, IP or IPX protocols inside PPP datagrams.

PPTP Encryption

The PPP frame is encrypted with Microsoft Point-to-Point Encryption (MPPE) by using encryption keys generated from the MS-CHAP V2 or EAP authentication process.

Layer 2 Tunneling Protocol

L2TP is an Internet tunneling protocol with roughly the same functionality as PPTP. The Windows XP implementation of L2TP is designed to run natively over IP networks.

L2TP Encryption

The L2TP message is encrypted with IPSec encryption mechanisms by using encryption keys generated from the IPSec certificates. The portion of the packet from the UDP header to the IPSec ESP Trailer inclusive is encrypted by IPSec.

Connecting to Computers by Using Dial-Up Networking

Dial-up networking enables you to extend your network to unlimited locations. A dial-up connection connects your computer to a private network or the Internet (through an Internet service provider) to a private network through the public Internet, using a secure Virtual Private Network (VPN) connection, or to an RAS server using the Microsoft RAS protocol. The Microsoft RAS protocol is a proprietary protocol that supports the NetBIOS standard.

The dial-up connection can be made by a modem over the public switched network (also known as the Plain Old Telephone System, or POTS) or through a cable modem, xDSL service, an X.25 interface, or high-speed ISDN line. The incoming connections can also be made by Point-to-Point (PPP) or Serial Line Internet Protocol (SLIP) to support dial-up connections to SLIP servers.

Installing VPN Connections

A VPN connection is configured running the New Connection Wizard (Create a New Connection) in the Network Connections applet in the Control Panel. A VPN is created by selecting the option Connect to the Network at My Workplace. The connection can be configured to dial to an Internet service provider (ISP) or to connect directly to a VPN server if your computer is directly connected to the Internet.

The type of connection (PPTP or L2TP) is defined by the server to which you are connecting. In any case, the connection and security are negotiated automatically.

Dial-Up to the Internet

Dial-up networking enables you to extend your network to unlimited locations. A dial-up connection connects your computer to a private network or the

Internet (through an Internet service provider) to a private network through the public Internet using a secure Virtual Private Network (VPN) connection, or to an RAS server using the Microsoft RAS Protocol. The Microsoft RAS protocol is a proprietary protocol that supports the NetBIOS standard.

Connect to the Internet

This option is used to connect to an Internet service provider (ISP). You can choose to pick an Internet service provider from a list or use a wizard to find one for you, or you can use a CD provided by your ISP. The third way of connecting to the Internet is to manually enter the configuration values. The configuration options include the following:

◆ Naming the provider

◆ Entering the phone number

◆ Providing the logon user ID and password (usually provided by the ISP)

◆ Configuring the personal Firewall

Connect to the Network at My Workplace

This option provides for a secure Virtual Private Network (VPN) connection over the public Internet. This type of network connection allows you to select a dial-up connection to establish first; or, if you already have a persistent connection to the Internet through a LAN connection (for example, a cable modem), the VPN can be established using the local connection. The remote VPN server computer's name or IP address is added to complete the configuration.

Internet Connection Sharing

With the Internet connection–sharing feature of Network and Dial-Up Connections, you can use Windows XP to connect your home network or small office network to the Internet.

A computer with Internet connection sharing needs two connections: one to the internal LAN and one to the Internet. Internet connection sharing is enabled on the Internet connection. This shared connection will allow your internal network to receive its addresses using DHCP, provide a DNS service to resolve names, and provide a gateway service to access computer systems outside your home network. The network address translation (NAT) service allows your home network to use any addressing scheme you want because the internal addresses are not broadcast onto the Internet.

The NAT is transparent to both the client and the server. The client appears to be talking directly with the external server and the external server behaves as though the NAT is the end client. To the client, the NAT might be its default gateway (as is the case with Internet connection sharing) or, in a larger network, the router that connects to the Internet.

When the NAT is performing address and port translation, all internal addresses will be mapped to the single IP address of the NAT's external network card or dial-up interface. Ports will be mapped so that they remain unique.

Accessing Files Using Internet Explorer

You can use Internet Explorer to access files on your computer, or on a remote computer on your Internet by using the address format:

```
file://drive:/filepath/filename.ext
```

For example, you might want to look at a text file `example.txt` that is located in a subdirectory named FTP on your local machine. The address you would provide to Internet Explorer would be

```
file://C:/FTP/example.txt
```

Internet Explorer would display that file in Notepad (probably) due to the affinity of Notepad to the .txt extension.

If the file is on a share on some other server in your network, the command format would be

```
file://server/share/filename.ext
```

In the previous example, the command

```
file://gordb3/FTP/example.txt
```

would also display the file in Notepad (provided that the FTP subdirectory is a share).

Finding and Installing Printers from Internet Explorer

Occasionally, you might need to find a printer while you are inside Internet Explorer. Normally, you would search for a printer using the Add a Printer command inside Printers and Faxes in the Control Panel. You also can install printers on your local system from within Internet Explorer.

If you know the name of your local print server, you can retrieve a list of the printers that are located on the server.

The command

```
http://printserver/printers
```

will display a list of printers defined on the server named *printserver*. By clicking the Connect link, you will install the correct printer drivers on your computer and create a new entry for the printer in Printers and Faxes in Control Panel.

Internet Information Services

When Web sites were first gaining acceptance, they were always run on dedicated servers. Now, Web sites are ubiquitous and are used to store files (in Web folders) or to access information (from SQL databases) and display data (through Visual InterDev and ASP pages) and static content (using FrontPage).

Windows XP Professional allows you to configure one Web site on your computer. Each Web site can, of course, have many virtual directories to access other information.

Virtual Directories

Virtual directories provide a mechanism to include content on your Web site that's stored in a directory structure under root. For example, if you have a computer called *TestWeb1* and you create a virtual directory called *WebProject1* under the default Web site, the default page (if you create one) would be addressed as `http://TestWeb1/WebProject1/default.htm`. Similarly, a second virtual directory called `SQLProject` would have its default Web page addressed as `http://TestWeb1/SQLProject/default.htm`. In this way, it appears that you have more than one Web site running on your computer when in fact you are addressing different content in different virtual folders.

You create virtual directories in the IIS snap-in by right-clicking the default Web site and selecting New. The Virtual Directory Creation Wizard guides you through selecting an alias for this directory and where to put the physical files. Normally, the alias is what you want to address the Web page as and the physical files are placed in a subdirectory under `InetPub/wwwroot`.

The Web page then becomes available under the address

```
http://machinename/alias
```

where `machinename` is the name of your Windows XP Professional computer and `alias` is the name chosen for the Web page.

Configuring Remote Desktop

Remote Desktop is configured in the System Applet in Control Panel. The Remote tab will display a Remote Desktop window. Ensure the check box labeled "Allow users to connect remotely to this computer" is checked to enable Remote Desktop.

By default, your domain user ID is enabled for Remote Desktop. That means you can remotely use your computer when you are at a different computer. By default, as well, any user who is also in the administrators group has administrative access to your computer.

You can use the Select Remote Users button to add additional users who will have remote access to your machine.

Configure Remote Assistance

Remote Assistance is configured in the System Applet in Control Panel. The Remote tab will display a Remote Assistance window. Ensure the check box labeled Allow Remote Assistance Invitations to Be Sent from This Computer is checked to enable Remote Assistance. Select the Advanced button to view the Remote Assistance Setting screen. Ensure the check box labeled Allow This Computer to Be Controlled Remotely is checked.

Requests for Assistance and Offering Help

There are two ways in which a friend can assist you in solving your problem; you can email an invitation or your friend can offer remote assistance.

A request for assistance can be done through two mechanisms. The first is the help system (Help and Support). The main screen is Help, and Support has a link under Ask for Assistance that is labeled Invite a

Friend to Connect to Your Computer with Remote Assistance. This link will take you to a screen to request Remote Assistance and to monitor outstanding invitations.

Internet Connection Firewall

A firewall is a service that intercepts network traffic and applies a set of rules to decide whether the packets should be allowed or denied passage. The information used to make this determination comes from the packet header and includes source and destination addresses, ports, and other information.

A Stateful Packet Filter

Internet Connection Firewall is more than just a static packet filter that decides to drop or pass a packet solely on its addressing information. ICF bases its decision in context with an established session. This allows the rules to be more comprehensive than those in a static filter.

State, for a connection-oriented protocol such as TCP, is the equivalent of the protocol's definition of a session, where the connection is opened and closed. For a connectionless protocol such as UDP, state is maintained as long as information flows between two endpoints without interruption for a given period of time.

This concept of state allows three primary rules to be defined:

◆ Any packet that matches an established connection is forwarded.

◆ Any packet sent that does not match an established connection will create a new entry in the state table, and the packet is forwarded.

◆ Any packet received that does not match an established connection is dropped.

This policy allows for normal client Internet access and prevents packets that are not expected (or desired) from accessing the network.

ICF also performs additional duties such as dropping packets that have contradictory flags set and enforcing the TCP three-way handshake for open ports. This reduces the effectiveness of some scanning techniques and denial-of-service attacks that rely on sending large numbers of random packets.

Internet Connection Firewall (ICF) opens and closes ports dynamically depending on the services you are accessing; however, there are a few exceptions.

Windows Messenger versions 4.0 and 4.5 both include the capability to transfer files. By default, ICF blocks file transfer and you will need to open a port for Messenger to accomplish this. The process is similar if you require additional ports to support multiple simultaneous File Transfers (ports 6891-6900).

ICF and Policies

Although Active Directory Group Policies are generally out of sight to a Windows XP Professional user, there is one situation in which a Group Policy should be understood.

ICF comes with a Group Policy that allows Domain Administrators to shut down ICF running in their domain. ICF can be configured to run when the PC is not on the network but this policy disables it when the PC is connected to the network.

This means that you can have ICF enabled all the time, but your Domain Administrators disable it when you are connected to the corporate LAN. If, for example, you go to a conference that is running an Internet Cafe or Wireless hotspot, ICF will be recognize that it is not on the Corporate LAN anymore and be enabled. When you return to work and reconnect to the Corporate LAN, ICF will shut down again.

Troubleshooting TCP/IP Connections

The first thing to do when troubleshooting TCP/IP networking connections is to use IPCONFIG /all to obtain the local TCP/IP configuration.

Typical problems found in the configuration are duplicate IP addresses with other computers on the network, or a subnet mask of 0.0.0.0.

PING is a tool that will help to verify connectivity at the IP level. The best process to follow when using PING to detect network problems is to use IP addresses only (so as not to confuse name resolution errors with network errors) and to ping progressively more remote computers.

Using Tracert

The Tracert diagnostic utility determines the route taken to a destination by sending Internet Control Message Protocol (ICMP) echo packets with varying IP Time-to-Live (TTL) values to the destination. Each router along the path is required to decrement the TTL on a packet by at least 1 before forwarding it. When the TTL on a packet reaches 0, the router should send an ICMP Time Exceeded message back to the source computer.

Resolve a NetBIOS Name to an IP Address

Resolving a NetBIOS name means successfully mapping a 16-byte NetBIOS name to an IP address. The File and Printer Sharing for Microsoft Networks service in Windows XP Professional uses NetBIOS name resolution. When your computer starts up, this service registers a unique NetBIOS name based on the name of your computer (padded out to 15 characters if it's shorter than that) with 0x20 as the 16th character.

Resolve a Host- or Domain Name to an IP Address

Hostnames are resolved by using the HOSTS file or by querying a DNS server. Problems in the HOSTS file usually involve spelling errors and duplicate entries. The Nslookup utility or the Netdiag resource kit utility can be used to diagnose hostname resolution problems.

Determine Whether the Address Is Local

The subnet mask along with the IP address are used to determine whether the IP address is local or on a remote subnet.

A misconfigured subnet mask can result in the system's inability to access any other system on the local subnet while still being able to communicate with remote systems.

If the IP address is local, ARP is used to identify the destination MAC address.

Determine the Correct Gateway

If the IP address is remote from the local subnet, the gateway to use to reach the remote address must be determined. If the network has a single router, this problem is straightforward. In a network with more than one router connected, additional steps must be taken.

To solve this problem, the system uses the routing table. The entries in the routing table enable IP to determine which gateway to send outgoing traffic through. The routing table has many entries for individual routes, each one consisting of a destination, network mask, gateway interface, and hop count (metric).

IMPLEMENTING, MONITORING, AND TROUBLESHOOTING SECURITY

A user account contains information about a person who can gain access to your network. Information stored in a user account includes the user's name and password as well as other information that describes the configuration of the user. User accounts are used to represent people in your networked environment. Accounts allow users to identify themselves when they log on to the local computer or domain. Users accounts are also used to grant (or deny) access to resources. Through user accounts, you can control how a user gains access to a resource.

The Workgroup Model

Under the Workgroup model, each computer in your environment is responsible for the management of its own local account database. Local user accounts contain information that defines users for the local computer. With a local user account, a user can log on to the local computer and gain access to local resources. To gain access to resources on another computer, a user must use an account on the other computer.

The Domain Model

Under the Domain model, a centralized database of user accounts is managed for a grouping (or domain) of computers. Domain user accounts contain information that defines users within the domain.

User Accounts

Windows XP automatically creates two user accounts called *built-in accounts* when it is installed. The Administrator account is the account that is used to manage the configuration of the computer and users stored on the computer. The Administrator account has the capability to manage all aspects of the computer so access to this account must be protected. You can rename the Administrator account but it cannot be deleted. Guest is also a built-in account. The Guest account can be used to grant occasional users access to resources. The Guest account is disabled by default.

Local User Accounts

Local user accounts are typically associated with the Workgroup model. Local user accounts can be used to access the computer on which the account physically resides and resources on the local machine. Local user accounts are limited to local resources.

Groups

Groups are used to simplify the overall management of accounts in your environment. In most environments users can be grouped into categories of user account (such as Accountants, Sales People, and so on). These categories of user accounts generally define common access needs for groups of users in your environment. Being a member of a group automatically grants you the same rights as the group object.

Built-In Groups

Windows XP systems have a number of built-in groups associated with them. These groups provide a powerful tool for the management of resources on the local system/domain. Membership in one (or more) of these groups gives users rights to access (and manage) the local operating system depending on the group. Each group is, by default, assigned a useful collection of rights and privileges.

The five built-in local groups added during installation are as follows:

◆ **Administrators**—Membership in the Administrators group allows a user to manage all aspects of the local operating system. Members of this group have the ability to manage user accounts, load and unload system drivers, and perform backups and restores of file systems.

◆ **Backup Operators**—Regular users have the ability to back up and restore files that they have permission to access without being part of this group. In most environments, however, backups are managed centrally so that they can be completed by set intervals with a high degree of reliability.

◆ **Guests**—The guests group is used to give someone limited access to resources on the system. The guest account is automatically added to this group.

◆ **Power Users**—Members of the Power Users group have more permission than members of the Users group and less permission than members of the Administrators group. Power Users can perform most operating system tasks (share resources, install or remove applications, and customize system resources).

◆ **Users**—By default, all users (with the exception of the built-in Administrator and Guest accounts) created on the local system are made members of the Users group. The Users group provides the user with all the necessary rights to run the computer as an end user.

User Rights

Table 4 lists the rights assigned to the various built-in groups.

TABLE 4
RIGHTS FOR THE VARIOUS BUILT-IN GROUPS

User Right	Description	Granted To
Access This Computer from the Network	Allows you to access resources from the computer over the network but does not give you the capability to access resources that your user account has not been given permission to use.	Everyone, Users, Power Users, Backup Operators, Administrators
Back Up Files and Directories	Allows you to back up file system resources regardless of permissions held by the user.	Backup Operators, Administrators
Bypass Traverse Checking	Gives you the ability to access a file resource deep in a directory structure even if the user does not have permission to the file's parent directory.	Everyone, Users, Power Users, Backup Operators, Administrators
Change the System Time	Allows you to change system time.	Power Users, Administrators
Create a Pagefile	Allows you to configure the virtual memory management of a system.	Administrators
Deny Access to This Computer from the Network	Restricts a user from accessing this computer over the network regardless of group membership.	None
Deny Logon Locally	Explicitly restricts a user from logging on to a system from the local console.	None
Force Shutdown from a Remote System	Allows a user to remotely shut down a system using a remote shutdown utility.	Administrators

User Right	Description	Granted To
Increase Quotas	Allows users to modify quota settings for NTFS-formatted partitions.	Administrators
Increase Scheduling Priority	Allows you to reschedule jobs that have been submitted to the scheduling service.	Administrators
Load and Unload Drivers	Allows you to load and unload device drivers.	Administrators
Log On Locally	Allows you to log on at the computer from the local computer console.	Guests, Users, Power Users, Backup Operators, Administrators
Manage Auditing and Security	Allows a user to specify what type of resource access will be audited.	Administrators
Remove Computer from Docking Station	Allows a user to undock a laptop from its docking station.	Users, Power Users, Administrators
Restore File and Directories	Allows users to restore a backup of a file system of permissions held by the user.	Backup Operators, Administrators
Shut Down the System	Allows a user to shut down the local system.	Users, Power Users, Backup Operators, Administrators. (On Windows 2000 Server, members of the Users group do not have this ability.)
Take Ownership of Files of Other Objects	Allows a user to take ownership of files, directories, printers and other objects on the computer. This right supersedes permissions protecting objects.	Administrators

Audit Policies

An audit policy defines the categories of user activities that Windows XP records in the security logs on each computer. Audit policies are set up to track authorized and unauthorized access to resources.

Categories of Security Events

Security events are divided into categories. This allows the system administrator to configure audit policies to specific categories of events (based on your organization's auditing and security plan). When viewing the event logs, you can search for specific categories of events.

Object Access Events

An audit policy can be configured to monitor access to objects such as files and folders, printers, and other objects. The audit policy defines what events will be entered in the event log.

Windows XP Security Configurations

Windows XP Professional manages security configurations through the use of templates. There are nine predefined templates, with four that relate to Windows XP Professional. They define default, compatible, secure, and highly secure configurations. The default configuration can be used to return your computer to the default Windows XP security configuration. The compatible template provides NT 4.0 backward compatibility for the Power Users group (for development of applications destined to run on Windows NT 4.0). The secure template implements all recommended security settings for Windows XP Professional. The highly secure configuration provides the greatest protection for Network traffic. This is reserved for Windows XP to Windows XP communication and will not allow your computer to communicate with NT 4.0 or Windows 9x machines.

Encrypting File System

Encrypting File System (EFS) allows the owner of a file system resource to encrypt it. The service is based on public/private encryption technology and is managed by the Windows XP Public Key Infrastructure (PKI) services.

The technology is based on a public key–based structure. Each user has a public and private key. The keys were created in such a way that anything encrypted using the private key can be decrypted only using the public key and anything encrypted using the public key can be decrypted only using the private key.

When the owner of a file encrypts a file system resource, a file encryption key is generated and used to encrypt the file. The file encryption keys are based on a fast symmetric key designed for bulk encryption. The file is encrypted in blocks with a different key for each block. All the file encryption keys are then stored with the file (as part of the header of the file).

When a file is accessed, EFS detects the access attempt and locates the user's certificate from the Windows XP PKI and the user's associated private key. The private key is then used to decrypt the Data Decryption Field (DDF) to retrieve the file encryption keys used to encrypt each block of the file. The only key in existence with the ability to decrypt the DDF information is the private key of the owner of the file. Access to the file is denied to anyone else, as they do not hold the private key required for decrypting the file encryption keys.

File encryption can be managed using Windows Explorer or the CYPHER program.

This element of the book provides you with some general guidelines for preparing for a certification exam. It is organized into four sections. The first section addresses your learning style and how it affects your preparation for the exam. The second section covers your exam preparation activities and general study tips. This is followed by an extended look at the Microsoft Certification exams, including several specific tips that apply to the various Microsoft exam formats and question types. Finally, changes in Microsoft's testing policies, and how these might affect you, are discussed.

LEARNING STYLES

To better understand the nature of preparation for the test, it is important to understand learning as a process. You probably are aware of how you best learn new material. You might find that outlining works best for you, or, as a visual learner, you might need to "see" things. Whatever your learning style, test preparation takes place over time. Obviously, you shouldn't start studying for these exams the night before you take them; it is very important to understand that learning is a developmental process. Understanding it as a process helps you focus on what you know and what you have yet to learn.

Thinking about how you learn should help you recognize that learning takes place when you are able to match new information to old. You have some previous experience with computers and networking; now you are preparing for this certification exam. Using this book, software, and supplementary materials will not just add incrementally to what you know; as you study, the organization of your knowledge actually restructures as you integrate new information into your existing knowledge base. This will lead you to a more comprehensive understanding of the tasks and concepts

Study and Exam Prep Tips

outlined in the objectives and of computing in general. Again, this happens as a result of a repetitive process rather than a singular event. Keep this model of learning in mind as you prepare for the exam, and you will make better decisions concerning what to study and how much more studying you need to do.

STUDY TIPS

There are many ways to approach studying just as there are many different types of material to study. However, the tips that follow should work well for the type of material covered on the certification exams.

Study Strategies

Although individuals vary in the ways they learn information, some basic principles of learning apply to everyone. You should adopt some study strategies that take advantage of these principles. One of these principles is that learning can be broken into various depths. Recognition (of terms, for example) exemplifies a more surface level of learning in which you rely on a prompt of some sort to elicit recall. Comprehension or understanding (of the concepts behind the terms, for example) represents a deeper level of learning. The ability to analyze a concept and apply your understanding of it in a new way represents a further depth of learning.

Your learning strategy should enable you to know the material at a level or two deeper than mere recognition. This will help you perform well on the exams. You will know the material so thoroughly that you can easily handle the recognition-level types of questions used in multiple-choice testing. You also will be able to apply your knowledge to solve new problems.

Macro and Micro Study Strategies

One strategy that can lead to this deeper learning includes preparing an outline that covers all the objectives and subobjectives for the particular exam on which you are working. You should delve a bit further into the material and include a level or two of detail beyond the stated objectives and subobjectives for the exam. Then, expand the outline by coming up with a statement of definition or a summary for each point in the outline.

An outline provides two approaches to studying. First, you can study the outline by focusing on the organization of the material. Work your way through the points and subpoints of your outline with the goal of learning how they relate to one another. For example, be sure you understand how each of the main objective areas is similar to and different from another. Then, do the same thing with the subobjectives; be sure you know which subobjectives pertain to each objective area and how they relate to one another.

Next, you can work through the outline, focusing on learning the details. Memorize and understand terms and their definitions, facts, rules and strategies, advantages and disadvantages, and so on. In this pass through the outline, attempt to learn detail rather than the big picture (the organizational information that you worked on in the first pass through the outline).

Research has shown that attempting to assimilate both types of information at the same time seems to interfere with the overall learning process. Separate your studying into these two approaches, and you will perform better on the exam.

Active Study Strategies

The process of writing down and defining objectives, subobjectives, terms, facts, and definitions promotes a more active learning strategy than merely reading the material does. In human information-processing terms, writing forces you to engage in more active encoding of the information. Simply reading over it exemplifies more passive processing.

Next, determine whether you can apply the information you have learned by attempting to create examples and scenarios on your own. Think about how or where you could apply the concepts you are learning. Again, write down this information to process the facts and concepts in a more active fashion.

The hands-on nature of the step-by-step tutorials and exercises at the ends of the chapters provide further active learning opportunities that will reinforce concepts as well.

Common-Sense Strategies

Finally, you should also follow common-sense practices when studying. Study when you are alert, reduce or eliminate distractions, and take breaks when you become fatigued.

Pretesting Yourself

Pretesting allows you to assess how well you are learning. One of the most important aspects of learning is what has been called "meta-learning." Meta-learning has to do with realizing when you know something well or when you need to study some more. In other words, you recognize how well or how poorly you have learned the material you are studying.

For most people, this can be difficult to assess objectively on their own. Practice tests are useful in that they reveal more objectively what you have learned and what you have not learned. You should use this information to guide review and further studying. Developmental learning takes place as you cycle through studying, assessing how well you have learned, then reviewing, and assessing again until you feel you are ready to take the exam.

You might have noticed the practice exam included in this book. Use it as part of the learning process. The *ExamGear, Training Guide Edition* test simulation software included on the CD also provides you with an excellent opportunity to assess your knowledge.

You should set a goal for your pretesting. A reasonable goal would be to score consistently in the 90-percent range.

See Appendix D, "Using the *ExamGear, Training Guide Edition* Software," for further explanation of the test-simulation software.

EXAM PREP TIPS

Having mastered the subject matter, the final preparatory step is to understand how the exam will be presented. Make no mistake: A Microsoft Certified Professional (MCP) exam will challenge both your knowledge and your test-taking skills. This section starts with the basics of exam design, reviews a new type of exam format, and concludes with hints targeted to each of the exam formats.

The MCP Exam

Every MCP exam is released in one of three basic formats. What's being called exam format here is really little more than a combination of the overall exam structure and the presentation method for exam questions.

Understanding the exam formats is key to good preparation because the format determines the number of questions presented, the difficulty of those questions, and the amount of time allowed to complete the exam.

Each exam format uses many of the same types of questions. These types or styles of questions include several types of traditional multiple-choice questions, multiple-rating (or scenario-based) questions, and simulation-based questions. Some exams include other types of questions that ask you to drag and drop objects on the screen, reorder a list, or categorize things. Still other exams ask you to answer these types of questions in response to a case study you have read. It's important that you understand the types of questions you will be asked and the actions required to properly answer them.

The rest of this section addresses the exam formats and then tackles the question types. Understanding the formats and question types will help you feel much more comfortable when you take the exam.

Exam Format

As previously mentioned, there are three basic formats for the MCP exams: the traditional fixed-form exam, the adaptive form, and the case study form. As its name implies, the fixed-form exam presents a fixed set of questions during the exam session. The adaptive form, however, uses only a subset of questions drawn from a larger pool during any given exam session. The case study form includes case studies that serve as the basis for answering the various types of questions.

Fixed-Form

A fixed-form computerized exam is based on a fixed set of exam questions. The individual questions are presented in random order during a test session. If you take the same exam more than once, you won't necessarily see the exact same questions. This is because two or three final forms are typically assembled for every fixed-form exam Microsoft releases. These are usually labeled Forms A, B, and C.

The final forms of a fixed-form exam are identical in terms of content coverage, number of questions, and allotted time, but the questions are different. You might notice, however, that some of the same questions appear on, or rather are shared among, different final forms. When questions are shared among multiple final forms of an exam, the percentage of sharing is generally small. Many final forms share no questions, but some older exams may have a 10%–15% duplication of exam questions on the final exam forms.

Fixed-form exams also have a fixed time limit in which you must complete the exam. The *ExamGear, Training Guide Edition* software on the CD-ROM that accompanies this book provides fixed-form exams.

Finally, the score you achieve on a fixed-form exam, which is always reported for MCP exams on a scale of 0 to 1,000, is based on the number of questions you answer correctly. The passing score is the same for all final forms of a given fixed-form exam.

The typical format for a fixed-form exam is as follows:

◆ 50–60 questions

◆ 75–90-minute testing time

◆ Question review is allowed, including the opportunity to change your answers

Adaptive Form

An adaptive-form exam has the same appearance as a fixed-form exam, but its questions differ in quantity and process of selection. Although the statistics of adaptive testing are fairly complex, the process is concerned with determining your level of skill or ability with the exam subject matter. This ability assessment begins with the presentation of questions of varying levels of difficulty and ascertaining at what difficulty level you can reliably answer them. Finally, the ability assessment determines whether that ability level is above or below the level required to pass that exam.

Examinees at different levels of ability will see quite different sets of questions. Examinees who demonstrate little expertise with the subject matter will continue to be presented with relatively easy questions. Examinees who demonstrate a high level of expertise will be presented progressively more difficult questions. Individuals of both levels of expertise may answer the same number of questions correctly, but because the higher-expertise examinee can correctly answer more difficult questions, he or she will receive a higher score and is more likely to pass the exam.

The typical design for the adaptive form exam is as follows:

◆ 20–25 questions

◆ 90-minute testing time (although this is likely to be reduced to 45–60 minutes in the near future)

◆ Question review is not allowed, providing no opportunity for you to change your answers

The Adaptive-Exam Process

Your first adaptive exam will be unlike any other testing experience you have had. In fact, many examinees have difficulty accepting the adaptive testing process because they feel that they were not provided the opportunity to adequately demonstrate their full expertise.

You can take consolation in the fact that adaptive exams are painstakingly put together after months of data gathering and analysis and that adaptive exams are just as valid as fixed-form exams. The rigor introduced through the adaptive testing methodology means that there is nothing arbitrary about the exam items you'll see. It is also a more efficient means of testing, requiring less time to conduct and complete than traditional fixed-form exams.

As you can see in Figure 1, a number of statistical measures drive the adaptive examination process. The measure most immediately relevant to you is the ability

estimate. Accompanying this test statistic are the standard error of measurement, the item characteristic curve, and the test information curve.

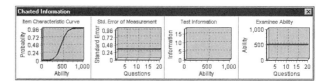

FIGURE 1
Microsoft's adaptive testing demonstration program.

The standard error, which is the key factor in determining when an adaptive exam will terminate, reflects the degree of error in the exam ability estimate. The item characteristic curve reflects the probability of a correct response relative to examinee ability. Finally, the test information statistic provides a measure of the information contained in the set of questions the examinee has answered, again relative to the ability level of the individual examinee.

When you begin an adaptive exam, the standard error has already been assigned a target value below which it must drop for the exam to conclude. This target value reflects a particular level of statistical confidence in the process. The examinee ability is initially set to the mean possible exam score (500 for MCP exams).

As the adaptive exam progresses, questions of varying difficulty are presented. Based on your pattern of responses to these questions, the ability estimate is recalculated. At the same time, the standard error estimate is refined from its first estimated value of one toward the target value. When the standard error reaches its target value, the exam is terminated. Thus, the more consistently you answer questions of the same degree of difficulty, the more quickly the standard error estimate drops, and the fewer questions you will end up seeing during the exam session. This situation is depicted in Figure 2.

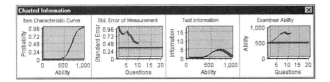

FIGURE 2
The changing statistics in an adaptive exam.

As you might suspect, one good piece of advice for taking an adaptive exam is to treat every exam question as if it were the most important. The adaptive scoring algorithm attempts to discover a pattern of responses that reflects some level of proficiency with the subject matter. Incorrect responses almost guarantee that additional questions must be answered (unless, of course, you get every question wrong). This is because the scoring algorithm must adjust to information that is not consistent with the emerging pattern.

Case Study Form

The case study–based format first appeared with the advent of the 70-100 exam (Solution Architectures). The questions in the case study format are not the independent entities that they are in the fixed and adaptive formats. Instead, questions are tied to a case study, a long scenario-like description of an information technology situation. As the test taker, your job is to extract from the case study the information that needs to be integrated with your understanding of Microsoft technology. The idea is that a case study will provide you with a situation that is even more like a "real-life" problem situation than the other formats provide.

The case studies are presented as *testlets*. These are sections within the exam in which you read the case study, and then answer 10 to 15 questions that apply to the case study. When you finish that section, you move on to another testlet with another case study and its associated questions. There can be as many as five of these

testlets that compose the overall exam. You will be given more time to complete such an exam because it takes time to read through the cases and analyze them. You might have as much as three hours to complete the exam—and you might need all of it. The case studies are always available through a linking button while you are in a testlet. However, after you leave a testlet, you cannot come back to it.

Figure 3 provides an illustration of part of such a case study.

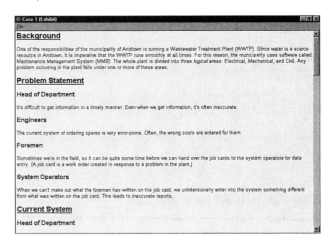

FIGURE 3
An example of a case study.

Question Types

A variety of question types can appear on MCP exams. Examples of many of the various types appear in this book and the *ExamGear, Training Guide Edition* software. We have attempted to cover all the types that were available at the time of this writing. Most of the question types discussed in the following sections can appear in each of the three exam formats.

The typical MCP exam question is based on the idea of measuring skills or the ability to complete tasks.

Therefore, most of the questions are written so as to present you with a situation that includes a role (such as a system administrator or technician), a technology environment (100 computers running Windows 98 on a Windows 2000 Server network), and a problem to be solved (the user can connect to services on the LAN but not the intranet). The answers indicate actions that you might take to solve the problem or create setups or environments that would function correctly from the start. Keep this in mind as you read the questions on the exam. You might encounter some questions that just call for you to regurgitate facts, but these will be relatively few and far between.

In the following sections, we will look at the different question types.

Multiple-Choice Questions

Despite the variety of question types that now appear in various MCP exams, the multiple-choice question is still the basic building block of the exams. The multiple-choice question comes in three varieties:

◆ **Regular multiple-choice**—Also referred to as an alphabetic question, it asks you to choose one answer as correct.

◆ **Multiple-answer multiple-choice**—Also referred to as a multi-alphabetic question, this version of a multiple-choice question requires you to choose two or more answers as correct. Typically, you are told precisely the number of correct answers to choose.

◆ **Enhanced multiple-choice**—This is simply a regular or multiple-answer question that includes a graphic or table to which you must refer to answer the question correctly.

Examples of such questions appear at the end of each chapter.

Simulation Questions

Simulation-based questions reproduce the look and feel of key Microsoft product features for the purpose of testing. The simulation software used in MCP exams has been designed to look and act, as much as possible, just like the actual product. Consequently, answering simulation questions in an MCP exam entails completing one or more tasks just as if you were using the product itself.

The format of a typical Microsoft simulation question consists of a brief scenario or problem statement, along with one or more tasks that you must complete to solve the problem. An example of a simulation question for MCP exams is shown in the following section.

A Typical Simulation Question

It sounds obvious, but your first step when you encounter a simulation question is to carefully read the question (see Figure 4). Do not go straight to the simulation application! You must assess the problem that's presented and identify the conditions that make up the problem scenario. Note the tasks that must be performed or outcomes that must be achieved to answer the question, and then review any instructions you're given on how to proceed.

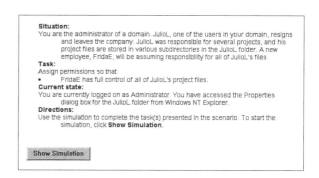

FIGURE 4
Typical MCP exam simulation question with directions.

The next step is to launch the simulator by using the button provided. After clicking the Show Simulation button, you will see a feature of the product, as shown in the dialog box in Figure 5. The simulation application will partially obscure the question text on many test center machines. Feel free to reposition the simulator and to move between the question text screen and the simulator by using hotkeys or point-and-click navigation, or even by clicking the simulator's launch button again.

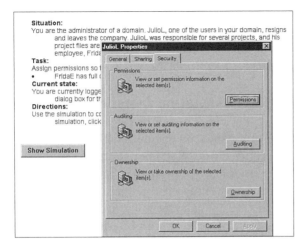

FIGURE 5
Launching the simulation application.

It is important for you to understand that your answer to the simulation question will not be recorded until you move on to the next exam question. This gives you the added capability of closing and reopening the simulation application (using the launch button) on the same question without losing any partial answer you might have made.

The third step is to use the simulator as you would the actual product to solve the problem or perform the defined tasks. Again, the simulation software is designed to function—within reason—just as the product does. But don't expect the simulator to reproduce product behavior perfectly. Most importantly, do not

allow yourself to become flustered if the simulator does not look or act exactly like the product.

Figure 6 shows the solution to the example simulation problem.

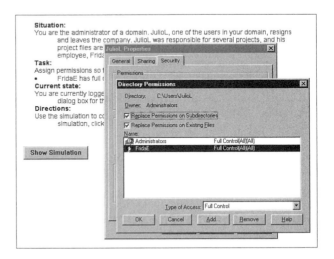

FIGURE 6
The solution to the simulation example.

Two final points will help you tackle simulation questions. First, respond only to what is being asked in the question; do not solve problems that you are not asked to solve. Second, accept what is being asked of you. You might not entirely agree with conditions in the problem statement, the quality of the desired solution, or the sufficiency of defined tasks to adequately solve the problem. Always remember that you are being tested on your ability to solve the problem as it is presented.

The solution to the simulation problem shown in Figure 6 perfectly illustrates both of those points. As you'll recall from the question scenario (refer to Figure 4), you were asked to assign appropriate permissions to a new user, Frida E. You were not instructed to make any other changes in permissions. Thus, if you were to modify or remove the administrator's permissions, this item would be scored wrong on an MCP exam.

Hot Area Question

Hot area questions call for you to click on a graphic or diagram to complete some task. You are asked a question that is similar to any other, but rather than clicking an option button or check box next to an answer, you click the relevant item in a screen shot or on a part of a diagram. An example of such an item is shown in Figure 7.

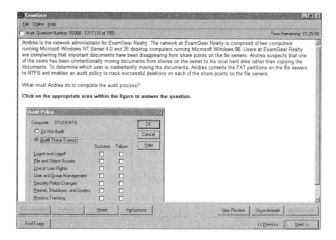

FIGURE 7
A typical hot area question.

Drag-and-Drop–Style Questions

Microsoft has used two different types of drag-and-drop questions in exams. The first is a select-and-place question. The other is a drop-and-connect question. Both are covered in the following sections.

Select and Place

Select-and-place questions typically require you to drag and drop labels on images in a diagram so as to correctly label or identify some portion of a network. Figure 8 shows you the actual question portion of a select-and-place item.

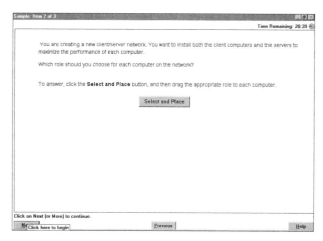

FIGURE 8
A select-and-place question.

Figure 9 shows the window you would see after you chose Select and Place. It contains the actual diagram in which you would select and drag the various server roles and match them up with the appropriate computers.

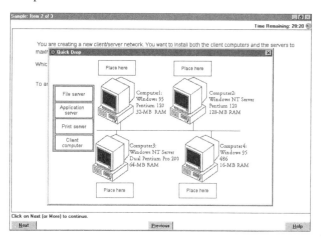

FIGURE 9
The window containing the diagram.

Drop and Connect

Drop-and-connect questions provide a different spin on the drag-and-drop question. The question provides you with the opportunity to create boxes that you can label, as well as connectors of various types with which to link them. In essence, you are creating a model or diagram in order to answer the question. You might have to create a network diagram or a data model for a database system. Figure 10 illustrates the idea of a drop-and-connect question.

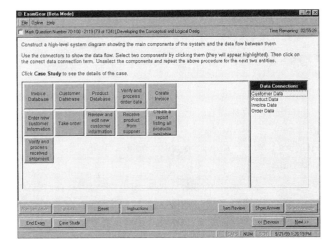

FIGURE 10
A drop-and-connect question.

Ordered-List Questions

Ordered-list questions simply require you to consider a list of items and place them in the proper order. You select items and then use a button to add them to a new list in the correct order. You have another button that you can use to remove the items in the new list in case you change your mind and want to reorder things. Figure 11 shows an ordered-list item.

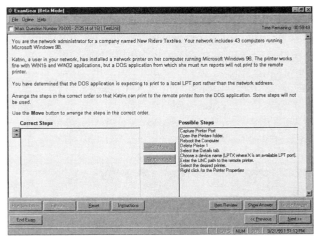

FIGURE 11
An ordered-list question.

Tree Questions

Tree questions require you to think hierarchically and categorically. You are asked to place items from a list into categories that are displayed as nodes in a tree structure. Such questions might ask you to identify parent-child relationships in processes or the structure of keys in a database. You also might be required to show order within the categories much as you would in an ordered-list question. Figure 12 shows a typical tree question.

As you can see, Microsoft is making an effort to utilize question types that go beyond asking you to simply memorize facts. These question types force you to know how to accomplish tasks and understand concepts and relationships. Study so that you can answer these types of questions rather than those that simply ask you to recall facts.

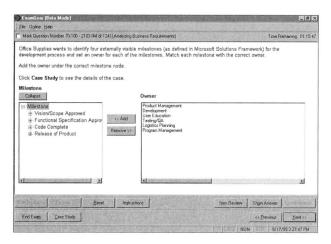

FIGURE 12
A tree question.

Putting It All Together

Given all these different pieces of information, the task now is to assemble a set of tips that will help you successfully tackle the different types of MCP exams.

More Exam-Preparation Tips

Generic exam-preparation advice is always useful. Tips include the following:

◆ Become familiar with the product. Hands-on experience is one of the keys to success on any MCP exam. Review the exercises and the Step by Steps in the book.

◆ Review the current exam-preparation guide on the Microsoft MCP Web site. The documentation Microsoft makes available over the Web identifies the skills every exam is intended to test.

◆ Memorize foundational technical detail, but remember that MCP exams are generally heavier on problem solving and application of knowledge than on questions that require only rote memorization.

◆ Take any of the available practice tests. We recommend the one included in this book and the ones you can create using the *ExamGear* software on the CD-ROM. As a supplement to the material bound with this book, try the free practice tests available on the Microsoft MCP Web site.

◆ Look on the Microsoft MCP Web site for samples and demonstration items. These tend to be particularly valuable for one significant reason: They help you become familiar with new testing technologies before you encounter them on MCP exams.

During the Exam Session

The following generic exam-taking advice that you've heard for years also applies when you're taking an MCP exam:

◆ Take a deep breath and try to relax when you first sit down for your exam session. It is very important that you control the pressure you may (naturally) feel when taking exams.

◆ You will be provided scratch paper. Take a moment to write down any factual information and technical detail that you committed to short-term memory.

◆ Carefully read all information and instruction screens. These displays have been put together to give you information relevant to the exam you are taking.

◆ Accept the nondisclosure agreement and preliminary survey as part of the examination process. Complete them accurately and quickly move on.

◆ Read the exam questions carefully. Reread each question to identify all relevant detail.

◆ Tackle the questions in the order in which they are presented. Skipping around won't build your confidence; the clock is always counting down (at least, in the fixed-form exams).

◆ Don't rush, but also don't linger on difficult questions. The questions vary in degree of difficulty. Don't let yourself be flustered by a particularly difficult or wordy question.

Fixed-Form Exams

Building from this basic preparation and test-taking advice, you also need to consider the challenges presented by the different exam designs. Because a fixed-form exam is composed of a fixed, finite set of questions, add these tips to your strategy for taking a fixed-form exam:

◆ Note the time allotted and the number of questions on the exam you are taking. Make a rough calculation of how many minutes you can spend on each question, and use this figure to pace yourself through the exam.

◆ Take advantage of the fact that you can return to and review skipped or previously answered questions. Record the questions you can't answer confidently on the scratch paper provided, noting the relative difficulty of each question. When you reach the end of the exam, return to the more difficult questions.

◆ If you have session time remaining after you complete all the questions (and if you aren't too fatigued!), review your answers. Pay particular attention to questions that seem to have a lot of detail or that require graphics.

◆ As for changing your answers, the general rule of thumb here is *don't*! If you read the question carefully and completely and you felt like you knew

the right answer, you probably did. Don't second-guess yourself. If, as you check your answers, one clearly stands out as incorrect, however, of course you should change it. But if you are at all unsure, go with your first impression.

Adaptive Exams

If you are planning to take an adaptive exam, keep these additional tips in mind:

◆ Read and answer every question with great care. When you're reading a question, identify every relevant detail, requirement, or task you must perform and double-check your answer to be sure you have addressed every one of them.

◆ If you cannot answer a question, use the process of elimination to reduce the set of potential answers, and then take your best guess. Stupid mistakes invariably mean that additional questions will be presented.

◆ You cannot review questions and change answers. When you leave a question, whether you've answered it or not, you cannot return to it. Do not skip any question, either; if you do, it's counted as incorrect.

Case Study Exams

This new exam format calls for unique study and exam-taking strategies. When you take this type of exam, remember that you have more time than in a typical exam. Take your time and read the case study thoroughly. Use the scrap paper or whatever medium is provided to you to take notes, diagram processes, and actively seek out the important information. Work through each testlet as if each were an independent exam. Remember, you cannot go back after you have left a testlet. Refer to the case study as often as you need to, but do not use that as a substitute for reading it carefully initially and for taking notes.

This format has appeared most often in the exams with a "Design" designation.

FINAL CONSIDERATIONS

Finally, a number of changes in the MCP program will impact how frequently you can repeat an exam and what you will see when you do.

◆ Microsoft has instituted a new exam retake policy. The new rule is "two and two, then one and two." That is, you can attempt any exam twice with no restrictions on the time between attempts. But after the second attempt, you must wait two weeks before you can attempt that exam again. After that, you will be required to wait two weeks between subsequent attempts. Plan to pass the exam in two attempts or plan to increase your time horizon for receiving the MCP credential.

◆ New questions are always being seeded into the MCP exams. After performance data is gathered on new questions, the examiners will replace older questions on all exam forms. This means that the questions appearing on exams will regularly change.

◆ Many of the current MCP exams may be republished in adaptive form. The exception to this may be the case study exams because the adaptive approach might not work with that format.

These changes mean that the brute-force strategies for passing MCP exams have lost their viability. So, if you don't pass an exam on the first or second attempt, it is likely that the exam's form could change significantly by the next time you take it. It could be updated from fixed-form to adaptive, or it could have a different set of questions or question types.

Microsoft's intention is not to make the exams more difficult by introducing unwanted change, but to create and maintain valid measures of the technical skills and knowledge associated with the different MCP credentials. Preparing for an MCP exam has always involved not only studying the subject matter but also planning for the testing experience itself. With the continuing changes, this is now more applicable than ever.

This exam consists of 60 questions reflecting the material you have covered in the chapters and which are representative of the types you should expect to see on the actual exam.

The answers to all questions appear in their own section following the exam. It's strongly suggested that when you take this exam, you treat it just as you would the actual exam at the test center. Time yourself, read carefully, and answer all the questions to the best of your ability.

Most of the questions do not simply require you to recall facts but require deduction on your part to come up with the best answer. Most questions require you to identify the best course of action to take in a given situation. Many of the questions are verbose, requiring you to read them carefully and thoroughly before you attempt to answer them. Run through the exam, and for questions you miss, review any material associated with them.

Practice Exam

EXAM QUESTIONS

1. A brand-new top-of-the-line workstation has just arrived in your office and you are about to install Windows XP Professional for the first time. The system contains a new SCSI controller interface that is not on the HCL, but the system's manufacturer has provided a driver. You tried to install Windows XP following the basic steps, but each time the system restarts, it stops. It seems the system cannot access any of the SCSI drives because the driver is not installed. What should you do to load the new SCSI driver during the installation of Windows XP?

   A. Boot from the driver disk that the manufacturer provided. Windows XP will recognize the SCSI devices and continue with the setup properly.

   B. During the final phase of setup, press F8 to install additional drivers for mass storage.

   C. During the first phase of setup, press F6 to load additional drivers for mass storage.

   D. Install the manufacturer's drivers on the boot disk using the makeboot.exe utility.

   E. Windows XP cannot be installed on a system with hardware that is not on the HCL.

2. Your new summer intern has been asked to prepare unattended answer files to help in the installation of Windows XP on several new computers. However, he cannot find the Setup Manager utility on the Windows XP Professional computer you provided for him. Where can you tell him to look to find this utility? Select the best answer.

   A. The utility is found in the winnt\system32 directory. It does not have an icon in the Start menu. Simply change to this directory and run Setupmgr.exe.

   B. Setup Manager is available only on a Windows 2000 server. You must install the Windows 2000 Server Tools on the Windows XP Professional system to have access to Setupmgr.exe.

   C. Setup Manager must be downloaded from the Microsoft Web site.

   D. Setup Manager is part of the resource kit. Simply install the resource kit and the utility will show up under Start, Programs.

   E. Setup Manager is part of the add-ons that are available in the add-on folder of the Windows XP Professional CD.

3. A new technician in the company has read all about RIS-automated installs and would like to implement the procedure in your network. What basic components must be present in the network to allow an RIS-based implementation? Select three answers.

   A. A DHCP server

   B. A DNS server

   C. A WINS server

   D. A server running Active Directory

   E. A Browser server

   F. An IPSec server

4. A small computer training company has decided to install the software and operating system needed every day for the next day's class. This process involves 125 identical computers that need Windows XP Professional and Office 2000. The setup process manually takes more than eight hours to perform. What should you do that would allow you to rebuild these machines in the quickest fashion?

A. Use Sysprep to develop an image of the system that can be cloned. Remove the drives from each system and copy the image to the drive of the new machine.

B. Use Riprep to prepare an image with Office 2000 installed for installation. Use Remote Installation Services to install the images to each computer.

C. Use Setup Manager to create an unattended installation file for the setup. Burn that installation file along with the distribution files to a CD.

D. Use Setup Manager to create an unattended installation file for setup. Place the unattended installation file and the distribution files on a network share.

5. You want to safely upgrade your 50 Windows 95 computers to Windows XP Professional. What steps could you take to ensure that the computers are compatible with Windows XP before performing the upgrade? Select all possible answers.

A. Run the `HCL.exe` program to create a compatibility report.

B. Run `Winnt.exe` or `Winnt32.exe` with the `/upgradetest` switch.

C. Run `Winnt32.exe` with the `/checkupgradeonly` switch.

D. Use the `Checkupgrade.exe` utility from the resource kit.

E. Use the `Chkupgrd.exe` utility from the resource kit.

F. Run a trial upgrade using `Winnt.exe` or `Winnt32.exe` with the `/trial` switch.

6. A client tries to upgrade his Windows 98 computer to Windows XP Professional. The client calls you at the help desk and asks you why he was unable to join the domain. He is using the same domain, computer, and username as he had in Windows 98. What should you tell him?

A. The Windows XP Professional system must be upgraded by administrators only.

B. A computer account must be created in the domain to allow the Windows XP Professional system to join.

C. You cannot use the same computer name for Windows XP that you had for Windows 98. Computer names are registered in the domain and cannot be shared.

D. Microsoft is marketing Windows 98 and Windows XP Professional to two very separate segments of the market. They are not compatible and therefore you cannot upgrade a Windows 98 computer to Windows XP Professional.

E. To upgrade to Windows XP Professional, an upgrade file must be copied to the client system. You will send him one today and he should copy it to the `%systemroot%` folder.

7. As the administrator of a network with a large number of aging systems that are being replaced this year with new machines, you're being asked to develop a plan for the migration. Despite the policy indicating that all files should be saved to the network, you know that many of your users are saving files to their local hard drives. You're particularly concerned about the output of a custom application that your company has written. It saves some important configuration information in MCF files. How should you migrate the

user environment from their existing system to the new systems that you're deploying?

A. Use the File and Settings Transfer Wizard to transfer settings and files from the old system to the new system.

B. Use the User State Migration Tool to transfer settings and files from the old system to the new system.

C. Remove the hard drive from the old system and put it in the new system. Upgrade the new system to Windows XP.

D. Use Remote Installation Services to back up the information from the old machine and copy it to the new machine.

8. Sara needs to update all the Windows XP Professional computers in her network to the latest service pack of the operating system. What method of deployment can she use? Select all that apply.

A. Windows Installer

B. Microsoft's SMS software

C. Windows XP Professional Update Manager

D. Windows XP group policies

E. Microsoft's Site Server software

9. During a planning session, you are asked what would be the best way to allow clients to have access to their files from any system in the network while still maintaining a secured environment. What would you propose? Select two answers.

A. Set up roaming profiles.

B. Have all users save their files in the Mydocuments folder.

C. Set up a home share on an NTFS partition on the server. Allow everyone full control over the share.

D. Configure each user with a Home directory that points to *server**home*\\%username%, where *server* is a network server and *home* is a shared folder.

E. Set up a home share on a FAT partition. Allow everyone full control over the share.

F. Configure each user account to use redirected folders as their home directories.

10. Alexander is a member of the Sales and the Accounting groups. You have given the Sales group Read permission and the Accounting group Change permission. Alexander is unable to access the folder. What is the most likely cause of the problem?

A. The folder is marked as Read Only at the NTFS level.

B. The files in the folder are marked as Read Only at the NTFS level.

C. Alexander has not been added to the list of users with at least Read access.

D. Alexander must have No Access assigned to his user account.

E. The group Everyone has been removed from the list of users with access.

11. You are the network administrator for Balzac Petroleum. You are concerned that certain files are being accessed on your network without proper permissions. What can you do to prevent unauthorized users access?

A. Change the default permission to Everyone Denied Access and add groups only as needed with the appropriate permissions.

B. Remove the default group Everyone and delete the Guest account.

C. Remove the default group Everyone and add groups only as needed with the appropriate permissions.

D. Remove the default Guest Accounts permissions on all files and add groups only as needed with the appropriate permissions.

E. Remove the default group Authenticated Users and add groups only as needed with the appropriate permissions.

12. You receive a call from the help desk staff that there is a user who is unable to access a file. They gave the user's account access to the file directly but he still can't access it. What are the possible reasons? Choose all that apply.

A. The user is a member of a group that has the Deny Access permission.

B. The file was encrypted by another user.

C. The user doesn't have access to the directory where the file resides.

D. The user has turned off Secure file access.

13. You store your sensitive documents on a file server in your private directory but you are concerned that other people might have access to your directory. Because of that, you have decided to encrypt your entire directory. In the middle of the encryption process, you receive a message that the disk is full. What's the most likely cause of this message?

A. Other users of the server have filled the drive. You should ask the administrator to make more space available.

B. The encryption process creates a separate copy of every file that it encrypts. You temporarily used double the space that you normally would.

C. You accidentally deselected the compression option for the files.

D. The files were automatically decompressed before encryption.

14. A client would like to send you a report but tells you her email is unavailable, although she still has access to the Internet for Web browsing. You do not want her to dial in to your office. How can she send you a copy of the report without the risk of sending a virus to your servers?

A. She can connect to your Web server and upload the file.

B. She can connect to your FTP site and upload the file.

C. She can connect to your intranet site server and upload the file.

D. She can print to one of your office printers that has been shared over the Internet.

E. She cannot send the report until her email has been fixed.

15. There are several users and several identical printers in an office. You need to be sure that if your printer is unavailable, the other printers will take over. You also need to be sure that the executives in the company never have to wait for a print job. What can you do to accommodate everyone? Select two answers.

A. Create a print job with high priority for executives.

B. Create a printer redirection on all printers to one another.

C. Set up a printer pool with several print devices of the same type.

D. Create a second printer with a higher job priority and share it only to executives.

E. Set up one printer exclusively for executives and one printer for all users.

16. Your office is setting up several new laptop computers with Windows XP Professional for the VPs in the company. The CIO is concerned someone might steal a laptop and copy files to a FAT partition and read its content. How can you be sure the files are secure? Select all that apply.

A. Install Windows XP Professional using RIS.

B. Be sure all local drives on the laptop computers are NTFS.

C. Enable DFS on the files you want protected.

D. Be sure all local drives are configured so only Owners have full access.

E. Enable EFS on all folders you want protected.

17. In what situations should the APM support be disabled? Select three.

A. The computer is a desktop.

B. The laptop computer is set up to dual-boot with Windows 98 and Windows XP Professional.

C. The computer has multiple CPUs.

D. The computer has multiple video devices.

E. The laptop is running a lot of software as background applications.

F. The laptop is always used as a standalone unit.

18. A new Windows XP Professional system has arrived in your office with a DVD drive. What are the names of the new formats used for hardware decoders providing full-motion video and surround-sound capability used by DVDs? Select all that apply.

A. DVD

B. NTFS

C. UDF

D. MPEG-2

E. AC-3

19. While working with disk partitions, you notice your disk administrator showing that you have a Basic disk. What features are not supported by a Basic disk? Select three.

A. Create and delete primary and extended partitions and logical drives.

B. Mark a partition as active.

C. Create simple, spanned, striped, mirrored, and RAID-5 volumes.

D. Delete spanned volumes, striped volumes, mirrored volumes, and RAID-5 volumes.

E. Break a mirror from a mirrored volume.

F. Extend volumes and volume sets.

G. Add a mirror to a simple volume.

20. You have installed a PCI video adapter in your new Windows XP Professional computer that already had an onboard video adapter. Which of the following statements is true?

A. The onboard video adapter will be the primary adapter.

B. The onboard video adapter will be the secondary adapter.

C. Windows XP Professional can configure each adapter to be primary or secondary using the Display applet in the Control Panel.

D. The system's BIOS must be used to set the onboard adapter as secondary; otherwise, it will be primary.

E. PCI cards cannot be used in a multiadapter implementation.

21. You receive a call from a user who's just installed a new scanner. Everything appeared to go fine until she shut down the computer last night and turned it on this morning. The system won't reboot. The driver she installed was a third-party driver that caused problems on her system. What should be done to allow the user the most flexibility for supporting herself and preventing support problems?

A. Revoke the user's ability to install new hardware. Require that help desk staff or network administrators install new hardware.

B. Set Windows XP to block the installation of unsigned drivers.

C. Turn on Remote Assistance.

D. Always boot the computer in Safe Mode.

22. You have been monitoring your Windows XP Professional system and want to verify whether the processor is overburdened. What counters would you be looking at, and what values would help you decide whether another processor is required?

A. If processor time is more than 90% and the interrupt time is greater than 15%.

B. If the system time is more than 90%.

C. If the processor time is more than 90% and the hard page faults are greater than 2.

D. If the percentage of user time is more than 90%.

E. If processor time is more than 90% and the average queue length is more than 1.

23. A user calls the help desk for help in setting up a digital camera on a Windows XP Professional computer. He tells you the device is PnP, and has plugged it into the system, but he is getting errors such as `You do not have sufficient rights to perform such a task`. What could be the problem and how would you solve it?

A. The user is unable to access the Windows XP Professional source files on the server with his logon name. Change the shared permission to allow this user access to the files.

B. Plug and Play assumes the user's logon rights. You must be logged on as an administrator to install hardware.

C. Disconnect the device and install the drivers first. After the drivers are on the computer, plug in the device and Plug and Play will connect properly.

D. Windows XP Professional does not support Plug and Play. Disable the PnP on the camera and reinstall.

E. All digital cameras use the Infrared protocol. Be sure it's installed first, and then install the camera.

24. As a junior network administrator, you have been asked to install Windows XP Professional on several types of laptop computers. You notice that the APM features are enabled on some laptops and disabled on others. What could be the reason for this inconsistency? Select two answers.

    A. The laptop computer is ACPI compliant only.

    B. The laptop computer's BIOS must be upgraded to a Windows XP Professional–compatible version.

    C. Microsoft has determined that some laptop computers will not support APM properly and therefore does not install APM support.

    D. During the installation, some laptop computers must have been set up with the Mobile option, whereas others were set up using the Typical setting.

    E. The Windows XP Professional software was not installed for mobile users. Rerun the setup and choose Mobile Users.

25. A client has installed several new drivers from Microsoft and a few third-party ones without realizing it. One of the new third-party drivers has caused damage to his Windows XP Professional computer. He calls you at the help desk and asks, "Why did the system not warn me when I installed this third-party driver?" How should you respond?

    A. Driver verification is done automatically and the system did not find any errors with the third-party drivers.

    B. A policy governing whether the verification of signatures is to be applied is not enabled.

    C. Each driver must be tested manually before being installed. The Windows XP Professional operating system cannot verify each file as it is installed.

    D. All drivers in Windows XP are pretested by Microsoft and will not install otherwise. He must be mistaken; there were no third-party drivers installed.

    E. Windows XP Professional will repair any damaged files if he uses the repair process off the emergency repair disk.

26. You are responsible for all new drivers that are introduced into your network composed of 100 Windows XP Professional computers. How can you ensure that only drivers that have been tested by Microsoft are installed?

    A. From the System icon in the Control Panel, set the digital signature to Block—Prevent the installation of all unsigned files.

    B. From the Security icon in the Control Panel, set the digital signature to Block—Prevent the installation of all unsigned files.

    C. From the System icon in the Control Panel, set the digital signature to Warn—Display a message before installing unsigned files.

    D. From the Security icon in the Control Panel, set the digital signature to Warn—Display a message before installing unsigned files.

    E. This cannot be done. You cannot prevent non-Microsoft driver files from being installed.

27. Your predecessor had created a series of automated tasks that are running on your Windows XP Professional system each day. You are using the Find command to locate these task files on the workstation. What file extension are you looking for?

    A. .Tas

    B. .Job

    C. .At

D. `.Inf`

E. `.Bat`

28. To maintain systems, your IT department chooses to use automated tasks. Using the Task Scheduler in Windows XP Professional and the AT command, entries are added to various systems. On occasion, you try to modify an existing task using the AT command, but are unable to. This problem does not seem to appear for all tasks. What could be the problem and how would you solve it?

   A. The AT command is a Windows NT 4.0 command and will not work in Windows XP Professional.

   B. The AT command cannot edit a task that was scheduled with the Tasks Scheduler. After a task has been created or modified using Windows XP Professional Tasks Scheduler, you must continue to use it.

   C. The Windows XP Professional Task Scheduler can be configured to maintain backward compatibility with the AT command. After this option is set, you will be able to edit and view all tasks using either tool.

   D. Use the WINAT command from the resource kit. It can read or edit any type of task that was created or edited by any tool.

29. The administrator from your remote office sends you the following screen capture as shown in Figure PE.1. What type of bottleneck is present, if any?

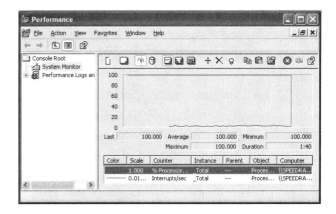

FIGURE PE.1
Figure for question 29.

   A. There is no bottleneck.

   B. A Process bottleneck.

   C. A Disk bottleneck.

   D. A Processor bottleneck.

   E. A memory bottleneck.

30. For most Internet sites, you don't allow the download of ActiveX controls, but your sister organization has developed a Web site that uses ActiveX controls. How would you allow Internet Explorer to download and run ActiveX controls from the sister organization's Web site but not others on the Internet?

   A. Create a new Internet Explorer security zone, add the sister organization's Web site to the zone, and set the zone security to allow the download of ActiveX controls.

   B. Add the sister organization to the trusted zone and make sure that the trusted zone security allows the download of ActiveX controls.

C. Add the sister organization to the restricted zone and make sure that the restricted zone security allows the download of ActiveX controls.

D. Have the sister organization use SSL certificates to encrypt the ActiveX control.

31. A client sends you her system and tells you there are several errors coming up when she starts up. You believe it is a faulty driver for a new piece of hardware she installed. How can you best troubleshoot the problem? Select two answers.

   A. Create a hardware profile called *test*.

   B. Boot the system in the test profile and disable the device and/or services you believe to be at fault.

   C. Boot the system in safe mode and disable the device and/or service you believe to be at fault.

   D. Create a drivers disk to update all drivers to the latest for each device.

   E. Create a hardware service called *test*.

32. You need to decide the type of media to use to perform your daily backups. What media type does Windows XP Professional support? Select all that apply.

   A. CD-ROMs

   B. Hard drives

   C. Floppy disk drives

   D. Network drives

   E. Tape drives

   F. Modems

   G. DVD-ROM drives

33. As the administrator of a small legal firm, you want to maintain certain desktop configuration standards in the organization. What tool can you use to maintain control?

   A. Group policy

   B. Remote access control

   C. System management

   D. IntelliMirror

   E. Roaming profiles

34. You have decided to implement policies that will allow users to maintain a certain desktop configuration standard. You want to allow users the ability to change some personal settings, however. What do you need to do to make sure each user maintains his own settings if he shares a computer?

   A. Change each user to roaming profiles.

   B. Do nothing; roaming profiles are on by default.

   C. Do nothing; local profiles will take care of each user's settings.

   D. Each user must save his settings to his home folder.

   E. This cannot be done. All users on a system will share settings.

35. Two users are sharing a Windows XP account. You want to prevent the two from changing the settings that might confuse the other. What can you do?

   A. Change `NTUser.dat` to `Ntuser.one`.

   B. Restrict roaming profiles.

   C. Disable profiles.

   D. Copy `NTUser.dat` to `Ntuser.man`.

   E. Rename `Ntuser.dat` to `Ntuser.man`.

36. You've set up account policies such that the users must change their passwords periodically and that those passwords must be sufficiently complex. You've even gone so far as to implement a password history. However, you're still finding users that always use the same password on the network. How can you prevent the users from using the same password all the time?

    A. Set the minimum password age account policy to 1 day.

    B. Set the maximum password age account policy to 1 day.

    C. Set the password history to 32.

    D. Set the never reuse password policy.

37. Your sales force does some traveling, but they are not on the road all the time. They work mainly from their office computers, but when they do travel, they take out laptops from the IT laptop pool. Because the laptops are pooled, you want them to have a consistent desktop configuration and not allow changes. What should you do?

    A. Set up the laptops with local profiles.

    B. Do nothing; roaming profiles are on by default.

    C. Set up the laptops with roaming, mandatory profiles.

    D. Set up the laptops with roaming, personal profiles.

38. Several hearing-impaired individuals in your department have approached you about the benefits of Windows XP. What new features can you tell them about that would improve their working conditions? Select all that apply.

    A. Surround-sound setups

    B. Dictation software

    C. ShowSounds

    D. SoundSentry

    E. Auto volume control

39. You need to make sure that all users have the same applications ready to use regardless of which computer they use in the office. Which Windows XP Professional feature would you implement?

    A. Group policy

    B. Remote software installation

    C. System management server installations

    D. RIS (Remote Installation Server)

    E. Roaming profiles

40. Windows XP Professional systems can be controlled with custom desktops through Active Directory. Which other operating systems can be controlled in the same way? Select all that apply.

    A. Unix

    B. Novell NetWare

    C. Windows NT 4.0

    D. Apple Macintosh

    E. Windows 95

41. You are in charge of configuring TCP/IP for all the clients and servers on your network. All clients are DHCP enabled. When you first installed the DCHP Server, a Class B subnet mask was chosen. You have reconfigured the DHCP server to use a Class C subnet mask. A user calls and says she cannot connect to any servers on the network. What command would you tell the user to type to find out her IP Address?

A. `Nbtstat -c.`

B. `Ipconfig /all`

C. `Ipconfig /release`

D. Ping Servers

42. You are troubleshooting a connectivity problem and a Windows XP Professional computer. Using the `PING` command, what would you do first?

    A. Ping the remote host.

    B. Ping the address of 127.0.0.1.

    C. Ping the local host.

    D. Ping the gateway.

43. One of your servers, Server A, manages file and print services for the administrative staff. You recently rebooted Server B, which handles DNS. Since that time, some users have mentioned that they're having trouble accessing Server A. Other than rebooting, what can be done to allow users to access Server A without problems?

    A. Run `IPCONFIG/FLUSHDNS` on each client that is having problems.

    B. Run `IPCONFIG/REGISTERDNS` on each client that is having problems.

    C. Run `IPCONFIG/FLUSHDNS` on Server A.

    D. Run `IPCONFIG/REGISTERDNS` on Server A.

44. You are an administrator of a small office. There are 10 Windows XP Professional computers. To connect to the Internet, you have shared an Internet connection. One of the users in the office cannot connect to your computer to access the Internet. When you run `ipconfig` on his computer, you see that the address assigned to his computer is 10.1.54.232. Which of the following address ranges should his IP address fall between?

A. 1.0.0.1 and 1.255.255.254

B. 192.168.0.1 and 192.168.255.254

C. 191.191.0.1 and 191.194.255.254

D. 224.224.244.1 and 224.224.244.254

45. You are the network administrator for a network that has 50 users who dial in from home. A help desk analyst has asked you to explain the differences between SLIP and PPP. Which of the following would you tell the analyst apply only to PPP? Select two.

    A. Supports TCP/IP, IPX, and NetBEUI.

    B. Passwords are sent as clear text.

    C. Usually needs scripting to complete log on.

    D. Supports encryption for authentication.

    E. No error detection.

    F. Can be used only for dial out.

46. As the help manager, you need to explain to all the new help desk support staff the different ways to resolve computer names. Which of the following would you tell them can be used for NetBIOS name resolution? Choose all that apply.

    A. `lmhosts`

    B. `wins`

    C. `lmhosts.sam`

    D. hosts cache

    E. names

    F. DHCP

    G. hosts

47. You have an environment that consists of both Novell 4.1 and Windows 2000 servers. Your clients also need to access the Internet. Which protocols should each client have installed?

A. TCP/IP

B. NWLink (IPX/SPX)

C. NetBEUI

D. DLC

48. You are the network administrator of a network that spans two cities. There are 10 Windows 2000 servers and 200 Windows XP Professional computers. To implement name resolution, you decided on LMHOSTS files. Users are complaining that when they try to connect to a server called \\vcrmail in a remote location, it takes a long time to connect. Which of the following could you add to the LMHOSTS file to make the connections faster? Select the best answer.

A. `121.45.6.201     vcrmail       #load`

B. `121.45.6.201     #PRE          vcrmail`

C. `#Dom             121.45.6.201  vcrmail`

D. `121.45.6.201     vcrmail       #PRE`

49. A small office has one Windows 2000 server and four Windows XP Professional workstations. What should you do to set up the best configuration?

A. Set up the Windows 2000 Server as a domain controller. Set up each workstation individually.

B. Set up the Windows 2000 Server as a domain controller and each Windows XP Professional workstation as a member of the domain.

C. Set up the Windows 2000 Server as a member server in a workgroup. Add each Windows XP Professional machine to the workgroup.

D. Set up the Windows 2000 Server as a member server in a workgroup. Set up each workstation individually.

50. You are a network administrator. Jane Smith in accounting has moved on to new opportunities. Fred Jones, a new employee, has replaced Jane in accounting. Which one of the following actions would you take to allow Fred access to all of Jane's resources?

A. Delete Jane's account and create Fred's account.

B. Rename Jane's account to Fred's name.

C. Tell Fred to use Jane's account and password.

D. Create an account for Fred and tell him to re-create everything.

51. You are a local network administrator. Your network is made up of three active directory domains with 2000 Windows XP Professional computers and 250 Windows 2000 Server computers. The local HR manager has asked you to configure his Windows XP Professional computer so that people across the enterprise can access a specific folder called statsdata. What should you tell him?

A. Windows XP Professional cannot share folders.

B. Windows XP Professional cannot share folders when a member of a domain.

C. Create the share and give the domain users group permission to read the directory.

D. You must establish trust relationships between the three active directory domains (if they are not in the same forest) and then add each of the domain users groups from each of the three domains with read access to the folder.

52. You installed Windows XP Professional in a dual-boot environment with Windows 98. Someone converted the boot partition to NTFS from FAT32. Windows 98 will no longer boot. How can you fix this?

A. Convert the NTFS partition back to FAT32.

B. Convert the Dynamic Disk back to a Basic Disk.

C. Reinstall Windows 98.

D. Reinstall Windows 98 and Windows XP.

53. You are an administrator of a network that consists of 50 Windows XP Professional computers and 6 Windows 2000 Server computers. The network was just upgraded to Windows XP from Windows NT 4.0. The users are complaining that they cannot run all the applications that used to run on their Windows NT 4.0 workstations. What group would you add them to so they can run all the applications that they used to run?

A. Users

B. Guests

C. Backup Operators

D. Power Users

54. You are the help desk manager. You are creating a chart that will allow the help desk analysts to understand the differences between built-in global groups and built-in local groups. Which of the following are built-in local groups? Select all that apply.

A. Guests

B. Administrators

C. Domain Admins

D. Power Users

E. Everyone

F. Domain Users

G. Managers

55. As the network administrator, you are auditing specific folders on users' Windows XP Professional computers. A user asks you to explain where she can find out who has been accessing the audited folder on her computer. You tell her about Event view and the security log. When she tries to read the security log, it denies the user access. To what group would she have to be added so she can access the security log?

A. Guest

B. Administrators

C. Auditors

D. Power Users

56. Your accounting department is still running a special program to support an online service that was designed prior to the Internet. The last time their program was updated was right after the release of Windows 95. Their systems were running Windows 98 but you've just replaced them with Windows XP Professional machines. When users try to use the application, they are receiving odd errors and in some cases garbled displays. What should be done to resolve this problem?

A. Reinstall the application.

B. Install Windows 98 on top of Windows XP on their new systems.

C. Use the Program Compatibility options to have the system emulate a Windows 98 machine.

D. Use the Program Compatibility options to emulate Windows 98 for the application that is having trouble.

57. You receive a message that Internet Explorer cannot display an ActiveX control because of security settings. What could cause this error? Choose all that apply.

A. The administrator has blocked access to the site through the proxy server.

B. The site is not in your trusted site list that you have set to low security.

C. The ActiveX control is not compiled for Windows XP.

D. The site is listed in the restricted sites list on the computer.

58. You are a desktop support analyst. A user has asked for EFS to be configured on his Windows XP Professional computer. What would you enable on the computer to be able to unencrypt files if the user's private key has been deleted?

A. unecrypt.exe

B. recovery agent

C. unlock files agent

D. decrypt agent

59. In a small network, you installed Windows XP on a few machines. Approximately 30 days later, you've begun receiving calls that the users can't log on to the workstations. What is the most likely cause?

A. Product Activation for Windows XP Professional wasn't completed.

B. The DNS entries for the workstations have expired.

C. The DHCP addresses for the workstations have expired.

D. The users have filled the hard drive.

60. Your organization has three executives who have to print cover letters for the board of directors and want priority access to the printer so these letters will print out first. The other users of the printer often print large-print documents. You've

set up another printer for use by the executives and have set appropriate permissions. How should you set up the executive printer object so they will always have first access to the printer?

A. Set the priority of the printer to 1.

B. Set the priority of the printer to 99.

C. Set the priority of the default job to 1.

D. Set the priority of the default job to 99.

ANSWERS TO EXAM QUESTIONS

1. **C**. There will always be new devices introduced and Windows XP will be compatible with them if the manufacturer provides the appropriate drivers. In the first phase, the installation program will try to detect the SCSI interface and will fail. At this point, you can press the F6 key to install additional drivers. The boot disk created with Makeboot.exe cannot be altered with any new drivers. For more information, see "Installing Windows XP Professional Manually" in Chapter 1, "Installing Windows XP Professional."

2. **D**. After the resource kit is installed, the Setup Manager will be listed in the Resource Kit menu within the Start program's menu. The correct file name is setupmgr.exe. You can also install this file from the XP Professional CD from the \SUPPORT\TOOLS\DEPLOY.CAB file. For more information, see "Using the Setup Manager" in Chapter 1, "Installing Windows XP Professional."

3. **A, B, D**. The RIS server will require a DHCP server to hand out TCP/IP addresses and allow clients to boot up. It will also require a DNS

server to locate the RIS server and a server running Active Directory to determine what operating system image to install. For more information, see "Remote Installation Services" in Chapter 1, "Installing Windows XP Professional."

4. **B**. All the options are solutions but only RIS has the capability to send an image to a large number of PCs with minimal interaction. For more information, see "Automating the Installation Process" in Chapter 1, "Installing Windows XP Professional."

5. **C, E**. `Winnt32.exe` using the `/checkupgradeonly` switch as well as the `Chkupgrd.exe` utility will generate a report showing any incompatibilities. No software will be installed onto the existing Windows 95 computer. For more information, see "Upgrading to Windows XP Professional" in Chapter 1, "Installing Windows XP Professional."

6. **B**. Windows 95 and 98 systems are not really part of the domain and, therefore, do not require a computer account. Windows NT 4.0, 2000, and XP must have a valid computer account or user account capable of adding a computer account before a client can join the domain. For more information, see "Upgrading to Windows XP Professional" in Chapter 1, "Installing Windows XP Professional."

7. **B**. The File and Settings Transfer Wizard is good for a few computers but it is difficult to automate and will require more time than the User State Migration Tool for larger environments. Additionally, the User State Migration Tool allows you to add other files, file extensions, and settings that will be moved with the settings. Because the question asked about a custom application's data, you should assume that you'll need the extra flexibility that the User State Migration Tool provides. It is a bad idea to move a hard

drive from one system to another without a completely new installation. RIS cannot be used to back up configuration data from a machine. For more information, see "Migrating User Environments" in Chapter 1, "Installing Windows XP Professional."

8. **B, D**. The Windows Installer can be used only for applications, not operating systems. SMS can deploy any type of package, including service packs. Windows XP group policies have a section on deploying software to systems based on usernames or computer names. Site Server is to configure and manage Web sites. For more information, see "Service Pack Deployment" in Chapter 1, "Installing Windows XP Professional."

9. **C, D**. Using an NTFS share and `%username%` will create a folder for each user with full control assigned only to them. The shared folder on the server does not need to be protected much because the local NTFS permissions are more restrictive. Roaming profiles and Mydocuments would allow users to access files, but this is an unsecured method and copies all files to and from the server each time the clients log on or off the system. This can be very slow. For more information, see "Developing an Efficient Directory Structure" in Chapter 2, "Implementing and Conducting Administration of Resources."

10. **D**. A No Access setting will override any other permissions. The Sales and Accounting groups would give Alexander an effective permission of Change; however, No Access will override that. For more information, see "File Resources" in Chapter 2, "Implementing and Conducting Administration of Resources."

11. **C**. The default permission on all shares is Everyone Has Full Control; this includes the guest account as well. Remove this permission

and add only groups with the appropriate permissions. For more information, see "File Resources" in Chapter 2, "Implementing and Conducting Administration of Resources."

12. **A, B, C**. The Deny Access permission supersedes all other permissions including those assigned directly to the user. If the file is encrypted by a user, no other user can view its contents. If the user doesn't have the Bypass Traverse Checking user right and they don't have access to the directory, they won't be able to access a file in the directory—even if they have permission. There is no such option as Secure File Access. For more information, see "File Resources" in Chapter 2, "Implementing and Conducting Administration of Resources."

13. **D**. Encrypted files cannot be compressed. If a compressed file is encrypted, it is decompressed first—automatically. It is possible that other users filled the file server; however, it's unlikely because the user was performing a "batch" operation on a large number of files. The encryption process does not create another copy of the file. For more information, see "File Encryption" in Chapter 2, "Implementing and Conducting Administration of Resources."

14. **D**. Sending the file through the Web or FTP servers will carry the risk of sending a virus. Using Internet-based printing, the report can be sent safely. For more information, see "The Print Environment" in Chapter 2, "Implementing and Conducting Administration of Resources."

15. **C, D**. All print devices can be set up and shared in a printer pool, which would prevent any one print device failure from causing downtime. The same print device can be set up with two printers, each with different permissions and properties. The Executives will print with a higher priority and therefore will jump the queue. For more

information, see "The Print Environment" in Chapter 2, "Implementing and Conducting Administration of Resources."

16. **B, E**. NTFS can be used to implement local permissions on files. With the help of EFS, additional encryption can be added to files so that, even if they are copied to a FAT partition, they cannot be viewed by anyone but the owner. For more information, see "Managing File Resources" in Chapter 2, "Implementing and Conducting Administration of Resources."

17. **A, C, D**. A desktop will not need to conserve energy because it is not running on batteries. Multiple CPUs and multiple video cards are not stable under the APM environment. Windows 98 and Windows XP Professional both support APM. For more information, see "Power Management" in Chapter 3, "Implementing, Managing, Monitoring, and Troubleshooting Hardware Devices and Drivers."

18. **D, E**. MPEG-2 and AC-3 are decoder formats that allow DVDs to bypass the standard PCI controllers and access the display adapters. For more information, see "Installing Hardware" in Chapter 3, "Implementing, Managing, Monitoring, and Troubleshooting Hardware Devices and Drivers."

19. **C, F, G**. Basic disks are supported for backward compatibility. They cannot be used to create mirrors or volumes. For more information, see "Installing Hardware" in Chapter 3, "Implementing, Managing, Monitoring, and Troubleshooting Hardware Devices and Drivers."

20. **B**. There are no configuration tools to change the primary adapter. It will be the first PCI card detected. Some systems' BIOSs can be set to deactivate the onboard card but not to set it as primary. It will always be a secondary adapter.

For more information, see "Display Devices" in Chapter 3, "Implementing, Managing, Monitoring, and Troubleshooting Hardware Devices and Drivers."

21. **B**. If you were to revoke the user's ability to install hardware, it would prevent bad driver installation but would also increase administration. Forcing XP to prevent the installation of unsigned drivers will limit the number of bad drivers installed while still allowing users to support themselves. Remote assistance will be of no use if the computer doesn't boot. Booting the computer in safe mode will prevent many operations from working and is not a recommended mode for running the system. For more information, see "Managing Driver Signing" in Chapter 3, "Implementing, Managing, Monitoring, and Troubleshooting Hardware Devices and Drivers."

22. **A**. If the processor is busy with any type of activity at a level of 90% or more over an extended period of time, it is common to have the processor spike to 100%. The interrupts per second show how many requests are coming in. The queue length should not be more than 2 for any long period of time. For more information, see "Monitoring Multiple CPUs" in Chapter 3, "Implementing, Managing, Monitoring, and Troubleshooting Hardware Devices and Drivers."

23. **B**. You must be logged on with a user ID that has administrator privileges to complete this procedure. If your camera supports Plug and Play, Windows XP Professional will detect it and install the correct drivers automatically. For more information, see "Cameras" in Chapter 3, "Implementing, Managing, Monitoring, and Troubleshooting Hardware Devices and Drivers."

24. **A, C**. On the Windows XP Professional CD, a file called `Biosinfo.inf` has a list of laptops that will be set up with AutoEnable and AutoDisable

for APM. ACPI-only systems do not support APM, either. For more information, see "Power Management" in Chapter 3, "Implementing, Managing, Monitoring, and Troubleshooting Hardware Devices and Drivers."

25. **B**. The system must be configured to prevent installation or provide a warning when an unsigned file is being installed. For more information, see "Managing and Troubleshooting Driver Signing" in Chapter 4, "Monitoring and Optimizing System Performance and Reliability."

26. **A**. All drivers and files that are signed will be installed automatically. Nonsigned files may be blocked or the installer will get a warning if the signature policy is in place. For more information, see "Managing and Troubleshooting Driver Signing" in Chapter 4, "Monitoring and Optimizing System Performance and Reliability."

27. **B**. Search for files with a `.Job` extension in the `Winnt\tasks` folder. For more information, see "Configuring, Managing, and Troubleshooting the Task Scheduler" in Chapter 4, "Monitoring and Optimizing System Performance and Reliability."

28. **B**. Windows XP Professional will continue to accept and allow you to edit tasks using the `AT` command. However, after the tasks are modified in the Task Scheduler, their format is changed and can no longer be read by the older `AT` command. For more information, see "Configuring, Managing, and Troubleshooting the Task Scheduler" in Chapter 4, "Monitoring and Optimizing System Performance and Reliability."

29. **D**. A processor bottleneck occurs if the percentage of processor time is above 90% and the processor queue length is above 2. For more information, see "Optimizing and Troubleshooting Performance of the Windows

XP Professional Desktop" in Chapter 4, "Monitoring and Optimizing System Performance and Reliability."

30. **B**. You can add trusted organizations into the trusted zone and set security options differently for the trusted zone. You cannot set up a new zone for a specific site and you should not set up trusted sites in the restricted zone. It is, however, technically possible to do so. For more information, see "Configuring Internet Options" in Chapter 7, "Implementing, Monitoring, and Troubleshooting Security."

31. **A, B**. By creating a test hardware profile, you do not risk losing the original configuration. After the system has been restarted in the test configuration, you can disable devices or services. If the desired results occur, you make these changes permanent in the original configuration. For more information, see "Managing Hardware Profiles" in Chapter 4, "Monitoring and Optimizing System Performance and Reliability."

32. **B, C, D, E**. CD-ROMs and DVD-ROMs are read only and therefore cannot be written to from the backup utility. Modems cannot be used in backup at this point. Windows XP Professional can be configured to use any writable device connected to the system. For more information, see "Recovering System and User Data by Using Windows Backup" in Chapter 4, "Monitoring and Optimizing System Performance and Reliability."

33. **A**. Group policies from Active Directory can help maintain a standard desktop and reduce administration cost. For more information, see "The Desktop Environment" in Chapter 5, "Configuring and Troubleshooting the Desktop Environment."

34. **C**. Local profiles are always enabled on a Windows XP Professional system. As long as the users do not change computers, roaming profiles are not needed. For more information, see "Configuring and Managing User Profiles" in Chapter 5, "Configuring and Troubleshooting the Desktop Environment."

35. **E**. `Ntuser.dat` can be renamed to `NTUser.man` and it will make the profile mandatory. Users can change settings but will not be able to save them upon exiting. Unlike Windows 9x, you cannot disable profiles in Windows XP Professional. For more information, see "Mandatory User Profiles" in Chapter 5, "Configuring and Troubleshooting the Desktop Environment."

36. **A**. Enforcing a password history is the first step of preventing the user from using the same password again. The minimum password age is required to prevent the user from changing their password over and over again until they can change it back to the original password. Setting the maximum password age to 1 day would require the user to change their password every day. Changing the length of the password history won't solve the problem because they can still change their passwords enough times that they will be able to use their original password again. There is no option to prevent a user from using a password over again—you can control only the number of new passwords that must be used before they resume the original password. For more information, see "Password Policies" in Chapter 7, "Implementing, Monitoring, and Troubleshooting Security."

37. **C**. The two different types of user profiles are local and roaming. Roaming profiles can be further divided into either personal (which allow the users' changes to be saved) or mandatory (which do not save the users' changes). For more information see "User Profile Types" in Chapter 5,

"Configuring and Troubleshooting the Desktop Environment."

38. **C, D**. ShowSounds and SoundSentry give people with hearing impairments control of their audio environments. For more information, see "Accessibility Benefits with Windows XP" in Chapter 5, "Configuring and Troubleshooting the Desktop Environment."

39. **A**. Group policies from Active Directory can help publish and assign applications to users. For more information, see "The Desktop Environment" in Chapter 5, "Configuring and Troubleshooting the Desktop Environment."

40. **A, C**. Several operating systems other than Windows XP, including Unix and Windows NT 4.0, can be controlled. For more information, see "The Desktop Environment" in Chapter 5, "Configuring and Troubleshooting the Desktop Environment."

41. **B**. To find out IP information on a computer that is DHCP enabled, use the `ipconfig` command. The `/all` switch will show you all the IP information. For more information, see "Understanding DHCP" in Chapter 6, "Implementing, Managing, and Troubleshooting Network Protocols and Services."

42. **B**. The correct order is as follows:

Ping the address of 127.0.0.1.

Ping the local host.

Ping the gateway.

Ping the remote host.

The order reflects the path through which information must travel when communicating over TCP/IP: first the stack (127.0.0.1), then the card, the gateway, and the remote host. For more information, see "Configuring the TCP/IP Protocol"

in Chapter 6, "Implementing, Managing, and Troubleshooting Network Protocols and Services."

43. **D**. The `/FLUSHDNS` switch discards the DNS cache on the local machine. If the server IP address had changed, this might have been an appropriate option. `/REGISTERDNS` forces a server to reregister its DNS information. In this case, the command must be run on Server A so it can reregister its address with the DNS server. For more information, see "Domain Network Systems Server Address" in Chapter 6, "Implementing, Managing, and Troubleshooting Network Protocols and Services."

44. **B**. When you share an Internet connection on a Windows XP computer, it will automatically assign DHCP addresses to clients. The addresses that it assigns are between 192.168.0.1 and 192.168.255.254. For more information, see "Internet Connection Sharing" in Chapter 6, "Implementing, Managing, and Troubleshooting Network Protocols and Services."

45. **A, D**. Only PPP supports IPX and NetBEUI as well as TCP/IP. PPP also supports encryption of logon information if configured. For more information, see "Serial Line Internet Protocol" and "Point-to-Point Protocol" in Chapter 6, "Implementing, Managing, and Troubleshooting Network Protocols and Services."

46. **A, B, G**. The `LMHOSTS` file is used to statically map IP addresses to NetBIOS names. WINS is a service that is installed on a server to create a database, a NetBIOS name, and associated IP addresses. Clients can query the database to find name-to-IP-address mappings. If the first two methods fail, Windows will read the `HOST` file to see whether there is a hostname that is the same as the NetBIOS name. For more information, see "Resolve a NetBIOS Name to an IP Address" in

Chapter 6, "Implementing, Managing, and Troubleshooting Network Protocols and Services."

47. **A, B**. The Novell 4.1 servers will require NWLink (IPX/SPX). The Internet requires TCP/IP. Windows 2000 can use either protocol. You do not want to install NetBEUI because it is unneeded, or DLC because it's not a protocol capable of carrying file and print traffic to a server. For more information, see "Network Protocols" in Chapter 6, "Implementing, Managing, and Troubleshooting Network Protocols and Services."

48. **D**. By adding the `#PRE` switch to the end of the line, you are telling Windows to load the name mapping into the NetBIOS name cache. This cache can be checked running the `nbtstat -c` command. For more information, see "`LMHOSTS` File Errors" and "Understanding DHCP" in Chapter 6, "Implementing, Managing, and Troubleshooting Network Protocols and Services."

49. **B**. Setting up a domain and making the workstations a member of that domain allows you to set up a single-user account that works across multiple machines. All other configurations require that each user have an account established on each machine. For more information, see "User Accounts" in Chapter 7, "Implementing, Monitoring, and Troubleshooting Security."

50. **B**. The correct method is to rename Jane's account to Fred's login name. Because user access is really controlled by SID, the name is just to make it easier to see and control. Answer A is incorrect because Fred will not have access to Jane's resources. B is incorrect because it is a security risk. Answer D is too much work. For more information, see "Groups" in Chapter 7,

"Implementing, Monitoring, and Troubleshooting Security."

51. **D**. Access must be assigned individually for each domain. For more information, see "Groups" in Chapter 7, "Implementing, Monitoring, and Troubleshooting Security."

52. **D**. Windows XP can convert partition formats from FAT32 to NTFS, but not the other way around. If the disk was a dynamic disk, you could not convert it back to basic without deleting all partitions on the disk and reinstalling both operating systems. Reinstalling Windows 98 will not allow it to see the NTFS partition. For more information, see "Windows XP File Systems" in Chapter 1, "Installing Windows XP Professional."

53. **D**. Applications that were written for Windows NT 4.0 do not know about the Windows XP security model. By adding the users into the Power Users group, they should be able to run all applications. For more information, see "Groups" in Chapter 7, "Implementing, Monitoring, and Troubleshooting Security."

54. **A, B, D**. Answers C and F are built-in Global groups. Everyone is a System group. Managers is not a built-in group; it is a group that was created by an administrator. For more information, see "Create and Manage Local Users and Groups" in Chapter 6, "Implementing, Managing, and Troubleshooting Network Protocols and Services."

55. **B**. Only administrators can access the security log on Windows XP Professional computers. For more information, see "Setting Up Auditing" in Chapter 7, "Implementing, Monitoring, and Troubleshooting Security."

56. **D**. Windows XP's Program Compatibility options can emulate any operating system Windows 95 or later. This is set on a program-by-program basis

and is the best thing to attempt first for programs that have run on previous versions of Windows. For more information, see "Program Compatibility Options" in Chapter 5, "Configuring and Troubleshooting the Desktop Environment."

57. **B, D**. One of the Internet Explorer settings is whether to allow ActiveX controls to be downloaded. If a site is not in your trusted sites list, and your Internet sites list security is set too high, or if the site is listed in the restricted list, it's possible that you will not be able to load the ActiveX controls that the site uses. If the administrator had blocked access at the Proxy server, you wouldn't have been able to access any part of the site, not just the ActiveX control. ActiveX controls are not compiled for a specific operating system; however, they are compiled for a specific processor type. For more information, see "Configuring Internet Options" in Chapter 7, "Implementing, Monitoring, and Troubleshooting Security."

58. **B**. The recovery agent must be configured in the security policies of the local computer for it to work. For more information, see "Encrypting File System" in Chapter 7, "Implementing, Monitoring, and Troubleshooting Security."

59. **A**. The product activation mechanism will prevent users from logging on if the product hasn't been activated after 30 days. Both DHCP and DNS automatically refresh and wouldn't prevent logon to the system. For more information, see "Post-Installation Tasks" in Chapter 1, "Installing Windows XP Professional."

60. **B**. The higher the number, the higher the priority in print jobs. The priority is set on the printer, not the default print job. For more information, see "Setting Print Priority and Printer Availability" in Chapter 2, "Implementing and Conducting Administration of Resources."

APPENDIXES

Glossary

accessibility options   Settings in Windows 2000 and XP that enable you to configure the environment for users with special requirements, such as mobility or sensory challenges. These options enable these users to more effectively interact with the system.

account policy   Account policies enable administrative control over such things as passwords and lockouts.

activation   The process of binding a product key to a machine. Microsoft's new copyright protection scheme. Retail versions of Windows XP must be activated within 30 days.

Active Directory   In Microsoft Windows 2000 Server, Active Directory provides a central repository of network objects for the purposes of administration and organization. This is the primary tool for consolidating Windows 2000 networks into a unified whole.

Advanced Configuration and Power Interface (ACPI)   This power scheme supersedes APM and offers a greater set of features to manage power.

Advanced Power Management (APM)   APM is an older power management system that is based on a BIOS approach to managing power.

answer file   Another name for an unattended text file. See *unattended text file.*

auditing   Auditing tracks authorized and unauthorized access to resources.

basic disks   A standard hard-drive configuration that supports four primary partitions or three primary partitions and one extended partition.

boot partition   The disk partition that contains the installation of Windows XP.

bootable disk   A floppy disk that can be used to boot a computer.

Briefcase   A feature, initially included with Windows 95, that allows the manual synchronization of files on a notebook with files on a network. Used to maintain copies of files while not connected to the network. Largely replaced by offline files.

built-in group   Built-in groups are automatically created at the time of installation and represent a collection of rights and privileges. Built-in groups are specific to the installation type.

Built-in groups for workstations and member servers include Administrators, Backup Operators, Guests, HelpServicesGroup, Network Configuration Operators, Power Users, Remote Desktop Users, Replicator, and Users.

DHCP (Dynamic Host Configuration Protocol)   Part of the TCP/IP suite, the purpose of DHCP is to enable a server to be configured in such a way that stations requiring an IP address can contact the server to attain one. These servers (appropriately named DHCP servers) can maintain a series of IP addresses and other network configuration settings, called *scopes*, which they hand out on an as-needed basis to systems requesting them.

disk duplexing   A form of mirroring in which the controller that reads and writes the hard drives is also duplicated so that should one controller fail, the other is able to continue. This eliminates the disk controller from being a single point of failure for the system and creates better fault tolerance.

disk partition   Hard disks can be partitioned so that one physical hard disk can be broken into multiple logical disks. Each partition can be assigned a drive letter and formatted with a separate file system. Partitions infer a basic disk organizational structure.

distribution groups   Distribution groups are used to organize users together for non–security-related administration.

DNS (Domain Name Service and Domain Name System)   These two terms often are used interchangeably. The Domain Name System refers to the structure that enables hosts to have names on the Internet that are associated with IP addresses so that they can be found. An example would be newriders.com. The Domain Name Service is a utility that acts as an enabler for the Domain Name *System*, which is sometimes referred to as Name Servers or DNS Servers. The key to remembering the difference is to think of the system as the entire process and the service as a part of the whole.

domain   A group of computers that share a security policy and a *user account* database. Well-suited to larger environments, domains enable many thousands of computers and user accounts to be centrally managed and controlled. Users need to remember only one name and password and administrators can then assign them access to whatever resources are appropriate.

dual-boot system   A system that is configured to support more than one operating system. When a dual-boot system starts, the user can choose which system to use.

dynamic disks   A new disk organizational structure available under Windows 2000 and Windows XP. A hard disk can be defined as either a basic disk or a dynamic disk, but not both. After a hard disk is defined as a dynamic disk, primary and extended partitions are no longer required. Instead, volumes are created, and you can have as many volumes as you want within your system.

Encrypting File System (EFS)   A system service that allows the user to encrypt file system resources so that access is restricted to the user only and protected from others. They are based on public key encryption schemes and provide security that is transparent to the user.

event logs   Event logs contain records of system events related to security, system events, and application events.

extended partition   An area of space on a hard disk that can be used for the creation of logical drives. The use of an extended partition enables users to create more than four drives out of one physical hard disk device. You can have only one extended partition per physical hard disk.

Extensible Authentication Protocol (EAP)   An extension to the Point-to-Point Protocol (PPP) that allows for arbitrary authentication mechanisms to be employed for the validation of a PPP connection.

FAT   An older formatting system still in widespread use. Originally designed for use with DOS (Disk Operating System), this file system, despite its limitations, has remained popular for a long time and is still used on many systems. Security is weak; compatibility is high.

FAT32   Introduced in the second edition of Windows 95 (OSR/2), this file format was designed to support larger hard drives in a more efficient manner. Optional for use under Windows 98, Windows Me, Windows 2000, and Windows XP.

File and Settings Transfer Wizard (FAST)   A graphical utility designed to move files and settings from an old machine to a new machine. Moves all office files, all files in the My Documents folder, and most settings.

Folder share   A share created on a computer that gives other computers on the network access to a folder resource. Permissions assigned to a folder share accommodate various levels of permission to the resources contained in the folder.

group   A collection of users, computers, or other objects with similar administrative requirements collected together for the purpose of administration.

group policy   A security policy that requires Active Directory and that enables an administrator to control the environment of several users. It allows control of many behaviors in their environment. A very powerful feature, it is not covered as part of the Professional Training courses, but falls into Server Training.

Hardware Abstraction Layer (HAL)   A layer of software provided by the hardware manufacturer that hides, or abstracts, hardware differences from higher layers of the operating system. Different types of hardware are made to look alike to the operating system.

hardware profiles   Hardware profiles tell your Windows XP Professional computer what devices to start and what setting to use for each device. These profiles are useful if you have a portable computer, for example, and use it in a variety of locations. In general, hardware profiles enable you to maintain different configurations of available peripherals.

Hypertext Transport Protocol (HTTP)   The standard Web transfer protocol. The transfer consists of a request and a response.

Internet Connection Firewall (ICF)   A firewall service that is used to set restrictions on what information is communicated from your home or small office network to and from the Internet to your network.

Internet Connection Sharing (ICS)   A Windows 2000 or Windows XP computer can be used as a gateway to the Internet if it has two network adapters. ICS is enabled on the adapter connected to the Internet, which creates a DHCP scope and DNS proxy for the machines connected to the internal network.

Internet Explorer (IE)   One of a class of applications known as browsers. With Internet Explorer and an Internet connection, you can search for and view information on the World Wide Web. You can type the address of the Web page you want to visit into the address bar, or click an address from your list of Favorites. Internet Explorer also lets you search the Internet for people, businesses, and information about subjects that interest you.

Internet Information Server (IIS)   A set of software services that support Web site creation, configuration, and management, along with other Internet functions. Internet Information Services include Network News Transfer Protocol (NNTP), File Transfer Protocol (FTP), and Simple Mail Transfer Protocol (SMTP).

IPSec (Internet Protocol Security)   Designed to allow for end-to-end security, IPSec is an Internet Engineering Task Force (IETF) standard that defines how security is configured. This is done through public key cryptography and controlled by the administrator through policies. Windows XP enables you to use an MMC console to configure IPSec and also has predefined IPSec policies that you can use, as well as the custom policies you create and configure yourself.

IPX/SPX (Internetwork Packet Exchange/Sequenced Packet Exchange)   Novell NetWare uses this protocol stack at the Network and Transport layers. Novell now supports TCP/IP, but IPX/SPX is still very important because a large installed base of Novell systems uses it, and some companies prefer to use it internally on newer Novell Servers. IPX and SPX correspond to IP and TCP, respectively, in the TCP/IP protocol stack.

IrDA devices   IrDA devices use infrared signals to communicate. This can be quite advantageous in a laptop system where you can use an IrDA interface to print or transfer data without the need for cables.

LastKnownGood configuration   Saved in the Registry of Windows XP, the LastKnownGood configuration is a Registry snapshot of the system configuration as it was the last time the system successfully started and a login was performed. As soon as you log in to the system, the current configuration becomes the LastKnownGood configuration. In the event you restart the system and a failure occurs with the configuration that prevents you from logging in, you can then use the configuration to restore your system to its previous state.

libraries   Each media device in a media pool belongs to a library, which is a named collection of media. Libraries come in two varieties: robotic, which are automated units that can hold multiple media, and standalone, which are single-slot CD-ROM or tape devices holding a single piece of media.

Local Group Policy   Local Group Policies are stored on the local system and are used to control components, such as Administrative Templates, Software Settings, Security Settings, Scripts, and Folder Redirection. Local Group Policy is a powerful control feature that is part of an Active Directory implementation and is beyond the scope of this course.

local groups   Local groups are used to assign permissions to resources that are on a workstation or a member server.

local profile   A set of user preferences that are stored on the machine being referenced. For example, if a user known as John has a profile on a computer known as System1, System1 has a record of John's configuration preferences, which are then referred to as being *local*.

logical drive   An area of hard disk space within an extended partition that has been defined as a drive.

mandatory profile   In this case, the configuration options of a user are set, and each time that user logs on to a computer, the profile is loaded. If the user makes changes, these are not retained, and the options set as mandatory are loaded at next login. This can prevent users from making changes that are not approved or that might cause problems in an environment.

media pools   A logical collection of similar media with similar properties.

mirrored   A fault-tolerant scheme in which two drives are entered into a relationship such that any data written to one drive is also written to the other. This results in a set of data that is equal on both drives and is hence referred to as *mirrored*. The same disk controller in mirroring serves both of these disks, so the disk controller represents a single point of failure.

MS-CHAP   A mutual authentication protocol. This means that both the client and the server prove that they have knowledge of the user's password. The remote access server asks for proof by sending a challenge to the remote access client. The remote access client asks for proof by sending a challenge to the remote access server. If the server cannot prove that it has knowledge of the user's password by correctly answering the client's challenge, the client terminates the connection. Without mutual authentication, a remote access client could not detect a connection to an impersonating remote access server.

NetBEUI (NetBIOS Enhanced User Interface)   Developed by IBM and Microsoft and originally used in LAN Manager Server and Windows for Workgroups 3.11, this protocol was designed for LAN traffic in smaller environments. It was developed at a time when the Internet was not seen as something every home user and office user would use, so it has limitations. As an example, you are unable to use this protocol in a routed network. Not supported in Windows XP.

NetBIOS (Network Basic Input/Output Service) A standard set of protocols designed by IBM and used to resolve names for computers on a network. Enhanced by Microsoft over the last 10 years.

NT File System See *NTFS*.

NTFS A file system supported by Windows NT, Windows 2000, and Windows XP. Starting with Windows 2000, a version known as NTFS5 is supported. With NTFS, security can be set at the file or folder level. NTFS also supports encryption, mount points, compression, and larger volume/partition sizes.

NTFS permissions A more complex and powerful method of controlling access to resources both over a network and locally on the computer. The preferred method of control in higher-security environments, NTFS permissions require that the format of the hard drive be NTFS.

offline files A feature of Windows 2000 and Windows XP that allows mobile users to travel with the files that they need most. Offline files are files that exist on the network that the local computer makes a cached copy of that the user can use when the network is not available. The files are later synchronized with the network.

performance counter A measured performance statistic that resides within a performance object. As an example, the processor object has several counters related to it, such as % Processor Time and % User Time. There are literally hundreds of performance counters underneath dozens of performance objects in Windows XP. Many programs add performance objects and the associated counters during installation so that you can monitor that application's performance.

Performance Monitor The Performance Monitor is a tool designed to monitor how the operating system and any applications or services, including disks, memory, processors, and network components, use the resources of the system. The statistics usually measured are throughput, queues, and response times that represent resource usage. Performance data is defined in terms of objects, counters, and instances. An object is any resource, application, or service that you can measure. You can view this information graphically or in the form of reports. Alerts and captures can also be run to advise you when conditions have exceeded or fallen below a user-defined level, and captures can be run to monitor system information over time.

Plug and Play A term used to describe the process whereby a new hardware device can be added to a system and be recognized and assigned resources without user intervention. In reality, for this to occur, the device must identify itself to the system, which must support this functionality (through the BIOS and/or the OS). Therefore, older devices are often not plug and play because they cannot identify and receive this automatic configuration.

primary partition A disk partition that can be set active on a hard disk. Most disk configurations support a maximum of four primary partitions (only one can be set active at a time).

print device The hardware on which the requested print job is created. Also refers to the physical destination of the printer.

print driver Often provided by the manufacturer of the print device, print drivers translate requests to print into a format understood by the print device.

print server The computer that receives the printing requests from other computers and forwards them to an appropriate or defined printer.

printer A software representation of a physical print device or devices. Print jobs are sent to printers on a computer and then to print devices. It is worth noting that a single physical print device may serve the needs of several software printers. Microsoft does not consider the printer to be hardware. See also *print device*.

printer permissions   Permissions that control access to printer use.

printer share   A printer resource that has been shared to allow access over the network. Printer shares may also be controlled using a Web browser, and access can be controlled via permissions.

RAID-5   RAID refers to a Redundant Array of Inexpensive Disks. RAID-5 refers to a specific methodology that uses an array of disks. Data is striped across them, and write parity provides fault tolerance. Requiring three disks at a minimum and up to 32 disks at a maximum, RAID-5 can be implemented at a software or hardware level. Typically, a larger computing environment would invest in a hardware implementation of RAID-5.

Recovery Console   The Windows XP Recovery Console is a tool that enables you to start a system that cannot load Windows XP and have access to a command prompt. This command prompt can then be used to copy files from a floppy disk or CD-ROM to your hard drive and otherwise attempt to repair the failed or damaged installation.

Remote Access Service (RAS)   A Windows-based computer running the Routing and Remote Access service and configured to provide remote networking for telecommuters, mobile workers, and system administrators who monitor and manage servers at multiple branch offices. Users with a computer running Windows and Network Connections can dial in to an RAS server to remotely access their networks for services.

Remote Installation Services (RIS)   A service that can be used to manage Windows 2000 and Windows XP installation images from a central location.

roaming profile   A set of configuration preferences that are stored on a network share and are accessible from several machines. When the user logs on to a

computer, this share is accessed and the configuration options are loaded to the local machine. In this way, the profile follows the user from machine to machine and is said to be *roaming*.

security groups   Security groups are used to organize *user accounts* to give permissions to a resource.

security template   Security templates are provided by Windows 2000 and Windows XP for common security scenarios. These templates can be assigned to the computer or modified to meet unique security requirements.

simple volumes   A simple volume is created on dynamic disks and does not span to other disks. See also *spanned volumes*.

spanned volumes   Spanning is a process in which a volume or partition is extended across different disks. Spanning can be used to combine free space on several different drives and to capture this free space into one volume or drive. Space on each drive does not have to be of the same size.

striped volumes   Striping is a process whereby several drives are combined into a set to which data is written across all the drives in a sequential manner from drive to drive. This provides speed improvements and can provide fault tolerance when done with parity (as in RAID-5). Striped sets must be created using equal space on each of the participating drives.

synchronization   Synchronization occurs when you are using offline files and you reconnect to the network. Your system copies any locally changed files to the network and the network copies any network files that have been changed to your system. In the event of a conflict, such as when a file has been changed in both locations, you are asked what action you would like to take.

system partition   The disk partition used to start a computer system.

Task Scheduler   The Task Scheduler enables you to select programs and batch files to run at different times. These tasks can be run once, on a schedule, when a condition is met, at login, or at startup. You are able to specify the account used to start the task and this information is stored with the task so that it can be copied to another computer.

TCP/IP (Transmission Control Protocol/Internet Protocol)   This networking protocol stack was developed by the Department of Defense (DoD) to enable communication between computer systems. It has since become the de facto standard for the Internet. Note: Even though it was developed in the 1960s, TCP/IP as a protocol stack (or suite) saw its use really boom in the early to mid-1980s.

unattended text file   A text file that contains answers to the user prompts required during the Windows XP installation process.

UNC (Uniform Naming Convention)   This is sometimes referred to as Universal Naming Convention. This is a method of specifying a file on a system in such a way that the path to the file is described completely, including the computer on which it resides, the share in which it is contained, and the path to it. For example, if I had a file called `Trivia.txt` in a share called History on a computer called Study, the path that file would be `\\Study\History\Trivia.txt`. This corresponds to the `\\Server\Share\File` structure.

Uniqueness Definition File (UDF)   A text file, used in conjunction with an unattended text file, that enables unique computer settings to be fed into the automated installation process.

universal groups   Used to assign permissions to resources located in multiple domains.

USB devices   As the number of devices that users attached to their systems increased, a method of

providing high-speed, low-latency connections was needed. A solution (Universal Serial Bus, or USB) allows for up to 127 devices to be attached to a Windows XP system in a dynamic manner (you can plug in and unplug devices without shutting down the system).

user account   A name and password the user uses to gain access to a system and, through the account, access to resources.

User State Migration Tool (USMT)   A set of command-line tools that move user files and settings from one computer to another, similar to the File and Settings Transfer Wizard (see definition). The USMT tools are designed to be customized so they can be used to move custom configuration information and special files.

VPN (Virtual Private Network)   Nodes on remote networks are connected in such a way that the connections they use appear to be part of the same network. This enables them to use a public system, such as the Internet, as the medium through which to route traffic, while they still appear to have a point-to-point connection to one another or the servers they are accessing. In a private network setting, VPNs are used to group computers or users together so that they appear to be a network unto themselves. In Windows XP, VPNs refer to networks that are formed by the process of tunneling through the Internet or some other public network.

Windows Installer   A tool that can be used to set up applications on a system. Unlike setup programs of the past, the Windows Installer is a collection of files that describe how and from where an application should be installed. This enables an application's files to be installed, repaired, and reinstalled. In this way, an application can "follow" a user from desktop to desktop and be installed only on demand. Also, if a user accidentally harms program files, the application can be reinstalled the next time the user goes to use it.

WINS   Windows Internet Naming Service. Occasionally, I have seen this referred to as INS (without the *W* in front). This service also is used for location of nodes on a network. WINS resolves NetBIOS names to IP addresses.

workgroup   A collection of computers in which each computer is participating in the network, and each is responsible for the management of its own shares and security. This effectively creates a situation in which every computer operator is the administrator of his or her own system. This results in a situation in which users must remember login names and passwords for several systems and administration becomes distributed. This solution is best suited to small environments only (50 or fewer systems).

Overview of the Certification Process

You must pass rigorous certification exams to become a Microsoft Certified Professional. These closed-book exams provide a valid and reliable measure of your technical proficiency and expertise. Developed in consultation with computer industry professionals who have experience with Microsoft products in the workplace, the exams are conducted by two independent organizations. Virtual University Enterprises (VUE) testing centers offer exams at more than 3,000 locations in 120 countries. Sylvan Prometric offers the exams at many Authorized Prometric Testing Centers around the world as well.

To schedule an exam, call VUE at 800-837-8734 (or register online at `http://www.vue.com/` or Sylvan Prometric Testing Centers at 800-755-EXAM (3926) (or register online at `http://www.2test.com/register`).

TYPES OF CERTIFICATION

◆ **Microsoft Certified Professional (MCP)**—The Microsoft Certified Professional (MCP) credential is for professionals who have the skills to successfully implement a Microsoft product or technology as part of a business solution in an organization.

◆ **Microsoft Certified Database Administrator (MCDBA) on Microsoft SQL Server 2000**—Qualified individuals can derive physical database designs, develop logical data models, create physical databases, create data services by using Transact-SQL, manage and maintain databases, configure and manage security, monitor and optimize databases, and install and configure Microsoft SQL Server.

◆ **Microsoft Certified Systems Administrator (MCSA)**—This credential certifies that the individual has the skills to successfully implement, manage, and troubleshoot the ongoing needs of Microsoft Windows 2000-based operating environments, including Windows .NET Server.

◆ **Microsoft Certified Systems Engineer (MCSE) on Microsoft Windows 2000**—These individuals are qualified to analyze the business requirements for a system architecture; design solutions; deploy, install, and configure architecture components; and troubleshoot system problems.

◆ **Microsoft Certified Solution Developer (MCSD)**—These individuals are qualified to design and develop custom business solutions by using Microsoft development tools, technologies, and platforms. The new track includes certification exams that test users' abilities to build Web-based, distributed, and commerce applications by using Microsoft products such as Microsoft SQL Server, Microsoft Visual Studio, and Microsoft Component Services.

◆ **Microsoft Certified Application Developer (MCAD)**—The Microsoft Certified Application Developer (MCAD) for Microsoft .NET credential is for professionals who use Microsoft technologies to develop and maintain department-level applications, components, Web or desktop clients, or back-end data services.

◆ **Microsoft Certified Trainer (MCT)**—Persons with this credential are instructionally and technically qualified by Microsoft to deliver Microsoft Education Courses at Microsoft-authorized sites. An MCT must be employed by a Microsoft Solution Provider Authorized Technical Education Center or a Microsoft Authorized Academic Training site.

NOTE

For up-to-date information about each type of certification, visit the Microsoft Training and Certification World Wide Web site at `http://www.microsoft .com/train-cert/`. You also may contact Microsoft through the following sources:

◆ Microsoft Certified Professional Program: 800-636-7544

◆ `http://register.microsoft.com/contactus/contactus.asp`

NOTE

Although most exams are no longer available for the following certifications, individuals who earned them remain certified as of Summer of 2002:

• Microsoft Certified Professional + Internet (MCP+I)

• Microsoft Certified Professional + Site Building (MCP+SB)

• Microsoft Certified Systems Engineer + Internet (MCSE+I)

CERTIFICATION REQUIREMENTS

An asterisk following an exam in any of the following lists means that it is slated for retirement.

How to Become a Microsoft Certified Professional

To become certified as an MCP, you need only to pass any Microsoft exam (with the exception of Microsoft Windows 2000 Accelerated Exam for MCPs Certified on Microsoft Windows NT 4.0, #70-240).

How to Become a Microsoft Certified Database Administrator on Microsoft SQL Server 2000

To achieve the MCDBA certification, you need to pass three core exams and one elective exam.

Core Exams

The core exams must come from three areas:

◆ *Administration Exams*

Administering Microsoft SQL Server 7.0, #70-028

OR Installing, Configuring, and Administering Microsoft SQL Server 2000, Enterprise Edition, #70-228

◆ *Design Exams*

Designing and Implementing Databases with Microsoft SQL Server 7.0, #70-029

OR Designing and Implementing Databases with Microsoft SQL Server 2000, Enterprise Edition, #70-229

◆ *Networking Systems Exams*

Installing, Configuring, and Administering Microsoft Windows 2000 Server, #70-215

OR Installing, Configuring, and Administering Microsoft .NET Enterprise Servers, #70-275

OR Microsoft Windows 2000 Accelerated Exam for MCPs Certified on Microsoft Windows NT 4.0, #70-240 (only for those who have passed exams #70-067, #70-068, and #70-073)

Elective Exams

You also must pass one elective exam from the following list (note that #70-240 can be counted twice—as both a core and elective exam in the MCDBA track):

◆ Designing and Implementing Distributed Applications with Microsoft Visual C++ 6.0, #70-015

◆ Designing and Implementing Data Warehouses with Microsoft SQL Server 7.0 and Microsoft Decision Support Services 1.0, #70-019

◆ Designing and Implementing Distributed Applications with Microsoft Visual FoxPro 6.0, #70-155

◆ Designing and Implementing Distributed Applications with Microsoft Visual Basic 6.0, #70-175

◆ Implementing and Administering a Microsoft Windows 2000 Network Infrastructure, #70-216 (only for those who have *NOT* already passed #70-067*, #70-068*, and #70-073*)

OR Implementing and Administering a Microsoft Windows .NET Server Network Infrastructure, #70-276

OR Microsoft Windows 2000 Accelerated Exam for MCPs Certified on Microsoft Windows NT 4.0, #70-240 (only for those who have passed exams #70-067*, #70-068*, and #70-073*)

How to Become a Microsoft Certified Systems Administrator

To become certified as an MCSA, you must pass three core exams and one elective exam. The core exams must consist of one client operating system exam and two networking system exams. Exam #70-240 can count as both a core and an elective.

Core Exams

◆ Client Operating System Exams

Installing, Configuring, and Administering Microsoft Windows 2000 Professional, #70-210

OR Installing, Configuring, and Administering Microsoft Windows XP Professional, #70-270

OR Microsoft Windows 2000 Accelerated Exam for MCPs Certified on Microsoft Windows NT 4.0, #70-240 (only for those who have passed exams #70-067*, #70-068*, and #70-073*)

◆ Networking System Exams

Installing, Configuring, and Administering Microsoft Windows 2000 Server, #70-215

OR Installing, Configuring, and Administering Microsoft Windows .NET Server, #70-275

OR Microsoft Windows 2000 Accelerated Exam for MCPs Certified on Microsoft Windows NT 4.0, #70-240 (only for those who have passed exams #70-067*, #70-068*, and #70-073*)

Managing a Microsoft Windows 2000 Network Environment, #70-218

Managing a Microsoft Windows .NET Server Network Environment, #70-278

Elective Exams

◆ Administering Microsoft SQL Server 7.0, #70-028

◆ Implementing and Supporting Microsoft Exchange Server 5.5, #70-081

◆ Implementing and Supporting Microsoft Systems Management Server 2.0, #70-086

◆ Implementing and Administering a Microsoft Windows 2000 Network Infrastructure, #70-216

OR Microsoft Windows 2000 Accelerated Exam for MCPs Certified on Microsoft Windows NT 4.0, #70-240 (only for those who have passed exams #70-067*, #70-068*, and #70-073*)

◆ Installing, Configuring, and Administering Microsoft Exchange 2000 Server, #70-224

◆ Installing, Configuring, and Administering Microsoft Internet Security and Acceleration (ISA) Server 2000, Enterprise Edition, #70-227

◆ Installing, Configuring, and Administering Microsoft SQL Server 2000, Enterprise Edition, #70-228

◆ Supporting and Maintaining a Microsoft Windows NT Server 4.0 Network, #70-244

◆ CompTIA A+ and CompTIA Network+

  OR CompTIA A+ and CompTIA Server+

How to Become a Microsoft Certified Systems Engineer

You must pass four core operating system exams, one core design exam, and two elective exams to become an MCSE. You must also pass two elective exams.

Core Exams

The Windows 2000 Track core requirements for MCSE certification include the following for those who have *NOT* passed #70-067,#70-068, and #70-073:

◆ Installing, Configuring, and Administering Microsoft Windows 2000 Professional, #70-210

◆ Installing, Configuring, and Administering Microsoft Windows 2000 Server, #70-215

◆ Implementing and Administering a Microsoft Windows 2000 Network Infrastructure, #70-216

◆ Implementing and Administering a Microsoft Windows 2000 Directory Services Infrastructure, #70-217

The Windows 2000 Track core requirements for MCSE certification include the following for those who have passed #70-067*, #70-068*, and #70-073*:

◆ Microsoft Windows 2000 Accelerated Exam for MCPs Certified on Microsoft Windows NT 4.0, #70-240

All candidates must pass one of these additional core exams:

◆ Designing a Microsoft Windows 2000 Directory Services Infrastructure, #70-219

◆ *OR* Designing Security for a Microsoft Windows 2000 Network, #70-220

◆ *OR* Designing a Microsoft Windows 2000 Infrastructure, #70-221

◆ *OR* Designing Highly Available Web Solutions with Microsoft Windows 2000 Server Technologies, #70-226

  (This exam is in development. It is expected to be released in its beta version in May 2001.)

Elective Exams

You must pass two elective exams. Exams 70-219,70-220, 70-221, and 70-226 may count as an elective exam as long as they are not already being used as an additional core exam. The elective exams are as follows:

◆ Implementing and Supporting Microsoft SNA Server 4.0, 70-085

◆ Implementing and Supporting Microsoft Systems Management Server 2.0, 70-086

◆ Designing and Implementing Data Warehouses with Microsoft SQL Server 7.0, 70-019

◆ Designing and Implementing Databases with Microsoft SQL Server 7.0, 70-029

  OR Designing and Implementing Databases with Microsoft SQL Server 2000 Enterprise Edition, 70-229

◆ Administering Microsoft SQL Server 7.0, 70-028

OR Installing, Configuring, and Administering Microsoft SQL Server 2000 Enterprise Edition, 70-228

◆ Implementing and Supporting Web Sites Using Microsoft Site Server 3.0, 70-056

◆ Implementing and Supporting Microsoft Exchange Server 5.5, 70-081

OR Installing, Configuring, and Administering Microsoft Exchange 2000 Server, 70-224

◆ Implementing and Supporting Microsoft Proxy Server 2.0, 70-088

OR Installing, Configuring, and Administering Microsoft Internet Security and Acceleration (ISA) Server 2000, Enterprise Edition, 70-227

◆ Implementing and Supporting Microsoft Internet Explorer 5.0 by Using the Microsoft Internet Explorer, Administration Kit, 70-080

◆ Managing a Microsoft Windows 2000 Network Environment, 70-218

◆ Designing a Microsoft Windows 2000 Directory Services Infrastructure, 70-219

◆ Designing Security for a Microsoft Windows 2000 Network, 70-220

◆ Designing a Microsoft Windows 2000 Network Infrastructure, 70-221

◆ Migrating from Microsoft Windows NT 4.0 to Microsoft Windows 2000, 70-222

◆ Installing, Configuring, and Administering Microsoft Clustering Services by Using Microsoft Windows 2000 Advanced Server, 70-223

◆ Designing and Deploying a Messaging Infrastructure with Microsoft Exchange 2000 Server, 70-225

◆ Designing Highly Available Web Solutions with Microsoft Windows 2000 Server Technologies, 70-226

◆ Designing and Implementing Solutions with Microsoft BizTalk Server 2000, Enterprise Edition, 70-230

◆ Implementing and Maintaining Highly Available Web Solutions with Microsoft Windows 2000 Server Technologies and Microsoft Application Center 2000, 70-232

◆ Designing and Implementing Solutions with Microsoft Commerce Server 2000, 70-234

◆ Supporting and Maintaining a Microsoft Windows NT Server 4.0 Network, 70-244

How to Become a Microsoft Certified Solution Developer

The MCSD certification is outlined as follows. Undoubtedly, changes will come to this certification as the .NET framework continues to unfold. However, no changes had yet been announced at the time of this writing.

You must pass three core exams and one elective exam. The three core exam areas are listed as follows, as are the elective exams from which you can choose.

Core Exams

The core exams include the following:

◆ *Desktop Applications Development (one required)*

Designing and Implementing Desktop Applications with Microsoft Visual C++ 6.0, #70-016

OR Designing and Implementing Desktop Applications with Microsoft Visual FoxPro 6.0, #70-156

OR Designing and Implementing Desktop Applications with Microsoft Visual Basic 6.0, #70-176

◆ *Distributed Applications Development (one required)*

Designing and Implementing Distributed Applications with Microsoft Visual C++ 6.0, #70-015

OR Designing and Implementing Distributed Applications with Microsoft Visual FoxPro 6.0, #70-155

OR Designing and Implementing Distributed Applications with Microsoft Visual Basic 6.0, #70-175

◆ *Solution Architecture (required)*

Analyzing Requirements and Defining Solution Architectures, #70-100

Elective Exam

You must pass one of the following elective exams:

◆ Designing and Implementing Distributed Applications with Microsoft Visual C++ 6.0, #70-015

◆ Designing and Implementing Desktop Applications with Microsoft Visual C++ 6.0, #70-016

◆ Designing and Implementing Data Warehouses with Microsoft SQL Server 7.0, #70-019

◆ Designing and Implementing Databases with Microsoft SQL Server 7.0, #70-029

◆ Designing and Implementing Commerce Solutions with Microsoft Site Server 3.0, Commerce Edition, #70-057

◆ Designing and Implementing Solutions with Microsoft Office 2000 and Microsoft Visual Basic for Applications, #70-091

◆ Designing and Implementing Collaborative Solutions with Microsoft Outlook 2000 and Microsoft Exchange Server 5.5, #70-105

◆ Designing and Implementing Web Solutions with Microsoft Visual InterDev 6.0, #70-152

◆ Designing and Implementing Distributed Applications with Microsoft Visual FoxPro 6.0, #70-155

◆ Designing and Implementing Desktop Applications with Microsoft Visual FoxPro 6.0, #70-156

◆ Designing and Implementing Distributed Applications with Microsoft Visual Basic 6.0, #70-175

◆ Designing and Implementing Desktop Applications with Microsoft Visual Basic 6.0, #70-176

◆ Designing and Implementing Databases with Microsoft SQL Server 2000 Enterprise Edition, #70-229

◆ Designing and Implementing Solutions with Microsoft BizTalk Server 2000 Enterprise Edition, #70-230

◆ Designing and Implementing Solutions with Microsoft Commerce Server 2000, #70-234

How to Become a Microsoft Certified Application Developer

The following bullets describe what you need to accomplish in order to achieve the MCAD certification:

◆ **Core Exams (2 Exams Required)**—To fulfill the core certification requirements, pass one exam focused on either Web Application Development or XML Windows Application Development in the language of your choice. Then pass one Web Services and Server Components exam.

◆ **Elective Exams (1 Exams Required)**—In addition to the core exam requirements, you must also pass one elective exam that provides proof of expertise with a specific Microsoft server product.

Core Exams

◆ **Exam 70–305***: Developing and Implementing Web Applications with Microsoft Visual Basic® .NET and Microsoft Visual Studio® .NET

◆ **Exam 70–306***: Developing and Implementing Windows-based Applications with Microsoft Visual Basic .NET and Microsoft Visual Studio .NET

◆ **Exam 70–315***: Developing and Implementing Web Applications with Microsoft Visual C#™ .NET and Microsoft Visual Studio .NET

◆ **Exam 70–316***: Developing and Implementing Windows-based Applications with Microsoft Visual C# .NET and Microsoft Visual Studio .NET

◆ **Exam 70–310***: Developing XML Web Services and Server Components with Microsoft Visual Basic .NET and the Microsoft .NET Framework

◆ **Exam 70–320***: Developing XML Web Services and Server Components with Microsoft Visual C# and the Microsoft .NET Framework

Elective Exams

◆ **Exam 70–229**: Designing and Implementing Databases with Microsoft SQL Server™ 2000 Enterprise Edition

◆ **Exam 70–230**: Designing and Implementing Solutions with Microsoft BizTalk Server® 2000 Enterprise Edition

◆ **Exam 70–234**: Designing and Implementing Solutions with Microsoft Commerce Server 2000

◆ **Exam 70-305*, 70-306*, 70-315*, or 70-316***

If you use Exam 70-305 or 70-315 to satisfy the core exam requirement, you may use either Exam 70-306 or 70-316 as an elective.

If you use Exam 70-306 or 70-316 to satisfy the core exam requirement, you may use either Exam 70-305 or 70-315 as an elective.

Becoming a Microsoft Certified Trainer

As of January 1, 2001, all MCTs must hold a premier Microsoft Certified Professional (MCP) certification (Microsoft Certified Systems Engineer, Microsoft Certified Solution Developer, or Microsoft Certified Database Administrator). To fully understand the requirements and process for becoming an MCT, you need to obtain the Microsoft Certified Trainer Guide document from `http://www.microsoft.com/train-ingandservices/content/downloads/MCT_guide.doc`.

At this site, you can read the document as a Web page or display and download it as a Word file. You also can download the application form from the site. The MCT Guide explains the process for becoming an MCT. The general steps for the MCT certification are as follows:

1. Complete and mail a Microsoft Certified Trainer application to Microsoft. You must include proof of your skills for presenting instructional material. The options for doing so are described in the MCT Guide.

2. Obtain and study the Microsoft Trainer Kit for the Microsoft Official Curricula (MOC) courses for which you want to be certified. Microsoft Trainer Kits can be ordered by calling 800-688-0496 in North America. Those of you in other regions should review the MCT Guide for information on how to order a Trainer Kit.

3. Take and pass any required prerequisite MCP exam(s) to measure your current technical knowledge.

4. Prepare to teach an MOC course. Begin by attending the MOC course for the course for which you want to be certified. This is required so you understand how the course is structured, how labs are completed, and how the course flows.

5. Pass any additional exam requirement(s) to measure any additional product knowledge that pertains to the course.

6. Submit your course preparation checklist to Microsoft so that your additional accreditation may be processed and reflected on your transcript.

WARNING

The Exact Process for Obtaining Your MCT You should consider the preceding steps a general overview of the MCT certification process. The precise steps that you need to take are described in detail on the Web site mentioned earlier. Do not misinterpret the preceding steps as the exact process you must undergo.

If you are interested in becoming an MCT, you can obtain more information by visiting the Microsoft Certified Training WWW site at `http://www.microsoft.com/traincert/` and choosing MCT under Technical Certifications or by calling 800-688-0496.

What's on the CD-ROM

This appendix is a brief rundown of what you'll find on the CD-ROM that comes with this book. For a more detailed description of the PrepLogic Practice Tests, Preview Edition exam simulation software, see Appendix D, "Using the *PrepLogic, Preview Edition* Software." In addition to the *PrepLogic Practice Tests, Preview Edition*, the CD-ROM includes the electronic version of the book in Portable Document Format (PDF), several utility and application programs, and a complete listing of test objectives and where they are covered in the book.

PrepLogic Practice Tests, Preview Edition

PrepLogic is a leading provider of certification training tools. Trusted by certification students worldwide, we believe PrepLogic is the best practice exam software available. In addition to providing a means of evaluating your knowledge of the Training Guide material, *PrepLogic Practice Tests, Preview Edition* features several innovations that help you to improve your mastery of the subject matter.

For example, the practice tests allow you to check your score by exam area or domain to determine which topics you need to study more. Another feature allows you to obtain immediate feedback on your responses in the form of explanations for the correct and incorrect answers.

PrepLogic Practice Tests, Preview Edition exhibits most of the full functionality of the *Premium Edition* but offers only a fraction of the total questions. To get the complete set of practice questions and exam functionality, visit PrepLogic.com and order the *Premium Edition* for this and other challenging exam titles.

Again, for a more detailed description of the *PrepLogic Practice Tests, Preview Edition* features, see Appendix D.

Exclusive Electronic Version of Text

The CD-ROM also contains the electronic version of this book in Portable Document Format (PDF). The electronic version comes complete with all figures as they appear in the book. You will find that the search capabilities of the reader come in handy for study and review purposes.

Using the *PrepLogic, Preview Edition Software*

This Training Guide includes a special version of *PrepLogic Practice Tests*—a revolutionary test engine designed to give you the best in certification exam preparation. PrepLogic offers sample and practice exams for many of today's most in-demand and challenging technical certifications. This special *Preview Edition* is included with this book as a tool to use in assessing your knowledge of the Training Guide material, while also providing you with the experience of taking an electronic exam.

This appendix describes in detail what *PrepLogic Practice Tests, Preview Edition* is, how it works, and what it can do to help you prepare for the exam. Note that although the *Preview Edition* includes all the test simulation functions of the complete, retail version, it contains only a single practice test. The *Premium Edition*, available at PrepLogic.com, contains the complete set of challenging practice exams designed to optimize your learning experience.

Exam Simulation

One of the main functions of *PrepLogic Practice Tests, Preview Edition* is exam simulation. PrepLogic is designed to offer the most effective exam simulation available in order to prepare you to take the actual vendor certification exam.

Question Quality

The questions provided in the *PrepLogic Practice Tests, Preview Edition* are written to the highest standards of technical accuracy. The questions tap the content of the Training Guide chapters and help you to review and assess your knowledge before you take the actual exam.

Interface Design

The *PrepLogic Practice Tests, Preview Edition* exam simulation interface provides you with the experience of taking an electronic exam. This allows you to effectively prepare yourself for taking the actual exam by making the test experience a familiar one. Using this test simulation can help to eliminate the sense of surprise or anxiety you might experience in the testing center because you will already be acquainted with computerized testing.

Effective Learning Environment

The *PrepLogic Practice Tests, Preview Edition* interface provides a learning environment that not only tests you through the computer, but also teaches the material you need to know to pass the certification exam. Each question comes with a detailed explanation of the correct answer and often provides reasons the other options are incorrect. This information helps to reinforce the knowledge you already have and also provides practical information you can use on the job.

Software Requirements

PrepLogic Practice Tests requires a computer with the following:

◆ Microsoft Windows 98, Windows Me, Windows NT 4.0, Windows 2000, or Windows XP

◆ A 166 MHz or faster processor is recommended

◆ A minimum of 32MB of RAM

◆ As with any Windows application, the more memory, the better your performance

◆ 10MB of hard drive space

Installing *PrepLogic Practice Tests, Preview Edition*

Install *PrepLogic Practice Tests, Preview Edition* by running the setup program on the *PrepLogic Practice Tests, Preview Edition* CD. Follow these instructions to install the software on your computer.

1. Insert the CD into your CD-ROM drive. The Autorun feature of Windows should launch the software. If you have Autorun disabled, click the Start button and select Run. Go to the root directory of the CD and select setup.exe. Click Open, and then click OK.

2. The Installation Wizard copies the *PrepLogic Practice Tests, Preview Edition* files to your hard drive; adds *PrepLogic Practice Tests, Preview Edition* to your Desktop and Program menu; and installs test engine components to the appropriate system folders.

Removing *PrepLogic Practice Tests, Preview Edition* from Your Computer

If you elect to remove the *PrepLogic Practice Tests, Preview Edition* product from your computer, an uninstall process has been included to ensure that it is removed from your system safely and completely. Follow these instructions to remove *PrepLogic Practice Tests, Preview Edition* from your computer:

1. Select Start, Settings, Control Panel.

2. Double-click the Add/Remove Programs icon.

3. You are presented with a list of software currently installed on your computer. Select the appropriate *PrepLogic Practice Tests, Preview Edition* title you wish to remove. Click the Add/Remove button. The software is then removed from you computer.

Using *PrepLogic Practice Tests, Preview Edition*

PrepLogic is designed to be user friendly and intuitive. Because the software has a smooth learning curve, your time is maximized, as you will start practicing almost immediately. *PrepLogic Practice Tests, Preview Edition* has two major modes of study: Practice Test and Flash Review.

Using Practice Test mode, you can develop your test-taking abilities, as well as your knowledge through the use of the Show Answer option. While you are taking the test, you can reveal the answers along with a detailed explanation of why the given answers are right or wrong. This gives you the ability to better understand the material presented.

Flash Review is designed to reinforce exam topics rather than quiz you. In this mode, you will be shown a series of questions, but no answer choices. Instead, you will be given a button that reveals the correct answer to the question and a full explanation for that answer.

Starting a Practice Test Mode Session

Practice Test mode enables you to control the exam experience in ways that actual certification exams do not allow:

- ◆ **Enable Show Answer Button**—Activates the Show Answer button, allowing you to view the correct answer(s) and a full explanation for each question during the exam. When not enabled, you must wait until after your exam has been graded to view the correct answer(s) and explanation(s) .

- ◆ **Enable Item Review Button**—Activates the Item Review button, allowing you to view your answer choices, marked questions, and facilite navigation between questions.

- ◆ **Randomize Choices**—Randomize answer choices from one exam session to the next; makes memorizing question choices more difficult, therefore keeping questions fresh and challenging longer.

To begin studying in Practice Test mode, click the Practice Test radio button from the main exam customization screen. This will enable the options detailed above.

To your left, you are presented with the options of selecting the pre-configured Practice Test or creating your own Custom Test. The pre-configured test has a fixed time limit and number of questions. Custom Tests allow you to configure the time limit and the number of questions in your exam.

The *Preview Edition* included with this book includes a single pre-configured Practice Test. Get the compete set of challenging PrepLogic Practice Tests at `PrepLogic.com` and make certain you're ready for the big exam.

Click the Begin Exam button to begin your exam.

Starting a Flash Review Mode Session

Flash Review mode provides you with an easy way to reinforce topics covered in the practice questions. To begin studying in Flash Review mode, click the Flash Review radio button from the main exam customization screen. Select either the pre-configured Practice Test or create your own Custom Test.

Click the Best Exam button to begin your Flash Review of the exam questions.

Standard *PrepLogic Practice Tests, Preview Edition* Options

The following list describes the function of each of the buttons you see. Depending on the options, some of the buttons will be grayed out and inaccessible or missing completely. Buttons that are accessible are active. The buttons are as follows:

◆ **Exhibit**—This button is visible if an exhibit is provided to support the question. An exhibit is an image that provides supplemental information necessary to answer the question.

◆ **Item Review**—This button leaves the question window and opens the Item Review screen. From this screen you will see all questions, your answers, and your marked items. You will also see correct answers listed here when appropriate.

◆ **Show Answer**—This option displays the correct answer with an explanation of why it is correct. If you select this option, the current question is not scored.

◆ **Mark Item**—Check this box to tag a question you need to review further. You can view and navigate your Marked Items by clicking the Item Review button (if enabled). When grading your exam, you will be notified if you have marked items remaining.

◆ **Previous Item**—This option allows you to view the previous question.

◆ **Next Item**—This option allows you to view the next question.

◆ **Grade Exam**—When you have completed your exam, click this button to end your exam and view your detailed score report. If you have unanswered or marked items remaining you will be asked if you would like to continue taking your exam or view your exam report.

Time Remaining

If the test is timed, the time remaining is displayed on the upper right corner of the application screen. It counts down the minutes and seconds remaining to complete the test. If you run out of time, you will be asked if you want to continue taking the test or if you want to end your exam.

Your Examination Score Report

The Examination Score Report screen appears when the Practice Test mode ends—as the result of time expiration, completion of all questions, or your decision to terminate early.

This screen provides you with a graphical display of your test score with a breakdown of scores by topic domain. The graphical display at the top of the screen compares your overall score with the PrepLogic Exam Competency Score.

The PrepLogic Exam Competency Score reflects the level of subject competency required to pass this vendor's exam. While this score does not directly translate to a passing score, consistently matching or exceeding this score does suggest you possess the knowledge to pass the actual vendor exam.

Review Your Exam

From Your Score Report screen, you can review the exam that you just completed by clicking on the View Items button. Navigate through the items viewing the questions, your answers, the correct answers, and the explanations for those answers. You can return to your score report by clicking the View Items button.

Get More Exams

Each *PrepLogic Practice Tests, Preview Edition* that accompanies your Training Guide contains a single PrepLogic Practice Test. Certification students worldwide trust PrepLogic Practice Tests to help them pass their IT certification exams the first time. Purchase the *Premium Edition* of PrepLogic Practice Tests and get the entire set of all new challenging Practice Tests for this exam. PrepLogic Practice Tests—Because You Want to Pass the First Time.

Contacting PrepLogic

If you would like to contact PrepLogic for any reason, including information about our extensive line of certification practice tests, we invite you to do so. Please contact us online at `http://www.preplogic.com`.

Customer Service

If you have a damaged product and need a replacement or refund, please call the following phone number:

800-858-7674

Product Suggestions and Comments

We value your input! Please email your suggestions and comments to the following address:

`feedback@preplogic.com`

License Agreement

YOU MUST AGREE TO THE TERMS AND CONDITIONS OUTLINED IN THE END USER LICENSE AGREEMENT ("EULA") PRESENTED TO YOU DURING THE INSTALLATION PROCESS. IF YOU DO NOT AGREE TO THESE TERMS DO NOT INSTALL THE SOFTWARE.

NUMBERS

16-bit applications (application performance), 292

SYMBOLS

* (asterisks), 448
? (question marks), 176

A

Above Normal CPU scheduling priority (application performance), 290
Accelerated Graphics Port (AGP), multiple-display support, 204
access
　granting, resources (Guest account), 493
　resources, preventing (Authenticated Users group), 507
　rights. *See* permissions
Access Control Settings dialog box, 527
Access this computer from the network (user right), 510
accessibility options, 366-368
Accessibility Options applet, keyboards (customizing), 218
Accessibility Wizard, accessibility program, 367
accessing
　data (application performance), 292
　EFS (Encrypting File System) files, 504
　Event Viewer, 520
　files
　　Internet Explorer, 427
　　NTFS (Users group), 507
　　NWLink, 395
　　Offline Files, 127
　folders, Offline Files, 127
　installation files, 26
　local systems, shared folders, 105
　media, libraries (media pools), 200
　printers, NWLink, 395
　remote computers, Terminal Services, 435
　removable media, 198

　resources
　　Administrators group, 504
　　Guests group, 505
　roaming user profiles, 355
　Security property page, 115
　Web site, Internet Explorer, 428-430
Account Is Disabled, configuration option (local user account), 498
Account Lockout Duration, account lockout policy (local Account Policy), 519
account lockout policies (local Account Policy), 518-519
Account Lockout Threshold, account lockout policy (local Account Policy), 519
Account Logon (security event category), 523
Account Management (security event category), 523
accounts. *See also* group accounts; local users, accounts
　Administrator account, built-in account, 493
　administrator user accounts, 504
　built-in accounts, 493
　computer accounts
　　Active Directory, 66
　　domain model requirement (network security group), 25
　Guest account, built-in account, 493
　HelpAssistant accounts, 493
　IUSR_%COMPUTERNAME% accounts, 493
　IUSR_computername, 505
　IWAM_%COMPUTERNAME% accounts, 493
　IWAM_computername, 505
　machine accounts, joining domains (security), 405
　SUPPORT accounts
　　HelpServicesGroup, 505
　　local user accounts, 493
ACPI (Advanced Configuration and Power Interface)
　APM (Advanced Power Management), 209
　BIOS, 173
　configuring, 210-211
　HAL (Hardware Abstraction Layer), 173

B

How can we make this index more useful? Email us at indexes@quepublishing.com

J-K

M

managing
    ownership, 120
    resource owners, 115
multiple share permissions, shared folders, 104
NTFS
    assigning, 111
    permissions, file resources, 111-126
    shared folders (file resources), 122-123
print jobs, managing, 150
printing (Creator Owner group), 507
resources, security identifier (SID), 492
share permissions, shared folders, 103-105
shared folders, 106
special permissions
    files, 116-121
    folders, 116-121
    modifying, 120
testing, 114
Permissions button, 106
Permissions for, security setting (NTFS), 115
personal roaming user profiles, 358-360
personalized settings, copying (updating Windows), 77
phases, installations (Windows XP), 26
Phone and Modem Options link, 224
PhysicalDisk object, disk counters, 283
Ping, diagnostic utility (TCP/IP), 466
PING command, connectivity (TCP/IP connections), 446-447
pinging
    computers (ICMP), 444
    remote hosts, 447
pipes, implementing, 399
PKI (Public Key Infrastructure)
    EFS (Encrypting File System), 536
    file encryption, 135
PnP (Plug and Play)
    ACPI (Advanced Configuration Power Interface), 210
    BIOS, 173
    CD-ROM devices, 181
    DVD devices, 181
    hardware, 173-175
    IrDA devices, installing, 226
    modems, installing, 224
    NDIS 5.0, 391

network adapters, 236
scanners, installing, 217
smart card readers, installing, 222
USB devices, 230
video adapters (display device), 207
Point-to-Point (PPP), line protocol, 420
Point-to-Point Tunneling Protocol (PPTP)
    encryptions, 417
    line protocol, 420
    VPN (Virtual Private Network), 416
points
    restore points
        creating (System Restore), 304
        System Restore, 302-305
    share points, networks (UNC), 403
policies
    account lockout policies (local Account Policy security), 518-519
    audit policies
        enabling, 524
        security events, 522-528
    ICF (Internet Connection Firewall), 444
    local Account Policy, security, 517-519
    local Group Policy, security, 516
    password policies (local Account Policy security), 517-518
Policy Change (security event category), 523
Pool Nonpaged Bytes counter (application performance), 291
Pool Nonpaged Bytes counter (memory shortages), 272
Pool Paged Bytes counter (application performance), 291
Pool Paged Bytes counter (memory shortages), 272
pooling printers, 148
pools, memory, 268
port mapping, ICF (Internet Connection Firewall), 441-442
Port Name dialog box, 150
portable computers. *See* Power Management
ports
    connecting, 229
    hardware installations, 178
    infrared ports, handheld devices, 228, 232
    input/output (I/O), 174
    IrDA, 226
    Messenger File Transfer, opening, 441

jobs
    canceling, 151
    managing, 150-152
    notifications, setting, 151
    pausing, 151
    priority print times, setting, 151
    processing, 138
    restarting, 151
    spooling, 213
local printers, 141-143
managing, 144-150, 214, 428
naming, 140
NWLink, accessing, 395
pausing, 145
permissions (Creator Owner group), 507
pooling, 148
ports, 140, 148
Printer Spooler Service, 146
priority, printers (managing), 146-148
redirecting, 148-150
remote printers, connecting, 143
resources, 138-153
restarting, 145
servers, print environment, 138
setting, 144, 152
shared printers, connecting, 143
sharing, 140
spoolers, client side, 214
spooling, 147
test pages, 141
troubleshooting, 214-216
Printers and Other Hardware link, 224, 227, 239
Printers command (Setting menu), 215
priorities, CPU scheduling priorities (application performance), 290
Priority option (print jobs), 152
priority print times, print jobs, 151
private key, encryption, 135, 536
% Privilege Time counter (application performance), 291
Privilege Use (security event category), 524
% Privileged Time (processor counter), 278
privileges
    administrative

domains (joining), 405
hardware profiles, 297
ICF (Internet Connection Firewall), 440
Windows Update, 240
Driver Signing, 241
installing, 217, 223
updating, 239
users, Network Identification Wizard, 29
Process (_Total)/Page File Bytes counter (paging files), 269
Process object (application performance), 290
Process Tracking (security event category), 523
processing, distributed processing (IPC), 398
processor, bottlenecks (processor queues), 279
Processor Queue Length (processor counter), 278-279
processor queues (processor bottlenecks), 279
processor scheduling (Performance Options page), 271
% Processor Time (processor counter), 278-279, 291
processors. *See also* **CPUs**
    bottlenecks, 278, 281-282
    counters (processor performance), 277-279
    desktop, performance, 277-282
    hardware component, installation preparations, 19
    performance, 280
product family, 16-18
Product Registration Wizard, 654
Profile 1, hardware profile (mobile computers), 295
Profile Path box, 356, 359
Profile tab, 356, 359, 500
profiles. *See also* **users, profiles**
    hardware profiles, 295-297
    roaming profiles, FAST and USMT, 77
Program Compatibility Wizard, 369
Program to Run option (Scheduled Task Wizard), 293
program updates
    upgrades, 82
Programs, Accessories command (Start menu), 129, 436
Programs, Administrative Tools command (Start menu), 433, 495
programs
    accessibility, 367
    compatibility options (desktop), 368
    protection, features, 17
    setup programs

S

command-line
   Disk Management, 190
   DISKPART (extending volumes), 193
   LoadState.EXE (USMT), 81
   ScanState.EXE (USMT), 81
  converting, 137
  determining (hostnames), 457
  diagnostic utilities, TCP/IP, 466
  FTOnline, fault-tolerated disks, 187
  managing, 21, 134, 369-372
  Net View, name resolutions (identifying), 461
  Nslookup, DNS error messages (identifying name resolutions), 464
  Route utility, command-line arguments, 458
Utility Manager, accessibility program, 367

V

variables, creating (roaming user profiles), 357
verifying
  file signatures (Driver Signing), 241
  upgrade paths, updating Windows, 71-72
versions, NTFS, 24
video
  adapters
   BIOS (multiple-display support), 204
   display device, 207-208
   multiple-display support, 204
  resolutions, 636-364
  settings (desktop), 362-364
View
  link, 354
  menu commands
   Choose Columns, 521
   Filter, 521
   Resources by Connection, 179
  tab, 115, 329, 355
view settings, modifying (Windows Explorer), 355
viewing
  directories, user profiles, 350
  event logs (Event Viewer), 520-522
  hidden files (Recovery Console), 329
  Local Computer Policy settings, 508

  local user profiles, 355
  Performance Monitor, 267
  Security tab, 115
virtual desktops, 204
virtual directories, 434
Virtual Directory Creation Wizard, 434
virtual DOS machine (NTVDM), 16-bit applications, 292
virtual memory space, paging files, 268
Virtual Private Network. See VPN
viruses, scanning (Trend Micro), 74
volume
  sets
   basic disks, 187
   media devices, 192-198
  troubleshooting, 197-198
volume shadow copy, backup mode, 307
Volume tab, 184
volumes
  boot partitions, 191
  configuring (Disk Management), 189
  converted basic disks, 191
  DFS (Distributed File System), disk space, 285
  disk counters, 284
  dynamic, 191-192
   disks, 187
   storage, 20
  extending, 194
  mirrored volumes (RAID-1), 194
  partitions, 193
  RAID-5 volumes, 195-197
  simple volumes, 193
  spanned volumes, deleting, 193
  status, Disk Management, 191, 197
  striped volumes (RAID-0), 193
VPN (Virtual Private Network)
  connections, installing, 418
  Internet Connection sharing, 425
  L2TP (Layer 2 Tunneling Protocol), 417
  network connections, My Workplace, 423
  Point-to-Point Tunneling Protocol (PPTP), 420
  PPTP (Point-to-Point Tunneling Protocol), 416
  TCP/IP configurations, 415-418
VUE, contact information, 641
VUE Web site, 641

How can we make this index more useful? Email us at indexes@quepublishing.com